READINGS IN THE HISTORY OF
CHRISTIAN THOUGHT

Robert L. Ferm
POMONA COLLEGE

READINGS
IN THE HISTORY OF
CHRISTIAN THOUGHT

HOLT, RINEHART AND WINSTON, INC.

New York · Chicago · San Francisco

Toronto · London

for Mother and Dad

and the riches

of Beall and Mercer

PREFACE

This volume is designed as a source book for the history of Christian thought. Its purpose is to bring within easy reach the obvious and central sources of the western theological heritage, not to offer the new or the unusual. Though this means that frequently provocative and illuminating byways are ignored and that the history of the church and related aspects of intellectual and cultural history are not included, it does not imply that such study is peripheral; space is the limiting factor.

The focus of attention is on four general topics. Part I is concerned with "methods" in theology. Representatives of the whole spectrum of theological inquiry, from the rigorous separation of philosophy and theology of Tertullian to the "rational" theology of William Ellery Channing, are included. Part II offers early church documents relating to the development of the doctrine of the Trinity and the person of Christ, and the early and continuing interpretations of the atoning work of Christ. In Part III the problems of original sin, free will, and justification by faith are considered. The selections in Part IV are organized around the topic of the church and, especially, sacramental theory. An additional table of contents, organized chronologically, is included for the convenience of those who deal with the sources of Christian thought historically rather than topically.

With the exception of the work of William Ellery Channing, no document is included that was written after 1800. The nineteenth century brought a reorientation in traditional theological formulation and the ever increasing availability of source material in the more recent period makes advisable drawing an arbitrary line at 1800. Neither is any material included from the Apostolic Fathers, largely because of the readily available collections of material from this period.

The editor's introductions to the selections are purposely kept brief and descriptive. There are available useful histories of the church and

Christian thought that the reader should consult. For classroom use, lectures on the development of theological formulation and church history should properly supply contextual information. In this task it is the editor's judgment to remain in the background.

As one reads in the rich variety of Christian theology, it becomes ever more apparent that there can be no one normative theological position; the breadth of historical affirmations continues to shed new light and shadows on the search of man to articulate his relation to the God of Christian faith and to the tradition that is his. The faithful reader of history cannot become provincial. Those who are versed in the traditional theological issues soon realize the many sidedness of solutions, the tentative nature of human answers. Though the past cannot be the norm, history does provide the anchor.

R. L. F.

Claremont, California
November 1963

TABLE OF CONTENTS

Preface   vii

Chronological Table of Contents   xv

PART I

Methods in Christian Theology:
The Knowledge of God

SELECTION

1 TERTULLIAN
   The Prescription Against Heretics   3

2 CLEMENT OF ALEXANDRIA
   The Stromata   11

3 ORIGEN
   De Principiis [On the Interpretation of Scripture] 19

4 AUGUSTINE
   A. *Letter 120*   26
   B. *God—The Eternal Creator*   32

5 ANSELM
   Proslogium   37

6 THOMAS AQUINAS
   Summa Theologica   45

7 MEISTER ECKHART
   The Nobility of the Soul   59

8   MARTIN LUTHER
The Letter and the Spirit   64

9   JOHN CALVIN
Institutes of the Christian Religion   71

10   The Council of Trent (1545–1563)   87

11   WILLIAM ELLERY CHANNING
Unitarian Christianity   90

PART II

The Person and Work of Christ: The Person of Christ

12   A. Old Roman Symbol   105
    B. The Apostles' Creed   106

13   TERTULLIAN
Against Praxeas   107

14   ORIGEN
De Principiis   117

15   DIONYSIUS OF ROME
A Letter Concerning Sabellianism   124

16   DIONYSIUS OF ALEXANDRIA
A Letter to Dionysius of Rome   125

17   ARIUS
A. A Letter to Alexander, Bishop of Alexandria   127
B. A Letter to Eusebius, Bishop of Nicomedia   128

18   CONSTANTINE
A Letter to Alexander of Alexandria and Arius   130

19   ALEXANDER, BISHOP OF ALEXANDRIA
A Letter to the Church   132

20   COUNCIL OF NICAEA
A. Eusebius of Caesarea, A Letter Including the Creeds of
    Caesarea and Nicaea   136
B. The Council's Letter to the Church at Alexandria   139

21 CONSTANTINE
    A Letter to the Church of Alexandria   141

22 The Dedicatory Creed, Antioch (341)   142

23 Council of Sirmium (357)   144

24 The Council of Sirmium (359): The Dated Creed   146

25 ATHANASIUS
    A. Against the Arians   148
    B. On Homoiousions   149
    C. Statement of Faith   151

26 Nicene-Constantinopolitan Creed   154

27 GREGORY OF NAZIANZEN
    A Letter to Cledonius [On Apollinarianism]   155

28 CYRIL; NESTORIUS
    A. A Letter to Nestorius   159
    B. Council of Ephesus (431): The Anathemas   162
    C. Council of Ephesus (431): Decree Against Nestorius   166
    D. Council of Ephesus (431): Decree Against Cyril   167
    E. Council of Antioch (433): Creed   168

29 EUTYCHES; LEO I; Council of Chalcedon (451)
    A. Council of Constantinople (448): Condemnation of
       Eutyches   169
    B. Tome of Leo I   170
    C. Council of Chalcedon (451): The Definition of Faith 175

30 Council of Constantinople (680–681): The Definition of
    Faith   179

The Work of Christ

31 IRENAEUS
    Against Heresies   185

32 ATHANASIUS
    The Incarnation of the Word of God   192

33 GREGORY OF NYSSA
    The Great Catechism   197

34 AUGUSTINE
    A. On the Trinity   205
    B. On the Gospel of John   210

35 ANSELM
    Cur Deus Homo (Why God Man?)   214

36 PETER ABAILARD
    Exposition of the Epistle to the Romans   240

37 The Racovian Catechism   244

38 HUGO GROTIUS
    A Defence of the Catholic Faith Concerning the Satisfac-
       tion of Christ   253

PART III

The Human Condition
and Its Remedy

39 AUGUSTINE
    A. Letter 217   266
    B. A Treatise on Rebuke and Grace   270
    C. Four Books Against the Pelagians   282

40 PELAGIUS
    A. Letter to Demetrias   291
    B. [Excerpts from] Expositions of Thirteen Epistles of St.
       Paul   297

41 JOHN CASSIAN
    The Third Conference of Abbot Chaeremon   300

42 Council of Orange (529)   305

43 PETER ABAILARD
    Know Thyself   308

44   THOMAS AQUINAS
    Summa Theologica   314

45   MARTIN LUTHER
    A. *A Treatise on Christian Liberty*   333
    B. *Preface to the Epistle to the Romans*   340
    C. *The Bondage of the Will*   351

46   JOHN CALVIN
    Institutes of the Christian Religion   357

47   ANONYMOUS (ANABAPTIST)
    Concerning the Satisfaction of Christ   373

48   *The Council of Trent (1545–1563)*   381

49   JAMES ARMINIUS
    Declaration of Sentiments   390

50   *The Remonstrance: 1610*   397

51   *The Canons of the Synod of Dort*   399

52   JOHN WESLEY
    A. *Free Grace*   407
    B. *The Scripture Way of Salvation*   412

53   WILLIAM ELLERY CHANNING
    A. *The Moral Argument Against Calvinism*   418
    B. *Likeness to God*   422

PART IV

The Church and the Sacraments

54   CYPRIAN, BISHOP OF CARTHAGE
    The Unity of the Catholic Church   431

55   AUGUSTINE
    A. *On Baptism*   438
    B. *The City of God*   442

56   *The Donation of Constantine*   448

57   POPE GREGORY VII
    A Letter to Hermann, Bishop of Metz   451

58   PASCHASIUS RADBERTUS
     The Lord's Body and Blood   455

59   RATRAMNUS
     Christ's Body and Blood   460

60   THOMAS AQUINAS
     On the Truth of the Catholic Faith [Summa Contra
     Gentiles]   466

61   BONIFACE VIII
     Unam Sanctam   480

62   JOHN HUSS
     The Church   483

63   MARTIN LUTHER
     The Babylonian Captivity of the Church   496

64   HULDREICH ZWINGLI
     Exposition of the Christian Faith   515

65   SWISS ANABAPTISTS
     The Schleitheim Confession of Faith   528

66   JOHN CALVIN
     Institutes of the Christian Religion   535

67   The Council of Trent (1545–1563)   552

68   Profession of the Tridentine Faith   567

69   MENNO SIMONS
     Foundation of Christian Doctrine [On Baptism]   569

70   The Thirty-nine Articles of the Church of England   574

71   RICHARD HOOKER
     Laws of Ecclesiastical Polity   578

72   The Racovian Catechism   587

73   The Cambridge Platform   593

74   JOHN WINTHROP
     A Model of Christian Charity   604

BIBLIOGRAPHY   611

CHRONOLOGICAL
TABLE OF CONTENTS

	SELECTION	PAGE
IRENAEUS *Against Heresies*	31	185
TERTULLIAN *The Prescription Against Heretics*	1	3
Against Praxeas	13	107
CLEMENT OF ALEXANDRIA *The Stromata*	2	11
ORIGEN *De Principiis* [On the Interpretation of Scripture]	3	19
De Principiis	14	117
Old Roman Symbol	12 A	105
CYPRIAN, BISHOP OF CATHAGE *The Unity of the Catholic Church*	54	431
DIONYSIUS OF ROME *A Letter Concerning Sabellianism*	15	124
DIONYSIUS OF ALEXANDRIA *A Letter to Dionysius of Rome*	16	125
ARIUS *A Letter to Alexander, Bishop of Alexandria*	17 A	127
A Letter to Eusebius, Bishop of Nicomedia	17 B	128
ALEXANDER, BISHOP OF ALEXANDRIA *A Letter to the Church*	19	132

CONSTANTINE
A Letter to Alexander of Alexandria and Arius   18   130
A Letter to the Church of Alexandria   21   141

EUSEBIUS OF CAESAREA
A Letter Including the Creeds of Caesarea and Nicaea   20 A   136

The Council's [Nicaea] Letter to the Church of
   Alexandria   20 B   139

The Dedicatory Creed, Antioch (341)   22   142

Council of Sirmium, 357   23   144

The Council of Sirmium, 359: The Dated Creed   24   146

ATHANASIUS
Against the Arians   25 A   148
On Homoiousions   25 B   149
Statement of Faith   25 C   151
The Incarnation of the Word of God   32   192

GREGORY OF NYSSA
The Great Catechism   33   197

GREGORY OF NAZIANZEN
A Letter to Cledonius [On Apollinarianism]   27   155

Nicene-Constantinopolitan Creed   26   154

AUGUSTINE
Letter 120   4 A   26
God—The Eternal Creator   4 B   32
On the Trinity   34 A   205
On the Gospel of John   34 B   210
Letter 217   39 A   266
A Treatise on Rebuke and Grace   39 B   270
Four Books Against the Pelagians   39 C   282
On Baptism   55 A   438
The City of God   55 B   442

PELAGIUS
Letter to Demetrias   40 A   291
[Excerpts from] Expositions of Thirteen Epistles of St.
   Paul   40 B   297

JOHN CASSIAN
The Third Conference of Abbot Chaeremon   41   300

CYRIL
A Letter to Nestorius   28 A   159

Council of Ephesus (431): The Anathemas   28 B   162
                            Decree Against Nestorius   28 C   166
                            Decree Against Cyril   28 D   167

Council of Antioch (433): Creed   28 E   168

*Council of Constantinople (448): Condemnation of
    Eutyches*   29 A   169

LEO I
Tome   29 B   170

*The Council of Chalcedon (451): The Definition of
    Faith*   29 C   175

Council of Orange, 529   42   305

*Council of Constantinople (680–681): The Definition
    of Faith*   30   179

The Apostles' Creed   12 B   106

The Donation of Constantine   56   448

PASCHASIUS RADBERTUS
The Lord's Body and Blood   58   455

RATRAMNUS
Christ's Body and Blood   59   460

GREGORY VII
A Letter to Hermann, Bishop of Metz   57   451

ANSELM,
Proslogium   5   37
Cur Deus Homo (Why God Man?)   35   214

PETER ABAILARD
Exposition of the Epistle to the Romans   36   240
Know Thyself   43   308

THOMAS AQUINAS
Summa Theologica   6   45
Summa Theologica   44   314
*On the Truth of the Catholic Faith
    [Summa Contra Gentiles]*   60   466

BONIFACE VIII
Unam Sanctam   61   480

MEISTER ECKHART
The Nobility of the Soul   7   59

JOHN HUSS
The Church   62   483

MARTIN LUTHER
The Letter and the Spirit   8   64
A Treatise on Christian Liberty   45 A   333
Preface to the Epistle to the Romans   45 B   340
The Bondage of the Will   45 C   351
The Babylonian Captivity of the Church   63   496

ANONYMOUS (ANABAPTIST)
Concerning the Satisfaction of Christ   47   373

SWISS ANABAPTISTS
The Schleitheim Confession of Faith   65   528

HULDREICH ZWINGLI
Exposition of the Christian Faith   64   515

MENNO SIMONS
Foundation of Christian Doctrine [On Baptism]   69   569

JOHN CALVIN
Institutes of the Christian Religion   9   71
Institutes of the Christian Religion   46   357
Institutes of the Christian Religion   66   535

The Council of Trent (1545–1563)   10   87
The Council of Trent (1545–1563)   48   381
The Council of Trent (1545–1563)   67   552

Profession of the Tridentine Faith   68   567

The Thirty-nine Articles of the Church of England   70   574

RICHARD HOOKER
Laws of Ecclesiastical Policy   71   578

The Racovian Catechism   37   244
The Racovian Catechism   72   587

JAMES ARMINIUS
Declaration of Sentiments   49   390

The Remonstrance: 1610   50   397

The Canons of the Synod of Dort   51   399

HUGO GROTIUS
A Defence of the Catholic Faith Concerning the Satis-
faction of Christ   38   253

JOHN WINTHROP
A Model of Christian Charity   74   604

The Cambridge Platform   73   593

JOHN WESLEY
Free Grace   52 A   407
The Scripture Way of Salvation   52 B   412

WILLIAM ELLERY CHANNING
Unitarian Christianity   11   90
The Moral Argument Against Calvinism   53 A   418
Likeness to God   53 B   422

PART I

Methods in Christian Theology:
The Knowledge of God

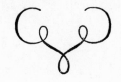

1

TERTULLIAN, BORN probably between the years 150–155 at Carthage, in North Africa, left his mark on many facets of early Christian theology. He was educated in Rome where he practiced law until his conversion to Christianity about 190, a date that marked the beginning of his intense study and prolific writing. In the first decade of the second century, Tertullian joined the heretical Montanist movement, a group that affirmed the approaching end of the age, the inauguration of the dispensation of the Holy Spirit, and encouraged an ascetic and celibate life. Though he was regarded as "heretical," he wrote forceful denunciations of other "heresies," for example, *Against Praxeas, Five Books Against Marcion,* and these served to shape the lines along which major theological issues were to develop.

The following selection from his *The Prescription Against Heretics* illustrates a sharp difference between early Western and Eastern (See Clement, *The Stromata* [Selection 2]) Christian theological methodology. Tertullian's sharp disjunction of theology and philosophy is characteristic of one strain in Christian theology.[1]

The Prescription Against Heretics *

TERTULLIAN

1. THE WAY OF THE HERETIC

The character of the times in which we live is such as to call forth from us even this admonition, that we ought not to be astonished at the heresies (which abound) neither ought their existence to surprise us, for it was foretold that they should come to pass; nor the fact that they subvert the faith of some, for their final cause is, by affording a trial to faith, to give it also the opportunity of being "approved." Groundless, therefore,

* From *The Ante-Nicene Fathers,* Vol. III, Alexander Roberts and James Donaldson, eds. Grand Rapids, Michigan: Wm. B. Eerdmans Publishing Co., 1951. [The titles for the sections are supplied by the editor.]

[1] See also *Against Praxeas,* Selection 13.

3

and inconsiderate is the offense of the many who are scandalized by the very fact that heresies prevail to such a degree. . . .

It is usual, indeed, with persons of a weaker character, to be so built up (in confidence) by certain individuals who are caught by heresy, as to topple over into ruin themselves. How comes it to pass, (they ask), that this woman or this man, who were the most faithful, the most prudent, and the most approved in the church, have gone over to the other side? Who that asks such a question does not in fact reply to it himself, to the effect that men whom heresies have been able to pervert ought never to have been esteemed prudent, or faithful, or approved? This again is, I suppose, an extraordinary thing, that one who has been approved should afterwards fall back? Saul, who was good beyond all others, is afterwards subverted by envy. David, a good man "after the Lord's own heart," is guilty afterwards of murder and adultery. Solomon, endowed by the Lord with all grace and wisdom, is led into idolatry by women. For the Son of God alone was it reserved to persevere to the last without sin. But what if a bishop, if a deacon, if a widow, if a virgin, if a doctor, if even a martyr, have fallen from the rule (of faith), will heresies on that account appear to possess the truth? Do we prove the faith by the persons, or the persons by the faith? No one is wise, no one is faithful, no one excels in dignity, but the Christian; and no one is a Christian but he who perseveres even to the end. . . . Let the chaff of a fickle faith fly off as much as it will at every blast of temptation, all the purer will be that heap of corn which shall be laid up in the garner of the Lord. Did not certain of the disciples turn back from the Lord Himself, when they were offended? Yet the rest did not therefore think that they must turn away from following Him, but because they knew that He was the Word of Life, and was come from God, they continued in His company to the very last, after He had gently inquired of them whether they also would go away. . . .

These [pagan philosophies] are "the doctrines" of men and "of demons" produced for itching ears of the spirit of this world's wisdom: this the Lord called "foolishness," and "chose the foolish things of the world" to confound even philosophy itself. For (philosophy) it is which is the material of the world's wisdom, the rash interpreter of the nature and the dispensation of God. Indeed heresies are themselves instigated by philosophy. . . . Writing to the Colossians, he [Paul] says, "See that no one beguile you through philosophy and vain deceit, after the tradition of men, and contrary to the wisdom of the Holy Ghost." He had been at Athens, and had in his interviews (with its philosophers) become acquainted with that human wisdom which pretends to know the truth, whilst it only corrupts it, and is itself divided into its own manifold heresies, by the variety of its mutually repugnant sects. What indeed has Athens to do with Jerusalem? What concord is there between the Academy and the Church? what between heretics and Christians? Our instruction comes from "the porch of Solomon," who had himself taught that "the Lord should be sought in simplicity of heart." Away with all attempts to produce a mottled Christianity of Stoic, Platonic, and dialectic composition! We want no curious disputation after possessing Christ Jesus, no inquisition after enjoying the gospel! With our faith, we desire no further belief. For this is our palmary faith, that there is nothing which we ought to believe besides. . . .

2. "SEEK, AND YOU SHALL FIND"

I come now to the point which (is urged both by our own brethren and by the heretics). Our brethren adduce it as a pretext for entering on curious inquiries, and the heretics insist on it for importing the scrupulosity (of their unbelief). It is written, they say, "Seek, and ye shall find." Let us remember at what time the Lord said this. I think it was at the very outset of His teaching, when there was still a doubt felt by all whether He were the Christ, and when even Peter had not yet declared Him to be the Son of God, and John (Baptist) had actually ceased to feel assurance about Him. With good reason, therefore, was it then said, "Seek, and ye shall find," when inquiry was still to be made of Him who was not yet become known. Besides, this was said in respect to the Jews. For it is to them that the whole matter of this reproof pertains, seeing that they had (a revelation) where they might seek Christ. "They have," says He, "Moses and Elias,"—in other words, the law and the prophets, which preach Christ; as also in another place He says plainly, "Search the Scriptures, in which ye expect (to find) salvation; for they testify of me;" which will be the meaning of "Seek, and ye shall find." For it is clear that the next words also apply to the Jews: "Knock, and it shall be opened unto you." The Jews had formerly been in covenant with God; but being afterwards cast off on account of their sins, they began to be without God. The Gentiles, on the contrary, had never been in covenant with God; they were only as "a drop from a bucket," and "as dust from the threshing floor," and were ever outside the door. Now, how shall he who was always outside knock at the place where he never was? What door does he know of, when he has passed through none, either by entrance or ejection? Is it not rather he who is aware that he once lived within and was thrust out, that (probably) found the door and knocked thereat? In like manner, "Ask, and ye shall receive," is suitably said to one who was aware from whom he ought to ask,—by whom also some promise had been given; that is to say, "the God of Abraham, of Isaac, and of Jacob." Now the Gentiles knew nothing either of Him, or of any of His promises. Therefore it was to Israel that He spake when He said, "I am not sent but to the lost sheep of the house of Israel. . . ."

Now the reason of this saying ["Seek, and ye shall find"] is comprised in three points: in the matter, in the time, in the limit. In the matter, so that you must consider *what it is* you have to seek; in the time, *when you* have to seek; in the limit, *how long.* What you have "to seek," then, is that which Christ has taught, (and you must go on seeking) of course for such times as you fail to find,—until indeed you find it. But you have succeeded in finding when you have believed. For you would not have believed if you had not found; as neither would you have sought except with a view to find. Your object, therefore, in seeking was to find; and your object in finding was to believe. All further delay for seeking and finding you have prevented by believing. The very fruit of your seeking has determined for you this limit. This boundary has He set for you Himself, who is unwilling that you should believe anything else than what He has taught or, therefore, even seek for it. If however, because so many other things have been taught by one and another, we are on that account bound to go on seeking, so long as we are able to find anything, we must (at that rate) be ever seeking, and never believe anything at all. For where shall be the end of seeking? Where the stop in believing? where the completion in finding? (Shall it be) with Marcion? But even Valentinus proposes (to us the) maxim, "Seek, and ye shall find. . . ." Thus I shall be nowhere, and still be encountering (that challenge), "Seek, and ye shall find," precisely as if I had no resting-place; as if (indeed) I had never found that which Christ has taught—that which ought to be sought, that which must needs be believed. . . .

But yet, if I have believed what I was bound to believe, and then afterwards think that there is something new to be sought after, I of course expect that there is something else to be found, although I should by no means entertain such expectation, unless it were because I either had not believed, although I apparently had become a believer, or else have ceased to believe. If I thus desert my faith, I am found to be a denier thereof. Once for all I would say, No man seeks, except him who either never possessed, or else has lost (what he sought). The old woman (in the Gospel) had lost one of her ten pieces of silver, and therefore she sought it; when, however, she found it, she ceased to look for it. The neighbor was without bread, and therefore he knocked; but as soon as the door was opened to him, and he received the bread, he discontinued knocking. The widow kept asking to be heard by the judge, because she was not admitted; but when her suit was heard, thenceforth she was silent. So that there is a limit both to seeking and to knocking, and to asking. "For to every one that asketh," says He, "it shall be given, and to him that knocketh it shall be opened, and by him that seeketh it shall be found." Away with the man who is ever seeking because he never finds; for he seeks there where nothing can be found. Away with him who is always knocking because it will never be opened to him; for he knocks where there is none (to open). Away with him who is always asking because he will never be heard; for he asks of one who does not hear. . . . Let our "seeking" therefore be in that which is our own, and from those who are our own, and concerning that which is our own—that, and only that, which can become an object of inquiry without impairing the rule of faith. . . .

3. THE RULE OF FAITH

Now, with regard to this rule of faith—that we may from this point acknowledge what it is which we defend—it is, you must know, that which prescribes the belief that there is one only God, and that He is none other than the Creator of the world, who produced all things out of nothing through His own Word, first of all sent forth; that this Word is called His Son, and, under the name of God, was seen in diverse manners by the patriarchs, heard at all times in the prophets, at last brought down by the Spirit and Power of the Father into the Virgin Mary, was made flesh in her womb, and, being born of her, went forth as Jesus Christ; thenceforth he preached the new law and the new promise of the kingdom of heaven, worked miracles; having been crucified, He rose again the third day; (then) having ascended into the heavens, He sat at the right hand of the Father; sent instead of Himself the Power of the Holy Ghost to lead such as believe; will come with glory to take the saints to the enjoyment of everlasting life and of the heavenly promises, and to condemn the wicked to everlasting fire, after the resurrection of both these classes shall have happened, together with the restoration of their flesh. This rule, as it will be proved, was taught by Christ, and raises amongst ourselves no other questions than those which heresies introduce, and which make men heretics.

. . . the apostle, forbids us to enter on "questions," or to lend our ears to newfangled statements, or to consort with a heretic "after the first and second admonition," not, (be it observed,) after discussion. Discussion he has inhibited in this way, by designating admonition as the purpose of dealing with a heretic, and the first one too, because he is not a Christian; in order that he might not, after the manner of a Christian, seem to require correction again and again, and "before two or three witnesses," seeing that he ought to be corrected, for the very reason that he is not to be disputed with; and in the next place, because a controversy over the Scriptures, clearly, produce no other effect than help to upset either the stomach or the brain. . . .

Our appeal, therefore, must not be made to the Scriptures; nor must controversy be admitted on points in which victory will either be impossible, or uncertain, or not certain enough. But even if a discussion from the Scriptures should not turn out in such a way as to place both sides on a par, (yet) the natural order of things would require that this point should be first proposed, which is now the only one which we must discuss: "With whom lies that very faith to which the Scriptures belong. From what and through whom, and when, and to whom, has been handed down that rule, by which men become Christians?" For wherever it shall be manifest that the true Christian rule and faith shall be, there will likewise be the true Scriptures and expositions thereof, and all the Christian traditions.

Christ Jesus our Lord . . . did, whilst He lived on earth, Himself declare what He was, what He had been, what the Father's will was which He was administering, what the duty of man was which He was prescribing; (and this declaration He made,) either openly to the people, or privately to His disciples, of whom He had chosen the twelve chief ones to be at His side, and whom He destined to be the teachers of the nations. Accordingly, after one of these had been struck off, He commanded the eleven others, on His departure to the Father, to "go and teach all nations, who were to be baptized into the Father, and into the Son, and into the Holy Ghost." . . . and after first bearing witness to the faith in Jesus Christ throughout Judaea, and founding churches (there), they next went forth into the world and preached the same doctrine of the same faith to the nations. They then in like manner founded churches, one after another, derived the tradition of the faith, and the seeds of the doctrine, and are every day deriving them, that they may become churches. Indeed, it is on this account only that they will be able to deem themselves apostolic, as being the offspring of apostolic churches. Every sort of thing must necessarily revert to its original for its classification. Therefore the churches, although they are so many and so great, comprise but the one primitive church, (founded) by the apostles, from which they all (spring). In this way all are primitive, and all are apostolic, whilst they are all proved to be one, in (unbroken) unity, by their peaceful communion, and title of brotherhood, and bond of hospitality,—privileges which no other rule directs than the one tradition of the selfsame mystery.

From this, therefore, do we draw up our rule. Since the Lord Jesus Christ sent the apostles to preach, (our rule is) that no others ought to be received as preachers than those whom Christ appointed; for "no man knoweth the Father save the Son, and he to whomsoever the Son will reveal Him." Nor does the Son seem to have revealed Him to any other than the apostles, whom He sent forth to preach—that, of course, which He revealed to them. Now, what that was which they preached—in other words, what it was which Christ revealed to them—can, as I must here likewise prescribe, properly be proved in no other way than by those very churches which the apostles founded in person, by declaring the gospel to them directly themselves, both *viva voce*, as the phrase is, and subsequently by their epistles. . . .

But if there be any (heresies) which are bold enough to plant themselves in the midst of the apostolic age, that they may thereby seem to have been handed down by the apostles, we can say: Let them produce the original records of their churches; let them unfold the roll of their bishops, running down in due succession from the beginning in such a manner that (that first bishop of their) bishop shall be able to show for his ordainer and predecessor some one of the apostles or of apostolic men,—a man, moreover, who continued stedfast with the apostles. For this is the manner in which the apostolic churches transmit their registers: as the church of Smyrna, which records that Polycarp was placed therein by John; as also the church of Rome, which makes Clement to have been ordained in like manner by Peter. In exactly the same way the other churches likewise exhibit (their several worthies), whom, as having been appointed to their episcopal places by apostles, they regard as transmitters of the apostolic seed. Let the heretics contrive something of the same kind. For after their blasphemy, what is there that is unlawful for them (to attempt)? But should they even effect the contrivance, they will not advance a step. For their very doctrine, after comparison with that of the apostles, will declare, by its own diversity and contrariety, that it had for its author neither an apostle nor an apostolic man; because, as the apostles would never have taught things which were self-contradictory, so the apostolic men would not have inculcated teaching different from the apostles, unless they who received their instruction from the apostles went and preached in a contrary manner. To this test, therefore will they be submitted for proof by those churches, who, although they derive not their founder from apostles or apostolic men (as being of much later date, for they are in fact being founded daily), yet, since they agree in the same faith, they are accounted as not less apostolic because they are akin in doctrine. Then let all the heresies, when challenged to these two tests by our apostolic church, offer their proof of how they deem themselves to be apostolic. But in truth they neither are so, nor are they able to prove themselves to be what they are not. Nor are they admitted to peaceful relations and communion by such churches as are in any way connected with apostles, inasmuch as they are in no sense themselves apostolic because of their diversity as to the mysteries of the faith. . . .

It has also been a subject of remark, how extremely frequent is the intercourse which heretics hold with magicians, with mountebanks, with astrologers, with philosophers; and the reason is, that they are men who devote themselves to curious questions. "Seek, and ye shall find," is everywhere in their minds. Thus, from the very nature of their conduct, may be estimated the quality of their faith. In their discipline we have an index of their doctrine. They say that God is not to be feared; therefore all things are in their view free and unchecked. Where, however is God not feared, except where He is not? Where God is not, there truth also is not. Where there is no truth, then, naturally enough, there is also such a discipline as theirs. But where God is, there exists "the fear of God which is the beginning of wisdom." Where the fear of God is, there is seriousness, an honourable and yet thoughtful diligence, as well as an anxious carefulness and a well-considered admission (to the sacred ministry) and a safely-guarded communion, and promotion after good service, and a scrupulous submission (to authority), and a devout attendance, and a modest gait, and a united church, and God in all things.

2

TITUS FLAVIUS CLEMENS (Clement of Alexandria) was born near the middle of the second century, probably in Athens. Under the tutelage of Greek teachers, Clement was introduced to the literary, philosophical, and cultural legacies of the Hellenistic world. The prominence of the mystery religions, especially the Mysteries of Eleusis, gave a character to his thought that was to be carried through his life's work —a mystical bent of mind, insistence on purity, and interest in gnostic philosophy. Somewhere about the age of twenty, Clement was converted to Christianity and noting the character of his early training, it is likely that his change was on intellectual rather than emotional grounds. Shortly after leaving Athens, he became interested in the catechetic school at Alexandria and its main teacher, Pantaenus. The school had been formed to train converts to Christianity and to instruct those who were inquiring about the substance of the Christian faith. Though the school was associated with the church, it was not under its formal control or authority. The cosmopolitan character of Alexandria must have contributed to Clement's willingness to settle down; its museum and library were among the best; its harbor made the town a center of commerce and thus attracted visitors from other cultural centers. Clement was associated with the school for twenty years, assuming Pantaenus' responsibilities about 189 when the founder of the school left for a missionary journey. Clement was forced to leave Alexandria about 202–203 during the severe persecution of Severus. The details of the remainder of his life are clouded, though it appears that he survived the persecution and resumed his travels, with his death occurring about 213.

By the second century, the time of Clement, Christianity

had become gradually organized with ecclesiastical order achieving some degree of stability and theological concerns beginning to assume central importance. Many schemes competed for the attention and allegiance of men. Misconceptions of Christian faith abounded; aberrations of Christianity were plentiful. Clement's vocation as a teacher is reflected throughout his writing in his *Protrepticus, Paedagogus,* and *The Stromata.* His task was to interpret doctrine in an attractive way to "inquirers," and in doing so he sought to apply the methods of intellectual endeavor current in the day. Clement did not demean philosophy, but regarded it as a proper, though incomplete, starting point for an understanding of the "gospel." The "true Gnostic" does not shun such labor, but eagerly and rightly adopts its tasks and concerns. But even the learned Greeks should remember that they derived much from Moses; the tradition of the Hebrew-Christian has antiquity on its side. Even the adherent of Christianity must be reminded, however, that wisdom from other sources is still wisdom and cannot be neglected or ignored because its auspices are other than those of the gospel. Gold *is* gold wherever you find it.

The selections from *The Stromata* that follow are part of a lengthy essay, made up of seven books and dealing with a variety of topics. "Stromata" has happily been translated as "carpet bags." The reader should note in these passages the task of a learned mind concerned for the intelligible interpretation of Christian faith and confronted by open and conflicting discussions of truth. Clement's position represents a recurring one in the history of Christian thought.

The Stromata*

CLEMENT OF ALEXANDRIA

1. PHILOSOPHY, THE HANDMAID OF THEOLOGY

The STROMATA will contain the truth mixed up in the dogmas of philosophy, or rather covered over and hidden, as the edible part of the nut

* From *The Ante-Nicene Fathers,* Vol. II, Bks. 1, 2, 5, 6, Alexander Roberts and James Donaldson, eds. Grand Rapids, Mich.: Wm. B. Eerdmans Publishing Co., 1951. [The titles for the sections are supplied by the editor.]

in the shell. For, in my opinion, it is fitting that the seeds of truth be kept for the husbandmen of faith, and no others. I am not oblivious of what is babbled by some, who in their ignorance are frightened at every noise, and say that we ought to occupy ourselves with what is most necessary, and which contains the faith; and that we should pass over what is beyond and superfluous, which wears out and detains us to no purpose, in things which conduce nothing to the great end. Others think that philosophy was introduced into life by an evil influence, for the ruin of men, by an evil inventor. But I shall show, throughout the whole of these *Stromata*, that evil has an evil nature, and can never turn out the producer of aught that is good; indicating that philosophy is in a sense a work of Divine Providence.

. . . philosophy does not ruin life by being the originator of false practices and base deeds, although some have calumniated it, though it be the clear image of truth, a divine gift to the Greeks; nor does it drag us away from the faith, as if we were bewitched by some delusive art, but rather, so to speak, by the use of an ampler circuit, obtains a common exercise demonstrative of the faith.

. . . before the advent of the Lord, philosophy was necessary to the Greeks for righteousness. And now it becomes conducive to piety; being a kind of preparatory training to those who attain to faith through demonstration. "For thy foot," it is said, "will not stumble, if thou refer what is good, whether belonging to the Greeks or to us, to Providence."[1] For God is the cause of all good things; but of some primarily, as of the Old and the New Testament; and of others by consequence, as philosophy. Perchance, too, philosophy was given to the Greeks directly and primarily, till the Lord should call the Greeks. For this was a schoolmaster to being "the Hellenic mind," as the law, the Hebrews, "to Christ." Philosophy, therefore, was a preparation, paving the way for him who is perfected in Christ. "Now, says Solomon, "defend wisdom, and it will exalt thee, and it will shield thee with a crown of pleasure." For when thou has strengthened wisdom with a cope by philosophy, and with right expenditure, thou wilt preserve it unassailable by sophists. The way of truth is therefore one. . . .

The Greek preparatory culture, therefore, with philosophy itself, is shown to have come down from God to men, not with a definite direction, but in the way in which showers fall down on the good land, and on the dunghill, and on the houses. And similarly both the grass and the wheat sprout; and the figs and any other reckless trees grow on sepulchres. And things that grow, appear as a type of truths. For they enjoy the same influence of the rain. But they have not the same grace as those which spring up in rich soil, inasmuch as they are withered or plucked up. And here we are aided by the parable of the sower, which the Lord interpreted. For the

[1] Proverbs iii, 23.

husbandman of the soil which is among men is one; He who from the beginning, from the foundation of the world, sowed nutritious seeds; He who in each age rained down the Lord, the Word. . . .

Some, who think themselves naturally gifted, do not wish to touch either philosophy or logic; nay more, they do not wish to learn natural science. They demand base faith alone, as if they wished, without bestowing any care on the vine, straightway to gather clusters from the first. Now the Lord is figuratively described as the vine, from which, with pains and the art of husbandry, according to the word, the fruit is to be gathered.

We must lop, dig, bind, and perform the other operations. The pruning-knife, I should think, and the pick-axe, and the other agricultural implements, are necessary for the culture of the vine, so that it may produce eatable fruit. And as in husbandry, so also in medicine: he has learned to purpose, who has practiced the various lessons, so as to be able to cultivate and to heal. So also here, I call him truly learned who brings everything to bear on the truth; so that, from geometry, and music, and grammar, and philosophy itself, culling what is useful, he guards the faith against assault. . . . And he who brings everything to bear on a right life, procuring examples from the Greeks and barbarians, this man is an experienced searcher after truth, and in reality a man of much counsel, like the touchstone (that is, the Lydian) which is believed to possess the power of distinguishing the spurious from the genuine gold. . . .

As many men drawing down the ship, cannot be called many causes, but one cause consisting of many;—for each individual by himself is not the cause of the ship being drawn, but along with the rest;—so also philosophy, being the search for truth, contributes to the comprehension of truth; not as being the cause of comprehension, but a cause along with other things, and cooperator; perhaps also a joint cause. . . . But if philosophy contributes remotely to the discovery of truth, by reaching, by diverse essays, after the knowledge which touches close on the truth, the knowledge possessed by us, it aids him who aims at grasping it, in accordance with the Word, to apprehend knowledge. But the Hellenic truth is distinct from that held by us (although it has got the same name), both in respect of extent of knowledge, certainly of demonstration, divine power, and the like. For we are taught of God, being instructed in the truly "sacred letters" by the Son of God. Whence those, to whom we refer, influence souls not in the way we do, but by different teaching. And if, for the sake of those who are fond of fault-finding, we must draw a distinction, by saying that philosophy is a concurrent and cooperating cause of true apprehension, being the search for truth, then we shall avow it to be a preparatory training for the enlightened man. . . . Since almost all of us, without training in arts and sciences, and the Hellenic philosophy, and some even without learning at all, through the influence of a philosophy divine and barbarous, and by power, have through faith received the Word concerning God, trained by self-operating wisdom. But that which acts in conjunction with something else, being of itself incapable of operating by itself, we describe as cooperating and concausing, and say that it becomes a cause only in virtue of its being a joint-cause, and receives the name of cause only in respect of its concurring with something else, but that it cannot by itself produce the right effect . . . the truth which is according to faith is as necessary for life as bread; while the preparatory discipline is like sauce and sweetmeats.

2. THE WAY OF FAITH

. . . faith, which the Greeks disparage, deeming it futile and barbarous, is a voluntary preconception, the assent of piety—"the subject of things hoped for, the evidence of things not seen," according to the divine apostle. . . . If then it be choice, being desirous of something, the desire is in this instance intellectual. And since choice is the beginning of action, faith is discovered to be the beginning of action, being the foundation of rational choice in the case of any one who exhibits to himself the previous demonstration through faith. Voluntarily to follow what is useful, is the first principle of understanding. Unswerving choice, then, gives considerable momentum in the direction of knowledge. The exercise of faith directly becomes knowledge, reposing on a sure foundation. Knowledge, accordingly, is defined by the sons of the philosophers as a habit, which cannot be overthrown by reason. Is there any other true condition such as this, except piety, of which alone the Word is teacher? I think not.

. . . faith is something superior to knowledge, and is its criterion. Conjecture, which is only a feeble supposition, counterfeits faith; as the flatterer counterfeits a friend, and the wolf the dog. And as the workman sees that by learning certain things he becomes an artificer, and the helmsman by being instructed in the art will be able to steer; he does not regard the mere wishing to become excellent and good enough, but he must learn it by the exercise of obedience. But to obey the Word, whom we call Instructor, is to believe Him, going against Him in nothing. For how can we take up a position of hostility to God? Knowledge, accordingly, is characterized by faith; and faith, by a kind of divine mutual and reciprocal correspondence, becomes characterized by knowledge. . . .

How can one, without a preconceived idea of what he is aiming after, learn about that which is the subject of his investigation? He, again, who has learned has already turned his preconception into comprehension. And if he who learns, learns not without a preconceived idea which takes in what is expressed, that man has ears to hear the truth. And happy is the man that speaks to the ears of those who hear; as happy certainly also is he who is a child of obedience. Now to hear is to understand. If then, faith is nothing else than a preconception of the mind in regard to what is the subject of discourse, and obedience is so called, and understanding and persuasion; no one shall learn aught without faith, since no one (learns aught) without preconception. . . .

And He who communicated to us being and life, has communicated to us also reason, wishing us to live rationally and rightly. For the Word of the Father of the universe is not the uttered word, but the wisdom and most manifest kindness of God, and His power too, which is almighty and truly divine, and not incapable of being conceived by those who do not confess—the all-potent will. But since some are unbelieving, and some are disputatious, all do not attain to the perfection of the good. For neither is it possible to attain it without the exercise of free choice; nor does the whole depend on our own purpose; as, for example, what is destined to happen. "For by grace we are saved:" not, indeed, without good works; but we must, by being formed for what is good, acquire an inclination for it. And we must possess the healthy mind which is fixed on the pursuit of the good; in order to which we have the greatest need of divine grace, and of right teaching, and of holy susceptibility, and of the drawing of the Father to Him. For, bound in this earthly body, we apprehend the objects of sense by means of the body; but we grasp intellectual objects by means of the logical faculty itself. But if one expects to apprehend all things by the senses, he has fallen far from the truth. Spiritually, therefore, the apostle writes respecting the knowledge of God, "For now we see as through a glass, but then face to face." For the vision of truth is given but to few. Accordingly, Plato says in the *Epinomis*, "I do not say that it is possible for all to be blessed and happy; only a few. Whilst we live, I pronounce this to be the case. But there is a good hope that after death I shall attain all." To the same effect is what we find in Moses: "No man shall see My face and live." For it is evident that no one during the period of life has been able to apprehend God clearly. But, "the pure in heart shall see God," when they arrive at the final perfection. For since the soul became too enfeebled for the apprehension of realities, we needed a divine teacher. The Saviour is sent down—a teacher and leader in the acquisition of the good—the secret and sacred token of the great Providence. "Where, then, is the scribe? where is the searcher of this world? Hath not God made foolish the wisdom of this world?" it is said. And again, "I will destroy the wisdom of the wise, and bring to nothing the understanding of the prudent," plainly of those wise in their own eyes, and disputatious. . . . And on learning the way of truth, let us walk on the right way, without turning till we attain to what we desire. . . .

This discourse respecting God is most difficult to handle. For since the first principle of everything is difficult to find out, the absolutely first and oldest principle, which is the cause of all other things being and having been, is difficult to exhibit. For how can that be expressed which is neither genus, nor difference, nor species, nor individual, nor number; nay more, is neither an event, nor that to which an event happens? No one can rightly express Him wholly. For on account of His greatness He is ranked as the All, and is the Father of the universe. Nor are any parts to be predicated of Him. For the One is indivisible; wherefore also it is infinite, not considered with reference to inscrutability, but with reference to its being without dimensions, and not having a limit. And therefore it is without form and name. And if we name it, we do not do so properly, terming it either the One, or the Good, or Mind, or Absolute Being, or Father, or God, or Creator, or Lord. We speak not as supplying His name; but for want, we use good names, in order that the mind may have these as points of support, so as not to err in other respects. For each one by itself does not express God; but all together are indicative of the power of the Omnipotent. For predicates are expressed either from what belongs to things themselves, or from their mutual relation. But none of these are admissible in reference to God. Nor any more is He apprehended by the science of demonstration. For it depends on primary and better known principles. But there is nothing antecedent to the Unbegotten.

It remains that we understand, then, the Unknown, by divine grace, and by the word alone that proceeds from Him; as Luke in the Acts of the Apostles relates that Paul said, "Men of Athens, I perceive that in all things ye are too superstitious. For in walking about, and beholding the objects of your worship, I found an altar on which was inscribed, "To the Unknown God. Whom therefore ye ignorantly worship, Him declare I unto you. . . ."

3. THE TRUE GNOSTIC

As we have long ago pointed out, what we propose as our subject is not the discipline which obtains in each sect, but that which is really philosophy, strictly systematic Wisdom, which furnishes acquaintance with the things which pertain to life. And we define Wisdom to be certain knowledge, being a sure and irrefragable apprehension of things divine and human, comprehending the present, past and future, which the Lord hath taught us, both by His advent and by the prophets. . . .

Now those are called philosophers, among us, who love Wisdom, the Creator and Teacher of all things, that is, the knowledge of the Son of God; and among the Greeks those who undertake arguments on virtue. Philosophy, then, consists of such dogmas found in each sect (I mean those of philosophy) as cannot be impugned, with a corresponding life, collected into one selection; and these, stolen from the Barbarian God-given grace, have been adorned by Greek speech. For some they have borrowed, and others they have misunderstood. And in the case of others, what they have spoken, in consequence of being moved, they have not yet perfectly worked out; and others by human conjecture and reasoning, in which also they stumble. And they think that they have hit the truth perfectly; but as we understand them, only partially. They know, then, nothing more than this world. And it is just like geometry, which treats of measures and magnitudes and forms, by delineation on plane-surfaces; and just as painting appears to take in the whole field of view in the scenes represented. But it gives a false description of the view, according to the rules of the art, employing the signs that result from the incidents of the lines of vision. By this means, the higher and lower points in the view, and those between, are preserved; and some objects seem to appear in the foreground, and others in the background, and others to appear in some other way, on the smooth and level surface. So also the philosophers copy the truth, after the manner of painting. And always in the case of each one of them, their self-love is the cause of all their mistakes. Wherefore one ought not, in the desire for the glory that terminates in men, to be animated by self-love; but loving God, to become really holy with wisdom.

For Paul too, in the Epistles, plainly does not disparage philosophy; but deems it unworthy of the man who has attained to the elevation of the Gnostic, any more to go back to the Hellenic "phliosophy," figuratively calling it "the rudiments of this world," as being most rudimentary, and a preparatory training for the truth. Wherefore also, writing to the Hebrews, who were declining again from faith to the law, he says, "Have ye not need again of one to teach you which are the first principles of the oracles of God, and are become such as have need of milk, and not of strong meat?" So also to the Colossians, who were Greek converts, "Beware lest any man spoil you by philosophy and vain deceit, after the tradition of men, after the rudiments of this world, and not after Christ,"—enticing them again to return to philosophy, the elementary doctrine.

And should one say that it was through human understanding that philosophy was discovered by the Greeks, still I find the Scriptures saying that understanding is sent by God. . . .

Philosophy is not then false . . . but what is said must be looked at, to see if it keep by the truth. And in general terms we shall not err in alleging that all things necessary and profitable for life came to us from God, and that philosophy more especially was given to the Greeks, as a covenant peculiar to them—being as it is, a stepping-stone to the philosophy which is according to Christ—although those who applied themselves to the philosophy of the Greeks shut their ears voluntarily to the truth. . . .

For to him knowledge is the principle thing. Consequently, therefore, he applies to the subjects that are a training for knowledge, taking from each branch of study its contribution to the truth. Prosecuting, then, the proportion of harmonies in music; and in arithmetic noting the increasing and decreasing of numbers, and their relations to one another, and how the most of things fall under some proportion of numbers; studying geometry which is abstract essence, he perceives a continuous distance, and an immutable essence which is different from these bodies. And by astronomy, again, raised from the earth in his mind, he is elevated along with heaven, and will revolve with its revolution; studying ever divine things, and their harmony with each other; from which Abraham starting, ascended to the knowledge of Him who created them. Further, the Gnostic will avail himself of dialectics, fixing on the distinction of genera into species, and will master the distinction of existences, will he come to what are primary and simple. . . .

Though men's actions are ten thousand in number, the sources of all sin are but two, ignorance and inability. And both depend on ourselves; inasmuch as we will not learn, nor, on the other hand, restrain lust. And of these, the one is that, in consequence of which people do not judge well, and the other that, in consequence of which they cannot comply with right judgments. For neither will one who is deluded in his mind be able to act rightly, though perfectly able to do what he knows; nor, though capable of judging what is requisite, will he keep himself free of blame, if destitute of power in action. Consequently, then, there are assigned two kinds of correction applicable to both kinds of sin: for the one, knowledge and clear demonstration from the testimony of the scriptures; and for the other, the training according to the Word, which is regulated by the discipline of faith and fear. And both develop into perfect love. For the end of the Gnostic here is, in my judgment, twofold,—partly scientific contemplation, partly action. . . .

Our Gnostic then alone, having grown old in the scriptures, and maintaining apostolic and ecclesiastic orthodoxy in doctrines, lives most correctly in accordance with the Gospel, and discovers the proofs, for which he may have made search (sent forth as he is by the Lord), from the law and the prophets. For the life of the Gnostic, in my view, is nothing but deeds and words corresponding to the tradition of the Lord.

3 ORIGEN (185–254) STANDS OUT as one of the major theologians of the early church. At the age of eighteen he became the head of the catechetical school in Alexandria, the successor of Clement (150–213?). He was forced to leave Alexandria for Caesarea (Palestine) during a severe persecution in 215. His ordination in 230 by the bishops of

Caesarea and Jerusalem, while still associated with the Alexandria Church, resulted in his condemnation and banishment by the Bishop of Alexandria, Demetrius. From 230 until his death in 254, probably as a result of cruelties inflicted upon him during the Decian persecution in 250, he lived and wrote in Caesarea and enjoyed the respect of Eastern churchmen.

Many noteworthy treatises have come from his pen: the *Hexapla*, a comparative edition of the Bible; *De Principiis*, a systematic statement of Christian faith; *Contra Celsum*; *De Oratione*; plus commentaries on biblical books.

In the following selection from Book IV of *De Principiis* we have Origen's interpretation of scripture. His use of the allegorical method allowed considerable freedom in exegesis.[1]

De Principiis[*]

[On the Interpretation of Scripture]

ORIGEN

The way . . . in which we ought to deal with the scriptures, and extract from them their meaning, is the following, which has been ascertained from the scriptures themselves. By Solomon in the Proverbs we find some such rule as this enjoined respecting the divine doctrines of scripture: "And do thou portray them in a threefold manner, in counsel and knowledge, to answer words of truth to them who propose them to thee." The individual ought, then, to portray the ideas of holy Scripture in a threefold manner upon his own soul; in order that the simple man may be edified by the "flesh," as it were, of the scripture, for so we name the obvious sense; while he who has ascended a certain way (may be edified) by the "soul," as it were. The perfect man, again, and he who resembles those spoken of by the apostle, when he says, "We speak wisdom among them that are perfect, but not the wisdom of the world, nor of the rulers of this world, who come to nought; but we speak the wisdom of God in a

* From *The Ante-Nicene Fathers*, Vol. IV, Alexander Roberts and James Donaldson, eds. Grand Rapids, Mich.: Wm. B. Eerdmans Publishing Co., 1951.

[1] See also *De Principiis*, Selection 14.

mystery, the hidden wisdom, which God hath ordained before the ages, unto our glory," (may receive edification) from the spiritual law, which has a shadow of good things to come. For as man consists of body, and soul, and spirit, so in the same way does scripture, which has been arranged to be given by God for the salvation of men. And therefore we deduce this also from a book which is despised by some—*The Shepherd*—in respect of the command given to Hermas to write two books, and after so doing to announce to the presbyters of the Church what he had learned from the Spirit. The words are as follows: "You will write two books, and give one to Clement, and one to Grapte. And Grapte shall admonish the widows and the orphans, and Clement will send to the cities abroad, while you will announce to the presbyters of the Church." Now Grapte, who admonishes the widows and the orphans, is the mere letter (of scripture), which admonishes those who are yet children in soul, and not able to call God their Father, and who are on that account styled orphans,—admonishing, moreover, those who no longer have an unlawful bridegroom, but who remain widows, because they have not yet become worthy of the (heavenly) Bridegroom; while Clement, who is already beyond the letter, is said to send what is written to the cities abroad, as if we were to call these the "souls," who are above (the influence of) bodily (affections) and degraded ideas,— the disciple of the Spirit himself being enjoined to make known, no longer by letters, but by living words, to the presbyters of the whole Church of God, who have become grey through wisdom.

But as there are certain passages of scripture which do not at all contain the "corporeal" sense, as we shall show in the following (paragraphs), there are also places where we must seek only for the "soul," as it were, and "spirit" of scripture. And perhaps on this account the water-vessels containing two or three firkins a-piece are said to lie for the purification of the Jews, as we read in the Gospel according to John: the expression darkly intimating, with respect to those who (are called) by the apostle "Jews" secretly, that they are purified by the word of scripture, receiving sometimes two firkins, i.e., so to speak, the "psychical" and "spiritual" sense; and sometimes three firkins, since some have, in addition to those already mentioned, also the "corporeal" sense, which is capable of (producing) edification. And six water-vessels are reasonably (appropriate) to those who are purified in the world, which was made in six days—the perfect number. That the first "sense," then, is profitable in this respect, that it is capable of imparting edification, is testified by the multitudes of genuine and simple believers; while of that interpretation which is referred back to the "soul," there is an illustration in Paul's first Epistle to the Corinthians. The expression is, "Thou shalt not muzzle the mouth of the ox that treadeth out the corn"; to which he adds, "Doth God take care of oxen? or saith He it altogether for our sakes? For our sakes, no doubt, this was written: that he that plougheth should plough in hope, and that he who thresheth, in hope of partaking." And there are numerous interpretations adapted to the multitude which are in circulation, and which edify those who are unable to understand profounder meanings, and which have somewhat the same character.

But the interpretation is "spiritual," when one is able to show of what heavenly things the Jews "according to the flesh" served as an example and a shadow, and of what future blessings the law contains a shadow. And, generally, we must investigate, according to the apostolic promise, "the wisdom in a mystery, the hidden wisdom which God ordained before the world for the glory" of the just, which "none of the princes of this world knew." And the same apostle says somewhere, after referring to certain events mentioned as occurring in Exodus and Numbers, "that these things happened to them figuratively, but that they were written on our account, on whom the ends of the world are come." And he gives an opportunity for ascertaining of what things these were patterns, when he says: "For they drank of the spiritual Rock that followed them, and that Rock was Christ." And in another Epistle, when sketching the various matters relating to the tabernacle, he used the words: "Thou shalt make everything according to the pattern showed thee in the mount." Moreover, in the Epistle to the Galatians, as if upbraiding those who think that they read the law, and yet do not understand it, judging that those do not understand it who do not reflect that allegories are contained under what is written, he says: "Tell me, ye that desire to be under the law, do ye not hear the law? For it is written, Abraham had two sons; the one by the bond-maid, the other by the free woman. But he who was by the bond-maid was born according to the flesh; but he of the free woman was by promise. Which things are an allegory: for these are the two covenants," and so on. Now we must carefully observe each word employed by him. He says: "Ye who desire to be under the law," not "Ye that are under the law;" and, "Do ye not hear the law?"—"hearing" being understood to mean "comprehending" and "knowing." And in the Epistle to the Colossians, briefly abridging the meaning of the whole legislation, he says: "Let no man therefore judge you in meat, or in drink, or in respect of a festival, or of a new moon, or of Sabbaths, which are a shadow of things to come." Moreover, in the Epistle to the Hebrews, discoursing of those who belong to the circumcision, he writes: "who serve for an ensample and shadow of heavenly things." Now it is probable that, from these illustrations, those will entertain no doubt with respect to the five books of Moses, who have once given in their adhesion to the apostle, as divinely inspired; but do you wish to know, with regard to the rest of the history, if it also happened as a pattern? We must note, then, the expression in the Epistle to the Romans, "I have left to myself seven thousand men, who have not bowed the knee to Baal," quoted from the third book of Kings, which Paul has understood as equivalent (in meaning) to those who are Israelites according to election, because not only were the Gentiles benefited by the advent of Christ, but also certain of the race of God.

This being the state of the case, we have to sketch what seem to us to be the marks of the (true) understanding of scriptures. And, in the first place, this must be pointed out, that the object of the Spirit, which by the providence of God, through the Word who was in the beginning with God, illuminated the ministers of truth, the prophets and apostles, was especially (the communication) of ineffable mysteries regarding the affairs of men (now by men I mean those souls that make use of bodies), in order that he who is capable of instruction may by investigation, and by devoting himself to the study of the profundities of meaning contained in the words, become a participator of all the doctrines of his counsel. And among those matters which relate to souls (who cannot otherwise obtain perfection apart from the rich and wise truth of God), the (doctrines) belonging to God and His only-begotten Son are necessarily laid down as primary, viz., of what nature He is, and in what manner He is the Son of God, and what are the causes of His descending even to (the assumption of) human flesh, and of complete humanity; and what, also, is the operation of this (Son), and upon whom and when exercised. And it was necessary also that the subject of kindred beings, and other rational creatures, both those who are divine and those who have fallen from blessedness, together with the reasons of their fall, should be contained in the divine teaching; and also that of the diversities of souls, and of the origin of these diversities, and of the nature of the world, and the cause of its existence. We must learn also the origin of the great and terrible wickedness which overspreads the earth, and whether it is confined to this earth only, or prevails elsewhere. Now, while these and similar objects were present to the Spirit, who enlightened the souls of the holy ministers of the truth, there was a second object, for the sake of those who were unable to endure the fatigue of investigating matters so important, viz., to conceal the doctrine relating to the previously mentioned subjects, in expressions containing a narrative which conveyed an announcement regarding the things of the visible creation, the creation of man, and the successive descendants of the first men until they became numerous; and other histories relating the acts of just men, and the sins occasionally committed by these same men as being human beings, and the wicked deeds, both of unchastity and vice, committed by sinful and ungodly men. And what is most remarkable, by the history of wars, and of the victors, and the vanquished, certain mysteries are indicated to those who are able to test these statements. And more wonderful still, the laws of truth are predicted by the written legislation;—all these being described in a connected series, with a power which is truly in keeping with the wisdom of God. For it was intended that the covering also of the spiritual truths—I mean the "bodily" part of scripture—should not be without profit in many cases, but should be capable of improving the multitude, according to their capacity.

But since, if the usefulness of the legislation, and the sequence and beauty of the history, were universally evident of itself, we should not believe that any other thing could be understood in the scriptures save what was obvious, the word of God has arranged that certain stumbling-blocks, as it were, and offences, and impossibilities, should be introduced into the midst of the law and the history, in order that we may not, through being drawn away in all directions by the merely attractive nature of the language, either altogether fall away from the (true) doctrines, as learning nothing worthy of God, or, by not departing from the letter, come to the knowledge of nothing more divine. And this also we must know, that the principal aim being to announce the "spiritual" connection in those things that are done, and that ought to be done, where the Word found that things done according to the history could be adapted to these mystical senses, He made use of them, concealing from the multitude the deeper meaning; but where, in the narrative of the development of super-sensual things, there did not follow the performance of those certain events, which was already indicated by the mystical meaning, the scripture interwove in the history (the account of) some event that did not take place, sometimes what could not have happened; sometimes what could, but did not. And sometimes a few words are interpolated which are not true in their literal acceptation, and sometimes a larger number. And a similar practice also is to be noticed with regard to the legislation, in which is often to be found what is useful in itself, and appropriate to the times of the legislation; and sometimes also what does not appear to be of utility; and at other times impossibilities are recorded for the sake of the more skilful and inquisitive, in order that they may give themselves to the toil of investigating what is written, and thus attain to a becoming conviction of the manner in which a meaning worthy of God must be sought out in such subjects.

It was not only, however, with the (scriptures composed) before the advent (of Christ) that the Spirit thus dealt; but as being the same Spirit, and (proceeding) from the one God, He did the same thing both with the evangelists and the apostles,—as even these do not contain throughout a pure history of events, which are interwoven indeed according to the letter, but which did not actually occur. Nor even do the law and the command-ments wholly convey what is agreeable to reason. For who that has under-standing will suppose that the first, and second, and third day, and the evening and the morning, existed without a sun, and moon, and stars? and that the first day was, as it were, also without a sky? And who is so foolish as to suppose that God, after the manner of a husbandman, planted a para-dise in Eden, towards the east, and placed in it a tree of life, visible and palpable, so that one tasting of the fruit by the bodily teeth obtained life? and again, that one was a partaker of good and evil by masticating what was taken from the tree? And if God is said to walk in the paradise in the evening, and Adam to hide himself under a tree, I do not suppose that any one doubts that these things figuratively indicate certain mysteries, the history having taken place in appearance, and not literally. Cain also, when going forth from the presence of God, certainly appears to thoughtful men as likely to lead the reader to inquire what is the presence of God, and what is the meaning of going out from Him. And what need is there to say more, since those who are not altogether blind can collect countless instances of a similar kind recorded as having occurred, but which did not literally take place? Nay, the Gospels themselves are filled with the same kind of narratives; e.g., the devil leading Jesus up into a high mountain, in order to show him from thence the kingdoms of the whole world, and the glory of them. For who is there among those who do not read such accounts carelessly, that would not condemn those who think that with the eye of the body—which requires a lofty height in order that the parts lying (immediately) under and adjacent may be seen—the kingdoms of the Persians, and Scythians, and Indians, and Parthians, were beheld, and the manner in which their princes are glorified among men? And the attentive reader may notice in the Gospels innumerable other passages like these, so that he will be convinced that in the histories that are literally recorded, circumstances that did not occur are inserted.

And if we come to the legislation of Moses, many of the laws manifest the irrationality, and others the impossibility, of their literal observance. The irrationality (in this), that the people are forbidden to eat vultures, although no one even in the direst famines was (ever) driven by want to have recourse to this bird; and that children eight days old, which are uncircumcised, are ordered to be exterminated from among their people, it being necessary, if the law were to be carried out at all literally with regard to these, that their fathers, or those with whom they are brought up, should be commanded to be put to death. Now the scripture says: "Every male that is uncircumcised, who shall not be circumcised on the eighth day, shall be cut off from among his people." And if you wish to see impossibilities contained in the legislation, let us observe that the goat-stag is one of those animals that cannot exist, and yet Moses commands us to offer it as being a clean beast; whereas a griffin, which is not recorded ever to have been subdued by man, the lawgiver forbids to be eaten. Nay, he who carefully considers (the famous injunction relating to) the Sabbath, "Ye shall sit each one in your dwellings: let no one go out from his place on the seventh day," will deem it impossible to be literally observed: for no living being is able to sit throughout a whole day, and remain without moving from a sitting position. And therefore those who belong to the circumcision, and all who desire that no meaning should be exhibited, save the literal one, do not investigate at all such subjects as those of the goat-stag and griffin and vulture, but indulge in foolish talk on certain points, multiplying words and adducing tasteless traditions; as, for example, with regard to the Sabbath, saying that two thousand cubits is each one's limit. Others, again, among whom is Dositheus the Samaritan, condemning such an interpretation, think that in the position in which a man is found on the Sabbath-day, he is to remain until evening. Moreover, the not carrying of a burden on the Sabbath-day is an impossibility; and therefore the Jewish teachers have fallen into countless absurdities, saying that a shoe of such a kind was a burden, but not one of another kind; and that a sandal which had nails was a burden, but not one that was without them; and in like manner what was borne on one shoulder (was a load), but not that which was carried on both. . . .

All these statements have been made by us, in order to show that the design of that divine power which gave us the sacred scriptures is, that we should not receive what is presented by the letter alone (such things being sometimes not true in their literal acceptation, but absurd and impossible), but that certain things have been introduced into the actual history and into the legislation that are useful in their literal sense.

. . . the exact reader must, in obedience to the Saviour's injunction to "search the scriptures," carefully ascertain in how far the literal meaning is true, and in how far impossible; and so far as he can, trace out, by means of similar statements, the meaning everywhere scattered through scripture of that which cannot be understood in a literal signification.

Since, therefore, as will be clear to those who read, the connection taken literally is impossible, while the sense preferred is not impossible, but even the true one, it must be our object to grasp the whole meaning, which connects the account of what is literally impossible in an intelligible manner with what is not only not impossible, but also historically true, and which is allegorically understood, in respect of its not having literally occurred. For, with respect to Holy Scripture, our opinion is that the whole of it has a "spiritual," but not the whole a "bodily" meaning, because the bodily meaning is in many places proved to be impossible.

AUGUSTINE (354–430), BISHOP OF HIPPO (in Africa), has had seminal influence on many different problems in Christian theology. He was baptised in 387 and ordained a priest in 391, after having been involved in his earlier years in

Manichaeism and neo-Platonism. His *Confessions* are indispensable for understanding his personal pilgrimage.

The first selection is a letter addressed to Consentius, about whom little is now known. In a letter to Augustine, Consentius had asked him to discuss the Trinity and to assist in making it understandable to human reason. Augustine's letter in reply offers a concise statement of his approach to theological issues; it was written between 408 and 412 A.D.

The second selection is from Book XI of *The City of God*, the section of that major work where Augustine begins to describe the "earthly and heavenly cities."[1]

Letter 120 *

AUGUSTINE

God forbid that He should hate in us that faculty by which He made us superior to all other living beings. Therefore, we must refuse so to believe as not to receive or seek a reason for our belief, since we could not believe at all if we did not have rational souls. So, then, in some points that bear on the doctrine of salvation, which we are not yet able to grasp by reason —but we shall be able to sometime—let faith precede reason, and let the heart be cleansed by faith so as to receive and bear the great light of reason; this is indeed reasonable. Therefore the Prophet said with reason: "If you will not believe, you will not understand"; thereby he undoubtedly made a distinction between these two things and advised us to believe first so as to be able to understand whatever we believe. It is, then, a reasonable requirement that faith precede reason, for, if this requirement is not reasonable, then it is contrary to reason, which God forbid. But, if it is reasonable that faith precede a certain great reason which cannot yet be grasped, there is no doubt that, however slight the reason which proves this, it does precede faith.

That is why the Apostle warns us that we ought to be ready to give an answer to anyone who asks us a reason for our faith and hope, since, if

* From *The Fathers of the Church*, Vol. XVIII, *St. Augustine Letters*, Vol. II, tr. by Sister Wilfred Parsons. Washington, D.C.: The Catholic University of America Press, 1953.

1 See also *On The Trinity*, Selection 34A; *On The Gospel of John*, Selection 34B; *Letter 217*, Selection 39A; *A Treatise on Rebuke and Grace*, Selection 39B; *Against The Pelagians*, Selection 39C; *On Baptism*, Selection 55A; *The City of God*, Selection 55B.

an unbeliever asks me a reason for my faith and hope, and I see that he cannot accept it until he believes, I give him that very reason, so that he may see how absurd it is for him to ask a reason for things which he cannot grasp until he believes. But, if a believer asks a reason that he may understand what he believes, his mental ability is to be considered and then, when the reason for his faith has been given according to it, he may draw as much understanding as he can, more if he is capable of more, less if he is less capable, but with the provision that, to the extent that he attains to the fullness and perfection of knowledge, he does not withdraw from the way of faith. On this point the Apostle says: "And if in anything you be otherwise minded, this also God will reveal to you; nevertheless whereunto we are come, let us walk in the same." If, then, we are faithful now, we shall attain to the way of faith, and, if we do not leave it, we shall unfailingly come not only to a great understanding of incorporeal and unchanging things, such as cannot be reached by all in this life, but even to the height of contemplation, which the Apostle calls "face to face." For, some have very little knowledge, yet by walking with great perseverance in the way of faith they attain to that most blessed contemplation; whereas others, although they know even now what the invisible, unchanging, and incorporeal nature is, and what way leads to the abode of such happiness, cannot attain to it because the way, which is Christ crucified, seems foolish to them, and they refuse to withdraw to the innermost chamber of that repose by whose light their mind is stunned as by a far-shining radiance.

There are, however, some things which we are not able to believe when we hear them, because we do not apply our faith to them, yet when a reason for them is given, we recognize it as true. Thus, none of the miracles of God is believed by infidels because the reason for them is not evident; as a matter of fact, there are things for which no reason can be given, but that does not mean there is none, for God made nothing in the universe without reason. Of certain of His wonderful works it is better sometimes for the reason to be hidden; otherwise, our minds, weighed down with weariness, might hold them cheap if we had knowledge of their causes. There are others, and they are many, who are more impressed by wonder at the objects than by a knowledge of their causes, and, when miracles cease to be wonderful, they have to be roused to faith in the invisible by visible wonders. Thus they may be cleansed and purified by charity, and may return to the point they had left when they ceased to wonder, through familiarity with truth. In the theatre, men wonder at the rope-dancer, and take pleasure in the musicians: in the former case, the difficulty of the act rouses awe; in the latter, pleasure sustains and nourishes them.

I should like to say these things to rouse your faith to a love of understanding to which true reason leads the mind and for which faith prepares it. For, that reasoning which argues about the Trinity, which is God, that the Son is not co-eternal with the Father, or that He is of another substance, and that the Holy Spirit is unlike Him in some way and therefore inferior, and that reasoning which claims that the Father and the Son are of one and the same substance, but that the Holy Spirit is of another, are to be avoided and detested, not because they are reasoning but because they are false reasoning; for, if the reasoning were true, it would surely not go wrong. Therefore, just as you ought not to give up all speech because there is false speech, so you ought not to turn against all reasoning because there is false reasoning. I would say the same of wisdom: that wisdom is not to be avoided because there is also false wisdom, to which Christ crucified is foolishness, though He is "the power of God and the wisdom of God," and, therefore, "by the foolishness of our preaching it pleased God to save them that believe; for the foolishness of God is wiser than men." This truth could not be made acceptable to some of the philosophers and orators who followed a way that was not the true one, but an imitation of the true one, and who deceived themselves and others on it. But by others it could be accepted, and to those who could accept it Christ crucified was neither a stumbling-block nor foolishness: among them are those that are called, both Jews and Greeks, "to whom he is the power of God and the wisdom of God." In this way, that is, in the faith of Christ crucified, those who were able by the grace of God to embrace His upright code of conduct, even though they are called Philosophers or orators, certainly confessed with humble piety that the fishermen who preceded them were far superior to themselves, both in the steadfast strength of their belief, and in the unerring truth of their understanding. For, when they had learned that the foolish and weak things of the world had been chosen for this purpose that the wise and strong things might be confounded, and when they understood that their own wisdom was folly and their strength weakness, they were confounded for their own salvation and made foolish and weak, that by the foolish and weak thing of God, which is wiser and stronger than men, they might be chosen among the foolish and weak things and might become truly wise and effectually strong.

But, the devout believer is ashamed of any but the truest reasoning; therefore, let us not be slow to overthrow a sort of idolatry which the frailty of human thought is prone to set up in our hearts, in consequence of our customary dealing with visible things, and let us not make bold to believe that the Trinity, which we worship as invisible, incorporeal, and unchangeable, is like three great living objects, which though immense and beautiful, are bounded by the proper limits of their own spaces, touching each other because they are ranged close together, either with one of them in the middle, so as to separate the two joined to it on either side, or in the fashion of a triangle, with each one touching the other two, and none separated from any. Let us not believe, either, that the huge mass of these three great Persons, which are limited on however large a scale from above and below and round about, have a single godhead as if it were a fourth person, not like any one of them, whereas it is common to all as the divinity of all and in all, and wholly in each one; through which sole Godhead the same Trinity is said to be God. And we must not believe that His three Persons are nowhere but in heaven, while that Divinity is not in any one place but is present everywhere, and for that reason it would be right to say that God is in heaven and on earth, because of the Godhead which is everywhere and is common to the Three, but it would not be right to say that the Father is on earth or the Son or the Holy Spirit, since the abode of this Trinity is only in heaven. When true reasoning begins to break down that train of carnal thought, that vain imagining, with His interior help and light —since He does not dwell in our hearts with such idols—we make haste to shatter them and, so to speak, to shake our faith free of them, so that we do not allow even the dust of such fancies to remain there.

Therefore, should we not listen in vain to what is true, unless faith which clothes us with piety had preceded reason, through whose outward argument, together with the light of truth within us, we are roused to perceive that these idols are false? Thus, when faith acts in its own sphere, reason following after finds something of what faith was seeking, and true reason is to be preferred to false reason because it makes us understand what we believe, but faith in things not yet understood is undoubtedly even more to be preferred. It is better to believe in something true but not yet seen, than to take the false thing one sees for true. For, faith has its own eyes with which it sees, so to speak, that what it does not yet see is true, and with which it most certainly sees that it does not yet see what it believes. Moreover, he who now understands by a true reasoning what he only believed a while ago is emphatically to be preferred to the one who wishes to understand now what he believes, but, if he does not also have a desire for the things which are to be understood, he considers them an object of belief only, and he fails to grasp the advantage of faith, for a devout faith does not wish to be without hope and without charity. So, then, a faithful man ought to believe what he does not yet see, so as to hope for and love the fulfillment of vision.

As a matter of fact, we hold things visible but past by faith alone, since there is no hope of seeing again what has slipped away with time. They are regarded as finished and gone by, as it is expressed in the words: "Christ died once for our sins, and rose again and dieth now no more: death shall no more have dominion over him." The things which are not yet in existence, but are to come, such as the resurrection of our spiritual bodies, are believed in such wise that we hope to see them, but they cannot be experienced now.

And of the things which are such that they are neither past nor future, but remain forever, some are invisible, like justice and wisdom, and some are visible, like the Body of Christ, now immortal. But, "the invisible things are clearly seen, being understood," and in that way they are also seen in a special and appropriate manner. And, when they are seen, they are much more certain than the objects of the bodily sense, but they are said to be visible because they cannot, in any way, be seen by these mortal eyes. On the other hand, those living things which are visible and perpetual can be seen even by these mortal eyes, if they are made manifest; as the Lord showed Himself to the disciples after His Resurrection, and even after His Ascension, to the Apostle Paul and to the deacon Stephen.

Therefore, we believe in those visible and perpetual things in such wise that, even if they are not manifested to us, we hope we shall see them some day, and we do not make an effort to understand them by reasoning and thought, except that we make a distinction in our thought between these visible things and invisible ones, and we imagine to ourselves in thought what they are like, although we know quite well that they are not known to us. Thus, I think in one way of Antioch, a city unknown to me, and in another way of Carthage, which I do know; my mind makes an image of the former but recalls the latter. There is, however, no doubt in my mind that my belief about the former is based on the evidence of numerous witnesses, but about the latter on my own sense-impressions. Nevertheless, we do not form an image of justice and wisdom or anything else of this sort, in any other way, but we see them differently; we behold these invisible qualities by a simple intellectual attention of the mind and reason, without any forms or physical bulk, without any features or appearance of parts, without any locality, whether limited or of unbounded space. The light itself by which we distinguish all this, by which we are made aware of what we believe without knowing it, that we hold as objects of knowledge, what physical shape we recall, what one we imagine, what the sense-organ perceives, what the mind imagines in the likeness of a body, what is present to the intellect as certain yet totally unlike any physical object, this light by which all these mental acts are differentiated, is not diffused in any special place, like the brilliance of this sun or of any physical light, and does not illumine our mind as if it were a visible brightness, but it shines invisibly and indescribably, yet intelligibly, and it is as certain a fact itself as are the realities which we see as certain by means of it.

We have, then, three classes of objects which are seen: the first, of material things, such as heaven and earth and everything the physical sense-organ perceives or experiences in them; the second, of representations of material things, such as those we picture to ourselves in thought by means of our imagination, whether we behold them inwardly as remembered or as imagined objects. In this class are visions, such as occur either in sleep or in some state of ecstasy, and are presented in these spatial dimensions. The third class is different from both the former, and consists of things which are not corporeal and have no corporeal representation: for example, wisdom, which is perceived by the understanding and by whose light all these other things are correctly estimated. But, in which class we are to believe that the Trinity, which we wish to know about, is included? Obviously, in some one of them or in none. If in some one, it must be the one which is superior to the other two, namely, the one in which wisdom is included. But, if His gift is in us, and if it is a lesser thing than that supreme and unchangeable wisdom which is said to be of God—I suppose we should not rate the giver as lower than his gift—if some of His light is in us and is called our wisdom, in so far as we can grasp anything of Him, "through a glass in a dark manner," then we must distinguish that wisdom from all material objects and from all representations of material objects.

But, if the Trinity is not to be included in any of those classes, and if it is so far invisible that it is not seen by the mind, we have no reason at all to believe that it is like either material objects or the representations of material objects. It is not in the beauty of its shape nor in its immensity that it surpasses material things, but in the difference and complete dissimilarity of its nature. It is also remote from any comparison with our spiritual goods, such as wisdom, justice, charity, chastity, and other like qualities, which we certainly do not value for their physical size, nor do we endow them in our thoughts with bodily shapes, but, when we understand them properly, we behold them by the light of our mind without bodily attributes or any likeness of bodily attributes. How much more, then, must we refrain from any comparison of physical qualities and dimensions in thinking of the Trinity! But the Apostle is witness that our mind is not to shrink away from it entirely, when he says: "For the invisible things of him from the creation of the world are clearly seen, being understood by the things that are made; his eternal power also and divinity." Consequently, since the same Trinity created both body and soul, it is evidently superior to both. And, if the soul so considered, especially the human, rational, and intellectual soul, which was made in His image, does not elude our thoughts and understanding; if, by mind and understanding, we are able to grasp its excellence, which is to say, the mind itself and the understanding, it will not perhaps be unreasonable for us to try to raise our soul to the understanding of its Creator, with His help. But, if it fails in that and falls back on itself, let it be satisfied with devout faith, as long as it is a wanderer from the Lord, until He acts to fulfill His promise in man, as the Apostle says: "Who is able to do all things more abundantly than we desire or understand. . . ."

God—The Eternal Creator[*]

AUGUSTINE

It is a great and very rare thing for a man, after he has contemplated the whole creation, corporeal and incorporeal, and has discerned its mutability, to pass beyond it, and, by the continued soaring of his mind, to attain to the unchangeable substance of God, and, in that height of contemplation, to learn from God Himself that none but He has made all that is not of the divine essence. For God speaks with a man not by means of some audible creature dinning in his ears, so that atmospheric vibrations connect Him that makes with him that hears the sound, nor even by means of a spiritual being with the semblance of a body, such as we see in dreams or similar states; for even in this case He speaks as if to the ears of the body, because it is by means of the semblance of a body He speaks, and with the appearance of a real interval of space,—for visions are exact representations of bodily objects. Not by these, then, does God speak, but by the truth itself, if any one is prepared to hear with the mind rather than with the body. For He speaks to that part of man which is better than all else that is in him, and than which God Himself alone is better. For since man is most properly understood (or, if that cannot be, then, at least, *believed*) to be made in God's image, no doubt it is that part of him by which he rises above those lower parts he has in common with the beasts, which brings him nearer to the Supreme. But since the mind itself, though naturally capable of reason and intelligence, is disabled by besotting and inveterate vices not merely from delighting and abiding in, but even from tolerating His unchangeable light, until it has been gradually healed, and renewed, and made capable of such felicity, it had, in the first place, to be impregnated with faith, and so purified. And that in this faith it might advance the more confidently towards the truth, the truth itself, God, God's Son, assuming humanity without destroying His divinity, established and founded this faith, that there might be a way for man to man's God through a God-man. For this is the Mediator between God and men, the man Christ Jesus. For it is as man that He is the Mediator and the Way. Since, if the way lieth between him who goes, and the place whither he goes, there is hope of his reaching it; but if there be no way, or if he know not where it is, what boots it to know whither he should go? Now the only way that is infallibly secured against all mistakes, is when the very same person is at once God and man, God our end, man our way.

[*] From *The City of God*, Vol. I, Book XI, Chaps. 2–6, tr. by Marcus Dods. Edinburgh: T. & T. Clark, 1872. [The title is supplied by the editor.]

This Mediator, having spoken what He judged sufficient, first by the prophets, then by His own lips, and afterwards by the apostles, has besides produced the Scripture which is called canonical, which has paramount authority, and to which we yield assent in all matters of which we ought not to be ignorant, and yet cannot know of ourselves. For if we attain the knowledge of present objects by the testimony of our own senses, whether internal or external, then, regarding objects remote from our own senses, we need others to bring their testimony, since we cannot know them by our own, and we credit the persons to whom the objects have been or are sensibly present. Accordingly, as in the case of visible objects which we have not seen, we trust those who have, (and likewise with all sensible objects,) so in the case of things which are perceived by the mind and spirit, i.e. which are remote from our own interior sense, it behoves us to trust those who have seen them set in that incorporeal light, or abidingly contemplate them. . . .

Of all visible things, the world is the greatest; of all invisible, the greatest is God. But, that the world is, we see; that God is, we believe. That God made the world, we can believe from no one more safely than from God Himself. But where have we heard Him? Nowhere more distinctly than in the Holy Scriptures, where His prophets said, "In the beginning God created the heavens and the earth." Was the prophet present when God made the heavens and the earth? No; but the wisdom of God, by whom all things were made, was there, and wisdom insinuates itself into holy souls, and makes them the friends of God and His prophets, and noiselessly informs them of His works. They are taught also by the angels of God, who always behold the face of the Father, and announce His will to whom it befits. Of these prophets was he who said and wrote, "In the beginning God created the heavens and the earth." And so fit a witness was he of God, that the same Spirit of God, who revealed these things to him, enabled him also so long before to predict that our faith also would be forthcoming.

But why did God choose then to create the heavens and earth which up to that time He had not made? If they who put this question wish to make out the the world is eternal and without beginning, and that consequently it has not been made by God, they are strangely deceived, and rave in the incurable madness of impiety. For, though the voices of the prophets were silent, the world itself, by its well-ordered changes and movements, and by the fair appearance of all visible things, bears a testimony of its own, both that it has been created, and also that it could not have been created save by God, whose greatness and beauty are unutterable and invisible. As for those[2] who own, indeed, that it was made by God, and yet ascribe to it not a temporal but only a creational beginning,

2 The neo-Platonists.

so that in some scarcely intelligible way the world should always have existed a created world, they make an assertion which seems to them to defend God from the charge of arbitrary hastiness, or of suddenly conceiving the idea of creating the world as a quite new idea, or of casually changing His will, though He be unchangeable. But I do not see how this supposition of theirs can stand in other respects, and chiefly in respect of the soul; for if they contend that it is co-eternal with God, they will be quite at a loss to explain whence there has accrued to it new misery, which through a previous eternity had not existed. For if they said that its happiness and misery ceaselessly alternate, they must say, further, that this alternation will continue for ever; whence will result this absurdity, that, though the soul is called blessed, it is not so in this, that it foresees its own misery and disgrace. And yet, if it does not foresee it, and supposes that it will be neither disgraced nor wretched, but always blessed, then it is blessed because it is deceived; and a more foolish statement one cannot make. But if their idea is that the soul's misery has alternated with its bliss during the ages of the past eternity, but that now, when once the soul has been set free, it will return henceforth no more to misery, they are nevertheless of opinion that it has never been truly blessed before, but begins at last to enjoy a new and uncertain happiness; that is to say, they must acknowledge that some new thing, and that an important and signal thing, happens to the soul which never in a whole past eternity happened to it before. And if they deny that God's eternal purpose included this new experience of the soul, they deny that He is the Author of its blessedness, which is unspeakable impiety. If, on the other hand, they say that the future blessedness of the soul is the result of a new decree of God, how will they show that God is not chargeable with that mutability which displeases them? Further, if they acknowledge that it was created in time, but will never perish in time, —that it has, like number,[3] a beginning but no end,—and that, therefore, having once made trial of misery, and been delivered from it, it will never again return thereto, they will certainly admit that this takes place without any violation of the immutable counsel of God. Let them, then, in like manner believe regarding the world that it too could be made in time, and yet that God, in making it, did not alter His eternal design. . . .

Next, we must see what reply can be made to those who agree that God is the Creator of the world, but have difficulties about the time of its creation, and what reply, also, they can make to difficulties we might raise about the place of its creation. For, as they demand why the world was created then and no sooner, we may ask why it was created just here where it is, and not elsewhere. For if they imagine infinite spaces of time before the world, during which God could not have been idle, in like manner they may conceive outside the world infinite realms of space, in which, if

[3] Number begins at one, but runs on infinitely.

any one says that the Omnipotent cannot hold His hand from working, will it not follow that they must adopt Epicurus' dream of innumerable worlds with this difference only, that he asserts that they are formed and destroyed by the fortuitous movements of atoms, while they will hold that they are made by God's hand, if they maintain that, throughout the boundless immensity of space, stretching interminably in every direction round the world, God cannot rest, and that the worlds which they suppose Him to make cannot be destroyed. For here the question is with those who, with ourselves, believe that God is spiritual, and the Creator of all existences but Himself. As for others, it is a condescension to dispute with them on a religious question, for they have acquired a reputation only among men who pay divine honours to a number of gods, and have become conspicuous among the other philosophers for no other reason than that, though they are still far from the truth, they are near it in comparison with the rest. While these, then, neither confine in any place, nor limit, nor distribute the divine substance, but, as is worthy of God, own it to be wholly though spiritually present everywhere, will they perchance say that this substance is absent from such immense spaces outside the world, and is occupied in one only, (and that a very little one compared with the infinity beyond,) the one, namely, in which is the world? I think they will not proceed to this absurdity. Since they maintain that there is but one world, of vast material bulk, indeed, yet finite, and in its own determinate position, and that this was made by the working of God, let them give the same account of God's resting in the infinite times before the world as they give of His resting in the infinite spaces outside of it. And as it does not follow that God set the world in the very spot it occupies and no other by accident rather than by divine reason, although no human reason can comprehend why it was so set, and though there was no merit in the spot chosen to give it the precedence of infinite others, so neither does it follow that we should suppose that God was guided by chance when He created the world in that and no earlier time, although previous times had been running by during an infinite past, and though there was no difference by which one time could be chosen in preference to another. But if they say that the thoughts of men are idle when they conceive infinite places, since there is no place beside the world, we reply that, by the same showing, it is vain to conceive of the past times of God's rest, since there is no time before the world. . . .

For if eternity and time are rightly distinguished by this, that time does not exist without some movement and transition, while in eternity there is no change, who does not see that there could have been no time had not some creature been made, which by some motion could give birth to change,—the various parts of which motion and change, as they cannot be simultaneous, succeed one another,—and thus, in these shorter or longer intervals of duration, time would begin? Since then, God, in whose eternity is no change at all, is the Creator and Ordainer of time, I do not see how He can be said to have created the world after spaces of time had elapsed, unless it be said that prior to the world there was some creature by whose movement time could pass. And if the sacred and infallible scriptures say that in the beginning God created the heavens and the earth, in order that it may be understood that He had made nothing previously,—for if He had made anything before the rest, this thing would rather be said to have been made "in the beginning,"—then assuredly the world was made, not in time, but simultaneously with time. For that which is made in time is made both after and before some time,—after that which is past, before that which is future. But none could then be past, for there was no creature by whose movements its duration could be measured. But simultaneously with time the world was made, if in the world's creation change and motion were created, as seems evident from the order of the first six or seven days. For in these days the morning and evening are counted, until, on the sixth day, all things which God then made were finished, and on the seventh the rest of God was mysteriously and sublimely signalized. What kind of days these were it is extremely difficult, or perhaps impossible for us to conceive, and how much more to say!

5

THE WORK of Anselm (1033–1109) has been of central importance to the history of philosophy and theology. His early life was spent in the monastery at Bec where he served as abbot and director of its school. In 1093 he became the Archbishop of Canterbury.

His ontological argument for the existence of God is found in the *Proslogium*, portions of which follow. Also included is the reply to this work by Gaunilon, a contemporary monk, and Anselm's counter response.[1]

1 See also *Why God Man* (*Cur Deus Homo*), Selection 35.

Proslogium*

ANSELM

. . . I have written the following treatise in the person of one who strives to lift his mind to the contemplation of God, and seeks to understand what be believes. . . .

CHAPTER 1

Lord, I acknowledge and I thank thee that thou hast created me in this thine image, in order that I may be mindful of thee, may conceive of thee, and love thee; but that image has been so consumed and wasted away by vices, and obscured by the smoke of wrong-doing, that it cannot achieve that for which it was made, except thou renew it, and create it anew. I do not endeavor, O Lord, to penetrate thy sublimity, for in no wise do I compare my understanding with that; but I long to understand in some degree thy truth, which my heart believes and loves. For I do not seek to understand that I may believe, but I believe in order to understand. For this also I believe,—that unless I believed, I should not understand.

CHAPTER 2

Truly there is a God, although the fool hath said in his heart, there is no God.

And so, Lord, do thou, who dost give understanding to faith, give me, so far as thou knowest it to be profitable, to understand that thou art as we believe; and that thou art that which we believe. And, indeed, we believe that thou art a being than which nothing greater can be conceived. Or is there no such nature, since the fool hath said in his heart, there is no God? (Psalms xiv. 1). But at any rate, this very fool, when he hears of this being of which I speak—a being than which nothing greater can be conceived—understands what he hears, and what he understands is in his understanding; although he does not understand it to exist.

For, it is one thing for an object to be in the understanding, and another to understand that the object exists. When a painter first conceives of what he will afterwards perform, he has it in his understanding, but he does not yet understand it to be, because he has not yet performed it. But

* From Sidney Norton Deane, tr., St. Anselm Proslogium; Monologium; An Appendix in Behalf of the Fool by Gaunilon; Cur Deus Homo. La Salle, Ill.: The Open Court Publishing Company, 1954.

after he has made the painting, he both has it in his understanding, and he understands that it exists, because he has made it.

Hence, even the fool is convinced that something exists in the understanding, as least, than which nothing greater can be conceived. For, when he hears of this, he understands it. And whatever is understood, exists in the understanding. And assuredly that, than which nothing greater can be conceived, cannot exist in the understanding alone. For, suppose it exists in the understanding alone: then it can be conceived to exist in reality; which is greater.

Therefore, if that, than which nothing greater can be conceived, exists in the understanding alone, the very being, than which nothing greater can be conceived, is one, than which a greater can be conceived. But obviously this is impossible. Hence, there is no doubt that there exists a being, than which nothing greater can be conceived, and it exists both in the understanding and in reality.

CHAPTER 3

God cannot be conceived not to exist.—God is that, than which nothing greater can be conceived.—That which can be conceived not to exist is not God.

And it assuredly exists so truly, that it cannot be conceived not to exist. For, it is possible to conceive of a being which cannot be conceived not to exist; and this is greater than one which can be conceived not to exist. Hence, if that, than which nothing greater can be conceived, can be conceived not to exist, it is not that, than which nothing greater can be conceived. But this is an irreconcilable contradiction. There is, then, so truly a being than which nothing greater can be conceived to exist, that it cannot even be conceived not to exist; and this being thou art, O Lord, our God.

So truly, therefore, dost thou exist, O Lord, my God, that thou canst not be conceived not to exist; and rightly. For, if a mind could conceive of a being better than thee, the creature would rise above the Creator; and this is most absurd. And, indeed, whatever else there is, except thee alone, can be conceived not to exist. To thee alone, therefore, it belongs to exist more truly than all other beings, and hence in a higher degree than all others. For, whatever else exists does not exist so truly, and hence in a less degree it belongs to it to exist. Why, then, has the fool said in his heart, there is no God (Psalms xiv. 1), since it is so evident, to a rational mind, that thou dost exist in the highest degree of all? Why, except that he is dull and a fool?

CHAPTER 4

How the fool has said in his heart what cannot be conceived.—A thing may be conceived in two ways: (1) when the word signifying it is conceived; (2) when the thing itself is understood. As far as the word goes, God can be conceived not to exist; in reality he cannot.

But how has the fool said in his heart what he could not conceive; or how is it that he could not conceive what he said in his heart? since it is the same to say in the heart, and to conceive.

But, if really, nay, since really, he both conceived, because he said in his heart; and did not say in his heart, because he could not conceive; there is more than one way in which a thing is said in the heart or conceived. For, in one sense, an object is conceived, when the word signifying it is conceived; and in another, when the very entity, which the object is, is understood.

In the former sense, then, God can be conceived not to exist; but in the latter, not at all. For no one who understands what fire and water are can conceive fire to be water, in accordance with the nature of the facts themselves, although this is possible according to the words. So, then, no one who understands what God is can conceive that Goes does not exist; although he says these words in his heart, either without any, or with some foreign, signification. For, God is that than which a greater cannot be conceived. And he who thoroughly understands this, assuredly understands that this being so truly exists, that not even in concept can it be non-existent. Therefore, he who understands that God so exists, cannot conceive that he does not exist.

I thank thee, gracious Lord, I thank thee; because what I formerly believed by thy bounty, I now so understand by thine illumination, that if I were unwilling to believe that thou dost exist, I should not be able not to understand this to be true. . . .

Appendix

IN BEHALF OF THE FOOL

AN ANSWER TO THE ARGUMENT OF ANSELM IN THE PROSLOGIUM BY GAUNILON A MONK OF MARMOUTIER

If one doubts or denies the existence of a being of such a nature that nothing greater than it can be conceived, he receives this answer:

The existence of this being is proved, in the first place, by the fact that he himself, in his doubt or denial regarding this being, already has it in his understanding; for in hearing it spoken of he understands what is spoken of. It is proved, therefore, by the fact that what he understands must exist not only in his understanding, but in reality also.

And the proof of this is as follows.—It is a greater thing to exist both in the understanding and in reality than to be in the understanding alone. And if this being is in the understanding alone, whatever has even in the past existed in reality will be greater than this being. And so that which was greater than all beings will be less than some being, and will not be greater than all: which is a manifest contradiction.

And hence, that which is greater than all, already proved to be in the understanding, must exist not only in the understanding, but also in reality: for otherwise it will not be greater than all other beings.

The fool might make this reply:

This being is said to be in my understanding already, only because I understand what is said. Now could it not with equal justice be said that I have in my understanding all manner of unreal objects, having absolutely no existence in themselves, because I understand these things if one speaks of them, whatever they may be? . . .

For, suppose that I should hear something said of a man absolutely unknown to me, of whose very existence I was unaware. Through that special or general knowledge by which I know what man is, or what men are, I could conceive of him also, according to the reality itself, which man is. And yet it would be possible, if the person who told me of him deceived me, that the man himself, of whom I conceived, did not exist; since that reality according to which I conceived of him, though a no less indisputable fact, was not that man, but any man. . . .

[Or] for example: it is said that somewhere in the ocean is an island, which, because of the difficulty, or rather the impossibility, of discovering what does not exist, is called the lost island. And they say that this island has an inestimable wealth of all manner of riches and delicacies in greater abundance than is told of the Islands of the Blest; and that having no owner or inhabitant, it is more excellent than all other countries, which are inhabited by mankind, in the abundance with which it is stored.

Now if some one should tell me that there is such an island, I should easily understand his words, in which there is no difficulty. But suppose that he went on to say, as if by a logical inference: "You can no longer doubt that this island which is more excellent than all lands exists somewhere, since you have no doubt that it is in your understanding. And since it is more excellent not to be in the understanding alone, but to exist both in the understanding and in reality, for this reason it must exist. For if it does not exist, any land which really exists will be more excellent than it; and so the island already understood by you to be more excellent will not be more excellent."

If a man should try to prove to me by such reasoning that this island truly exists, and that its existence should no longer be doubted, either I should believe that he was jesting, or I know not which I ought to regard as the greater fool: myself, supposing that I should allow this proof; or him, if he should suppose that he had established with any certainty the existence of this island. For he ought to show first that the hypothetical excellence of this island exists as a real and indubitable fact, and in no wise as any unreal object, or one whose existence is uncertain, in my understanding. . . .

ANSELM'S APOLOGETIC

IN REPLY TO GAUNILON'S ANSWER IN BEHALF OF THE FOOL

It was a fool against whom the argument of my Proslogium was directed. Seeing, however, that the author of these objections is by no means a fool, and is a Catholic, speaking in behalf of the fool, I think it sufficient that I answer the Catholic.

CHAPTER 1

A general refutation of Gaunilon's argument. It is shown that a being than which a greater cannot be conceived exists in reality.

You say—whosoever you may be, who say that a fool is capable of making these statements—that a being than which a greater cannot be conceived is not in the understanding in any other sense than that in which a being that is altogether inconceivable in terms of reality, is in the understanding. You say that the inference that this being exists in reality, from the fact that it is in the understanding, is no more just than the inference that a lost island most certainly exists, from the fact that when it is described the hearer does not doubt that it is in his understanding.

But I say: if a being than which a greater is inconceivable is not understood or conceived, and is not in the understanding or in concept, certainly either God is not a being than which a greater is inconceivable, or else he is not understood or conceived, and is not in the understanding or in concept. But I call on your faith and conscience to attest that this is most false. Hence, that than which a greater cannot be conceived is truly understood and conceived, and is in the understanding and in concept. Therefore either the grounds on which you try to controvert me are not true, or else the inference which you think to base logically on those grounds is not justified.

But you hold, moreover, that supposing that a being than which a greater cannot be conceived is understood, it does not follow that this being is in the understanding; nor, if it is in the understanding, does it therefore exist in reality.

In answer to this, I maintain positively: if that being can be even conceived to be, it must exist in reality. For that than which a greater is inconceivable cannot be conceived except as without beginning. But whatever can be conceived to exist, and does not exist, can be conceived to exist through a beginning. Hence what can be conceived to exist, but does not exist, is not the being than which a greater cannot be conceived. Therefore, if such a being can be conceived to exist, necessarily it does exist.

Furthermore: if it can be conceived at all, it must exist. For no one who denies or doubts the existence of a being than which a greater is inconceivable, denies or doubts that if it did exist, its non-existence, either in reality or in the understanding, would be impossible. For otherwise it would not be a being than which a greater cannot be conceived. But as to whatever can be conceived, but does not exist—if there were such a being, its non-existence, either in reality or in the understanding, would be possible. Therefore if a being than which a greater is inconceivable can be even conceived, it cannot be non-existent. . . .

CHAPTER 3

A criticism of Gaunilon's example, in which he tries to show that in this way the real existence of a lost island might be inferred from the fact of its being conceived.

But, you say, it is as if one should suppose an island in the ocean, which surpasses all lands in its fertility, and which, because of the difficulty, or rather the impossibility, of discovering what does not exist, is called a lost island; and should say that there can be no doubt that this island truly exists in reality, for this reason, that one who hears it described easily understands what he hears.

Now I promise confidently that if any man shall devise anything existing either in reality or in concept alone (except that than which a greater cannot be conceived) to which he can adapt the sequence of my reasoning, I will discover that thing, and will give him his lost island, not to be lost again.

But it now appears that this being than which a greater is inconceivable cannot be conceived not to be, because it exists on so assured a ground of truth; for otherwise it would not exist at all.

Hence, if any one says that he conceives this being not to exist, I say that at the time when he conceives of this either he conceives of a being than which a greater is inconceivable, or he does not conceive at all. If he does not conceive, he does not conceive of the non-existence of that of which he does not conceive. But if he does conceive, he certainly conceives of a being which cannot be even conceived not to exist. For if it could be conceived not to exist, it could be conceived to have a beginning and an end. But this is impossible.

He, then, who conceives of this being conceives of a being which cannot be even conceived not to exist; but he who conceives of this being does not conceive that it does not exist; else he conceives what is inconceivable.

The non-existence, then, of that than which a greater cannot be conceived is inconceivable.

CHAPTER 4

The difference between the possibility of conceiving of non-existence, and understanding non-existence.

You say, moreover, that whereas I assert that this supreme being cannot be *conceived* not to exist, it might better be said that its non-existence, or even the possibility of its non-existence, cannot be *understood*.

But it was more proper to say, it cannot be conceived. For if I had said that the object itself cannot be understood not to exist, possibly you yourself, who say that in accordance with the true meaning of the term what is unreal cannot be understood, would offer the objection that nothing which is can be understood not to be, for the non-existence of what exists is unreal: hence God would not be the only being of which it could be said, it is impossible to understand its non-existence. For thus one of those beings which most certainly exist can be understood not to exist in the same way in which certain other real objects can be understood not to exist.

But this objection, assuredly, cannot be urged against the term *conception*, if one considers the matter well. For although no objects which exist can be understood not to exist, yet all objects, except that which exists in the highest degree, can be conceived not to exist. For all those objects, and those alone, can be conceived not to exist, which have a beginning or end or composition of parts: also, as I have already said, whatever at any place or at any time does not exist as a whole.

That being alone, on the other hand, cannot be conceived not to exist, in which any conception discovers neither beginning nor end nor composition of parts, and which any conception finds always and everywhere as a whole.

Be assured, then, that you can conceive of your own non-existence, although you are most certain that you exist. I am surprised that you should have admitted that you are ignorant of this. For we conceive of the non-existence of many objects which we know to exist, and of the existence of many which we know not to exist; not by forming the opinion that they so exist, but by imagining that they exist as we conceive of them.

And indeed, we can conceive of the non-existence of an object, although we know it to exist, because at the same time we can conceive of the former and know the latter. And we cannot conceive of the non-existence of an object, so long as we know it to exist, because we cannot conceive at the same time of existence and non-existence.

If, then, one will thus distinguish these two senses of this statement, he will understand that nothing, so long as it is known to exist, can be conceived not to exist; and that whatever exists, except that being than which a greater cannot be conceived, can be conceived not to exist, even when it is known to exist.

So, then, of God alone it can be said that it is impossible to conceive of his non-existence; and yet many objects, so long as they exist, in one sense cannot be conceived not to exist. But in what sense God is to be conceived not to exist, I think has been shown clearly enough in my book. . . .

CHAPTER 10

The certainty of the foregoing argument.—The conclusion of the book.

I believe that I have shown by an argument which is not weak, but sufficiently cogent, that in my former book I proved the real existence of a being than which a greater cannot be conceived; and I believe that this argument cannot be invalidated by the validity of any objection. For so great force does the signification of this reasoning contain in itself, that this being which is the subject of discussion, is of necessity, from the very fact that it is understood or conceived, proved also to exist in reality, and to be whatever we should believe of the divine substance.

For we attribute to the divine substance anything of which it can be conceived that it is better to be than not to be that thing. For example: it is better to be eternal than not eternal; good, than not good; nay, goodness itself, than not goodness itself. But it cannot be that anything of this nature is not a property of the being than which a greater is inconceivable. Hence, the being than which a greater is inconceivable must be whatever should be attributed to the divine essence.

6   THE *Summa Theologica* of Thomas Aquinas (1225–1274) is a work of lasting importance. This Dominican friar wedded the revival of Aristotelian philosophy with an elaborate statement of Christian faith that has served as the main exposition of Roman Catholic theology. Aquinas' systematic work became the basis for the Council of Trent (1545–1563)[1] and was considered to be by Pope Leo XIII in his Encyclical, *Aeterni Patris* (1879), "the special bulwark and glory of the Catholic faith."

[1] See also *On the Truth of the Catholic Faith*, Selection 60, and *Council of Trent*, Selections 10, 48, 67.

The following selections from the *Summa Theologica*
deal with Aquinas' understanding of the theological task
and his arguments for the existence of God.

Summa Theologica*

THOMAS AQUINAS

Question One

WHAT SACRED DOCTRINE IS, AND WHAT IT CONCERNS

In order to confine our purpose within definite limits, we must first
inquire into sacred doctrine itself, what it is and what it concerns. Ten
questions are asked. 1. Whether sacred doctrine is necessary. 2. Whether
it is a science. 3. Whether it is one science, or several. 4. Whether it is
speculative or practical. 5. How it is related to other sciences. 6. Whether
it is wisdom. 7. What is its subject-matter. 8. Whether it proceeds by argument. 9. Whether it ought to make use of metaphors or figures of speech.
10. Whether the sacred Scriptures of this doctrine should be expounded in
several ways.

Article One

**WHETHER ANOTHER DOCTRINE IS NECESSARY, BESIDES THE PHILOSOPHICAL
SCIENCES**

We proceed to the first article thus:

1. It seems that there is no need for any other doctrine besides the
philosophical sciences. Man should not strive to know what is above reason,
since it is said in Ecclesiasticus 3:22: "seek not to know what is higher than
thyself." Now what is within the reach of reason is adequately dealt with in
the philosophical sciences. It seems superfluous, therefore, that there should
be another doctrine besides the philosophical sciences.

2. Again, a doctrine can be concerned only with "what is," since only
what is true can be known, and whatever is true, is. Now all things which
"are" are dealt with in the philosophical sciences, which treat even of God,
wherefore one part of philosophy is called theology, or the science of divine

* From *Nature and Grace*, Vol. XI, LCC. Tr. A. M. Fairweather. Published 1954
by The Westminster Press. Used by permission. Also by permission of Student Christian
Movement Press Limited.

things, as the philosopher[2] says in 6 *Metaph*. (Commentary II). There was therefore no need for another doctrine, besides the philosophical sciences.

On the other hand: it is said in II Tim. 3:16: "All scripture is given by inspiration of God, and is profitable for doctrine, for reproof, for correction, for instruction in righteousness. . . ."[3] Now the divinely inspired scriptures are quite distinct from the philosophical sciences, which are devised by human reason. It is therefore expedient that there should be another science which is divinely inspired, besides the philosophical sciences.

I answer: it was necessary for man's salvation that there should be a doctrine founded on revelation, as well as the philosophical sciences discovered by human reason. It was necessary, in the first place, because man is ordained to God as his end, who surpasses the comprehension of reason, according to Isa. 64:4: "neither hath the eye seen, O God, besides thee, what he hath prepared for him that waiteth for him." Men must have some foreknowledge of the end to which they ought to direct their intentions and actions. It was therefore necessary that some things which transcend human reason should be made known through divine revelation. It was necessary also that man should be instructed by divine revelation even in such things concerning God as human reason could discover. For such truth about God as could be discovered by reason would be known only by the few, and that after a long time, and mixed with many errors. Now the whole salvation of man, which lies in God, depends on the knowledge of this truth. It was therefore necessary that men should be instructed in divine things through divine revelation, in order that their salvation might come to pass the more fittingly and certainly. It was necessary, therefore, that there should be a sacred doctrine given through revelation, as well as the philosophical sciences discovered by reason.

On the first point: although things which are beyond human knowledge are not to be sought by man through reason, such things are revealed by God, and are to be accepted by faith. Hence Ecclesiasticus adds in the same passage: "many things beyond human understanding have been revealed unto thee" (3:25).

On the second point: sciences are distinguished by their different ways of knowing. The astronomer and the naturalist prove the same thing, for example, that the world is round. But the astronomer proves it by mathematics, without reference to matter, whereas the naturalist proves it by examining the physical. There is no reason, then, why the same things, which the philosophical sciences teach as they can be known by the light of

[2] I.e., Aristotle. [For page references from Aristotle's works, the reader is referred to the index of the volume from which these selections are taken: Vol. XI, The Library of Christian Classics. Ed.].

[3] Scriptural passages are quoted from the Authorized Version, any significant divergences in the text being indicated by footnotes.

natural reason, should not also be taught by another science as they are known through divine revelation. The theology which depends on sacred scripture is thus generically different from the theology which is a part of philosophy.

Article Two

WHETHER SACRED DOCTRINE IS A SCIENCE

We proceed to the second article thus:

1. It seems that sacred doctrine is not a science. For every science depends on principles which are self-evident, whereas sacred doctrine depends on articles of faith which are not self-evident, since they are not conceded by everybody. As is said in II Thess. 3:2: "all men have not faith." Hence sacred doctrine is not a science.

2. Again, there is no science of particulars.[4] But sacred doctrine is concerned with particulars, such as the deeds of Abraham, Isaac, Jacob, and others. It is not therefore a science.

On the other hand: Augustine says (14 *De Trin.* 1): "by this science only is faith begun, nourished, defended, and strengthened." Now this is true of no science except sacred doctrine. Sacred doctrine is therefore a science.

I answer: sacred doctrine is a science. But we must realize that there are two kinds of sciences. Some of them, such as arithmetic, geometry, and the like, depend on principles known by the natural light of reason. Others depend on principles known through a higher science. Thus the science of perspective depends on principles known through geometry, and music on principles known through arithmetic. Sacred doctrine is a science of the latter kind, depending on principles known through a higher science, namely the science of God and the blessed. Just as music accepts the principles given to it by arithmetic, so does sacred doctrine accept the principles revealed to it by God.

On the first point: the principles of any science are either self-evident, or derived from what is known through a higher science. The principles of sacred doctrine are so derived, as we have said.

On the second point: sacred doctrine does not narrate particular things because it is principally concerned with them. It introduces them as examples to follow, as do the moral sciences; and also as proofs of the authority of those through whom the divine revelation, on which sacred scripture and sacred doctrine are founded, reaches us.

---

[4] Aristotle held that the sheer individuality of a particular, its "primary substance," could never be an object of science because it could never be a predicate. Only the "secondary substance," or essence, comprising the universals which must apply to a particular of a certain kind, could be known scientifically. Cf. *Categories* V.

Article Three

WHETHER SACRED DOCTRINE IS A SINGLE SCIENCE

We proceed to the third article thus:

1. It seems that sacred doctrine is not a single science. As the philosopher says: "one science treats of one kind of subject only" (I *Post An.*, Text 43). Now sacred doctrine treats of the Creator and also of creatures, and these do not belong to one kind of subject. Hence it is not a single science.

2. Again, sacred doctrine treats of angels, of creatures with bodies, and of the customs of men. These belong to different philosophical sciences. Hence sacred doctrine is not a single science.

On the other hand: sacred scripture speaks of these things as of a single science, for it is said in Wisdom 10:10: "She hath given him the science of holy things."

I answer: sacred doctrine is a single science. The unity of a power or habit[5] is indeed to be judged by its object, but by the formal nature of its object, not by the material nature of it. For example, man, ass, and stone agree in possessing the formal nature of "the coloured," which is the object of sight. Now since sacred doctrine treats of things as divinely revealed, as we said in the previous article, all things which are divinely revealed agree in the one formal nature which is the object of this science. They are therefore comprehended under sacred doctrine as a single science.

On the first point: sacred doctrine is not concerned with God and with creatures equally. It is concerned with God fundamentally, and with creatures in so far as they relate to God as their beginning or end. Thus the unity of the science is not destroyed.

On the second point: there is nothing to prevent lower powers or habits being differentiated in their relation to matters which yet go together for a higher power or habit, because a higher power or habit comprehends its object under a more universal aspect. Thus the object of the common sense is "the sensible," which includes both the "visible" and the "audible." Common sense is a single power which comprehends all objects of the five senses. Similarly, sacred doctrine remains a single science while it treats under one aspect, in so far as they are all revealed by God, matters which are dealt with by separate philosophical sciences. Sacred doctrine is thus like an imprint of God's knowledge, which is one and undivided, yet is knowledge of all things.

Article Four

WHETHER SACRED DOCTRINE IS A PRACTICAL SCIENCE

We proceed to the fourth article thus:

1. It seems that sacred doctrine is a practical science. For "the end of practical knowledge is action," according to the philosopher (2 *Metaph.*,

[5] See note to 12ae, Q. 82, Art. 1.

Text 3), and sacred doctrine is concerned with action, according to James 1:22: "Be ye doers of the word, and not hearers only." Sacred doctrine is therefore a practical science.

2. Again, sacred doctrine is divided into the Old and the New Law, and the Law has to do with the science of morals, which is practical. Sacred doctrine is therefore a practical science.

On the other hand: every practical science is concerned with the works of men. Ethics is concerned with their actions, and architecture with their buildings. But sacred doctrine is concerned principally with God, whose works men are. Hence it is not a practical science. Rather is it speculative.

I answer: as was said in the preceding article, sacred doctrine embraces matters dealt with by separate philosophical sciences while it itself remains one, because the formal nature to which it attends in diverse things is their being made known by the divine light. Hence even though some matters in the philosophical sciences are speculative and some practical, sacred doctrine includes them all within itself, just as God knows both himself and his works by the same knowledge. But sacred doctrine is more speculative than practical, since it is concerned with divine things more fundamentally than with the actions of men, in which it is interested in so far as through them men are brought to the perfect knowledge of God in which their eternal happiness consists. The answer to the objections is then obvious.

Article Five
WHETHER SACRED DOCTRINE IS NOBLER THAN OTHER SCIENCES

We proceed to the fifth article thus:

1. It seems that sacred doctrine is not nobler than other sciences. For the dignity of a science is indicated by its certainty, and other sciences whose principles cannot be doubted appear to be more certain than sacred doctrine, whose principles, i.e., the articles of faith, are the subject of debate. Thus it seems that other sciences are nobler.

2. Again, a lower science depends on a higher, as music depends on arithmetic. Now sacred doctrine derives something from the philosophical sciences. Hieronymus, indeed, says that "the ancient teachers filled their books with so many philosophical doctrines and opinions that one does not know which to admire the more, their secular learning or their knowledge of the scriptures" (Epist. 84 to Magnus the Roman orator). Sacred doctrine is therefore lower than other sciences.

On the other hand: other sciences are said to be subsidiary to this doctrine in Prov. 9:3: "She hath sent forth her maidens: she crieth upon the highest places of the city."

I answer: since sacred doctrine is speculative in some things and practical in others, it transcends all other sciences, whether speculative or practical. One speculative science is said to be nobler than another either because it is more certain, or because it treats of a nobler subject. Sacred doctrine surpasses other speculative sciences in both respects. It is more certain, since the certainty of other sciences depends on the natural light of human reason, which is liable to err, whereas its own certainty is founded on the light of divine knowledge, which cannot be deceived. Its subject is also nobler, since it is concerned principally with things above reason, whereas other sciences deal with things within the reach of reason. Finally, one practical science is nobler than another if it serves a more ultimate end. Politics is nobler than military science, because the good of an army is subsidiary to the good of the state. Now in so far as sacred doctrine is practical, its end is eternal happiness, and all other ends of the practical sciences are subsidiary to this as their ultimate end. It is plain, then, that it is nobler than the others in every way.

On the first point: there is nothing to prevent what is in itself the more certain from appearing to us to be the less certain, owing to the weakness of the intellect, "which is to the things most manifest to nature like the eyes of a bat to the light of the sun," as is said in *Metaph.* 2. The doubt felt by some in respect of the articles of faith is not due to any uncertainty in the thing itself. It is due to the weakness of human understanding. Nevertheless, the least knowledge which one can have of higher things is worth more than the most certain knowledge of lesser things, as is said in the *De Partibus Animalium* (bk. 1, ch. 5).

On the second point: this science can make use of the philosophical sciences in order to make what it teaches more obvious, not because it stands in need of them. It does not take its principles from other sciences, but receives them directly from God through revelation. It thus derives nothing from other sciences as from superiors, but uses them as ancillary inferiors, as the master sciences use subsidiary sciences, or as politics uses military science. Its use of them is not due to any defect or inadequacy in itself. It is due to the limitation of our understanding. We are more easily led from what is known by natural reason, on which other sciences depend, to the things above reason which this science teaches us. . . .

Article Eight

WHETHER SACRED DOCTRINE PROCEEDS BY ARGUMENT

We proceed to the eighth article thus:

1. It seems that sacred doctrine does not proceed by argument. For Ambrose says: "where faith is sought, eschew arguments" (*De Fid. Cath.*), and it is especially faith that is sought in this doctrine. As it is said in John 20:31: "these are written, that ye might believe." It follows that sacred doctrine does not proceed by argument.

2. Again, if sacred doctrine proceeded by argument, it would argue either on the ground of authority or on the ground of reason. But to argue from authority would be beneath its dignity, since "authority is the weakest

kind of proof," as Boethius says (*Topica* 6), and to argue by reason would be unworthy of its end, since "faith has no merit when human reason proves it by test," as Gregory says (*Hom. in Evang.* 26). It follows that sacred doctrine does not proceed by argument.

On the other hand: Titus 1:9 says of a bishop, "holding fast the faithful word as he hath been taught, that he may be able by sound doctrine both to exhort and to convince the gainsavers."

I answer: just as other sciences do not argue to prove their own principles, but argue from their principles to prove other things which the sciences include, so neither deos this doctrine argue to prove its principles, which are the articles of faith, but argues from these to prove other things. Thus in I Cor. 15 the apostle argues from the resurrection of Christ to prove the general resurrection. We must remember, however, that the inferior philosophical sciences do not prove their own principles, nor defend them against one who denies them. They leave this to a higher science. The highest of them, metaphysics, does argue in defence of its principles, provided that he who denies them concedes anything at all. But it cannot argue with him if he concedes nothing, although it can refute his reasoning. Now sacred doctrine, which has no superior, likewise argues at times with one who denies its principles, provided that its adversary concedes something of what is received through revelation. Thus we argue from the authority of sacred doctrine against heretics, and from the authority of one article of faith against those who deny another. But when an adversary believes nothing at all of what has been revealed, there is no way of proving the articles of faith by argument, except by disproving any grounds which he may bring against the faith. For since faith takes its stand on infallible truth, the contrary of which cannot possibly be demonstrated, it is obvious that proofs cited against the faith are not demonstrative, but answerable.

On the first point: although arguments of human reason cannot suffice to prove matters of faith, sacred doctrine argues from the articles of faith to other things, as said above.

On the second point: proof by authority is especially characteristic of this science, because its principles are obtained through revelation. The authority of those who received revelation has to be believed. But this does not detract from the dignity of the science. Appeal to an authority which depends on human reason is the weakest kind of proof. Appeal to an authority founded on divine revelation is the most telling. Yet sacred doctrine does make use of human reason, not indeed to prove the faith (which would take away its merit), but to clarify certain points of doctrine. Since grace does not supplant nature, but perfects it, reason ought to be the servant of faith in the same way as the natural inclination of the will is the servant of charity—"bringing into captivity every thought to the obedience of Christ," as the apostle says in II Cor. 10:5. Sacred doctrine uses even the authority of philosophers in this way, wherever they have been able to know the truth through natural reason. In Acts 17:28, for example, Paul quotes the words of Aratus: "as certain also of your poets have said, For we also are his offspring." Sacred doctrine uses such authorities, however, as supporting and probable arguments. It uses the canonical scriptures as the proper authority from which it is bound to argue, and uses other teachers of the Church as authorities from which one may indeed argue with propriety, yet only with probability.

Article Nine

WHETHER SACRED DOCTRINE SHOULD USE METAPHORS

We proceed to the ninth article thus:

1. It seems that sacred doctrine should not use metaphors. What is fitting for lesser doctrines would appear to be inappropriate to this doctrine, which holds the supreme place among the sciences, as was said in the preceding article. Now to proceed by various similies and figures is fitting for poetry, the least of all doctrines. Hence this doctrine should not use metaphors.

2. Again, the purpose of this doctrine is, apparently, to explain the truth, since a reward is promised to those who explain it. "They who explain me shall have eternal life" (Ecclesiasticus 24:21). Now truth is obscured by metaphors. This doctrine should not, therefore, record divine things under the form of corporeal things.

3. Again, the more sublime are creatures, the greater their likeness to God. Hence if any of them are to be used in the manifestation of God, it ought to be the more sublime creatures especially—not the lowest, as is often the case in scripture.

On the other hand: it is said in Hos. 12:10: "I have multiplied visions, and used similitudes, by the ministry of the prophets." Now to declare something by a similitude is to use a metaphor. The use of metaphors therefore befits sacred doctrine.

I answer: it is fitting that sacred scripture should declare divine and spiritual things by means of material similies. God provides for all things according to the capacity of their nature, and it is natural for man to reach intelligible things through sensible things, since all his knowledge begins from sense. Hence spiritual things are appropriately given to us by scripture in material metaphors. This is what Dionysius is saying in 2 Coel. Hier.: "It is impossible for the divine ray to lighten us unless it is shaded by a variety of sacred veils." It is also appropriate that the sacred scriptures which are given for all alike ("I am debtor . . . both to the wise and to the unwise," Rom. 1:14), should expound spiritual things by means of material similitudes, so that simple people who cannot understand intelligible things as they are should at least be able to understand them in this way.

On the first point: poetry uses metaphors to depict, since men naturally find pictures pleasing. But sacred doctrine uses them because they are necessary and useful.

On the second point: as Dionysius says, the ray of divine revelation is not destroyed by the sensible images which veil it (2 Coel Hier.). It remains in its truth, not allowing the minds of men to rest in the images, but raising them to know intelligible things.[6] It instructs others also in intelligible things, through those to whom the revelation is made. Thus what is veiled by metaphor in one passage of scripture is declared more explicitly in others. This veiling in metaphors is useful for stimulating the thoughtful, and useful also against unbelievers, of whom it is said in Matt. 7:6: "Give not that which is holy unto the dogs."

On the third point: as Dionysius says, it is more fitting that scripture should declare divine things in simple than in higher corporeal forms (2 Coel. Hier.). There are three reasons for this. First, the human mind is the more saved from error when it is abundantly plain that these forms are not a proper signification of divine things. This might be doubtful if divine things were described in terms of higher corporeal forms, especially with those who cannot think beyond higher corporeal things. Secondly, it is better suited to the knowledge of God which we have in this life. We know what God is not, better than we know what he is. Likenesses of things farther removed from him lead us to appreciate the more truly that God transcends whatever we say or think about him. Thirdly, divine things are the better hidden from the unworthy.

Whatever we say or think about him. Thirdly, divine things are the better hidden from the unworthy.

Question Two

THE EXISTENCE OF GOD

Three questions are asked concerning the existence of God.
1. Whether it is self-evident that God exists. 2. Whether the existence of God can be demonstrated. 3. Whether God exists.

Article One

WHETHER IT IS SELF-EVIDENT THAT GOD EXISTS

We proceed to the first article thus:
1. It seems to be self-evident that God exists: Things are said to be self-evident when the knowledge of them is naturally in us, as is obviously

---

[6] According to the De Adhaerendo Deo, of Albertus Magnus, the mind should strive to pass entirely beyond the images of sensible things in its contemplation of God. It seems to have been acknowledged, however, that the human mind cannot dispense with such images altogether.

the case with first principles. Now the Damascene says that "the knowledge that God exists is naturally inborn in all men" (1 *De Fid. Orth.* 1, 3). It is therefore self-evident that God exists.

2. Again, as the philosopher says of the first principles of demonstration, whatever is known as soon as the terms are known is self-evident (1 *Post. An.*, ch. 2). Thus we know that any whole is greater than its part as soon as we know what a whole is, and what a part is. Now when it is understood what the term "God" signifies, it is at once understood that God exists. For the term "God" means that than which nothing greater can be signified, and that which exists in reality is greater than that which exists only in the intellect. Hence since "God" exists in the intellect as soon as the term is understood, it follows that God exists also in reality. It is therefore self-evident that God exists.

3. Again, it is self-evident that truth exists. For truth exists if anything at all is true, and if anyone denies that truth exists, he concedes that it is true that it does not exist, since if truth does not exist it is then true that it does not exist. Now God is truth itself, according to John 14:6: "I am the way, and the truth, and the life." It is therefore self-evident that God exists.

On the other hand: no one can conceive the opposite of what is self-evident, as the philosopher explains in dealing with the first principles of demonstration (4 *Metaph.*, text 9; 1 *Post. An.*, texts 5 and *ult.*). Now the opposite of "God exists" can be conceived, according to Ps. 53:1: "The fool hath said in his heart, There is no God." It follows that it is not self-evident that God exists.

I answer: there are two ways in which a thing may be self-evident. It may be self-evident in itself, but not self-evident to us. It may also be self-evident both in itself and to us. A proposition is self-evident when its predicate is contained in the meaning of its subject. For example, the proposition "man is an animal" is self-evident, because "animal" is contained in the meaning of "man." Hence if the predicate and the subject are known to everyone, the proposition will be self-evident to everyone. This is obviously the case with regard to the first principles of demonstration, whose terms are universals known to everyone, such as being and not-being, whole, part, and the like. But when there are some to whom the predicate and the subject are unknown, the proposition will not be self-evident to them, however self-evident it may be in itself. Thus Boethius says (*Lib. de Hebd.*— Whether all Existence is Good): "it happens that some universal concepts of mind are self-evident only to the wise, e.g., that the incorporeal is not in space." I say, then, that this proposition "God exists" is self-evident in itself, since its predicate is the same with its subject. For God is his existence, as we shall show in Q. 3, Art. 4. But since we do not know what God is, it is not self-evident to us, but must be proved by means of what is better known to us though less well known to nature,[7] i.e., by means of the effects of God.

On the first point: the knowledge that God exists is inborn in us in a general and somewhat confused manner. For God is the final beatitude of man, and a man desires beatitude naturally, and is also naturally aware of what he desires. But this is not absolute knowledge that God exists, any more than to know that someone is coming is to know that Peter is coming, even though it should actually be Peter who comes. Many indeed think that riches are man's perfect good, and constitute his beatitude. Others think that pleasures are his perfect good, and others again something else.

On the second point: he who hears the term "God" may not understand it to mean that than which nothing greater can be conceived, since some have believed that God is a body. But given that one understands the term to mean this, it does not follow that he understands that that which the term signifies exists in the nature of things, but only that it exists in the intellect. Neither can it be argued that God exists in reality, unless it is granted that that than which nothing greater can be conceived exists in reality, which is not granted by those who suppose that God does not exist.

On the third point: it is self-evident that truth in general exists. But it is not self-evident to us that the first truth exists.

Article Two

WHETHER GOD'S EXISTENCE CAN BE DEMONSTRATED

We proceed to the second article thus:

1. It seems that God's existence cannot be demonstrated. God's existence is an article of faith. But matters of faith cannot be demonstrated, since demonstration makes a thing to be known, whereas the apostle makes it clear that faith is of things not seen (Heb., ch. 11). It follows that God's existence cannot be demonstrated.

2. Again the medium of demonstration is the essence. But as the Damascene says (1 De. Fid. Orth. 4), we cannot know what God is, but only what he is not. It follows that we cannot demonstrate that God exists.

3. Again, God's existence could be demonstrated only from his effects. But his effects are not proportionate to God himself, since God is infinite while they are finite, and the finite is not proportionate to the infinite. Now a cause cannot be demonstrated from an effect which is not proportionate to itself. It follows that God's existence cannot be demonstrated.

On the other hand: the apostle says in Rom. 1:20: "the invisible things

[7] According to 1 Post. An., chs. 2, 3, the ultimate grounds of scientific proof must be self-evident principles which are "better known to nature," i.e., first in the order of nature, and thus naturally prior to the conclusions drawn from them. The order of our knowing is then the same as the order of being, so that we understand things through their causes. This is obviously impossible in the present instance. Cf. Art. 2.

of him . . . are clearly seen, being understood by the things that are made."
Now this is possible only if God's existence can be demonstrated from the
things that are made. For the first thing that is understood about anything
is its existence.

I answer: there are two kinds of demonstration. There is demonstration
through the cause, or, as we say, "from grounds," which argues from what
comes first in nature. There is also demonstration by means of effects, or
"proof by means of appearances," which argues from what comes first for
ourselves. Now when an effect is more apparent to us than its cause, we
reach a knowledge of the cause through its effect. Even though the effect
should be better known to us, we can demonstrate from any effect that its
cause exists, because effects always depend on some cause, and a cause must
exist if its effect exists. We can demonstrate God's existence in this way,
from his effects which are known to us, even though we do not know his
essence.

On the first point: the existence of God, and similar things which can
be known by natural reason as Rom., ch. 1, affirms, are not articles of faith,
but preambles to the articles. Faith presupposes natural knowledge as grace
presupposes nature, and as perfection presupposes what can be perfected.
There is no reason, however, why what is in itself demonstrable and know-
able should not be accepted in faith by one who cannot understand the
demonstration of it.

On the second point: when a cause is demonstrated by means of its
effect, we are bound to use the effect in place of a definition of the cause in
proving the existence of the cause. This is especially the case with regard to
God. For in proving that something exists, we are bound to accept the
meaning of the name as the medium of demonstration, instead of the
essence, since the question of what a thing is must follow the question of its
existence. Since the names applied to God are derived from his effects, as
we shall show in Q. 13, Art. 1, we may use the name "God" as the medium
in demonstrating God's existence from his effect.

On the third point: effects which are not proportionate to their cause
do not give us perfect knowledge of their cause. Nevertheless, it can be
clearly demonstrated from any effect whatever that its cause exists, as we
have said. In this way we can prove God's existence from his effects, even
though we cannot know his essence perfectly by means of them.

Article Three

WHETHER GOD EXISTS

We proceed to the third article thus:

1. It seems that God does not exist. If one of two contraries were to be
infinite, the other would be wholly excluded. Now the name "God" means
that he is infinite good. There would therefore be no evil if God were to
exist. But there is evil in the world. It follows that God does not exist.

2. Again, what can be explained by comparatively few principles is not the consequence of a greater number of principles. Now if we suppose that God does not exist, it appears that we can still account for all that we see in the world by other principles, attributing all natural things to nature as their principle, and all that is purposive to human reason or will. There is therefore no need to suppose that God exists.

On the other hand: in Ex. 3:14 God says in person: "I AM THAT I AM."

I answer: God's existence can be proved in five ways. The first and clearest proof is the argument from motion.[8] It is certain, and in accordance with sense experience, that some things in this world are moved. Now everything that is moved is moved by something else, since nothing is moved unless it is potentially that to which it is moved, whereas that which moves is actual. To move is nothing other than to bring something from potentiality to actuality, and a thing can be brought from potentiality to actuality only by something which is actual. Thus a fire, which is actually hot, makes wood, which is potentially hot, to be actually hot, so moving and altering it. Now it is impossible for the same thing to be both actual and potential in the same respect, although it may be so in different respects. What is actually hot cannot at the same time be potentially hot, although it is potentially cold. It is therefore impossible that, in the same respect and in the same way, anything should be both mover and moved, or that it should move itself. Whatever is moved must therefore be moved by something else. If, then, that by which it is moved is itself moved, this also must be moved by something else, and this in turn by something else again. But this cannot go on forever, since there would then be no first mover, and consequently no other mover, because secondary movers cannot move unless moved by a first mover, as a staff cannot move unless it is moved by the hand. We are therefore bound to arrive at a first mover which is not moved by anything, and all men understand that this is God.

The second way is from the nature of an efficient cause. We find that there is a sequence of efficient causes in sensible things. But we do not find that anything is the efficient cause of itself. Nor is this possible, for the thing would then be prior to itself, which is impossible. But neither can the sequence of efficient causes be infinite, for in every sequence the first efficient cause is the cause of an intermediate cause, and an intermediate cause is the cause of the ultimate cause, whether the intermediate causes be many, or only one. Now if a cause is removed, its effect is removed. Hence if there were no first efficient cause, there would be no ultimate cause, and no intermediate cause. But if the regress of efficient causes were infinite, there would

[8] This paragraph may be compared with Aristotle's *Physics*, bk. 7, ch. 1, 242a; bk. 8, ch. 4, 254b, ch. 5, 256a. Cf. also S. *Contra Gentiles* I, ch. 13, which contains all except the third way. The third way is contained with slight variations in *ibid.* I, ch. 15, II, ch. 15.

be no first efficient cause. There would consequently be no ultimate effect, and no intermediate causes. But this is plainly false. We are therefore bound to suppose that there is a first efficient cause. And all men call this God.

The third way is from the nature of possibility and necessity. There are some things which may either exist or not exist, since some things come to be and pass away, and may therefore be or not be. Now it is impossible that all of these should exist at all times, because there is at least some time when that which may possibly not exist does not exist. Hence if all things were such that they might not exist, at some time or other there would be nothing. But if this were true there would be nothing existing now, since what does not exist cannot begin to exist, unless through something which does exist. If there had been nothing existing it would have been impossible for anything to begin to exist, and there would now be nothing at all. But this is plainly false, and hence not all existence is merely possible. Something in things must be necessary. Now everything which is necessary either derives its necessity from elsewhere, or does not. But we cannot go on to infinity with necessary things which have a cause of their necessity, any more than with efficient causes, as we proved. We are therefore bound to suppose something necessary in itself, which does not owe its necessity to anything else, but which is the cause of the necessity of other things. And all men call this God.

The fourth way is from the degrees that occur in things, which are found to be more and less good, true, noble, and so on. Things are said to be more and less because they approximate in different degrees to that which is greatest. A thing is the more hot the more it approximates to that which is hottest. There is therefore something which is the truest, the best, and the noblest, and which is consequently the greatest in being, since that which has the greatest truth is also greatest in being, as is said in 2 *Metaph.*, text 4. Now that which most thoroughly possesses the nature of any genus is the cause of all that the genus contains. Thus fire, which is most perfectly hot, is the cause of all hot things, as is said in the same passage. There is therefore something which is the cause of the being of all things that are, as well as of their goodness and their every perfection. This we call God.

The fifth way is from the governance of things. We see how some things, like natural bodies, work for an end even though they have no knowledge. The fact that they nearly always operate in the same way, and so as to achieve the maximum good, makes this obvious, and shows that they attain their end by design, not by chance. Now things which have no knowledge tend towards an end only through the agency of something which knows and also understands, as an arrow through an archer. There is therefore an intelligent being by whom all natural things are directed to their end. This we call God.

On the first point: as Augustine says (*Enchirid.* II): "since God is supremely good, he would not allow any evil thing to exist in his works, were he not able by his omnipotence and goodness to bring good out of evil." God's infinite goodness is such that he permits evil things to exist, and brings good out of them.

On the second point: everything that can be attributed to nature must depend on God as its first cause, since nature works for a predetermined end through the direction of a higher agent. Similarly, whatever is due to purpose must depend on a cause higher than the reason or will of man, since these are subject to change and defect. Anything which is changeable and subject to defect must depend on some first principle which is immovable and necessary in itself, as we have shown.

7 MEISTER ECKHART (1260–1327) is a central representative of the mystic strain in medieval theology. He was a member of the Dominican order and thoroughly versed in the theological work of Thomas Aquinas. Eckhart conceived of the fully developed religious life as the union of the soul with God. He himself struggled to achieve this full human-divine communion, though in so doing he undercut many ecclesiastical practices. In his later life he was charged with heresy; his excommunication from the church did not occur until two years after his death.

The Nobility of the Soul[*]

MEISTER ECKHART

Whosoever would attain to the summit of his noble nature and to the vision of the sovran good, which is God himself, must have profoundest knowledge of himself and of things above himself. Thus he reaches the supreme. Beloved, learn to know thyself, it shall profit thee more than any craft of creatures. How to know thyself, of this now learn two ways.

First, see that thy outward senses are properly controlled. Reflect, as regards these outward senses, that to the eye evil presents itself no less than

[*] From, Franz Pfeiffer, *Meister Eckhart*, tr. by C. de B. Evans, Vol. I. London: John M. Watkins, 1924.

good. The ear is importuned by one as well as the other and so with the other senses. Wherefore it behoves thee strictly to confine thyself and with all diligence to those things which are good. So much for the outward senses.

Now turn to the inward senses or noble powers of the soul, lower and higher. Take the lower powers first. These are intermediate between the higher powers and the outward senses. They are excited by the outward senses: what the eye sees, what the ear hears, they offer forthwith to desire. This offers it again, in the ordinary course, to the second power, called judgment, which considers it and once more passes it on to the third power, reckoning or reason. In this way it is clarified before it arrives at the higher faculties. So exalted is the power of the soul that she can seize it minus form or image and carry it in this state up into her higher powers. Here it is stored in the memory, mastered in the intellect and consummated in the will. These are the superior powers of the soul and they are one in nature. What the soul does is done by this simple nature in her powers.

Now it may be asked, What is this nature of the soul?—It is the consciousness (the spark or synteresis) in the soul, that is the impartible nature of the soul. So subtile is this nature of the soul that space might not exist at all for all it troubles her. For instance, if one has a friend a thousand leagues away, thither flows the soul with the best part of her powers, loving her friend there. St. Augustine testifies to this. He says, 'The soul is where she loves rather than where she is giving life.' The simple nature of the soul is in no way hampered by place. So much for the nature of the soul.

Next consider her higher powers, so orderly appointed, so admirably adapted to their several functions albeit of one nature. Memory is the power of storing up what the other powers bring in, that is its function.—The second power is understanding. This is so exalted that in its understanding of the highest good, God namely, all the other powers must subserve it to the best of their ability.—The third faculty is will. It is lordly enough to bid what it will and forbid what it will not; from things it does not will it is altogether free. So much for the superior powers of the soul and the rôle assigned to each.

Doctors dispute as to whether understanding is the nobler or the will The position is this. Understanding sees things beyond this mundane level, that is its prerogative. But to will alone are all things possible. As St. Paul declares, 'I can do all things in God who strengtheneth me.' When understanding comes to the end of its tether, up soars the will transcendent in the light and power of faith. Here will surpasses understanding. This is the prerogative of will. But mind you, though the will is free to do and leave undone exactly as it will, this upward flight is not achieved by its own power alone: help comes from the other powers and from faith as well. What help we shall now see. The powers have in common their impartible nature, and to this is due the transcension of the will. The other powers are the cause of this transcension in virtue of identity of nature. That is one help.

Then comes the question, which is the power in the psychic Trinity wherein faith first appears?—The middle one: it springs from understanding but it is fortified in will and will is fortified by faith. Thus the light of faith contributes to this ascent of will. That is the second help. And of still another it remains to tell. Intellect projects itself to hear and understand. It analyses, orders, synthesises. But even when working to perfection, always there is something on beyond which it cannot penetrate and which it recognizes as belonging to a higher order. This it communicates to will, in their common nature, not in its individual capacity. This communication gives will an upward swing which displaces it into that higher order—always in their common nature. Here understanding is superior to will. But to will as individual a certain superiority belongs at the summit of its nature where it receives from the highest good, from very God.—What does it receive?— It receives grace and in grace the highest good itself. What soul receives she receives willingly or not at all. Not that will as such receives this light: to receive is not its part; but by the grace of the sovran good the other powers are strengthened in their common nature. This light is kindled in that second power, in the Holy Ghost. It is in this light that all works are wrought in the soul. As Isaiah says, 'All our works are wrought by God.' This light is gracious light, and any light outside this light is the light of nature. It is a sure sign of this light when of his own free will a person turns from mortal things to the highest good, God namely. We are in duty bound to love him for conferring on the soul such great perfection. When she has reached her limit of endeavour then will as such is free to leap over to that gnosis which is God himself. A somersault which lands the soul at the summit of her power. A marvel, truly, God has made from naught in the image of himself!

See now how the soul rises to sovran rank and to the zenith of her power. One master says, God is conveyed into the soul and there implanted. Whence there arises in the soul a divine love-spring which bears the soul back into God. Mark how. According to one holy man, 'Whatever we can say of God, that God is not.' According to another, 'Whatever we can say of God, God is.' And an eminent authority declares that both are right. With these three holy men even so I say, that when with her own understanding the soul receives divine understanding it is offered forthwith to her will. Will accepting it grows one with what it has accepted and finally takes it and puts it away in the memory. Thus God is conveyed and implanted in the soul. Then as to the divine love-spring. This overflowing in the soul causes her higher powers to flood the lower ones and the lower ones flood the outward man who, borne above all nether things, is incapable save of what is spiritual. As the spirit works by divine energy even so the outward man is driven by the spirit.

Oh wonder of wonders! When I think of the union of the soul with God! He makes the soul to flow out of herself in joyful ecstasy, for no named things content her. And since she is herself a nature named therefore she fails to content herself. The divine love-spring surges over the soul sweeping her out of herself into the unnamed being in her original source, for that is all God is. Creatures have given him names, but in himself he is nameless essence. Thus the soul arrives at the height of her perfection.

Further as concerns the noble nature of the soul. St. Augustine says, 'As with God so with the soul.' Had God not made the soul in the likeness of himself, to be God by grace, she could never be God above grace. Her likeness to the pattern of the blessed Trinity we see by comparing her with God.

God is threefold in Person and onefold in his nature. God is in all places and in each place whole. In other words, all places are the place of God. And the same with her. God has prevision of all things and everything is pictured in his providence. This is natural to God. And also to the soul. She too is threefold in her powers and simple in her nature. She too exists in all her members and in each member whole. So that all her members are the place of the soul. She too has foresight and imagines such things as she is able. To anything that we can predicate of God, soul has a certain likeness. Or, in the words of St. Augustine, 'Like God like the soul.' God has endowed the soul with his own likeness which did she not possess she could not be God by grace nor above grace either; whereas in this likeness she is able to attain to being God by grace and also above grace. And she must equal him in divine love and divine activity. So much for the soul as being God by grace.

The soul who abides in this perfect likeness and in this noble nature God has given her, and at the same time rises to higher rank and higher, to her, what time she leaves the body, and at that very point, eternal life is open and in the opening she is encompassed with divine light, and enveloped in this divine light she is absorbed and transformed into God. Now each of the powers of the soul is endowed with the likeness of a divine Person: will receives the likeness of the Holy Ghost; understanding receives the likeness of the Son; memory the likeness of the Father and (her nature the likeness of the) divine nature withal remaining undivided.—That is as far as I can understand it.

In the third place let us see how the soul becomes God above grace. What God has given her is changeless for she has reached a height where she has no further need of grace. In this exalted state she has lost her proper self and is flowing full-flood into the unity of the divine nature. But what, you may ask, is the fate of this lost soul: does she find herself or not? My answer is, it seems to me that she does find herself and that at the point where every intelligence sees itself with itself. For though she sink all sinking in the oneness of divinity she never touches bottom. Wherefore God has left her one little point from which to get back to herself and find herself and know herself as creature. For it is of the very essence of the soul that she is powerless to plumb the depths of her creator. Henceforth I shall not speak about the soul, for she has lost her name yonder in the oneness of divine essence. There she is no more called soul: she is called infinite being. . . .

Now we will speak about the union of the soul with God. There are those who say, nothing unites the soul so much as knowledge. Others again aver the same of love. And yet a third school teaches that nothing unites like use (i.e. actual enjoyment). Now I put one question regarding these three things. What is the property of each? Each is its own peculiar property. But at the summit of its property (its nature) each of them approaches so closely to the rest that they are virtually the same: threefold yet one in nature. This, to be sure, is not strictly true, but in the higher reaches of their nature, where they are verging on each other, knowledge enhances love and love enjoyment. Each one, however, does its own appropriate work. Knowledge raises the soul to the rank of God; love unites the soul with God; use perfects the soul to God. These three transport the soul right out of time into eternity. There the spirit in perfect freedom enjoys in its origin the height of bliss. Love and the sweetness of its uses have lured forth the soul to its naked spark. What is her fortune there? All I can say is this: the glance, out of the spirit, which pierces without stop into naked Godhead; the flow, out of the Godhead, into the naked spirit, these are but one form which conforms and unites the spirit to God in form and oneness so that it receives as like from like. How spirit fares in this exalted state I know not, nor can I tell at all more than to say that the spirit is then at the summit of its power and its welfare is supreme.

Peradventure you will say, 'It is all very well to talk, my friend, but how do I arrive at this exalted state you have described?'—See. God is what he is and what he is is mine and what is mine I love and what I love loves me and absorbs me and what absorbs me that I am rather than my own self. By loving God therefore ye may become God with God.

8

MARTIN LUTHER remains among the most provocative of Christian theologians. Though he did not have the systematic interest of John Calvin, his zealous and spirited writings have continued to be a seminal influence in Christian thought.

Born in 1483, educated at the University of Erfurt, Luther entered an Augustinian monastery as fulfillment of a vow made during a moment of personal trial. The rigorous study and disciplined life of a monk left him still concerned about his status before God. After a period at the University of Wittenberg, where he lectured on the Old and New Testaments, he began his critique of Roman Catholicism. Enjoying the protection of his political overlord, Frederick the Wise, his reforming labors increased in scope and intensity—an attack on abuses of the church and a reconsideration of fundamental elements in the Roman Catholic interpretation of the Christian faith. His death occurred in 1546.

The following selection is taken from: *Dr. Martin Luther's Answer to the Super Christian, Superspiritual, and Superlearned Book of Goat Emser of Leipzig*, written in 1521. Jerome Emser, a teacher of Luther and a stalwart defender of the papacy, engaged in a verbal and written controversy with the Wittenberg reformer after the publication of Luther's *Address to the Christian Nobility of the German Nation*. An excerpt from Luther's counterresponse follows, showing his stress on the sole authority of scripture in matters of faith in contrast to the traditional and complementary relation of scripture and tradition in Catholicism.[1]

The Letter and the Spirit*

MARTIN LUTHER

The Holy Spirit is the plainest writer and speaker in heaven and earth, and therefore His words cannot have more than one, and that the very simplest, sense, which we call the literal, ordinary, natural, sense. That the things indicated by the simple sense of His simple words should signify something further and different, and therefore one thing should always signify another, is more than a question of words or of language. For the same is true of all other things outside of the scriptures, since all of God's works

* From Works of Martin Luther, Vol. III. Philadelphia: A. J. Holman Co., 1930. Used by permission of The Board of Publications of the Lutheran Church in America.

[1] See also, *The Treatise on Christian Liberty*, Selection 45A; *Preface to Romans*, Selection 45B; *The Bondage of The Will*, Selection 45C; *The Babylonian Captivity of the Church*, Selection 63. Also, *Council of Trent*, Selection 10.

and creatures are living signs and words of God, as St. Augustine and all the teachers declare. But we are not on that account to say that the scriptures or the Word of God have more than one meaning.

A painted picture of a living man signifies a person, without need of a word of explanation. But that does not cause you to say that the word "picture" has a twofold sense, a literal sense, meaning the picture, and a spirtual sense, meaning the living person. Now, although the things described in the scriptures have a further significance, the scriptures do not on that account have a twofold sense, but only the one which the words give. Beyond that we can give permission to speculative minds to seek and chase after the various significations of the things mentioned, provided they take care not to go too far or too high, as sometimes happens to the chamois hunters and did happen to Origen. It is much surer and safer to abide by the words in their simple sense; they furnish the real pasture and right dwelling-places for all minds.

Now see the lofty way in which Emser comes along with his double Bible and brings uncertainty upon both parts. When St. Peter says: "We are all priests," he declares, this is said in the spiritual, not in the literal, sense. But when I ask, why not in the literal sense? Emser answers: Because the literal sense killeth. He does not understand one iota of what he says, nor does he see how he himself brings shame upon his own priesthood by teaching clearly that it is not the living, spiritual priesthood, but the literal, harmful, deadly priesthood, so that it would indeed be better to be a mythical priest than such a literal priest. If whatever is not spirit has no life and has no spiritual meaning, it must surely be harmful, deadly, and worse than heathenish, and must be understood literally, if indeed the high, superspiritual Emserian theology is to stand. 'Twere well if a smith remained a smith and a poetaster stayed a poetaster, and left the wielding of the spiritual sword to such as have strong fists and powerful arms. The scriptures do not tolerate such a separation of the letter and the spirit as Emser so wantonly teaches; they know but one priesthood and have but one meaning.

Many sensible men have made the mistake of calling the "letter" a figure of speech, Augustine among them. As if I were to say, Emser is a stupid ass, and a simple-minded man hearing these words, would understand that Emser were actually an ass with long ears and four legs. The man would have been deceived by the letter, whereas I wanted to convey, through the figure of speech, what a blockhead Emser is. Figures of speech are a subject of study in the schools and are called in Greek *schemata*, and in Latin *figurae*, because they are a decking out of speech, even as you adorn the body with jewels. The scriptures are full of such figures of speech, particularly the books of the prophets. John and Christ in Luke iii call the Jews *genimina viperarum*, generation of vipers. St. Paul in Colossians ii calls them dogs. Psalm cix says: "The dew of thy children shall come out of the womb of

the morning." Again: "God shall send the rod of thy strength out of Zion."
That means the children of Christ are born, not physically from a mother's
womb, but without the work of man, like the dew from heaven, out of the
morning of the Christian church. Further, Christ says, Matthew v: "Ye are
the salt of the earth and the light of the world." But this is not what St. Paul
means by the word "letter." This belongs to the study of grammar in the
schools.

If you can humble yourself and not despise me altogether, I will do
what out of Christian duty I owe to my enemy, and not withhold from you
God's gift to me. I will give you better instruction in this matter—I say this
without boasting—than any you have received heretofore from any teacher
except St. Augustine, if perchance you have read his *De Spiritu et Litera*.
None of the others will teach you aright. You will not find a single letter in
the whole Bible that agrees with what you, together with Origen and
Jerome, call the spiritual sense. St. Paul calls it a mystery, a secret, hidden
sense, wherefore the earliest of the fathers called it an anagogical, that is, a
more remote sense, a meaning by itself, and sometimes also an allegory, St.
Paul himself using the latter term in Galatians iv. But that is not yet the
"spirit," although the Spirit has given it as well as the letter and all the gifts,
as we see from I Corinthians xiv: "The Spirit speaketh mysteries." Some,
however, because they did not understand this matter, ascribed a fourfold
sense to scripture, the literal, the allegorical, the anagogical, and the tropo-
logical, for which there is no foundation whatever.

It is therefore not well named the literal sense, for by letter Paul means
something quite different. They do much better who call it the grammatical,
historical sense. It would be well to call it the speaking or language sense
as St. Paul does in I Corinthians xiv, because it is understood by every-
boy in the sense of the spoken language. He who hears the words that
Abraham had two sons by two wives, receives them in that sense and has no
further thoughts than those indicated by the language, until the Spirit
goes farther and reveals the hidden sense concerning Christ and the two
covenants and peoples. Such hidden meanings are then called mysteries, just
as St. Paul in Ephesians v calls the union of Christ and the Church in one
body a mystery, although the letter of the scriptures in Genesis ii speaks of
man and wife. Great care is necessary however, that not everyone shall of
himself invent mysteries, as some have done and still do. The Spirit must
do it Himself or one must prove them by scripture, as I said in the treatise
on the *Papacy*.

Therefore the text of St. Paul in II Corinthians iv, "The letter killeth
but the spirit giveth life," squares with this twofold sense, the spiritual and
the literal, as perfectly as Emser's head squares with philosophy and theology. How and why Origen, Jerome, and some other fathers also turned and
twisted this text in the same manner I will not discuss now. It is generally

known and can easily be proved that they treated other passages in the same way in order to refute the Jews and the heretics. But we ought to excuse them for that and not follow them here like unclean animals who gulp down everything they find and make no distinctions in the work and teaching of the fathers, until at last we follow them only in those things wherein the beloved fathers—as human beings—erred, and depart from them in the things they did well. I could prove this easily from the teachings and the lives of all who now are considered the very worthiest among them.

Let us now consider the text concerning the letter and the spirit. In that passage St. Paul does not write one iota about these two senses, but declares that there are two kinds of preaching or ministries. One is that of the Old Testament, the other that of the New Testament. The Old Testament preaches the letter, the New Testament the spirit. But in order that I may not, like Goat Emser, tell my own dream, let us hear in the clear words of the apostle himself that he speaks of the ministers or preachers of the New Testament in II Corinthians iv. They read as follows: "Ye are an epistle of Christ, through our ministry, written not with ink, but with the Spirit of the living God; not in tables of stone, but in fleshy tables of the heart. Therefore we needed not epistles of commendation to you. And such trust have we to God through Christ, not that we are sufficient of ourselves to think anything of ourselves, but our sufficiency is of God; who also hath made us able ministers and preachers of the New Testament, not of the letter, but of the spirit; for the letter killeth, but the spirit giveth life," etc.

Is that not a clear statement concerning preaching? We see clearly that St. Paul speaks of two tables and two kinds of preaching. The tables of Moses were of stone, on which the law was inscribed by God's finger, Exodus xx. The tables of Christ, or the epistles of Christ, as he calls them here, are the hearts of Christians, in which are written, not letters as on Moses' tables, but the spirit of God, through the preaching of the Gospel and the ministry of the apostles. Now, just what does this mean? The letter is naught else but the divine law and commandment which is given in the Old Testament, through Moses, and is taught and proclaimed through Aaron's priesthood. It is called "letter" because it is written with letters on the tables of stone and in books. A letter it must ever remain; it never gives anything except its command. For no man is made better by the law, but only worse, for the law does not give help or grace; it merely commands and demands that a man do what a man never willingly does, and indeed, cannot do. But the spirit, which is divine grace, gives strength and power to the heart, yea, creates a new man, who grows to love God's command- ments and does with joy all that he ought to do.

This spirit cannot be contained in any letter, it cannot be written with ink, on stone, or in books, as the law can be, but is written only in the heart, a living writing of the Holy Spirit who uses no means at all. Therefore St.

Paul calls it Christ's epistle, not Moses' tables; it is written not with ink, but with the Spirit of God. By this spirit or grace a man does what the law commands and satisfies it. In this manner he becomes free from the letter that kills him and lives through the grace of the Spirit. Everyone that does not have this grace of the living Spirit is dead, although he makes a fine show in the outward keeping of the whole law. For this reason the apostle says of the law that it kills, that it makes no one alive and would keep one eternally in bondage to death unless grace comes to set him free and to give him life.

These, then, are the two ministries. The priests, preachers, and ministries of the Old Testament deal with naught else but the law of God; they have as yet no open proclamation of the spirit and of grace. But in the New Testament all the preaching is of grace and the spirit given to us through Christ. For the preaching of the New Testament is naught else but an offering and presentation of Christ to all men out of the pure mercy of God, in such wise that all who believe in Him receive God's grace and the Holy Spirit, by which all sin is forgiven, all law is fulfilled, they become God's children, and have eternal salvation. Therefore St. Paul here calls the New Testament proclamation *ministerium spiritus*, a ministry of the spirit, i.e., a ministry by which the spirit and grace of God are presented and offered to all who by the law have been burdened, killed, and made to long for grace. The law he calls *ministerium literae*, a ministry of the letter, i.e., a ministry which offers nothing but the letter or the law, that produces no life nor a fulfillment of the law whose demands no man can satisfy. Therefore it must needs remain a letter, and as a letter it can accomplish nothing more than to kill a man, i.e., it shows him what he ought to do and yet cannot do; this makes him realize that he is in disgrace and dead before God, whose commandments he does not keep and yet must keep.

This makes it clear that the word of the apostle, "The letter killeth, the spirit giveth life," might be expressed in other words, thus: "The law killeth, but the grace of God giveth life," or: "Grace gives help and does all that the law demands and of itself cannot do." For this reason St. Paul calls God's law a law of death and of sin, and declares, Romans viii: "The law of the living spirit in Christ has redeemed me from the law of sin and death. For the law could not help me—it made things worse through the wickedness of the sinful flesh—therefore God sent his own son into our flesh, and let him become like unto our sinful flesh and thus blotted out our sins through Christ's assumption of sin in his suffering, that thereby the righteousness of the law might be fulfilled in us." Here we see how excellently St. Paul teaches us to understand aright, Christ, God's grace, and the New Testament. It is all comprised in the fact that Christ came unto our sin, bore it in His body on the cross, and blotted it out, so that all who believed on Him were rid of their sin and received grace henceforth to satisfy God's law and the letter that killeth, and thus were made partakers of eternal life. See, that is what is meant by *ministerium spiritus, non literae*, the preaching of the spirit, the preaching of grace, the preaching of a right indulgence, the preaching of Christ, i.e., the New Testament, of which much could be said if the evil spirit had not blinded the world through the pope, and by man-teaching had led it into the abyss of outermost darkness.

Now we see that all commandments lead unto death, since even divine commandments mean death, for everything that is not spirit or grace means death. It is, therefore, monstrous ignorance to call allegories, tropologies, and the like, spirit. They can all be encompassed in language and do not give life, but grace has no receptacle save the heart. And just as not all men take up this life of the spirit, nay, most of them let the ministers of the spirit preach and offer them such rich grace in vain, and believe not the Gospel, so likewise not all receive the ministry of the letter or preaching of the law, they do not want to be put under death, i.e., they understand not God's law, and go along without receiving either letter or spirit. And to pursue Goat Emser's blind perversion still further: he thinks we should avoid the letter and flee the death of the letter. That is what happens when one reads only the books of the fathers and puts the scriptures aside, juggles with spears and daggers, and makes a dense fog of the scriptures, but a bright light of the teachings of the fathers. . . .

My counsel therefore was and is, that we do not make a pretense of reforming these man-made teachings and the canon law, as Emser foolishly suggests, for that is impossible, but that we burn them up, cast them out, destroy them, overturn them entirely, or at least as much of them as we can, and then restore simply the two ministries of the letter and the spirit, which cannot be exercised unless the teachings of men are put away. It is surely proper that they give way to God's letter and spirit, to which they are a hindrance and obstruction. To preach the letter and the spirit gives us more to do than we are equal to, even if we began at the beginning of the world and kept on until doomsday.

Through we now live in the New Testament and should have only the preaching of the spirit, yet we are still clothed in flesh and blood, and therefore the preaching of the letter is needed too, first of all through the law to bring the people unto death and destroy their self-confidence, that they may know themselves and become hungry for the spirit and thirsty for grace, and so to prepare them for the preaching of the spirit, as it is written of St. John that he prepared the people for Christ by preaching repentance, which was the ministry of the letter, and then led them unto Christ and said: "Behold the lamb of God, that taketh away the sin of the whole world," which was the ministry of the spirit. These are the two works of God commended so often in the scriptures: He kills and makes alive, He wounds and He heals, He destroys and builds up, He condemns and pardons, He

brings low and lifts up, He rebukes and brings to honor, as it is recorded in
Deuteronomy xxxii, I Samuel ii, Psalm cxi, and other places. These works
He performs through the two ministries, the one by the letter, the second
by the Spirit. By the letter no one can abide in the presence of His wrath,
by the spirit no one can perish in the presence of His grace. O what an
abundance of riches is here! One could go on speaking about it forever,
and yet the pope and the precepts of men have hidden it and fastened an
iron curtain before it, that it cries to heaven. Amen.

9 JOHN CALVIN (1509–1564), the father of the Reformed tradition within Protestantism, was the major systematic
theologian of the sixteenth-century Reformation. Trained
in the legal profession, he gave an articulate and detailed
expression of his understanding of the Christian faith in his
major work, *Institutes of the Christian Religion*. The *Institutes* went through several editions, the first was published
in 1536; the last edition (1559), selections from which follow, was considerably expanded and developed. The work
is comprised of four books: I, "On the Knowledge of God
the Creator"; II, "On the Knowledge of God the Redeemer";
III, "On the Manner of Receiving the Grace of Christ";
IV, "On the External Means or Aids by Which God calls Us
into Communion with Christ." Calvin was a prolific writer;
his biblical commentaries serve to add richness to the closely
argued *Institutes*.

The following selection offers this Genevan theologian's
characteristically Reformed view of man's original ability
to derive knowledge of God from the natural world, yet
warped by sin, man must now put on the "spectacles of
scripture" to make evident what has become obscure.[1]

[1] See also selections from the *Institutes*, Selections 46, 66.

Institutes of the Christian Religion*

JOHN CALVIN

BOOK 1

CHAPTER 1

The connection between the knowledge of God and the knowledge of ourselves

True and substantial wisdom principally consists of two parts, the knowledge of God, and the knowledge of ourselves. But, while these two branches of knowledge are so intimately connected, which of them precedes and produces the other, is not easy to discover. For, in the first place, no man can take a survey of himself but he must immediately turn to the contemplation of God, in whom he "lives and moves;" since it is evident that the talents which we possess are not from ourselves, and that our very existence is nothing but a subsistence in God alone. These bounties, distilling to us by drops from heaven, form, as it were, so many streams conducting us to the fountain-head. Our poverty conduces to a clearer display of the infinite fulness of God. Especially, the miserable ruin, into which we have been plunged by the defection of the first man, compels us to raise our eyes towards heaven, not only as hungry and famished, to seek thence a supply for our wants, but, aroused with fear, to learn humility. For, since man is subject to a world of miseries, and has been spoiled of his divine array, this melancholy exposure discovers an immense mass of deformity: every one, therefore, must be so impressed with a consciousness of his own infelicity, as to arrive at some knowledge of God. Thus a sense of our ignorance, vanity, poverty, infirmity, depravity, and corruption, leads us to perceive and acknowledge that in the Lord alone are to be found true wisdom, solid strength, perfect goodness, and unspotted righteousness; and so, by our imperfections, we are excited to a consideration of the perfections of God. Nor can we really aspire toward him, till we have begun to be displeased with ourselves. For who would not gladly rest satisfied with himself? where is the man not actually absorbed in self-complacency, while he remains unacquainted with his true situation, or content with his own endowments, and ignorant or forgetful of his own misery? The knowledge of ourselves, therefore, is not only an incitement to seek after God, but likewise a considerable assistance towards finding him.

On the other hand, it is plain that no man can arrive at the true knowl-

* From John Calvin, *Institutes of the Christian Religion*, Vol. I, Bk. I, tr. by John Allen. Philadelphia: Presbyterian Board of Christian Education, 1936.

edge of himself, without having first contemplated the divine character, and then descended to the consideration of his own. For, such is the native pride of us all, we invariably esteem ourselves righteous, innocent, wise, and holy, till we are convinced, by clear proofs, of our unrighteousness, turpitude, folly, and impurity. But we are never thus convinced, while we confine our attention to ourselves, and regard not the Lord, who is the only standard by which this judgment ought to be formed. Because, from our natural proneness to hypocrisy, any vain appearance of righteousness abundantly contents us instead of the reality; and, every thing within and around us being exceedingly defiled, we are delighted with what is least so, as extremely pure, while we confine our reflections within the limits of human corruption. So the eye, accustomed to see nothing but black, judges that to be very white, which is but whitish, or perhaps brown. Indeed, the senses of our bodies may assist us in discovering how grossly we err in estimating the powers of the soul. For if at noon-day we look either on the ground, or at any surrounding objects, we conclude our vision to be very strong and piercing; but when we raise our eyes and steadily look at the sun, they are at once dazzled and confounded with such a blaze of brightness, and we are constrained to confess, that our sight, so piercing in viewing terrestrial things, when directed to the sun, is dimness itself. Thus also it happens in the consideration of our spiritual endowments. For as long as our views are bounded by the earth, perfectly content with our own righteousness, wisdom, and strength, we fondly flatter ourselves, and fancy we are little less than demigods. But, if we once elevate our thoughts to God, and consider his nature, and the consummate perfection of his righteousness, wisdom, and strength, to which we ought to be conformed,—what before charmed us in ourselves under the false pretext of righteousness, will soon be loathed as the greatest iniquity; what strangely deceived us under the title of wisdom, will be despised as extreme folly; and what wore the appearance of strength, will be proved to be most wretched impotence. So very remote from the divine purity is what seems in us the highest perfection.

Hence that horror and amazement with which the scripture always represents the saints to have been impressed and disturbed, on every discovery of the presence of God. For when we see those, who before his appearance stood secure and firm, so astonished and affrighted at the manifestation of his glory, as to faint and almost expire through fear,—we must infer that man is never sufficiently affected with a knowledge of his own meanness, till he has compared himself with the Divine Majesty. Of this consternation we have frequent examples in the Judges and Prophets; so that it was a common expression among the Lord's people—"We shall die, because we have seen God." Therefore the history of Job, to humble men with a consciousness of their pollution, impotence, and folly, derives its principal argument from a description of the Divine purity, power, and wisdom. And not without reason. For we see how Abraham, the nearer he approached to behold the glory of the Lord, the more fully acknowledged himself to be but "dust and ashes"; and how Elias could not bear his approach without covering his face, his appearance is so formidable. And what can man do, all vile and corrupt, when fear constrains even the cherubim themselves to veil their faces? This is what the prophet Isaiah speaks of—"the moon shall be confounded, and the sun ashamed, when the Lord of hosts shall reign:" that is, when he shall make a fuller and nearer exhibition of his splendour, it shall eclipse the splendour of the brightest object besides. But, though the knowledge of God and the knowledge of ourselves be intimately connected, the proper order of instruction requires us first to treat of the former, and then to proceed to the discussion of the latter.

CHAPTER 2

The nature and tendency of the knowledge of God

By the knowledge of God, I intend not merely a notion that there is such a Being, but also an acquaintance with whatever we ought to know concerning Him, conducing to his glory and our benefit. For we cannot with propriety say, there is any knowledge of God where there is no religion or piety. I have no reference here to that species of knowledge by which men, lost and condemned in themselves, apprehend God the Redeemer in Christ the Mediator; but only to that first and simple knowledge, to which the genuine order of nature would lead us, if Adam had retained his innocence. For though, in the present ruined state of human nature, no man will ever perceive God to be a Father, or the Author of salvation, or in any respect propitious, but as pacified by the mediation of Christ; yet it is one thing to understand, that God our Maker supports us by his power, governs us by his providence, nourishes us by his goodness, and follows us with blessings of every kind, and another to embrace the grace of reconciliation proposed to us in Christ. Therefore, since God is first manifested, both in the structure of the world and in the general tenor of scripture, simply as the Creator, and afterwards reveals himself in the person of Christ as a Redeemer, hence arises a twofold knowledge of him; of which the former is first to be considered, and the other will follow in its proper place. For though our mind cannot conceive of God, without ascribing some worship to him, it will not be sufficient merely to apprehend that he is the only proper object of universal worship and adoration, unless we are also persuaded that he is the fountain of all good, and seek for none but in him. This I maintain, not only because he sustains the universe, as he once made it, by his infinite power, governs it by his wisdom, preserves it by his goodness, and especially reigns over the human race in righteousness and judgment, exercising a merciful forbearance, and defending them by his protection; but because there cannot be found the least particle of wisdom, light, righteousness, power, rectitude, or sincere truth which does not proceed from him, and claim him for its author: we should therefore learn to expect and supplicate all these things from him, and thankfully to acknowledge what he gives us. For this sense of the divine perfections is calculated to teach us piety, which produces religion. By piety, I mean a reverence and love of God arising from a knowledge of his benefits. For, till men are sensible that they owe every thing to God, that they are supported by his paternal care, that he is the Author of all the blessings they enjoy, and that nothing should be sought independently of him, they will never voluntarily submit to his authority; they will never truly and cordially devote themselves to his service, unless they rely upon him alone for true felicity.

Cold and frivolous, then, are the speculations of those who employ themselves in disquisitions on the essence of God, when it would be more interesting to us to become acquainted with his character, and to know what is agreeable to his nature. For what end is answered by professing, with Epicurus, that there is a God, who, discarding all concern about the world, indulges himself in perpetual inactivity? What benefit arises from the knowledge of a God with whom we have no concern? Our knowledge of God should rather tend, first, to teach us fear and reverence; and, secondly, to instruct us to implore all good at his hand, and to render him the praise of all that we receive, For how can you entertain a thought of God without immediately reflecting, that, being a creature of his formation, you must, by right of creation, be subject to his authority? that you are indebted to him for your life, and that all your actions should be done with reference to him? If this be true, it certainly follows that your life is miserably corrupt, unless it be regulated by a desire of obeying him, since his will ought to be the rule of our conduct. Nor can you have a clear view of him without discovering him to be the fountain and origin of all good. This would produce a desire of union to him, and confidence in him, if the human mind were not seduced by its own depravity from the right path of investigation. For, even at the first, the pious mind dreams not of any imaginary deity, but contemplates only the one true God; and, concerning him, indulges not the fictions of fancy, but, content with believing him to be such as he reveals himself, uses the most diligent and unremitting caution, lest it should fall into error by a rash and presumptuous transgression of his will. He who thus knows him, sensible that all things are subject to his control, confides in him as his Guardian and Protector, and unreservedly commits himself to his care. Assured that he is the author of all blessings, in distress or want he immediately flies to his protection, and expects his aid. Persuaded of his goodness and mercy, he relies on him with unlimited confidence, nor doubts of finding in his clemency a remedy provided for all his evils. Knowing him to be his Lord and Father, he concludes that he ought to mark his government in all things, revere his majesty, endeavour to promote his glory, and obey his commands. Perceiving him to be a just judge, armed with severity for the punishment of crimes, he keeps his tribunal always in view, and is restrained by fear from provoking his wrath. Yet he is not so terrified at the apprehension of his justice, as to wish to evade it, even if escape were possible; but loves him as much in punishing the wicked as in blessing the pious, because he believes it as necessary to his glory to punish the impious and abandoned, as to reward the righteous with eternal life. Besides, he restrains himself from sin, not merely from a dread of vengeance, but because he loves and reveres God as his Father, honours and worships him as his Lord, and, even though there were no hell, would shudder at the thought of offending him. See, then, the nature of pure and genuine religion. It consists in faith, united with a serious fear of God, comprehending a voluntary reverence, and producing legitimate worship agreeable to the injunctions of the law. And this requires to be the more carefully remarked, because men in general render to God a formal worship, but very few truly reverence him; while great ostentation in ceremonies is universally displayed, but sincerity of heart is rarely to be found.

CHAPTER 3

The human mind naturally endued with the knowledge of God

We lay it down as a position not to be controverted, that the human mind, even by natural instinct, possesses some sense of a Deity. For that no man might shelter himself under the pretext of ignorance, God hath given to all some apprehension of his existence, the memory of which he frequently and insensibly renews; so that, as men universally know that there is a God, and that he is their Maker, they must be condemned by their own testimony, for not having worshipped him and consecrated their lives to his service. If we seek for ignorance of a Deity, it is nowhere more likely to be found, than among tribes the most stupid and furthest from civilization. But, as the celebrated Cicero observes, there is no nation so barbarous, no race so savage; as not to be firmly persuaded of the being of a God. Even those who in other respects appear to differ but little from brutes, always retain some sense of religion; so fully are the minds of men possessed with this common principle, which is closely interwoven with their original composition. Now, since there has never been a country or family, from the beginning of the world, totally destitute of religion, it is a tacit confession, that some sense of the Divinity is inscribed on every heart. Of this opinion, idolatry itself furnishes ample proof. For we know how reluctantly man would degrade himself to exalt other creatures above him. His preference of worshipping a piece of wood or stone, to being thought to have no god, evinces the impression of a Deity on the human mind to be very strong, the obliteration of which is more difficult than a total change of the natural disposition; and this is certainly changed, whenever man leaves his natural pride, and voluntarily descends to such meannesses under the notion of worshipping God.

It is most absurd, then, to pretend, as is asserted by some, that religion was the contrivance of a few subtle and designing men, a political machine to confine the simple multitude to their duty, while those who inculcated the worship of God on others, were themselves far from believing that any god existed. I confess, indeed, that artful men have introduced many inventions into religion, to fill the vulgar with reverence, and strike them with terror, in order to obtain the greater command over their minds. But this they never could have accomplished, if the minds of men had not previously been possessed of a firm persuasion of the existence of God, from which the propensity to religion proceeds. And that they who cunningly imposed on the illiterate, under the pretext of religion, were themselves wholly destitute of any knowledge of God, is quite incredible. For though there were some in ancient times, and many arise in the present age, who deny the existence of God, yet, in spite of their reluctance, they are continually receiving proofs of what they desire to disbelieve. We read of no one guilty of more audacious or unbridled contempt of the Deity than Caligula; yet no man ever trembled with greater distress at any instance of Divine wrath, so that he was constrained to dread the Divinity whom he professed to despise. This you may always see exemplified in persons of similar character. For the most audacious contemners of God are most alarmed, even at the noise of a falling leaf. Whence arises this, but from the vengeance of the Divine Majesty, smiting their consciences the more powerfully in proportion to their efforts to fly from it? They try every refuge to hide themselves from the Lord's presence, and to efface it from their minds; but their attempts to elude it are all in vain. Though it may seem to disappear for a moment, it presently returns with increased violence; so that, if they have any remission of the anguish of conscience, it resembles the sleep of persons intoxicated, or subject to frenzy, who enjoy no placid rest while sleeping, being continually harassed with horrible and tremendous dreams. The impious themselves, therefore, exemplify the observation, that the idea of a God is never lost in the human mind.

It will always be evident to persons of correct judgment, that the idea of a Deity impressed on the mind of man is indelible. That all have by nature an innate persuasion of the Divine existence, a persuasion inseparable from their very constitution, we have abundant evidence in the contumacy of the wicked, whose furious struggles to extricate themselves from the fear of God are unavailing. Though Diagoras, and others like him, turn to ridicule what all ages have believed of religion; though Dionysius scoff at the judgment of Heaven,—it is but a forced laughter, for the worm of a guilty conscience torments them within, worse than if they were seared with hot irons. I agree not with Cicero, that errors in process of time become obsolete, and that religion is increased and ameliorated daily. For the world, as will shortly be observed, uses its utmost endeavours to banish all knowledge of God, and tries every method of corrupting his worship. I only maintain, that while the stupid insensibility which the wicked wish to acquire, to promote their contempt of God, prey upon their minds, yet the sense of a Deity, which they ardently desire to extinguish is still strong, and frequently discovers itself. Whence we infer, that this is a doctrine, not first to be learned in the schools, but which every man from his birth is self-taught, and which, though many strain every nerve to banish if from them, yet nature itself permits none to forget. Now, if the end for which all men are born and live, be to know God,—and unless the knowledge of God have reached this point, it is uncertain and vain,—it is evident, that all who direct not every thought and action of life to this end, are degenerated from the law of their creation. Of this the heathen philosophers themselves were not ignorant. This was Plato's meaning, when he taught that the chief good of the soul consists in similitude to God, when the soul, having a clear knowledge of him, is wholly transformed into his likeness. The reasoning also of Gryllus, in Plutarch, is very accurate, when he affirms, that men entirely destitute of religion, not only do not excel the brutes, but are in many respects far more wretched, being obnoxious to evil under so many forms, and always dragging on a tumultuous and restless life. The worship of God is therefore the only thing which renders men superior to brutes, and makes them aspire to immortality.

CHAPTER 4

This knowledge extinguished or corrupted, partly by ignorance, partly by error

While experience testifies that the seeds of religion are sown by God in every heart, we scarcely find one man in a hundred who cherishes what he he has received, and not one in whom they grow to maturity, much less bear fruit in due season. Some perhaps grow vain in their own superstitions, while others revolt from God with intentional wickedness; but all degenerate from the true knowledge of him. The fact is, that no genuine piety remains in the world. But, in saying that some fall into superstition through error, I would not insinuate that their ignorance excuses them from guilt; because their blindness is always connected with pride, vanity, and contumacy. Pride and vanity are discovered, when miserable men, in seeking after God, rise not, as they ought, above their own level, but judge of him according to their carnal stupidity, and leave the proper path of investigation in pursuit of speculations as vain as they are curious. Their conceptions of him are formed, not according to the representations he gives of himself, but by the inventions of their own presumptuous imaginations. This gulf being opened, whatever course they take, they must be rushing forwards to destruction. None of their subsequent attempts for the worship or service of God can be considered as rendered to him; because they worship not him, but a figment of their own brains in his stead. This depravity Paul expressly remarks: "Professing themselves to be wise, they become fools." He had before said, "they became vain in their imaginations." But lest any should exculpate them, he adds that they were deservedly blinded, because, not content within the bounds of sobriety, but arrogating to themselves more than was right, they wilfully darkened, and even infatuated themselves with pride, vanity, and perverseness. Whence it follows, that their folly is inexcusable, which originates not only in a vain curiosity, but in false confidence, and an immoderate desire to exceed the limits of human knowledge.

David's assertion, that "the fool hath said in his heart, There is no God," is primarily, as we shall soon see in another place, to be restricted to those who extinguish the light of nature, and wilfully stupefy themselves. For we see many, become hardened by bold and habitual transgressions, striving to banish all remembrance of God, which the instinct of nature is still suggesting to their minds. To render their madness more detestable, he introduces them as expressly denying the existence of God; not that they deprive him of his being, but because they rob him of his justice and providence, shutting him up as an idler in heaven. Now, as nothing would be more inconsistent with Deity, than to abandon the government of the world, leave it to fortune, and connive at the crimes of men, that they might wanton with impunity,—whoever extinguishes all fear of the heavenly judgment, and indulges himself in security, denies that there is any God. After the impious have wilfully shut their own eyes, it is the righteous vengeance of God upon them, to darken their understandings, so that, seeing, they may not perceive. David is the best interpreter of his own meaning, in another place, where he says, "The wicked have no fear of God before their eyes;" and again, that they encourage themselves in their iniquities with the flattering persuasion that God doth not see them. Though they are constrained to acknowledge the existence of God, yet they rob him of his glory, by detracting from his power. For as God, according to the testimony of Paul, "cannot deny himself," because he perpetually remains like himself,—those who feign him to be a vain and lifeless image, are truly said to deny God. It must also be remarked, that, though they strive against their own natural understanding, and desire not only to banish him thence, but even to annihilate him in heaven, their insensibility can never prevail so as to prevent God from sometimes recalling them to his tribunal. But as no dread restrains them from violent opposition to the divine will, it is evident, as long as they are carried away with such a blind impetuosity, that they are governed by a brutish forgetfulness of God.

Thus is overthrown the vain excuse pleaded by many for their superstition; for they satisfy themselves with any attention to religion, however preposterous, not considering that the Divine Will is the perpetual rule to which true religion ought to be conformed; that God ever continues like himself; that he is no spectre of phantasm, to be metamorphosed according to the fancy of every individual. It is easy to see how superstition mocks God with hypocritical services, while it attempts to please him. For, embracing only those things which he declares he disregards, it either contemptuously practises, or even openly rejects, what he prescribes and declares to be pleasing in his sight. Persons who introduce newly-invented methods of worshipping God, really worship and adore the creature of their distempered imaginations; for they would never have dared to trifle in such a manner with God, if they had not first feigned a god conformable to their own false and foolish notions. Wherefore the apostle pronounces a vague and unsettled notion concerning the Deity to be ignorance of God. "When ye knew not God, (says he,) ye did service unto them which by nature were no gods." And in another place he speaks of the Ephesians as having been "without God," while they were strangers to a right knowledge of the only true God. Nor, in this respect, is it of much importance, whether you imagine to yourself one god or more; for in either case you depart and revolt from the true God, and, forsaking him, you have nothing left you but an execrable idol. We must therefore decide, with Lactantius, that there is no legitimate religion unconnected with truth.

Another sin is, that they never think of God but against their inclinations, nor approach him till their reluctance is overcome by constraint; and then they are influenced, not by a voluntary fear, proceeding from reverence of the Divine Majesty, but by a servile and constrained fear, extorted by the divine judgment, which they dread because it is inevitable, at the same time that they hate it. Now, to impiety, and to this species of it alone, is applicable that assertion of Statius, that fear first made gods in the world. They, whose minds are alienated from the righteousness of God, earnestly desire the subversion of that tribunal, which they know to be established for the punishment of transgressions against it. With this disposition, they wage war against the Lord, who cannot be deprived of his judgment; but when they apprehend his irresistible arm to be impending over their heads, unable to avert or evade it, they tremble with fear. That they may not seem altogether to despise him, whose majesty troubles them, they practise some form of religion; at the same time not ceasing to pollute themselves with vices of every kind, and to add one flagitious act to another, till they have violated every part of God's holy law, and dissipated all its righteousness. It is certain, at least, that they are not prevented by that pretended fear of God from enjoying pleasure and satisfaction in their sins, practising self-adulation, and preferring the indulgence of their own carnal intemperance to the salutary restraints of the Holy Spirit. But that being a false and vain shadow of religion, and scarcely worthy even to be called its shadow,—it is easy to infer the wide difference between such a confused notion of God, and the piety which is instilled only into the minds of the faithful, and is the source of religion. Yet hypocrites, who are flying from God, resort to the artifices of superstition, for the sake of appearing devoted to him. For whereas the whole tenor of their life ought to be a perpetual course of obedience to him, they make no scruple of rebelling against him in almost all their actions, only endeavouring to appease him with a few paltry sacrifices. Whereas he ought to be served with sanctity of life and integrity of heart, they invent frivolous trifles and worthless observances, to conciliate his favour. They abandon themselves to their impurities with the greater licentiousness, because they confide in being able to discharge all their duty to him by ridiculous expiations. In a word, whereas their confidence ought to be placed on him, they neglect him, and depend upon themselves or on other creatures. At length they involve themselves in such a vast accumulation of errors, that those sparks which enable them to discover the glory of God are smothered, and at last extinguished by the criminal darkness of iniquity. That seed, which it is impossible to eradicate, a sense of the existence of a Deity, yet remains; but so corrupted as to produce only the worst of fruits. Yet this is a further proof of what I now contend for, that an idea of God is naturally engraved on the hearts of men, since necessity extorts a confession of it, even from reprobates themselves. In the moment of tranquillity, they facetiously mock the Divine Being, and with loquacious impertinence derogate from his power. But if any despair oppress them, it stimulates them to seek him, and dictates concise prayers, which prove that they are not altogether ignorant of God, but that what ought to have appeared before had been suppressed by obstinacy.

CHAPTER 5

The knowledge of God conspicuous in the formation and continual government of the world

. . . Of his wonderful wisdom, both heaven and earth contain innumerable proofs; not only those more abstruse things, which are the subjects of astronomy, medicine, and the whole science of physics, but those things which force themselves on the view of the most illiterate of mankind, so that they cannot open their eyes without being constrained to witness them. Adepts, indeed, in those liberal arts, or persons just initiated into them, are thereby enabled to proceed much further in investigating the secrets of Divine Wisdom. Yet ignorance of those sciences prevents no man from such a survey of the workmanship of God, as is more than sufficient to excite his admiration of the Divine Architect. In disquisitions concerning the motions of the stars, in fixing their situations, measuring their distances, and distinguishing their peculiar properties, there is need of skill, exactness, and industry; and the providence of God being more clearly revealed by these discoveries, the mind ought to rise to a sublimer elevation for the contemplation of his glory. But since the meanest and most illiterate of mankind, who are furnished with no other assistance than their own eyes, cannot be ignorant of the excellence of the Divine skill, exhibiting itself in that endless, yet regular variety of the innumerable celestial host,—it is evident, that the Lord abundantly manifests his wisdom to every individual on earth. Thus it belongs to a man of preëminent ingenuity to examine, with the critical exactness of Galen, the connection, the symmetry, the beauty, and the use of the various parts of the human body. But the composition of the human body is universally acknowledged to be so ingenious, as to render its Maker the object of deserved admiration. . . .

But herein appears the vile ingratitude of men—that, while they ought to be proclaiming the praises of God for the wonderful skill displayed in their formation, and the inestimable bounties he bestows on them, they are only inflated with the greater pride. They perceive how wonderfully God works within them, and experience teaches them what a variety of blessings they receive from his liberality. They are constrained to know, whether willingly or not, that these are proofs of his divinity: yet they suppress this knowledge in their hearts. Indeed, they need not go out of themselves, provided they do not, by arrogating to themselves what is given from heaven, smother the light which illuminates their minds to a clearer discovery of God. Even in the present day, there are many men of monstrous dispositions, who hesitate not to pervert all the seeds of divinity sown in the nature of man, in order to bury in oblivion the name of God. How detestable is this frenzy, that man, discovering in his body and soul a hundred vestiges of God, should make this very excellence a pretext for the denial of his being! They will not say that they are distinguished from the brutes by chance; but they ascribe it to nature, which they consider as the author of all things, and remove God out of sight. They perceive most exquisite workmanship in all their members, from the head to the feet. Here also they substitute nature in the place of God. But above all, the rapid motions of the soul, its noble faculties, and excellent talents, discover a Divinity not easily concealed; unless the Epicureans, like the Cyclops, from this eminence should audaciously wage war against God. Do all the treasures of heavenly wisdom concur in the government of a worm five feet in length? and shall the universe be destitute of this privilege? To state that there is in the soul a certain machinery corresponding to every part of the body, is so far from obscuring the divine glory, that it is rather an illustration of it. Let Epicurus answer; what concourse of atoms in the concoction of food and drink distributes part into excrements and part into blood, and causes the several members to perform their different offices with as much diligence as if so many souls by common consent governed one body? . . .

Let us remember, then, in every consideration of our own nature, that there is one God, who governs all natures, and who expects us to regard him, to direct our faith to him, to worship and invoke him. For nothing is more preposterous than to enjoy such splendid advantages, which proclaim within us their divine origin, and to neglect the Author who bountifully bestows them. . . .

But, notwithstanding the clear representations given by God in the mirror of his works, both of himself and of his everlasting dominion, such is our stupidity, that, always inattentive to these obvious testimonies, we derive no advantage from them. For, with regard to the structure and very beautiful organization of the world, how few of us are there, who, when lifting up their eyes to heaven, or looking round on the various regions of the earth, direct their minds to the remembrance of the Creator, and do not rather content themselves with a view of his works, to the total neglect of their Author! And with respect to those things that daily happen out of the ordinary course of nature, is it not the general opinion, that men are rolled and whirled about by the blind temerity of fortune, rather than governed by the providence of God? Or if, by the guidance and direction of these things, we are ever driven (as all men must sometimes be) to the considera- tion of a God, yet, when we have rashly conceived an idea of some deity, we soon slide into our own carnal dreams, or depraved inventions, corrupting by our vanity the purity of divine truth. We differ from one another, in that each individual imbibes some peculiarity of error; but we perfectly agree in a universal departure from the one true God, to preposterous trifles. This disease affects, not only the vulgar and ignorant, but the most eminent, and those who, in other things, discover peculiar sagacity. How abundantly have all the philosophers, in this respect, betrayed their stupidity and folly! For, to spare others, chargeable with greater absurdities, Plato him- self, the most religious and judicious of them all, loses himself in his round globe. And what would not befall others, when their principal men, whose place it was to enlighten the rest, stumble upon such gross errors! So also, while the government of human actions proves a providence too plainly to admit of a denial, men derive no more advantage from it, than if they believed all things to be agitated forwards and backwards by the uncertain caprice of fortune; so great is our propensity to vanity and error! I speak exclusively of the excellent of mankind, not of the vulgar, whose madness in the profanation of divine truth has known no bounds. . . .

But whatever deficiency of natural ability prevents us from attaining the pure and clear knowledge of God, yet, since that deficiency arises from our own fault, we are left without any excuse. Nor indeed can we set up any pretence of ignorance, that will prevent our own consciences from per- petually accusing us of indolence and ingratitude. Truly it would be a defence worthy to be admitted, if a man should plead that he wanted ears to hear the truth, for the publication of which even the mute creatures are supplied with most melodious voices; if he should allege that his eyes are not capable of seeing what is demonstrated by the creatures without the help of the eyes; if he should plead mental imbecility, while all the irrational creatures instruct us. Wherefore we are justly excluded from all excuse for our uncertain and extravagant deviations, since all things conspire to show us the right way. But, however men are chargeable with sinfully corrupting the seeds of divine knowledge, which, by the wonderful operation of nature, are sown in their hearts, so that they produce no good and fair crop, yet it is beyond a doubt, that the simple testimony magnificently borne by the creatures to the glory of God, is very insufficient for our instruction. For as soon as a survey of the world has just shown us a deity, neglecting the true God, we set up in his stead the dreams and phantasms of our own brains; and confer on them the praise of righteousness, wisdom, goodness, and power, due to him. We either obscure his daily acts, or pervert them by an erroneous estimate; thereby depriving the acts themselves of their glory, and their Author of his deserved praise.

CHAPTER 6

The guidance and teaching of the scripture necessary to lead to the knowl-edge of God the Creator

Though the light which presents itself to all eyes, both in heaven and in earth, is more than sufficient to deprive the ingratitude of men of every excuse, since God, in order to involve all mankind in the same guilt, sets before them all, without exception, an exhibition of his majesty, delineated in the creatures,—yet we need another and better assistance, properly to direct us to the Creator of the world. Therefore he hath not unnecessarily added the light of his word, to make himself known unto salvation, and hath honoured with this privilege those whom he intended to unite in a more close and familiar connection with himself. For, seeing the minds of all men to be agitated with unstable dispositions, when he had chosen the Jews as his peculiar flock, he enclosed them as in a fold, that they might not wander after the vanities of other nations. And it is not without cause that he preserves us in the pure knowledge of himself by the same means; for, otherwise, they who seem comparatively to stand firm, would soon fall. For, as persons who are old, or whose eyes are by any means become dim, if you show them the most beautiful book, though they perceive something writ-ten, but can scarcely read two words together, yet, by the assistance of spectacles, will begin to read distinctly,—so the scripture, collecting in our minds the otherwise confused notions of Deity, dispels the darkness, and gives us a clear view of the true God. This, then, is a singular favour, that, in the instruction of the Church, God not only uses mute teachers, but even opens his own sacred mouth; not only proclaims that some god ought to be worshipped, but at the same time pronounces himself to be the Being to whom this worship is due; and not only teaches the elect to raise their view to a Deity, but also exhibits himself as the object of their contemplation. This method he hath observed toward his Church from the beginning; beside those common lessons of instruction, to afford them also his word; which furnishes a more correct and certain criterion to distinguish him from all fictitious deities. And it was undoubtedly by this assistance that Adam, Noah, Abraham, and the rest of the patriarchs, attained to that familiar knowledge which distinguished them from unbelievers. I speak not yet of the peculiar doctrine of faith which illuminated them into the hope of eternal life. For, to pass from death to life, they must have known God, not only as the Creator, but also as the Redeemer; as they certainly obtained both from his word. For that species of knowledge, which related to him as the Creator and Governor of the world, in order, preceded the other. To this was afterwards added the other internal knowledge, which alone vivifies dead souls, and apprehends God, not only as the Creator of the world, and as the sole Author and Arbiter of all events, but also as the Redeemer in the person of the Mediator. But, being not yet come to the fall of man and the corruption of nature, I also forbear to treat of the remedy. Let the reader remember, therefore, that I am not yet treating of that covenant by which God adopted the children of Abraham, and of that point of doctrine by which believers have always been particularly separated from the profane nations, since that is founded on Christ; but am only showing how we ought to learn from the scripture, that God, who created the world, may be certainly distinguished from the whole multitude of fictitious deities. The series of subjects will, in due time, lead us to redemption. But, though we shall adduce many testimonies from the New Testament, and some also from the Law and the Prophets, in which Christ is expressly mentioned, yet they will all tend to prove, that the scripture discovers God to us as the Creator of the world, and declares what sentiments we should form of him, that we may not be seeking after a deity in the labyrinth of uncertainty.

But, whether God revealed himself to the patriarchs by oracles and visions, or suggested, by means of the ministry of men, what should be handed down by tradition to their posterity, it is beyond a doubt that their minds were impressed with a firm assurance of the doctrine, so that they were persuaded and convinced that the information they had received came from God. For God always secured to his word an undoubted credit, superior to all human opinion. At length, that the truth might remain in the world in a continual course of instruction to all ages, he determined that the same oracles which he had deposited with the patriarchs should be committed to public records. With this design the Law was promulgated, to which the Prophets were afterwards annexed, as its interpreters.—For, though the uses of the law were many, as will be better seen in the proper place; and particularly the intention of Moses, and of all the prophets, was to teach the mode of reconciliation between God and man, (whence also Paul calls Christ "the end of the law,")—yet I repeat again, that, beside the peculiar doctrine of faith and repentance, which proposes Christ as the Mediator, the scripture distinguishes the only true God by certain characters and titles, as the Creator and Governor of the world, that he may not be confounded with the multitude of false gods. Therefore, though every man should seriously apply himself to a consideration of the works of God, being placed in this very splendid theatre to be a spectator of them, yet he ought principally to attend to the word, that he may attain superior advantages. And, therefore, it is not surprising, that they who are born in darkness grow more and more hardened in their stupidity; since very few attend to the word of God with teachable dispositions, to restrain themselves within the limits which it prescribes, but rather exult in their own vanity. This, then, must be considered as a fixed principle, that, in order to enjoy the light of true religion, we ought to begin with the doctrine of heaven; and that no man can have the least knowledge of true and sound doctrine, without having been a disciple of the scripture. Hence originates all true wisdom, when we embrace with reverence the testimony which God hath been pleased therein to deliver concerning himself. For obedience is the source, not only of an absolutely perfect and complete faith, but of all right knowledge of God. And truly in this instance God hath, in his providence, particularly consulted the true interests of mankind in all ages.

For, if we consider the mutability of the human mind,—how easy its lapse into forgetfulness of God; how great its propensity to errors of every kind; how violent its rage for the perpetual fabrication of new and false religions,—it will be easy to perceive the necessity of the heavenly doctrine being thus committed to writing, that it might not be lost in oblivion, or evaporate in error, or be corrupted by the presumption of men. Since it is evident, therefore, that God, foreseeing the inefficacy of his manifestation of himself in the exquisite structure of the world, hath afforded the assistance of his word to all those to whom he determined to make his instructions effectual,—if we seriously aspire to a sincere contemplation of God, it is necessary for us to pursue this right way. We must come, I say, to the word, which contains a just and lively description of God as he appears in his works, when those works are estimated, not according to our depraved judgment, but by the rule of eternal truth. If we deviate from it, as I have just observed, though we run with the utmost celerity, yet, being out of the course, we shall never reach the goal. For it must be concluded; that the light of the Divine countenance, which even the Apostle says "no man can approach unto," is like an inexplicable labyrinth to us, unless we are directed by the line of the word; so that it were better to halt in this way, than to run with the greatest rapidity out of it. Therefore David, inculcating the necessity of the removal of superstitions out of the world, that pure religion may flourish, frequently introduces God as "reigning;" by the word "reigning," intending, not the power which he possesses, and which he exercises in the universal government of nature, but the doctrine in which he asserts his legitimate sovereignty; because errors can never be eradicated from the human heart, till the true knowledge of God is implanted in it.

Therefore the same Psalmist, having said, that "the heavens declare the glory of God, and the firmament showeth his handywork; day unto day uttereth speech, and night unto night showeth knowledge," afterwards proceeds to the mention of the word: "The law of the Lord is perfect, converting the soul: the testimony of the Lord is sure, making wise the simple: the statutes of the Lord are right, rejoicing the heart: the commandment of the Lord is pure, enlightening the eyes." For, though he also comprehends other uses of the law, yet he suggests, in general, that, since God's invitation of all nations to him by the view of heaven and earth is ineffectual, this is the peculiar school of the children of God. The same is adverted to in the twenty-ninth Psalm, where the Psalmist, having preached the terrors of the Divine voice which in thunders, in winds, in showers, in whirlwinds, and in tempests, shakes the earth, makes the mountains tremble, and breaks the cedars, adds, at length, towards the close, "in his temple doth every one speak of his glory;" because unbelievers are deaf to all the voices of God, which resound in the air. So, in another Psalm, after describing the terrible waves of the sea, he concludes thus: "Thy testimonies are very sure; holiness becometh thine house, O Lord, for ever." Hence also proceeds the observation of Christ to the Samaritan woman, that her nation and all others worshipped they knew not what; and that the Jews were the only worshippers of the true God. For, since the human mind is unable, through its imbecility, to attain any knowledge of God without the assistance of his sacred word, all mankind, except the Jews, as they sought God without the word, must necessarily have been wandering in vanity and error.

10   THE COUNCIL OF TRENT was held intermittently from 1545 to 1563. It was the effort of the Roman Catholic Church to define dogma and, in the Canons, to make explicit rejection of Protestant affirmations. The decisions at the council made secure the theological separation between the Roman Catholic Church and the developing Protestant traditions.[1]

In the selections that follow, the council defined the Catholic position on the relation of scripture and tradition.

[1] See also Council of Trent, Selections 48, 67.

The Council of Trent (1545–1563)*

THIRD SESSION: FEBRUARY 4, 1546

DECREE TOUCHING THE SYMBOL OF FAITH

In the name of the Holy and Undivided Trinity, Father, and Son, and Holy Ghost.

This sacred and holy, oecumenical, and general Synod of Trent,—lawfully assembled in the Holy Ghost, the same three legates of the Apostolic See presiding therein,—considering the magnitude of the matters to be treated of, especially of those comprised under the two heads, of the extirpating of heresies, and the reforming of manners, for the sake of which chiefly it is assembled, and recognizing with the apostles, that its "wrestling is not against flesh and blood, but against the spirits of wickedness in the high places," exhorts, with the same apostle, all and each, above all things, to be "strengthened in the Lord, and in the might of his power, in all things taking the shield of faith, wherewith they may be able to extinguish all the fiery darts of the most wicked one, and to take the helmet of salvation, with the sword of the Spirit, which is the word of God." Wherefore, that this its pious solicitude may begin and proceed by the grace of God, it ordains and decrees that, before all other things, a confession of faith is to be set forth; following herein the examples of the Fathers, who have been wont, in the most sacred councils, at the beginning of the Actions thereof, to oppose this shield against heresies; and with this alone, at times, have they drawn the unbelieving to the faith, overthrown heretics, and confirmed the faithful. For which cause, this Council has thought good, that the Symbol of faith which the holy Roman Church makes use of,—as being that principle wherein all who profess the faith of Christ necessarily agree, and that firm and alone foundation "against which the gates of hell shall never prevail",—be expressed in the very same words in which it is read in all the churches. Which Symbol is as follows:

I believe in one God, the Father Almighty, Maker of heaven and earth, of all things visible and invisible; and in one Lord Jesus Christ, the only-begotten Son of God, and born of the Father before all ages; God of God, light of light, true God of true God; begotten, not made, consubstantial with the Father, by whom all things were made: who for us men, and for our salvation, came down from the heavens, and was incarnate by the Holy Ghost of the Virgin Mary, and was made man: crucified also for us under Pontius Pilate, he suffered and was buried; and he rose again

* From Philip Schaff, The Creeds of Christendom, Vol. II. New York: Harper and Row Publishers, 1919. Used by permission of Mary L. Schaff.

on the third day, according to the scriptures; and he ascended into heaven, sitteth at the right hand of the Father; and again he will come with glory to judge the living and the dead; of whose kingdom there shall be no end: and in the Holy Ghost, the Lord, and the giver of life, who proceedeth from the Father and the Son; who with the Father and the Son together is adored and glorified; who spoke by the prophets: and one holy Catholic and Apostolic Church. I confess one baptism for the remission of sins; and I look for the resurrection of the dead, and the life of the world to come. Amen.

FOURTH SESSION: APRIL 8, 1546

DECREE CONCERNING THE CANONICAL SCRIPTURES

The sacred and holy, oecumenical, and general Snyod of Trent,—lawfully assembled in the Holy Ghost, the same three legates of the Apostolic See presiding therein,—keeping this always in view, that, errors being removed, the purity itself of the Gospel be preserved in the Church: which (Gospel), before promised through the prophets in the Holy Scriptures, our Lord Jesus Christ, the Son of God, first promulgated with His own mouth, and then commanded to be preached by His Apostles to every creature, as the fountain of all, both saving truth, and moral discipline; and seeing clearly that this truth and discipline are contained in the written books, and the unwritten traditions which, received by the Apostles from the mouth of Christ himself, or from the Apostles themselves, the Holy Ghost dictating, have come down even unto us, transmitted as it were from hand to hand: [the Synod] following the examples of the orthodox Fathers, receives and venerates with an equal affection of piety and reverence, all the books both of the Old and of the New Testament—seeing that one God is the author of both—as also the said traditions, as well those appertaining to faith as to morals, as having been dictated, either by Christ's own word of mouth, or by the Holy Ghost, and preserved in the Catholic Church by a continuous succession.

And it has thought it meet that a list of the sacred books be inserted in this decree, lest a doubt may arise in any one's mind, which are the books that are received by this Synod. They are as set down here below: of the Old Testament: the five books of Moses, to wit, Genesis, Exodus, Leviticus, Numbers, Deuteronomy; Josue, Judges, Ruth, four books of Kings, two of Paralipomenon, the first book of Esdras, and the second which is entitled Nehemias; Tobias, Judith, Esther, Job, the Davidical Psalter, consisting of a hundred and fifty psalms, the Proverbs, Ecclesiastes, the Canticle of Canticles, Wisdom, Ecclesiasticus, Isaias, Jeremias, with Baruch; Ezechiel, Daniel; the twelve minor prophets, to wit, Osee, Joel, Amos, Abdias, Jonas, Micheas, Nahum, Habacuc, Sophonias, Aggaeus, Zacharias, Malachias; two books of the Machabees, the first and the second. Of the New Testament: the four Gospels, according to Matthew, Mark,

Luke, and John; the Acts of the Apostles written by Luke the Evangelist; fourteen epistles of Paul the apostle, (one) to the Romans, two to the Corinthians, (one) to the Galatians, to the Ephesians, to the Philippians, to the Colossians, two to the Thessalonians, two to Timothy, (one) to Titus, to Philemon, to the Hebrews; two of Peter the apostle, three of John the apostle, one of the apostle James, one of Jude the apostle, and the Apocalypse of John the apostle.

But if any one receive not, as sacred and canonical, the said books entire with all their parts, as they have been used to be read in the Catholic Church, and as they are contained in the old Latin vulgate edition; and knowingly and deliberately contemn the traditions aforesaid; let him be anathema. Let all, therefore, understand, in what order, and in what manner, the said synod, after having laid the foundation of the Confession of faith, will proceed, and what testimonies and authorities it will mainly use in confirming dogmas, and in restoring morals in the Church.

DECREE CONCERNING THE EDITION, AND THE USE, OF THE SACRED BOOKS

Moreover, the same sacred and holy synod,—considering that no small utility may accrue to the Church of God, if it be made known which out of all Latin editions, now in circulation, of the sacred books, is to be held as authentic,—ordains and declares, that the said old and vulgate edition, which, by the lengthened usage of so many ages, has been approved of in the Church, be, in public lectures, disputations, sermons, and expositions, held as authentic; and that no one is to dare, or presume to reject it under any pretext whatever.

Furthermore, in order to restrain petulant spirits, it decrees, that no one, relying on his own skill, shall,—in matters of faith, and of morals pertaining to the edification of Christian doctrine,—wresting the sacred scripture to his own senses, presume to interpret the said sacred scripture contrary to that sense which holy mother Church,—whose it is to judge of the true sense and interpretation of the holy scriptures,—hath held and doth hold; or even contrary to the unanimous consent of the Fathers; even though such interpretations were never [intended] to be at any time published. Contraveners shall be made known by their Ordinaries, and be punished with the penalties by law established.

11 WILLIAM ELLERY CHANNING (1780–1842) was the first major spokesman for American Unitarianism. His early theological training was among the New England Calvinists, the heirs of Jonathan Edwards (1703–1758), but the new interests

of the Enlightenment and the new spirit of American independence brought Channing's rejection of his Calvinistic heritage. Reliance on reason, stress on the benevolence of God, and confidence in an inner moral sense were marks of all his theological writings.

As a distinct movement, American Unitarianism was a product of the nineteenth century. In 1805 the Hollis Professorship of Divinity at Harvard University was given to a Unitarian, Henry Ware; Channing's essay, *Unitarian Christianity*, first delivered in 1819, became the credo for many Unitarians. In the following selection, Channing outlined his theological methodology and its application to the traditional trinitarian affirmation.[1]

Unitarian Christianity[*]

WILLIAM ELLERY CHANNING

I. We regard the scriptures as the records of God's successive revelations to mankind, and particularly of the last and most perfect revelation of his will by Jesus Christ. Whatever doctrines seem to us to be clearly taught in the scriptures, we receive without reserve or exception. We do not, however, attach equal importance to all the books in this collection. Our religion, we believe, lies chiefly in the New Testament. The dispensation of Moses, compared with that of Jesus, we consider as adapted to the childhood of the human race, a preparation for a nobler system, and chiefly useful now as serving to confirm and illustrate the Christian scriptures. Jesus Christ is the only master of Christians, and whatever he taught, either during his personal ministry or by his inspired Apostles, we regard as of divine authority and profess to make the rule of our lives.

This authority which we give to the scriptures is a reason, we conceive, for studying them with peculiar care and for inquiring anxiously into the principles of interpretation by which their true meaning may be ascertained. The principles adopted by the class of Christians in whose name I speak need to be explained because they are often misunderstood. We are particularly accused of making an unwarrantable use of reason in the interpretation of scripture. We are said to exalt reason above revelation, to prefer

---

* From *The Works of William E. Channing*. Boston: American Unitarian Association, 1891.

[1] See also *Moral Argument Against Calvinism*, Selection 53A; *Likeness to God*, Selection 53B.

our own wisdom to God's. Loose and undefine charges of this kind are circulated so freely that we think it due to ourselves, and to the cause of truth, to express our views with some particularity.

Our leading principle in interpreting scripture is this, that the Bible is a book written for men, in the language of men, and that its meaning is to be sought in the same manner as that of other books. We believe that God, when He speaks to the human race, conforms, if we may so say, to the established rules of speaking and writing. How else would the scriptures avail us more than if communicated in an unknown tongue?

Now all books and all conversation require in the reader or hearer the constant exercise of reason; or their true import is only to be obtained by continual comparison and inference. Human language, you well know, admits various interpretations; and every word and every sentence must be modified and explained according to the subject which is discussed, according to the purposes, feelings, circumstances, and principles of the writer, and according to the genius and idioms of the language which he uses. These are acknowledged principles in the interpretation of human writings; and a man whose words we should explain without reference to these principles would reproach us justly with a criminal want of candor and an intention of obscuring or distorting his meaning.

Were the Bible written in a language and style of its own, did it consist of words which admit but a single sense and of sentences wholly detached from each other, there would be no place for the principles now laid down. We could not reason about it as about other writings. But such a book would be of little worth; and perhaps, of all books, the scriptures correspond least to this description. The word of God bears the stamp of the same hand which we see in his works. It has infinite connections and dependences. Every proposition is linked with others, and is to be compared with others, that its full and precise import may be understood. Nothing stands alone. The New Testament is built on the Old. The Christian dispensation is a continuation of the Jewish, the completion of a vast scheme of providence requiring great extent of view in the reader. Still more, the Bible treats of subjects on which we receive ideas from other sources besides itself—such subjects as the nature, passions, relations, and duties of man—and it expects us to restrain and modify its language by the known truths which observation and experience furnish on these topics.

We profess not to know a book which demands a more frequent exercise of reason than the Bible. In addition to the remarks now made on its infinite connections, we may observe that its style nowhere affects the precision of science or the accuracy of definition. Its language is singularly glowing, bold, and figurative, demanding more frequent departures from the literal sense than that of our own age and country, and consequently demanding more continual exercise of judgment. We find, too, that the different portions of this book, instead of being confined to general truths, refer perpetually to the times when they were written, to states of society, to modes of thinking, to controversies in the church, to feelings and usages which have passed away, and without the knowledge of which we are constantly in danger of extending to all times and places what was of temporary and local application. We find, too, that some of these books are strongly marked by the genius and character of their respective writers, that the Holy Spirit did not so guide the Apostles as to suspend the peculiarities of their minds, and that a knowledge of their feelings, and of the influences under which they were placed, is one of the preparations for understanding their writings. With these views of the Bible, we feel it our bounden duty to exercise our reason upon it perpetually, to compare, to infer, to look beyond the letter to the spirit, to seek in the nature of the subject and the aim of the writer his true meaning; and, in general, to make use of what is known for explaining what is difficult and for discovering new truths.

Need I descend to particulars to prove that the scriptures demand the exercise of reason? Take, for example, the style in which they generally speak of God, and observe how habitually they apply to him human passions and organs. Recollect the declarations of Christ: that he came not to send peace but a sword; that unless we eat his flesh and drink his blood we have no life in us; that we must hate father and mother, and pluck out the right eye; and a vast number of passages equally bold and unlimited. Recollect the unqualified manner in which it is said of Christians that they possess all things, know all things, and can do all things. Recollect the verbal contradiction between Paul and James, and the apparent clashing of some parts of Paul's writings with the general doctrines and end of Christianity. I might extend the enumeration indefinitely; and who does not see that we must limit all these passages by the known attributes of God, of Jesus Christ, and of human nature, and by the circumstances under which they were written, so as to give the language a quite different import from what it would require had it been applied to different beings, or used in different connections.

Enough has been said to show in what sense we make use of reason in interpreting scripture. From a variety of possible interpretations we select that which accords with the nature of the subject and the state of the writer, with the connection of the passage, with the general strain of scripture, with the known character and will of God, and with the obvious and acknowledged laws of nature. In other words, we believe that God never contradicts in one part of scripture what He teaches in another; and never contradicts in revelation what He teaches in his works and providence. And we therefore distrust every interpretation which, after deliberate attention, seems repugnant to any established truth. We reason about the Bible precisely as civilians do about the constitution under which we live; who, you know, are accustomed to limit one provision of that venerable instrument by others, and to fix the precise import of its parts by inquiring into its general spirit, into the intentions of its authors, and into the prevalent feelings, impressions, and circumstances of the time when it was framed. Without these principles of interpretation, we frankly acknowledge that we cannot defend the divine authority of the scriptures. Deny us this latitude, and we must abandon this book to its enemies.

We do not announce these principles as original or peculiar to ourselves. All Christians occasionally adopt them, not excepting those who most vehemently decry them when they happen to menace some favorite article of their creed. All Christians are compelled to use them in their controversies with infidels. All sects employ them in their warfare with one another. All willingly avail themselves of reason when it can be pressed into the service of their own party, and only complain of it when its weapons wound themselves. None reason more frequently than those from whom we differ. It is astonishing what a fabric they rear from a few slight hints about the fall of our first parents; and how ingeniously they extract from detached passages mysterious doctrines about the divine nature. We do not blame them for reasoning so abundantly but for violating the fundamental rules of reasoning, for sacrificing the plain to the obscure and the general strain of scripture to a scanty number of insulated texts.

We object strongly to the contemptuous manner in which human reason is often spoken of by our adversaries because it leads, we believe, to universal skepticism. If reason be so dreadfully darkened by the fall that its most decisive judgments on religion are unworthy of trust, then Christianity, and even natural theology, must be abandoned; for the existence and veracity of God, and the divine original of Christianity, are conclusions of reason and must stand or fall with it. If revelation be at war with this faculty, it subverts itself, for the great question of its truth is left by God to be decided at the bar of reason. It is worthy of remark how nearly the bigot and the skeptic approach. Both would annihilate our confidence in our faculties, and both throw doubt and confusion over every truth. We honor revelation too highly to make it the antagonist of reason or to believe that it calls us to renounce our highest powers.

We indeed grant that the use of reason in religion is accompanied with danger. But we ask any honest man to look back on the history of the church and say whether the renunciation of it be not still more dangerous. Besides, it is a plain fact that men reason as erroneously on all subjects as on religion. Who does not know the wild and groundless theories which have been framed in physical and political science? But who ever supposed that we must cease to exercise reason on nature and society because men have erred for ages in explaining them? We grant that the passions continually, and sometimes fatally, disturb the rational faculty in its inquiries into revelation.

The ambitious contrive to find doctrines in the Bible which favor their love of dominion. The timid and dejected discover there a gloomy system, and the mystical and fanatical a visionary theology. The vicious can find examples or assertions on which to build the hope of a late repentance or of acceptance on easy terms. The falsely refined contrive to light on doctrines which have not been soiled by vulgar handling. But the passions do not distract the reason in religious any more than in other inquiries which excite strong and general interest; and this faculty, of consequence, is not to be renounced in religion unless we are prepared to discard it universally. The true inference from the almost endless errors which have darkened theology is, not that we are to neglect and disparage our powers, but to exert them more patiently, circumspectly, uprightly—the worst errors, after all, having sprung up in that church which proscribes reason and demands from its members implicit faith. The most pernicious doctrines have been the growth of the darkest times, when the general credulity encouraged bad men and enthusiasts to broach their dreams and inventions and to stifle the faint remonstrances of reason by the menaces of everlasting perdition. Say what we may, God has given us a rational nature and will call us to account for it. We may let it sleep, but we do so at our peril. Revelation is addressed to us as rational beings. We may wish, in our sloth, that God had given us a system demanding no labor of comparing, limiting, and inferring. But such a system would be at variance with the whole character of our present existence; and it is the part of wisdom to take revelation as it is given to us, and to interpret it by the help of the faculties which it everywhere supposes and on which it is founded.

To the views now given an objection is commonly urged from the character of God. We are told that, God being infinitely wiser than men, his discoveries will surpass human reason. In a revelation from such a teacher we ought to expect propositions which we cannot reconcile with one another, and which may seem to contradict established truths; and it becomes us not to question or explain them away, but to believe and adore, and to submit our weak and carnal reason to the divine word. To this objection we have two short answers. We say, first, that it is impossible that a teacher of infinite wisdom should expose those whom he would teach to infinite error. But if once we admit that propositions which in their literal sense appear plainly repugnant to one another, or to any known truth, are still to be literally understood and received, what possible limit can we set to the belief of contradictions? What shelter have we from the wildest fanaticism, which can always quote passages that, in their literal and obvious sense, give support to its extravagances? How can the Protestant escape from transubstantiation, a doctrine most clearly taught us, if the submission of reason, now contended for, be a duty? How can we even hold fast the truth of revelation; for if one apparent contradiction may be true, so may another, and the proposition that Christianity is false, though involving inconsistency, may still be a verity?

We answer again that, if God be infinitely wise, He cannot sport with the understandings of his creatures. A wise teacher discovers his wisdom in adapting himself to the capacities of his pupils, not in perplexing them with what is unintelligible, not in distressing them with apparent contradictions, not in filling them with a skeptical distrust of their own powers. An infinitely wise teacher, who knows the precise extent of our minds and the best method of enlightening them, will surpass all other instructors in bringing down truth to our apprehension, and in showing its loveliness and harmony. We ought, indeed, to expect occasional obscurity in such a book as the Bible, which was written for past and future ages as well as for the present. But God's wisdom is a pledge that whatever is necessary for us, and necessary for salvation, is revealed too plainly to be mistaken, and too consistently to be questioned, by a sound and upright mind. It is not the mark of wisdom to use an unintelligible phraseology, to communicate what is above our capacities, to confuse and unsettle the intellect by appearances of contradiction. We honor our Heavenly Teacher too much to ascribe to him such a revelation. A revelation is a gift of light. It cannot thicken our darkness and multiply our perplexities.

II. Having thus stated the principles according to which we interpret scripture, I now proceed to the second great head of this discourse, which is to state some of the views which we derive from that sacred book, particularly those which distinguish us from other Christians.

1. In the first place, we believe in the doctrine of God's UNITY, or that there is one God and one only. To this truth we give infinite importance, and we feel ourselves bound to take heed lest any man spoil us of it by vain philosophy. The proposition that there is one God seems to us exceedingly plain. We understand by it that there is one being, one mind, one person, one intelligent agent, and one only, to whom underived and infinite perfection and dominion belong. We conceive that these words could have conveyed no other meaning to the simple and uncultivated people who were set apart to be the depositaries of this great truth and who were utterly incapable of understanding those hairbreadth distinctions between being and person which the sagacity of later ages has discovered. We find no intimation that this language was to be taken in an unusual sense, or that God's unity was a quite different thing from the oneness of other intelligent beings.

We object to the doctrine of the Trinity that, while acknowledging in words, it subverts in effect the unity of God. According to this doctrine, there are three infinite and equal persons possessing supreme divinity, called the Father, Son, and Holy Ghost. Each of these persons, as described by theologians, has his own particular consciousness, will, and perceptions. They love each other, converse with each other, and delight in each other's society. They perform different parts in man's redemption, each having his appropriate office and neither doing the work of the other. The Son is mediator, and not the Father. The Father sends the Son, and is not himself sent; nor is He conscious, like the Son, of taking flesh. Here, then, we have three intelligent agents, possessed of different consciousnesses, different wills, and different perceptions, performing different acts and sustaining different relations; and if these things do not imply and constitute three minds or beings, we are utterly at a loss to know how three minds or beings are to be formed. It is difference of properties and acts and consciousness which leads us to the belief of different intelligent beings, and, if this mark fails us, our whole knowledge falls; we have no proof that all the agents and persons in the universe are not one and the same mind. When we attempt to conceive of three Gods, we can do nothing more than represent to ourselves three agents, distinguished from each other by similar marks and peculiarities to those which separate the persons of the Trinity; and when common Christians hear these persons spoken of as conversing with each other, loving each other, and performing different acts, how can they help regarding them as different beings, different minds?

We do, then, with all earnestness, though without reproaching our brethren, protest against the irrational and unscriptural doctrine of the Trinity. "To us," as to the Apostle and the primitive Christians, "there is one God, even the Father." With Jesus, we worship the Father as the only living and true God. We are astonished that any man can read the New Testament and avoid the conviction that the Father alone is God. We hear our Saviour continually appropriating this character to the Father. We find the Father continually distinguished from Jesus by this title. "God sent his Son." "God anointed Jesus." Now, how singular and inexplicable is this phraseology, which fills the New Testament, if this title belong equally to Jesus, and if a principal object of this book is to reveal him as God, as partaking equally with the Father in supreme divinity! We challenge our opponents to adduce one passage in the New Testament where the word God means three persons, where it is not limited to one person, and where, unless turned from its usual sense by the connection, it does not mean the Father. Can stronger proof be given that the doctrine of three persons in the Godhead is not a fundamental doctrine of Christianity?

This doctrine, were it true, must, from its difficulty, singularity, and importance, have been laid down with great clearness, guarded with great care, and stated with all possible precision. But where does this statement appear? From the many passages which treat of God, we ask for one, one only, in which we are told that He is a threefold being, or that He is three persons, or that He is Father, Son, and Holy Ghost. On the contrary, in the

New Testament, where, at least, we might expect many express assertions of this nature, God is declared to be one, without the least attempt to prevent the acceptation of the words in their common sense; and He is always spoken of and addressed in the singular number, that is, in language which was universally understood to intend a single person, and to which no other idea could have been attached without an express admonition. So entirely do the scriptures abstain from stating the Trinity that when our opponents would insert it into their creeds and doxologies they are compelled to leave the Bible and to invent forms of words altogether unsanctioned by scriptural phraseology. That a doctrine so strange, so liable to misapprehension, so fundamental as this is said to be, and requiring such careful exposition should be left so undefined and unprotected, to be made out by inference, and to be hunted through distant and detached parts of scripture—this is a difficulty which, we think, no ingenuity can explain.

We have another difficulty. Christianity, it must be remembered, was planted and grew up amidst sharp-sighted enemies who overlooked no objectionable part of the system and who must have fastened with great earnestness on a doctrine involving such apparent contradictions as the Trinity. We cannot conceive an opinion against which the Jews, who prided themselves on an adherence to God's unity, would have raised an equal clamor. Now, how happens it that in the apostolic writings, which relate so much to objections against Christianity and to the controversies which grew out of this religion, not one word is said implying that objections were brought against the gospel from the doctrine of the Trinity, not one word is uttered in its defense and explanation, not a word to rescue it from reproach and mistake? This argument has almost the force of demonstration. We are persuaded that, had three divine persons been announced by the first preachers of Christianity, all equal and all infinite, one of whom was the very Jesus who had lately died on the cross, this pecularity of Christianity would have almost absorbed every other, and the great labor of the Apostles would have been to repel the continual assaults which it would have awakened. But the fact is that not a whisper of objection to Christianity on that account reaches our ears from the apostolic age. In the Epistles we see not a trace of controversy called forth by the Trinity.

We have further objections to this doctrine, drawn from its practical influence. We regard it as unfavorable to devotion, by dividing and distracting the mind in its communion with God. It is a great excellence of the doctrine of God's unity, that it offers to us ONE OBJECT of supreme homage, adoration, and love, One Infinite Father, one Being of beings, one original and fountain, to whom we may refer all good, in whom all our powers and affections may be concentrated, and whose lovely and venerable nature may pervade all our thoughts. True piety, when directed to an undivided Deity, has a chasteness, a singleness, most favorable to religious awe and love. Now, the Trinity sets before us three distinct objects of supreme adoration; three infinite persons, having equal claims on our hearts; three divine agents, performing different offices and to be acknowledged and worshiped in different relations. And is it possible, we ask, that the weak and limited mind of man can attach itself to these with the same power and joy as to One Infinite Father, the only First Cause, in whom all the blessings of nature and redemption meet as their center and source? Must not devotion be distracted by the equal and rival claims of three equal persons, and must not the worship of the conscientious, consistent Christian be disturbed by an apprehension lest he withhold from one or another of these his due proportion of homage!

We also think that the doctrine of the Trinity injures devotion, not only by joining to the Father other objects of worship, but by taking from the Father the supreme affection which is his due and transferring it to the Son. This is a most important view. That Jesus Christ, if exalted into the infinite Divinity, should be more interesting than the Father, is precisely what might be expected from history and from the principles of human nature. Men want an object of worship like themselves, and the great secret of idolatry lies in this propensity. A God clothed in our form and feeling our wants and sorrows speaks to our weak nature more strongly than a Father in heaven, a pure spirit, invisible and unapproachable save by the reflecting and purified mind. We think, too, that the peculiar offices ascribed to Jesus by the popular theology make him the most attractive person in the Godhead. The Father is the depository of the justice, the vindicator of the rights, the avenger of the laws of the Divinity. On the other hand, the Son, the brightness of the divine mercy, stands between the incensed Deity and guilty humanity, exposes his meek head to the storms and his compassionate breast to the sword of the divine justice, bears our whole load of punishment, and purchases with his blood every blessing which descends from heaven. Need we state the effect of these representations, especially on common minds, for whom Christianity was chiefly designed and whom it seeks to bring to the Father as the loveliest being? We do believe that the worship of a bleeding, suffering God tends strongly to absorb the mind and to draw it from other objects, just as the human tenderness of the Virgin Mary has given her so conspicuous a place in the devotions of the church of Rome. We believe, too, that this worship, though attractive, is not most fitted to spiritualize the mind, that it awakens human transport rather than that deep veneration of the moral perfections of God which is the essence of piety.

2. Having thus given our views of the unity of God, I proceed, in the second place, to observe that we believe in the unity of Jesus Christ. We believe that Jesus is one mind, one soul, one being, as truly one as we are, and equally distinct from the one God. We complain of the doctrine of the Trinity that, not satisfied with making God three beings, it makes Jesus

Christ two beings, and thus introduces infinite confusion into our conceptions of his character. This corruption of Christianity, alike repugnant to common sense and to the general strain of scripture, is a remarkable proof of the power of a false philosophy in disfiguring the simple truth of Jesus.

According to this doctrine, Jesus Christ, instead of being one mind, one conscious, intelligent principle whom we can understand, consists of two souls, two minds; the one divine, the other human; the one weak, the other almighty; the one ignorant, the other omniscient. Now we maintain that this is to make Christ two beings. To denominate him one person, one being, and yet to suppose him made up of two minds, infinitely different from each other, is to abuse and confound language and to throw darkness over all our conceptions of intelligent natures. According to the common doctrine, each of these two minds in Christ has its own consciousness, its own will, its own perceptions. They have, in fact, no common properties. The divine mind feels none of the wants and sorrows of the human, and the human is infinitely removed from the perfection and happiness of the divine. Can you conceive of two beings in the universe more distinct? We have always thought that one person was constituted and distinguished by one consciousness. The doctrine that one and the same person should have two consciousnesses, two wills, two souls, infinitely different from each other, this we think an enormous tax on human credulity.

We say that if a doctrine so strange, so difficult, so remote from all the previous conceptions of men be indeed a part, and an essential part, of revelation, it must be taught with great distinctness, and we ask our brethren to point to some plain, direct passage where Christ is said to be composed of two minds infinitely different yet constituting one person. We find none. Other Christians, indeed, tell us that this doctrine is necessary to the harmony of the scriptures, that some texts ascribe to Jesus Christ human, and others divine properties, and that to reconcile these we must suppose two minds, to which these properties may be referred. In other words, for the purpose of reconciling certain difficult passages, which a just criticism can in a great degree, if not wholly, explain, we must invent a hypothesis vastly more difficult, and involving gross absurdity. We are to find our way out of a labyrinth by a clue which conducts us into mazes infinitely more inextricable.

Surely, if Jesus Christ felt that he consisted of two minds, and that this was a leading feature of his religion, his phraseology respecting himself would have been colored by this pecularity. The universal language of men is framed upon the idea that one person is one person, is one mind and one soul; and when the multitude heard this language from the lips of Jesus, they must have taken it in its usual sense, and must have referred to a single soul all which he spoke, unless expressly instructed to interpret it differently. But where do we find this instruction? Where do you meet, in the New

Testament, the phraseology which abounds in Trinitarian books and which necessarily grows from the doctrine of two natures in Jesus? Where does this divine teacher say, "This I speak as God, and this as man; this is true only of my human mind, this only of my divine"? Where do we find in the Epistles a trace of this strange phraseology? Nowhere. It was not needed in that day. It was demanded by the errors of a later age.

We believe, then, that Christ is one mind, one being, and, I add, a being distinct from the one God. That Christ is not the one God, not the same being with the Father, is a necessary inference from our former head, in which we saw that the doctrine of three persons in God is a fiction. But on so important a subject I would add a few remarks. We wish that those from whom we differ would weigh one striking fact. Jesus, in his preaching, continually spoke of God. The word was always in his mouth. We ask, does he by this word ever mean himself? We say, never. On the contrary, he most plainly distinguishes between God and himself, and so do his disciples. How this is to be reconciled with the idea that the manifestation of Christ as God was a primary object of Christianity, our adversaries must determine.

If we examine the passages in which Jesus is distinguished from God, we shall see that they not only speak of him as another being, but seem to labor to express his inferiority. He is continually spoken of as the Son of God, sent of God, receiving all his powers from God, working miracles because God was with him, judging justly because God taught him, having claims on our belief because he was anointed and sealed by God, and as able of himself to do nothing. The New Testament is filled with this language. Now we ask what impression this language was fitted and intended to make? Could any who heard it have imagined that Jesus was the very God to whom he was so industriously declared to be inferior; the very Being by whom he was sent, and from whom he professed to have received his message and power? Let it here be remembered that the human birth, and bodily form, and humble circumstances, and mortal sufferings of Jesus must all have prepared men to interpret, in the most unqualified manner, the language in which his inferiority to God was declared. Why, then, was this language used so continually, and without limitation, if Jesus were the Supreme Deity, and if this truth were an essential part of his religion? I repeat it, the human condition and sufferings of Christ tended strongly to exclude from men's minds the idea of his proper Godhead; and, of course, we should expect to find in the New Testament perpetual care and effort to counteract this tendency, to hold him forth as the same being with his Father, if this doctrine were, as is pretended, the soul and center of his religion. We should expect to find the phraseology of scripture cast into the mold of this doctrine, to hear familiarly of God the Son, of our Lord God Jesus, and to be told that to us there is one God, even Jesus. But, instead of this, the inferiority of Christ pervades the New Testament. It is not only implied in the general phraseology, but repeatedly and decidedly expressed, and unaccompanied with any admonition to prevent its application to his whole nature. Could it, then, have been the great design of the sacred writers to exhibit Jesus as the Supreme God?

I am aware that these remarks will be met by two or three texts in which Christ is called God, and by a class of passages, not very numerous, in which divine properties are said to be ascribed to him. To these we offer one plain answer. We say that it is one of the most established and obvious principles of criticism that language is to be explained according to the known properties of the subject to which it is applied. Every man knows that the same words convey very different ideas when used in relation to different beings. Thus, Solomon *built* the temple in a different manner from the architect whom he employed; and God *repents* differently from man. Now we maintain that the known properties and circumstances of Christ, his birth, sufferings, and death, his constant habit of speaking of God as a distinct being from himself, his praying to God, his ascribing to God all his power and offices—these acknowledged properties of Christ, we say, oblige us to interpret the comparatively few passages which are thought to make him the Supreme God in a manner consistent with his distinct and inferior nature. It is our duty to explain such texts by the rule which we apply to other texts in which human beings are called gods and are said to be partakers of the divine nature, to know and possess all things and to be filled with all God's fullness. These latter passages we do not hesitate to modify and restrain and turn from the most obvious sense, because this sense is opposed to the known properties of the beings to whom they relate; and we maintain that we adhere to the same principle, and use no greater latitude, in explaining as we do the passages which are thought to support the Godhead of Christ.

Trinitarians profess to derive some important advantages from their mode of viewing Christ. It furnishes them, they tell us, with an infinite atonement, for it shows them an infinite being suffering for their sins. The confidence with which this fallacy is repeated astonishes us. When pressed with the question whether they really believe that the infinite and unchangeable God suffered and died on the cross, they acknowledge that this is not true, but that Christ's human mind alone sustained the pains of death. How have we, then, an infinite sufferer? This language seems to us an imposition on common minds, and very derogatory to God's justice, as if this attribute could be satisfied by a sophism and a fiction.

We are also told that Christ is a more interesting object, that his love and mercy are more felt, when he is viewed as the Supreme God who left his glory to take humanity and to suffer for men. That Trinitarians are strongly moved by this representation we do not mean to deny; but we think their

emotions altogether founded on a misapprehension of their own doctrines.
They talk of the second person of the Trinity's leaving his glory and his
Father's bosom to visit and save the world. But this second person, being
the unchangeable and infinite God, was evidently incapable of parting with
the least degree of his perfection and felicity. At the moment of his taking
flesh, he was as intimately present with his Father as before, and equally
with his Father filled heaven, and earth, and immensity. This Trinitarians
acknowledge; and still they profess to be touched and overwhelmed by the
amazing humiliation of this immutable being! But not only does their doctrine, when fully explained, reduce Christ's humiliation to a fiction, it
almost wholly destroys the impressions with which his cross ought to be
viewed. According to their doctrine, Christ was comparatively no sufferer
at all. It is true, his human mind suffered; but this, they tell us, was an
infinitely small part of Jesus, bearing no more proportion to his whole nature
than a single hair of our heads to the whole body, or than a drop to the
ocean. The divine mind of Christ, that which was most properly himself,
was infinitely happy at the very moment of the suffering of his humanity.
While hanging on the cross, he was the happiest being in the universe, as
happy as the infinite Father; so that his pains, compared with his felicity,
were nothing. This Trinitarians do, and must, acknowledge. It follows necessarily from the immutableness of the divine nature which they ascribe to
Christ; so that their system, justly viewed, robs his death of interest, weakens
our sympathy with his sufferings, and is, of all others, most unfavorable to
a love of Christ founded on a sense of his sacrifices for mankind. We esteem
our own views to be vastly more affecting. It is our belief that Christ's
humiliation was real and entire, that the whole Saviour, and not a part of
him, suffered, that his crucifixion was a scene of deep and unmixed agony.
As we stand round his cross, our minds are not distracted, nor our sensibility
weakened, by contemplating him as composed of incongruous and infinitely
differing minds, and as having a balance of infinite felicity. We recognize in
the dying Jesus but one mind. This, we think, renders his sufferings, and
his patience and love in bearing them, incomparably more impressive and
affecting than the system we oppose.

PART II

The Person and Work
of Christ

THE PERSON OF CHRIST

12 The Christian church developed "rules of faith" or baptismal formulae as statements of Christian belief for instructional purposes and as guides lines for theological affirmations. The *Old Roman Symbol*, which formed the basic structure for the later Apostles' Creed, was one such statement. This formula was the product of many minds and its precise original form is difficult to determine. From the fourth century we have early texts in Latin and Greek, from Rufinus and Marcellus of Ancyra respectively, though the *Old Roman Symbol* probably dates from the middle of the second century. It has been suggested that the Docetist heresy, which affirmed that Christ's life was not a real and full human existence, and Ebionite affirmations, which ignored the divinity of Christ, were causes for the formation of the *Old Roman Symbol*; each of these positions was ruled out in the language of the statement. As the years passed, further additions were made to the basic structure and by the late seventh or early eighth century *The Apostles' Creed* in its present form was stabilized.

A. Old Roman Symbol*

1. I believe in God the Father Almighty.
2. And in Jesus Christ, his only Son, our Lord;
3. Who was born by the Holy Ghost of the Virgin Mary;
4. Was crucified under Pontius Pilate and was buried;
5. The Third day he rose from the dead;
6. He ascended into heaven; and sitteth on the right hand of the Father;
7. From thence he shall come to judge the quick and the dead.
8. And in the Holy Ghost;
9. The Holy Church;
10. The forgiveness of Sins;
11. The resurrection of the body (flesh).

* From Philip Schaff, *The Creeds of Christendom*, Vol. I. New York: Harper and Row Publishers, 1919. Used by permission of Mary L. Schaff.

B. The Apostles' Creed*¹

1. I believe in God the Father Almighty [Maker of heaven and earth].
2. And in Jesus Christ, his only Son, our Lord;
3. Who was [conceived] by the Holy Ghost, born of the Virgin Mary;
4. [Suffered]; under Pontius Pilate, was crucified [dead], and buried [He descended into Hell];
5. The third day he rose from the dead;
6. He ascended into heaven; and sitteth on the right hand of [God] the Father [Almighty];
7. From thence he shall come to judge the quick and the dead.
8. [I believe] in the Holy Ghost;
9. The Holy [Catholic] Church; [The Communion of saints];
10. The forgiveness of sins;
11. The resurrection of the body (flesh);
12. [And the life everlasting].

13 No ONE NAME is more central in the development of early Christological doctrine than that of Tertullian. His legal training, his Latin proficiency, and his incisive and influential essays have led later men to call him the father of Latin Christianity. Throughout his writing, his penchant for precise definition and clarity of expression is evident. In his later life he undertook to defend Christianity against Praxeas, a proponent of modalistic monarchianism. The Modalistic Monarchians asserted that Father, Son, and Holy Spirit were three modes, faces, or aspects of the Godhead, with no clear distinction among them. This position led to the heresy of patripassionism or, to use the name taken from one of its leaders, Sabellianism (Sabellius), which stated that the Father was indistinguishable from the Son and, therefore, was born of the Virgin Mary and suffered on the cross. In his essay, *Against Praxeas*, Tertullian developed

* *Ibid.*

1 The additional phrases are enclosed in brackets.

a position on the relation of Father, Son, and Holy Spirit that became influential in Western Christianity and had great bearing on the decision made at Nicaea in 325.[1] His formulae, **una substantia** (one substance) **tres personae** (three persons), and **una persona** (one person) **duae naturae** (two natures) served as a norm for later Christological discussion.[2]

Against Praxeas[*]

TERTULLIAN

CHAPTER 2

We . . . believe that there is one only God, but under the following dispensation, or οἰκονομία, as it is called, that this one only God has also a Son, His Word, who proceeded from Himself, by whom all things were made, and without whom nothing was made. Him we believe to have been sent by the Father into the Virgin, and to have been born of her—being both Man and God, the Son of Man and the Son of God, and to have been called by the name of Jesus Christ; we believe Him to have suffered, died, and been buried, according to the scriptures, and, after He had been raised again by the Father and taken back to heaven, to be sitting at the right hand of the Father, and that He will come to judge the quick and the dead; who sent also from heaven from the Father, according to His own promise, the Holy Ghost, the Paraclete, the sanctifier of the faith of those who believe in the Father, and in the Son, and in the Holy Ghost. . . . All are of One, by unity (that is) of substance; while the mystery of the dispensation is still guarded, which distributes the Unity into a Trinity, placing in their order the three Persons—the Father, the Son, and the Holy Ghost: three, however, not in condition, but in degree; not in substance, but in form; not in power, but in aspect; yet of one substance, and of one condition, and of one power, inasmuch as He is one God, from whom these degrees and forms and aspects are reckoned, under the name of the Father, and of the Son, and of the Holy Ghost. How they are susceptible of number without division, will be shown as our treatise proceeds.

---

* From The Ante-Nicene Fathers, Vol. III, Alexander Roberts and James Donaldson, eds. Grand Rapids, Mich.: Wm. B. Eerdmans Publishing Co., 1951. For Tertullian's further discussion of the relation of human and divine natures in the person of Christ see: Tertullian, On the Flesh of Christ, in The Ante-Nicene Fathers, Vol. III.

[1] See also Council of Nicaea, Selection 20.
[2] See also The Prescription Against Heretics, Selection 1.

CHAPTER 3

The simple, indeed, (I will not call them unwise and unlearned) who always constitute the majority of believers, are startled at the dispensation [οἰκονομία] (of the Three in One), on the ground that their very rule of faith withdraws them from the world's plurality of gods to the one only true God; not understanding that, although He is the one only God, He must yet be believed in with His own οἰκονομία [dispensation]. The numerical order and distribution of the Trinity they assume to be a division of the Unity; whereas the Unity which derives the Trinity out of its own self is so far from being destroyed, that it is actually supported by it. They are constantly throwing out against us that we are preachers of two gods and three gods, while they take to themselves pre-eminently the credit of being worshippers of the One God; just as if the Unity itself with irrational deductions did not produce heresy, and the Trinity rationally considered constitute the truth. We, say they, maintain the Monarchy (or, sole government of God). And so, as far as the sound goes, do even Latins (and ignorant ones too) pronounce the word in such a way that you would suppose their understanding of the μοναρχία (or Monarchy) was as complete as their pronunciation of the term. Well, then Latins take pains to pronounce the μοναρχία (or Monarchy), while Greeks actually refuse to understand the οἰκονομία, or Dispensation (of the Three in One). As for myself, however, if I have gleaned any knowledge of either language, I am sure that μοναρχία (or Monarchy) has no other meaning than single and individual rule; but for all that, this monarchy does not, because it is the government of one, preclude him whose government it is, either from having a son, or from having made himself actually a son to himself, or from ministering his own monarchy by whatever agents he will. Nay more, I contend that no dominion so belongs to one only, as his own, or is in such a sense singular, or is in such a sense a monarchy, as not also to be administered through other persons most closely connected with it, and whom it has itself provided as officials to itself. If, moreover, there be a son belonging to him whose monarchy it is, it does not forthwith become divided and cease to be a monarchy, if the son also be taken as a sharer in it; but it is as to its origin equally his, by whom it is communicated to the son; and being his, it is quite as much a monarchy (or sole empire), since it is held together by two who are so inseparable. Therefore, inasmuch as the Divine Monarchy also is administered by so many legions and hosts of angels, according as it is written, "Thousand thousands ministered unto Him, and ten thousand times ten thousand stood before Him;" and since it has not from this circumstance ceased to be the rule of one (so as no longer to be a monarchy), because it is administered by so many thousands of powers; how comes it to pass that God should be thought to suffer division and severance in the Son and in the Holy Ghost, who have the second and third places assigned to them, and who are so closely joined with the Father in His substance, when He suffers no such (division and severance) in the multitude of so many angels? Do you really suppose that Those, who are naturally members of the Father's own substance, pledges of His love, instruments of His might, nay, His power itself and the entire system of His monarchy, are the overthrow and destruction thereof? You are not right in so thinking. I prefer your exercising yourself on the meaning of the thing rather than on the sound of the word. Now you must understand the overthrow of a monarchy to be *this*, when another dominion, which has a framework and a state peculiar to itself (and is therefore a rival), is brought in over and above it: when, e.g., some other god is introduced in opposition to the Creator, as in the opinions of Marcion; or when many gods are introduced, according to your Valentinuses and your Prodicuses. Then it amounts to an overthrow of the Monarchy, since it involves the destruction of the Creator.

CHAPTER 4

But as for me, who derive the Son from no other source but from the substance of the Father, and (represent Him) as doing nothing without the Father's will, and as having received all power from the Father, how can I be possibly destroying the Monarchy from the faith, when I preserve it in the Son just as it was committed to Him by the Father? The same remark (I wish also to be formally) made by me with respect to the third degree *in the Godhead*, because I believe the Spirit *to proceed* from no other source than from the Father through the Son. . . . We thus see that the Son is no obstacle to the Monarchy, although it is now administered by the Son; because with the Son it is still in its own state, and with its own state will be restored to the Father by the Son. No one, therefore, will impair it, on account of admitting the Son (to it), since it is certain that it has been committed to Him by the Father, and by and by has to be again delivered up by Him to the Father. Now, from this one passage of the epistle of the *inspired* apostle, we have been already able to show that the Father and the Son are two *separate Persons*, not only by the mention of their separate names as Father and the Son, but also by the fact that He who delivered up the kingdom, and He to whom it is delivered up—and in like manner, He who subjected (all things), and He to whom they were subjected—must necessarily be two different Beings.

CHAPTER 5

But since they will have the Two to be but One, so that the Father shall be deemed to be the same as the Son, it is only right that the whole question respecting the Son should be examined, as to whether He exists, and who He is and the mode of His existence. Thus shall the truth itself secure its own sanction from the scriptures, and the interpretations which guard them. There are some who allege that even Genesis opens thus in Hebrew: "In the beginning God made for Himself a Son." As there is no ground for this, I am led to other arguments derived from God's own dispensation, in which He existed before the creation of the world, up to the generation of the Son. For before all things God was alone—being in Himself and for Himself universe, and space, and all things. Moreover, He was alone, because there was nothing external to Him but Himself. Yet even not then was He alone; for He had with Him that which He possessed in Himself, that is to say, His own Reason. For God is rational, and Reason was first in Him; and so all things were from Himself. This Reason is His own Thought (or Consciousness) which the Greeks call λόγος [logos], by which term we also designate Word or *Discourse* and therefore it is now usual with our people, owing to the mere simple interpretation of the term, to say that the Word was in the beginning with God; although it would be more suitable to regard Reason as the more ancient; because God had not Word from the beginning, but He had Reason even before the beginning; because also Word itself consists of Reason, which it thus proves to have been the prior existence as being its own substance. Not that this distinction is of any practical moment. For although God had not yet sent out His Word, He still had Him within Himself, both in company with and included within His very Reason, as He silently planned and arranged within Himself everything which He was afterwards about to utter through His Word. Now, whilst He was thus planning and arranging with His own Reason, He was actually causing that to become Word which He was dealing with in the way of Word or *Discourse*. And that you may the more readily understand this, consider first of all, from your own self, who are made "in the image and likeness of God," for what purpose it is that you also possess reason in yourself, who are a rational creature, as being not only made by a rational Artificer, but actually animated out of His substance. Observe, then, that when you are silently conversing with yourself, this very process is carried on within you by your reason, which meets you with a word at every movement of your thought, at every impulse of your conception. Whatever you think, there is a word; whatever you conceive, there is reason. You must needs speak it in your mind; and while you are speaking, you admit speech as an interlocutor with you, involved in which there is this very reason, whereby, while in thought you are holding converse with your word, you are (by reciprocal action) producing thought by means of that converse with your word. Thus, in a certain sense, the word is a second *person* within you, through which in thinking you utter speech, and through which also, (by reciprocity of process,) in uttering speech you generate thought. The word is itself a different thing from yourself. Now how much more fully is all this transacted in God, whose image and likeness even you are regarded as being, inasmuch as He has reason within Himself even while He is silent, and involved in that Reason His Word! I may therefore without rashness first lay this down (as a fixed principle) that even then before the creation of the universe God was not alone, since He had within Himself both Reason, and, inherent in Reason, His Word, which He made second to Himself by agitating it within Himself.

CHAPTER 6

This power and disposition of the Divine Intelligence is set forth also in the scripture under the name of Σοφία, Wisdom; for that can be better entitled to the name of Wisdom than the Reason or the Word of God? Listen therefore to Wisdom herself, constituted in the character of a Second Person: "At the first the Lord created me as the beginning of His ways, with a view to His own works, before He made the earth, before the mountains were settled; moreover, before all the hills did He beget me;" (Prov. viii, 22–25) that is to say, He created and generated me in His own intelligence. Then, again, observe the distinction between them implied in the companionship of Wisdom with the Lord. "When He prepared the heaven," says Wisdom, "I was present with Him; and when He made His strong places upon the winds, which are the clouds above; and when He secured the fountains, (and all things) which are beneath the sky, I was by, arranging all things with Him; I was by, in whom He delighted; and daily, too, did I rejoice in His presence." (Prov. viii, 27–30). Now, as soon as it pleased God to put forth into their respective substances and forms the things which He had planned and ordered within Himself, in conjunction with His Wisdom's Reason and Word, He first put forth the Word Himself, having within Him His own inseparable Reason and Wisdom, in order that all things might be made through Him through whom they had been planned and disposed, yea, and already made, so far forth as (they were) in the mind and intelligence of God. This, however, was still wanting to them, that they should also be openly known, and kept permanently in their proper forms and substances. . . .

CHAPTER 8

With us, however, the Son alone knows the Father, and has Himself unfolded "the Father's bosom." He has also heard and seen all things with the Father; and what He has been commanded by the Father, that also does He speak. And it is not His own will, but the Father's, which He has accomplished, which He had known most intimately, even from the beginning. . . . For God sent forth the Word, as the Paraclete also declares, just as the root puts forth the tree, and the fountain the river, and the sun the ray. . . . I should not hesitate, indeed, to call the tree the son or off-spring of the root, and the river of the fountain, and the ray of the sun; because every original source is a parent, and everything which issues from the origin is an offspring. Much more is (this true of) the Word of God, who has actually received as His own peculiar designation the name of Son. But still the tree is not severed from the root, nor the river from the fountain, nor the ray from the sun; nor, indeed, is the Word separated from God. Following, therefore, the form of these analogies, I confess that I call God and His Word—the Father and His Son—two. For the root and the tree are distinctly two things, but correlatively joined; the fountain and the river are also two forms, but indivisible; so likewise the sun and the ray are two forms, but coherent ones. Everything which proceeds from something else must needs be second to that from which it proceeds, without being on that account separated. Where, however, there is a second, there must be two; and where there is a third, there must be three. Now the Spirit indeed is third from God and the Son; just as the fruit of the tree is third from the root, or as the stream out of the river is third from the fountain, or as the apex of the ray is third from the sun. Nothing, however, is alien from that original source whence it derives its own properties. In like manner the Trinity, flowing down from the Father through intertwined and connected steps, does not at all disturb the Monarchy, [or oneness of the divine essence], whilst it at the same time guards the state of the Economy.

CHAPTER 9

Bear always in mind that this is the rule of faith which I profess; by it I testify that the Father, and the Son, and the Spirit are inseparable from each other, and so will you know in what sense this is said. Now, observe, my assertion is that the Father is one, and the Son is one, and the Spirit one, and that They are distinct from Each Other. This statement is taken in a wrong sense by every uneducated as well as every perversely disposed person, as if it predicated a diversity in such a sense as to imply a separation among the Father, and the Son, and the Spirit. I am, moreover, obliged to say this, when (extolling the Monarchy at the expense of the Economy) they con-tend for the identity of the Father and Son and Spirit, that it is not by way of diversity that the Son differs from the Father, but by distribution: it is not by division that He is different, but by distinction; because the Father is not the same as the Son, since they differ one from the other in the mode of their being. For the Father is the entire substance, but the Son is a derivation and portion of the whole, as He Himself acknowledges: "My Father is greater than I. . . ." Thus the Father is distinct from the Son, being greater than the Son, inasmuch as He who begets is one, and He who is begotten is another; He, too, who sends is one, and He who is sent is another; and He, again, who makes is one, and He through whom the thing is made is another. Happily the Lord Himself employs this expression of the person of the Paraclete, so as to signify not a division or severance, but a disposition (of mutual relations in the Godhead); for He says, "I will pray the Father, and He shall send you another Comforter . . . even the Spirit of truth," thus making the Paraclete distinct from Himself, even as we say that the Son is also distinct from the Father; so that He showed a third degree in the Paraclete, as we believe the second degree is in the Son, by reason of the order observed in the *Economy*. Besides, does not the very fact that they have the distinct names of *Father* and *Son* amount to a declaration that they are distinct in personality? For, of course, all things will be what their names represent them to be; and what they are and ever will be, that will they be called; and the distinction indicated by the names does not at all admit of any confusion, because there is none in the things which they designate. "Yes is yes, and no is no; for what is more than these, cometh of evil." (Math. V, 37). . . .

CHAPTER 13

For we, who by the grace of God possess an insight into both the times and the occasions of the Sacred Writings, especially we who are followers of the Paraclete, not of human *teachers*, do indeed definitively declare that *Two* Beings are God, the Father and the Son, and, with the addition of the Holy Spirit, even *Three*, according to the principle of the *divine* economy, which introduces *number*, in order that the Father may not, as you perversely infer, be Himself believed to have been born and to have suffered, which it is not lawful to believe, forasmuch as it has not been so handed down. That there are, however, two Gods or two Lords, is a statement which at no time proceeds out of our mouth: not as if it were untrue that the Father is God, and the Son is God, and the Holy Ghost is God, and each is God; but because in earlier times Two were actually spoken of as God, and two as Lord, that when Christ should come He might be both acknowledged as God and designated as Lord, being the Son of Him who is both God and Lord. Now, if there were found in the scriptures but one Personality of Him who is God and Lord, Christ would justly enough be inadmissible to the title of God and Lord: for (in the scriptures) there was declared to be none other than One God and One Lord, and it must have followed that the Father should Himself seem to have come down (to earth), inasmuch as only One God and One Lord was ever read of (in the scriptures), and His entire *Economy* would be involved in obscurity, which has been planned and arranged with so clear a foresight in *His providential dispensa-*

tion as matter for our faith. As soon, however, as Christ came, and was recognized by us as the very Being who had from the beginning caused plurality (in the Divine Economy), being the *second* from the Father, and with the Spirit the *third*, and Himself declaring and manifesting the Father more fully (than He had ever been before), the title of Him who is God and Lord was at once restored to the Unity (of the Divine Nature), even because the Gentiles would have to pass from the multitude of their idols to the One Only God, in order that a difference might be distinctly settled between the worshippers of One God and the votaries of polytheism. For it was only right that Christians should shine in the world as "children of light," adoring and invoking Him who is the One God and Lord as "the light of the world." Besides, if, from that perfect knowledge which assures us that the title of God and Lord is suitable both to the Father, and to the Son, and to the Holy Ghost, we were to invoke a *plurality of gods and lords*, we should quench our torches, and we should become less courageous to endure the martyr's sufferings, from which an easy escape would everywhere lie open to us, as soon as we swore by a *plurality of gods and lords*, as sundry heretics do, who hold more gods than One. I will therefore not speak of gods at all, nor of lords, but I shall follow the apostle; so that if the Father and the Son, are alike to be invoked, I shall call the Father "God", and invoke Jesus Christ as "Lord." But when Christ alone (is mentioned), I shall be able to call Him "God", as the same apostle says: "Of whom is Christ, who is over all, God blessed for ever." For I should give the name of "sun" even to a sunbeam, considered in itself; but if I were mentioning the sun from which the ray emanates, I certainly should at once withdraw the name of sun from the mere beam. For although I make not two suns, still I shall reckon both the sun and its ray to be as much two things and two forms of one undivided substance, as God and His Word, as the Father and the Son. . . .

CHAPTER 27

But why should I linger over matters which are so evident, when I ought to be attacking points on which they seek to obscure the plainest proof? For, confuted on all sides on the distinction between the Father and the Son, which we maintain without destroying their inseparable union—as (by the examples) of the sun and the ray, and the fountain and the river—yet, by help of (their conceit) an indivisible number (with issues) of two and three, they endeavour to interpret this distinction in a way which shall nevertheless tally with their own opinions: so that, all in one Person, they distinguish two, Father and Son, understanding the Son to be flesh, that is man, that is Jesus; and the Father to be spirit, that is God, that is Christ. Thus they, while contending that the Father and the Son are one and the same, do in fact begin by dividing them rather than uniting them. For if Jesus is one, and Christ is another, then the Son will be different from the Father, because the Son is Jesus, and the Father is Christ. Such a monarchy as this they learnt, I suppose, in the school of Valentinus, making two—Jesus and Christ. But this conception of theirs has been, in fact, already confuted in what we have previously advanced, because the Word of God or the Spirit of God is also called the power of the Highest, whom they make the Father; whereas these relations are not themselves the same as He whose relations they are said to be, but they proceed from Him and appertain to Him. However, another refutation awaits them on this point of their heresy. See, say they, it was announced by the angel: "Therefore that Holy Things which shall be born of thee shall be called the Son of God." Therefore, (they argue,) as it was the flesh that was born, it must be the flesh that is the Son of God. Nay, (I answer,) this is spoken concerning the Spirit of God. For it was certainly of the Holy Spirit that the virgin conceived; and that which he conceived, she brought forth. That, therefore, had to be born which was conceived and was to be brought forth; that is to say, the Spirit, whose "name should be called Emmanuel which being interpreted, is, God with us." Besides, the flesh is not God, so that it could not have been said concerning it, "That Holy Thing shall be called the Son of God," but only that Divine Being who was born in the flesh, of whom the psalm also says, "Since God became man in the midst of it, and established it by the will of the Father." Now what Divine Person was born in it? The Word, and the Spirit which became incarnate with the Word by the will of the Father. The Word, therefore, is incarnate; and this must be the point of our inquiry: How the Word became flesh,—whether it was by having been transfigured, as it were, in the flesh, or by having really clothed Himself in flesh. Certainly it was by a real clothing of Himself in flesh. For the rest, we must needs believe God to be unchangeable, and incapable of form, as being eternal. But transfiguration is the destruction of that which previously existed. For whatsoever is transfigured into some other thing ceases to be that which it had been, and begins to be that which it previously was not. God, however, neither ceases to be what He was, nor can He be any other thing than what He is. The Word is God, and "the Word of the Lord remaineth for ever,"—even by holding on unchangeably in His own proper form. Now, if He admits not of being transfigured, it must follow that He be understood in this sense to have become flesh, when He comes to be in the flesh, and is manifested, and is seen, and is handled by means of the flesh; since all the other points likewise require to be thus understood. For if the Word became flesh by a transfiguration and change of substance, it follows at once that Jesus must be a substance compounded of two substances—of flesh and spirit,—a kind of mixture, like electrum, composed of gold and silver; and it begins to be neither gold (that is to say, spirit) nor silver (that is to say, flesh),—the one being changed by the other, and a third substance produced. Jesus, therefore, cannot at this rate be God, for He has ceased to be the Word, which was made flesh; nor can He be Man incarnate, for He is not properly flesh, and it was flesh which the Word became. Being compounded, therefore, of both, He actually is neither; He is rather some third substance, very different from either. But the truth is, we find that He is expressly set forth as both God and Man; the very psalm which we have quoted intimating (of the flesh), that "God became Man in the midst of it, He therefore established it by the will of the Father,"—certainly in all respects as the Son of God and the Son of Man, being God and Man, differing no doubt according to each substance in its own especial property, inasmuch as the Word is nothing else but God, and the flesh nothing else but Man. Thus does the aspostle also teach respecting His two substances, saying, "who was made of the seed of David;" in which words He will be Man and Son of Man. "Who was declared to be the Son of God, according to the Spirit;" in which words He will be God, and the Word—the Son of God. We see plainly the twofold state, which is not confounded, but conjoined in One Person—Jesus, God and Man. Concerning Christ, indeed, I defer what I have to say. (I remark here), that the property of each nature is so wholly preserved, that the Spirit on the one hand did all things in Jesus suitable to Itself, such as miracles, and mighty deeds, and wonders; and the Flesh, on the other hand, exhibited the affections which belong to it. It was hungry under the devil's temptation, thirsty with the Samaritan woman, wept over Lazarus, was troubled even unto death, and at last actually died. If, however, it was only a *tertium quid*, some composite essence formed out of the Two substances, like the *electrum* (which we have mentioned), there would be no distinct proofs apparent of either nature. But by a transfer of functions, the Spirit would have done things to be done by the Flesh, and the Flesh such as are effected by the Spirit; or else such things as are suited neither to the Flesh nor to the Spirit, but confusedly of some third character. Nay more, on this supposition, either the Word underwent death, or the flesh did not die, if so be the Word was converted into flesh; because either the flesh was immortal, or the Word was mortal. Forasmuch, however, as the two substances acted distinctly, each in its own character, there necessarily accrued to them severally their own operations, and their own issues. Learn then, together with Nicodemus, that "that which is born in the flesh is flesh, and that which is born of the Spirit is Spirit." Neither the flesh becomes Spirit, nor the Spirit flesh. In one *Person* they no doubt are well able to be co-existent. Of them Jesus consists—Man, of the flesh; of the Spirit, God—and the angel designated Him as "the Son of God," in respect of that nature, in which He was Spirit, reserving for the flesh the appellation "Son of Man." In like manner, again, the apostle calls Him "the Mediator between God and Men," and so affirmed His participation of both substances. Now, to end the matter, will you, who interpret the Son of God to be flesh, be so good as to show us what the Son of Man is? Will He then, I want to know, be the Spirit? But you insist upon it that the Father Himself is the Spirit, on the ground that "God is a Spirit," just as if we did not read also that there is "the Spirit of God;" in the same manner as we find that as "the Word was God," so also there is "the Word of God."

14   In *De Principiis* Origen (185–254) considered a variety of theological problems, including an exposition of his Christological position. While seeking to defend the "unity" of the Trinity, he used terms that were later interpreted by some as emphasizing the subordination of the Son to the Father. Later Arians looked to Origen for support, though with some injustice to the intent of his work[1]

De Principiis*

ORIGEN

In the first place, we must note that the nature of that deity which is in Christ in respect of His being the only-begotten Son of God is one thing, and that human nature which He assumed in these last times for the purposes of the dispensation (of grace) is another. And therefore we have first to ascertain what the only-begotten Son of God is, seeing He is called by many different names, according to the circumstances and views of individuals. For He is termed Wisdom, according to the expression of Solomon: "The Lord created me—the beginning of His ways, and among His works, before He made any other thing; He founded me before the ages. In the beginning, before He formed the earth, before He brought forth the fountains of waters, before the mountains were made strong, before all the hills, He brought me forth." (Prov. viii, 22–25). He is also styled First-born, as the apostle has declared: "who is the first-born of every creature." (Cor.

* From *The Ante-Nicene Fathers*, Vol. IV, Bk. I., Ch. II. Grand Rapids, Mich.: Wm. B. Eerdmans Publishing Co., 1951.

1 See also, *De Principiis*, Selection 3 and Arius, Selection 17.

i. 15). The first-born, however, is not by nature a different person from the Wisdom, but one and the same. Finally, the Apostle Paul says that "Christ (is) the power of God and the wisdom of God." (I Cor. i. 24).

Let no one, however, imagine that we mean anything impersonal when we call Him the wisdom of God; or suppose, for example, that we understand Him to be, not a living being endowed with wisdom, but something which makes men wise, giving itself to, and implanting itself in, the minds of those who are made capable of receiving His virtues and intelligence. If, then, it is once rightly understood that the only-begotten Son of God is His wisdom hypostatically existing, I know not whether our curiosity ought to advance beyond this, or entertain any suspicion that that ὑπόστασις or *substantia* contains anything of a bodily nature, since everything that is corporeal is distinguished either by form, or colour, or magnitude. And who in his sound senses ever sought for form, or colour, or size, in wisdom, in respect of its being wisdom? And who that is capable of entertaining reverential thoughts or feelings regarding God, can suppose or believe that God the Father ever existed, even for a moment of time, without having generated this Wisdom? For in that case he must say either that God was unable to generate Wisdom before He produced her, so that He afterwards called into being her who formerly did not exist, or that He possessed the power indeed, but—what cannot be said of God without impiety—was unwilling to use it; both of which suppositions, it is patent to all, are alike absurd and impious: for they amount to this, either that God advanced from a condition of inability to one of ability, or that, although possessed of the power, He concealed it, and delayed the generation of Wisdom. Wherefore we have always held that God is the Father of His only-begotten Son, who was born indeed of Him, and derives from Him what He is, but without any beginning, not only such as may be measured by any divisions of time, but even that which the mind alone can contemplate within itself, or behold, so to speak, with the naked powers of the understanding. And therefore we must believe that Wisdom was generated before any beginning that can be either comprehended or expressed. And since all the creative power of the coming creation was included in this very existence of Wisdom (whether of those things which have an original or of those which have a derived existence), having been formed beforehand and arranged by the power of foreknowledge; on account of these very creatures which had been described, as it were, and prefigured in Wisdom herself, does Wisdom say, in the words of Solomon, that she was created the beginning of the ways of God, inasmuch as she contained within herself either the beginnings, or forms, or species of all creation.

Now, in the same way in which we have understood that Wisdom was the beginning of the ways of God, and is said to be created, forming beforehand and containing within herself the species and beginnings of all creatures, must we understand her to be the Word of God, because of her disclosing to all other beings, i.e., to universal creation, the nature of the mysteries and secrets which are contained within the divine wisdom; and on this account she is called the Word, because she is, as it were, the interpreter of the secrets of the mind. . . . John, however, . . . says in the beginning of his Gospel, when defining God by a special definition to be the Word, "And God was the Word, and this was in the beginning with God." Let him, then, who assigns a beginning to the Word or Wisdom of God, take care that he be not guilty of impiety against the unbegotten Father Himself, seeing he denies that He had always been a Father, and had generated the Word, and had possessed wisdom in all preceding periods, whether they be called times or ages, or anything else that can be so entitled.

This Son, accordingly, is also the truth and life of all things which exist. And with reason. For how could those things which were created live, unless they derived their being from life? or how could those things which are, truly exist, unless they came down from the truth? or how could rational beings exist, unless the Word or reason had previously existed? or how could they be wise, unless there were wisdom? But since it was to come to pass that some also should fall away from life, and bring death upon themselves by their declension—for death is nothing else than a departure from life—and as it was not to follow that those beings which had once been created by God for the enjoyment of life should utterly perish, it was necessary that, before death, there should be in existence such a power as would destroy the coming death, and that there should be a resurrection, the type of which was in our Lord and Saviour, and that this resurrection should have its ground in the wisdom and word and life of God. And then, in the next place, since some of those who were created were not to be always willing to remain unchangeable and unalterable in the calm and moderate enjoyment of the blessings which they possessed, but, in consequence of the good which was in them being theirs not by nature or essence, but by accident, were to be perverted and changed, and to fall away from their position, therefore was the Word and Wisdom of God made the Way. And it was so termed because it leads to the Father those who walk along it.

Whatever, therefore, we have predicated of the wisdom of God, will be appropriately applied and understood of the Son of God, in virtue of His being the Life, and the Word, and the Truth, and the Resurrection: for all these titles are derived from His power and operations, and in none of them is there the slightest ground for understanding anything of a corporeal nature which might seem to denote either size, or form, or colour; for those children of men which appear among us, or those descendants of other living beings, correspond to the seed of those by whom they were begotten, or derive from those mothers, in whose wombs they are formed and nourished, whatever that is, which they bring into this life, and carry with them when they are born. But it is monstrous and unlawful to compare God the Father, in the generation of His only-begotten Son, and in the substance of the same, to any man or other living thing engaged in such an act; for we must of necessity hold that there is something exceptional and worthy of God which does not admit of any comparison at all, not merely in things, but which cannot even be conceived by thought or discovered by perception, so that a human mind should be able to apprehend how the unbegotten God is made the Father of the only-begotten Son. Because His generation is as eternal and everlasting as the brilliancy which is produced from the sun. For it is not by receiving the breath of life that He is made a Son, by any outward act, but by His own nature. . . .

Let us now see how we are to understand the expression "invisible image," that we may in this way perceive how God is rightly called the Father of His Son; and let us, in the first place, draw our conclusions from what are customarily called images among men. That is sometimes called an image which is painted or sculptured on some material substance, such as wood or stone; and sometimes a child is called the image of his parent, when the features of the child in no respect belie their resemblance to the father. I think, therefore, that that man who was formed after the image and likeness of God may be fittingly compared to the first illustration. Respecting him, however, we shall see more precisely, God willing, when we come to expound the passage in Genesis. But the image of the Son of God, of whom we are now speaking, may be compared to the second of the above examples, even in respect of this, that He is the invisible image of the invisible God, in the same manner as we say, according to the sacred history, that the image of Adam is his son Seth. The words are, "And Adam begat Seth in his own likeness, and after his own image." (Gen. v. 3). Now this image contains the unity of nature and substance belonging to Father and Son. For if the Son do, in like manner, all those things which the Father doth, then, in virtue of the Son doing all things like the Father, is the image of the Father formed in the Son, who is born of Him, like an act of His will proceeding from the mind. And I am therefore of opinion that the will of the Father ought alone to be sufficient for the existence of that which He wishes to exist. For in the exercise of His will He employs no other way than that which is made known by the counsel of His will. And thus also the existence of the Son is generated by Him. For this point must above all others be maintained by those who allow nothing to be unbegotten, i.e., unborn, save God the Father only. And we must be careful not to fall into the absurdities of those who picture to themselves certain emanations, so as to divide the divine nature into parts, and who divide God the Father as far as they can, since even to entertain the remotest suspicion of such a thing regarding an incorporeal being is not only the height of impiety, but

a mark of the greatest folly, it being most remote from any intelligent conception that there should be any physical division of any incorporeal nature.
Rather, therefore, as an act of the will proceeds from the understanding, and
neither cuts off any parts nor is separated or divided from it, so after some
such fashion is the Father to be supposed as having begotten the Son, His
own image; namely, so that, as He is Himself invisible by nature, He also
begat an image that was invisible. For the Son is the Word, and therefore
we are not to understand that anything in Him is cognisable by the senses.
He is wisdom, and in wisdom there can be no suspicion of anything corporeal. He is the true light, which enlightens every man that cometh into
this world; but He has nothing in common with the light of this sun.
Our Saviour, therefore, is the image of the invisible God, inasmuch as
compared with the Father Himself He is the truth; and as compared with
us, to whom He reveals the Father, He is the image by which we come to
the knowledge of the Father, whom no one knows save the Son, and he to
whom the Son is pleased to reveal Him. And the method of revealing Him
is through the understanding. For He by whom the Son Himself is understood, understands, as a consequence, the Father also, according to His
own words: "He that hath seen Me, hath seen the Father also. . . ." (John
xiv. 9).

In order, however, to arrive at a fuller understanding of the manner
in which the Saviour is the figure of the person or subsistence of God, let
us take an instance, which, although it does not describe the subject of
which we are treating either fully or appropriately, may nevertheless be seen
to be employed for this purpose only, to show that the Son of God, who was
in the form of God, divesting Himself (of His glory), makes it His object,
by this very divesting of Himself, to demonstrate to us the fulness of
His deity. For instance, suppose that there were a statue of so enormous a
size as to fill the whole world, and which on that account could be seen
by no one; and that another statue were formed altogether resembling it
in the shape of the limbs, and in the features of the countenance, and in
form and material, but without the same immensity of size, so that those
who were unable to behold the one of enormous proportions, should, on
seeing the latter, acknowledge that they had seen the former, because it
preserved all the features of its limbs and countenance, and even the very
form and material, so closely, as to be altogether undistinguishable from it;
by some such similitude, the Son of God, divesting Himself of His equality
with the Father, and showing to us the way to the knowledge of Him, is
made the express image of His person: so that we, who were unable to
look upon the glory of that marvellous light when placed in the greatness
of His Godhead, may, by His being made to us brightness, obtain the means
of beholding the divine light by looking upon the brightness. This comparison, of course, of statues, as belonging to material things, is employed

for no other purpose than to show that the Son of God, though placed in the very insignificant form of a human body, in consequence of the resemblance of His works and power to the Father, showed that there was in Him an immense and invisible greatness, inasmuch as He said to His disciples, "He who sees Me, sees the Father also;" and, "I and the Father are one." And to these belong also the similar expression, "The Father is in Me, and I in the Father. . . ."

That is properly termed everlasting or eternal which neither had a beginning of existence, nor can ever cease to be what it is. And this is the idea conveyed by John when he says that "God is light." Now His wisdom is the splendour of that light, not only in respect of its being light, but also of being everlasting light, so that His wisdom is eternal and everlasting splendour. If this be fully understood, it clearly shows that the existence of the Son is derived from the Father, but not in time, nor from any other beginning, except, as we have said, from God Himself.

But wisdom is also called the stainless mirror of the ἐνέργεια or working of God. We must first understand, then, what the working of the power of God is. It is a sort of vigour, so to speak, by which God operates either in creation, or in providence, or in judgment, or in the disposal and arrangement of individual things, each in its season. For as the image formed in a mirror unerringly reflects all the acts and movements of him who gazes on it, so would Wisdom have herself to be understood when she is called the stainless mirror of the power and working of the Father: as the Lord Jesus Christ also, who is the Wisdom of God, declares of Himself when He says, "The words which the Father doeth, these also doeth the Son likewise." (John v. 19). And again He says, that the Son cannot do anything of Himself, save what He sees the Father do. As therefore the Son in no respect differs from the Father in the power of His works, and the work of the Son is not a different thing from that of the Father, but one and the same movement, so to speak, is in all things, He therefore named Him a stainless mirror, that by such an expression it might be understood that there is no dissimilarity whatever between the Son and the Father. How, indeed, can those things which are said by some to be done after the manner in which a disciple resembles or imitates his master, or according to the view that those things are made by the Son in bodily material which were first formed by the Father in their spiritual essence, agree with the declarations of scripture, seeing in the Gospel the Son is said to do not similar things, but the same things in a similar manner?

It remains that we inquire what is the "image of His goodness;" and here, I think, we must understand the same thing which we expressed a little ago, in speaking of the image formed by the mirror. For He is the primal goodness, doubtless, out of which the Son is born, who, being in all respects the image of the Father, may certainly also be called with propriety the image of His goodness. For there is no other second goodness existing in the

Son, save that which is in the Father. And therefore also the Saviour Himself rightly says in the Gospel, "There is none good save one only, God the Father," (Luke, xviii, 19) that by such an expression it may be understood that the Son is not of a different goodness, but of that only which exists in the Father, of whom He is rightly termed the image, because He proceeds from no other source but from that primal goodness, lest there might appear to be in the Son a different goodness from that which is in the Father. Nor is there any dissimilarity or difference of goodness in the Son. And therefore it is not to be imagined that there is a kind of blasphemy, as it were, in the words, "There is none good save one only, God the Father," as if thereby it may be supposed to be denied that either Christ or the Holy Spirit was good. But, as we have already said, the primal goodness is to be understood as residing in God the Father, from whom both the Son is born and the Holy Spirit proceeds, retaining within them, without any doubt, the nature of that goodness which is in the source whence they are derived. And if there be any other things which in scripture are called good, whether angel, or man, or servant, or treasure, or a good heart, or a good tree, all these are so termed catachrestically, having in them an accidental, not an essential goodness. But it would require both much time and labour to collect together all the titles of the Son of God, such, e.g., as the true light, or the door, or the righteousness, or the sanctification, or the redemption, and countless others; and to show for what reasons each one of them is so given. Satisfied, therefore, with what we have already advanced, we go on with our inquiries into those other matters.

15

IN THE MID-THIRD CENTURY, the conflict over the interpretation of the relation of Father and Son in the Godhead broke out in the church at Alexandria. The bishop of the church, Dionysius, was concerned with the prominence of Sabellian sentiments in his congregation and in defending a line of Origenistic thought, he used terminology that seemed to assert the subordination of the Son to the Father. He likened the Son to a ship and the Father to the shipbuilder; the Son to a vine and the Father to the caretaker of the vineyard. Members of the Alexandrian Church wrote to Dionysius, Bishop of Rome, about the issue. In reply the Roman bishop said that Dionysius of Alexandria had used unfortunate language, though he was correct in attempting to point out the errors of the Sabellians. The outline of the position of

Dionysius of Rome is stated in the following letter. The problems about which Tertullian and Origen had written earlier were continuing to be of central theological concern.

A Letter Concerning Sabellianism[*]

DIONYSIUS OF ROME

Next, I may reasonably turn to those who divide and cut to pieces and destroy that most sacred doctrine of the Church of God, the divine Monarchy, making it as it were three powers and partitive subsistences and godheads three. I am told that some among you who are catechists and teachers of the Divine Word, take the lead in this tenet, who are diametrically opposed, so to speak, to Sabellius's opinions; for he blasphemously says that the Son is the Father, and the Father the Son, but they in some sort preach three Gods, as dividing the sacred Monad into three subsistences foreign to each other and utterly separate. For it must needs be that with the God of the Universe, the Divine Word is united, and the Holy Ghost must repose and habitate in God; thus in one as in a summit, I mean the God of the Universe, must the Divine Triad be gathered up and brought together. . . . Equally must one censure those who hold the Son to be a work, and consider that the Lord has come into being, as one of things which really came to be; whereas the divine oracles witness to a generation suitable to Him and becoming, but not to any fashioning or making. . . . For if He came to be Son, once He was not; but He was always, if (that is) He be in the Father, as He says Himself, and if the Christ be Word and Wisdom and Power (which, as ye know, divine scripture says), and these attributes be powers of God. If then the Son came into being, once these attributes were not; consequently there was a time, when God was without them; which is most absurd. . . . And one may say to them, O reckless men, is He a work, who is 'the First-born of every creature, who is born from the womb before the morning star,' who said, as Wisdom, 'Before all the hills He begets me?' And in many passages of the divine oracles is the Son said to have been generated, but nowhere to have come into being; which manifestly convicts those of misconception about the Lord's generation, who presume to call Him divine and ineffable generation a making. Neither then may we divide into three Godheads the wonderful and divine Monad; nor disparage with the name of 'work' the dignity and exceeding majesty of the Lord; but we must believe in

---

* From Athanasius, *Defense of the Nicene Definition*, tr. by Archibald Robertson, A Select Library of Nicene and Post-Nicene Fathers, Vol. IV, Second series. Grand Rapids, Mich.: Wm. B. Eerdmans Publishing Co., 1957.

God the Father Almighty, and in Christ Jesus His Son, and in the Holy Ghost, and hold that to the God of the universe the Word is united. For 'I,' says He, 'and the Father are one;' and, 'I in the Father and the Father in Me.' For thus both the Divine Triad, and the holy preaching of the Monarchy, will be preserved."

16 DIONYSIUS, BISHOP OF ALEXANDRIA (200–265), a student of Origen, became the Bishop of Alexandria in 248, after serving for some time as head of the Alexandrian catechetic school. His unguarded language in attacking the Sabellians in the church of Alexandria left him in a vulnerable position and the following excerpt from a letter to Dionysius of Rome indicates his own uneasiness with his choice of words. It is especially important to note that though he did not find the term, *homoousios*, (of the same substance)[1] in the scriptures to describe the relation between Father and Son, he was willing to use it to convey the meaning behind his position.

A Letter to Dionysius of Rome*

DIONYSIUS OF ALEXANDRIA

But when I spoke of things created, and certain works to be considered, I hastily put forward illustrations of such things, as it were little appropriate, when I said neither is the plant the same as the husbandman, nor the boat the same as the boatbuilder. But when I lingered rather upon things suitable and more adapted to the nature of the thing, and I unfolded in many words, by various carefully considered arguments, what things were more true; which things, moreover, I have set forth to you in another letter. And in these things I have also proved the falsehood of the charge which they bring against me—to wit, that I do not maintain that Christ is consubstantial with God. For although I say that I have never either found or read

* From *The Ante-Nicene Fathers*, Vol. VI. Grand Rapids, Mich.: Wm. B. Eerdmans Publishing Co., 1951.

[1] This term became of crucial importance in the Nicene decision of 325. See also Council of Nicaea, Selection 20.

this word in the sacred scriptures, yet other reasonings, which I immediately subjoined, are in no wise discrepant from this view, because I brought
forward as an illustration human offspring, which assuredly is of the same
kind as the begetter; and I said that parents are absolutely distinguished
from their children by the fact alone that they themselves are not their
children, or that it would assuredly be a matter of necessity that there would
neither be parents nor children. But, as I said before, I have not the letter
in my possession, on account of the present condition of affairs; otherwise
I would have sent you the very words that I then wrote, yea, and a copy of
the whole letter, and I will send it if at any time I shall have the opportunity. I remember, further, that I added many similitudes from things
kindred to one another. For I said that the plant, whether it grows up from
seed or from a root, is different from that whence it sprouted, although it is
absolutely of the same nature; and similarly, that a river flowing from a
spring takes another form and name: for that neither is the spring called
the river, nor the river the spring, but that these are two things, and that the
spring indeed is, as it were, the father, while the river is the water from the
spring. But they feign that they do not see these things and the like to
them which are written, as if they were blind; but they endeavour to assail
me from a distance with expressions too carelessly used, as if they were
stones, not observing that on things of which they are ignorant, and which
require interpretation to be understood, illustrations that are not only remote, but even contrary, will often throw light.

It was said above that God is the spring of all good things, but the
Son was called the river flowing from Him; because the word is an emanation
of the mind, and—to speak after human fashion—is emitted from the heart
by the mouth. But the mind which springs forth by the tongue is different
from the word which exists in the heart. For this latter, after it has emitted
the former, remains and is what it was before; but the mind sent forth flies
away, and is carried everywhere around, and thus each is in each although
one is from the other, and they are one although they are two. And it is
thus that the Father and the Son are said to be one, and to be in one another.

17   ARIUS, A PRESBYTER in the church of Alexandria, brought the
long germinating controversy concerning the relation of the
Father and Son to protracted eccleciastical discussion. Arius
received his training under Lucian of Antioch, a student of

Origen; both Lucian and his disciple emphasized the subordinationist strain of Origen's thought. Arius, conscious of continuing Sabellian tendencies in the Alexandrian Church, insisted that God the Father alone was without beginning; the Son was brought into being. Arius' position was in many respects ambiguous because the view he held of the Son was that of a being neither fully God nor fully man. It was his attempt to emphasize the unity of God, while at the same time to avoid a Sabellian interpretation. Thus Arius' position is similar to the subordinationist strain of Origen's Christology. Arius' bishop, Alexander of Alexandria, called a synod to deal with the issue the presbyter raised, with the result that Arius and his followers were condemned. In the two excerpts that follow we have, first, Arius' defense of his position made to his bishop, Alexander, and then his appeal for support sent to his fellow student of Lucian, Eusebius of Nicomedia.

A. A Letter to Alexander, Bishop of Alexandria*

ARIUS

Our faith from our forefather, which also we have learned from thee, Blessed Pope, is this:—We acknowledge One God, alone Ingenerate, alone Everlasting, alone Unbegun, alone True, alone having Immortality, alone Wise, alone Good, alone Sovereign; Judge, Governor, and Providence of all, unalterable and unchangeable, just and good, God of Law and Prophets and New Testament; who begat an Only-begotten Son before eternal times, through whom He has made both the ages and the universe; and begat Him, not in semblance, but in truth; and that He made Him subsist at His own will, unalterable and unchangeable; perfect creature of God, but not as one of the creatures; offspring, but not as one of things begotten; nor as Valentinus pronounced that the offspring of the Father was an issue; nor as Manichaeus taught that the offspring was a portion of the Father, one in essence; or as Sabellius, dividing the Monad, speaks of a Son-and-Father; nor as Hieracas, of one torch from another, or as a lamp divided into two;

* From Athanasius, De Synodis, tr. by Archibald Robertson, A Select Library of Nicene and Post-Nicene Fathers, Vol. IV, Second series. Grand Rapids, Mich.: Wm. B. Eerdmans Publishing Co., 1957.

nor that He who was before, was afterwards generated or new-created into a Son, as thou too thyself, Blessed Pope, in the midst of the Church and in session hast often condemned; but, as we say, at the will of God, created before times and before ages, and gaining life and being from the Father, who gave subsistence to His glories together with Him. For the Father did not, in giving to Him the inheritance of all things, deprive Himself of what He has ingenerately in Himself; for He is the Fountain of all things. Thus there are Three Subsistences. And God, being the cause of all things, is Unbegun and altogether Sole, but the Son being begotten apart from time by the Father, and being created and founded before ages, was not before His generation, but being begotten apart from time before all things, alone was made to subsist by the Father. For He is not eternal or co-eternal or co-unoriginate with the Father, nor has He His being together with the Father, as some speak of relations, introducing two ingenerate beginnings, but God is before all things as being Monad and Beginning of all. Wherefore also He is before the Son; as we have learned also from thy preaching in the midst of the Church. So far then as from God He has being, and glories, and life, and all things are delivered unto Him, in such sense is God His origin. For He is above Him, as being His God, and before Him. But if the terms 'from Him,' and 'from the womb,' and 'I came forth from the Father, and I am come,' be understood by some to mean as if a part of Him, one in essence or as an issue, then the Father is according to them compounded and divisible and alterable and material, and, as far as their belief goes, has the circumstances of a body, Who is the Incorporeal God.

B. A Letter to Eusebius, Bishop of Nicomedia[*]

ARIUS

To his very dear lord, the man of God, the faithful and orthodox Eusebius, Arius, unjustly persecuted by Alexander the Pope, on account of that all-conquering truth of which you also are a champion, sendeth greeting in the Lord.

* From Theodoret, *Ecclesiastical History*, tr. by Bloomfield Jackson, A Select Library of Nicene and Post-Nicene Fathers, Vol. III, Second series. Grand Rapids, Mich.: Wm. B. Eerdmans Publishing Co., 1952.

Ammonius, my father, being about to depart for Nicomedia, I considered myself bound to salute you by him, and withal to inform that natural affection which you bear towards the brethren for the sake of God and His Christ, that the bishop greatly wastes and persecutes us, and leaves no stone unturned against us. He has driven us out of the city as atheists, because we do not concur in what he publicly preaches, namely, God always, the Son always; as the Father so the Son; the Son co-exists unbegotten with God; He is everlasting; neither by thought nor by any interval does God precede the Son; always God, always Son; he is begotten of the unbegotten; the Son is of God Himself. Eusebius, your brother bishop of Caesarea, Theodotus, Paulinus, Athanasius, Gregorius, Aetius, and all the bishops of the East, have been condemned because they say that God had an existence prior to that of His Son; except Philogonius, Hellanicus, and Marcarius, who are unlearned men, and who have embraced heretical opinions. Some of them say that the Son is an eructation, others that He is a production, others that He is also unbegotten. These are impieties to which we cannot listen, even though the heretics threaten us with a thousand deaths. But we say and believe, and have taught, and do teach, that the Son is not unbegotten, nor in any way part of the unbegotten; and that He does not derive His subsistence from any matter; but that by His own will and counsel He has subsisted before time, and before ages, as perfect God, only begotten and unchangeable, and that before He was begotten, or created, or purposed, or established, He was not. For He was not unbegotten. We are persecuted, because we say that the Son has a beginning, but that God is without beginning. This is the cause of our persecution, and likewise, because we say that He is of the non-existent. And this we say, because He is neither part of God, nor of any essential being. For this are we persecuted; the rest you know. I bid thee farewell in the Lord, remembering our afflictions, my fellow-Lucianist, and true Eusebius.

18 In 312, CONSTANTINE was "converted" to Christianity. After the death of Galerius in 311 four leaders vied for the throne of the empire. Not until Constantine's defeat of Licinius in 323 was Constantine made the sole ruler of the empire. In solidifying his control it was apparent that the erupting and divisive theological struggle concerning the nature of the Godhead, then current in Alexandria and spreading throughout the empire, needed to be quelled. Thus Constantine sent

Hosius of Cordova, his trusted advisor, to Alexandria with a letter addressed to Alexander of Alexandria and Arius. (Hosius was steeped in the Western theological tradition stemming from Tertullian, a factor that was influential in the later decision at Nicaea.) The tone of the letter is remarkably calm when compared with Constantine's letter written after the Council of Nicaea. (See Selection 21).

A Letter to Alexander of Alexandria and Arius*

CONSTANTINE

I am informed that your present controversy originated thus. When you, Alexander, inquired of your presbyters what each thought on a certain inexplicable passage of the written Word, rather on a subject improper for discussion; and you, Arius, rashly gave expression to a view of the matter such as ought either never to have been conceived, or when suggested to your mind, it became you to bury it in silence. This dispute having thus been excited among you, communion has been denied; and the most holy people being rent into two factions, have departed from the harmony of the common body. Wherefore let each one of you, showing consideration for the other, listen to the impartial exhortation of your fellow-servant. And what counsel does he offer? It was neither prudent at first to agitate such a question, nor to reply to such a question when proposed: for the claim of no law demands the investigation of such subjects, but the idle useless talk of leisure occasions them. And even if they should exist for the sake of exercising our natural faculties, yet we ought to confine them to our own consideration, and not incautiously bring them forth in public assemblies, nor thoughtlessly confide them to the ears of everybody. Indeed how few are capable either of adequately expounding, or even accurately understanding the import of matters so vast and profound!

And even if any one should be considered able to satisfactorily accomplish this, how large a portion of the people would he succeed in convincing? Or who can grapple with the subtleties of such investigations without danger of lapsing into error? It becomes us therefore on such topics to check

* From Socrates, *Ecclesiastical History*, tr. by A. C. Zenos, in A Select Library of Nicene and Post-Nicene Fathers, Vol. II., Second series. Grand Rapids, Mich.: Wm. B. Eerdmans Publishing Co., 1952.

loquacity, lest either on account of the weakness of our nature we should be incompetent to explain the subject proposed; or the dull understanding of the audience should make them unable to apprehend clearly what is attempted to be taught: and in the case of one or the other of these failures, the people must be necessarily involved either in blasphemy or schism. Wherefore let an unguarded question, and an inconsiderate answer, on the part of each of you, procure equal forgiveness from one another. No cause of difference has been started by you bearing on any important precept contained in the Law; nor has any new heresy been introduced by you in connection with the worship of God; but ye both hold one and the same judgment on these points, which is the Creed. Moreover, while you thus pertinaciously contend with one another about matters of small or scarcely the least importance, it is unsuitable for you to have charge of so many people of God, because you are divided in opinion: and not only is it unbecoming, but it is also believed to be altogether unlawful.

In order to remind you of your duty by an example of an inferior kind, I may say: you are well aware that even the philosophers themselves are united under one sect. Yet they often differ from each other on some parts of their theories: but although they may differ on the very highest branches of science, in order to maintain the unity of their body, they still agree to coalesce. Now, if this is done amongst them, how much more equitable will it be for you, who have been constituted ministers of the Most High God, to become unanimous with one another in such a religious profession. . . . But in order that you may have some idea of my excessive grief on account of this unhappy difference, listen to what I am about to state. On my recent arrival at the city of Nicomedia, it was my intention immediately after to proceed into the East: but while I was hastening toward you, and had advanced a considerable distance on my way, intelligence of this affair altogether reversed my purpose, lest I should be obliged to see with my own eyes a condition of things such as I could scarcely bear the report of. Open to me therefore by your reconciliation henceforth, the way into the East, which ye have obstructed by your contentions against one another: and permit me speedily to behold both you and all the rest of the people rejoicing together; and to express my due thanks to the Divine Being, because of the general harmony and liberty of all parties, accompanied by the cordial utterance of your praise.

19   BISHOP ALEXANDER of Alexandria defended against Arius the line of thought stemming from Origen that stressed the coeternality of Father and Son. He vigorously attacked the Arian position in a letter to the bishops of the church, and at the Council of Nicaea he acted as a leader of the anti-Arian party.

A Letter to the Church[*]

ALEXANDER, BISHOP OF ALEXANDRIA

To our beloved and most honored fellow-Ministers of the Catholic Church everywhere, Alexander sends greetings in the Lord.

Inasmuch as the Catholic Church is one body, and we are commanded in the Holy Scriptures to maintain 'the bond of unity and peace,' it becomes us to write, and mutually acquaint one another with the condition of things among each of us, in order that 'if one member suffers or rejoices, we may either sympathize with each other, or rejoice together.' Know therefore that there have recently arisen in our diocese lawless and anti-christian men, teaching apostasy such as one may justly consider and denominate the forerunner of Antichrist. I wished indeed to consign this disorder to silence, that if possible the evil might be confined to the apostates alone, and not go forth into other districts and contaminate the ears of some of the simple. But since Eusebius, now in Nicomedia, thinks that the affairs of the Church are under his control because, forsooth, he deserted his charge at Berytus and assumed authority over the church at Nicomedia with impunity, and has put himself at the head of these apostates, daring even to send commendatory letters in all directions concerning them, if by any means he might inveigle some of the ignorant into this most impious and anti-christian heresy, I felt imperatively called on to be silent no longer, knowing what is written in the law, but to inform you of all these things, that ye might understand both who the apostates are, and also the contemptible character of their heresy, and pay no attention to anything that Eusebius should write to you. For now wishing to renew his former malevolence, which seemed to have been buried in oblivion by time, he affects to write in their behalf;

* From Socrates, *Ecclesiastical History*, tr. by A. C. Zenos, A Select Library of Nicene and Post-Nicene Fathers, Vol. II, Second series. Grand Rapids, Mich.: Wm. B. Eerdmans Publishing Co., 1952.

while the fact itself plainly shows that he does this for the promotion of his own purposes. These then are those who have become apostates: Arius, Achillas, Aithales, and Carpones, another Arius, Sarmates, Euzoïus, Lucius, Julian, Menas, Helladius, and Gaius; with these also must be reckoned Secundus and Theonas, who once were called bishops. The dogmas they have invented and assert, contrary to the scriptures, are these: That God was not always the Father, but that there was a period when he was not the Father; that the Word of God was not from eternity, but was made out of nothing; for that the ever-existing God ('the I AM'—the eternal One) made him who did not previously exist, out of nothing; wherefore there was a time when he did not exist, inasmuch as the Son is a creature and a work. That he is neither like the Father as it regards his essence, nor is by nature either the Father's true Word, or true Wisdom, but indeed one of his works and creatures, being erroneously called Word and Wisdom, since he was himself made by God's own Word and the Wisdom which is in God, whereby God both made all things and him also. Wherefore he is as to his nature mutable and susceptible of change, as all other rational creatures are: hence the Word is alien to and other than the essence of God; and the Father is inexplicable by the Son, and invisible to him, for neither does the Word perfectly and accurately know the Father, neither can he distinctly see him. The Son knows not the nature of his own essence: for he was made on our account, in order that God might create us by him, as by an instrument; nor would he ever have existed, unless God had wished to create us.

Some one accordingly asked them whether the Word of God could be changed, as the devil has been? and they feared not to say, 'Yes, he could; for being begotten, he is susceptible to change.' We then, with the bishops of Egypt and Libya, being assembled together to the number of nearly a hundred, have anathematized Arius for his shameless avowal of these heresies, together with all such as have countenanced them. Yet the partisans of Eusebius have received them; endeavoring to blend falsehood with truth, and that which is impious with what is sacred. But they shall not prevail, for the truth must triumph; and 'light has no fellowship with darkness, nor has Christ any concord with Belial.' Who ever heard such blasphemies? or what man of any piety is there now hearing them that is not horror-stuck, and stops his ears, lest the filth of these expressions should pollute his sense of hearing? Who that hears John saying, 'In the beginning was the Word,' does not condemn those that say, 'There was a period when the Word was not'? or who, hearing in the Gospel of 'the only-begotten Son,' and that 'all things were made by him,' will not adhor those that pronounce the Son to be one of the things made? How can he be one of the things which were made by himself? Or how can he be the only-begotten, if he is reckoned among created things? And how could he have had his existence from nonentities, since the Father has said, 'My heart has indited a good matter'; and 'I begat thee out of my bosom before the dawn'? Or how is he unlike the Father's essence, who is 'his perfect image,' and 'the brightness of his glory' and says: 'He that hath seen me, hath seen the Father'? Again, how if the Son is the Word and Wisdom of God, was there a period when he did not exist? for that is equivalent to their saying that God was once destitute both of Word and Wisdom. How can he be mutable and susceptible of change, who says of himself, 'I am in the Father, and the Father in me'; and 'I and the Father are one'; and again by the Prophet, 'Behold me because I am, and have not changed'? But if any one may also apply the expression to the Father himself, yet would it now be even more fitly said of the Word; because he was not changed by having become man, but as the Apostle says, 'Jesus Christ, the same yesterday, to-day, and forever.' But what could persuade them to say that he was made on our account, when Paul has expressly declared that 'all things are for him, and by him'? One need not wonder indeed at their blasphemous assertion that the Son does not perfectly know the Father; for having once determined to fight against Christ, they reject even the words of the Lord himself, when he says, 'As the Father knows me, even so know I the Father.' If therefore the Father but partially knows the Son, it is manifest that the Son also knows the Father but in part. But if it would be improper to affirm this, and it be admitted that the Father perfectly knows the Son, it is evident that as the Father knows his own Word, so also does the Word know his own Father, whose Word he is. . . . Many heresies have arisen before these, which exceeding all bounds in daring, have lapsed into complete infatuation: but these persons, by attempting in all their discourses to subvert the Divinity of The Word, as having made a nearer approach to Antichrist, have comparatively lessened the odium of former ones. Wherefore they have been publicly repudiated by the Church, and anathematized. We are indeed grieved on account of the perdition of these persons, and especially so because, after having been previously instructed in the doctrines of the Church, they have now apostatized from them. Nevertheless we are not greatly surprised at this, for Hymenaeus and Philetus fell in like manner (II Tim. 2, 17–18); and before them Judas, who had been a follower of the Saviour, but afterwards deserted him and became his betrayer. . . . [We were not] without forewarning respecting these very persons: for the Lord himself said: 'Take heed that no man deceive you: for many shall come in my name, saying, I am Christ: and shall deceive many'; and 'the time is at hand; Go ye not therefore after them.' And Paul, having learned these things from the Saviour, wrote, 'That in the latter times some should apostatize from the faith, giving heed to deceiving spirits, and doctrines of devils,' who pervert the truth. Seeing then that our Lord and Saviour Jesus Christ has himself enjoined this, and has also by the apostle given us intimation respecting such men, we having ourselves heard their impiety, have in consequence anathematized them, as we before said, and declared them to be alienated from the Catholic Church and faith. Moreover we have intimated this to your piety, beloved and most honored fellow-ministers, in order that ye might neither receive any of them, if they should presume to come to you, nor be induced to put confidence in Eusebius, or any other who may write to you about them. For it is incumbent on us who are Christians, to turn away from all those who speak or entertain a thought against Christ, as from those who are resisting God, and are destroyers of the souls of men: neither does it become us even 'to salute such men,' as the blessed John has prohibited, 'lest we should at any time be made partakers of their sins.' Greet the brethren which are with you; those who are with me salute you.

20

THE COUNCIL OF NICAEA was the first ecumenical gathering of the church. Its delegates had been summoned by the Emperor, Constantine, at public expense, to deal with the issues raised by Arius in the church at Alexandria. Though there were other matters considered, the decision concerning the relation between the Father and Son has been of lasting significance.

The council was made up of three groups: Arius and his defenders, led by Eusebius of Nicomedia; Alexander and the strong anti-Arians, including Hosius of Cordova, the confidant of Constantine; and a large majority of eastern bishops for whom Eusebius of Caesarea became the spokesman.

After recognizing that scriptural language was insufficient to resolve the issue, Eusebius of Caesarea proposed the creed in use in the Eastern churches as a basis for the council's deliberations. It was soon apparent, however, that Eusebius' creed could not prove to be satisfactory, since the Arians were quite willing to interpret it in line with their theological position. It contained some "Arian" phrases, such as, "first born of every creature," "Begotten of the Father before all worlds," and could generally be interpreted in a subordinationist manner. The creed, however, did serve as the basis for the Nicene Creed.

When the revised creed was presented to the council, the key additions were: the inclusion of the term, homoousion (of the same substance), which the Arians could not accept, and the important addition, "was made man," which ruled out the *tertium quid* Christ of the Arians. In addition, anathemas were added to make specific the Arian assertions that were condemned. It is reported that a key figure in the revision of the Caesarean Creed was Hosius of Cordova, the Spanish cleric well versed in Tertullian.

From the letter of Eusebius of Caesarea that follows, it is clear that the decision was not unanimous or fully comprehended by all the participants in the council. Word of the decision of the council must have reached Eusebius' church in Caesarea before he wrote, for his letter indicates that the church was not entirely satisfied with his decision to accept the Nicene statement. Though the doctrine of the Trinity was now declared to be normative doctrine, the church was entering a period of intense theological-ecclesiastical-political maneuvering; the three Arians banished by the Council and Eusebius of Nicomedia, who refused to sign the anathemas, sought to rally the Arians to a counter offensive.

A. Eusebius of Caesarea: A Letter Including the Creeds of Caesarea and Nicaea*

You will have probably learnt from other sources what was decided respecting the faith of the church at the general Council of Nicaea, for the fame of great transactions generally outruns the accurate account of them: but lest rumours not in accordance with the truth should reach you, I think it necessary to send to you, first, the formulary of faith originally proposed

* From Theodoret, *Ecclesiastical History*, tr. by Bloomfield Jackson, A Select Library of Nicene and Post-Nicene Fathers, Vol. III, Second series. Grand Rapids, Mich.: Wm. B. Eerdmans Publishing Co., 1952.

by us, and, next, the second, published with additions made to our terms. The following is our formulary, which was read in the presence of our most pious emperor, and declared to be couched in right and proper language.

[THE CREED OF CAESAREA]

'As in our first catechetical instruction, and at the time of our baptism, we received from the bishops who were before us and as we have learnt from the Holy Scriptures, and, alike as presbyters, and as bishops, were wont to believe and teach; so we now believe and thus declare our faith. It is as follows:—

'We believe in one God, Father Almighty, the Maker of all things, visible and invisible; and in one Lord Jesus Christ, the Word of God, God of God, Light of Light, Life of Life, Only-begotten Son, First-born of every creature, begotten of the Father before all worlds; by Whom all things were made; Who for our salvation was incarnate, and lived among men. He suffered and rose again the third day, and ascended to the Father; and He will come again in glory to judge the quick and the dead. We also believe in one Holy Ghost.

'We believe in the being and continual existence of each of these; that the Father is in truth the Father; the Son in truth the Son; the Holy Ghost in truth the Holy Ghost; as our Lord, when sending out His disciples to preach the Gospel, said, 'Go forth and teach all nations, baptizing them into the name of the Father, and of the Son, and of the Holy Ghost.' We positively affirm that we hold this faith, that we have always held it, and that we adhere to it even unto death, condemning all ungodly heresy. We testify, as before God the Almighty and our Lord Jesus Christ, that we have thought thus from the heart, and from the soul, ever since we have known ourselves; and we have the means of showing, and, indeed, of convincing you that we have always during the past thus believed and preached.'

When this formulary had been set forth by us, there was no room to gainsay it; but our beloved emperor himself was the first to testify that it was most orthodox, and that he coincided in opinion with it; and he exhorted the others to sign it, and to receive all the doctrine it contained, with the single addition of the one word—'consubstantial.' He explained that this term implied no bodily condition or change, for that the Son did not derive His existence from the Father either by means of division or of abscission, since an immaterial, intellectual, and incorporeal nature could not be subject to any bodily condition or change. These things must be understood as bearing a divine and mysterious signification. Thus reasoned our wisest and most religious emperor. The addition of the word consubstantial has given occasion for the composition of the following formulary:—

[THE CREED PUBLISHED BY THE COUNCIL–325]

'We believe in one God, Father Almighty, Maker of all things visible and invisible. And in one Lord Jesus Christ, the Son of God, begotten of the Father; only-begotten, that is, of the substance of the Father, God of God, Light of Light, Very God of very God, begotten not made, being of one substance with the Father: by Whom all things were made both in heaven and on earth: Who for us men, and for our salvation, came down from heaven, and was incarnate, and was made man; He suffered, and rose again the third day; He ascended into heaven, and is coming to judge both quick and dead. And we believe in the Holy Ghost. The holy Catholic and Apostolic Church anathematizes all who say that there was a time when the Son of God was not; that before He was begotten He was not; that He was made out of the non-existent; or that He is of a different essence and of a different substance from the Father; and that He is susceptible of variation or change.'

When they had set forth this formulary, we did not leave without examination of that passage in which it is said that the Son is of the substance of the Father, and consubstantial with the Father. Questions and arguments thence arose, and the meaning of the terms was exactly tested. Accordingly they were led to confess that the word consubstantial signifies that the Son is of the Father, but not as being a part of the Father. We deemed it right to receive this opinion; for that is sound doctrine which teaches that the Son is of the Father, but not part of His substance. From the love of peace, and lest we should fall from the true belief, we also accept this view, neither do we reject the term 'consubstantial.' For the same reason we admitted the expression, 'begotten, but not made;' for they alleged that the word 'made' applies generally to all things which were created by the Son, to which the Son is in no respect similar; and that consequently He is not a created thing, like the things made by Him, but is of a substance superior to all created objects. The Holy Scriptures teach Him to be begotten of the Father, by a mode of generation which is incomprehensible and inexplicable to all created beings. So also the term 'of one substance with the Father,' when investigated, was accepted not in accordance with bodily relations or similarity to mortal beings. For it was also shown that it does not either imply division of substance, nor abscission, nor any modification or change or diminution in the power of the Father, all of which are alien from the nature of the unbegotten Father. It was concluded that the expression, 'being of one substance with the Father,' implies that the Son of God does not resemble, in any one respect, the creatures which He has made; but that to the Father alone, who begat Him, He is in all points perfectly like: for He is of the essence and of the substance of none save of the Father. This interpretation having been given of the doctrine, it appeared right to us to assent to it, especially as we were aware that of the ancients some learned and celebrated bishops and writers have used the term 'consubstantial' with respect to the divinity of the Father and of the Son.

These are the circumstances which I had to communicate respecting the published formulary of the faith. To it we all agreed, not without investigation, but, after having subjected the views submitted to us to thorough examination in the presence of our most beloved emperor, for the above reasons we all acquiesced in it. We also allowed that the anathema appended by them to their formulary of faith should be accepted, because it prohibits the use of words which are not scriptural; through which almost all the disorder and troubles of the Church have arisen. And since no passage of the inspired scripture uses the terms 'out of the non-existent,' or that 'there was a time when He was not,' nor indeed any of the other phrases of the same class, it did not appear reasonable to assert or to teach such things. In this opinion, therefore, we judged it right to agree; since, indeed, we had never, at any former period been accustomed to use such terms. . . .

We have thought it requisite, beloved brethren, to transmit you an account of these circumstances, in order to show you what examination and investigation we bestowed on all the questions which we had to decide; and also to prove how at one time we resisted firmly, even to the last hour, when doctrines improperly expressed offended us, and, at another time, we, without contention, accepted the articles which contained nothing objectable, when after a thorough and candid investigation of their signification, they appeared perfectly comformable with what had been confessed by us in the formulary of faith which we had published.

B. The Council's Letter to the Church at Alexandria[*]

To the church of Alexandria which, by the grace of God, is great and holy, and to the beloved brethren in Egypt, Libya, and Pentapolis, the

* From Theodoret, *Ecclesiastical History*, tr. by Bloomfield Jackson, A Select Library of Nicene and Post-Nicene Fathers, Vol. III, Second series. Grand Rapids, Mich.: Wm. B. Eerdmans Publishing Co., 1952.

bishops who have been convened to the great and holy Council of Nicaea, send greeting in the Lord.

The great and holy Council of Nicaea having been convened by the grace of God, and by the most religious emperor, Constantine, who summoned us from different provinces and cities, we judge it requisite that a letter be sent from the whole Holy Synod to inform you also what questions have been mooted and debated, and what has been decreed and established.

In the first place, the impious doctrines of Arius were investigated before our most religious emperor Constantine; and his impiety was unanimously anathematized, as well as the blasphemous language and views which he had propounded, alleging that the Son of God was out of what was not, that before He was begotten He was not, that there was a period in which He was not, and that He can, according to His own freewill, be capable either of virtue or of vice. The holy council anathematized all these assertions, and even refused so much as to listen to such impious and foolish opinions, and such blasphemous expressions. The final decision concerning him you already know, or will soon hear; but we will not mention it now, lest we should appear to trample upon a man who has already received the recompense due to his sins. Such influence has his impiety obtained as to involve Theonas, Bishop of Marmarica, and Secundus, Bishop of Ptolemais, in his ruin, and they have shared his punishment. . . .

Rejoice, then, in the success of our undertakings, and in the general peace and concord, and in the extirpation of every heresy, and receive with still greater honour and more fervent love, Alexander, our fellow-minister and your bishop, who imparted joy to us by his presence, and who, at a very advanced age, has undergone so much fatigue for the purpose of restoring peace among you. Pray for us all, that what has been rightly decreed may remain steadfast, through our Lord Jesus Christ, being done, as we trust, according to the good pleasure of God and the Father in the Holy Ghost, to whom be glory for ever and ever. Amen.

21

A COMPARISON of this letter with Constantine's earlier letter to the church of Alexandria (See Selection 18) shows a decidedly more energetic defence of the anti-Arians.

A Letter to the Church of Alexandria*

CONSTANTINE

Constantine Augustus, to the Catholic church of the Alexandrians. Beloved brethren, hail! We have received from Divine Providence the inestimable blessing of being relieved from all error, and united in the acknowledgment of one and the same faith. The devil will no longer have any power against us, since all that which he had malignantly devised for our destruction has been entirely overthrown from the foundations. The splendor of truth has dissipated at the command of God those dissensions, schisms, tumults, and so to speak, deadly poisons of discord. Wherefore we all worship one true God, and believe that he is. But in order that this might be done, by divine admonition I assembled at the city of Nicaea most of the bishops; with whom I myself also, who am but one of you, and who rejoice exceedingly in being your fellow-servant, undertook the investigation of the truth. Accordingly, all points which seemed in consequence of ambiguity to furnish any pretext for dissension, have been discussed and accurately examined. And may the Divine Majesty pardon the fearful enormity of the blasphemies which some were shamelessly uttering concerning the mighty Saviour, our life and hope; declaring and confessing that they believe things contrary to the divinely inspired scriptures. While more than three hundred bishops remarkable for their moderation and intellectual keenness, were unanimous in their confirmation of one and the same faith, which according to the truth and legitimate construction of the law of God can only be the faith; Arius alone beguiled by the subtlety of the devil, was discovered to be the sole disseminator of this mischief, first among you, and afterwards with unhallowed purposes among others also. Let us therefore embrace that doctrine which the Almighty has presented to us: let us return to our beloved brethren from whom an irreverent servant of the devil has separated us: let us go with all speed to the common body and our own natural members. For this is becoming your penetration, faith and sanctity; that since the error has been proved to be due to him who is an enemy to the truth, ye should return to the divine favor. For that which has commended itself to the judgment of three hundred bishops cannot be other than the doctrine of God; seeing that the Holy Spirit dwelling in the minds of so many dignified persons has effectually enlightened them respecting the Divine will. Wherefore let no one vacillate or linger, but let

* From Socrates, *Ecclesiastical History*, tr. by A. C. Zenos, A Select Library of Nicene and Post-Nicene Fathers, Vol. II, Second series. Grand Rapids, Mich.: Wm. B. Eerdmans Publishing Co., 1952.

all with alacrity return to the undoubted path of duty; that when I shall arrive among you, which will be as soon as possible, I may with you return due thanks to God, the inspector of all things, for having revealed the pure faith, and restored to you that love for which ye have prayed. May God protect you, beloved brethren.

22

THE ARIANS did not remain in banishment long; by 335 Arius was restored to a position of authority. A decade after the Council of Nicaea, the theological and political winds had changed and some of the defenders of the Nicene decision were in exile, Athanasius by 336. The Arians, supported by those who had only reluctantly accepted the Nicene decision, sought to reformulate the creed. The term, *homoousion*, remained a bone of contention, many fearing that it led to Sabellianism. At the dedication of the new church in Antioch, some ninety bishops wrote *The Dedicatory Creed*, a more ambiguous and lengthy statement of the relation of Father and Son than the Nicene Creed and one that allowed for an Arian interpretation. Because it lacked the precision of the Nicene declaration, many who halfheartedly supported the decision of 325 welcomed the new statement.

The Dedicatory Creed, Antioch (341)*

We believe, comformably to the evangelical and apostolical tradition, in One God, the Father Almighty, the Framer, and Maker, and Provider of the Universe, from whom are all things.

And in One Lord Jesus Christ, His Son, Only-begotten God by whom are all things, who was begotten before all ages from the Father, God from

* From Athanasius, *De Synodis*, tr. by Archibald Robertson, A Select Library of Nicene and Post-Nicene Fathers, Vol. IV, Second series. Grand Rapids, Mich.: Wm. B. Eerdmans Publishing Co., 1957.

God, whole from whole, sole from sole, perfect from perfect, King from King, Lord from Lord, Living Word, Living Wisdom, true Light, Way, Truth, Resurrection, Shepherd, Door, both unalterable and unchangeable; exact Image of the Godhead, Essence, Will, Power and Glory of the Father; the first born of every creature, who was in the beginning with God, God the Word, as it is written in the Gospel, 'and the Word was God'; by whom all things were made, and in whom all things consist; who in the last days descended from above, and was born of a Virgin according to the scriptures, and was made Man, Mediator between God and man, and Apostle of our faith, and Prince of Life, as He says, 'I came down from heaven, not to do Mine own will, but the will of Him that sent Me'; who suffered for us and rose again on the third day, and ascended into heaven, and sat down on the right hand of the Father, and is coming again with glory and power, to judge quick and dead.

And in the Holy Ghost, who is given to those who believe for comfort, and sanctification, and initiation, as also our Lord Jesus Christ enjoined His disciples, saying, "Go ye, teach all nations, baptizing them in the Name of the Father, and the Son, and the Holy Ghost'; namely of a Father who is truly Father, and a Son who is truly Son, and of the Holy Ghost who is truly Holy Ghost, the names not being without meaning or effect, but denoting accurately the peculiar subsistence, rank, and glory of each that is named, so that they are three in subsistence, and in agreement one.

Holding then this faith, and holding it in the presence of God and Christ, from beginning to end, we anathematize every heretical heterodoxy. And if any teaches, beside the sound and right faith of the scriptures, that time, or season, or age, either is or has been before the generation of the Son, be he anathema. Or if any one says, that the Son is a creature as one of the creatures, or an offspring as one of the offsprings, or a work as one of the works, and not the aforesaid articles one after another, as the divine scriptures have delivered, or if he teaches or preaches beside what we received, be he anathema. For all that has been delivered in the divine scriptures, whether by Prophets or Apostles, do we truly and reverentially both believe and follow.

23 BY THE MID-FOURTH CENTURY, the Arians were becoming bolder. When in 350, Constantius, an Arian, became sole emperor, the extreme form of the movement developed. At the Council of Sirmium (357) and under the leadership of

the adamant Arians, Ursacius and Valens, a creed was formulated that stated their position in uncompromising terms.
This creed served to unite the anti-Arians and marked the
beginning of the demise of Arianism as a commanding
movement in the church.

Council of Sirmium, 357[*]

Since it appeared good that some deliberation respecting the faith
should be undertaken, all points have been carefully investigated and discussed at Sirmium, in presence of Valens, Ursacius, Germinius, and others.

It is evident that there is one God, the Father Almighty, according
as it is declared over the whole world; and his only-begotten Son Jesus
Christ, our Lord, God, and Saviour, begotten of him before the ages. But
we ought not to say that there are two Gods, since the Lord himself has said
'I go unto my Father and your Father, and unto my God and your God.'
(John xx, 17). Therefore he is God even of all, as the apostle also taught,
'Is he the God of the Jews only? Is he not also of the Gentiles? Yea of the
Gentiles also; seeing that it is one God who shall justify the circumcision by
faith.' (Romans iii, 29–30). And in all other matters there is agreement,
nor is there any ambiguity. But since it troubles very many to understand
about that which is termed *substantia* in Latin, and *ousia* in Greek; that
is to say, in order to mark the sense more accurately, the word *homoousion*
(of the same substance) or *homoiousion* (of like substance), it is altogether
desirable that none of these terms should be mentioned: nor should they be
preached on in the church, for this reason, that nothing is recorded concerning them in the Holy Scriptures; and because these things are above the
knowledge of mankind and human capacity, and that no one can explain
the Son's generation, of which it is written, "And who shall declare his
generation?" (Isaiah liii, 5). It is manifest that the Father only knows in
what way he begat the Son; and again the Son, how he was begotten by the
Father. But no one can doubt that the Father is greater in honor, dignity,
and divinity, and in the very name of Father; the Son himself testifying "My
Father who hath sent me is greater than I." (John xiv, 28). And no one is

* From Socrates, *Ecclesiastical History*, tr. by A. C. Zenos, A Select Library of
Nicene and Post-Nicene Fathers, Vol. II, Second series. Grand Rapids, Mich.: Wm. B.
Eerdmans Publishing Co., 1952. [This creed was frequently referred to as the "Blas-
phemy of Sirmium."]

ignorant that this is also catholic doctrine, that there are two persons of the Father and Son, and that the Father is the greater: but that the Son is subject, together with all things which the Father has subjected to him. That the Father had no beginning, and is invisible, immortal, and impassible: but that the Son was begotten of the Father, God of God, Light of Light; and that no one comprehends his generation, as was before said, but the Father alone. That the Son himself, our Lord and God, took flesh or a body, that is to say human nature, according as the angel brought glad tidings: and as the whole scripture teaches, and especially the apostle who was the great teacher of the Gentiles, Christ assumed the human nature through which he suffered, from the Virgin Mary. But the summary and confirmation of the entire faith is, that (the doctrine of) the Trinity should be always maintained, according as we have read in the gospel, "Go ye and disciple all nations, baptizing them in the name of the Father, and of the Son, and of the Holy Spirit." (Matthew xxviii, 19). Thus the number of the Trinity is complete and perfect. Now the Comforter, the Holy Spirit, sent by the Son, came according to his promise, in order to sanctify and instruct the apostles and all believers.

24 THE EXTREME ARIAN STATEMENT formulated at the Council of Sirmium (357) led to the formation of a new statement at another meeting at Sirmium in 359, called by the emperor, Constantius. At this council, the moderate defenders of Nicaea, those who were troubled by the term, *homoousion* (of the same substance), yet opposed to the Arian position, were in control. The creed formulated at this meeting has traditionally been called, "The Dated Creed," because its opening sentence reads: "The catholic faith was expounded . . . on the twenty-third of May." The group that led the council has been given the label, *Homoiousion,* from their insistence that the relation of the Son and the Father should be described as "like the Father essentially." When Constantius died two years later, in 361, and Athanasius returned from exile, the task of the opponents of Arianism was to unite the two groups that affirmed *homoousion* (of the same substance) and *homoiousion* (of like substance).

The Council of Sirmium, 359: The Dated Creed[*]

The catholic faith was expounded at Sirmium in presence of our lord Constantius, in the consulate of the most illustrious Flavius Eusebius, and Hypatius, on the twenty-third of May.

We believe in one only and true God, the Father Almighty, the Creator and Framer of all things: and in one only-begotten Son of God, before all ages, before all beginning, before all conceivable time, and before all comprehensible thought, begotten without passion: by whom the ages were framed, and all things made: who was begotten as the only-begotten of the Father, only of only, God of God, like to the Father who begat him, according to the scriptures: whose generation no one knows, but the Father who begat him. We know that this his only-begotten Son came down from the heavens by his Father's consent for the putting away of sin, was born of the Virgin Mary, conversed with his disciples, and fulfilled every dispensation according to the Father's will: as crucified and died, and descended into the lower parts of the earth, and disposed matters there; at the sight of whom the (door keepers of Hades trembled): having arisen on the third day, he again conversed with his disciples, and after forty days were completed he ascended into the heavens, and is seated at the Father's right hand; and at the last day he will come in his Father's glory to render to every one according to his works. (We believe) also in the Holy Spirit, whom the only-begotten Son of God Jesus Christ himself promised to send to the human race as the Comforter, according to that which is written: "I go away to my Father, and will ask him, and he will send you another Comforter, the Spirit of truth. He shall receive of mine, and shall teach you, and bring all things to your remembrance. As for the term, "substance," which was used by our fathers for the sake of greater simplicity, but not being understood by the people has caused offense on account of the fact that the scriptures do not contain it, it seemed desirable that it should be wholly abolished, and that in future no mention should be made of substance in reference to God, since the divine scriptures have nowhere spoken concerning the substance of the Father and the Son. But we say that the Son is in all things like the Father, as the Holy Scriptures affirm and teach.

* From Socrates, *Ecclesiastical History*, tr. by A. C. Zenos, A Select Library of Nicene and Post-Nicene Fathers, Vol. II, Second series. Grand Rapids, Mich.: Wm. B. Eerdmans Publishing Co., 1952.

25

ATHANASIUS WAS one of the major figures in the first centuries of Christianity. He was born at the end of the third century, probably in 298, and attended the famous catechetic school in Alexandria. Though he was present at the Council of Nicaea only as a nonvoting member, his concern with the Arian heresy was already uppermost in his mind; in 328 he succeeded Alexander as Bishop of Alexandria and remained in that position until his death in 373.

During his forty-five years as Bishop of Alexandria he was a central figure in the disputes arising from the Council of Nicaea (325). Though he is frequently remembered for his work, *On the Incarnation of God*, written early in his life, no one was more prominent as a defender of the Nicene decision or more involved in welding together a common front against resurgent Arianism. It was this later role that Athanasius played so well. After the Council of Sirmium (357) the Arians became increasingly bold and sought to overthrow the Nicene Creed with a new statement allowing for such latitude that their position would not be classified as heresy. Open support came from sympathizers with the Arian cause throughout the empire; hidden support came from the division within the ranks of the Nicene defenders. There were those who were reluctant to accept the term, *homoousion* (of the same substance), because of their fear of Sabellianism. Thus the orthodox ranks were divided. Athanasius sought to unite the *Homoousions* and the *Homoiousions*, the latter led by such men as the Cappadocian fathers: Basil of Ancyra, Gregory of Nyssa, and Gregory of Nazianzen. The following selections include excerpts from Athanasius, *Against the Arians, Statement of Faith*, and *De Synodis*, the latter dealing with his treatment of the *homoiousion* position developed at the Council of Sirmium, in 359.[1]

[1] See also Council of Sirmium (359), Selection 24.

A. Against the Arians[*]

ATHANASIUS

. . . if the Son were a creature, man had remained mortal as before, not being joined to God; for a creature had not joined creatures to God, as seeking itself one to join it; nor would a portion of the creation have been the creation's salvation, as needing salvation itself. To provide against this also, He sends His own Son, and He becomes Son of Man, by taking created flesh; that, since all were under sentence of death, He, being other than them all, might Himself for all offer to death His own body; and that henceforth, as if all had died through Him, the word of that sentence might be accomplished (for 'all died' in Christ), and all through Him might thereupon become free from sin and from the curse which came upon it, and might truly abide for ever, risen from the dead and clothed in immortality and incorruption. For, the Word being clothed in the flesh, as has many times been explained, every bite of the serpent began to be utterly staunched from out it; and whatever evil sprung from the motions of the flesh, to be cut away, and with these death also was abolished, the companion of sin, as the Lord Himself says, 'The prince of this world cometh, and findeth nothing in Me;' and 'For this end was He manifested,' as John has written, 'that He might destroy the works of the devil.' And these being destroyed from the flesh, we all were thus liberated by the kinship of the flesh, and for the future were joined, even we, to the Word. And being joined to God, no longer do we abide upon earth; but, as He Himself has said, where He is, there shall we be also; and henceforward we shall fear no longer the serpent, for he was brought to nought when he was assailed by the Saviour in the flesh, and heard Him say, 'Get thee behind Me, Satan,' and thus he is cast out of paradise into the eternal fire. Nor shall we have to watch against woman beguiling us, for 'in the resurrection they neither marry nor are given in marriage, but are as the Angels;' and in Christ Jesus it shall be 'a new creation,' and 'neither male nor female, but all and in all Christ;' and where Christ is, what fear, what danger can still happen?

But this would not have come to pass, had the Word been a creature; for with a creature, the devil, himself a creature, would have ever continued the battle, and man, being between the two, had been ever in peril of death, having none in whom and through whom he might be joined to God and delivered from all fear. Whence the truth shews us that the Word is not of

[*] From Athanasius, *Four Discourses Against the Arians*, tr. by Archibald Robertson, A Select Library of Nicene and Post-Nicene Fathers, Vol. IV, Second series. Grand Rapids, Mich.: Wm. B. Eerdmans Publishing Co., 1957.

things originate, but rather Himself their Framer. For therefore did He assume the body originate and human, that having renewed it as its Framer, He might deify it in Himself, and thus might introduce us all into the kingdom of heaven after His likeness. For man had not been deified if joined to a creature, or unless the Son were very God; nor had man been brought into the Father's presence, unless He had been His natural and true Word who had put on the body. And as we had not been delivered from sin and the curse, unless it had been by nature human flesh, which the Word put on (for we should have had nothing common with what was foreign), so also the man had not been deified, unless the Word who became flesh had been by nature from the Father and true and proper to Him. For therefore the union was of this kind, that He might unite what is man by nature to Him who is in the nature of the Godhead, and his salvation and deification might be sure. Therefore let those who deny that the Son is from the Father by nature and proper to His Essence, deny also that He took true human flesh of Mary Ever-Virgin; for in neither case had it been of profit to us men, whether the Word were not true and naturally Son of God, or the flesh not true which He assumed. But surely He took true flesh, though Valentinus rave; yea the Word was by nature Very God, through Ariomaniacs rave; and in that flesh has come to pass the beginning of our new creation, He being created man for our sake, and having made for us that new way, as has been said.

B. On Homoiousions*

ATHANASIUS

Those who deny the Council [Nicaea] altogether, are sufficiently exposed by these brief remarks; those, however, who accept everything else that was defined at Nicaea, and doubt only about the Coessential, must not be treated as enemies; nor do we here attack them as Ariomaniacs, nor as opponents of the Fathers, but we discuss the matter with them as brothers with brothers, who mean what we mean, and dispute only about the word. For, confessing that the Son is from the essence of the Father, and not from other subsistence, and that He is not a creature nor work, but His genuine and natural offspring, and that He is eternally with the Father as being His

* From Athanasius, *De Synodis*, tr. by Archibald Robertson, A Select Library of Nicene and Post-Nicene Fathers, Vol. IV, Second series. Grand Rapids, Mich.: Wm. B. Eerdmans Publishing Co., 1957.

Word and wisdom, they are not far from accepting even the phrase, 'Co-essential.' Now such is Basil, who wrote from Ancyra concerning the faith. For only to say 'like according to essence,' is very far from signifying 'of the essence,' by which, rather, as they say themselves, the genuineness of the Son to the Father is signified. Thus tin is only like to silver, a wolf to a dog, and gilt brass to the true metal; but tin is not from silver, nor could a wolf be accounted the offspring of a dog. But since they say that He is 'of the essence' and 'Like-in-essence,' what do they signify by these but 'Coessential?' For, while to say only 'Like-in-essence,' does not necessarily convey 'of the essence,' on the contrary, to say 'Coessential,' is to signify the meaning of both terms, 'Like-in-essence,' and 'of the essence.' And accordingly they themselves in controversy with those who say that the Word is a creature, instead of allowing Him to be genuine Son, have taken their proofs against them from human illustrations of son and father, with this exception that God is not as man, nor the generation of the Son as issue of man, but such as may be ascribed to God, and is fit for us to think. Thus they have called the Father of the Fount of Wisdom and Life, and the Son the Radiance of the Eternal Light, and the Offspring from the Fountain, as He says, 'I am the Life,' and 'I Wisdom dwell with Prudence.' But the Radiance from the Light, and Offspring from Fountain, and Son from Father, how can these be so fitly expressed as by 'Coessential?' And is there any cause of fear, lest, because the offspring from men are coessential, the Son, by being called Coessential, be Himself considered as a human offspring too? perish the thought! not so; but the explanation is easy. For the Son is the Father's Word and Wisdom, whence we learn the impassibility and indivisibility of such a generation from the Father. For not even man's word is part of him, nor proceeds from him according to passion; much less God's Word; whom the Father has declared to be His own Son, lest, on the other hand, if we merely heard of 'Word,' we should suppose Him, such as is the word of man, impersonal; but that, hearing that He is Son, we may acknowledge Him to be living Word, and substantive Wisdom.

Accordingly, as in saying 'offspring,' we have no human thoughts, and, though we know God to be a Father, we entertain no material ideas concerning Him, but while we listen to these illustrations and terms, we think suitably of God, for He is not as man, so in like manner, when we hear of 'coessential,' we ought to transcend all sense, and, according to the Proverb, 'understand by the understanding what is set before us'; so as to know, that not by will, but in truth, is He genuine from the Father, as Life from Fountain, and Radiance from Light, Else why should we understand 'offspring' and 'son,' in no corporeal way, while we conceive of 'coessential' as after the manner of bodies? especially since these terms are not here used about different subjects, but of whom 'offspring' is predicated, of Him is 'coessential' also. And it is but consistent to attach the same sense to both expressions as applied to the Saviour, and not to interpret 'offspring' in a good sense, and 'coessential' otherwise; since to be consistent, ye who are thus minded and who say that the Son is Word and Wisdom of the Father, should entertain a different view of these terms also, and understand Word in another sense, and Wisdom in yet another. But, as this would be absurd (for the Son is the Father's Word and Wisdom, and the Offspring from the Father is one and proper to His essence), so the sense of 'Offspring' and 'Coessential' is one, and whoso considers the Son an offspring, rightly considers Him also as 'coessential.'

This is sufficient to show that the meaning of the beloved ones is not foreign nor far from the 'Coessential.'

C. Statement of Faith[*]

ATHANASIUS

1. We believe in one Unbegotten God, Father Almighty, maker of all things both visible and invisible, that hath His being from Himself. And in one Only-begotten Word, Wisdom, Son, begotten of the Father without beginning and eternally; word not pronounced nor mental, nor an effluence of the Perfect, not a dividing of the impassible Essence, nor an issue; but absolutely perfect Son, living and powerful, the true Image of the Father, equal in honour and glory. For this, he says, 'is the will of the Father, that as they honour the Father, so they may honour the Son also': very God of very God, as John says in his general Epistles, 'And we are in Him that is true, even in His Son Jesus Christ: this is the true God and everlasting life': Almighty of Almighty. For all things which the Father rules and sways, the Son rules and sways likewise: wholly from the Whole, being like the Father as the Lord says, 'he that hath seen Me hath seen the Father'. But he was begotten ineffably and incomprehensibly, for 'who shall declare his generation?' in other words, no one can. Who, when at the consummation of the ages, He had descended from the bosom of the Father, took from the undefiled Virgin Mary our humanity, Christ Jesus, whom He delivered of His own will to suffer for us, as the Lord saith: 'No man taketh My life from Me. I have power to lay it down, and have power to take it again'. In which humanity He was crucified and died for us, and rose from the dead, and

* From Athanasius, Statement of Faith, tr. by Archibald Robertson, A Select Library of Nicene and Post-Nicene Fathers, Vol. IV, Second series. Grand Rapids, Mich.: Wm. B. Eerdmans Publishing Co., 1957.

was taken up into the heavens, having been created as the beginning of ways for us, when on earth He shewed us light from out of darkness, salvation from error, life from the dead, an entrance to paradise, from which Adam was cast out, and into which he again entered. . . . (He shewed us) also a way up to the heavens, whither the humanity of the Lord, in which He will judge the quick and the dead, entered as precursor for us. We believe, likewise, also in the Holy Spirit that searcheth all things, even the deep things of God, and we anathematise doctrines contrary to this.

2. For neither do we hold a Son-Father, as do the Sabellians, calling Him of one but not of the same essence, and thus destroying the existence of the Son. Neither do we ascribe the passible body which He bore for the salvation of the whole world to Father. Neither can we imagine three Subsistences separated from each other, as results from their bodily nature in the case of men, lest we hold a plurality of gods like the heathen. But just as a river, produced from a well, is not separate, and yet there are in fact two visible objects and two names. For neither is the Father the Son, nor the Son the Father. For the Father is Father of the Son, and the Son, Son of the Father. For like as the well is not a river, nor the river a well, but both are one and the same water which is conveyed in a channel from the well to the river, so the Father's deity passes into the Son without flow and without division. For the Lord says, 'I came out from the Father and am come'. But He is ever with the Father, for He is in the bosom of the Father, nor was ever the bosom of the Father void of the deity of the Son. For He says, 'I was by Him as one setting in order'. But we do not regard God the Creator of all, the Son of God, as a creature, or thing made, or as made out of nothing, for He is truly existent from Him who exists, alone existing from Him who alone exists, in as much as the like glory and power was eternally and conjointly begotten of the Father. For 'He that hath seen' the Son 'hath seen the Father. All things to wit were made through the Son; but He Himself is not a creature, as Paul says of the Lord: 'In Him were all things created, and He is before all'. Now He says not, 'was created' before all things, but 'is' before all things. To be created, namely, is applicable to all things, but 'is before all' applies to the Son only.

3. He is then by nature an Offspring, perfect from the Perfect, begotten before all the hills, that is before every rational and intelligent essence, as Paul also in another place calls Him 'first-born of all creation'. But by calling Him First-born, He shews that He is not a Creature, but Offspring of the Father. For it would be inconsistent with His deity for Him to be called a creature. For all things were created by the Father through the Son, but the Son alone was eternally begotten from the Father, whence God the Word is 'first-born of all creation,' unchangeable from unchangeable. However, the body which He wore for our sakes is a creature; concerning which Jeremiah says, according to the edition of the seventy translators: 'The Lord created for us for a planting a new salvation, in which salvation men shall go about:'

but according to Aquila the same text runs: 'The Lord created a new thing in woman.' Now the salvation created for us for a planting, which is new, not old, and for us, not before us, is Jesus, Who in respect of the Saviour was made man, and whose name is translated in one place Salvation, in another Saviour. But salvation proceeds from the Saviour, just as illumination does from the light. The salvation, then, which was from the Saviour, being created new, did, as Jeremiah says, 'create for us a new salvation,' and as Aquila renders: 'The Lord created a new thing in woman,' that is in Mary. For nothing new was created in woman, save the Lord's body, born of the Virgin Mary without intercourse, as also it says in the Proverbs in the person of Jesus: 'The Lord created me, a beginning of His ways for His works'. Now he does not say, 'created me before His works,' lest any should take the text of the deity of the Word.

4. Each text then which refers to the creature is written with reference to Jesus in a bodily sense. For the Lord's Humanity was created as 'a beginning of ways,' and He manifested it to us for our salvation. For by it we have our access to the Father. For He is the way which leads us back to the Father. And a way is a corporeal visible thing, such as is the Lord's humanity. Well, then, the Word of God created all things, not being a creature, but an offspring. For He created none of the created things equal or like unto Himself. But it is the part of a Father to beget, while it is a workman's part to create. Accordingly, that body is a thing made and created, which the Lord bore for us, which was begotten for us, as Paul says, 'wisdom from God, and sanctification and righteousness, and redemption;' while yet the Word was before us and before all Creation, and is, the Wisdom of the Father. But the Holy Spirit, being that which proceeds from the Father, is ever in the hands of the Father Who sends and of the Son Who conveys Him, by Whose means he filled all things. The Father, possessing His existence from Himself, begat the Son, as we said, and did not create Him, as a river from a well and as a branch from a root, and as brightness from a light, things which nature knows to be indivisible; through whom to the Father be glory and power and greatness before all ages, and unto all the ages of the ages. Amen.

26 THOUGH THE NICENE-CONSTANTINOPOLITAN CREED is referred to by some christian Churches as the Nicene Creed, it is probably based on a statement of faith of the Jerusalem Church and was formulated after the Council of Nicaea. One important difference from the Nicene Creed is that statement which sought to make clear that the Holy Spirit is not subordinate to the Father and the Son; some within the church, for example, the Macedonians, denied that the Holy Spirit was *homoousion* (of the same substance) with the Father.

Nicene-Constantinopolitan Creed[*]

We believe in one God, the Father Almighty, maker of heaven and earth and of all things visible and invisible. And in one Lord Jesus Christ, the only begotten Son of God, begotten of his Father before all worlds, Light of Light, very God of very God, begotten not made, being of one substance with the Father, by whom all things were made. Who for us men and for our salvation came down from heaven and was incarnate by the Holy Ghost and the Virgin Mary, and was made man, and was crucified also for us under Pontius Pilate. He suffered and was buried, and the third day he rose again according to the scriptures, and ascended into heaven, and sitteth at the Right Hand of the Father. And he shall come again with glory to judge both the quick and the dead. Whose kingdom shall have no end.

And (we believe) in the Holy Ghost, the Lord and Giver-of-Life, who proceedeth from the Father, who with the Father and the Son together is worshipped and glorified, who spake by the prophets. And (we believe) in one, holy, Catholic and Apostolic Church. We acknowledge one baptism for the remission of sins, (and) we look for the resurrection of the dead and the life of the world to come. Amen.

27   FOLLOWING THE REAFFIRMATION of the Nicene decision at the Council of Constantinople (381) the attention of the church leaders turned to a related problem: the relation of human and divine natures in the person of Christ.

    Apollinarius, Bishop of Laodicea and long a defender of

* From *The Seven Ecumenical Councils*, Henry Percival, ed., A Select Library of Nicene and Post-Nicene Fathers, Vol. XIV, Second series. Grand Rapids, Mich.: Wm. B. Eerdmans Publishing Co., 1956.

the Nicene Creed, sought to define this relation, though he did so in terms that were later regarded as heretical. Apollinarius was troubled by the idea of two full natures in Christ, especially if the human will could choose in opposition to the divine will. Apollinarius argued that since the distinctive characteristic of personality was the rational soul, the center of self-determination, Christ must have possessed only a divine, not a human soul. In the Logos of God there is a full divine nature united with a human body and animal soul (but not a rational soul), the divine rational soul becoming the controlling power of the human nature. Thus there was a union of human and divine natures in Christ, but a union that did not include complete human nature.

The following excerpt from a letter of Gregory of Nazianzen to a fellow cleric, Cledonius, offers a contemporary, critical description of the Apollinarian position. Gregory's analysis of Apollinarius centered on the soteriological problem: that which is most in need of redemption by Christ is man's rational soul, yet it is this which is missing in the union of human and divine nature in Christ, according to Apollinarius.

A Letter to Cledonius*

[On Apollinarianism]

GREGORY OF NAZIANZEN

I desire to learn what is this fashion of innovation in things concerning the Church, which allows anyone who likes, or the passerby, as the Bible says, to tear asunder the flock that has been well led, and to plunder it by larcenous attacks, or rather by piratical and fallacious teachings. . . . they also assert, as I am told, that they have been received by the Western Synod, by which they were formerly condemned, as is well known to everyone. If, however, these who hold the views of Apollinarius have either now or formerly been received, let them prove it and we will be content. For it is evident that they can only have been so received as assenting to the Ortho-

* From Gregory Nazianzen, *Selected Letters*, tr. by C. G. Browne, A Select Library of Nicene and Post-Nicene Fathers, Vol. VII, Second series. Grand Rapids, Mich.: Wm. B. Eerdmans Publishing Co., 1955.

dox Faith, for this were an impossibility on any other terms. . . . Do not let the men deceive themselves and others with the assertion that the "Man of the Lord," as they call Him, Who is rather our Lord and God, is without human mind. For we do not sever the Man from the Godhead, but we lay down as a dogma the Unity and Identity of Person, Who of old was not Man but God, and the Only Son before all ages, unmingled with body or anything corporeal; but Who in these last days has assumed Manhood also for our salvation; passible in His Flesh, impassible in His Godhead; circumspect in the body, uncircumscript in the Spirit; at once earthly and heavenly, tangible and intangible, comprehensible and incomprehensible; that by One and the Same Person, Who was perfect Man and also God, the entire humanity fallen through sin might be created anew.

If anyone does not believe that Holy Mary is the Mother of God, he is severed from the Godhead. If anyone should assert that He passed through the Virgin as through a channel, and was not at once divinely and humanly formed in her (divinely, because without the intervention of a man; humanly, because in accordance with the laws of gestation), he is in like manner godless. If any assert that the Manhood was formed and afterward was clothed with the Godhead, he too is to be condemned. For this were not a Generation of God, but a shirking of generation. If any introduce the notion of Two Sons, one of God the Father, the other of the Mother, and discredits the Unity and Identity, may he lose his part in the adoption promised to those who believe aright. For God and Man are two natures, as also soul and body are; but there are not two Sons or two Gods. For neither in this life are there two manhoods; though Paul speaks in some such language of the inner and outer man. And (if I am to speak concisely) the Saviour is made of elements which are distinct from one another (for the invisible is not the same with the visible, nor the timeless with that which is subject to time), yet He is not two Persons. God forbid! For both natures are one by the combination, the Deity being made Man, and the Manhood deified or however one should express it. And I say different Elements, because it is the reverse of what is the case in the Trinity; for There we acknowledge different Persons, so as not to confound the persons; but not different Elements, for the Three are One and the same in Godhead. . . .

If anyone has put his trust in Him as a Man without a human mind, he is really bereft of mind, and quite unworthy of salvation. For that which He has not assumed He has not healed; but that which is united to His Godhead is also saved. If only half Adam fell, then that which Christ assumes and saves may be half also; but if the whole of his nature fell, it must be united to the whole nature of Him that was begotten, and so be saved as a whole. Let them not, then, begrudge us our complete salvation, or clothe the Saviour only with bones and nerves and the portraiture of humanity. For if His Manhood is without soul, even the Arians admit this, that they may attribute His Passion to the Godhead, as that which gives motion to the body is also that which suffers. But if He has a soul, and yet is without a mind, how is He man, for man is not a mindless animal? And this would necessarily involve that while His form and tabernacle was human, His soul should be that of a horse or an ox, or some other of the brute creation. This, then, would be what He saves; and I have been deceived by the Truth, and let to boast of an honour which had been bestowed upon another. But if His Manhood is intellectual and not without mind, let them cease to be thus really mindless. But, says such an one, the Godhead took the place of the human intellect. How does this touch me? For Godhead joined to flesh alone is not man, nor to soul alone, nor to both apart from intellect, which is the most essential part of man. Keep then the whole man, and mingle Godhead therewith, that you may benefit me in my completeness. But, he asserts, He could not contain Two perfect Natures. Not if you only look at Him in a bodily fashion. For a bushel measure will not hold two bushels, nor will the space of one body hold two or more bodies. But if you will look at what is mental and incorporeal, remember that I in my own personality can contain soul and reason and mind and the Holy Spirit; and before me this world, by which I mean the system of things visible and invisible, contained Father, Son, and Holy Ghost. For such is the nature of intellectual Existences, that they can mingle with one another and with bodies, incorporeally and invisibly. . . .

Further let us see what is their account of the assumption of Manhood, or the assumption of Flesh, as they call it. If it was in order that God, otherwise incomprehensible, might be comprehended, and might converse with men through His Flesh as through a veil, their mask and the drama which they represent is a pretty one, not to say that it was open to Him to converse with us in other ways, as of old, in the burning bush and in the appearance of a man. But if it was that He might destroy the condemnation by sanctifying like by like, then as He needed flesh for the sake of the flesh which had incurred condemnation, and soul for the sake of our soul, so, too, He needed mind for the sake of mind, which not only fell in Adam, but was the first to be affected, as the doctors say of illnesses. For that which received the command was that which failed to keep the command, and that which failed to keep it was that also which dared to transgress; and that which transgressed was that which stood most in need of salvation; and that which needed salvation was that which also He took upon Him. Therefore, Mind was taken upon Him. This has now been demonstrated, whether they like it or no, by, to use their own expression, geometrical and necessary proofs. But you are acting as if, when a man's eye had been injured and his foot had been injured in consequence, you were to attend to the foot and leave the eye uncared for; or as if, when a painter had drawn something badly, you were to alter the picture, but to pass over the artist as if he had succeeded. But if they, overwhelmed by these arguments, take refuge in the proposition that it is possible for God to save man even apart from mind, why, I suppose that it would be possible for Him to do so also apart from flesh by a mere act of will, just as He works all other things, and has wrought them without body. Take away, then, the flesh as well as the mind, that your monstrous folly may be complete. But they are deceived by the latter, and, therefore, they run to the flesh, because they do not know the custom of scripture. We will teach them this also. For what need is there even to mention to those who know it, the fact that everywhere in scripture he is called Man, and the Son of man? . . .

Moreover, in no other way was it possible for the Love of God toward us to be manifested than by making mention of our flesh, and that for our sake He descended even to our lower part. For that flesh is less precious than soul, everyone who has a spark of sense will acknowledge. And so the passage, The Word was made Flesh, seems to me to be equivalent to that in which it is said that He was made sin, or a curse for us; not that the Lord was transformed into either of these, how could He be? But because by taking them upon Him He took away our sins and bore our iniquities. This, then, is sufficient to say at the present time for the sake of clearness and of being understood by the many. And I write it, not with any desire to compose a treatise, but only to check the progress of deceit; and if it is thought well, I will give a fuller account of these matters at greater length.

28 CYRIL (d.442), BISHOP OF ALEXANDRIA, and Nestorius (d.451), Patriarch of Constantinople, became the central figures in the controversy over the relation of the human and divine natures in the person of Christ. Cyril, representing the Alexandrian school, emphasized the divine nature of Christ, frequently to the point of tending to absorb the human in the divine. Nestorius, closely related to the Antioch school, sought to preserve the two natures in separation and to stress the humanity of Christ.

Theodore, Bishop of Mopsuestia, and teacher of Nestorius, described in his work, *On The Incarnation*, the relation of the divine and human in Christ as a "moral" union, frequently using the term conjunction ($\sigma\nu\nu\acute{\alpha}\phi\epsilon\iota\alpha$) rather than the more explicit word union ($\overset{"}{\epsilon}\nu\omega\sigma\iota\varsigma$).

The controversy broke out in Constantinople when

Nestorius and other leaders of the church said that the term, *theotokos* (Mother of God) was inappropriate to describe the Virgin Mary. The two natures were united morally, but not essentially; Mary was *Christotokos*, the Mother of Christ. Later in his life Nestorius, in clarifying his position, spoke of two *prosopa* (persons, referring especially to the appearance) before the incarnation, and one after the incarnation. Elsewhere he wrote of a divine nature (*ousia*) and a human nature (*ousia*) that were united in one person, a position which, though ambiguously written, was not dissimilar from Tertullian's earlier statement.

At Ephesus (431) a council was called to deal with the issue. In attendance were Nestorius, Cyril, and their respective followers; an important figure, John of Antioch, did not arrive in time for the opening meetings. Over the vehement protest of some of the delegates, Cyril called the council to order, and the council proceeded to excommunicate Nestorius. A few days later John of Antioch arrived and held a council that deposed Cyril and the Bishop of Ephesus, Memnon. The emperor confirmed both decisions and Cyril and Nestorius were imprisoned, an action that was soon reversed in the case of Cyril.

In 433 John of Antioch and Cyril agreed on the use of a creed that retained the term *theotokos* (Mother of God) and affirmed the union rather than the conjunction of human and divine natures in the person of Christ. The controversy subsided for a short time.

A. A Letter to Nestorius[*]

CYRIL

To the most religious and beloved of God, fellow minister Nestorius, Cyril sends greeting in the Lord.

I hear that some are rashly talking of the estimation in which I hold your holiness, and that this is frequently the case especially at the times that meetings are held of those in authority. And perchance they think in so doing to say something agreeable to you, but they speak senselessly, for they

* From *Ten Ecumenical Councils*, Henry R. Percival, ed., A Select Library of Nicene and Post-Nicene Fathers, Vol. XIV, Second series. Grand Rapids, Mich.: Wm. B. Eerdmans Publishing Co., 1956.

have suffered no injustice at my hands, but have been exposed by me only to their profit; this man as an oppressor of the blind and needy, and that as one who wounded his mother with a sword. Another because he stole, in collusion with his waiting maid, another's money, and had always laboured under the imputation of such like crimes as no one would wish even one of his bitterest enemies to be laden with. I take little reckoning of the words of such people, for the disciple is not above his Master, nor would I stretch the measure of my narrow brain above the Fathers, for no matter what path of life one pursues it is hardly possible to escape the smirching of the wicked, whose mouths are full of cursing and bitterness, and who at the last must give an account to the Judge of all.

But I return to the point which especially I had in mind. And now I urge you, as a brother in the Lord, to propose the word of teaching and the doctrine of the faith with all accuracy to the people, and to consider that the giving of scandal to one even of the least of those who believe in Christ, exposes a body to the unbearable indignation of God. And of how great diligence and skill there is need when the multitude of those grieved is so great, so that we may administer the healing word of truth to them that seek it. But this we shall accomplish most excellently if we shall turn over the words of the holy Fathers, and are zealous to obey their commands, proving ourselves, whether we be in the faith according to that which is written, and conform our thoughts to their upright and irreprehensible teaching.

The holy and great synod therefore says, that the only begotten Son, born according to nature of God the Father, very God of very God, Light of Light, by whom the Father made all things, came down, and was incarnate, and was made man, suffered, and rose again the third day, and ascended into heaven. These words and these decrees we ought to follow, considering what is meant by the Word of God being incarnate and made man. For we do not say that the nature of the Word was changed and became flesh, or that it was converted into a whole man consisting of soul and body; but rather that the Word having personally united to himself flesh animated by a rational soul, did in an ineffable and inconceivable manner become man, and was called the Son of Man, not merely as willing or being pleased to be so called, neither on account of taking to himself a person, but because the two natures being brought together in a true union, there is of both one Christ and one Son; for the difference of the natures is not taken away by the union, but rather the divinity and the humanity make perfect for us the one Lord Jesus Christ by their ineffable and inexpressible union. So then he who had an existence before all ages and was born of the Father, is said to have been born according to the flesh of a woman, not as though his divine nature received its beginning of existence in the holy Virgin, for it needed not any second generation after that of the Father (for it would be absurd and foolish to say that he who existed before all ages, coeternal with the Father, needed any second beginning of existence), but since, for us and for our salvation, he personally united to himself an human body, and came forth of a woman, he is in this way said to be born after the flesh; for he was not first born a common man of the holy Virgin, and then the Word came down and entered into him, but the union being made in the womb itself, he is said to endure a birth after the flesh, ascribing to himself the birth of his own flesh. On this account we say that he suffered and rose again; not as if God the Word suffered in his own nature stripes, or the piercing of the nails, or any other wounds, for the Divine nature is incapable of suffering, inasmuch as it is incorporeal, but since that which had become his own body suffered in this way, he is also said to suffer for us; for he who is in himself incapable of suffering was in a suffering body. In the same manner also we conceive respecting his dying; for the Word of God is by nature immortal and incorruptible, and life and life-giving; since, however, his own body did, as Paul says, by the grace of God taste death for every man, he himself is said to have suffered death for us, not as if he had any experience of death in his own nature (for it would be madness to say or think this), but because, as I have just said, his flesh tasted death. In like manner his flesh being raised again, it is spoken of as his resurrection, not as if he had fallen into corruption (God forbid), but because his own body was raised again. We, therefore, confess one Christ and Lord, not as worshipping a man *with* the Word (lest this expression "with the Word" should suggest to the mind the idea of division), but worshipping him as one and the same, forasmuch as the body of the Word, with which he sits with the Father, is not separated from the Word himself, not as if two sons were sitting with him, but one by the union with the flesh. If, however, we reject the personal union as impossible or unbecoming, we fall into the error of speaking of two sons, for it will be necessary to distinguish, and to say, that he who was properly man was honored with the appellation of Son, and that he who is properly the Word of God, has by nature both the name and the reality of Sonship. We must not, therefore, divide the one Lord Jesus Christ into two Sons. Neither will it at all avail to a sound faith to hold, as some do, an union of persons; for the scripture has not said that the Word united to himself the person of man, but that he was made flesh. This expression, however, "the Word was made flesh," can mean nothing else but that he partook of flesh and blood like to us; he made our body his own, and came forth man from a woman, not casting off his existence as God, or his generation of God the Father, but even in taking to himself flesh remaining what he was. This the declaration of the correct faith proclaims everywhere. This was the sentiment of the holy Fathers; therefore they ventured to call the holy Virgin, the Mother of God, not as if the nature of the Word or his divinity had its beginning from the holy Virgin, but because of her was born that holy body with a rational soul, to which the Word being personally united is said to be born according to the flesh. These things, therefore, I now write unto you for the love of Christ, beseeching you as a brother, and testifying to you before Christ and the elect angels, that you would both think and teach these things with us, that the peace of the Churches may be preserved and the bond of concord and love continue unbroken amongst the Priests of God.

B. Council of Ephesus (431): The Anathemas*

I

Cyril. If anyone will not confess that the Emmanuel is very God, and that therefore the Holy Virgin is the Mother of God, inasmuch as in the flesh she bore the Word of God made flesh (as it is written, "The Word was made flesh") : let him be anathema.

Nestorius. If anyone says that the Emmanuel is true God, and not rather God with us, that is, that he has united himself to a like nature with ours, which he assumed from the Virgin Mary, and dwelt in it; and if anyone calls Mary the mother of God the Word, and not rather mother of him who is Emmanuel; and if he maintains that God the Word has changed himself into the flesh, which he only assumed in order to make his Godhead visible, and to be found in form as a man, let him be anathema.

II

Cyril. If anyone shall not confess that the Word of God the Father is united hypostatically to flesh, and that with that flesh of his own, he is one only Christ both God and man at the same time: let him be anathema.

Nestorius. If anyone asserts that, at the union of the Logos with the flesh, the divine Essence moved from one place to another; or says that the flesh is capable of receiving the divine nature, and that it has been partially united with the flesh; or ascribes to the flesh, by reason of its reception of

* From *Ten Ecumenical Councils*, Henry R. Percival, ed., A Select Library of Nicene and Post-Nicene Fathers, Vol. XIV, Second series. Grand Rapids, Mich.: Wm. B. Eerdmans Publishing Co., 1956.

God, an extension to the infinite and boundless, and says that God and man are one and the same in nature; let him be anathema.

III

Cyril. If anyone shall after the (hypostatic) union divide the hypostases in the one Christ, joining them by that connexion alone, which happens according to worthiness, or even authority and power, and not rather by a coming together, which is made by natural union: let him be anathema.

Nestorius. If anyone says that Christ, who is also Emmanuel, is One, not (merely) in consequence of *connection*, but (also) in *nature*, and does not acknowledge the *connection* of the two natures, that of the Logos and of the assumed manhood, in one Son, as still continuing without *mingling*; let him be anathema.

IV

Cyril. If anyone shall divide between two persons or subsistences those expressions which are contained in the Evangelical and Apostolical writings, or which have been said concerning Christ by the Saints, or by himself, and shall apply some to him as to a man separate from the Word of God, and shall apply others to the only Word of God the Father, on the ground that they are fit to be applied to God: let him be anathema.

Nestorius. If anyone assigns the expressions of the Gospels and Apostolic letters, which refer to the two natures of Christ, to one only of those natures, and even ascribes suffering to the divine Word, both in the flesh and in the Godhead; let him be anathema.

V

Cyril. If anyone shall dare to say that the Christ is a Theophorus (that is, God-bearing) man and not rather that he is very God, as an only Son through nature, because "the Word was made flesh," and "hath a share in flesh and blood as we do:" let him be anathema.

Nestorius. If anyone ventures to say that, even after the assumption of human nature, there is only one Son of God, namely, he who is so in nature, while he (since the assumption of the flesh) is certainly Emmanuel: let him be anathema.

VI

Cyril. If anyone shall dare say that the Word of God the Father is the God of Christ or the Lord of Christ, and shall not rather confess him as at the same time both God and Man, since according to the scriptures, "The Word was made flesh"; let him be anathema.

Nestorius. If anyone, after the Incarnation calls another than Christ the Word, and ventures to say that the form of a servant is equally with the Word of God, without beginning and uncreated, and not rather that it is made by him as its natural Lord and Creator and God, and that he has promised to raise it again in the words: "Destroy this temple, and in three days I will build it up again"; let him be anathema.

VII

Cyril. If anyone shall say that Jesus as man is only energized by the Word of God, and that the glory of the only-begotten is attributed to him as something not properly his: let him be anathema.

Nestorius. If anyone says that the man who was formed of the Virgin is the Only-begotten, who was born from the bosom of the Father, before the morning star was, and does not rather confess that he has obtained the designation of Only-begotten on account of his connection with him who in nature is the Only-begotten of the Father; and besides, if anyone calls another than the Emmanuel Christ; let him be anathema.

VIII

Cyril. If anyone shall dare to say that the assumed man ought to be worshipped together with God the Word, and glorified together with him, and recognized together with him as God, and yet as two different things, the one with the other (for this "Together with" is added [i.e., by the Nestorians] to convey this meaning); and shall not rather with one adoration worship the Emmanuel and pay to him one glorification, as (it is written) "The Word was made flesh"; let him be anathema.

Nestorius. If anyone says that the form of a servant should, for its own sake, that is, in reference to its own nature, be reverenced, and that it is the ruler of all things, and not rather that (merely) on account of its connection with the holy and in itself universally-ruling nature of the Only-begotten, it is to be reverenced; let him be anathema.

IX

Cyril. If any man shall say that the one Lord Jesus Christ was glorified by the Holy Ghost, so that he used through him a power not his own and from him received power against unclean spirits and power to work miracles before men and shall not rather confess that it was his own Spirit through which he worked these divine signs; let him be anathema.

Nestorius. If anyone says that the form of a servant is of like nature with the Holy Ghost, and not rather that it owes its union with the Word which has existed since the conception, to his mediation, by which it works miraculous healings among men, and possesses the power of expelling demons; let him be anathema.

X

Cyril. Whosoever shall say that it is not the divine Word himself, when he was made flesh and had become man as we are, but another than he, a man born of a woman, yet different from him, who is become our Great High Priest and Apostle; or if any man shall say that he offered himself in sacrifice for himself and not rather for us, whereas, being without sin, he had no need of offering or sacrifice: let him be anathema.

Nestorius. If anyone maintains that the Word, who is from the beginning, has become the high priest and apostle of our confession, and has offered himself for us, and does not rather say that it is the work of Emmanuel to be an apostle; and if anyone in such a manner divides the sacrifice between him who united (the word) and him who was united (the manhood) referring it to a common sonship, that is, not giving to God that which is God's, and to man that which is man's; let him be anathema.

XI

Cyril. Whosoever shall not confess that the flesh of the Lord giveth life, and that it pertains to the Word of God the Father as his very own, but shall pretend that it belongs to another person who is united to him (i.e., the Word) only according to honour, and who has served as a dwelling for the divinity; and shall not rather confess, as we say, that that flesh giveth life because it is that of the Word who giveth life to all: let him be anathema.

Nestorius. If anyone maintains that the flesh which is united with God the Word is by the power of its own nature life-giving, whereas the Lord himself says, "It is the Spirit that quickeneth; the flesh profiteth nothing", let him be anathema. . . . If, then, anyone maintains that God the Logos has in a carnal manner, in his substance, become flesh, and persists in this with reference to the Lord Christ; who himself after his resurrection said to his disciples, "Handle me and see; for a spirit hath not flesh and bones, as ye behold me having" (Luke xxiv, 39); let him be anathema.

XII

Cyril. Whosoever shall not recognize that the Word of God suffered in the flesh, that he was crucified in the flesh, and that likewise in that same flesh he tasted death and that he is become the first-begotten of the dead, for, as he is God, he is the life and it is he that giveth life: let him be anathema.

Nestorius. If anyone, in confessing the sufferings of the flesh, ascribes these also to the Word of God as to the flesh in which he appeared, and thus does not distinguish the dignity of the natures; let him be anathema.

C. Council of Ephesus (431): Decree Against Nestorius *

As, in addition to other things, the impious Nestorius has not obeyed our citation, and did not receive the holy bishops who were sent by us to him, we were compelled to examine his ungodly doctrines. We discovered that he had held and published impious doctrines in his letters and treatises, as well as in discourses which he delivered in this city, and which have been testified to. Compelled thereto by the canons and by the letter of our most holy father and fellow-servant Coelestine, the Roman bishop, we have come, with many tears, to this sorrowful sentence against him, namely, that our Lord Jesus Christ, whom he has blasphemed, decrees by the holy synod that Nestorius be excluded from the episcopal dignity, and from all priestly communion.

* From Ten Ecumenical Councils, Henry R. Percival, ed., A Select Library of Nicene and Post-Nicene Fathers, Vol. XIV, Second series. Grand Rapids, Mich.: Wm. B. Eerdmans Publishing Co., 1956.

D. Council of Ephesus (431): Decree Against Cyril[*]

The holy synod assembled in Ephesus, by the grace of God and at the command of the pious emperors, declares: We should indeed have wished to be able to hold a synod in peace, according to the canons of the holy Fathers and the letters of our most pious and Christ-loving emperors; but because you held a separate assembly from a heretical, insolent, and obstinate disposition, although, according to the letters of our most pious emperors, we were in the neighborhood, and because you have filled both the city and the holy synod with every sort of confusion, in order to prevent the examination of points agreeing with the Apollinarian, Arian, and Eunomian heresies and impieties, and have not waited for the arrival of the most religious bishops summoned from all regions by our pious emperors, and when the most magnificent Count Candidianus warned you and admonished you in writing and verbally that you should not hear such a matter, but await the common judgment of all the most holy bishops; therefore know thou, O Cyril, Bishop of Alexandria, and thou, O Memnon, bishop of this city, that ye are dismissed and deposed from all sacerdotal functions as the originators and leaders of all this disorder and lawlessness, and those who have violated the canons of the Fathers and the imperial decrees. And all ye others who seditiously and wickedly, and contrary to all ecclesiastical sanctions and the royal decrees, gave your consent are excommunicated until you acknowledge your fault and reform and accept anew the faith set forth by the holy Fathers at Nicaea, adding to it nothing foreign or different, and until ye anathematize the heretical propositions of Cyril, which are plainly repugnant to evangelical and apostolic doctrine, and in all things comply with the letters of our most pious and Christ-loving emperors, who require a peaceful and accurate consideration of the dogma.

E. Council of Antioch (433): Creed[*]

We therefore acknowledge our Lord Jesus Christ, the Son of God, the only begotten, complete God and complete man, of a rational soul and body; begotten of the Father before the ages according to His godhead, but in the last days for us and for our salvation, of the Virgin Mary, according to the manhood; that He is of the same nature as the Father according to His godhead, and of the same nature with us according to His manhood; for a union of the two natures has been made; therefore we confess one Christ, one Son, one Lord. According to this conception of the unconfused union, we confess that the holy Virgin is Theotokos [Mother of God], because God the Word was made flesh and became man, and from her conception united with Himself the temple received from her. We recognize the evangelical and apostolic utterances concerning the Lord making common, as in one person, the divine and the human characteristics, but distinguishing them as in two natures; and teaching that the godlike traits are according to the godhead of Christ, and the humble traits according to His manhood.

29 THE ISSUE concerning the relation of the two natures, divine and human, in Christ was raised again when Dioscurus, who succeeded Cyril as Bishop of Alexandria, and Flavian, the successor of Nestorius in Constantinople, became involved in a dispute over the beliefs of Eutyches, the head of a monastery near Constantinople. Eutyches described the nature of Christ as being the same (*homoousion*) with God the Father but not with man. After the incarnation there was only one nature. This came to be known as the monophysite heresy. Dioscurus supported Eutyches. At a synod in Constantinople in 448 Flavian excommunicated Eutyches. The new Bishop of Rome, Leo I., supported Flavian and in a letter, the *Tome of Leo*, insisted that in

* Reprinted with the permission of Charles Scribner's Sons from *A Source Book for Ancient Church History* by J. C. Ayer. Copyright 1913 Charles Scribner's Sons; renewal copyright 1941 J. C. Ayer.

Christ there were two complete natures, divine and human. This letter became of crucial importance in the decision made at Chalcedon in 451. Before that meeting was held, however, the Emperor, Theodosius II, summoned a council to meet at Ephesus in 449. Theodosius supported Dioscurus and Eutyches and the council condemned Flavian; the *Tome of Leo* was not read to the assembled delegates. The council enunciated the position that after the incarnation no distinction between the natures existed. The procedure used at this 449 meeting has prompted others to call it the Robber Synod.

It was at the Council of Chalcedon, the Third Ecumenical Council, summoned by the new Empress, Pulcheria, a supporter of Leo I, that the decision of two natures, one person was affirmed.

A. Council of Constantinople (448): Condemnation of Eutyches*

Archbishop Flavian said: Do you confess that the one and the same Son, our Lord Jesus Christ, is consubstantial with His Father as to His divinity, and consubstantial with His mother as to His humanity?

Eutyches said: When I intrusted myself to your holiness I said that you should not ask me further what I thought concerning the Father, Son, and Holy Ghost.

The archbishop said: Do you confess Christ to be of two natures?

Eutyches said: I have never yet presumed to speculate concerning the nature of my God, the Lord of heaven and earth; I confess that I have never said that He is consubstantial with us. Up to the present day I have not said that the body of our Lord and God was consubstantial with us; I confess that the holy Virgin is consubstantial with us, and that of her our God was incarnate . . .

Florentius, the patrician, said: Since the mother is consubstantial with us, doubtless the Son is consubstantial with us.

Eutyches said: I have not said, you will notice, that the body of a man became the body of God, but the body was human, and the Lord was incarnate of the Virgin. If you wish that I should add to this that His body is consubstantial with us, I will do this; but I do not understand the term consubstantial in such a way that I do not deny that he is the Son of God. Formerly I spoke in general not of a consubstantiality according to the flesh; now I will do so, because your Holiness demands it. . . .

Florentius said: Do you or do you not confess that our Lord, who is of the Virgin, is consubstantial and of two natures after the incarnation?

Eutyches said: I confess that our Lord was of two natures before the union [i.e., the union of divinity and humanity in the incarnation], but after the union one nature. . . . I follow the teaching of the blessed Cyril and the holy Fathers and the holy Athanasius, because they speak of two natures before the union, but after the union and incarnation they speak not of two natures but of one nature.

[CONDEMNATION OF EUTYCHES]

Eutyches, formerly presbyter and archimandrite, has been shown, by what has taken place and by his own confession, to be infected with the heresy of Valentinus and Apollinaris, and to follow stubbornly their blasphemies, and rejecting our arguments and teaching, is unwilling to consent to true doctrines. Therefore, weeping and mourning his complete perversity, we have decreed through our Lord Jesus Christ, who has been blasphemed by him, that he be deprived of every sacerdotal office, that he be put out of our communion, and deprived of his position over a monastery. All who hereafter speak with him or associate with him, are to know that they also are fallen into the same penalty of excommunication.

B. Tome*

LEO 1

Leo [the bishop] to his [most] dear brother Flavian.

Having read your Affection's letter, the late arrival of which is matter of surprise to us, and having gone through the record of the proceedings of the bishops, we have now, at last, gained a clear view of the scandal which has risen up among you, against the integrity of the faith; and what at first

* From *Ten Ecumenical Councils*, Henry R. Percival, ed., A Select Library of Nicene and Post-Nicene Fathers, Vol. XIV, Second series. Grand Rapids, Mich.: Wm. B. Eerdmans Publishing Co., 1956.

seemed obscure has now been elucidated and explained. By this means Eutyches, who seemed to be deserving of honour under the title of Presbyter, is now shown to be exceedingly thoughtless and sadly inexperienced, so that to him also we may apply the prophet's words, "He refused to understand in order to act well: he meditated unrighteousness on his bed." What, indeed, is more unrighteous than to entertain ungodly thoughts, and not to yield to persons wiser and more learned? But into this folly do they fall who, when hindered by some obscurity from apprehending the truth, have recourse, not to the words of the Prophets, not to the letters of the Apostles, nor to the authority of the Gospels, but to themselves; and become teachers of error, just because they have not been disciples of the truth. For what learning has he received from the sacred pages of the New and the Old Testament, who does not so much as understand the very beginning of the Creed? And that which, all the world over, is uttered by the voices of all applicants for regeneration, is still not grasped by the mind of this aged man. If, then, he knew not what he ought to think about the Incarnation of the Word of God, and was not willing, for the sake of obtaining the light of intelligence, to make laborious search through the whole extent of the Holy Scriptures, he should at least have received with heedful attention that general Confession common to all, whereby the whole body of the faithful profess that they "believe in God the Father Almighty, and in Jesus Christ his only Son our Lord, who was born of the Holy Ghost and the Virgin Mary." By which three clauses the engines of almost all heretics are shattered. For when God is believed to be both "Almighty" and "Father," it is proved that the Son is everlasting together with himself, differing in nothing from the Father, because he was born as "God from God," Almighty from Almighty, Coeternal from Eternal; not later in time, not inferior in power, not unlike him in glory, not divided from him in essence, but the same Only-begotten and Everlasting Son of an Everlasting Parent was "born of the Holy Ghost and the Virgin Mary." This birth in time in no way detracted from, in no way added to, that divine and everlasting birth; but expended itself wholly in the work of restoring man, who had been deceived; so that it might both overcome death, and by its power "destroy the devil who had the power of death." For we could not have overcome the author of sin and of death, unless he who could neither be contaminated by sin, nor detained by death, had taken upon himself our nature, and made it his own. For, in fact, he was "conceived of the Holy Ghost" within the womb of a Virgin Mother, who bore him as she had conceived him, without loss of virginity. . . . Possibly his [Eutyches] reason for thinking that our Lord Jesus Christ was not of our nature was this—that the Angel who was sent to the blessed and ever Virgin Mary said, "The Holy Ghost shall come upon thee, and the power of the Highest shall overshadow thee, and therefore also that holy thing which shall be born of thee shall be called the Son of God;" as if, because the Virgin's conception was caused by a divine act, therefore the flesh of him whom she conceived was not of the nature of her who conceived him. But we are not to understand that "generation," peerlessly wonderful, and wonderfully peerless, in such a sense as that the newness of the mode of production did away with the proper character of the kind. For it was the Holy Ghost who gave fecundity to the Virgin, but it was from a body that a real body was derived; and "when Wisdom was building herself a house," the "Word was made flesh, and dwelt among us," that is, in that flesh which he assumed from a human being, and which he animated with the spirit of rational life. Accordingly, while the distinctness of both natures and substances was preserved, and both met in one Person, lowliness was assumed by majesty, weakness by power, mortality by eternity; and, in order to pay the debt of our condition, the inviolable nature was united to the passible, so that as the appropriate remedy for our ills, one and the same "Mediator between God and man, the Man Christ Jesus," might from one element be capable of dying and also from the other be incapable. Therefore in the entire and perfect nature of very man was born very God, whole in what was his, whole in what was ours. By "ours" we mean what the Creator formed in us at the beginning and what he assumed in order to restore; for of that which the deceiver brought in, and man, thus deceived, admitted, there was not a trace in the Saviour; and the fact that he took on himself a share in our infirmities did not make him a partaker in our transgressions. He assumed "the form of a servant" without the defilement of sin, enriching what was human, not impairing what was divine: because that "emptying of himself," whereby the Invisible made himself visible, and the Creator and Lord of all things willed to be one among mortals, was a stooping down in compassion, not a failure of power. Accordingly, the same who, remaining in the form of God, made man, was made man in the form of a servant. For each of the natures retains its proper character without defect; and as the form of God does not take away the form of a servant, so the form of a servant does not impair the form of God. . . . Accordingly, the Son of God, descending from his seat in heaven, and not departing from the glory of the Father, enters this lower world, born after a new order, by a new mode of birth. After a new order; because he who in his own sphere is invisible, became visible in ours; He who could not be enclosed in space, willed to be enclosed; continuing to be before times, he began to exist in time; the Lord of the universe allowed his infinite majesty to be overshadowed, and took upon him the form of a servant; the impassible God did not disdain to be passible Man, and the immortal One to be subjected to the laws of death. And born by a new mode of birth; because inviolate virginity, while ignorant of concupiscence, supplied the matter of his flesh. What was assumed from the Lord's mother was nature, not fault; nor does the wondrousness of the nativity of our Lord Jesus Christ, as born of a

Virgin's womb, imply that his nature is unlike ours. For the selfsame who is very God, is also very man; and there is no illusion in this union, while the lowliness of man and the loftiness of Godhead meet together. For as "God" is not changed by the compassion [exhibited], so "Man" is not consumed by the dignity [bestowed]. For each "form" does the acts which belong to it, in communion with the other; the Word, that is, performing what belongs to the Word, and the flesh carrying out what belongs to the flesh; the one of these shines out in miracles, the other succumbs to injuries. And as the Word does not withdraw from equality with the Father in glory, so the flesh does not abandon the nature of our kind. For, as we must often be saying, he is one and the same, truly Son of God, and truly Son of Man. God, inasmuch as "in the beginning was the Word, and the Word was with God, and the Word was God." Man, inasmuch as "the Word was made flesh, and dwelt among us." God, inasmuch as "all things were made by him, and without him nothing was made." Man, inasmuch as he was "made of a woman, made under the law." The nativity of the flesh is a manifestation of human nature; the Virgin's child-bearing is an indication of Divine power. . . . For although in the Lord Jesus Christ there is one Person of God and man, yet that whereby contumely attaches to both is one thing, and that whereby glory attaches to both is another; for from what belongs to us he has that manhood which is inferior to the Father; while from the Father he has equal Godhead with the Father. Accordingly, on account of this unity of Person which is to be understood as existing in both the natures, we read, on the one hand, that "the Son of Man came down from heaven," inasmuch as the Son of God took flesh from that Virgin of whom he was born; and on the other hand, the Son of God is said to have been crucified and buried, inasmuch as he underwent this, not in his actual Godhead; wherein the Only-begotten is coeternal and consubstantial with the Father, but in the weakness of human nature. . . . The properties of the Divine and the human nature might be acknowledged to remain in him without causing a division, and that we might in such sort know that the Word is not what the flesh is, as to confess that the one Son of God is both Word and flesh. On which mystery of the faith this Eutyches must be regarded as unhappily having no hold, who does not recognise our nature to exist in the Only-begotten Son of God, either by way of the lowliness of mortality, or of the glory of resurrection. Nor has he been overawed by the declaration of the blessed Apostle and Evangelist John, saying, "Every spirit that confesseth that Jesus Christ has come in the flesh is of God; and every spirit which dissolveth Jesus is not of God, and this is Antichrist." Now what is to dissolve Jesus, but to separate the human nature from him, and to make void by shameless inventions that mystery by which alone we have been saved? Moreover, being in the dark as to the nature of Christ's body, he must needs be involved in the like senseless blindness with regard to his

Passion also. For if he does not think the Lord's crucifixion to be unreal, and does not doubt that he really accepted suffering, even unto death, for the sake of the world's salvation; as he believes in his death, let him acknowledge his flesh also, and not doubt that he whom he recognises as having been capable of suffering is also Man with a body like ours; since to deny his true flesh is also to deny his bodily sufferings. If then he accepts the Christian faith, and does not turn away his ear from the preaching of the Gospel, let him see what nature it was that was transfixed with nails and hung on the wood of the cross; and let him understand whence it was that, after the side of the Crucified had been pierced by the soldier's spear, blood and water flowed out, that the Church of God might be refreshed both with a Laver and with a Cup. Let him listen also to the blessed Apostle Peter when he declares, that "sanctification by the Spirit" takes place through the "sprinkling of the blood of Christ," and let him not give a mere cursory reading to the words of the same Apostle, "Knowing that ye were not redeemed with corruptible things, as silver and gold, from your vain way of life received by tradition from your fathers, but with the precious blood of Jesus Christ as a Lamb without blemish and without spot." Let him also not resist the testimony of Blessed John the Apostle, "And the blood of Jesus the Son of God cleanseth us from all sin." And again, "This is the victory which overcometh the world, even our faith;" and, "who is he that overcometh the world, but he that believeth that Jesus is the Son of God? This is he that came by water and blood, even Jesus Christ; not in water only, but in water and blood; and it is the Spirit that beareth witness, because the Spirit is truth. For there are three that bear witness—the Spirit, the water, and the blood; and the three are one." That is, the Spirit of sanctification, and the blood of redemption, and the water of baptism; which three things are one, and remain undivided, and not one of them is disjoined from connection with the others; because the Catholic Church lives and advances by this faith, that in Christ Jesus we should believe neither manhood to exist without true Godhead, nor Godhead without true manhood. But when Euytches, on being questioned in your examination of him, answered, "I confess that our Lord was of two natures before the union, but after the union I confess one nature;" I am astonished that so absurd and perverse a profession as this of his was not rebuked by a censure on the part of any of his judges, and that an utterance extremely foolish and extremely blasphemous was passed over, just as if nothing had been heard which could give offence: seeing that it is as impious to say that the Only-begotten Son of God was of two natures before the Incarnation as it is shocking to affirm that, since the Word became flesh, there has been in him one nature only. But lest Eutyches should think that what he said was correct, or was tolerable, because it was not confuted by any assertion of yours, we exhort your earnest solicitude, dearly beloved brother, to see that, if by God's merciful inspiration the case is brought to a satisfactory issue, the inconsiderate and inexperienced man be cleansed also from this pestilent notion of his; seeing that, as the record of the proceedings has clearly shown, he had fairly begun to abandon his own opinion when on being driven into a corner by authoritative words of yours, he professed himself ready to say what he had not said before, and to give his adhesion to that faith from which he had previously stood aloof. But when he would not consent to anathematize the impious dogma you understood, brother, that he continued in his own misbelief, and deserved to receive sentence of condemnation. For which if he grieves sincerely and to good purpose, and understands, even though too late, how properly the Episcopal authority has been put in motion, or if, in order to make full satisfaction, he shall condemn *viva voce*, and under his own hand, all that he has held amiss, no compassion, to whatever extent, which can be shown him when he has been set right, will be worthy of blame, for our Lord, the true and good Shepherd, who laid down his life for his sheep, and who came to save men's souls and not to destroy them, wills us to imitate his own loving kindness; so that justice should indeed constrain those who sin, but mercy should not reject those who are converted. For then indeed is the true faith defended with the best results, when a false opinion is condemned even by those who have followed it. But in order that the whole matter may be piously and faithfully carried out, we have appointed our brethren, Julius, Bishop, and Reatus, Presbyter (of the title of St. Clement) and also my son Hilarus, Deacon, to represent us; and with them we have associated Dalcitius, our Notary, of whose fidelity we have had good proof: trusting that the Divine assistance will be with you, so that he who has gone astray may be saved by condemning his own unsound opinion. May God keep you in good health, dearly beloved brother. Given on the Ides of June, in the Consulate of the illustrious men, Asterius and Protogenes.

C. The Council of Chalcedon (451): The Definition of Faith[*]

The holy, great, and ecumenical synod, assembled by the grace of God and the command of our most religious and Christian Emperors, Marcian

[*] From *Ten Ecumenical Councils*, Henry R. Percival, ed., A Select Library of Nicene and Post-Nicene Fathers, Vol. XIV, Second series. Grand Rapids, Mich.: Wm. B. Eerdmans Publishing Co., 1956.

and Valentinan, Augusti, at Chalcedon, the metropolis of the Bithynian Province, in the martyry of the holy and victorious martyr Euphemia, has decreed as follows:

Our Lord and Saviour Jesus Christ, when strengthening the knowledge of the Faith in his disciples, to the end that no one might disagree with his neighbour concerning the doctrines of religion, and that the proclamation of the truth might be set forth equally to all men, said, "My peace I leave with you, my peace I give unto you." But, since the evil one does not desist from sowing tares among the seeds of godliness, but ever invents some new device against the truth; therefore the Lord, providing, as he ever does, for the human race, has raised up this pious, faithful, and zealous Sovereign, and has called together unto him from all parts the chief rulers of the priest-hood; so that, the grace of Christ our common Lord inspiring us, we may cast off every plague of falsehood from the sheep of Christ, and feed them with the tender leaves of truth. And this have we done with one unanimous consent, driving away erroneous doctrines and renewing the unerring faith of the Fathers, publishing to all men the Creed of the Three Hundred and Eighteen (Council of Nicea), and to their number adding, as their peers, the Fathers who have received the same summary of religion. Such are the One Hundred and Fifty holy Fathers who afterwards assembled in the great Constantinople and ratified the same faith. Moreover, observing the order and every form relating to the faith, which was observed by the holy synod formerly held in Ephesus, of which Celestine of Rome and Cyril of Alex-andria, of holy memory, were the leaders, we do declare that the exposition of the right and blameless faith made by the Three Hundred and Eighteen holy and blessed Fathers, assembled at Nice in the reign of Constantine of pious memory, shall be pre-eminent: and that those things shall be of force also, which were decreed by the One Hundred and Fifty holy Fathers at Constantinople, for the uprooting of the heresies which had then sprung up, and for the confirmation of the same Catholic and Apostolic Faith of ours. (The statements of Nicaea and Constantinople were included here—ed.)

This wise and salutary formula of divine grace sufficed for the perfect knowledge and confirmation of religion; for it teaches the perfect (doctrine) concerning the Father, Son, and Holy Ghost, and sets forth the Incarnation of the Lord to them that faithfully receive it. But, forasmuch as persons undertaking to make void the preaching of the truth have through their individual heresies given rise to empty babblings; some of them daring to corrupt the mystery of the Lord's incarnation for us and refusing (to use) the name Mother of God in reference to the Virgin, while others, bringing in a confusion and mixture, and idly conceiving that the nature of the flesh and of the Godhead is all one, maintaining that the divine Nature of the Only Begotten is, by mixture, capable of suffering; therefore this present holy, great, and ecumenical synod, desiring to exclude every device against the Truth, and teaching that which is unchanged from the beginning, has at the very outset decreed that the faith of the Three Hundred and Eighteen Fathers shall be preserved inviolate. And on account of them that contend against the Holy Ghost, it confirms the doctrine afterwards delivered concerning the substance of the Spirit by the One Hundred and Fifty holy Fathers who assembled in the imperial City; which doctrine they declared unto all men, not as though they were introducing anything that had been lacking in their predecessors, but in order to explain through written documents their faith concerning the Holy Ghost against those who were seeking to destroy his sovereignty. And, on account of those who have taken in hand to corrupt the mystery of the dispensation (i.e., the Incarnation) and who shamelessly pretend that he who was born of the holy Virgin Mary was a mere man, it receives the synodical letters of the Blessed Cyril, Pastor of the church of Alexandria, addressed to Nestorius and the Easterns, judging them suitable, for the refutation of the frenzied folly of Nestorius, and for the instruction of those who long with holy ardour for a knowledge of the saving symbol. And, for the confirmation of the orthodox doctrines, it has rightly added to these the letter of the President of the great and old Rome, the most blessed and holy Archbishop Leo, which was addressed to Archbishop Flavian of blessed memory, for the removal of the false doctrine of Eutyches, judging them to be agreeable to the confession of the great Peter, and as it were a common pillar against misbelievers. For it opposes those who would rend the mystery of the dispensation into a Duad of Sons; it repels from the sacred assembly those who dare to say that the Godhead of the Only Begotten is capable of suffering; it resists those who imagine a mixture or confusion of the two natures of Christ; it drives away those who fancy his form of a servant is of an heavenly or some substance other than that which was taken of us, and it anathematizes those who foolishly talk of two natures of our Lord before the union, conceiving that after the union there was only one.

Following the holy Fathers we teach with one voice that the Son (of God) and our Lord Jesus Christ is to be confessed as one and the same (Person), that he is perfect in Godhead and perfect in manhood, very God and very man, of a reasonable soul and (human) body consisting, consubstantial with the Father as touching his Godhead, and consubstantial with us as touching his manhood; made in all things like unto us, sin only excepted; begotten of his Father before the worlds according to his Godhead; but in these last days for us men and for our salvation born (into the world) of the Virgin Mary, the Mother of God according to his manhood. This one and the same Jesus Christ, the only-begotten Son (of God) must be confessed to be in two natures, unconfusedly, immutably, indivisibly, inseparably (united), and that without the distinction of natures being taken away by such union, but rather the peculiar property of each nature being preserved and being united in one Person and subsistence, not separated or divided into two persons, but one and the same Son and only-begotten, God the Word, our Lord Jesus Christ, as the Prophets of old time have spoken concerning him, and as the Lord Jesus Christ hath taught us, and as the Creed of the Fathers hath delivered to us.

These things, therefore, having been expressed by us with the greatest accuracy and attention, the holy Ecumenical Synod defines that no one shall be suffered to bring forward a different faith, nor to write, nor to put together, nor to excogitate, nor to teach it to others. But such as dare either to put together another faith, or to bring forward or to teach or to deliver a different Creed to such as wish to be converted to the knowledge of the truth from the Gentiles, or Jews or any heresy whatever, if they be bishops or clerics let them be deposed, the Bishops from the Episcopate, and the clerics from the clergy; but if they be monks or laics: let them be anathematized.

After the reading of the definition, all the most religious bishops cried out: This is the faith of the fathers: let the metropolitans forthwith subscribe it: let them forthwith, in the presence of the judges, subscribe it: let that which has been well defined have no delay: this is the faith of the Apostles: by this we all stand: thus we all believe.

30 THE CHALCEDONIAN CREED proved to be more acceptable to the churches in the West than to those in the Eastern part of the Empire. During the following two centuries, the monophysite position (one divine nature in Christ after the incarnation) and the monothelete position (one divine will in Christ after the incarnation) developed strength. At the Sixth Ecumenical Council in Constantinople (680–681) the church defined the orthodox position that there are two natures and two wills in the person of Christ. This decision was the culmination of the long series of councils working toward an orthodox definition of the person of Christ.

Council of Constantinople (680–681): The Definition of Faith*

The holy, great, and Ecumenical Synod which has been assembled by the grace of God, and the religious decree of the most religious and faithful and mighty Sovereign Constantine, in this God-protected and royal city of Constantinople, New Rome, in the Hall of the imperial Palace, called Trullus, has decreed as follows.

The only-begotten Son, and Word of God the Father, who was made man in all things like unto us without sin, Christ our true God, has declared expressly in the words of the Gospel, "I am the light of the world; he that followeth me shall not walk in darkness, but shall have the light of life." And again, "My peace I leave with you, my peace I give unto you." Our most gentle Sovereign, the champion of orthodoxy, and opponent of evil doctrine, being reverentially led by this divinely uttered doctrine of peace, and having convened this our holy and Ecumenical assembly, has united the judgment of the whole Church. Wherefore this our holy and Ecumenical Synod having driven away the impious error which had prevailed for a certain time until now, and following closely the straight path of the holy and approved Fathers, has piously given its full assent to the five holy and Ecumenical Synods . . . renewing in all things the ancient decrees of religion, and chasing away the impious doctrines of irreligion. And this our holy and Ecumenical Synod inspired of God has set its seal to the Creed which was put forth by the 318 Fathers [Nicaea], and again religiously confirmed by the 150 [Constantinople I], which also the other holy synods cordially received and ratified for the taking away of every soul-destroying heresy.

The holy and Ecumenical Synod further says, this pious and orthodox Creed of the Divine grace would be sufficient for the full knowledge and confirmation of the orthodox faith. But as the author of evil, who, in the beginning, availed himself of the aid of the serpent, and by it brought the poison of death upon the human race, has not desisted, but in like manner now, having found suitable instruments for working out his will . . . has actively employed them in raising up for the whole Church the stumbling

* From Ten Ecumenical Councils, Henry R. Percival, ed., A Select Library of Nicene and Post-Nicene Fathers, Vol. XIV, Second series. Grand Rapids, Mich.: Wm. B. Eerdmans Publishing Co., 1956.

blocks of one will and one operation in the two natures of Christ our true God, one of the Holy Trinity; thus disseminating, in novel terms, amongst the orthodox people, an heresy similar to the mad and wicked doctrine of the impious Apollinaris, Severus, and Themistius, and endeavouring craftily to destroy the perfection of the incarnation of the same our Lord Jesus Christ, our God, by blasphemy representing his flesh endowed with a rational soul as devoid of will or operation. . . . Following the five holy Ecumenical Councils and the holy and approved Fathers, with one voice defining that our Lord Jesus Christ must be confessed to be very God and very man, one of the holy and consubstantial and life-giving Trinity, perfect in Deity and perfect in humanity, very God and very man, of a reasonable soul and human body subsisting; consubstantial with the Father as touching his Godhead and consubstantial with us as touching his manhood; in all things like unto us, sin only excepted; begotten of his Father before all ages according to his Godhead, but in these last days for us men and for our salvation made man of the Holy Ghost and of the Virgin Mary, strictly and properly the Mother of God according to the flesh; one and the same Christ our Lord the only-begotten Son of two natures unconfusedly, unchangeably, inseparably, indivisibly to be recognized, the peculiarities of neither nature being lost by the union but rather the proprieties of each nature being preserved, concurring in one Person and in one subsistence, not parted or divided into two persons but one and the same only-begotten Son of God, the Word, our Lord Jesus Christ, according as to Prophets of old have taught us and as our Lord Jesus Christ himself hath instructed us, and the Creed of the holy Fathers hath delivered to us; defining all this we likewise declare that in him are two natural wills and two natural operations indivisibly, inconvertibly, inseparably, inconfusedly, according to the teaching of the holy Fathers. And these two natural wills are not contrary to one to the other (God forbid) as the impious heretics assert, but his human will follows and that not as resisting and reluctant, but rather as subject to his divine and omnipotent will. For it was right that the flesh should be moved but subject to the divine will, according to the most wise Athanasius. For as his flesh is called and is the flesh of God the Word, so also the natural will of his flesh is called and is the proper will of God the Word, as he himself says: "I came down from heaven, not that I might do mine own will but the will of the Father which sent me!" where he calls his own will the will of his flesh, inasmuch as his flesh was also his own. For as his most holy and immaculate animated flesh was not destroyed because it was deified but continued in its own state and nature, so also his human will, although deified, was not suppressed, but was rather preserved. . . .

We glorify two natural operations indivisibly, immutably, inconfusedly, inseparably in the same our Lord Jesus Christ our true God, that is to say a divine operation and a human operation, according to the divine preacher

Leo, who most distinctly asserts as follows: "For each form does in communion with the other what pertains properly to it, the Word, namely, doing that which pertains to the Word, and the flesh that which pertains to the flesh."

For we will not admit one natural operation in God and in the creature, as we will not exalt into the divine essence what is created, nor will we bring down the glory of the divine nature to the place suited to the creature.

We recognize the miracles and the sufferings as of one and the same [Person], but of one or of the other nature of which he is and in which he exists, as Cyril admirably says. Preserving therefore the inconfusedness and indivisibility, we make briefly this whole confession, believing our Lord Jesus Christ to be one of the Trinity and after the incarnation our true God, we say that his two natures shone forth in his one subsistence in which he both performed the miracles and endured the sufferings through the whole of his economic conversation, and that not in appearance only but in very deed, and this by reason of the difference of nature which must be recognized in the same Person, for although joined together yet each nature wills and does the things proper to it and that indivisibly and inconfusedly. Wherefore we confess two wills and two operations, concurring most fitly in him for the salvation of the human race.

These things, therefore, will all diligence and care having been formulated by us, we define that it be permitted to no one to bring forward, or to write, or to compose, or to think, or to teach a different faith. Whosoever shall presume to compose a different faith, or to propose, or teach, or hand to those wishing to be converted to the knowledge of the truth, from the Gentiles or Jews, or from any heresy, any different Creed; or to introduce a new voice or invention of speech to subvert these things which now have been determined by us, all these, if they be bishops or clerics let them be deposed, the bishops from the Episcopate, the clerics from the clergy; but if they be monks or laymen: let them be anathematized.

THE WORK OF CHRIST

31 IRENAEUS (c. 130–202) WAS BORN in Smyrna in Asia Minor and served for many years as the Bishop of Lugdunum (Lyons, France). In *Against Heresies* where he challenged some of the major "heretical" groups of the growing church, especially Gnosticism and Montanism, he developed his own theological affirmations.

Irenaeus' soteriological interest resulted in an engaging statement on the work of Christ. Two particular groups encountered his argument: the Docetists, who affirmed the "seeming" but not concrete existence of Christ, and the Ebionites, who viewed the work of Christ as a continuation of the Old Testament prophetic tradition. Irenaeus' "recapitulation" theory affirmed that Christ "summed up" human life and offered concrete union of God with human nature. What had been lost in Adam is now recovered, and man now confronts one in whom perfect obedience has been realized.

Against Heresies*

IRENAEUS

. . . in no other way could we have learned the things of God, unless our Master, existing as the Word, had become man. For no other being had the power of revealing to us the things of the Father, except His own proper Word. For what other person "knew the mind of the Lord," or who else "has become His counsellor?" Again, we could have learned in no other way than by seeing our Teacher, and hearing His voice with our own ears, that, having become imitators of His works as well as doers of His words, we may have communion with Him, receiving increase from the perfect One, and from Him who is prior to all creation. We—who were but lately created by the only best and good Being, by Him also who has the gift of immortality, having been formed after His likeness (predestinated, according to the prescience of the Father, that we, who had as yet no existence, might come into being), and made the first-fruits of creation—have received, in the times

* From *The Ante-Nicene Fathers*, Alexander Roberts and James Donaldson, eds., Vol. I. Grand Rapids, Mich.: Wm. B. Eerdmans Publishing Co., 1951.

known beforehand, [the blessings of salvation] according to the ministration of the Word, who is perfect in all things, as the mighty Word, and very man, who, redeeming us by His own blood in a manner consonant to reason, gave Himself as a redemption for those who had been led into captivity. And since the apostasy tyrannized over us unjustly, and, though we were by nature the property of the omnipotent God, alienated us contrary to nature, rendering us its own disciples, the Word of God, powerful in all things, and not defective with regard to His own justice, did righteously turn against that apostasy, and redeem from it His own property, not by violent means, as the [apostasy] had obtained dominion over us at the beginning, when it insatiably snatched away what was not its own, but by means of persuasion, as became a God of counsel, who does not use violent means to obtain what He desires; so that neither should justice be infringed upon, nor the ancient handiwork of God go to destruction. Since the Lord thus has redeemed us through His own blood, giving His soul for our souls, and His flesh for our flesh, and has also poured out the Spirit of the Father for the union and communion of God and man, imparting indeed God to men by means of the Spirit, and, on the other hand, attaching man to God by His own in-carnation, and bestowing upon us at His coming immortality durably and truly, by means of communion with God,—all the doctrines of the heretics fall to ruin.

Vain indeed are those who allege that He appeared in mere seeming. For these things were not done in appearance only, but in actual reality. But if He did appear as a man, when He was not a man, neither could the Holy Spirit have rested upon Him,—an occurrence which did actually take place—as the Spirit is invisible; nor, [in that case], was there any degree of truth in Him, for He was not that which He seemed to be. But I have already remarked that Abraham and the other prophets beheld Him after a prophetical manner, foretelling in vision what should come to pass. If, then, such a being has now appeared in outward semblance different from what he was in reality, there has been a certain prophetical vision made to men; and another advent of His must be looked forward to, in which He shall be such as He has now been seen in a prophetic manner. And I have proved already, that it is the same thing to say that He appeared merely to outward seeming, and [to affirm] that He received nothing from Mary. For He would not have been one truly possessing flesh and blood, by which He redeemed us, unless He had summed up in Himself the ancient formation of Adam. Vain therefore are the disciples of Valentinus who put forth this opinion, in order that they may exclude the flesh from salvation, and cast aside what God has fashioned.

Vain also are the Ebionites, who do not receive by faith into their soul the union of God and man, but who remain in the old leaven of [the natural] birth, and who do not choose to understand that the Holy Ghost came upon Mary, and the power of the Most High did overshadow her: wherefore also what was generated is a holy thing, and the Son of the Most High God the Father of all, who effected the incarnation of this being, and showed forth a new [kind of] generation; that as by the former generation we inherited death, so by this new generation we might inherit life. Therefore do these men reject the commixture of the heavenly wine, and wish it to be water of the world only, not receiving God so as to have union with Him, but they remain in that Adam who had been conquered and was expelled from Paradise: not considering that as, at the beginning of our formation in Adam, that breath of life which proceeded from God, having been united to what had been fashioned, animated the man, and manifested him as a being endowed with reason; so also, in [in times of] the end, the Word of the Father and the Spirit of God, having become united with the ancient substance of Adam's formation, rendered man living and perfect, receptive of the perfect Father, in order that as in the natural [Adam] we all were dead, so in the spiritual we may all be made alive. For never at any time did Adam escape the hands of God, to whom the Father speaking, said, "Let Us make man in Our image, after Our likeness." And for this reason in the last times (fine), not by the will of the flesh, nor by the will of man, but by the good pleasure of the Father, His hands formed a living man, in order that Adam might be created [again] after the image and likeness of God.

And vain likewise are those who say that God came to those things which did not belong to Him, as if covetous of another's property; in order that He might deliver up that man who had been created by another, to that God who had neither made nor formed anything, but who also was deprived from the beginning of His own proper formation of men. The advent, therefore, of Him whom these men represent as coming to the things of others, was not righteous; nor did He truly redeem us by His own blood, if He did not really become man, restoring to His own handiwork what was said [of it] in the beginning, that man was made after the image and likeness of God; not snatching away by stratagem the property of another, but taking possession of His own in a righteous and gracious manner. As far as concerned the apostasy, indeed, He redeems us righteously from it by His own blood; but as regards us who have been redeemed, [He does this] graciously. For we have given nothing to Him previously, nor does He desire anything from us, as if He stood in need of it; but we do stand in need of fellowship with Him. And for this reason it was that He graciously poured Himself out, that He might gather us into the bosom of the Father. . . .

And inasmuch as the apostle has not pronounced against the very substance of flesh and blood, that it cannot inherit the kingdom of God, the same apostle has everywhere adopted the term "flesh and blood" with regard to the Lord Jesus Christ, partly indeed to establish His human nature (for He did Himself speak of Himself as the Son of man), and partly that He might confirm the salvation of our flesh. For if the flesh were not in a position to be saved, the Word of God would in no wise have become flesh. And if the blood of the righteous were not to be inquired after, the Lord would certainly not have had blood [in His composition]. . . . Now this [blood] could not be required unless it also had the capability of being saved; nor would the Lord have summed up these things in Himself, unless He had Himself been made flesh and blood after the way of the original formation [of man], saving in his own person at the end that which had in the beginning perished in Adam.

But if the Lord became incarnate for any other order of things, and took flesh of any other substance, He has not then summed up human nature in His own person, nor in that case can He be termed flesh. For flesh has been truly made [to consist in] a transmission of that thing moulded originally from the dust. But if it had been necessary for Him to draw the material [of His body] from another substance, the Father would at the beginning have moulded the material [of flesh] from a different substance [than from what He actually did]. But now the case stands thus, that the Word has saved that which really was [created, viz.,] humanity which had perished, effecting by means of Himself that communion which should be held with it, and seeking out its salvation. But the thing which had perished possessed flesh and blood. For the Lord, taking dust from the earth, moulded man; and it was upon his behalf that all the dispensation of the Lord's advent took place. He had Himself, therefore, flesh and blood, recapitulating in Himself not a certain other, but that original handiwork of the Father, seeking out that thing which had perished. . . .

If, then, any one allege that in this respect the flesh of the Lord was different from ours, because it indeed did not commit sin, neither was deceit found in His soul, while we, on the other hand, are sinners, he says what is the fact. But if he pretends that the Lord possessed another substance of flesh, the sayings respecting reconciliation will not agree with that man. For that thing is reconciled which had formerly been in enmity. Now, if the Lord had taken flesh from another substance, He would not, by so doing, have reconciled that one to God which had become inimical through transgression. But now, by means of communion with Himself, the Lord has reconciled man to God the Father, in reconciling us to Himself by the body of His own flesh, and redeeming us by His own blood. . . .

He has therefore, in His work of recapitulation, summed up all things, both waging war against our enemy, and crushing him who had at the beginning led us away captives in Adam, and trampled upon his head, as thou canst perceive in Genesis that God said to the serpent, "And I will put enmity between thee and the woman, and between thy seed and her seed; He shall be on the watch for (*observabit*) thy head, and thou on the watch for His heel." For from that time, He who should be born of a woman, [namely] from the Virgin, after the likeness of Adam, was preached as keeping watch for the head of the serpent. This is the seed of which the apostle says in the Epistle to the Galatians, "that the law of works was established until the seed should come to whom the promise was made." This fact is exhibited in a still clearer light in the same Epistle, where he thus speaks: "But when the fulness of time was come, God sent forth His Son, made of a woman." For indeed the enemy would not have been fairly vanquished, unless it had been a man [born] of a woman who conquered him. For it was by means of a woman that he got the advantage over man at first, setting himself up as man's opponent. And therefore does the Lord profess Himself to be the Son of man, comprising in Himself that original man out of whom the woman was fashioned (ex quo ea quæ secundum mulierem est plasmatio facta est), in order that, as our species went down to death through a vanquished man, so we may ascend to life again through a victorious one; and as through a man death received the palm [of victory] against us, so again by a man we may receive the palm against death.

Now the Lord would not have recapitulated in Himself that ancient and primary enmity against the serpent, fulfilling the promise of the Creator (Demiurgi), and performing His command, if He had come from another Father. But as He is one and the same, who formed us at the beginning, and sent His Son at the end, the Lord did perform His command, being made of a woman, by both destroying our adversary, and perfecting man after the image and likeness of God. And for this reason He did not draw the means of confounding him from any other source than from the words of the law, and made use of the Father's commandment as a help toward the destruction and confusion of the apostate angel. Fasting forty days, like Moses and Elias, He afterwards hungered, first, in order that we may perceive that He was a real and substantial man—for it belongs to a man to suffer hunger when fasting; and secondly, that His opponent might have an opportunity of attacking Him. For as at the beginning it was by means of food that [the enemy] persuaded man, although not suffering hunger, to transgress God's commandments, so in the end he did not succeed in persuading Him that was an hungered to take that food which proceeded from God. For, when tempting Him, he said, "If thou be the Son of God, command that these stones be made bread." But the Lord repulsed him by the commandment of the law, saying, "It is written, Man doth not live by bread alone." As to those words [of His enemy,] "If thou be the Son of God," [the Lord] made no remark; but by thus acknowledging His human nature He baffled His adversary, and exhausted the force of his first attack by means of His Father's word. The corruption of man, therefore, which occurred in paradise by both [of our first parents] eating, was done away with by [the Lord's] want of food in this world. But he, being thus vanquished by the law, endeavoured again to make an assault by himself quoting a commandment of the law. For, bringing Him to the highest pinnacle of the temple, he said to Him, "If thou are the Son of God, cast thyself down. For it is written, That God shall give His angels charge concerning thee, and in their hands they shall bear thee up, lest perchance thou dash thy foot against a stone;" thus concealing a falsehood under the guise of scripture, as is done by all the heretics. For that was indeed written [namely], "That He hath given His angels charge concerning Him;" but "cast thyself down from hence" no scripture said in reference to Him: this kind of persuasion the devil produced from himself. The Lord therefore confuted him out of the law, when He said, "It is written again, Thou shalt not tempt the Lord thy God;" pointing out by the word contained in the law that which is the duty of man, that he should not tempt God; and in regard to Himself, since He appeared in human form, [declaring] that He would not tempt the Lord his God. The pride of reason, therefore, which was in the serpent, was put to nought by the humility found in the man [Christ], and now twice was the devil conquered from scripture, when he was detected as advising things contrary to God's commandment, and was shown to be the enemy of God by [the expression of] his thoughts. He then, having been thus signally defeated, and then, as it were, concentrating his forces, drawing up in order all his available power for falsehood, in the third place "showed Him all the kingdoms of the world, and the glory of them," saying, as Luke relates, "All these will I give thee,—for they are delivered to me; and to whom I will, I give them,—if thou wilt fall down and worship me." The Lord then, exposing him in his true character, says, "Depart, Satan; for it written, Thou shalt worship the Lord thy God, and Him only shalt thou serve." He both revealed him by this name, and showed [at the same time] who He Himself was. For the Hebrew word "Satan" signifies an apostate. And thus, vanquishing him for the third time, He spurned him from Him finally as being conquered out of the law; and there was done away with that infringement of God's commandment which had occurred in Adam, by means of the precept of the law, which the Son of man observed, who did not transgress the commandment of God.

Who, then, is this Lord God to whom Christ bears witness, whom no man shall tempt, whom all should worship, and serve Him alone? It is, beyond all manner of doubt, that God who also gave the law. For these things had been predicted in the law, and by the words (sententiam) of the law the Lord showed that the law does indeed declare the Word of God from the Father; and the apostate angel of God is destroyed by its voice, being exposed in his true colours, and vanquished by the Son of man keeping the commandment of God. For as in the beginning he enticed man to transgress his Maker's law, and thereby got him into his power; yet his power consists in transgression and apostasy, and with these he bound man [to himself]; so again, on the other hand, it was necessary that through man himself he should, when conquered, be bound with the same chains with which he had bound man, in order that man, being set free, might return to his Lord, leaving to him (Satan) those bonds by which he himself had been fettered, that is, sin. For when Satan is bound, man is set free; since "none can enter a strong man's house and spoil his goods, unless he first bind the strong man himself." The Lord therefore exposes him as speaking contrary to the word of that God who made all things, and subdues him by means of the commandment. Now the law is the commandment of God. The Man proves him to be a fugitive from and a transgressor of the law, an apostate also from God. After [the Man had done this], the Word bound him securely as a fugitive from Himself, and made spoil of his goods,—namely, those men whom he held in bondage, and whom he unjustly used for his own purposes. And justly indeed is he led captive, who had led men unjustly into bondage; while man, who had been led captive in times past, was rescued from the grasp of his possessor, according to the tender mercy of God the Father, who had compassion on His own handiwork, and gave to it salvation, restoring it by means of the Word—that is, by Christ—in order that men might learn by actual proof that he receives incorruptibility not of himself, but by the free gift of God.

23

ATHANASIUS (b. 298) WAS a stalwart defender of the Nicene Creed (325) and until his death in 373, much of his administrative and theological energy was given to the task of uniting the various theological factions combatting Arianism. His theological critique of Arianism was based on soteriological grounds, a being who, as the Arians insisted, was neither fully God nor fully man could not be the saviour of man. The following selections from his essay must be read with the Arian position in mind.[1]

[1] See also *Against the Arians, On Homoiousions, Statement of Faith*, Selection 25.

The Incarnation of the Word of God[*]

ATHANASIUS

. . . because death and corruption were gaining ever firmer hold on them, the human race was in process of destruction. Man, who was created in God's image and in his possession of reason reflected the very Word Himself, was disappearing, and the work of God was being undone. The law of death, which followed from the Transgression, prevailed upon us, and from it there was no escape. The thing that was happening was in truth both monstrous and unfitting. It would, of course, have been unthinkable that God should go back upon His word and that man, having transgressed, should not die; but it was equally monstrous that beings which once had shared the nature of the Word should perish and turn back again into nonexistence through corruption. It was unworthy of the goodness of God that creatures made by Him should be brought to nothing through the deceit wrought upon man by the devil; and it was supremely unfitting that the work of God in mankind should disappear, either through their own negligence or through the deceit of evil spirits. As, then, the creatures whom He had created reasonable, like the Word, were in fact perishing, and such noble works were on the road to ruin, what then was God, being Good, to do? Was He to let corruption and death have their way with them? In that case, what was the use of having made them in the beginning? Surely it would have been better never to have been created at all than, having been created, to be neglected and perish; and, besides that, such indifference to the ruin of His own work before His very eyes would argue not goodness in God but limitation, and that far more than if He had never created men at all. It was impossible, therefore, that God should leave man to be carried off by corruption, because it would be unfitting and unworthy of Himself. . . .

What—or rather Who was it that was needed for such grace and such recall as we require? Who, save the Word of God Himself, Who also in the beginning had made all things out of nothing? His part it was, and His alone, both to bring again the corruptible to incorruption and to maintain for the Father His consistency of character with all. For He alone, being Word of the Father and above all, was in consequence both able to re-create all, and worthy to suffer on behalf of all and to be an ambassador for all with the Father.

* Reprinted with permission of the publisher from The Incarnation of the Word of God Being the Treatise of St. Athanasius by St. Athanasius, tr. by a Religious of CSMV. Copyright 1946 by The Macmillan Company. Also with permission of Geoffrey Bles Ltd.

For this purpose, then, the incorporeal and incorruptible and immaterial Word of God entered our world. In one sense, indeed, He was not far from it before, for no part of creation had ever been without Him Who, while ever abiding in union with the Father, yet fills all things that are. But now He entered the World in a new way, stooping to our level in His love and Self-revealing to us. He saw the reasonable race, the race of men that, like Himself, expressed the Father's Mind, wasting out of existence, and death reigning over all in corruption. He saw that corruption held us all the closer, because it was the penalty for the Transgression; He saw, too, how unthinkable it would be for the law to be repealed before it was fulfilled. He saw how unseemly it was that the very things of which He Himself was the Artificer should be disappearing. He saw how the surpassing wickedness of men was mounting up against them; He saw also their universal liability to death. All this He saw and, pitying our race, moved with compassion for our limitation, unable to endure that death should have the mastery, rather than that His creatures should perish and the work of His Father for us men come to nought, He took to Himself a body, a human body even as our own. Nor did He will merely to become embodied or merely to appear; had that been so, He could have revealed His divine majesty in some other and better way. No, He took our body, and not only so, but He took it directly from a spotless, stainless virgin, without the agency of human father—a pure body, untainted by intercourse with man. He, the Mighty One, the Artificer of all, Himself prepared this body in the virgin as a temple for Himself, and took it for His very own, as the instrument through which He was known and in which He dwelt. Thus, taking a body like our own, because all our bodies were liable to the corruption of death, He surrendered His body to death instead of all, and offered it to the Father. This He did out of sheer love for us, so that in His death all might die, and the law of death thereby be abolished because, having fulfilled in His body that for which it was appointed, it was thereafter voided of its power for men. This He did that He might turn again to incorruption men who had turned back to corruption, and make them alive through death by the appropriation of His body and by the grace of His resurrection. Thus He would make death to disappear from them as utterly as straw from fire.

The Word perceived that corruption could not be got rid of otherwise than through death; yet He Himself, as the Word, being immortal and the Father's Son, was such as could not die. For this reason, therefore, He assumed a body capable of death, in order that it, through belonging to the Word Who is above all, might become in dying a sufficient exchange for all, and, itself remaining incorruptible through His indwelling, might thereafter put an end to corruption for all others as well, by the grace of the resurrection. It was by surrendering to death the body which He had taken, as an offering and sacrifice free from every stain, that He forthwith abolished death for His human brethren by the offering of the equivalent. For naturally, since the Word of God was above all, when He offered His own temple and bodily instrument as a substitute for the life of all, He fulfilled in death all that was required. Naturally also, through this union of the immortal Son of God with our human nature, all men were clothed with incorruption in the promise of the resurrection. For the solidarity of mankind is such that, by virtue of the Word's indwelling in a single human body, the corruption which goes with death has lost its power over all. You know how it is when some great king enters a large city and dwells in one of its houses; because of his dwelling in that single house, the whole city is honoured, and enemies and robbers cease to molest it. Even so is it with the King of all; He has come into our country and dwelt in one body amidst the many, and in consequence the designs of the enemy against mankind have been foiled, and the corruption of death, which formerly held them in its power, has simply ceased to be. For the human race would have perished utterly had not the Lord and Saviour of all, the Son of God, come among us to put an end to death. . . .

What, then, was God to do? What else could He possibly do, being God, but renew His Image in mankind, so that through it men might once more come to know Him? And how could this be done save by the coming of the very Image Himself, our Saviour Jesus Christ? Men could not have done it, for they are only made after the Image; nor could angels have done it, for they are not the images of God. The Word of God came in His own Person, because it was He alone, the Image of the Father, Who could re-create man made after the Image.

. . . when writers on this sacred theme speak of Him as eating and drinking and being born, they mean that the body, as a body, was born and sustained with the food proper to it nature; while God the Word, Who was united with it, was at the same time ordering the universe and revealing Himself through His bodily acts as not man only but God. Those acts are rightly said to be His acts, because the body which did them did indeed belong to Him and none other; moreover, it was right that they should be thus attributed to Him as Man, in order to show that His body was a real one and not merely an appearance. From such ordinary acts as being born and taking food, He was recognised as being actually present in the body; but by the extraordinary acts which He did through the body He proved Himself to be the Son of God. That is the meaning of His words to the unbelieving Jews: "If I do not the works of My Father, believe Me not; but if I do, even if ye believe not Me, believe My works, that ye may know that the Father is in Me and I in the Father."

Invisible in Himself, He is known from the works of creation; so also, when His Godhead is veiled in human nature, His bodily acts still declare Him to be not man only, but the Power and Word of God. To speak authoritatively to evil spirits, for instance, and to drive them out, is not human but divine; and who could see Him curing all the diseases to which mankind is prone, and still deem Him mere man and not also God? He cleansed lepers, He made the lame to walk, He opened the ears of the deaf and the eyes of the blind, there was no sickness or weakness that He did not drive away. Even the most casual observer can see that these were acts of God. The healing of the man born blind, for instance, who but the Father and Artificer of man, the Controller of his whole being, could thus have restored the faculty denied at birth? He Who did thus must surely be Himself the Lord of birth. This is proved also at the outset of His becoming Man. He formed His own body from the virgin; and that is no small proof of His Godhead, since He Who made that was the Maker of all else. And would not anyone infer from the fact of that body being begotten of a virgin only, without human father, that He Who appeared in it was also the Maker and Lord of all beside? . . .

All these things the Saviour thought fit to do, so that, recognising His bodily acts as works of God, men who were blind to His presence in creation might regain knowledge of the Father. For, as I said before, who that saw His authority over evil spirits and their response to it could doubt that He was, indeed, the Son, the Wisdom and the Power of God? Even the very creation broke silence at His behest and, marvellous to relate, confessed with one voice before the cross, that monument of victory, that He Who suffered thereon in the body was not man only, but Son of God and Saviour of all. The sun veiled his face, the earth quaked, the mountains were rent asunder, all men were stricken with awe. These things showed that Christ on the cross was God, and that all creation was His slave and was bearing witness by its fear to the presence of its Master.

Thus, then, God the Word revealed Himself to men through His works. We must next consider the end of His earthly life and the nature of His bodily death. This is, indeed, the very centre of our faith, and everywhere you hear men speak of it; by it, too, no less than by His other acts, Christ is revealed as God and Son of God.

We have dealt as far as circumstances and our own understanding permit with the reason for His bodily manifestation. We have seen that to change the corruptible to incorruption was proper to none other than the Saviour Himself, Who in the beginning made all things out of nothing; that only the Image of the Father could re-create the likeness of the Image in men, that none save our Lord Jesus Christ could give to mortals immortality, and that only the Word Who orders all things and is alone the Father's true and sole-begotten Son could teach men about Him and abolish the worship of idols. But beyond all this, there was a debt owing which must needs be paid; for, as I said before, all men were due to die. Here, then, is the second reason why the Word dwelt among us, namely that having proved His Godhead by His works, He might offer the sacrifice on behalf of all, surrendering His own temple to death in place of all, to settle man's account with death and free him from the primal transgression. In the same act also He showed Himself mightier than death, displaying His own body incorruptible as the first-fruits of the resurrection.

You must not be surprised if we repeat ourselves in dealing with this subject. We are speaking of the good pleasure of God and of the things which He in His loving wisdom thought fit to do, and it is better to put the same thing in several ways than to run the risk of leaving something out. The body of the Word, then, being a real human body, in spite of its having been uniquely formed from a virgin, was of itself mortal and, like other bodies, liable to death. But the indwelling of the Word loosed it from this natural liability, so that corruption could not touch it. Thus it happened that two opposite marvels took place at once: the death of all was consummated in the Lord's body; yet, because the Word was in it, death and corruption were in the same act utterly abolished. Death there had to be, and death for all, so that the due of all might be paid. Wherefore, the Word, as I said, being Himself incapable of death, assumed a mortal body, that He might offer it as His own in place of all, and suffering for the sake of all through His union with it, "might bring to nought Him that had the power of death, that is, the devil, and might deliver them who all their lifetime were enslaved by the fear of death."

Have no fear, then. Now that the common Saviour of all has died on our behalf, we who believe in Christ no longer die, as men die aforetime, in fulfillment of the threat of the law. That condemnation has come to an end; and now that, by the grace of the resurrection, corruption has been banished and done away, we are loosed from our mortal bodies in God's good time for each, so that we may obtain thereby a better resurrection. Like seeds cast into the earth, we do not perish in our dissolution, but like them shall rise again, death having been brought to nought by the grace of the Saviour. That is why blessed Paul, through whom we all have surety of the resurrection, says: "This corruptible must put on incorruption and this mortal must put on immortality; but when this corruptible shall have put on incorruption and this mortal shall have put on immortality, then shall be brought to pass the saying that is written, 'Death is swallowed up in victory. O Death, where is thy sting? O Grave, where is thy victory?'"

33 GREGORY OF NYSSA'S "FISH HOOK" interpretation is one of the clearest statements of the "ransom to the devil" theory of the atonement. Gregory was Bishop of the Cappadocian town, Nyssa, from 372 to his death about 395. He, his brother,

Basil of Caesarea, and Gregory of Nazianzen were the leaders of the Cappadocian school of thought that became so influential in the post-Nicene years. On the doctrine of the atonement, however, these men did not agree. Gregory of Nazianzen wrote against Gregory of Nyssa's suggestion that the Devil "swallowed" the bait, the God-man, and through God's deception of the Devil, man was released from bondage. The Bishop of Nyssa saw no alternative, despite the unhappy imagery, to a theory that would do full justice to God's wisdom and justice.

The Great Catechism*

GREGORY OF NYSSA

CHAPTER 20

The object of our inquiry in the case of God is before all things the indications of His goodness. And what testimony to His goodness could there be more palpable than this, viz. His regaining to Himself the allegiance of one who had revolted to the opposite side, instead of allowing the fixed goodness of His nature to be affected by the variableness of the human will? . . . For, as in the case of persons who are in a sickly condition, there are probably many who wish that a man were not in such evil plight, but it is only they in whom there is some technical ability operating in behalf of the sick, who bring their good-will on their behalf to a practical issue, so it is absolutely needful that wisdom should be conjoined with goodness. In what way, then, is wisdom contemplated in combination with goodness; in the actual events, that is, which have taken place? because one cannot observe a good purpose in the abstract; a purpose cannot possibly be revealed unless it has the light of some events upon it. Well, the things accomplished, progressing as they did in orderly series and sequence, reveal the wisdom and the skill of the Divine economy. And, since, as has been before remarked, wisdom, when combined with justice, then absolutely becomes a virtue, but, if it be disjoined from it, cannot in itself alone be good, it were well moreover in this discussion of the Dispensation in regard to man, to consider attentively in the light of each other these two qualities; I mean, its wisdom and its justice.

* From Gregory of Nyssa, "The Great Catechism," tr. by William Moore and H. A. Wilson, A Select Library of Nicene and Post-Nicene Fathers, Vol. V, Second series. Grand Rapids, Mich.: Wm. B. Eerdmans Publishing Co., 1954.

CHAPTER 21

What, then, is justice? We distinctly remember what in the course of our argument we said in the commencement of this treatise; namely, that man was fashioned in imitation of the Divine nature, preserving his resemblance to the Deity as well in other excellences as in possession of freedom of the will, yet being of necessity of a nature subject to change. For it was not possible that a being who derived his origin from an alteration should be altogether free from this liability. For the passing from a state of non-existence into that of existence is a kind of alteration; when being, that is, by the exercise of Divine power takes the place of nonentity. In the following special respect, too, alteration is necessarily observable in man, namely, because man was an imitation of the Divine nature, and unless some distinctive difference had been occasioned, the imitating subject would be entirely the same as that which it resembles; but in this instance, it is to be observed, there is a difference between that which "was made in the image" and its pattern; namely this, that the one is not subject to change, while the other is (for, as has been described, it has come into existence through an alteration), and being thus subject to alteration does not always continue in its existing state. For alteration is a kind of movement ever advancing from the present state to another; and there are two forms of this movement; the one being ever towards what is good, and in this the advance has no check, because no goal of the course to be traversed can be reached, while the other is in the direction of the contrary, and of it this is the essence, that it has no subsistence; for, as has been before stated, the contrary state to goodness conveys some such notion of opposition, as when we say, for instance, that that which is is logically opposed to that which is not, and that existence is so opposed to non-existence. Since, then, by reason of this impulse and movement of changeful alteration it is not possible that the nature of the subject of this change should remain self-centered and unmoved, but there is always something towards which the will is tending, the appetency for moral beauty naturally drawing it on to movement, this beauty is in one instance really such in its nature, in another it is not so, only blossoming with an illusive appearance of beauty; and the criterion of these two kinds is the mind that dwells within us. Under these circumstances it is a matter of risk whether we happen to choose the real beauty, or whether we are diverted from its choice by some deception arising from appearance, and thus drift away to the opposite; as happened, we are told in the heathen fable, to the dog which looked askance at the reflection in the water of what it carried in its mouth, but let go the real food, and, opening its mouth wide to swallow the image of it, still hungered. Since, then, the mind has been disappointed in its craving for the real good, and diverted to that which is not such, being persuaded, through the deception of the great advocate and inventor of vice, that that was beauty which was just the opposite (for this deception would never have succeeded, had not the glamour of beauty been spread over the hook of vice like a bait),—the man, I say, on the one hand, who had enslaved himself by indulgence to the enemy of his life, being of his own accord in this unfortunate condition, —I ask you to investigate, on the other hand, those qualities which suit and go along with our conception of the Deity, such as goodness, wisdom, power, immortality, and all else that has the stamp of superiority. As good, then, the Deity entertains pity for fallen man; as wise He is not ignorant of the means for his recovery; while a just decision must also form part of that wisdom; for no one would ascribe that genuine justice to the absence of wisdom.

CHAPTER 22

What, then, under these circumstances is justice? It is the not exercising any arbitrary sway over him who has us in his power, nor, by tearing us away by a violent exercise of force from his hold, thus leaving some colour for a just complaint to him who enslaved man through sensual pleasure. For as they who have bartered away their freedom for money are the slaves of those who have purchased them (for they have constituted themselves their own sellers, and it is not allowable either for themselves or any one else in their behalf to call freedom to their aid, not even though those who have thus reduced themselves to this sad state are of noble birth; and, if any one out of regard for the person who has so sold himself should use violence against him who has bought him, he will clearly be acting unjustly in thus arbitrarily rescuing one who has been legally purchased as a slave, whereas, if he wishes to pay a price to get such a one away, there is no law to prevent that), on the same principle, now that we had voluntarily bartered away our freedom, it was requisite that no arbitrary method of recovery, but the one consonant with justice should be devised by Him Who in His goodness had undertaken our rescue. Now this method is in a measure this; to make over to the master of the slave whatever ransom he may agree to accept for the person in his possession.

CHAPTER 23

What, then, was it likely that the master of the slave would choose to receive in his stead? It is possible in the way of inference to make a guess as to his wishes in the matter, if, that is, the manifest indications of what we are seeking for should come into our hands. He then, who, as we before stated in the beginning of this treatise, shut his eyes to the good in his envy of man in his happy condition, he who generated in himself the murky cloud of wickedness, he who suffered from the disease of the love of rule, that primary and fundamental cause of propension to the bad and the mother, so to speak, of all the wickedness that follows,—what would he ac- cept in exchange for the thing which he held, but something, to be sure, higher and better, in the way of ransom, that thus, by receiving a gain in the exchange, he might foster the more his own special passion of pride? Now unquestionably in not one of those who had lived in history from the beginning of the world had been been conscious of any such circum- stance as he observed to surround Him Who then manifested Himself, i.e., conception without carnal connection, birth without impurity, motherhood with virginity, voices of the unseen testifying from above to a transcendent worth, the healing of natural disease, without the use of means and of an extraordinary character, proceeding from Him by the mere utterance of a word and exercise of His will, the restoration of the dead to life, the absolu- tion of the damned, the fear with which He inspired devils, His power over tempests, His walking through the sea, not by the waters separating on either side, and, as in the case of Moses' miraculous power, making bare its depths for those who passed through, but by the surface of the water present- ing solid ground for His feet, and by a firm and hard resistance supporting His steps; then, His disregard for food as long as it pleased Him to abstain, His abundant banquets in the wilderness wherewith many thousands were fully fed (though neither did the heavens pour down manna on them, nor was their need supplied by the earth producing corn for them in its natural way, but that instance of munificence came out of the ineffable store-houses of His Divine power), the bread ready in the hands of those who distributed it, as if they were actually reaping it, and becoming more, the more the eaters were filled; and then, the banquet on the fish; not that the sea sup- plied their need, but He Who had stocked the sea with its fish. But how is it possible to narrate in succession each one of the Gospel miracles? The Enemy, therefore, beholding in Him such power, saw also in Him an oppor- tunity for an advance, in the exchange, upon the value of what he held. For this reason, he chooses Him as a ransom for those who were shut up in the prison of death. But it was out of his power to look on the unclouded aspect of God; he must see in Him some portion of that fleshly nature which through sin he had so long held in bondage. Therefore it was that the Deity was invested with the flesh, in order, that is, to secure that he, by looking upon something congenial and kindred to himself, might have no fears in approaching that supereminent power; and might yet by per- ceiving that power, showing as it did, yet only gradually, more and more splendour in the miracles, deem what was seen an object of desire rather than of fear. Thus, you see how goodness was conjoined with justice, and how wisdom was not divorced from them. For to have devised that the Divine power should have been containable in the envelopment of a body, to the end that the Dispensation in our behalf might not be thwarted through any fear inspired by the Deity actually appearing, affords a demonstration of all these qualities at once—goodness, wisdom, justice. His choosing to save man is a testimony of his goodness; His making the redemption of the captive a matter of exchange exhibits His justice, while the invention whereby He enabled the Enemy to apprehend that of which he was before incapable, is a manifestation of supreme wisdom.

CHAPTER 24

But possibly one who has given his attention to the course of the preceding remarks may inquire: "wherein is the power of the Deity, wherein is the imperishableness of that Divine power, to be traced in the processes you have described?" In order, therefore, to make this also clear, let us take a survey of the sequel of the Gospel mystery, where that Power conjoined with Love is more especially exhibited. In the first place, then, that the omnipotence of the Divine nature should have had strength to descend to the humiliation of humanity, furnishes a clearer proof of that omnipotence than even the greatness and supernatural character of the miracles. For that something pre-eminently great should be wrought out by Divine power is, in a manner, in accordance with, and consequent upon the Divine nature; nor is it startling to hear it said that the whole of the created world, and all that is understood to be beyond the range of visible things, subsists by the power of God, His will giving it existence according to His good pleasure. But this His descent to the humility of man is a kind of superabundant exercise of power, which thus finds no check even in directions which contravene nature. It is the peculiar property of the essence of fire to tend upwards; no one, therefore, deems it wonderful in the case of flame to see that natural operation. But should the flame be seen to stream downwards, like heavy bodies, such a fact would be regarded as a miracle; namely, how fire still remains fire, and yet, by this change of direction in its motion, passes out of its nature by being borne downward. In like manner, it is not the vastness of the heavens, and the bright shining of its constellations, and the order of the universe, and the unbroken administration over all existence that so manifestly displays the transcendent power of the Deity, as this condescension to the weakness of our nature; the way, in fact, in which sublimity, existing in lowliness, is actually seen in lowliness, and yet descends not from its height, and in which Deity, entwined as it is with the nature of man, becomes this, and yet still is that. For since, as has been said before, it was not in the nature of the opposing power to come in contact with the undiluted presence of God, and to undergo His unclouded manifestation, therefore, in order to secure that the ransom in our behalf might be easily accepted by him who required it, the Deity was hidden under the veil of our nature, that so, as with ravenous fish, the hook of the Deity might be gulped down along with the bait of flesh, and thus, life being introduced into the house of death, and light shining in darkness, that which is diametically opposed to light and life might vanish; for it is not in the nature of darkness to remain when light is present, or of death to exist when life is active. Let us, then, by way of summary take up the train of the argument for the Gospel mystery, and thus complete our answer to those who question this Dispensation of God, and show them on what ground it is that the Deity by a personal intervention works out the salvation of man. It is certainly most necessary that in every point the conceptions we entertain of the Deity should be such as befit the subject, and not that, while one idea worthy of His sublimity should be retained, another equally belonging to that estimate of Deity should be dismissed from it; on the contrary, every exalted notion, every devout thought, must most surely enter into our belief in God, and each must be made dependent on each in a necessary sequence. Well, then; it has been pointed out that His goodness, wisdom, justice, power, incapability of decay, are all of them in evidence in the doctrine of the Dispensation in which we are. His goodness is caught sight of in His election to save lost man; His wisdom and justice have been displayed in the method of our salvation; His power, in that, though born in the likeness and fashion of a man, on the lowly level of our nature, and in accordance with that likeness raising the expectation that he could be overmastered by death, he, after such a birth, nevertheless produced the effects peculiar and natural to Him. Now it is the peculiar effect of light to make darkness vanish, and of life to destroy death. Since, then, we have been led astray from the right path, and diverted from that life which was ours at the beginning, and brought under the sway of death, what is there improbable in the lesson we are taught by the Gospel mystery, if it be this; that cleansing reaches those who are befouled with sin, and life the dead, and guidance the wanderers, in order that defilement may be cleansed, error corrected, and what was dead restored to life?

CHAPTER 25

That Deity should be born in our nature, ought not reasonably to present any strangeness to the minds of those who do not take too narrow a view of things. For who, when he takes a survey of the universe, is so simple as not to believe that there is Deity in everything, penetrating it, embracing it, and seated in it? For all things depend on Him Who is, nor can there be anything which has not its being in Him Who is. If, therefore, all things in Him, and He in all things, why are they scandalized at the plan of Revelation, when it teaches that God was born among men, that same God Whom we are convinced is even now not outside mankind? For although this last form of God's presence amongst us is not the same as that former presence, still His existence amongst us equally both then and now is evidenced; only now He Who holds together Nature in existence is transfused in us; while at that other time He was transfused throughout our nature, in order that our nature might by this transfusion of the Divine become itself divine, rescued as it was from death, and put beyond the reach of the caprice of the antagonist. For His return from death becomes to our mortal race the commencement of our return to the immortal life.

CHAPTER 26

Still, in his examination of the amount of justice and wisdom discoverable in this Dispensation a person is, perhaps, induced to entertain the thought that it was by means of a certain amount of deceit that God carried out this scheme on our behalf. For that not by pure Deity alone, but by Deity veiled in human nature, God, without the knowledge of His enemy, got within the lines of him who had man in his power, is in some measure a fraud and a surprise; seeing that it is the peculiar way with those who want to deceive to divert in another direction the expectations of their intended victims, and then to effect something quite different from what these latter expected. But he who has regard for truth will agree that the essential qualities of justice and wisdom are before all things these; viz. of justice, to give to every one according to his due; of wisdom, not to pervert justice, and yet at the same time not to dissociate the benevolent aim of the love of mankind from the verdict of justice, but skilfully to combine both these requisites together, in regard to justice returning the due recompense, in regard to kindness not swerving from the aim of that love of man. Let us see, then, whether these two qualities are not to be observed in that which took place. That repayment, adequate to the debt, by which the deceiver was in his turn deceived, exhibits the justice of the dealing, while the object aimed at is a testimony to the goodness of Him who effected it. It is, indeed, the property of justice to assign to every one those particular results of which he has sunk already the foundations and the causes, just as the earth returns its harvests according to the kinds of seeds thrown into it; while it is the property of wisdom, in its very manner of giving equivalent returns, not to depart from the kinder course. Two persons may both mix poison with food, one with the design of taking life, the other with the design of saving that life; the one using it as a poison, the other only as an antidote to poison; and in no way does the manner of the cure adopted spoil the aim and purpose of the benefit intended; for although a mixture of poison with the food may be effected by both of these persons alike, yet looking at their intention we are indignant with the one and approve the other; so in this instance, by the reasonable rule of justice, he who practised deception receives in return that very treatment, the seeds of which he had himself sown of his own free will. He who first deceived man by the bait of sensual pleasure is himself deceived by the presentment of the human form. But as regards the aim and purpose of what took place, a change in the direction of the nobler is involved; for whereas he, the enemy, effected his deception for the ruin of our nature, He who is at once the just, and good, and wise one, used His device, in which there was deception, for the salvation of him who had perished, and thus not only conferred benefit on the lost one, but on him, too, who had wrought our ruin. For from this approximation of death to life, of darkness to light, of corruption to incorruption, there is effected an obliteration of what is worse, and a passing away of it into nothing, while benefit is conferred on him who is freed from those evils. For it is as when some worthless material has been mixed with gold, and the gold-refiners burn up the foreign and refuse part in the consuming fire, and so restore the more precious substance to its natural lustre: (not that the separation is effected without difficulty, for it takes time for the fire by its melting force to cause the baser matter to disappear; but for all that, this melting away of the actual thing that was embedded in it to the injury of its beauty is a kind of healing of the gold.) In the same way when death, and corruption, and darkness, and every other offshoot of evil had grown into the nature of the author of evil, the approach of the Divine power, acting like fire, and making that unnatural accretion to disappear, thus by purgation of the evil becomes a blessing to that nature, though the separation is agonizing. Therefore even the adversary himself will not be likely to dispute that what took place was both just and salutary, that is, if he shall have attained to a perception of the boon. For it is now as with those who for their cure are subjected to the knife and the cautery; they are angry with the doctors, and wince with the pain of the incision; but if recovery of health be the result of this treatment, and the pain of the cautery passes away, they will feel grateful to those who have wrought this cure upon them. In like manner, when, after long periods of time, the evil of our nature, which now is mixed up with it and has grown with its growth, has been expelled, and when there has been a restoration of those who are now lying in Sin to their primal state, a harmony of thanksgiving will arise from all creation, as well from those who in the process of the purgation have suffered chastisement, as from those who needed not any purgation at all. These and the like benefits the great mystery of the Divine incarnation bestows. For in those points in which He was mingled with humanity, passing as He did through all the accidents proper to human nature, such as birth, rearing, growing up, and advancing even to the taste of death, He accomplished all the results before mentioned, freeing both man from evil, and healing even the introducer of evil himself. For the chastisement, however painful, of moral disease is a healing of its weakness.

3 4

Augustine's treatise, *On The Trinity*, is an extensive and elaborate theological work, touching on many of the traditional problems. It is approximately 180,000 words and the fifteen books were written during the first and second decades of the fifth century, after the Council of Nicaea (325) and before the Council of Chalcedon (451). Throughout the work Augustine makes clear that the trinitarian doctrine is inseparable from the affirmation of the unity of God; Augustine cannot write about the unity of God without considering its trinitarian character. By examination of human analogies, he sought to throw light on this affirmation of the church.[1]

The second selection is from Tractate XXXVI of Augustine's commentary *On the Gospel of John* where he deals with Chapter VIII, verses 15–18.

A. On the Trinity*

AUGUSTINE

BOOK 9

1. We certainly seek a trinity,—not any trinity, but that Trinity which is God, and the true and supreme and only God. Let my hearers then wait, for we are still seeking. And no one justly finds fault with such a search, if at least he who seeks that which either to know or to utter is most difficult, is steadfast in the faith. . . . For a certain faith is in someway the starting-point of knowledge; but a certain knowledge will not be made perfect, except after this life, when we shall see face to face. Let us therefore be thus minded, so as to know that the disposition to seek the truth is more safe than that which presumes things unknown to be known. Let us therefore so seek as if we should find, and so find as if we were about to seek . . . let

* From Augustine, *On The Trinity*, tr. by A. W. Haddan, A Select Library of Nicene and Post-Nicene Fathers, Vol. III, First series. Grand Rapids, Mich.: Wm. B. Eerdmans Publishing Co., 1956.

[1] See also *Letter 120*, Selection 4A; "God—the Eternal Creator," *The City of God*, Selection 4B; *Letter 217*, Selection 39A; *A Treatise on Rebuke and Grace*, Selection 39B; *Against the Pelagians*, Selection 39C; *On Baptism*, Selection 55A; *The City of God*, Selection 55B.

us believe that the Father, and the Son, and the Holy Spirit is one God, the Creator and Ruler of the whole creature; and that the Father is not the Son, nor the Holy Spirit either the Father or the Son, but a trinity of persons mutually interrelated, and a unity of an equal essence. And let us seek to understand this, praying for help from Himself, whom we wish to understand; and as much as He grants, desiring to explain what we understand with so much pious care and anxiety, that even if in any case we say one thing for another, we may at least say nothing unworthy. As, for the sake of example, if we say anything concerning the Father that does not properly belong to the Father, or does belong to the Son, or to the Holy Spirit, or to the Trinity itself; and if anything of the Son which does not properly suit with the Son, or at all events which does suit with the Father, or with the Holy Spirit, or with the Trinity; or if, again, anything concerning the Holy Spirit, which is not fitly a property of the Holy Spirit, yet is not alien from the Father, or from the Son, or from the one God the Trinity itself. Even as now our wish is to see whether the Holy Spirit is properly that love which is most excellent; which if He is not, either the Father is love, or the Son, or the Trinity itself; since we cannot withstand the most certain faith and weighty authority of scripture, saying, "God is love." And yet we ought not to deviate into profane error, so as to say anything of the Trinity which does not suit the Creator, but rather the creature, or which is feigned outright by mere empty thought.

2. And this being so, let us direct our attention to those three things which we fancy we have found. We are not yet speaking of heavenly things, nor yet of God the Father, and Son, and Holy Spirit, but of that inadequate image, which yet is an image, that is, man; for our feeble mind perhaps can gaze upon this more familiarly and more easily. Well then, when I, who make this inquiry, love anything, there are three things concerned— myself, and that which I love, and love itself. For I do not love love, except I love a lover; for there is no love where nothing is loved. Therefore there are three things—he who loves, and that which is loved, and love. But what if I love none except myself? Will there not then be two things—that which I love, and love? For he who loves and that which is loved are the same when any one loves himself; just as to love and to be loved, in the same way, is the very same thing when any one loves himself. Since the same thing is said, when it is said, he loves himself, and he is loved by himself. For in that case to love and to be loved are not two different things; just as he who loves and he who is loved are not two different persons. But yet, even so, love and what is loved are still two things. For there is no love when any one loves himself, except when love itself is loved. But it is one thing to love one's self, another to love one's own love. For love is not loved, unless as already loving something; since where nothing is loved, there is no love. Therefore there are two things when any one loves himself—love, and that

which is loved. For then he that loves and that which is loved are one. Whence it seems that it does not follow that three things are to be understood wherever love is. For let us put aside from the inquiry all the other many things of which a man consists; and in order that we may discover clearly what we are now seeking, as far as in such a subject is possible, let us treat of the mind alone. The mind, then, when it loves itself, discloses two things—mind and love. But what is to love one's self, except to wish to help one's self to the enjoyment of self? And when any one wishes himself to be just as much as he is, then the will is on a par with the mind, and the love is equal to him who loves. And if love is a substance, it is certainly not body, but spirit; and the mind also is not body, but spirit. Yet love and mind are not two spirits, but one spirit; nor yet two essences, but one: and yet here are two things that are one, he that loves and love; or, if you like so to put it, that which is loved and love. And these two, indeed, are mutually said relatively. Since he who loves is referred to love, and love to him who loves. For he who loves, loves with some love, and love is the love of some one who loves. But mind and spirit are not said relatively, but express essence. For mind and spirit do not exist because the mind and spirit of some particular man exists. For if we subtract the body from that which is man, which is so called with the conjunction of body, the mind and spirit remain. But if we subtract him that loves, then there is no love; and if we subtract love, then there is no one that loves. And therefore, in so far as they are mutually referred to one another, they are two; but whereas they are spoken in respect to themselves, each are spirit, and both together also are one spirit; and each are mind, and both together one mind. Where, then, is the Trinity? Let us attend as much as we can, and let us invoke the everlasting light, that He may illuminate our darkness, and that we may see in ourselves, as much as we are permitted, the image of God.

3. For the mind cannot love itself, except also it know itself; for how can it love what it does not know? Or if any body says that the mind, from either general or special knowledge, believes itself of such a character as it has by experience found others to be, and therefore loves itself, he speaks most foolishly. For whence does a mind know another mind, if it does not know itself? For the mind does not know other minds and not know itself, as the eye of the body sees other eyes and does not see itself; for we see bodies through the eyes of the body, because, unless we are looking into a mirror, we cannot refract and reflect the rays into themselves, which shine forth through those eyes, and touch whatever we discern,—a subject, indeed, which is treated of most subtly and obscurely, until it be clearly demonstrated whether the fact be so, or whether it be not. But whatever is the nature of the power by which we discern through the eyes, certainly, whether it be rays or anything else, we cannot discern with the eyes that power itself; but we inquire into it with the mind, and if possible, understand

even this with the mind. As the mind, then, itself gathers the knowledge of corporeal things through the senses of the body, so of incorporeal things through itself. Therefore it knows itself also through itself, since it is incorporeal; for if it does not know itself, it does not love itself.

4. But as there are two things (duo quaedam), the mind and the love of it, when it loves itself; so there are two things, the mind and the knowledge of it, when it knows itself. Therefore the mind itself, and the love of it, and the knowledge of it, are three things (tria quaedam), and these three are one; and when they are perfect they are equal. For if one loves himself less than as he is,—as for example, suppose that the mind of a man only loves itself as much as the body of a man ought to be loved, whereas the mind is more than the body,—then it is in fault, and its love is not perfect. Again, if it loves itself more than as it is,—as if, for instance, it loves itself as much as God is to be loved, whereas the mind is incomparably less than God,—here also it is exceedingly in fault, and its love of self is not perfect. But it is in fault more perversely and wrongly still, when it loves the body as much as God is to be loved. Also, if knowledge is less than that thing which is known, and which can be fully known, then knowledge is not perfect; but if it is greater, then the nature which knows is above that which is known, as the knowledge of the body is greater than the body itself, which is known by that knowledge. For knowledge is a kind of life in the reason of the knower, but the body is not life; and any life is greater than any body, not in bulk, but in power. But when the mind knows itself, its own knowledge does not rise above itself, because itself knows, and itself is known. When, therefore, it knows itself entirely, and no other thing with itself, then its knowledge is equal to itself; because its knowledge is not from another nature, since it knows itself. And when it perceives itself entirely, and nothing more, then it is neither less nor greater. We said therefore rightly, that these three things, [mind, love, and knowledge], when they are perfect, are by consequence equal. . . . [18]. And so there is a kind of image of the Trinity in the mind itself, and the knowledge of it, which is its offspring and its word concerning itself, and love as a third, and these three are one, and one substance. Neither is the offspring less, since the mind knows itself according to the measure of its own being; nor is the love less, since it loves itself according to the measure both of its own knowledge and of its own being. . . .

BOOK 10

17. . . . let us especially consider and discuss these three—memory, understanding, will [the image of the Trinity in the mind]. For we may commonly discern in these three the character of the abilities of the young also; since the more tenaciously and easily a boy remembers, and the more

acutely he understands, and the more ardently he studies, the more praise-worthy is he in point of ability. But when the question is about any one's learning, then we ask not how solidly and easily he remembers, or how shrewdly he understands; but what it is that he remembers, and what it is that he understands. And because the mind is regarded as praiseworthy, not only as being learned, but also as being good, one gives heed not only to what he remembers and what he understands, but also to what he wills (velit); not how ardently he wills, but first what it is he wills, and then how greatly he wills it. For the mind that loves eagerly is then to be praised, when it loves that which ought to be loved eagerly. Since, then, we speak of these three—ability, knowledge, use—the first of these is to be considered under the three heads, of what a man can do in memory, and understanding, and will. The second of them is to be considered in regard to that which any one has in his memory and in his understanding, which he has attained by a studious will. But the third, viz. use, lies in the will, which handles those things that are contained in the memory and under-standing, whether it refer them to anything further, or rest satisfied with them as an end. For to use, is to take up something into the power of the will; and to enjoy, is to use with joy, not any longer of hope, but of the actual thing. Accordingly, every one who enjoys, uses; for he takes up some-thing into the power of the will, wherein he also is satisfied as with an end. But not everyone who uses, enjoys, if he has sought after that, which he takes up into the power of the will, not on account of the thing itself, but on account of something else.

18. Since, then, these three, memory, understanding, will, are not three lives, but one life; nor three minds, but one mind; it follows certainly that neither are they three substances, but one substance. Since memory, which is called life, and mind, and substance, is so called in respect to itself; but it is called memory, relatively to something. And I should say the same also of understanding and of will, since they are called understanding and will relatively to something; but each in respect to itself is life, and mind, and essence. And hence these three are one, in that they are one life, one mind, one essence; and whatever else they are severally called in respect to them-selves, they are called also together, not plurally, but in the singular num-ber. But they are three, in that wherein they are mutually referred to each other; and if they were not equal, and this not only each to each, but also each to all, they certainly could not mutually contain each other; for not only is each contained by each, but also all by each. For I remember that I have memory and understanding, and will; and I understand that I under-stand, and will, and remember; and I will that I will, and remember, and understand; and I remember together my whole memory, and understand-ing, and will. For that of my memory which I do not remember, is not in my memory; and nothing is so much in the memory as memory itself.

Therefore I remember the whole memory. Also, whatever I understand I know that I understand, and I know that I will whatever I will; but whatever I know I remember. Therefore I remember the whole of my understanding, and the whole of my will. Likewise, when I understand these three things, I understand them together as whole. For there is none of things intelligible which I do not understand, except what I do not know; but what I do not know, I neither remember, nor will. Therefore, whatever of things intelligible I do not understand, it follows also that I neither remember nor will. And whatever of things intelligible I remember and will, it follows that I understand. My will also embraces my whole understanding and my whole memory, whilst I use the whole that I understand and remember. And, therefore, while all are mutually comprehended by each, and as wholes, each as a whole is equal to each as a whole, and each as a whole at the same time to all as wholes; and these three are one, one life, one mind, one essence.

B. On the Gospel of John*

AUGUSTINE

In the four Gospels, or rather in the four books of the one Gospel, Saint John the apostle, not undeservedly in respect of his spiritual understanding compared to the eagle, has elevated his preaching higher and far more sublimely than the other three; and in this elevating of it he would have our hearts likewise lifted up. For the other three evangelists walked with the Lord on earth as with a man; concerning His divinity they have said but little; but this evangelist, as if he disdained to walk on earth, just as in the very opening of his discourse he thundered on us, soared not only above the earth and above the whole compass of air and sky, but even above the whole army of angels and the whole order of invisible powers, and reached to Him by whom all things were made; saying, "In the beginning was the Word, and the Word was with God, and the Word was God. This was in the beginning with God. All things were made by Him, and without Him was nothing made." To this so great sublimity of his beginning all the rest of his preaching well agrees; and he has spoken concerning the divinity of the Lord as none other has spoken. What he had drunk in, the same he gave forth. For it is not without reason that it is recorded of him in this

* From, *Lectures or Tractates on the Gospel According to St. John*, by John Gibb, Vol. I. Edinburgh: T. & T. Clark, 1873.

very Gospel, that at supper he reclined on the Lord's bosom. From that breast then he drank in secret; but what he drank in secret he gave forth openly, that there may come to all nations not only the incarnation of the Son of God, and His passion and resurrection, but also what He was before His incarnation, the only Son of the Father, the Word of the Father, co-eternal with Him that begat, equal with Him by whom He was sent; but yet in that very sending made less, that the Father might be greater.

Whatever, then, you have heard stated in lowly manner concerning the Lord Jesus Christ, think of that economy by which He assumed flesh; but whatever you hear, or read, stated in the Gospel concerning Him that is sublime and high above all creatures, and divine, and equal and coeternal with the Father, be sure that this which you read appertains to the form of God, not to the form of the servant. For if you hold this rule, you who can understand it (inasmuch as you are not all able to understand it, but you are all bound to trust it)—if, I say, you hold this rule, as men walking in the light, you will fight against the calumnies of heretical darkness without fear. For there have not been wanting those who, in reading the Gospel, followed only those testimonies that concern the humility of Christ, and have been deaf to those which have declared His divinity; deaf for this reason, that they may be full of evil words. There have likewise been some, who, giving heed only to those which speak of the excellency of the Lord, even though they have read of His mercy in becoming man for our sakes, have not believed the testimonies, but accounted them false and invented by men; contending that our Lord Jesus Christ was only God, not also man. Some in this way, some in that; both in error. But the Catholic faith, holding from both the truths which each holds and preaching the truth which each believes, as both understood that Christ is God and also believed Him to be man: for each is written and each is true. Shouldst thou assert that Christ is only God, thou deniest the medicine whereby thou wast healed: shouldst thou assert that Christ is only man, thou deniest the power whereby thou wast created. Hold therefore both. O faithful soul and Catholic heart, hold both, believe both, faithfully confess both. Christ is both God and also man. How is Christ God? Equal with the Father, one with the Father. How is Christ man? Born of a virgin, taking upon Himself mortality from man, but not taking iniquity. . . .

"Because I am not alone, but I and the Father that sent me." If He is with Thee, how has He sent Thee? And has He sent Thee, and yet is He also with Thee? Is it so that having been sent, Thou hast not departed from Him? And didst thou come to us, and yet abide there? How is this to be believed, how apprehended? To these two questions I answer: Thou sayest rightly, how is it to be apprehended; how believed, thou sayest not rightly. Rather, for that reason is it right to believe it, because it is not immediately to be apprehended; for if it were a thing to be immediately apprehended, there would be no need to believe it, because it would be seen. It is because thou dost not apprehend that thou believest; but by believing thou art made capable of apprehending. For if thou dost not believe, thou wilt never apprehend, since thou wilt remain less capable. Let faith then purify thee, that understanding may fill thee. "My judgment is true," saith He, "because I am not alone, but I and the Father that sent me." Therefore, O Lord our God, Jesus Christ, Thy sending is Thy incarnation. So I see, so I understand: in short, so I believe, in case it may smack of arrogance to say, so I understand. Doubtless the Lord Jesus Christ is even here; rather, *was* here as to His flesh, *is* here now as to His Godhead: He was both with the Father and had not left the Father. Hence, in that He is said to have been sent and to have come to us, His incarnation is set forth to us, for the Father did not take flesh.

For there are certain heretics called Sabellians, who are also called Patripassians, who affirm that it was the Father Himself that had suffered. Do not thou so affirm, O Catholic; for if thou wilt be a Patripassian, thou wilt not be sane. Understand, then, that the incarnation of the Son is termed the sending of the Son; and do not believe that the Father was incarnate, but do not yet believe that He departed from the incarnate Son. The Son carried flesh, the Father was with the Son. If the Father was in heaven, the Son on earth, how was the Father with the Son? Because both Father and Son were everywhere: for God is not in such manner in heaven as not to be on earth. Hear him who would flee from the judgment of God, and found not a way to flee by: "Whither shall I go," saith he, "from Thy Spirit; and whither shall I flee from Thy face? If I ascend up into heaven; Thou art there." The question was about the earth; hear what follows: "If I descend unto hell, Thou art there." If, then, He is said to be present even in hell, what in the universe remains where He is not present? For the voice of God with the prophet is, "I fill heaven and earth." Hence He is everywhere, who is confined by no place. Turn not thou away from Him, and He is with thee. If thou wouldst come to Him, be not slow to love; for it is not with feet but with affections thou runnest. Thou comest while remaining in one place, if thou believest and lovest. Wherefore He is everywhere; and if everywhere, how not also with the Son? Is it so that He is not with the Son, while, if thou believest, He is even with thee?

How, then, is His judgment true, but because the Son is true? For this He said: "And if I judge, my judgment is true; because I am not alone, but I and the Father that sent me." Just as if He had said, "My judgment is true," because I am the Son of God. How dost Thou prove that Thou art the Son of God? "Because I am not alone, but I and the Father that sent me." Blush, Sabellian; thou hearest the Son, thou hearest the Father. Father is Father, Son is Son. He said not, I am the Father, and I the same am the

Son; but He saith, "I am not alone." Why art Thou not alone? Because the Father is with me. "I am, and the Father that sent me"; thou hearest, "I am, and He that sent me." Lest thou lose sight of the person, distinguish the persons. Distinguished by understanding, do not separate by faithlessness; lest again, fleeing as it were Charybdis, thou rush upon Scylla. For the whirlpool of the impiety of the Sabellians was swallowing thee, to say that the Father is the same who is Son: just now thou hast learned, "I am not alone, but I and the Father that sent me." Thou dost acknowledge that the Father is Father, and that the Son is Son; thou dost rightly acknowledge: but do not say the Father is greater, the Son is less; do not say, the Father is gold, the Son is silver. There is one substance, one Godhead, one co-eternity, perfect equality, no unlikeness.

For if thou only believe that Christ is another, not the same person that the Father is, but yet imagine that in respect of His nature He is somewhat different from the Father, thou hast indeed escaped Charybdis, but thou hast been wrecked on the rocks of Scylla. Steer the middle course, avoid each of the two perilous sides. Father is Father, Son is Son. Thou sayest now, Father is Father, Son is Son: thou hast fortunately escaped the danger of the absorbing whirl; why wouldst thou go unto the other side to say, the Father is this, the Son that? The Son is another person than the Father is, this thou sayest rightly; but that He is different in nature, thou sayest not rightly. Certainly the Son is another person, because He is not the same who is Father; and the Father is another person, because He is not the same who is Son: nevertheless, they are not different in nature, but the self-same is both Father and Son. What means the self-same? God is one. Thou hast heard, "Because I am not alone, but I and the Father that sent me": hear how thou mayest believe Father and Son; hear the Son Himself, "I and the Father are one." He said not, I am the Father; or, I and the Father is one person; but when He says, "I and the Father are one," hear both, both the one, unum, and the are, sumus, and thou shalt be delivered both from Charybdis and from Scylla. In these two words, in that He said one, He delivers thee from Arius; in that He said are, He delivers thee from Sabellius. If one, therefore not diverse; if are, therefore both Father and Son. For He would not say are of one person; but, on the other hand, He would not say one of diverse. Hence the reason why He says, "my judgment is true," is, that thou mayest hear it briefly, because I am the Son of God. But I would have thee in such wise believe that I am the Son of God, that thou mayest understand that the Father is with me: I am not Son in such manner as to have left Him; I am not in such manner here that I should not be with Him; nor is He in such manner there as not to be with me: I have taken to me the form of a servant, yet have I not lost the form of God; therefore He saith, "I am not alone, but I and the Father that sent me."

35

ANSELM'S STATEMENT of the "satisfaction" theory of the atonement is a major document in Christian theology. The essay consists of two parts. The first deals with the unbeliever's critique of Christianity; the second argues that without the God-man, Christ, immortality cannot be obtained. The dialogue form of the essay provides a neat way for Anselm to state his position. Through his naive questioner, Boso, he was able to discuss many of the traditional problems and positions. Anselm sought to show that satisfaction is paid to God, not to the Devil as the "ransom to the devil" theory had stated. Man deserves to be punished; his sin is an infinite sin because it is a sin against God. Man owes all he has to God, all he can do, but God's justice also needs to be satisfied and this man cannot do. Salvation can come only through one who is both God, able to offer satisfaction, and man, responsible for the debt. There is a similarity between Anselm's thesis concerning satisfaction and the concept of sovereignty and justice of feudal society. Sin is essentially rebellion against the sovereign Lord, a refusal of man to render his all to God. The "king" of the universe, as the king of the earthly realm, demands justice and satisfaction for the injury done to his creation. That is man's plight; Anselm offers one interpretation of the restoration of man's relationship with God.

Cur Deus Homo (Why God Man?)[*]

ANSELM

FIRST BOOK

CHAPTER 1

The question on which the whole work rests.

I have been often and most earnestly requested by many, both personally and by letter, that I would hand down in writing the proofs of a certain doctrine of our faith, which I am accustomed to give to inquirers; for they

* From Sidney Norton Deane, tr., St. Anselm Proslogium; Monologium; An Appendix in Behalf of the Fool by Gaunlion; Cur Deus Homo. La Salle, Ill.: The Open Court Publishing Company, 1954.

say that these proofs gratify them, and are considered sufficient. This they ask, not for the sake of attaining to faith by means of reason, but that they may be gladdened by understanding and meditating on those things which they believe; and that, as far as possible, they may be always ready to convince any one who demands of them a reason of that hope which is in us. And this question, both infidels are accustomed to bring up against us, ridiculing Christian simplicity as absurd; and many believers ponder it in their hearts; for what cause or necessity, in sooth, God became man, and by his own death, as we believe and affirm, restored life to the world; when he might have done this, by means of some other being, angelic or human, or merely by his will. Not only the learned, but also many unlearned persons interest themselves in this inquiry and seek for its solution. Therefore, since many desire to consider this subject, and, though it seem very difficult in the investigation, it is yet plain to all in the solution, and attractive for the value and beauty of the reasoning; although what ought to be sufficient has been said by the holy fathers and their successors, yet I will take pains to disclose to inquirers what God has seen fit to lay open to me. And since investigations, which are carried on by question and answer, are thus made more plain to many, and especially to less quick minds, and on that account are more gratifying, I will take to argue with me one of those persons who agitate this subject; one, who among the rest impels me more earnestly to it, so that in this way Boso may question and Anselm reply.

CHAPTER 2

How those things which are to be said should be received.

Boso. As the right order requires us to believe the deep things of Christian faith before we undertake to discuss them by reason; so to my mind it appears a neglect if, after we are established in the faith, we do not seek to understand what we believe. Therefore, since I thus consider myself to hold the faith of our redemption, by the prevenient grace of God, so that, even were I unable in any way to understand what I believe, still nothing could shake my constancy; I desire that you should discover to me, what, as you know, many besides myself ask, for what necessity and cause God, who is omnipotent, should have assumed the littleness and weakness of human nature for the sake of its renewal?

Anselm. You ask of me a thing which is above me, and therefore I tremble to take in hand subjects too lofty for me, lest, when some one may have thought or even seen that I do not satisfy him, he will rather believe that I am in error with regard to the substance of the truth, than that my intellect is not able to grasp it.

Boso. You ought not so much to fear this, because you should call to mind, on the other hand, that it often happens in the discussion of some question that God opens what before lay concealed; and that you should hope for the grace of God, because if you liberally impart those things which you have freely received, you will be worthy to receive higher things to which you have not yet attained. . . .

CHAPTER 3

Objections of infidels and replies of believers.

Boso. Infidels ridiculing our simplicity charge upon us that we do injustice and dishonor to God when we affirm that he descended into the womb of a virgin, that he was born of woman, that he grew on the nourishment of milk and the food of men; and, passing over many other things which seem incompatible with Deity, that he endured fatigue, hunger, thirst, stripes and crucifixion among thieves.

Anselm. We do no injustice or dishonor to God, but give him thanks with all the heart, praising and proclaiming the ineffable height of his compassion. For the more astonishing a thing it is and beyond expectation, that he has restored us from so great and deserved ills in which we were, to so great and unmerited blessings which we had forfeited; by so much the more has he shown his more exceeding love and tenderness towards us. For did they but carefully consider how fitly in this way human redemption is secured, they would not ridicule our simplicity, but would rather join with us in praising the wise beneficence of God. For, as death came upon the human race by the disobedience of man, it was fitting that by man's obedience life should be restored. And, as sin, the cause of our condemnation, had its origin from a woman, so ought the author of our righteousness and salvation to be born of a woman. And so also was it proper that the devil, who, being man's tempter, had conquered him in eating of the tree, should be vanquished by man in the suffering of the tree which man bore. Many other things also, if we carefully examine them, give a certain indescribable beauty to our redemption as thus procured. . . .

CHAPTER 5

How the redemption of man could not be effected by any other being but God.

Boso. If this deliverance were said to be effected somehow by any other being than God (whether it were an angelic or a human being), the mind of man would receive it far more patiently. For God could have made some man without sin, not of a sinful substance, and not a descendant of any man, but just as he made Adam, and by this man it should seem that the work we speak of could have been done.

Anselm. Do you not perceive that, if any other being should rescue man from eternal death, man would rightly be adjudged as the servant of that being? Now if this be so, he would in no wise be restored to that dignity which would have been his had he never sinned. For he, who was to be through eternity only the servant of God and an equal with the holy angels, would now be the servant of a being who was not God, and whom the angels did not serve. . . .

CHAPTER 7

How the devil had no justice on his side against man; and why it was, that he seemed to have had it, and why God could have freed man in this way.

Moreover, I do not see the force of that argument, which we are wont to make use of, that God, in order to save men, was bound, as it were, to try a contest with the devil in justice, before he did in strength, so that, when the devil should put to death that being in whom there was nothing worthy of death, and who was God, he should justly lose his power over sinners; and that, if it were not so, God would have used undue force against the devil, since the devil had a rightful ownership of man, for the devil had not seized man with violence, but man had freely surrendered to him. It is true that this might well enough be said, if the devil or man belonged to any other being than God, or were in the power of any but God. But since neither the devil nor man belong to any but God, and neither can exist without the exertion of Divine power, what cause ought God to try with his own creature (de suo, in suo), or what should he do but punish his servant, who had seduced his fellow-servant to desert their common Lord and come over to himself; who, a traitor, had taken to himself a fugitive; a thief, had taken to himself a fellow-thief, with what he had stolen from his Lord. For when one was stolen from his Lord by the persuasions of the other, both were thieves. For what could be more just than for God to do this? Or, should God, the judge of all, snatch man, thus held, out of the power of him who holds him so unrighteously, either for the purpose of punishing him in some other way than by means of the devil, or of sparing him, what injustice would there be in this? For, though man deserved to be tormented by the devil, yet the devil tormented him unjustly. For man merited punishment, and there was no more suitable way for him to be punished than by that being to whom he had given his consent to sin. But the infliction of punishment was nothing meritorious in the devil; on the other hand, he was even more unrighteous in this, because he was not led to it by a love of justice, but urged on by a malicious impulse. For he did not do this at the command of God, but God's inconceivable wisdom, which happily controls even wickedness, permitted it. . . . For by the just judgment of God it was decreed, and, as it were, confirmed by writing, that, since man had sinned, he should not henceforth of himself have the power to avoid sin or the punishment of sin; for the spirit is out-going and not returning (est enim spiritus vadens et non rediens); and he who sins ought not to escape with impunity, unless pity spare the sinner, and deliver and restore him. Wherefore we ought not to believe that, on account of this writing, there can be found any justice on the part of the devil in his tormenting man. In fine, as there is never any injustice in a good angel, so in an evil angel there can be no justice at all. There was no reason, therefore, as respects the devil, why God should not make use of his own power against him for the liberation of man.

CHAPTER 8

How, although the acts of Christ's condescension which we speak of do not belong to his divinity, it yet seems improper to infidels that these things should be said of him even as a man; and why it appears to them that this man did not suffer death of his own will.

Anselm. The will of God ought to be a sufficient reason for us, when he does anything, though we cannot see why he does it. For the will of God is never irrational.

Boso. That is very true, if it be granted that God does wish the thing in question; but many will never allow that God does wish anything if it be inconsistent with reason.

Anselm. What do you find inconsistent with reason, in our confessing that God desired those things which make up our belief with regard to his incarnation?

Boso. This in brief: that the Most High should stoop to things so lowly, that the Almighty should do a thing with such toil.

Anselm. They who speak thus do not understand our belief. For we affirm that the Divine nature is beyond doubt impassible, and that God cannot at all be brought down from his exaltation, nor *toil* in anything which he wishes to effect. But we say that the Lord Jesus Christ is very God and very man, one person in two natures, and two natures in one person. When, therefore, we speak of God as enduring any humiliation or infirmity, we do not refer to the majesty of that nature, which cannot suffer; but to the feebleness of the human constitution which he assumed. And so there remains no ground of objection against our faith. For in this way we intend no debasement of the Divine nature, but we teach that one person is both Divine and human. In the incarnation of God there is no lowering of the Deity; but the nature of man we believe to be exalted.

Boso. Be it so; let nothing be referred to the Divine nature, which is spoken of Christ after the manner of human weakness; but how will it ever be made out a just or reasonable thing that God should treat or suffer to be treated in such a manner, that man whom the Father called his beloved Son in whom he was well pleased, and whom the Son made himself? For what justice is there in *his* suffering death for the sinner, who was the most just of all men? What man, if he condemned the innocent to free the guilty, would not himself be judged worthy of condemnation? And so the matter seems to return to the same incongruity which is mentioned above.

For if he could not save sinners in any other way than by condemning the just, where is his omnipotence? If, however, he could, but did not wish to, how shall we sustain his wisdom and justice?

Anselm. God the Father did not treat that man as you seem to suppose, nor put to death the innocent for the guilty. For the Father did not compel him to suffer death, or even allow him to be slain, against his will, but of his own accord he endured death for the salvation of men.

Boso. Though it were not against his will, since he agreed to the will of the Father; yet the Father seems to have bound him, as it were, by his injunction. For it is said that Christ "humbled himself, being made obedient to the Father even unto death, and that the death of the cross." . . . it would rather appear that Christ endured death by the constraint of obedience, than by the inclination of his own free will.

CHAPTER 9

How it was of his own accord that he died, and what this means: "he was made obedient even unto death;" and: "for which cause God hath highly exalted him;" and: "I came not to do my own will;" and: "he spared not his own son;" and: "not as I will, but as thou wilt."

Anselm. It seems to me that you do not rightly understand the difference between what he did at the demand of obedience, and what he suffered, not demanded by obedience, but inflicted on him, because he kept his obedience perfect.

Boso. I need to have you explain it more clearly.

Anselm. Why did the Jews persecute him even unto death?

Boso. For nothing else, but that, in word and in life, he invariably maintained truth and justice.

Anselm. I believe that God demands this of every rational being, and every being owes this in obedience to God.

Boso. We ought to acknowledge this.

Anselm. That man, therefore, owed this obedience to God the Father, humanity to Deity; and the Father claimed it from him.

Boso. There is no doubt of this.

Anselm. Now you see what he did, under the demand of obedience.

Boso. Very true, and I see also what infliction he endured, because he stood firm in obedience. For death was inflicted on him for his perseverance in obedience and he endured it; but I do not understand how it is that obedience did not demand this.

Anselm. Ought man to suffer death, if he had never sinned, or should God demand this of him?

Boso. It is on this account that we believe that man would not have been subject to death, and that God would not have exacted this of him; but I should like to hear the reason of the thing from you.

Anselm. You acknowledge that the intelligent creature was made holy, and for this purpose, viz., to be happy in the enjoyment of God.

Boso. Yes.

Anselm. You surely will not think it proper for God to make his creature miserable without fault, when he had created him holy that he might enjoy a state of blessedness. For it would be a miserable thing for man to die against his will.

Boso. It is plain that, if man had not sinned, God ought not to compel him to die.

Anselm. God did not, therefore, compel Christ to die; but he suffered death of his own will, not yielding up his life as an act of obedience, but on account of his obedience in maintaining holiness; for he held out so firmly in this obedience that he met death on account of it. It may, indeed be said, that the Father commanded him to die, when he enjoined that upon him on account of which he met death. It was in this sense, then, that "as the Father gave him the commandment, so he did, and the cup which He gave to him, he drank; and he was made obedient to the Father, even unto death;" and thus "he learned obedience from the things which he suffered," that is, how far obedience should be maintained. . . . For it is not meant that he could not have attained his exaltation in any other way but by obedience unto death; nor is it meant that his exaltation was conferred on him, only as a reward of his obedience . . . but the expression is used because he had agreed with the Father and the Holy Spirit, that there was no other way to reveal to the world the height of his omnipotence, than by his death. . . . Again, when he says: "Father, if it be passible, let this cup pass from me; nevertheless not as I will, but as thou wilt;" and "If this cup may not pass from me, except I drink it, thy will be done;" he signifies by his own will the natural desire of safety, in accordance with which human nature shrank from the anguish of death. But he speaks of the will of the Father, not because the Father preferred the death of the Son to his life; but because the Father was not willing to rescue the human race, unless man were to do even as great a thing as was signified in the death of Christ. Since reason did not demand of another what he could not do, therefore, the Son says that he desires his own death. For he preferred to suffer, rather than that the human race should be lost; as if he were to say to the Father: "Since thou dost not desire the reconciliation of the world to take place in any other way, in this respect, I see that thou desirest my death; let thy will, therefore, be done, that is, let my death take place, so that the world may be reconciled to thee. . . ." So the Father desired the death of the Son, because he was not willing that the world should be saved in any other way, except by man's doing so great a thing as that which I have mentioned. And this, since none other could accomplish it, availed as much with the Son, who so earnestly desired the salvation of man, as if the Father had commanded him to die; and, therefore, "as the Father gave him commandment, so he did, and the cup which the Father gave to him he drank, being obedient even unto death."

CHAPTER 10

Likewise on the same topics; and how otherwise they can be correctly explained.

. . . Since, therefore, the will of the Son pleased the Father, and he did not prevent him from choosing, or from fulfilling his choice, it is proper to say that he wished the Son to endure death so piously and for so great an object, though he was not pleased with his suffering. Moreover, he said that the cup must not pass from him, except he drank it, not because he could not have escaped death had he chosen to; but because, as has been said, the world could not otherwise be saved; and it was his fixed choice to suffer death, rather than that the world should not be saved. It was for this reason, also, that he used those words, viz., to teach the human race that there was no other salvation for them but by his death; and not to show that he had no power at all to avoid death. For whatsoever things are said of him, similar to these which have been mentioned, they are all to be explained in accordance with the belief that he died, not by compulsion, but of free choice. For he was omnipotent, and it is said of him, when he was offered up, that he desired it. And he says himself: "I lay down my life that I may take it again; no man taketh it from me, but I lay it down of myself; I have power to lay it down, and I have power to take it again." A man cannot, therefore, be properly said to have been driven to a thing which he does of his own power and will. . . .

Anselm. Let us suppose, then, that the incarnation of God, and the things that we affirm of him as man, had never taken place; and be it agreed between us that man was made for happiness, which cannot be attained in this life, and that no being can ever arrive at happiness, save by freedom from sin, and that no man passes this life without sin. Let us take for granted, also, the other things, the belief of which is necessary for eternal salvation.

Boso. I grant it; for in these there is nothing which seems unbecoming or impossible for God.

Anselm. Therefore, in order that man may attain happiness, remission of sin is necessary.

Boso. We all hold this.

CHAPTER 11

What is it to sin, and to make satisfaction for sin.

Anselm. We must needs inquire, therefore, in what manner God puts away men's sins; and, in order to do this more plainly, let us first consider what it is to sin, and what it is to make satisfaction for sin.

Boso. It is yours to explain and mine to listen.

Anselm. If man or angel always rendered to God his due, he would never sin.

Boso. I cannot deny that.

Anselm. Therefore to sin is nothing else than not to render to God his due.

Boso. What is the debt which we owe to God?

Anselm. Every wish of a rational creature should be subject to the will of God.

Boso. Nothing is more true.

Anselm. This is the debt which man and angel owe to God, and no one who pays this debt commits sin; but every one who does not pay it sins. This is justice, or uprightness of will, which makes a being just or upright in heart, that is, in will; and this is the sole and complete debt of honor which we owe to God, and which God requires of us. For it is such a will only, when it can be exercised, that does works pleasing to God; and when this will cannot be exercised, it is pleasing of itself alone, since without it no work is acceptable. He who does not render this honor which is due to God, robs God of his own and dishonors him; and this is sin. Moreover, so long as he does not restore what he has taken away, he remains in fault; and it will not suffice merely to restore what has been taken away, but, considering the contempt offered, he ought to restore more than he took away. For as one who imperils another's safety does not enough by merely restoring his safety, without making some compensation for the anguish incurred; so he who violates another's honor does not enough by merely rendering honor again, but must, according to the extent of the injury done, make restoration in some way satisfactory to the person whom he has dishonored. We must also observe that when any one pays what he has unjustly taken away, he ought to give something which could not have been demanded of him, had he not stolen what belonged to another. So then, every one who sins ought to pay back the honor of which he has robbed God; and this is the satisfaction which every sinner owes to God.

Boso. Since we have determined to follow reason in all these things, I am unable to bring any objection against them, although you somewhat startle me.

CHAPTER 12

Whether it were proper for God to put away sins by compassion alone, without any payment of debt.

Anselm. Let us return and consider whether it were proper for God to put away sins by compassion alone, without any payment of the honor taken from him.

Boso. I do not see why it is not proper.

Anselm. To remit sin in this manner is nothing else than not to punish;

and since it is not right to cancel sin without compensation or punishment; if it be not punished, then is it passed by undischarged.

Boso. What you say is reasonable.

Anselm. It is not fitting for God to pass over anything in his kingdom undischarged.

Boso. If I wish to oppose this, I fear to sin.

Anselm. It is, therefore, not proper for God thus to pass over sin unpunished.

Boso. Thus it follows.

Anselm. There is also another thing which follows if sin be passed by unpunished, viz., that with God there will be no difference between the guilty and the not guilty; and this is unbecoming to God.

Boso. I cannot deny it.

Anselm. Observe this also. Every one knows that justice to man is regulated by law, so that, according to the requirements of law, the measure of award is bestowed by God.

Boso. This is our belief.

Anselm. But if sin is neither paid for nor punished, it is subject to no law.

Boso. I cannot conceive it to be otherwise.

Anselm. Injustice, therefore, if it is cancelled by compassion alone, is more free than justice, which seems very inconsistent. And to these is also added a further incongruity, viz., that it makes injustice like God. For as God is subject to no law, so neither is injustice.

Boso. I cannot withstand your reasoning. But when God commands us in every case to forgive those who trespass against us, it seems inconsistent to enjoin a thing upon us which it is not proper for him to do himself.

Anselm. There is no inconsistency in God's commanding us not to take upon ourselves what belongs to Him alone. For to execute vengeance belongs to none but Him who is Lord of all; for when the powers of the world rightly accomplish this end, God himself does it who appointed them for the purpose.

Boso. You have obviated the difficulty which I thought to exist; but there is another to which I would like to have your answer. For since God is so free as to be subject to no law, and to the judgment of no one, and is so merciful as that nothing more merciful can be conceived; and nothing is right or fit save as he wills; it seems a strange thing for us to say that he is wholly unwilling or unable to put away an injury done to himself, when we are wont to apply to him for indulgence with regard to those offences which we commit against others.

Anselm. What you say of God's liberty and choice and compassion is true; but we ought so to interpret these things as that they may not seem to interfere with His dignity. For there is no liberty except as regards what is best or fitting; nor should that be called mercy which does anything improper for the Divine character. Moreover, when it is said that what God wishes is just, and that what He does not wish is unjust, we must not understand that if God wished anything improper it would be just, simply because he wished it. For if God wishes to lie, we must not conclude that it is right to lie, but rather that he is not God. For no will can ever wish to lie, unless truth in it is impaired, nay, unless the will itself be impaired by forsaking truth. When, then, it is said: "If God wishes to lie," the meaning is simply this: "If the nature of God is such as that he wishes to lie;" and, therefore, it does not follow that falsehood is right, except it be understood in the same manner as when we speak of two impossible things: "If this be true, then that follows; because neither *this* nor *that* is true;" as if a man should say: "Supposing water to be dry, and fire to be moist;" for neither is the case. Therefore, with regard to these things, to speak the whole truth: If God desires a thing, it is right that he should desire that which involves no unfitness. For if God chooses that it should rain, it is right that it should rain; and if he desires that any man should die, then is it right that he should die. Wherefore, if it be not fitting for God to do anything unjustly, or out of course, it does not belong to his liberty or compassion or will to let the sinner go unpunished, who makes no return to God of what the sinner has defrauded him.

Boso. You remove from me every possible objection which I had thought of bringing against you. . . .

CHAPTER 13

How nothing less was to be endured, in the order of things, than that the creature should take away the honor due the Creator and not restore what he takes away.

Anselm. In the order of things, there is nothing less to be endured than that the creature should take away the honor due the Creator, and not restore what he has taken away.

Boso. Nothing is more plain than this. . . .

Anselm. Therefore the honor taken away must be repaid, or punishment must follow; otherwise, either God will not be just to himself, or he will be weak in respect to both parties; and this it is impious even to think of.

Boso. I think that nothing more reasonable can be said.

CHAPTER 14

How the honor of God exists in the punishment of the wicked.

Boso. But I wish to hear from you whether the punishment of the sinner is an honor to God, or how it is an honor. For if the punishment of the sinner is not for God's honor when the sinner does not pay what he took away, but is punished, God loses his honor so that he cannot recover it. And this seems in contradiction to the things which have been said.

Anselm. It is impossible for God to lose his honor; for either the sinner pays his debt of his own accord, or, if he refuse, God takes it from him. For either man renders due submission to God of his own will, by avoiding sin or making payment, or else God subjects him to himself by torments, even against man's will, and thus shows that he is the Lord of man, though man refuses to acknowledge it of his own accord. And here we must observe that as man in sinning takes away what belongs to God, so God in punishing gets in return what pertains to man. For not only does that belong to a man which he has in present possession, but also that which it is in his power to have. Therefore, since man was so made as to be able to attain happiness by avoiding sin; if, on account of his sin, he is deprived of happiness and every good, he repays from his own inheritance what he has stolen, though he repay it against his will. For although God does not apply what he takes away to any object of his own, as man transfers the money which he has taken from another to his own use; yet what he takes away serves the purpose of his own honor, for this very reason, that it is taken away. For by this act he shows that the sinner and all that pertains to him are under his subjection. . . .

CHAPTER 19

How man cannot be saved without satisfaction for sin.

Anselm. It was fitting for God to fill the places of the fallen angels from among men.

Boso. That is certain.

Anselm. Therefore there ought to be in the heavenly empire as many men taken as substitutes for the angels as would correspond with the number whose place they shall take, that is, as many as there are good angels now; otherwise they who fell will not be restored, and it will follow that God either could not accomplish the good which he begun, or he will repent of having undertaken it; either of which is absurd.

Boso. Truly it is fitting that men should be equal with good angels.

Anselm. Have good angels ever sinned?

Boso. No.

Anselm. Can you think that man, who has sinned, and never made satisfaction to God for his sin, but only been suffered to go unpunished, may become the equal of an angel who has never sinned?

Boso. These words I can both think of and utter, but can no more perceive their meaning than I can make truth out of falsehood.

Anselm. Therefore it is not fitting that God should take sinful man without an atonement, in substitution for lost angels; for truth will not suffer man thus to be raised to an equality with holy beings.

Boso. Reason shows this.

Anselm. Consider, also, leaving out the question of equality with the angels, whether God ought, under such circumstances, to raise man to the same or a similar kind of happiness as that which he had before he sinned.

Boso. Tell your opinion, and I will attend to it as well as I can.

Anselm. Suppose a rich man possessed a choice pearl which had never been defiled, and which could not be taken from his hands without his permission; and that he determined to commit it to the treasury of his dearest and most valuable possessions.

Boso. I accept your supposition.

Anselm. What if he should allow it to be struck from his hand and cast in the mire, though he might have prevented it; and afterwards taking it all soiled by the mire and unwashed, should commit it again to his beautiful and loved casket; will you consider him a wise man?

Boso. How can I? for would it not be far better to keep and preserve his pearl pure, than to have it polluted?

Anselm. Would not God be acting like this, who held man in paradise, as it were in his own hand, without sin, and destined to the society of angels, and allowed the devil, inflamed with envy, to cast him into the mire of sin, though truly with man's consent? For, had God chosen to restrain the devil, the devil could not have tempted man. Now I say, would not God be acting like this, should he restore man, stained with the defilement of sin, unwashed, that is, without any satisfaction, and always to remain so; should He restore him at once to paradise, from which he had been thrust out?

Boso. I dare not deny the aptness of your comparison, were God to do this, and therefore do not admit that he can do this. For it should seem either that he could not accomplish what he designed, or else that he repented of his good intent, neither of which things is possible with God.

Anselm. Therefore, consider it settled that, without satisfaction, that is, without voluntary payment of the debt, God can neither pass by the sin unpunished, nor can the sinner attain that happiness, or happiness like that, which he had before he sinned; for man cannot in this way be restored, or become such as he was before he sinned.

Boso. I am wholly unable to refute your reasoning. .

CHAPTER 20

That satisfaction ought to be proportionate to guilt; and that man is of himself unable to accomplish this.

Anselm. Neither, I think, will you doubt this, that satisfaction should be proportionate to guilt.

Boso. Otherwise sin would remain in a manner exempt from control (*inordinatum*), which cannot be, for God leaves nothing uncontrolled in his kingdom. But this is determined, that even the smallest unfitness is impossible with God.

Anselm. Tell me, then, what payment you make God for your sin?

Boso. Repentance, a broken and contrite heart, self-denial, various bodily sufferings, pity in giving and forgiving, and obedience.

Anselm. What do you give to God in all these?

Boso. Do I not honor God, when, for his love and fear, in heartfelt contrition I give up worldly joy, and despise, amid abstinence and toils, the delights and ease of this life, and submit obediently to him, freely bestowing my possessions in giving to and releasing others?

Anselm. When you render anything to God which you owe him, irrespective of your past sin, you should not reckon this as the debt which you owe for sin. But you owe God every one of those things which you have mentioned. For, in this mortal state, there should be such love and such desire of attaining the true end of your being, which is the meaning of prayer, and such grief that you have not yet reached this object, and such fear lest you fail of it, that you should find joy in nothing which does not help you or give encouragement of your success. For you do not deserve to have a thing which you do not love and desire for its own sake, and the want of which at present, together with the great danger of never getting it, causes you no grief. This also requires one to avoid ease and worldly pleasures such as seduce the mind from real rest and pleasure, except so far as you think suffices for the accomplishment of that object. But you ought to view the gifts which you bestow as a part of your debt, since you know that what you give comes not from yourself, but from him whose servant both you are and he also to whom you give. And nature herself teaches you to do to your fellow servant, man to man, as you would be done by; and that he who will not bestow what he has ought not to receive what he has not. Of forgiveness, indeed, I speak briefly, for, as we said above, vengeance in no sense belongs to you, since you are not your own, nor is he who injures you yours or his, but you are both the servants of one Lord, made by him out of nothing. And if you avenge yourself upon your fellow servant, you proudly assume judgment over him when it is the peculiar right of God, the judge of all. But what do you give to God by your obedience, which is not owed him already, since he demands from you all that you are and have and can become?

Boso. Truly I dare not say that in all these things I pay any portion of my debt to God.

Anselm. How then do you pay God for your transgression?

Boso. If in justice I owe God myself and all my powers, even when I do not sin, I have nothing left to render to him for my sin.

Anselm. What will become of you then? How will you be saved?

Boso. Merely looking at your arguments, I see no way of escape. But, turning to my belief, I hope through Christian faith, "which works by love," that I may be saved, and the more, since we read that if the sinner turns from his iniquity and does what is right, all his transgressions shall be forgotten.

Anselm. This is only said of those who either looked for Christ before his coming, or who believe in him since he has appeared. But we set aside Christ and his religion as if they did not exist, when we proposed to inquire whether his coming were necessary to man's salvation.

Boso. We did so.

Anselm. Let us then proceed by reason simply.

Boso. Though you bring me into straits, yet I very much wish you to proceed as you have begun.

CHAPTER 21

How great a burden sin is.

Anselm. So heinous is our sin whenever we knowingly oppose the will of God even in the slightest thing; since we are always in his sight, and he always enjoins it upon us not to sin.

Boso. I cannot deny it.

Anselm. Therefore you make no satisfaction unless you restore something greater than the amount of that obligation, which should restrain you from committing the sin.

Boso. Reason seems to demand this, and to make the contrary wholly impossible.

Anselm. Even God cannot raise to happiness any being bound at all by the debt of sin, because He ought not to.

Boso. This decision is most weighty.

Anselm. Listen to an additional reason which makes it no less difficult for man to be reconciled to God.

Boso. This alone would drive me to despair, were it not for the consolation of faith.

Anselm. But listen.

Boso. Say on.

CHAPTER 22

What contempt man brought upon God, when he allowed himself to be conquered by the devil; for which he can make no satisfaction.

Anselm. Man being made holy was placed in paradise, as it were in the place of God, between God and the devil, to conquer the devil by not yielding to his temptation, and so to vindicate the honor of God and put the devil to shame, because that man, though weaker and dwelling upon earth, should not sin though tempted by the devil, while the devil, though stronger and in heaven, sinned without any to tempt him. And when man could have easily effected this, he, without compulsion and of his own accord, allowed himself to be brought over to the will of the devil, contrary to the will and honor of God.

Boso. To what would you bring me?

Anselm. Decide for yourself if it be not contrary to the honor of God for man to be reconciled to Him, with this calumnious reproach still heaped upon God; unless man first shall have honored God by overcoming the devil, as he dishonored him in yielding to the devil. Now the victory ought to be of this kind, that, as in strength and immortal vigor, he freely yielded to the devil to sin, and on this account justly incurred the penalty of death; so, in his weakness and mortality, which he had brought upon himself, he should conquer the devil by the pain of death, while wholly avoiding sin. But this cannot be done, so long as from the deadly effect of the first transgression, man is conceived and born in sin.

Boso. Again I say that the thing is impossible, and reason approves what you say. . . .

CHAPTER 23

What man took from God by his sin, which he has no power to repay.

Anselm. . . . man cannot and ought not by any means to receive from God what God designed to give him, unless he return to God everything which he took from him; so that, as by man God suffered loss, by man, also, He might recover His loss. But this cannot be effected except in this way: that, as in the fall of man all human nature was corrupted, and, as it were, tainted with sin, and God will not choose one of such a race to fill up the number in his heavenly kingdom; so, by man's victory, as many men may be justified from sin as are needed to complete the number which man was made to fill. But a sinful man can by no means do this, for a sinner cannot justify a sinner.

Boso. There is nothing more just or necessary; but, from all these things, the compassion of God and the hope of man seems to fail, as far as regards that happiness for which man was made.

Anselm. Yet wait a little.

Boso. Have you anything further?

CHAPTER 24

How, as long as man does not restore what he owes God, he cannot be happy, nor is he excused by want of power.

Anselm. If a man is called unjust who does not pay his fellow-man a debt, much more is he unjust who does not restore what he owes God.

Boso. If he can pay and yet does not, he is certainly unjust. But if he be not able, wherein is he unjust?

Anselm. Indeed, if the origin of his inability were not in himself, there might be some excuse for him. But if in this very impotence lies the fault, as it does not lessen the sin, neither does it excuse him from paying what is due. Suppose one should assign his slave a certain piece of work, and should command him not to throw himself into a ditch, which he points out to him and from which he could not extricate himself; and suppose that the slave, despising his master's command and warning, throws himself into the ditch before pointed out, so as to be utterly unable to accomplish the work assigned; think you that his inability will at all excuse him for not doing his appointed work?

Boso. By no means, but will rather increase his crime, since he brought his inability upon himself. For doubly hath he sinned, in not doing what he was commanded to do and in doing what he was forewarned not to do.

Anselm. Just so inexcusable is man, who has voluntarily brought upon himself a debt which he cannot pay, and by his own fault disabled himself, so that he can neither escape his previous obligation not to sin, nor pay the debt which he has incurred by sin. For his very inability is guilt, because he ought not to have it; nay, he ought to be free from it; for as it is a crime not to have what he ought, it is also a crime to have what he ought not. Therefore, as it is a crime in man not to have that power which he received to avoid sin, it is also a crime to have that inability by which he can neither do right and avoid sin, nor restore the debt which he owes on account of his sin. For it is by his own free action that he loses that power, and falls into this inability. For not to have the power which one ought to have, is the same thing as to have the inability which one ought not to have. Therefore man's inability to restore what he owes to God, an inability brought upon himself for that very purpose, does not excuse man from paying; for the result of sin cannot excuse the sin itself.

Boso. This argument is exceedingly weighty, and must be true.

Anselm. Man, then, is unjust in not paying what he owes to God.

Boso. This is very true; for he is unjust, both in not paying, and in not being able to pay. . . .

Anselm. I do not deny that God is merciful, who preserveth man and beast, according to the multitude of his mercies. But we are speaking of that exceeding pity by which he makes man happy after this life. And I think that I have amply proved, by the reasons given above, that happiness ought not to be bestowed upon any one whose sins have not been wholly put away; and that this remission ought not to take place, save by the payment of the debt incurred by sin, according to the extent of sin. And if you think that any objections can be brought against these proofs, you ought to mention them.

Boso. I see not how your reasons can be at all invalidated.

Anselm. Nor do I, if rightly understood. But even if one of the whole number be confirmed by impregnable truth, that should be sufficient. For truth is equally secured against all doubt, if it be demonstrably proved by one argument as by many.

Boso. Surely this is so. But how, then, shall man be saved, if he neither pays what he owes, and ought not to be saved without paying? Or, with what face shall we declare that God, who is rich in mercy above human conception, cannot exercise this compassion?

Anselm. This is the question which you ought to ask of those in whose behalf you are speaking, who have no faith in the need of Christ for man's salvation, and you should also request them to tell how man can be saved without Christ. But, if they are utterly unable to do it, let them cease from mocking us, and let them hasten to unite themselves with us, who do not doubt that man can be saved through Christ; else let them despair of being saved at all. And if this terrifies them, let them believe in Christ as we do, that they may be saved. . . .

SECOND BOOK

CHAPTER 4

How God will complete, in respect to human nature, what he has begun.

Anselm. . . . we can easily see that God will either complete what he has begun with regard to human nature, or else he has made to no end so lofty a nature, capable of so great good. Now if it be understood that God has made nothing more valuable than rational existence capable of enjoying him; it is altogether foreign from his character to suppose that he will suffer that rational existence utterly to perish.

Boso. No reasonable being can think otherwise.

Anselm. Therefore is it necessary for him to perfect in human nature what he has begun. But this, as we have already said, cannot be accomplished save by a complete expiation of sin, which no sinner can effect for himself.

Boso. I now understand it to be necessary for God to complete what he has begun, lest there be an unseemly falling off from his design. . . .

CHAPTER 6

How no being, except the God-man, can make the atonement by which man is saved.

Anselm. But this cannot be effected, except the price paid to God for the sin of man be something greater than all the universe besides God.

Boso. So it appears.

Anselm. Moreover, it is necessary that he who can give God anything of his own which is more valuable than all things in the possession of God, must be greater than all else but God himself.

Boso. I cannot deny it.

Anselm. Therefore none but God can make this satisfaction.

Boso. So it appears.

Anselm. But none but a man ought to do this, otherwise man does not make the satisfaction.

Boso. Nothing seems more just.

Anselm. If it be necessary, therefore, as it appears, that the heavenly kingdom be made up of men, and this cannot be effected unless the aforesaid satisfaction be made, which none but God can make and none but man ought to make, it is necessary for the God-man to make it.

Boso. Now blessed be God! we have made a great discovery with regard to our question. Go on, therefore, as you have begun. For I hope that God will assist you.

Anselm. Now must we inquire how God can become man.

CHAPTER 7

How necessary it is for the same being to be perfect God and perfect man.

Anselm. The Divine and human natures cannot alternate, so that the Divine should become human or the human Divine; nor can they be so commingled as that a third should be produced from the two which is neither wholly Divine nor wholly human. For, granting that it were possible for either to be changed into the other, it would in that case be only God and not man, or man only and not God. Or, if they were so commingled that a third nature sprung from the combination of the two (as from two animals, a male and a female of different species, a third is produced, which does not preserve entire the species of either parent, but has a mixed nature derived from both), it would neither be God nor man. Therefore the God-man, whom we require to be of a nature both human and Divine, cannot be produced by a change from one into the other, nor by an imperfect commingling of both in a third; since these things cannot be, or, if they could be, would avail nothing to our purpose. Moreover, if these two complete natures are said to be joined somehow, in such a way that one may be Divine while the other is human, and yet that which is God not be the same with that which is man, it is impossible for both to do the work necessary to be accomplished. For God will not do it, because he has no debt to pay; and man will not do it, because he cannot. Therefore, in order that the God-man may perform this, it is necessary that the same being should be perfect God and perfect man, in order to make this atonement. For he cannot and ought not to do it, unless he be very God and very man. Since, then, it is necessary that the God-man preserve the completeness of each nature, it is no less necessary that these two natures be united entire in one person, just as a body and a reasonable soul exist together in every human being; for otherwise it is impossible that the same being should be very God and very man.

Boso. All that you say is satisfactory to me.

CHAPTER 8

How it behoved God to take a man of the race of Adam, and born of a woman.

Anselm. It now remains to inquire whence and how God shall assume human nature. For he will either take it from Adam, or else he will make a new man, as he made Adam originally. But, if he makes a new man, not of Adam's race, then this man will not belong to the human family, which descended from Adam, and therefore ought not to make atonement for it, because he never belonged to it. For, as it is right for man to make atonement for the sin of man, it is also necessary that he who makes the atonement should be the very being who has sinned, or else one of the same race. Otherwise, neither Adam nor his race would make satisfaction for themselves. Therefore, as through Adam and Eve sin was propagated among all men, so none but themselves, or one born of them, ought to make atonement for the sin of men. And, since they cannot, one born of them must fulfil this work. Moreover, as Adam and his whole race, had he not sinned, would have stood firm without the support of any other being, so, after the fall, the same race must rise and be exalted by means of itself. For, whoever restores the race to its place, it will certainly stand by that being who has made this restoration. Also, when God created human nature in Adam alone, and would only make woman out of man, that by the union of both sexes there might be increase, in this he showed plainly that he wished to produce all that he intended with regard to human nature from man alone. Wherefore, if the race of Adam be reinstated by any being not of the same race, it will not be restored to that dignity which it would have had, had not Adam sinned, and so will not be completely restored; and, besides, God will seem to have failed of his purpose, both which suppositions are incongruous. It is, therefore, necessary that the man by whom Adam's race shall be restored be taken from Adam.

Boso. If we follow reason, as we proposed to do, this is the necessary result. . . .

Anselm. In four ways can God create man, viz., either of man and woman, in the common way; or neither of man nor woman, as he created Adam; or of man without woman, as he made Eve; or of woman without man, which thus far he has never done. Wherefore, in order to show that this last mode is also under his power, and was reserved for this very purpose, what more fitting than that he should take that man whose origin we are seeking from a woman without a man? Now whether it be more worthy that he be born of a virgin, or one not a virgin, we need not discuss, but must affirm, beyond all doubt, that the God-man should be born of a virgin.

Boso. Your speech gratifies my heart. . . .

CHAPTER 11

How Christ dies of his own power, and how mortality does not inhere in the essential nature of man.

Anselm. Now, also, it remains to inquire whether, as man's nature is, it is possible for that man to die?

Boso. We need hardly dispute with regard to this, since he will be really man, and every man is by nature mortal.

Anselm. I do not think mortality inheres in the essential nature of man, but only as corrupted. Since, had man never sinned, and had his immortality been unchangeably confirmed, he would have been as really man; and, when the dying rise again, incorruptible, they will no less be really men. For, if mortality was an essential attribute of human nature, then he who was immortal could not be man. Wherefore, neither corruption nor incorruption belong essentially to human nature, for neither makes nor destroys a man; but happiness accrues to him from the one, and misery from the other. But since all men die, mortality is included in the definition of man, as given by philosophers, for they have never even believed in the possibility of man's being immortal in all respects. And so it is not enough to prove that that man ought to be subject to death, for us to say that he will be in all respects a man.

Boso. Seek then for some other reason, since I know of none, if you do not, by which we may prove that he can die.

Anselm. We may not doubt that, as he will be God, he will possess omnipotence.

Boso. Certainly.

Anselm. He can, then, if he chooses, lay down his life and take it again.

Boso. If not, he would scarcely seem to be omnipotent.

Anselm. Therefore is he able to avoid death if he chooses, and also to die and rise again. Moreover, whether he lays down his life by the intervention of no other person, or another causes this, so that he lays it down by permitting it to be taken, it makes no difference as far as regards his power.

Boso. There is no doubt about it.

Anselm. If, then, he chooses to allow it, he could be slain; and if he were unwilling to allow it, he could not be slain.

Boso. To this we are unavoidably brought by reason.

Anselm. Reason has also taught us that the gift which he presents to God, not of debt but freely, ought to be something greater than anything in the possession of God.

Boso. Yes.

Anselm. Now this can neither be found beneath him nor above him.

Boso. Very true.

Anselm. In himself, therefore, must it be found.

Boso. So it appears.

Anselm. Therefore will he give himself, or something pertaining to himself.

Boso. I cannot see how it should be otherwise.

Anselm. Now must we inquire what sort of a gift this should be? For he may not give himself to God, or anything of his, as if God did not have what was his own. For every creature belongs to God.

Boso. This is so.

Anselm. Therefore must this gift be understood in this way, that he somehow gives up himself, or something of his, to the honor of God, which he did not owe as a debtor.

Boso. So it seems from what has been already said.

Anselm. If we say that he will give himself to God by obedience, so as, by steadily maintaining holiness, to render himself subject to his will, this will not be giving a thing not demanded of him by God as his due. For every reasonable being owes his obedience to God.

Boso. This cannot be denied.

Anselm. Therefore must it be in some other way that he gives himself, or something belonging to him, to God.

Boso. Reason urges us to this conclusion.

Anselm. Let us see whether, perchance, this may be to give up his life or to lay down his life, or to deliver himself up to death for God's honor. For God will not demand this of him as a debt; for, as no sin will be found, he ought not to die, as we have already said.

Boso. Else I cannot understand it.

Anselm. But let us further observe whether this is according to reason.

Boso. Speak you, and I will listen with pleasure.

Anselm. If man sinned with ease, is it not fitting for him to atone with difficulty? And if he was overcome by the devil in the easiest manner possible, so as to dishonor God by sinning against him, is it not right that man, in making satisfaction for his sin, should honor God by conquering the devil with the greatest possible difficulty? Is it not proper that, since man has departed from God as far as possible in his sin, he should make to God the greatest possible satisfaction?

Boso. Surely, there is nothing more reasonable.

Anselm. Now, nothing can be more severe or difficult for man to do for God's honor, than to suffer death voluntarily when not bound by obligation; and man cannot give himself to God in any way more truly than by surrendering himself to death for God's honor.

Boso. All these things are true.

Anselm. Therefore, he who wishes to make atonement for man's sin should be one who can die if he chooses.

Boso. I think it is plain that the man whom we seek for should not only be one who is not necessarily subject to death on account of his omnipotence, and one who does not deserve death on account of his sin, but also one who can die of his own free will, for this will be necessary.

Anselm. There are also many other reasons why it is peculiarly fitting for that man to enter into the common intercourse of men, and maintain a likeness to them, only without sin. And these things are more easily and clearly manifest in his life and actions than they can possibly be shown to be by mere reason without experience. For who can say how necessary and wise a thing it was for him who was to redeem mankind, and lead them back by his teaching from the way of death and destruction into the path of life and eternal happiness, when he conversed with men, and when he taught them by personal intercourse, to set them an example himself of the way in which they ought to live? But how could he have given this example to weak and dying men, that they should not deviate from holiness because of injuries, or scorn, or tortures, or even death, had they not been able to recognise all these virtues in himself?

CHAPTER 12

How, though he share in our weakness, he is not therefore miserable.

Boso. All these things plainly show that he ought to be mortal and to partake of our weaknesses. But all these things are our miseries. Will he then be miserable?

Anselm. No, indeed! For as no advantage which one has apart from his choice constitutes happiness, so there is no misery in choosing to bear a loss, when the choice is a wise one and made without compulsion.

Boso. Certainly, this must be allowed. . . .

CHAPTER 14

How his death outweighs the number and greatness of our sins.

Boso. Now I ask you to tell me how his death can outweigh the number and magnitude of our sins, when the least sin we can think of you have shown to be so monstrous that, were there an infinite number of worlds as full of created existence as this, they could not stand, but would fall back into nothing, sooner than one look should be made contrary to the just will of God.

Anselm. Were that man here before you, and you knew who he was, and it were told you that, if you did not kill him, the whole universe, except God, would perish, would you do it to preserve the rest of creation?

Boso. No! not even were an infinite number of worlds displayed before me.

Anselm. But suppose you were told: "If you do not kill him, all the sins of the world will be heaped upon you."

Boso. I should answer, that I would far rather bear all other sins, not only those of this world, past and future, but also all others that can be conceived of, than this alone. And I think I ought to say this, not only with regard to killing him, but even as to the slightest injury which could be inflicted on him.

Anselm. You judge correctly; but tell me why it is that your heart recoils from one injury inflicted upon him as more heinous than all other sins that can be thought of, inasmuch as all sins whatsoever are committed against him?

Boso. A sin committed upon his person exceeds beyond comparison all the sins which can be thought of, that do not affect his person.

Anselm. What say you to this, that one often suffers freely certain evils in his person, in order not to suffer greater ones in his property?

Boso. God has no need of such patience, for all things lie in subjection to his power, as you answered a certain question of mine above.

Anselm. You say well; and hence we see that no enormity or multitude of sins, apart from the Divine person, can for a moment be compared with a bodily injury inflicted upon that man.

Boso. This is most plain.

Anselm. How great does this good seem to you, if the destruction of it is such an evil?

Boso. If its existence is as great a good as its destruction is an evil, then is it far more a good than those sins are evils which its destruction so far surpasses.

Anselm. Very true. Consider, also, that sins are as hateful as they are evil, and that life is only amiable in proportion as it is good. And, therefore, it follows that that life is more lovely than sins are odious.

Boso. I cannot help seeing this.

Anselm. And do you not think that so great a good in itself so lovely, can avail to pay what is due for the sins of the whole world?

Boso. Yes! it has even infinite value.

Anselm. Do you see, then, how this life conquers all sins, if it be given for them?

Boso. Plainly.

Anselm. If, then, to lay down life is the same as to suffer death, as the gift of his life surpasses all the sins of men, so will also the suffering of death. . . .

CHAPTER 19

How human salvation follows upon his death.

Anselm. Let us now observe, if we can, how the salvation of men rests on this.

Boso. This is the very wish of my heart. For, although I think I understand you, yet I wish to get from you the close chain of argument.

Anselm. There is no need of explaining how precious was the gift which the Son freely gave.

Boso. That is clear enough already.

Anselm. But you surely will not think that he deserves no reward, who freely gave so great a gift to God.

Boso. I see that it is necessary for the Father to reward the Son; else he is either unjust in not wishing to do it, or weak in not being able to do it; but neither of these things can be attributed to God.

Anselm. He who rewards another either gives him something which he does not have, or else remits some rightful claim upon him. But anterior to the great offering of the Son, all things belonging to the Father were his, nor did he ever owe anything which could be forgiven him. How then can a reward be bestowed on one who needs nothing, and to whom no gift or release can be made?

Boso. I see on the one hand a necessity for a reward, and on the other it appears impossible; for God must necessarily render payment for what he owes, and yet there is no one to receive it.

Anselm. But if a reward so large and so deserved is not given to him or any one else, then it will almost appear as if the Son had done this great work in vain.

Boso. Such a supposition is impious.

Anselm. The reward then must be bestowed upon some one else, for it cannot be upon him.

Boso. This is necessarily so.

Anselm. Had the Son wished to give some one else what was due to him, could the Father rightfully prevent it, or refuse to give it to the other person?

Boso. No! but I think it would be both just and necessary that the gift should be given by the Father to whomsoever the Son wished; because the Son should be allowed to give away what is his own, and the Father cannot bestow it at all except upon some other person.

Anselm. Upon whom would he more properly bestow the reward accruing from his death, than upon those for whose salvation, as right reason teaches, he became man; and for whose sake, as we have already said, he left an example of suffering death to preserve holiness? For surely in vain will men imitate him, if they be not also partakers of his reward. Or whom could he more justly make heirs of the inheritance, which he does not need, and of the superfluity of his possessions, than his parents and brethren? What more proper than that, when he beholds so many of them weighed down by so heavy a debt, and wasting through poverty, in the depth of their miseries, he should remit the debt incurred by their sins, and give them what their transgressions had forfeited?

Boso. The universe can hear of nothing more reasonable, more sweet, more desirable. And I receive such confidence from this that I cannot describe the joy with which my heart exults. For it seems to me that God can reject none who come to him in his name.

Anselm. Certainly not, if he come aright. And the scriptures, which rest on solid truth as on a firm foundation, and which, by the help of God, we have somewhat examined,—the scriptures, I say, show us how to approach in order to share such favor, and how we ought to live under it. . . .

CHAPTER 22

How the truth of the Old and New Testament is shown in the things which have been said.

Boso. All things which you have said seem to me reasonable and incontrovertible. And by the solution of the single question proposed do I see the truth of all that is contained in the Old and New Testament. For, in proving that God became man by necessity, leaving out what was taken from the Bible, viz., the remarks on the persons of the Trinity, and on Adam, you convince both Jews and Pagans by the mere force of reason. And the God-man himself originates the New Testament and approves the Old. And, as we must acknowledge him to be true, so no one can dissent from anything contained in these books.

Anselm. If we have said anything that needs correction, I am willing to make the correction if it be a reasonable one. But, if the conclusions which we have arrived at by reason seem confirmed by the testimony of the truth, then ought we to attribute it, not to ourselves, but to God, who is blessed forever.

36 PETER ABAILARD (1079–1142) has remained a figure of controversy in the history of Christian thought. The story of his love affair with Heloise, his theological battles with Bernard of Clairvaux (1090–1153), his condemnation by the Synod of Soissons in 1121, has been told, and frequently romanticised, by many.

Abailard's theory of the atonement, standing in sharp contrast to Anselm's "satisfaction" or the older "ransom to the devil" interpretations, was developed in his *Exposition of the Epistle to the Romans.* His thesis has frequently been called the "moral influence" theory, a label that is open to misinterpretation. The term "moral" in the label tends to obscure the decidedly religious element in his position. Abailard insisted that the work of Christ was to demonstrate the need for human response to the grace of God shown in Christ. His statement, therefore, must be studied in relation to his understanding of man and the nature of sin. (See Selection 43.)

Exposition of the Epistle to the Romans*

PETER ABAILARD

A most pressing problem obtrudes itself at this point, as to what that redemption of ours through the death of Christ may be, and in what way the apostle declares that we are justified by his blood—we who appear to be worthy of still greater punishment, seeing that we are the wicked servants who have committed the very things for which our innocent Lord was slain. And so it seems that we must first investigate why it was necessary for God to take human nature upon him so that he might redeem us by dying in the flesh; and from what person holding us captive, either justly or by fraud, he has redeemed us; and by what standard of justice he has liberated us from the dominion of that person who has given commands to which he willingly submitted in order to set us free.

Indeed, it is said that he has redeemed us from the dominion of Satan; that it was Satan who (because the first man had sinned and had yielded himself by voluntary obedience to him) was exercising a total dominion over man; and that he would always exercise the same unless a deliverer came. But since he has delivered his elect only, when, either in this age or in the age to come, did Satan or will Satan possess them more than he does now? Did the devil torment that beggar who rested on Abraham's bosom as he did Dives who is damned, although he may have tortured him less? Or had he power even over Abraham and the rest of the elect? When did that wicked torturer have power over him who is described as being

* From Peter Abailard "Exposition of the Epistle to the Romans," in A *Scholastic Miscellany,* tr. by Eugene Fairweather, Library of Christian Classics, Vol. X. London: Student Christian Movement Press Limited; Philadelphia: Westminster Press, 1956.

carried by the angels into Abraham's bosom—concerning whom Abraham himself pays testimony in the words, "But now he is comforted and thou are tormented"? Moreover, he declares that a great gulf has been fixed between the elect and the wicked so that the latter can never cross over to the former. Still less may the devil, who is more evil than all, acquire any power in that place where no wicked person has a place or even entry.

And what right to possess mankind could the devil possibly have unless perhaps he had received man for purposes of torture through the express permission, or even the assignment, of the Lord? For if any slave wanted to forsake his lord and put himself under the authority of another master, would he be allowed to act in such a way that his lord could not lawfully seek him out and bring him back, if he wanted to? Who indeed doubts that, if a slave of any master seduces his fellow slave by subtle suggestions and makes him depart from obedience to his true master, the seducer is looked upon by the slave's master as much more guilty than the seduced? And how unjust it would be that he who seduced the other should deserve, as a result, to have any special right or authority over him! And even if such a fellow had previously had any right over him, would he not deserve to lose that right? It is written, forsooth, "He who abuses authority committed to him deserves to lose any special rights." Where one slave was about to be set over the other and receive authority over him, it would never do for the more evil one who had absolutely no justification for preferment to be promoted; but it would be much more reasonable that the person who was seduced should possess a full claim for redress over the man who had caused the harm by his act of seduction. Furthermore, the devil could not grant that immortality which he promised man as a reward of transgression in the hope that in this way he might hold him fast by some sort of right.

And so from these reasonings it seems proved that the devil acquired no right against man whom he seduced simply by seducing him, except perhaps (as we said before) in so far as it was a case of the Lord's permitting it—by handing man over to the wretch who was to act as his jailer or torturer for punishment. For man had not sinned except against his own Lord, whose obedience he had forsaken. If, then, his Lord wanted to remit the sin, as was done to the Virgin Mary, and as Christ also did for many others before he underwent his Passion—as it is reported of Mary Magdalene, and as it is recorded that the Lord said to the paralytic, "Be of good heart, son, thy sins are fogiven thee"—if, I say, the Lord was willing to pardon sinful man apart from his Passion, and to say to his tormentor, "Do not punish him any further," how could the tormentor justly continue to torment him? For, as has been shown, he had received no absolute right of torture, but only such as came from express permission of the Lord.

So, if the Lord should cease to grant this permission, no right whatever would be left to the tormentor, and, if he should complain or murmur against the Lord, it would be quite appropriate for the Lord to reply, "Is thine eye evil because I am good?" The Lord inflicted no loss upon the devil when, from sinning humanity, he took upon himself pure flesh, and manhood free from all sin. Indeed, as man, he did not by his own merits ensure that he should be conceived, be born, and continue throughout his life without sin, but received this through the grace of the Lord upholding him. If, by the same grace, he wished to forgive sins to other men, could he not have delivered them from punishment? Assuredly, once the sins for which they were undergoing punishment have been forgiven, there appears to remain no reason why they should be any longer punished for them. Could not he, who showed such loving-kindness to man that he united him to his very self, extend to him a lesser boon by forgiving his sins?

So what compulsion, or reason, or need was there—seeing that by its very appearing alone the divine pity could deliver man from Satan—what need was there, I say, that the Son of God, for our redemption, should take upon him our flesh and endure such numerous fastings, insults, scourgings and spittings, and finally that most bitter and disgraceful death upon the cross, enduring even the cross of punishment with the wicked? In what way does the apostle declare that we are justified or reconciled to God through the death of his Son, when God ought to have been the more angered against man, inasmuch as men acted more criminally by crucifying his Son than they ever did by transgressing his first command in paradise through the tasting of a single apple? For the more men's sins were multiplied, the more just it would have been for God to be angry with men. And if that sin of Adam was so great that it could be expiated only by the death of Christ, what expiation will avail for that act of murder committed against Christ, and for the many great crimes committed against him or his followers? How did the death of his innocent Son so please God the Father that through it he should be reconciled to us—to us who by our sinful acts have done the very things for which our innocent Lord was put to death? Had not this very great sin been committed, could he not have pardoned the former much lighter sin? Had not evil deeds been multiplied, could he not have done such a good thing for man?

In what manner have we been made more righteous through the death of the Son of God than we were before, so that we ought to be delivered from punishment? And to whom was the price of blood paid for our redemption but to him in whose power we were—that is, to God himself, who (as we have said) handed us over to his torturer? For it is not the torturers but the masters of those who are held captive who arrange or receive such ransoms. Again, how did he release these captives for a price if he himself exacted or settled the price for release of the same? Indeed, how cruel and wicked it seems that anyone should demand the blood of an innocent person as the price for anything, or that it should in any way please him that an innocent man should be slain—still less that God should consider the death of his Son so agreeable that by it he should be reconciled to the whole world!

These, and like queries, appear to us to pose a considerable problem concerning our redemption or justification through the death of our Lord Jesus Christ.

Now it seems to us that we have been justified by the blood of Christ and reconciled to God in this way: through this unique act of grace manifested to us—in that his Son has taken upon himself our nature and persevered therein in teaching us by word and example even unto death—he has more fully bound us to himself by love; with the result that our hearts should be enkindled by such a gift of divine grace, and true charity should not now shrink from enduring anything for him.

And we do not doubt that the ancient Fathers, waiting in faith for this same gift, were aroused to very great love of God in the same way as men of this dispensation of grace, since it is written: "And they that went before and they that followed cried, saying: 'Hosanna to the Son of David,' " etc. Yet everyone becomes more righteous—by which we mean a greater lover of the Lord—after the Passion of Christ than before, since a realized gift inspires greater love than one which is only hoped for. Wherefore, our redemption through Christ's suffering is that deeper affection in us which not only frees us from slavery to sin, but also wins for us the true liberty of sons of God, so that we do all things out of love rather than fear— love to him who has shown us such grace that no greater can be found, as he himself asserts, saying, "Greater love than this no man hath, that a man lay down his life for his friends." Of this love the Lord says elsewhere, "I am come to cast fire on the earth, and what I will, but that it blaze forth?" So does he bear witness that he came for the express purpose of spreading this true liberty of love amongst men.

37 THE RACOVIAN CATECHISM (1605) was the doctrinal statement of the Socinians, centered at Rakow, Poland. The movement took its name from Lelio Sozzini (1525–1562) and his nephew, Fausto Sozzini (1539–1604), Italian émigrés who settled in Poland.

Socinianism was a combination of a rational theology

with strong insistence on the supernatural basis of Christianity. Scripture is the clear and authoritative record of God's revelation to man, though, carefully examined, it contains nothing contrary to reason. The life of Christ serves to display God's will for man and calls for man's faithful response and obedience. Christ is distinct from other men by the perfect obedience and holiness of His life and, therefore, can properly be called the only-begotten Son of God. Later Unitarians looked to the Socinians as their progenitors.

The Racovian Catechism*

SECTION IV. OF THE KNOWLEDGE OF CHRIST

CHAPTER 1

Of the person of Christ

As you have stated that there are some things relating to the Will of God, which were first revealed by Jesus Christ, and also asserted, at the commencement, that the way of salvation consisted in the knowledge of him,—I now wish you to specify what those particulars are, concerning Jesus Christ, which I ought to know?

Certainly: You must be informed, then, that there are some things relating to the PERSON, or nature, of Jesus Christ, and some, to his OFFICE, with which you ought to be acquainted.

What are the things relating to his Person, which I ought to know?

This one particular alone,—that by nature he was truly a man; a mortal man while he lived on earth, but now immortal. That he was a real man the scriptures testify in several places: Thus 1 Timothy ii. 5, "There is one God, and one mediator between God and men, the MAN Christ Jesus." 1 Corinthians xv. 21, 22, "Since by MAN came death, by MAN came also the resurrection of the dead. For as in ADAM all die, even so in CHRIST shall all be made alive." Romans v. 15, "If through the offence of one, many be dead, much more the grace of God, and the gift by grace, which is by one MAN, Jesus Christ, hath abounded unto many." John viii. 40, "But now ye seek to kill me, A MAN that hath told you the truth." See also Hebrews v. 1, &c. Such, besides, was the person whom God promised of old

* From *The Racovian Catechism*, tr. by Thomas Rees. London: Longman, Horst, Rees, Orme, and Brown, 1818.

by the prophets; and such also does the Creed called the Apostles', which all Christians, in common with ourselves, embrace, declare him to be.

Was, then, the Lord Jesus a mere or common man?

By no means: because, first, though by nature he was a man, he was nevertheless, at the same time, and even from his earliest origin, the only begotten Son of God. For being conceived of the Holy Spirit, and born of a virgin, without the intervention of any human being, he had properly no father besides God: though considered in another light, simply according to the flesh, without respect to the Holy Spirit, of which he was conceived, and with which he was anointed, he had David for his father, and was therefore his son. Concerning his supernatural conception, the angel thus speaks to Mary, Luke i. 35, "The Holy Ghost shall come upon thee, and the Power of the Highest shall overshadow thee; therefore also that holy thing which shall be born of thee shall be called the Son of God." Secondly, because, as Christ testifies of himself, he was sanctified and sent into the world by the Father; that is, being in a most remarkable manner separated from all other men, and, besides being distinguished by the perfect holiness of his life, endued with divine wisdom and power, was sent by the Father, with supreme authority, on an embassy to mankind. Thirdly, because, as the apostle Paul testifies, both in the Acts of the Apostles, and in his Epistle to the Romans, he was raised from the dead by God, and thus as it were begotten a second time;—particularly as by this event he became like God immortal. Fourthly, because by his dominion and supreme authority over all things, he is made to resemble, or, indeed, to equal God: on which account, "a king anointed by God," and "Son of God," are used in several passages of scripture as phrases of the same import. And the sacred author of the Epistle to the Hebrews (chap. i. ver. 5) shows from the words of the Psalmist (Psalm ii. 7), "Thou art my Son, this day have I begotten thee," that Christ was glorified by God, in order that he might be made a Priest, that is, the chief director of our religion and salvation,—in which office are comprised his supreme authority and dominion. He was, however, not merely the only begotten Son of God, but also A GOD, on account of the divine power and authority which he displayed even while he was yet mortal: much more may he be so denominated now that he has received all power in heaven and earth, and that all things, God himself alone excepted, have been put under his feet.—But of this you shall hear in its proper place.

But do you not acknowledge in Christ a divine, as well as a human nature or substance?

If by the terms divine nature or substance I am to understand the very essence of God, I do not acknowledge such a divine nature in Christ; for this were repugnant both to right reason and to the Holy Scriptures. But if, on the other hand, you intend by a divine nature the Holy Spirit which dwelt in Christ, united, by an indissoluble bond, to his human nature, and displayed in him the wonderful effects of its extraordinary presence; or if you understand the words in the sense in which Peter employs them (2 Peter i. 4), when he asserts that "we are partakers of a divine nature," that is, endued by the favour of God with divinity, or divine properties,—I certainly do so far acknowledge such a nature in Christ as to believe that next after God it belonged to no one in a higher degree.

Show me how the first mentioned opinion is repugnant to right reason?

First, on this account, That two substances endued with opposite and discordant properties, such as are God and man, cannot be ascribed to one and the same individual, much less be predicated the one of the other. For you cannot call one and the same thing first fire, and then water, and afterwards say that the fire is water, and the water fire. And such is the way in which it is usually affirmed;—first, that Christ is God, and afterwards that he is a man; and then that God is man, and that man is God.

But what ought to be replied, when it is alleged that Christ is constituted of a divine and human nature, in the same way as man is composed of a soul and body?

The cases are essentially different:—for it is stated that the two natures are so united in Christ, that he is both God and man: whereas the union between the soul and body is of such a kind that the man is neither the soul nor the body. Again, neither the soul nor the body, separately, constitutes a person: but as the divine nature, by itself, constitutes a person, so also must the human nature, by itself, constitute a person; since it is a primary or single intelligent substance. . . .

I perceive that Christ has not the divine nature which is claimed for him; but that he is a real man:—inform me now in what way the knowledge of this eminently conduces to salvation?

This you may perceive from hence: first, because the contrary opinion greatly tarnishes the glory of God; secondly, because it materially weakens and nearly destroys the certainty of our hope; and thirdly, because it makes one thing of Christ, and another of the Son of God; so that divine honour being transferred to the latter, the divine honour of him who is actually the Christ and the Son of God, is either taken away, or essentially impaired.

How does the opinion of our adversaries tarnish the glory of God?

Not only because the glory of the one God, which pertains to the Father alone, is transferred to another, concerning which I have already treated; but also because God is deprived of that glory which he seeks in the exaltation of Jesus Christ. For if Christ were the most high God, he could not be exalted; or if he could, his exaltation could refer to nothing but the reception of his divine nature entire. Paul, however, says (Ephes. i. 17–21) that "the God of our Lord Jesus Christ, the Father of Glory,—

wrought his mighty power in Christ, when he raised him from the dead, and set him at his own right hand in the heavenly places, far above all principality," &c. and also (Philipp. ii. 9, 10), that "God had highly exalted Christ, and given him a name which is above every name, that in the name of Jesus every knee should bow, and every tongue should confess that Jesus Christ is Lord to the glory of God the Father:" "To THE GLORY," the apostle writes, "OF GOD THE FATHER," who GAVE him such a name, and such glory.

How, secondly, does the opinion of our adversaries destroy or weaken our hope?

Because the greatest force which pertains to the resurrection of Christ, as a proof of our resurrection, is taken away by attributing this divine nature to him. For it would hence follow that Christ rose from the dead by virtue of his divine nature, as indeed is commonly maintained, and that, on this account, he could by no means be detained by death. But we have nothing in us by nature, which, after we are dead, can recall us to life, or which can in any way prevent our remaining dead perpetually. How then can the certainty of our resurrection be demonstrated from the example of Christ's resurrection, as the apostle Paul has done (1 Cor. xv.), when there exists such a disparity between Christ and us? And, indeed, if this opinion be admitted, Christ, in reality, could not die, and rise from the dead; since it would follow from it, that Christ was not a person, or, as they say, *suppositum humanum*, that is, a man subsisting of himself. But to die and to rise from the dead can comport with no other than a subject, [*suppositum*] or thing subsisting of itself. A divine person could not die. If therefore Christ was destitute of a human person, capable of dying and rising from the dead, how could he die, or rise from the dead? The same reason shows that Christ was not truly a man, since every one who is a real man is a human person. But that opinion which acknowledges Christ as subsisting of himself, and therefore truly a man, who was obedient to his Father unto death; and asserts and clearly determines that he died, was raised from the dead by God, and endowed with immortality; does in a wonderful manner sustain our hope of eternal salvation; placing before us the very image of the thing, and assuring us that we also, though we be mortal and die, shall nevertheless, if we follow his footsteps, be in due time raised from the dead, and be brought to a participation of the immortality which he now enjoys.

How, thirdly, does the opinion of our adversaries make one thing of Christ, and another of the Son of God?

Because it makes of Christ, the one God himself, and calls him the Son of God, who actually existed before the conception of the man Jesus by the Holy Spirit, and his birth of the Virgin, and indeed before all ages, and directs to the worship of him, our honour and faith:—while in the meantime, either he who is truly Christ and the Son of God, is to them an idol, if they worship him; or else it does not appear how he is at once the one God, and a man, and can be worshipped both as God, and as a man whom God has exalted. . . .

SECTION V. OF THE PROPHETIC OFFICE OF CHRIST

CHAPTER 8

The death of Christ

. . . But did not Christ die also, in order, properly speaking, to purchase our salvation, and literally to pay the debt of our sins?

Although Christians at this time commonly so believe, yet this notion is false, erroneous, and exceedingly pernicious; since they conceive that Christ suffered an equivalent punishment for our sins, and by the price of his obedience exactly compensated our disobedience. There is no doubt, however, but that Christ so satisfied God by his obedience, as that he completely fulfilled the whole of his will, and by his obedience obtained, through the grace of God, for all of us who believe in him, the remission of our sins, and eternal salvation.

How do you make it appear that the common notion is false and erroneous?

Not only because the scriptures are silent concerning it, but also because it is repugnant to the scriptures and to right reason.

Prove this, in order.

That nothing concerning it is to be found in the scriptures appears from hence; that they who maintain this opinion never adduce explicit texts of scripture in proof of it, but string together certain inferences by which they endeavour to maintain their assertions. But, besides that a matter of this kind, whereon they themselves conceive the whole business of salvation to turn, ought certainly to be demonstrated not by inferences alone but by clear testimonies of scripture, it might easily be shown that these inferences have no force whatever: otherwise, inferences which necessarily spring from the scriptures, I readily admit.

How is this opinion repugnant to the scriptures?

Because the scriptures everywhere testify that God forgives men their sins freely, and especially under the New Covenant (2 Cor. v. 19; Rom. iii. 24, 25; Matth. xviii. 23, &c.). But to a free forgiveness nothing is more opposite than such a satisfaction as they contend for, and the payment of an equivalent price. For where a creditor is satisfied, either by the debtor himself, or by another person on the debtor's behalf, it cannot with truth be said of him that he freely forgives the debt.

How is this repugnant to reason?

This is evident from hence; that it would follow that Christ, if he has satisfied God for our sins, has submitted to eternal death; since it appears that the penalty which men had incurred by their offences was eternal death; not to say that one death, though it were eternal in duration,—much less one so short,—could not of itself be equal to innumerable eternal deaths. For if you say that the death of Christ, because he was a God infinite in nature, was equal to the infinite deaths of the infinite race of men,—besides that I have already refuted this opinion concerning the nature of Christ,—it would follow that God's infinite nature itself suffered death. But as death cannot any way belong to the infinity of the divine nature, so neither, literally speaking (as much necessarily be done here where we are treating of a real compensation and payment), can the infinity of the divine nature any way belong to death. In the next place, it would follow that there was no necessity that Christ should endure such sufferings, and so dreadful a death; and that God—be it spoken without offence,—was unjust, who, when he might well have been contented with one drop (as they say) of the blood of Christ, would have him so severely tormented. Lastly, it would follow that we were more obliged to Christ than to God, and owed him more, indeed owed him every thing; since he, by this satisfaction, showed us much kindness; whereas God, by exacting his debt, showed us no kindness at all.

State in what manner this opinion is pernicious?

Because it opens a door to licentiousness, or, at least, invites men to indolence in the practice of piety, in what way soever they urge the piety of their patron. For if full payment have been made to God by Christ for all our sins, even those which are future, we are absolutely freed from all liability to punishment, and therefore no further condition can by right be exacted from us to deliver us from the penalties of sin. What necessity then would there be for living religiously? But the scripture testifies (Tit. ii. 14; Gal. i. 4; 1 Pet. i. 18; Heb. ix. 14; 2 Cor. v. 15; Eph. v. 26) that Christ died for this end, among others, that he might "redeem us from all iniquity, and purify us unto himself a peculiar people zealous of good works;" "that he might deliver us from the present evil world;" "might redeem us from our vain conversation, received by tradition from our fathers," in order that being "dead to sin" we might "live unto righteousness," that our consciences might be "purged from dead works to serve the living God."

But how do they maintain their opinion?

They endeavour to do this first by a certain reason, and then by the authority of scripture.

What is this reason?

They say that there are in God, by nature, justice and mercy: that as it is the property of mercy to forgive sins, so is it, they state, the property of justice to punish every sin whatever. But since God willed that both his mercy and justice should be satisfied together, he devised this plan, that Christ should suffer death in our stead, and thus satisfy God's justice in the human nature, by which he had been offended; and that his mercy should at the same time be displayed in forgiving sin.

What reply do you make to this reason?

This reason bears the appearance of plausibility, but in reality has in it nothing of truth or solidity; and indeed involves a self-contradiction. For although we confess, and hence exceedingly rejoice, that our God is wonderfully merciful and just, nevertheless we deny that there are in him the mercy and justice which our adversaries imagine, since the one would wholly annihilate the other. For, according to them, the one requires that God should punish no sin; the other, that he should leave no sin unpunished. If then it were naturally a property of God to punish no sin, he could not act against his nature in order that he might punish sin: in like manner also, if it were naturally a property of God to leave no sin unpunished, he could not, any more, contrary to his nature, refrain from punishing every sin. For God can never do any thing repugnant to those properties which pertain to him by nature. For instance, since wisdom belongs naturally to God, he can never do any thing contrary to it, but whatever he does he does wisely. But as it is evident that God forgives and punishes sins whenever he deems fit, it appears that the mercy which commands to spare, and the justice which commands to destroy, do so exist in him as that both are tempered by his will, and by the wisdom, the benignity, and holiness of his nature. Besides, the scriptures are not wont to designate the justice, which is opposed to mercy, and is discernible in punishments inflicted in wrath, by this term, but style it the SEVERITY, the ANGER, and WRATH of God:—indeed, it is attributed to the justice of God in the scriptures that he forgives sins: 1 John iv. 9; Rom. iii. 25, 26; and frequently in the Psalms.

What then is your opinion concerning this matter?

It is this;—that since I have shown that the mercy and justice which our adversaries conceive to pertain to God by nature, certainly do not belong to him, there was no need of that plan whereby he might satisfy such mercy and justice, and by which they might, as it were by a certain tempering, be reconciled to each other: which tempering nevertheless is such that it satisfies neither, and indeed destroys both;—For what is that justice, and what too that mercy, which punishes the innocent, and absolves the guilty? I do not, indeed, deny that there is a natural justice in God, which is called rectitude, and is opposed to wickedness: this shines in all his works, and hence they all appear just and right and perfect; and that, no less when he forgives than when he punishes our transgressions. . . .

But what do you conceive to be the meaning of the declaration,—that Christ has redeemed us and given himself a ransom for us?

The term REDEMPTION, in most passages of scripture, means simply LIBERATION; but by a more extended figure, it is put for that liberation for effecting which a certain price is paid. And it is said of the death of Christ that he has liberated us by it, because by means of it we have obtained our freedom both from our sins themselves, that we no longer serve them; and also from the punishment of them, that being snatched from the jaws of eternal death we may live for ever.

But why is this deliverance expressed by the term redemption?

Because there is a very great similarity between our deliverance and a redemption properly so called. For as in a proper redemption there must be a captive, the person who detains the captive, the redeemer, and lastly, the ransom, or price of the redemption; so also in our deliverance, if we speak of our sins themselves, man is the captive—they who detain him are sin, the world, the devil, and death: the redeemer of the captive are God and Christ; and the ransom, or price of the redemption, is Christ, or his soul paid by God and by Christ himself. The only difference lies here, that in this deliverance of us from our sins themselves, no one receives any thing under the name of ransom, which must always happen in a redemption properly so called. But if we speak of our deliverance from the punishment of our sins, we owe this to God, Christ having delivered us from it when, in compliance with the will of God, he gave himself up to death for us, and through his own blood entered into the heavenly place: which obedience of his son unto death, and the death of the cross, God accepted as an offering of all the most agreeable to him. But this is not to be understood nevertheless as importing that God, literally speaking, had received the full payment of our debts; since Christ was a victim of his own, provided by himself, as was also the case in the yearly sacrifice (the type of the sacrifice of Christ): and owed every thing to God through himself, and in his own name; and although his obedience was the highest and most perfect of any, yet he received an incomparably greater reward for it. Wherefore this ought to be ascribed to the unbounded grace and bounty of God; because he not only did not receive any part of what we owed to him, and because he not only forgave us all our debts; but also because he gave a victim of his own, and that his only-begotten and best-beloved son, that lamb without blemish, for us and our sins, not that he might pay himself any thing for us (for this would be a fictitious not a real payment), but might create for us so much greater and more certain a right to pardon and eternal life, and might bind himself by such a pledge to confer this upon us; and might also convert us to himself, and bless us with the other signal benefits of which we stood in need.

38   HUGO GROTIUS (1583–1645) was a Dutch historian, political
           theorist, and theologian. Though he is remembered most
           frequently for his *de Jure Belli et Pacis* (1624), a major
work in political theory, he was also involved in the Arminian controversy in the Dutch Reformed Church.[1] His defence of the Arminian position and protest against the
secular interference in religious affairs caused his imprisonment and later exile from the Netherlands.

His doctrine of the atonement, usually referred to as
the "governmental" theory, was developed in reaction to
the Socinian position.[2] In contrast to these sixteenth-century
"Unitarians," who viewed the work of Christ as an example
for man that commands an obedient response and to the
"satisfaction" theory of Anselm,[3] which suggested that
Christ satisfied man's debt to God, Grotius proposed that
the work of Christ was to uphold divine law and government.
God is the legal governor of the universe, the administrator
of law, but in the death of Christ God displayed His clemency, His hatred of sin, and His insistence on the authority
of divine law. The punishment due man for his sin could not
be ignored. Though God did not demand satisfaction, His
law must be preserved. This was the work of Christ. Grotius'
"governmental" theory had marked influence on Calvinism,
especially in eighteenth-century America.

[1] See also *Declaration of Sentiments*, Selection 49; *The Remonstrance: 1610*, Selection 50; *The Canons of the Synod of Dort*, Selection 51.
[2] See *The Racovian Catechism*, Selection 37.
[3] See Anselm, *Cur Deus Homo*, Selection 35.

A Defence of the Catholic Faith Concerning the Satisfaction of Christ*

GROTIUS

CHAPTER 1

To sum up what has been already said: since the scripture says that Christ was chastised by God, i.e., punished; that Christ bore our sins, i.e. the punishment of sins; was made sin, i.e. was subjected to the penalty of sins; was made a curse with God, or was exposed to the curse, that is, the penalty of the law; since, moreover, the very suffering of Christ, full of tortures, bloody, ignominious, is most appropriate matter of punishment; since, again, the scripture says that these were inflicted on him by God on account of our sins, i.e. our sins so deserving; since death itself is said to be the wages, i.e. the punishment of sin; certainly it can by no means be doubted that with reference to God the suffering and death of Christ had the character of a punishment. Nor can we listen to the interpretations of Socinus, which depart from the perpetual use of the words without authority, especially when no reason prevents us from retaining the received meaning of the words, as will be made plain below. There is, therefore, a punishment, in God actively, in Christ passively. Yet in the passion of Christ there is also a certain action, viz. the voluntary endurance of penal suffering.

THE END of the transaction of which we treat, in the intention of God and Christ, which, proposed in the act, may also be said to have been effected, is two-fold; namely, the exhibition of the divine justice, and the remission of sins with respect to us, i.e. our exemption from punishment. For if you take the exaction of punishment impersonally, its end is the exhibition of the divine justice; but if personally, i.e. why was Christ punished, the end is that we might be freed from punishment.

The former end is indicated by Paul when he says of Christ, "Whom God hath set forth to be a propitiation in his blood to declare his righteousness for the remission of sins that are past, through the forbearance of God." Then he adds, repeating almost the same words: "To declare, I say, at this time his righteousness, that he might be just and the justifier of him that

* From Hugo Grotius, A Defence of the Catholic Faith Concerning the Satisfaction of Christ, Against Faustus Socinus, tr. by Frank Hugh Foster. Andover: Warren F. Draper, 1889.

believeth in Jesus." Here, in close connection with the blood, i.e. the bloody death, stands the end, "to declare his righteousness."

By the expression "righteousness of God" is not to be understood that righteousness which God works in us, or which he imputes to us, but that which is in God. For he proceeds: "That he might be just," i.e. appear to be just. This justice of God, i.e. rectitude, for different objects has different effects. With reference to the good or evil deeds of a creature its effect, among other things, is retribution, with reference to which Paul said; "It is a righteous thing with God to recompense tribulation to them that trouble you." In another place: "Every transgression and disobedience received a just recompense of reward." And the following: "Whose damnation is just." The Syriac has it: "Whose condemnation is reserved for justice." So also, "day of wrath," and "day of just judgment" are the same. It is said that the final judgment will be "in equity." Elsewhere, "to judge in equity" is to take severe vengeance, which is shown by the additional words "make war," and much more by those that follow a little after: "And out of his mouth goeth a sharp sword, that with it he should smite the nations; and he shall rule them with a rod of iron; and he treadeth the wine-press of the fierceness and wrath of Almighty God." So both God is said to be just, and his punishments to be just, because he severely punishes sin. Vengeance is accordingly the name given now to the punitive justice of God, and now to the punishment inflicted by it. The judgment of God is explained by Paul to be this: that they who commit, or approve evil things, are worthy of death. Conjugate to these are "revenger" and "vengeance," the force of which is explained by the word "repay."

It is true that by the word *justice* is frequently meant *veracity*, frequently also *equity*. But since by this word, as has already been shown by many examples, that attribute of God is indicated which moves him to punish sin, and which is exhibited in this punishment of sin, we say that this is the proper signification of our passage. Different ages are set in opposition; e.g. the ages before Christ and that of Christ. To the former is attributed the passing over of sins, which is also explained by the word "forbearance." πάρεσις does not mean *remission*, but *passing over*, to which ἀνοχή, *forbearance*, is rightly added. By this word the Greeks designate a truce, because by it war was for a time kept in check. To this passing over and checking is opposed such a demonstration of justice that by it God may be, i.e. may appear, just. Once, when God passed over very many sins unpunished, his retributive justice did not sufficiently appear. At length, therefore, he showed how he was a just retributor when he determined that his own Son for this cause should shed his blood to become a propitiation for the human race, and to redeem all those who had ever believed, or should ever believe, in God. So the apostle has put the open demonstration in close connection with the grace, i.e. the divine goodness which is bestowed upon creatures, and with the justice of him who is the guardian of right order and also of retribution. Certainly the very word *blood,* the word *propitiation,* and even *redemption,* show that he is not engaged here with the simple testimony to goodness. He has also connected impetration with application. The impetration is through the blood; the application through faith. Rightly is that justice, of which we are treating, said to be made manifest through faith; that faith, namely, by which the blood of Christ is believed to have been shed to propitiate God; which faith entirely excludes all glory in works, all trust in the law.

This end, viz. the exhibition of the divine justice, is also rightly inferred from the form of the transaction of which we treat. For the end of punishment is the exhibition of retributive justice concerning sins, also upon antecedent cause, which we have above shown to be meritorious. But the impelling cause of an action cannot be meritorious except also the end be to make retribution.

. . . exemption from the punishment of our sins is the [second] end of the death of Christ, and the effect of that death. . . .

CHAPTER 3

. . . Having examined the part which God performs in this matter, we shall easily find a name for the act itself. And, first, since God, as we have proved, is to be considered here as a ruler, it follows that his act is an act of the administration of justice, generally so called. From this it follows that we are not treating here of acceptilation, as Socinus thinks, for that is not an act of the administration of justice. To designate the class of this act more particularly it may be considered either in relation to the divine sanction (or, as more recent jurists say, the penal law), or without regard to that relation. We add this specification because, even if the law had made no reference to punishment, yet, in the nature of things, man's act, either as having an intrinsic depravity from the immutable nature of the case, or also an extrinsic depravity on account of the contrary precept of God, deserved, on that very account, some punishment, and that, too, a grave one. That is, it was equitable to punish man as a sinner. If we take our stand here, the act of God of which we treat will be the punishment of one to obtain the impunity of another. Of the justice of this we shall soon treat. But if further we have regard to the sanction, or penal law, the act will be a method of relaxing or moderating the same law, which relaxation we call, in these days, dispensation. It may be defined: The act of a superior by which the obligation of an unabrogated law upon certain persons or things is removed. This is the sanction: the man that eateth of the forbidden tree shall surely die. In this passage by one species of sin every class of sin is indicated, as is expressed by the same law more clearly brought

out, "Cursed is every one that continueth not in all the precepts of the
law." By the words death and curse, in these passages, we understand especially eternal death. For this reason it is as if the law had been expressed in this manner: Every man that sinneth shall bear the punishment of eternal death.

There is, therefore, here no execution of that law; for if God always
executed the law no sinner could be saved from the penalty of eternal
death. But now we know that for believers there is no condemnation, because they are liberated from death and redeemed from the curse.

Again, this act is not an abrogation of the law; for abrogated law has
no binding force. But unbelievers are still exposed to the penalty of the
same law. Thus we find written that the wrath of God abideth upon them
that believe not, and that the wrath of God is come upon them to the
uttermost.

Again, it is not an interpretation of the law according to equity; for
that interpretation shows that some person or act never was comprehended
under the obligation of the law. Works of religion and mercy, for example,
were never comprehended under the interdiction of working upon the
Sabbath. But indeed all men (assuredly concluded under sin), even those
who are liberated, are, by nature or by act, children of wrath, that is, bound
by the sanction of the law. It is therefore not declared that there is no
obligation; but this is done that what was may be removed; that is, that a
relaxation or dispensation of the law may be made.

It may be asked here whether the penal law is relaxable? There are
certain irrelaxable laws, either absolutely or by hypothesis. Those are absolutely irrelaxable whose opposite involves, from the nature of the case,
immutable wickedness; as, for example, the law which forbids perjury, or
bearing false witness against one's neighbor. For, as we say that God cannot lie, or deny himself, so, no less rightly, do we say that God cannot
perform actions in themselves wicked, or approve them, or grant the right
to do them.

Those laws are irrelaxable of hypothesis which arise from a definite
decree; such as the law of condemning those who will not believe in Jesus
Christ.

But all positive laws are absolutely relaxable; and we are not compelled
to resort to hypothetical necessity, of a definite decree, where no mark of
such decree exists.

It is a great error to be afraid, as some are, lest in making such a concession we do injury to God, as if we made him mutable. The law is not
something internal within God, or the will of God itself, but only an effect
of that will. It is perfectly certain that the effects of the divine will are
mutable. By promulgating a positive law which at some time he may wish
to relax God does not signify that he wills anything but what he really

does will. God shows that he seriously wills that the law should be valid
and obligatory, yet with the reserved right of relaxing it. This inheres in
positive law, of its own nature, nor by any sign can it be understood to have
been abdicated by God. More than that, God does not deprive himself of
the right even of abrogating the law, as appears from the example of the
ceremonial law. To be sure it is a different thing, if with the positive law
be connected an oath, or a promise; for an oath is a sign of the immutability
of that with which it is joined. Moreover, a promise gives a right to the
party which cannot be taken away from it without injury. Wherefore,
although it is optional to promise, yet to break promises is not optional.
This is one of the cases, therefore, in which is involved immutable wickedness. God cannot break his promises, who is called faithful especially because he keeps them.

Let us therefore inquire whether there is anything in the said penal
law when promulgated which plainly repudiates relaxation.

First, it may be objected that it is just, in the nature of things, that
the wicked should themselves be punished with such a punishment as shall
correspond to their crime, and that this is, consequently, not subject to free-
will, and so not relaxable.

To answer this objection we must know that injustice does not result
from every negation of justice, even under the same circumstances. For as
it does not follow that if a king ought to be called liberal because he has
given a thousand talents to a certain man, he would therefore be illiberal
if he should not do so, so it is not a general rule that what may be done
justly cannot be omitted without injustice. Anything may be called natural in morals as well as in physics, properly or less properly. That is
properly natural in physics which necessarily coheres in the essence of anything, as feeling in a living object; but less properly that which is convenient to the nature of anything, and, as it were, accommodated to it, as
for a man to use his right arm. So in morals there are certain things properly
natural which necessarily follow from the relation of things to rational
natures, as that perjury is unlawful; and certain things improperly natural,
as that a son should succeed a father. According to this, that he who has
committed a crime, deserves punishment, and is on that account liable to
punishment, necessarily follows, from the very relation of sin and the
sinner to the superior, and is properly natural. But that all sinners should
be punished with a punishment corresponding to the crime is not simply
and universally necessary, nor properly natural, but only harmonious with
nature. Hence it follows that nothing prevents the law which demands this
from being relaxable.

The mark of definite decree, or of irrevocability, does not appear in
the law of which we are treating. Neither is the law a promise. Therefore
nothing prevents the relaxation of these things. For we should not admit

that a threat is equivalent to a promise. For from a promise a certain right is gained by him to whom the promise is made; but by a threat there is merely a more open declaration made of the desert of punishment in the sinner and the right of punishing in the threatener. Nor should we fear lest the veracity of God is impaired in any respect if he does not fulfill all his threats. For all threats which have not the sign of irrevocability must be understood, from their own nature, to diminish in no degree the right of the threatener to relax, as has been explained above. The example of the divine clemency towards the Ninevites proves this.

We must not omit here to show that the ancient philosophers judged by the light of nature that there was nothing more relaxable than a penal law. Aristotle says that the just man is inclined to forgive. Sopater, in his Epistle to Demetrius, says: "The right which is called equity, modifying the stern voice of the law, seems to me to be an irreprehensible class of genuine and liberal favors. That part of justice which reduces contracts to equity, entirely rejects every kind of favors. But that part which is engaged upon crimes does not disdain the mild and humane countenance of grace."

From what has already been said it appears that the positive and penal law of God was dispensable. But this does not prove that there were no reasons which (to stammer, as man must) might oppose their relaxation. These may be sought either in the nature of universal laws, or in the peculiar matter of the law. It is common to all laws that in relaxing, the authority of the law seems to be diminished in some respects. It is peculiar to this law that, although, as we have said, it is not of inflexible rectitude, yet it is entirely in harmony with the nature and order of things. Hence it follows, not that the law could not be relaxed at all, but that it could not be relaxed easily, or upon slight cause. And this has been followed by that sole all-wise Lawgiver. For he had a most weighty reason, when the whole human race had fallen into sin, for relaxing the law. If all sinners had been delivered over to eternal death, from the nature of the case, two most beautiful things would have entirely perished: on the part of men religion toward God, and on the part of God the declaration of especial favor toward men. God has not only followed reasons, and those most weighty, in relaxing the law, but he has also made use of a singular method of relaxation. For speaking of this a more suitable place will be found below. . . .

CHAPTER 5

. . . it will not be difficult to assign from the scriptures a sufficient cause, and, indeed, a most weighty cause, whether we inquire why God chose to remit to us eternal punishment, or why he did not choose to remit the same otherwise than by the punishment of Christ. The former has its cause in benevolence, which is, of all the attributes of God, most truly peculiar to him. For everywhere God describes himself chiefly by this attribute, that he is benignant and clement. Therefore, God is inclined to aid and bless men, but he cannot do this while that dreadful and eternal punishment remains. Besides, if eternal death should fall upon all, religion had totally perished through despair of felicity. There were, therefore, great reasons for sparing man.

On the other hand, those passages of scripture already adduced by us, which declare that Christ was delivered, suffered, died for our sins, show the reason why God imposed punishment upon Christ. This manner of speaking, as we have shown, points to the impulsive cause. It may be seen from what we have said of the end not only that there was a cause, but what it was, viz. that God was unwilling to pass over so many sins, and so great sins, without a distinguished example. This is so because every sin is seriously displeasing to God, and the more displeasing the more grave it is. Since God is active, and has created rational creatures in order to give more abundant testimony to his attributes, it is proper for him also to testify by some act how greatly he is displeased with sin. The act most suitable for this is punishment. Hence, arises that in God which the Sacred Writings, because there is no other more significant word, call wrath. God declares he is prevented by this wrath from blessing men.

Again, all neglect to punish sin leads per se to a lower estimation of sin, as, on the other hand, the most ready means of preventing sin is the fear of punishment. Hence, the well-known saying: "By bearing an old injury you invite a new." Therefore prudence also, on this account, invites the ruler to inflict punishment.

Moreover, the reasons for punishing are increased when a law has been published threatening punishment, for then the omission of punishment almost always detracts from the authority of the law among the subjects. Hence, the precept of politics: "Guard the established laws with the greatest care."

God has, therefore, most weighty reasons for punishing, especially if we are permitted to estimate the magnitude and multitude of sins. But because among all his attributes love of the human race is pre-eminent, God was willing, though he could have justly punished the sins of all men with deserved and legitimate punishment, that is, with eternal death, and had reasons for so doing, to spare those who believe in Christ. But since we must be spared either by setting forth, or not setting forth, some example against so many great sins, in his most perfect wisdom he chose that way by which he could manifest more of his attributes at once, viz. both clemency and severity, or his hate of sin and care for the preservation of his law.

So Aelianus, in commending the deed of Zaleucus, mentions two reasons for it, that the youth might not be made entirely blind, and that what had been once established should not become invalid. Of these reasons, the former operated to bring about some change in the law through clemency, the latter prevented too great a change. Those who have written on the relaxation of laws, observe that those are the best relaxations, which are accompanied by a commutation, or compensation. In this way the least injury is done to the law, and the particular precept is executed in some accordance with the reason upon which the law was founded. It is as if a man held to deliver a certain article should be excused upon paying the price. For the same thing and the same value are very nearly related.

Such commutation is admissable not only among things, but sometimes also among persons, provided that it can be done without injury to another. Thus sons are permitted to go into prison in place of their fathers, as Cimon for Miltiades. And not to go beyond penal judgments, and that too the divine, there exist in the Sacred Scriptures traces of a similar fact. To David, the homicide and adulterer, is pronounced at the command of God by Nathan: "The Lord hath put away thy sin (that is, the punishment of thy sin); thou shalt not die (which otherwise the law demanded); Howbeit because by this deed thou hast given great occasion to the enemies of the Lord to blaspheme, the child also that is born to thee (evidently since it is very closely connected with thee, and the substitute in thy punishment) shall surely die." Ahab had defiled himself with both murder and rapine. God announces to him through Elijah that the dogs will lick his blood. Yet immediately when his fear, and a certain reverence for the divine majesty was manifest, the same God said: "I will not bring the evil (viz. what both he had merited, and I threatened) in his days; but in his son's days (who shall bear not only his own, but also his father's punishment) will I bring the evil upon his house." In both cases God relaxes the law, or the threat of punishment, but not without some compensation, by transferring the punishment upon another. Thus at the same time he exhibits both his clemency and severity or hatred of sin. So, therefore, God, wishing to spare those who should believe in Christ, had sufficient, just, and great reasons for exacting of the willing Christ the punishment of our sins, viz. to use the words of Aelianus, "that what had been once established should not become invalid;" and that sin should not be thought of less importance, if so many great sins should be remitted without an example.

Further, God not only testified his own hatred of sin by this act, and so deterred us from sin (for it is an easy inference that if God would not remit the sins even of those who repented except Christ took their punishment, much less will he permit the contumacious to go unvisited); but more than that, he also declared in a marked way his great love for us in that we were spared by one to whom it was not a matter of indifference to punish sins, but who regarded it of so much importance that rather than dismiss them altogether unpunished, he delivered his only-begotten son to punishment for them! The ancients said of forgiveness that it was neither *according to* law, nor *against* law, but *above* law, and *for* law. So may we say with emphasis of this divine grace. It is *above* law, because we are not punished; *for* law, because punishment is not omitted; and remission is granted that we may live hereafter *to* the divine law.

PART III

The Human Condition
and Its Remedy

39 THE POSITION of Augustine (354–430) on the human condition and its remedy is many-sided and has shaped many aspects of Christian theology. His analysis cannot be found in any one essay, but develops in different form in nearly all his work.

The following selections are from three articles against the elusive Pelagian position. Pelagius (c. 360–c. 420) and his followers were not theologically united, but dealt in varying ways with the problems of human sin, human ability, and divine grace. The concerns of Pelagius were not always those of Augustine. Differing dispositions and interests frequently brought a theological conflict that was carried on in terms not congenial to the theological perspectives of the disputants. Pelagius was a moral reformer, seeking to commend and develop the monastic life. Some of his disciples, however, made a system out of his affirmations. For convenience in understanding the "Pelagian" position against which Augustine wrote, it is useful to use as summary points those that were condemned at the Council of Carthage (411–412): (1) Adam's sin did not affect the human race, only Adam; (2) each man is born in the same condition Adam enjoyed before the "fall"; (3) law and gospel are both designed for man's acceptance into the Kingdom of God; and (4) there were men without sin before the coming of Christ.

Letter 217, written about 426 to Vitalis ("a learned man in the church at Carthage") displays Augustine's concern for the inroads of Pelagianism in the Carthage Church and offers a summary of the twelve "truths that we know belong most firmly to the true and Catholic faith." *A Treatise on Rebuke and Grace* discusses the effect of Adam's sin and the freedom of the will. The selections from Books I, II, III of Augustine's *Four Books* against two letters of the Pelagians turns attention to the relation of grace and free will.[1]

---

[1] See also *Letter 120*, Selection 4A; "God—The Eternal Creator," *The City of God*, Selection 4B; *On The Trinity*, Selection 34A; *On the Gospel of John*, Selection 34B; *On Baptism*, Selection 55A; *The City of God*, Selection 55B.

A. Letter 217*

AUGUSTINE

. . . Since, therefore, by the favor of Christ, we are Catholic Christians:

We know that children not yet born have done nothing either good or evil in their own life, nor have they any merits of any previous life, which no individual can have as his own; that they come into the miseries of this life; that their carnal birth according to Adam involves them at the instant of nativity in the contagion of the primal death; that they are not delivered from the penalty of eternal death, which a just verdict passing from one lays upon all, unless they are born again in Christ through grace.

We know that the grace of God is given neither to children nor to adults according to their merits.

We know that in adults it is given for separate acts.

We know that it is not given to all men, and, where it is given, not only is it not given as a reward for good deeds, but it is not even given as a reward for good will in those to whom it is given, as is plainly evident in the case of children.

We know that, when it is not given, it is withheld by a just judgment of God.

We know that "we shall all stand before the judgment seat of Christ, that every one may receive the proper things of the body, according as he hath done whether it be good or evil," not according to what he would have done if he had lived longer.

We know that even children will receive either good or evil according to what they have done in the body. For they have done it, not by themselves but through those who answer for them when they are said to renounce the Devil and to believe in God. For this reason they are counted in the number of the faithful, as being referred to in the statement of the Lord when He said: "He that believeth and is baptized shall be saved." Therefore, those who do not receive this sacrament are subject to what follows: "But he that believeth not shall be condemned." Consequently even those, as I said, who die at that tender age are judged according to what they have done in the body, that is, in the time they have been in the body, when they believed or did not believe through the mouths and hearts of those who carried them when they were baptized or were not

* From *Saint Augustine: Letters*, Vol. V, tr. by Sister Wilfred Parsons. Washington, D.C.: The Catholic University of America Press, 1956.

baptized, when they ate the flesh of Christ or did not eat it, when they drank His Blood or did not drink it—according to these things which they have done in the body, not according to what they would have done if they had lived longer in this world.

We know that the dead who die in the Lord are blessed, and they have no concern with what they would have done if they had lived a longer time.

We know that those who believe in the Lord from their own heart do this of their own will and free choice.

We know that we who now believe act with an upright faith when we pray to God for those who refuse to believe, that they may will to do so.

We know that when some of these do believe we are accustomed, as we ought, to thank God uprightly and sincerely for this as a blessing from Him.

You recognize, I think, that among these things which I said we know I have not intended to enumerate everything which belongs to the Catholic faith but only those points which have to do with this question of the grace of God: whether this grace precedes or follows the will of man. That is, I wanted to explain more fully whether it is given to us because we will or whether God effects through it that we should will. If, then, you also, my brother, hold with us that those twelve statements of what I said we know belong to the correct Catholic faith, I give thanks to God, which certainly I could not truthfully do unless your holding them were a result of the grace of God; and if you do hold them, there is not a single difference left between us on this matter.

To run over these twelve with a brief explanation, how can grace follow the merit of the human will when it is given even to infants who cannot yet will or not will? How can the merits of the will even in adults be said to precede grace, if grace, in order to be truly grace, is not given according to our merits? Pelagius himself had such fear of this statement that he did not hesitate to condemn those who say that the grace of God is given according to our merits, lest he should be condemned by Catholic judges. How can the grace of God be identified with the nature of free will or with the law and doctrine when Pelagius himself repudiated that statement, thereby admitting without question that the grace of God is given to separate acts, especially in those who enjoy the use of free will?

How is it possible to say that all men would have received it if those to whom it is not given did not reject it of their own will, since "God will have all men to be saved," when there are many children to whom it is not given and many die without it, although they have no will opposed to it? Sometimes, even, their parents are in great desire and haste, with the ministers willing and ready, but as God does not will it, it is not given to them, and they die suddenly before it is given, although all haste was made for them to receive it? From this it is clear that those who resist this clear truth do not in the least understand the meaning of the saying that "God will have all men to be saved," when so many are not saved, not because they do not will it, but because God does not, which is evident without any shadow of doubt in the case of children. But, just as that saying: "In Christ all shall be made alive" although so many are punished with eternal death—means that all who receive eternal life receive it only in Christ, so also the saying, "God will have all men to be saved"—although He wills that so many should not be saved—means surely that all who are saved would not be so without His will, and if there is any other possible way of understanding those words of the Apostle, it cannot contradict this most evident truth by which we see that so many men are not saved because God does not will it, although men do.

How can the human will deserve to have grace given to it, if it is given freely to those to whom it is given, that it may be truly grace? What weight can the merits of the human will have in the matter, when those to whom this grace is not given differ by no merit, by no act of will, from those to whom it is given, but share with them the same just reason for receiving it, yet it is not given through a just judgment of God—for "there is no injustice with God"? Thus those to whom it is given are to understand how freely it is given to them, when it could equally justly be withheld, since it is justly withheld from those who have the same claim to it.

How is it possible to attribute to anything but the grace of God the will not only to believe, but also to persevere to the end, when the very end of this life depends on the power of God, not of man, and God could certainly bestow on one who would not persevere the blessing of hurrying him out of the body, "lest wickedness should alter his understanding"? For man will not receive either good or evil except according to what he has done in the body, not according to what he would have done if he had lived longer.

How can anyone say that the grace of God is not given to some children, but is given to others, destined to die, because God foresees the future will which they would have had if they had lived, when each one receives either good or evil, as the Apostle has defined, according to what he has done in the body, not according to what he would have done if he had remained longer in the body? How can men be judged according to the future will which, it is said, they would have had if they had been longer detained in the flesh, when scripture says: "Blessed are the dead who die in the Lord"? Undoubtedly, their happiness is neither certain nor secure if God will also judge the things they have not done, but which they would have done if they had had a more extended life. So, also, he who is carried off "lest wickedness should alter his understanding" receives no benefit, because he pays the penalty for that very wickedness from which, when it threatened him, he has probably been removed; and we should not rejoice over those who, as we know, have died in upright faith and a good life, because they may be judged according to some wicked deeds which they would perhaps have committed if they had lived. Those who have ended their life in unbelief and depraved morals should not be a subject of grief and destestation to us, because, perhaps, if they had lived they would have done penance and lived religiously, and so should be judged by this. In that the whole book *On Mortality* by the most blessed martyr Cyprian is to be censured and rejected, for in it his entire contention is that we know we should give thanks for the faithful who die a good death because they are taken away from the temptations of this life and will henceforth abide in assured blessedness. But since this is not false and the dead who die in the Lord certainly are blessed, there should be only mockery and execration for the erroneous opinion that men are to be judged according to their future will—which dying men will not have.

How can they say that it is a denial of the free choice of the will to admit that every man who believes in God in his heart believes only through his own free will, when those who attack the grace of God through which the will is free to choose and do good are, rather, the ones who attack the freedom of the will? How can they say that the fulfillment of the words of scripture: "The will is prepared by the Lord," is accomplished by the law of God and the doctrine of the scriptures and not, rather, by the secret prompting of the grace of God, when we pray to God with upright faith that those who contradict that same doctrine and refuse to believe may be willing to believe?

How can God wait on the will of men that they to whom He gives grace may forestall Him, when we give Him thanks—not without good reason—for those to whom He has advanced mercy, although they did not believe in Him and persecuted His doctrine with an evil will; whom He has converted to Himself with omnipotent ease, and whom from unbelievers He has made willing believers? Why give Him thanks for this if He has not done it? Why do we glorify Him in proportion to the joy we feel for those who had refused to believe but who have become believers, if the human will is not changed for the better by divine grace? The Apostle Paul says: "I was unknown by face to the Churches of Judea which are in Christ, but they had heard only that he who persecuted us in times past doth now preach the faith which once he impugned; and they magnified God in me." Why did they magnify God if God, in the goodness of His grace, had not converted the heart of that man to Himself, when, as he himself admits, he had "obtained mercy of the Lord to be faithful" to that faith which once he impugned? And by that word which he used, whom, if not God, does he declare to have wrought this great good? What is the meaning of "they magnified God" except "they pronounced God great in"? But how could they pronounce God great if He had not wrought that great deed of Paul's conversion, and how could He have done it but by changing his unwillingness into willingness to believe?

Assuredly, it is clear from those twelve statements—and you will not be allowed to deny that they form part of Catholic belief—that we confess the effect of them, separately and together, is to establish that the will of man is forestalled by the grace of God and that it is prepared by grace rather than rewarded in receiving it.

B. A Treatise on Rebuke and Grace[*]

AUGUSTINE

Now the Lord Himself not only shows us from what evil we should decline, and what good we should do, which is all that the letter of the law is able to effect; but He moreover helps us that we may decline from evil and do good, which none can do without the Spirit of grace; and if this be wanting, the law comes in merely to make us guilty and to slay us. It is on this account that the apostle says, "The letter killeth, but the Spirit giveth life." He, then, who lawfully uses the law learns therein evil and good, and if he do not confide in his own strength, flees to grace, by the help of which he may decline from evil and do good. But who is there who flees to grace except when "the steps of a man are ordered by the Lord, and He shall determine his way"? And by this means also the desire of the help of grace is the beginning of grace; of which, says he [the Psalmist], "And I said, Now I have begun; this is the change of the right hand of the Most High." It is to be confessed, therefore, that we have free choice to do both evil and good; but in doing evil every one is free from righteousness and a servant of sin, while in doing good no one can be free, unless he have been made free by Him who said, "If the Son shall make you free, then you shall be free indeed." Neither is it thus, that when any one has been made free from the dominion of sin, he no longer needs the help of his Deliverer; but rather thus, that hearing from Him, "With-

* From The Anti-Pelagian Works of St. Augustine, Vol. III, tr. by Peter Holmes and Robert E. Wallis. Edinburgh: T. & T. Clark, 1876.

out me ye can do nothing," he himself also says to Him, "Be thou my helper! Forsake me not." I rejoice that I have found in our brother Florus also this faith, which without doubt is THE TRUE AND PROPHETICAL AND APOSTOLICAL AND CATHOLIC FAITH; whence those are the rather to be corrected—whom indeed I now think to have been corrected by the favour of God—who did not understand him. . . .

For the grace of God through Jesus Christ our Lord must be apprehended,—as that by which alone men are delivered from evil, and without which they do absolutely no good thing, whether in thought, or will and affection, or in action; in order not only that they may know, by the manifestation of that grace, what should be done, but moreover that, by its enabling, they may do with love what they know. Certainly the apostle asked for this inspiration of good will and deed on behalf of those to whom he said, "Now we pray to God that ye do no evil, not that we should appear approved, but that ye should do that which is good." Who can hear this and not awake and confess that we have it from the Lord God that we turn aside from evil and do good?—since the apostle indeed says not, We admonish, we teach, we exhort, we rebuke; but he says, "We pray to God that ye do no evil, but that ye should do that which is good." And yet he was also in the habit of speaking to them, and doing all those things which I have mentioned,—he admonished, he taught, he exhorted, he rebuked. But he knew that all these things which he was doing in the way of planting and watering on the surface were of no avail unless He who giveth the increase in secret should give heed to his prayer on their behalf. Because, as the same teacher of the Gentiles says, "Neither is he that planteth anything, neither he that watereth, but God that giveth the increase. . . ."

Here, if I am asked why God should not have given them perseverance to whom He gave that love by which they might live as Christians, I answer that I do not know. For I do not speak arrogantly, but with acknowledgment of my small measure, when I hear the apostle saying, "O man, who art thou that repliest against God?" and, "O the depth of the riches of the wisdom and knowledge of God! how unsearchable are His judgments, and His ways untraceable!" So far, therefore, as He condescends to manifest His judgments to us, let us give thanks; but so far as [He thinks fit] to conceal them, let us not murmur against His counsel, but believe that this also is the most wholesome for us. But whoever you are that are hostile to His grace, and thus ask, what do you yourself say? it is well that you do not deny yourself to be a Christian and boast of being a Catholic. If, therefore, you confess that to persevere to the end in good is God's gift, I think that equally with me you are ignorant why one man should receive this gift and another should not receive it; and in this case we are both unable to penetrate the unsearchable judgments of God. Or if you say that it pertains to man's free choice—which you defend, not in accordance with God's grace, but in opposition to it—that any one should persevere in good, or should not persevere, not by the gift of God if he persevere, but by the action of human will, why will you strive against the words of Him who says, "I have prayed for thee, Peter, that thy faith fail not"? Will you dare to say that even when Christ prayed that Peter's faith might not fail, it would still have failed if Peter had willed it to fail; that is, if he had been unwilling that it should continue even to the end? As if Peter could in any measure will otherwise than Christ had asked for him that he might will. For who does not know that Peter's faith would then have perished if that will itself by which he was faithful should fail, and that it would have continued if that same will should abide? But because "the will is prepared by the Lord," therefore Christ's petition on his behalf could not be a vain petition. When, then, He prayed that his faith should not fail, what was it that he asked for, but that in his faith he should have a most free, strong, invincible, persevering will? Behold to what an extent the freedom of the will is defended in accordance with the grace of God, not in opposition to it; because the human will does not attain grace by freedom, but rather attains freedom by grace, and a delightful constancy, and an insuperable fortitude that it may persevere. . . .

Here arises another question, not reasonably to be slighted, but to be approached and solved in the help of the Lord in whose hand are both we and our discourses. For I am asked, in respect of this gift of God which is to persevere in good to the end, what I think of the first man himself, who assuredly was made upright without any fault. And I do not say: If he had not perseverance, how was he without fault, seeing that he was in want of so needful a gift of God? For to this interrogatory the answer is easy, that he had not perseverance, because he did not persevere in that goodness in which he was without sin; for he began to have sin from the point at which he fell; and if he began, certainly he was without sin before he had begun. For it is one thing not to have sin, and it is another not to abide in that goodness in which there is no sin. Because in that very fact, that he is not said never to have been without sin, but he is said not to have continued without sin, beyond all doubt it is demonstrated that he was without sin, seeing that he is blamed for not having continued in that goodness. But it should rather be asked and discussed with greater pains in what way we can answer those who say, If in that uprightness in which he was made without sin he had perseverance, beyond all doubt he persevered in it; and if he persevered, he certainly did not sin, and did not forsake that his uprightness. But that he did sin, and was a forsaker of goodness, the Truth declares. Therefore he had not perseverance in that goodness; and if he had it not, he certainly received it not.

For how should he have both received perseverance, and not have perse-vered? Further, if he had it not because he did not receive it, what sin did he commit by not persevering, if he did not receive perseverance? For it cannot be said that he did not receive it, for the reason that he was not separated by the bestowal of grace from the mass of perdition. Because that mass of perdition did not as yet exist in the human race before he had sinned from whom the corrupted source was derived. . . .

Wherefore we most wholesomely confess what we most accurately believe, that because the God and Lord of all things in His strength created all things good, and foreknew that evil things would arise out of good, and knew that it pertained to His most omnipotent goodness even to do good out of evil things rather than not to allow evil things to be at all, He so ordained the life of angels and men that in it He might first of all show what their free choice could do, and then what the kindness of His grace and judgment of His righteousness could do. Finally, certain angels, of whom the chief is he who is called the devil, became by free choice outcasts from the Lord God. Yet although they fled from His goodness, wherein they had been blessed, they could not flee from His judgment, by which they were made most wretched. Others, however, by the same free choice, stood fast in the truth, and merited the knowledge of that most certain truth that they should never fall. For if from the Holy Scriptures we have been able to attain the knowledge that none of the holy angels shall fall evermore, how much more have they themselves attained this knowledge by the truth more sub-limely revealed to them! Because to us is promised a blessed life without end, and equality with the angels, from which promise we certainly gather that when after judgment we shall have come to that life, we shall not fall from it; but if the angels are ignorant of this truth concerning themselves, we shall not be their equals, but more blessed than they. But the Truth has promised us equality with them. It is certain, then, that they have known this by sight, which we have known by faith, to wit, that there shall be now no more any fall of any holy angel. But to the devil and his angels, although they were blessed before they fell, and did not know that they should fall unto misery, there was still something which might be added to their blessed-ness, if of free will they had stood in the truth, until they should receive that fulness of the highest blessing as the reward of that very continuance of theirs; that is, that by the great abundance of the love of God, given by the Holy Spirit, they should absolutely not be able to fall any more, and that they should know this with the utmost certainty concerning themselves. They had not this plenitude of blessedness; but since they were ignorant of their future misery, they enjoyed a blessedness which was less, indeed, but still without any defect. For if they had known their future fall and eternal punishment, they certainly could not have been blessed, since the fear of so great an evil as this would compel them even then to be miserable. . . .

Thus also He [God] made man with free-will; and although ignorant of his future fall, yet therefore happy, because he thought it was in his own power both not to die and not to become miserable. In which state of uprightness and freedom from sin, if he had willed by his own free choice to continue, assuredly without any experience of death and of infelicity he would have received by the merit of that continuance the fulness of blessing with which the holy angels also are blessed; that is, the impossibility of falling any more, and the knowledge of this with absolute certainty. For even he himself could not be blessed although in Paradise, nay, he would not be there, where it would not become him to be miserable, if the foreknowledge of his fall made him wretched with the dread of such a disaster. But because of his free choice he forsook God, he experienced the just judgment of God, that with his whole race, which being as yet all constituted in him had sinned with him, he should be condemned. For as many of this race as are delivered by God's grace are certainly delivered from the condemnation in which they are already held bound. Whence, even if none should be delivered, no one could justly blame the judgment of God. That, therefore, in comparison of those that perish *few*, but in their absolute number *many*, are delivered, is effected by grace, is effected freely. Thanks must be given that it is effected that no one may be lifted up as of his own deserving, but that every mouth may be stopped, and he that glorieth may glory in the Lord. . . .

What then? Did not Adam have the grace of God? Yes, truly, he had it largely, but of a different kind. He was placed in the midst of benefits which he had received from the goodness of his Creator, for he had not procured those benefits by his own deservings; in which benefits he suffered absolutely no evil. But saints in this life, to whom pertains this grace of deliverance, are in the midst of evils out of which they cry to God, "Deliver us from evil." He [Adam] in those benefits needed not the death of Christ: the blood of that Lamb absolves *them* from guilt, as well inherited as their own. *He* had no need of that assistance which *they* implore when they say, "I see another law in my member warring against the law of my mind, and making me captive in the law of sin which is in my members. O wretched man that I am! who shall deliver me from the body of this death? The grace of God through Jesus Christ our Lord." Because in *them* the flesh lusteth against the spirit, and the spirit against the flesh, and as they labour and are imperilled in such a contest, they ask that by the grace of Christ the strength to fight and to conquer may be given them. He, however [*scil.* Adam], tempted and disturbed in no such conflict concerning himself against himself, in that position of blessedness enjoyed his peace with himself. . . .

The first man had not that grace by which he should never will to be evil; but assuredly he had that in which if he willed to abide he would never be evil, and without which, moreover, he could not of free choice be good, but which, nevertheless, by free choice he would forsake. God, therefore, did not will even him to be without His grace, which He left in his free choice; because free-will is sufficient for evil, but is of little avail for good, unless it is aided by Omnipotent Good. And if that man had not forsaken that assistance of his free-will, he would always have been good; but he forsook it, and he was forsaken. Because such was the nature of the aid, that he could forsake it when he would, and that he could continue in it when he would; but not such that he could be made to will his continuance. This first is the grace which was given to the first Adam; but more powerful than this is that in the second Adam. For the first is that whereby it is effected that a man may have righteousness if he will; the second, therefore, can do more than this, since by it it is even effected that he *will*, and wills so much, and loves with such ardour, that by the will of the Spirit he overcomes the will of the flesh, that lusteth in opposition to it. Nor was that, indeed, a small grace by which was demonstrated even the power of free choice, because man was so assisted that without this assistance he could not continue in good, but could forsake this assistance if he would. But this latter grace is by so much the greater, that it is a small matter for a man by its means to regain his lost freedom; it is of little account, finally, not to be able without it either to apprehend the good or to continue in good if he will, unless he is also *made to will*. . . .

At that time, therefore, God had given to man a good will[2] because in that will He had made him, since He had made him upright. He had given help without which he could not continue therein if he would; but that he should will, He left in his free choice. He could therefore continue if he would, because the help was not wanting whereby he could, and without which he could not, perseveringly hold fast the good which he would. But that he willed not to continue is absolutely the fault of him whose merit it would have been if he had willed to continue; as the holy angels did, who, while others fell of their own free choice, themselves by the same free choice stood, and deserved to receive the due reward of this continuance— to wit, such a fulness of blessing that by it they might have the fullest certainty of always abiding in it. If, however, this help had been wanting, either to angel or to man when they were first made, since their nature was not made such that without the divine help it could abide if it would, they certainly would not have fallen by their own fault, because the help would have been wanting without which they could not continue. Now, however, to those to whom such assistance is wanting, it is the penalty of sin; but to those to whom it is given, it is given of grace, not of debt; and by so much the more is given through Jesus Christ our Lord to those to whom it has

---

2 Some MSS. read, "a free-will."

pleased God to give it, that not only we have that help without which we cannot continue even if we will, but, moreover, we have so great and such a help as [to cause us] to *will*. Because by this grace of God there is caused in us, in the reception of good and in the persevering hold of it, not only to be able to do what we will, but even to will to do what we are able. But this was not the case in the first man; for the one of these things was in him, but the other was not. For he was not without the grace to receive good, because he had not yet lost it; but he was without the aid of grace to continue in it, and without this aid he could not do this at all; and he had received the ability if he would, but he had not the will to exercise the ability; for if he had possessed it, he would have persevered. For he could persevere if he would; but that he would not was the result of free choice, which at that time was in such wise free that he was capable of willing well and ill. For what shall be more free than free-will, when it shall not be able to serve sin? and this will be to man also as it has been made to the holy angels, the reward of deserving. But now that good deserving has been lost by sin in those who are delivered, that has become the gift of grace which would have been the reward of deserving. . . .

On which account we must consider with diligence and attention in what respect those two things differ from one another,—to be able not to sin, and not to be able to sin; to be able not to die, and not to be able to die; to be able not to forsake good, and not to be able to forsake good. For the first man was able not to sin, was able not to die, was able not to forsake good. Are we to say that he who had such a free-will could not sin? Or that he to whom it was said, "If thou shalt sin thou shalt die by 'death,'" could not die? Or could not he forsake good, when he would forsake this by sinning, and so die? Therefore the first liberty of the will was to be able not to sin, the last was much greater, not to be able to sin; the first immortality was to be able not to die, the last was much greater, not to be able to die; the first was the power of perseverance, to be able not to forsake good—the last was the felicity of perseverance, not to be able to forsake good. But because the last blessings were preferable and better, were those first ones, therefore, either no blessings at all, or trifling ones? . . .

Moreover, the helps themselves are to be distinguished. The assistance without which a thing does not come to pass is one thing, and the assistance with which a thing comes to pass is another. For without food we cannot live; and yet although food should be at hand, it would not cause a man to live who should will to die. Therefore the aid of food is that without which it does not come to pass that we live, not that with which it comes to pass that we live. But, indeed, when the blessedness which a man has not is given him, he becomes continually blessed. For the aid is not only that without which that does not happen, but also with which that does happen for the sake of which it is given. Wherefore this is an assistance both by which it comes to pass, and without which it does not come to pass; because, on the one hand, if blessedness should be given to a man, he becomes continually blessed; and, on the other, if it should never be given he will never be so. But food does not of necessity cause a man to live, and yet without it he cannot live. Therefore to the first man, who, in that [condition of] good in which he had been made upright, had received the ability not to sin, the ability not to die, the ability not to forsake that very [condition of] good, was given the aid of perseverance; not that by it it might come to pass that he should persevere, but because without it he could not of free-will persevere. But now to the saints predestinated to the kingdom of God by God's grace, the aid of perseverance that is given is not such as the former, but such that to them perseverance itself is bestowed; not only so that without that gift they cannot persevere, but, moreover, so that by means of this gift they cannot help persevering. For not only did He [Christ] say, "Without me ye can do nothing," but He also said, "Ye have not chosen me, but I have chosen you, and ordained you that ye should go and bring forth fruit, and that your fruit should remain." By which words He showed that He had given them not only righteousness, but perseverance therein. For when Christ thus ordained them that they should go and bring forth fruit, and that their fruit should remain, who would dare to say, It shall not remain? Who would dare to say, Perchance it will not remain? "For the gifts and calling of God are without repentance;" but the calling is of those who are called according to the purpose. When Christ intercedes, therefore, on behalf of these, that their faith should not fail, doubtless it will not fail unto the end. And thus it shall persevere even unto the end; nor shall the end of this life find it anything but continuing. . . .

Certainly a larger liberty is necessary in the face of so many and so great temptations, which had no existence in Paradise,—a liberty fortified and confirmed by the gift of perseverance, so that this world, with all its loves, its fears, its errors, may be overcome: the martyrdoms of the saints have taught this. In fine, he [Adam], not only with nobody to make him afraid, but, moreover, in spite of the authority of God's fear, availing himself of his free-will, did not continue in such a state of happiness, in such a facility of [not] sinning. But these [the saints], I say, not under the fear of the world, but in spite of the rage of the world lest they should stand, stood firm in the faith; while he could see the good things present which he was going to forsake, they could not see the good things future which they were going to receive. Whence is this, save by the gift of Him from whom they obtained mercy to be faithful; from whom they received the spirit, not of fear, whereby they would yield to the persecutors, but of power, and of love, and of continence, in which they could overcome all threatenings, all seductions, all torments? To him, therefore, without any sin, was given the free-will with which he was created; and he made it to serve sin. But although the will of these had been the servant of sin, it was delivered by Him who said, "If the Son shall make you free, then shall ye be free indeed." And by that grace they receive so great a freedom, that although as long as they live here they are fighting against sinful lusts, and some sins creep upon them unawares, on account of which they daily say, "Forgive us our debts," yet they do not any more obey the sin which is unto death, of which the Apostle John says, "There is a sin unto death: I do not say that he shall pray for it." Concerning which sin (since it is not expressed) many and different notions may be entertained. I, however, say, that that is the sin [in question], to forsake even unto death the faith which worketh by love. This sin they who are not free on the first condition, as Adam was, no further obey; for they are freed by the grace of God through the second Adam, and by that deliverance they have that free-will which enables them to serve God, not by which they may be made captive by the devil. From being made free from sin they have become the servants of righteousness, in which they will stand till the end, by the gift to them of perseverance from Him who foreknew them, and predestinated them, and called them according to His purpose, and justified them, and glorified them, since He has even already formed those things that are to come which He promised concerning them. And when He promised, "Abraham believed Him, and it was counted unto him for righteousness." For "he gave glory to God, most fully believing," as it is written, "that what He has promised He is able also to perform. . . ."

He Himself, therefore, makes those men good, to do good works. For He did not promise them to Abraham because He foreknew that of themselves they would be good. For if this were the case, what He promised was not *His*, but theirs. But it was not thus that Abraham believed, but "he was not weak in faith, giving glory to God; and most fully believing that what He has promised He is able also to perform." He does not say, What He foreknew, He is able to promise; nor what He foretold, He is able to manifest; nor what He promised, He is able to foreknow: but what He promised, He is able also to do. It is He, therefore, who makes them to persevere in good, who makes them good. But they who fall and perish have never been in the number of the predestinated. Although, then, the apostle might be speaking of all persons regenerated and living piously when he said, "Who art thou that judgest another man's servant? To his own master he standeth or falleth;" yet he continually had regard to the predestinated, and said, "But he shall stand;" and that they might not arrogate this to themselves, he says, "For God is able to make him stand." It is He Himself, therefore, that gives perseverance, who is able to establish those who stand, so that they may stand fast with the greatest perseverance; or to restore those who have fallen, for "the Lord setteth up those who are broken down. . . ."

As, therefore, the first man did not receive this gift of God,— that is, perseverance in goodness,—but it was left in his own choice to persevere or not to persevere, his will had such strength,—inasmuch as it had been created without any sin, and there was nothing in the way of concupiscence of himself that withstood it,—that the choice of persevering could worthily be entrusted to such goodness and to such facility in living well. But God at the same time foreknew what he would do in unrighteousness; foreknew, however, but did not force him to this; but at the same time He knew what He Himself would do in righteousness concerning him. But now, since that great freedom has been lost by the desert of sin, our weakness has remained to be aided by still greater gifts. For it pleased God, in order most effectually to quench the pride of human presumption, "that no flesh should glory in His presence"—that is, "no man." But whence should flesh not glory in His presence, save concerning its merits? Which, indeed, it might have had, but lost; and lost by that very means whereby it might have had them, that is, by its freewill; on account of which [loss] there remains nothing to those who are to be delivered, save the grace of the Deliverer. Thus, therefore, no flesh glories in His presence. For the unrighteous do not glory, since they have no ground of glory; nor the righteous, because they have a ground from Him, and have no glory of theirs, but Himself, to whom they say, "My glory, and the lifter up of my head." And thus it is that what is written pertains to every man, "that no flesh should glory in His presence." To the righteous, however, pertains that scripture: "He that glorieth, let him glory in the Lord." For this the apostle most manifestly showed, when, after saying "that no flesh should glory in His presence," lest the saints should suppose that they had been left without any glory, he presently added, "But of Him are ye in Christ Jesus, who of God is made unto us wisdom, and righteousness, and sanctification, and redemption: that, according as it is written, He that glorieth, let him glory in the Lord." Hence it is that in this abode of miseries, where trial is the life of man upon the earth, "strength is made perfect in weakness." What strength, save "that he that glorieth should glory in the Lord? . . ."

And thus God willed that His saints should not—even concerning perseverance itself in goodness—glory in their own strength, but in Himself, who not only gives them aid such as He gave to the first man, without which they cannot persevere if they will, but in them He also causes the will; that since they will not persevere unless they both can and will, both the capability and the will to persevere should be bestowed on them by the liberality of divine grace. Because by the Holy Spirit their will is so much enkindled that they therefore can, because they so *will*, they therefore so *will*, because God works in them to *will*. For if in so much weakness of this life (in which weakness, however, for the sake of checking pride, strength behoved to be perfected) their own will should be left to themselves, that they might, if they willed, continue in the help of God, without which they could not persevere, and God should not work in them to will, in the midst of so many and so great weaknesses their will itself would give way, and they would not be able to persevere, for the reason that failing from infirmity they would not *will*, or in the weakness of will they would not so will that they would be able. Therefore aid was brought to the infirmity of human will, so that it might be unchangeably and invincibly influenced by divine grace; and thus, although weak, it still might not fail, nor be overcome by any adversity. Thus it happened that man's will, weak and incapable, in good as yet small, persevered by God's strength; while the will of the first man, strong and healthful, having the power of free choice, did not persevere in a greater good; because although God's help was not wanting, without which it could not persevere if it would, yet it was not such a help as that by which God would work in man to *will*. Certainly to the strongest He yielded and permitted to do what He *willed*; to those that were weak He reserved that by His own gift they should most invincibly *will* what is good, and most invincibly refuse to forsake this. Therefore when Christ says, "I have prayed for thee that thy faith fail not," we may understand that it was said to him who is built upon the rock. And thus the man of God, not only because he has obtained mercy to be faithful, but also because faith itself does not fail, if he glories, must glory in the Lord. . . .

I speak thus of those who are predestinated to the kingdom of God, whose number is so certain that one can neither be added to them nor taken from them; not of those who, when He had announced and spoken of [the kingdom], were multiplied beyond number. For they may be said to be called but not chosen, because they are not called according to the purpose. But that the number of the elect is certain, and neither to be increased nor diminished,—although it is signified by John the Baptist when he says, "Bring forth, therefore, fruits meet for repentance: and think not to say within yourselves, We have Abraham to our father: for God is able of these stones to raise up children to Abraham." to show that those [whom he addressed] were in such wise to be cut off if they did not produce fruit, that the number which was promised to Abraham would not be wanting,— is yet more plainly declared in the Apocalypse: "Hold fast that which thou hast, lest another take thy crown." For if *another* would not receive unless *one* should have lost, the number is fixed. . . .

But, moreover, that such things as these are so spoken to Saints who will persevere, as if it were reckoned uncertain if they will persevere, is a reason that they ought not otherwise to hear these things, since it is well for them "not to be high-minded, but to fear." For who of the multitude of believers can presume, so long as he is living in this mortal state, that he is in the number of the predestinated? Because it is necessary that in this condition that should be kept hidden; since here we have to beware so much of pride, that even so great an apostle was buffeted by a messenger of Satan, lest he should be lifted up. Hence it was said to the apostles, "If ye abide in me;" and this He said who knew for a certainty that they would abide; and through the prophet, "If ye shall be willing, and will hear me," although He knew in whom He would work to will also. And many similar things are said. For the sake of the benefit of this secrecy, lest, perchance, any one should be lifted up, but that all, even although they are running well, should fear, in that it is not known who may attain,—for the sake of the advantage of this secrecy, it must be believed that some of the children of perdition, who have not received the gift of perseverance to the end, begin to live in the faith which worketh by love, and live for some time faithfully and righteously, and afterwards fall away, and are not taken away from this life before this happens to them. If this had happened to none of these, men would have that very wholesome fear, by which the sin of presumption is kept down, only so long as until they should attain to the grace of Christ by which to live piously, and afterwards would for time to come be secure that they would never fall away from Him. And such presumption in this condition of trials is not fitting, where there is so great weakness, that security may engender pride. Finally, this also shall be the case; but it shall be at that time, in men also as it already is in the angels, when there cannot be any pride. Therefore the number of the saints, by God's grace predestinated to God's kingdom, with the gift of perseverance to the end bestowed on them, shall be guided thither in its completeness, and there shall be at length without end preserved in its fullest completeness, most blessed, the mercy of their Saviour still cleaving to them, whether in their conversion, in their conflict, or in their crown. . . .

Hence, as far as concerns us, who are not able to distinguish those who are predestinated from those who are not, we ought on this very account to wish all men to be saved. Severe rebuke should be medicinally applied to all by us that they perish not themselves, or that they may not be the means of destroying others. It belongs to God, however, to make that rebuke useful to them whom He Himself has foreknown and predestinated to be conformed to the image of His Son. For, if at any time we abstain from rebuking, for fear lest by rebuke a man should perish, why do we not also rebuke, for fear lest a man should rather perish by our withholding it? For we have not greater bowels of love than the blessed apostle who says, "Rebuke those that are unruly; comfort the feeble-minded; support the weak; be patient towards all men. See that none render to any man evil for evil." Where it is to be understood that evil is then rather rendered for evil when one who ought to be rebuked is not rebuked, but by a wicked dissimulation is neglected. He says, moreover, "Them that sin rebuke before all, that others also may fear;" which must be received concerning those sins which are not concealed, lest he be thought to have spoken in opposition to the word of the Lord. For He says, "If thy brother shall sin against thee, rebuke him between thee and him." Notwithstanding, He Himself carries out the severity of rebuke to the extent of saying, "If he will not hear the church, let him be unto thee as a heathen man and a publican." And who loved the weak more than He who became weak for us all, and of that very weakness was crucified for us all? And since these things are so, grace neither restrains rebuke, nor does rebuke restrain grace; and on this account righteousness is so to be prescribed that we may ask in faithful prayer, that, by God's grace, what is prescribed may be done; and both of these things are in such wise to be done that righteous rebuke may not be neglected. But let all these things be done with charity, since, while charity does no sin, it covers the multitude of sins.

C. Four Books Against the Pelagians*

AUGUSTINE

BOOK 1

. . . by defending free-will they (Pelagians) are hastening to a confidence rather in doing righteousness of free-will than of God's aid, and so that every one may glory in himself, and not in the Lord. For which of us can say that by the sin of the first man free-will perished from the human race? Through sin liberty indeed perished, but it was that liberty which was in Paradise, of having a full righteousness with immortality; an account of which loss human nature is without divine grace, since the Lord says, "If the Son shall make you free, then shall ye be free indeed"—certainly free to live well and righteously. For free-will did not so far perish in the sinner, but that by it all sin,—especially they who sin with delight and with love of sin; they will what pleases them. Whence also the apostle says, "When ye were the servants of sin, ye were free from righteousness." Behold, they are shown to have been by no means able to serve sin except by another freedom. They are not, then, free from righteousness except by the choice of the will, but they do not become free from sin save by the grace of the Saviour. For which reason the admirable Teacher also distinguished these very words: "For when ye were the servants," says he, "of sin, ye were free from righteousness. What fruit had ye, then, in those things whereof ye are now ashamed? for the end of those things is death. But now being made free from sin and become servants to God, ye have your fruit unto holiness,

* From *The Anti-Pelagian Works of St. Augustine*, Vol. III, tr. by Peter Holmes & Robert E. Wallis. Edinburgh: T. & T. Clark, 1876.

and the end eternal life."[3] He called them free from righteousness, not freed; but from sin not free, lest they should attribute this to themselves; but most watchfully he preferred to say made free, referring this to that declaration of the Lord, "If the Son shall make you free, then shall ye be free indeed." Since, then, the sons of men do not live well unless they are made the sons of God, what is this but that He wills to give the power of good living to free-will, since this power is not given save by God's grace through Jesus Christ our Lord, as the gospel says: "And as many as received Him, to them gave He power to become the sons of God"?

But lest perchance they say that they are aided to the result of having power to become the sons of God, but that in order to deserve to receive this power they have first received Him by free-will with no assistance of grace, because this is the purpose of their endeavour to destroy grace, that they may contend that it is given according to our deservings; lest perchance, then, they so divide that evangelical statement as to refer merit to that portion of it wherein it is said, "But as many as received Him," and then say that in that which follows, grace is not given freely, but is repaid to this merit, "He gave them power to become the sons of God;" if it is asked of them what is the meaning of "received Him," will they say anything else than "believed on Him"? And in order, therefore, that they may know that this also pertains to grace, let them read what the apostle says: "And that ye be in nothing terrified by your adversaries, which indeed is to them a cause of perdition, but of your salvation, and that of God; for unto you it is given in the behalf of Christ not only to believe on Him, but also to suffer for His sake." Certainly he said that both were given. Let them read what he said also: "Peace be to the brethen, and love, with faith from God the Father and the Lord Jesus Christ." Let them also read what the Lord Himself says: "No man can come to me, except the Father who hath sent me shall draw him." Where, lest any one should suppose that anything else is said in the words "come to me" than "believe in me," a little after, when He was speaking of His body and blood, and many were offended at His discourse, He says, "The words which I have spoken unto you are spirit and life; but there are some of you which believe not." Then the Evangelist added, "For Jesus knew from the beginning who they were that believed, and who should betray Him. And He said, Therefore I said unto you that no man can come unto me except it were given him of my Father."[4] He repeated, to wit, the saying in which He had said, "No man can come unto me, except the Father who hath sent me shall draw him." And He declared that He said this for the sake of believers and unbelievers, explaining what He had said, "except the Father who hath sent me shall

[3] Romans, vi. 20.
[4] John, vi., 64 ff.

draw him," by repeating the very same thing in other words in that which He said, "except it were given him of my Father." Because he is drawn to Christ to whom it is given to believe on Christ. Therefore the power is given that they who believe on Him should become the sons of God, since this very thing is given, that they believe on Him. And unless this power be given from God, of free-will there can be none, because it will not be free in good if the deliverer have not made it free; but in evil he has a free-will in whom a deceiver, either secret or manifest, has grafted the love of wickedness, or he himself has persuaded himself of it.

It is not, therefore, true, as some affirm that we say . . . that "all are forced into sin," as if unwillingly, "by the necessity of their flesh"; but if they are already of the age to use the choice of their own mind, they are both retained in sin by their own will, and by their own will are hurried along from sin to sin. For even he who persuades and deceives does not act in them, except by ignorance of the truth or by delight in iniquity, or by both evils,—as well of blindness as of weakness. But this will, which is free in evil because it takes pleasure in evil, is not free in good, for the reason that it has not been made free. Nor can a man will any good thing unless he is aided by Him who cannot will evil,—that is, by the grace of God through Jesus Christ our Lord. For "everything which is not of faith is sin." And thus the good will which withdraws itself from sin is faithful, because the just by faith lives. And it pertains to faith to believe on Christ. And no man can believe on Christ—that is, come to Him—unless it be given to him. No man, therefore, can have a righteous will, unless, with no foregoing merits, he has received the true, that is, the gratuitous grace from above.

These proud and haughty people will not have this; and yet they do not maintain free-will by purifying it, but demolish it by exaggerating it. For they are angry with us who say these things, for no other reason than that they disdain to glory in the Lord. Yet Pelagius feared the episcopal judgment of Palestine; and when it was objected to him that he said that the grace of God is given according to our merits, he denied that he said so, and condemned those who said this with an anathema. And yet nothing else is found to be defended in the books which he afterwards wrote, thinking that he had put a deceit upon the men who were his judges, by lying or by hiding his meaning, I know not how, in ambiguous words. . . .

BOOK 2

. . . And now we must look to those things which they objected to us in their letters, gaining a brief advantage. And to these this is my answer. We do not say that by the sin of Adam free-will perished out of the nature of men, but that it is of force for sinning in men subjected to the devil; while it is not of avail for pious living, unless the will itself of man should be made free by God's grace, and assisted to every good movement of action, of speech, of thought. We say that no one but the Lord God is the maker of those who are born, and that marriage was ordained not by the devil, but by God Himself; yet that all are born under sin on account of the fault of the race, and that, therefore, all are under the devil until they are born again in Christ. Nor are we maintaining fate under the name of grace, because we say that the grace of God is preceded by no merits of man. If, however, it is agreeable to any to call the will of the Almighty God by the name of fate, while we indeed shun profane novelties of words, we have no desire to contend about words.

But, as I was somewhat more attentively considering for what reason they should think it well to object this to us, that we assert fate under the name of grace, I first of all looked into those words of theirs which follow. For thus they have thought that this was to be objected to us: "Under the name," say they, "of grace, they so assert fate as to say that unless God inspired man with the desire of good, unwilling and resisting, and that good imperfect, he would neither be able to decline from evil nor to lay hold of good." Then a letter after, where they themselves mention what they maintain, I gave heed to what was said by them about this matter. "We confess," say they, "that baptism is necessary for all ages, and that grace, moreover, assists the good purpose of everybody; but yet that it does not infuse the love of virtue into a reluctant mind, because there is no acceptance of persons with God." From these words of theirs, I perceive that for this reason they either think, or wish it to be thought, that we assert fate under the name of grace, because we say that God's grace is not given in respect of our merits, but according to His own most merciful will, in that He said, "I will be gracious to whom I will be gracious, and will show mercy on whom I will show mercy." Where, by way of consequence, it is added, "Therefore it is not of him that willeth, nor of him that meaneth, but of God that showeth mercy." Here any one might be equally foolish in thinking or saying that the apostle is an assertor of fate. But here these people sufficiently lay themselves open; for when they malign us by saying that we maintain fate under the name of grace, because we say that God's grace is not given in respect of our merits, beyond a doubt they confess that they themselves say that it is given in respect of our merits; thus their blindness could not conceal and dissimulate that they believe and think thus, although, when this view was objected to him, Pelagius, in the episcopal judgment of Palestine, with crafty fear condemned it. For it was objected to him from the words of his own disciple Coelestius, indeed, that he himself also was in the habit of saying that God's grace is given in respect to our merits. And he is abhorrence, or in pretended abhorrence of this, did not delay with his lips, at least, to anathematize it; but, as his later writings indicate, and the assertion of those followers of his makes evident, he kept in his deceitful heart until afterwards what the cunning of a denier had then hidden for fear, and moreover his boldness might put forth in letters. And still the Pelagian bishops do not dread, and at least are not ashamed, to send their letters to the Catholic Eastern bishops, in which they charge us with being assertors of fate because we do not say that even grace is given according to our merits; although Pelagius, fearing the Eastern bishops, did not dare to say this, and so was compelled to condemn it.

But is it thus, O children of pride, enemies of God's grace, new Pelagian heretics, that whoever says that all man's good deservings are preceded by God's grace, and that God's grace is not given to merits, lest it should not be grace if it is not given freely, but is repaid as due to those who deserve it, seems to you to assert fate? Do not you yourselves also say, whatever be your purpose, that baptism is necessary for all ages? Have you not written in this very letter of yours that opinion concerning baptism, and that concerning grace, side by side? Why did not baptism, which is given to infants, by that very juxtaposition admonish you what you ought to think concerning grace? For these are your words: "We confess that baptism is necessary for all ages, and that grace, moreover, assists the good purpose of everybody; but yet that it does not infuse the love of virtue into a reluctant mind, because there is no acceptance of persons with God." In all these words of yours, I for the meanwhile say nothing of what you have said concerning grace. But give a reason concerning baptism, why you should say that it is necessary for all ages; say why it is necessary for infants. Assuredly because it confers some good upon them; and that same something is neither small nor moderate, but of great account. For although you deny that they contract the original sin which is remitted in baptism, yet you do not deny that in that laver of regeneration they are adopted from the sons of men unto the sons of God; nay, you even preach this. Tell us, then, how the infants, whoever they are, that are baptized in Christ and have departed from the body, received so lofty a gift as this, and with what preceding merits. If you should say that they have deserved this by the piety of their parents, it will be replied to you, Why is this benefit sometimes denied to the children of pious people and given to the children of the wicked? For sometimes the offspring sprung from religious people, in tender age, and thus fresh from the womb, is forestalled by death before it can be washed in the laver of regeneration, and the infant born of Christ's foes is baptized in Christ by the mercy of Christians,—the baptized mother bewails her own little one not baptized, and the chaste virgin gathers in to be baptized a foreign offspring, exposed by an immodest mother. Here, certainly, the merits of parents are wanting, and even by your own confession the merits of the infants themselves are wanting also. For we know that you do not believe this of the human soul, that it has lived somewhere before it inhabited this earthly body, and has done something either of good or of evil for which it might deserve such difference in the flesh. What cause, then, has procured baptism for this infant, and has denied it to that? Do they themselves hold fate because they do not hold merit? or is there in these things acceptance of persons with God? For you have said both,—first fate, afterwards acceptance of persons,—that, since both must be refuted, there may remain the merit which you wish to introduce against grace. Answer, then, concerning the merits of infants, why some should depart from their bodies baptized, other not baptized, and neither possess nor want so excellent a gift by the merits of their parents, that they should become sons of God from sons of men, by no deserving of their parents, by no deservings of their own? You are silent, forsooth, and you find yourselves rather in the same position which you object to us. For if when there is no merit you say that consequently there is fate, and on this account wish the merit of man to be understood in the grace of God, lest you should be compelled to confess fate, see, you rather assert a fate in the baptism of infants, since you avow that in them there is no merit. But if, in the case of infants to be baptized, you deny that any merit at all precedes, and yet do not concede that there is a fate, why do you cry out, when we say that the grace of God is therefore given freely, lest it should not be grace, and is not repaid as if it were due to preceding merits, that we are assertors of fate?—not perceiving that in the justification of the wicked, as there are no merits because it is God's grace, so that it is not fate because it is God's grace, and so that it is not acceptance of persons because it is God's grace.

Because they who affirm fate contend that not only actions and events, but, moreover, our very wills themselves depend on the position of the stars at the time in which one is conceived or born; which positions they call constellations. But the grace of God surpasses not only all stars and all heavens, but, moreover, all angels. Hence the assertors of fate attribute both men's good and evil doings and fortunes to fate, but in the ill fortunes of men God is following up their merits with due retribution; but He bestows benefits by undeserved grace with a merciful will, doing both the one and the other not according to a seasonable conjunction of stars, but according to the eternal and deep counsel of His severity and goodness. We see, then, that neither belongs to fate. Here, if you answer that this very benevolence of God, by which He follows not merits, but bestows undeserved benefits with gratuitous bounty, should rather be called fate, when the apostle calls this grace, saying, "By grace are ye saved through faith; and that not of yourselves, but it is the gift of God; not of works, lest perchance any one should be lifted up," do you not consider—do you not perceive that it is not by us that fate is asserted under the name of grace, but it is rather by you that divine grace is called by the name of fate? . . .

BOOK 3

. . . "They assert," say they, "that baptism, moreover, does not make men new—that is, does not give full remission of sins; but they contend that they are partly made children of God and partly remain children of the world—that is, children of the devil." They lie; they lay traps; they shuffle; we do not say this. For we say that all men who are children of the devil are also children of the world; but not that all children of the world are also children of the devil. Far be it from us to say that the holy fathers Abraham, Isaac, and Jacob, and others of this kind, were children of the devil when they were begetting in marriage, and those believers who until now and still hereafter continue to beget. And yet we cannot contradict the Lord when He says, "The children of this world marry and give in marriage." Some, therefore, are children of this world, and yet are not children of the devil. For although the devil is the author and source of all sins, yet it is not every sin that makes children of the devil; for the children of God also sin, since if they say they have no sins they deceive themselves, and the truth is not in them. But they sin in virtue of that condition by which they are still children of this world; but by that grace wherewith they are the children of God they certainly sin not, because every one that is born of God sinneth not. But unbelief makes children of the devil; and unbelief is specially called sin, as if it were the only one, if it is not expressed what is the nature of the sin. As when the apostle is spoken of, if it be not expressed what apostle, none is understood but Paul; because he is better known by his many epistles, and he laboured more than they all. For which reason, in what the Lord said of the Holy Spirit, "He shall convict the world of sin." He meant to be understood unbelief; for He said this when He was explaining, "Of sin because they believed not on me," and when He says, "If I had not come and spoken to them, they should not have sin." For He meant not that before they had no sin, but He wished to indicate that very want of faith by which they neither believed Him when He was present to them and speaking to them; since they belonged to Him of whom the apostle says, "According to the prince of the power of the air, who now worketh in the children of unbelief." Therefore they in whom there is not faith are the children of the devil, because they have not in the inner man any reason why there should be forgiven them whatever is committed either by human infirmity, or by ignorance, or by any evil will whatever. But those are the children of God who certainly, if they should "say that they have no sin, deceive themselves, and the truth is not in them, but immediately" (as it continues) "when they confess their sins" (which the children of the devil do not do, or do not do according to the faith which is peculiar to the children of God), "He is faithful and just to forgive them their sins, and to cleanse them from all unrighteousness." And in order that what we say may be more fully understood, let Jesus Himself be heard, who certainly was speaking to the children of God when He said: "And if ye, being evil, know how to give good gifts to your children, how much more shall your Father which is in heaven give good things to them that ask Him." For if these were not the children of God, He would not say to them, "Your Father which is in heaven." And yet He says that they are evil, and that they know how to give good gifts to their children. Are they, then, evil in that they are the children of God? Away with the thought! But they are thence evil because they are still the children of this world, although now made children of God by the pledge of the Holy Spirit.

Baptism, therefore, washes away indeed all sins—absolutely all sins, whether of what are done or said or thought, whether original or added, whether such as are committed in ignorance or allowed in knowledge; but it does not take away the infirmity which the regenerate man resists when he fights the good fight, but to which he consents when as man he is overtaken in any fault; on account of the former, rejoicing with thanksgiving, but on account of the latter, groaning in the utterance of prayers. In respect of the former, saying, "What shall I render to the Lord for all which He has given me?" On account of the latter, saying, "Forgive us our debts." On account of the former, saying, "I will love Thee, O Lord, my strength." On account of the latter, saying, "Have mercy on me, O Lord; for I am weak." On account of the former, saying, "Mine eyes are ever towards the Lord; for He shall pluck my feet out of the net." On account of the latter, saying, "Mine eye is troubled with wrath." And innumerable passages with which the divine writings are filled, which alternately, either in exultation over God's benefits or in lamentation over our own evils, are uttered by children of God by faith as long as they are still children of this world in respect of the weakness of this life; whom, nevertheless, God distinguishes from the children of the devil, not only by the laver of regeneration, but moreover by the righteousness of that faith which worketh by love, because the just lives of faith. And this weakness with which we contend, with alternating failure and progress, even to the death of the body, and which is of great importance as to what it can overcome in us, shall be consumed by a second regeneration, of which the Lord says, "In the regeneration when the Son of man shall sit on the throne of His glory, ye also shall sit upon twelve thrones," etc. Certainly in this passage He calls without doubt the last resurrection the regeneration, which Paul the Apostle also calls both the adoption and the redemption, where he says, "But even we ourselves, which have the first-fruits of the Spirit ourselves, also groan within ourselves, waiting for the adoption—the redemption—of our body." Have we not been regenerated, adopted, and redeemed by the holy washing? And yet there remains a regeneration, an adoption, a redemption, which we ought now patiently to be waiting for as to come in the end, that we may then be in no degree any longer children of this world. Whosoever, then, takes away from baptism that which we only receive by its means, corrupts the faith; but whosoever attributes to it now that which we shall receive by its means indeed, but yet hereafter, cuts off hope. For if any one should ask of me whether we have been saved by baptism, I shall not be able to deny it, since the apostle says, "He saved us by the washing of regeneration and renewing of the Holy Ghost." But if he should ask whether by the same washing He has already absolutely in every way saved us, I shall answer: It is not so. Because the same apostle also says, "For we are saved by hope; but hope that is seen is not hope: for what a man seeth, why doth he yet hope for? But if we hope for that we see not, we with patience wait for it." Therefore the salvation of man is effected in baptism, because whatever sin he has derived from his parents is remitted, or whatever, moreover, he himself has sinned on his own account before baptism; but his salvation will hereafter be such that he cannot sin at all.

40 PELAGIUS (c. 360–c. 420), A BRITISH MONK, arrived in Rome near the end of the fourth century and was soon involved in controversy with Augustine (354–430). His critical reaction to the lax morality of Roman Christians and his own austere and rigorous life brought him to make theological affirmations concerning human ability and the relation of law and grace that aroused both support and condemnation. Pelagius' concerns centered on the need for a moral reform and yet he was drawn into debates that involved terms not of his own choosing. Though he was acquitted of error by a synod of the Eastern church, his followers became more inflexible in their affirmations and were later declared heretical.

In the *Letter to Demetrias* Pelagius was advising a Christian virgin of noble birth. Augustine was also in correspondence with this girl and Pelagius' letter did not escape the eye of Augustine.

In addition, the following selections include three brief excerpts from Pelagius' *Expositions of Thirteen Epistles of St. Paul.*

A. Letter to Demetrias[*]

PELAGIUS

CHAPTER 2

Whenever I have to speak about moral education and the conduct of a holy life, I usually point first to the strong stuff of which human nature is made and show what that nature is able to achieve. In this way I may stir my listener's mind toward a proper view of human virtue and prevent him from imagining in advance that he has been vainly called to impossible goals. We are never strong enough to enter upon the path of virtue without hope as our leader and companion. All struggle and longing are, to be sure, snuffed out by despair of achievement. Here especially I think I must follow the same order of exhortation which has characterized my other works. When it is a matter of entering upon the more perfect life, then our natural goodness[1] must be all the more fully proclaimed for two reasons: so that the soul will not be sluggish and negligent in the achievement of virtue only for the reason that it has no confidence in its ability to achieve it, and so that the soul will not in ignorance think that it does not possess what in fact does lie within it. It is always necessary to focus attention on that, whatever it is, which one desires to use. In testing and fulfilling any capability, we have first to state that which our natural goodness is able to accomplish. . . . In the case of a battle, that exhortation is the best and carries the most weight which reminds the combatant of his own physical powers.

First of all, then, you ought to measure the goodness of human nature by the author of that nature, namely God, who, when he made the world and the things that are in the world, is reported to have made them as good, in fact very good. Then think how much more excellent a creature he made man himself, for whose sake God is understood to have created all those things. By declaring his intention to make man in his own image and likeness, God made clear beforehand what sort of being he was about to create. He then put the whole animal world in subjection to man; he even constituted man as lord over beasts much mightier than he, whether in bulk of

[*] The translations are made by Professor Robert F. Evans of the University of Pennsylvania. All footnotes are his. Biblical references are to the Revised Standard Version. The Letter to Demetrias is translated from Migne, Patrologia Latina, Vol. XXX.

[1] Here Pelagius introduces what in his vocabulary amounts to a technical term—naturae bonum—which here has been translated throughout as "natural goodness." Human nature shares in the general goodness of creation as such but possesses in addition a peculiarly human goodness—that of will which is free for both moral good and evil. See Pelagius' discussion below in ch. 3.

body, physical prowess, or force of fang, and by all this he made amply clear how much more noble is man's created state. It was God's will that man, in pondering the mystery of mighty beasts in subjection to himself, should understand the dignity of his own nature. For God did not leave man destitute and without protection, did not leave him exposed and without recourse in the face of threatening dangers. To him whom he made without external armor God gave a better, internal weapon—that of reason and intelligence—with the end in view that through that very power of intellect by which he excelled the other animals man alone would know the maker of all things; in virtue of one and the same power of reason man was to be both servant of God and lord of the beasts. The Lord willed, however, that man should be a doer of righteousness of his own free will and not by compulsion, and he therefore "left man in the hand of his own counsel". He placed before man "life and death, good and evil, and whichever he chooses shall be given to him".[2] Accordingly we read in Deuteronomy: "I have set before you life and death, blessing and curse; therefore choose life, that you may live".[3]

CHAPTER 3

On this account you must now take care that you are not distracted by the thoughtless impiety of the ignorant throng. Do not think that man is therefore not made truly good just because he is able to do evil or because his violent nature is not bound fast in unchanging goodness. For if you would reconsider carefully and press your mind to a more subtle understanding, the condition of man would appear to you better and higher for the very reason that some take it to be inferior. The glory of the rational soul lies precisely in this decision over the twofold path, in this very freedom for both directions. In this, I say, consists the whole excellence of our nature, in this its dignity; and accordingly it is in virtue of this freedom that the best among us deserve praise and reward. There would be no virtue whatever in him who perseveres in the good if he were not able to change his course toward evil. God willed to bestow upon the rational creature the gift of voluntary goodness and the power of free choice. By planting within man the possibility of either course he made man's will to be autonomous, with the result that man has a natural capacity for both good and evil and may bend his will to either. God was not able to produce spontaneous goodness in any other way than in that creature that was able itself to produce evil. Our most excellent creator willed two things—that we should be able to do either, but that we should do one of them, namely the good which he commanded. He bestowed the capacity for evil for one purpose only—that we should do his will of our own

---

[2] This sentence and the previous one use phrases from the book of Ecclesiasticus or Sirach, ch. 15, vv. 14 and 17.
[3] Deut. 30:19.

will. That being the case, our very capacity to do evil acts is itself good. It is good, I say, because from it arises a superior kind of good, voluntary and autonomous, not bound by necessity but having the power of independent decision. For it is given to us to choose, to resist, to examine, to reject. The only reason why the rational creature is held in esteem above the others is that whereas all the others possess only a necessary goodness and a goodness that pertains to creation as such, this one creature possesses the goodness of will.

I am ashamed to say, however, that when the human condition is under discussion, a great many people, as if to find fault with the work of God, say irreverently and ignorantly that man ought to have been made in such a way that he would have been able to do no evil at all. Thus does the pot say to the potter, "Why did you make me like this?"[4] And we find the most wicked of men saying that they would prefer to have been made differently and pretending that they are really doing quite well with such a nature as the Creator has given them. In effect, those who have no intention of amending their lives give the appearance of wanting to amend their nature.

The goodness of this human nature has been implanted so widely in the totality of mankind that it sometimes shows itself even in heathen men who do not worship God at all. Of the philosophers whom we have heard, read, and seen ourselves, how many have been chaste, patient, temperate, generous, abstinent, kind, ornaments of the world and yet rejecting the world's pleasures, lovers of righteousness no less than of knowledge. Where, I ask, where is the source of such virtues in these strangers to God if not in natural goodness? Now whether we see all of these virtues of which I have spoken to be possessed by one man or single virtues by individual men, the point here is that since there is one nature common to all men, these people demonstrate by their example, each in his turn, that all such virtues can exist in all men. If even without God men show what manner of creature God has made them, see what Christians are able to do, whose nature and life have through Christ been instructed for the better and who are assisted also by the help of divine grace.

CHAPTER 4

Now let us come to the secrets of our own souls. Let each one turn most careful attention to himself. Let us ask what judgment is forthcoming from our own meditations on this subject. Let conscience itself give judgment on natural goodness. Let us be instructed by the internal teaching of the soul, and let us become acquainted with the endowments of our mind from no other source than from that mind itself. Why is it, I ask you, that in the

4 Rom. 9:20.

face of every sin we either blush with shame or are afraid? Why, having committed an offense, do we display now a crimson, now a pallid face, and flee with trembling heart from anyone who is witness to even our merest peccadillos? Why are we tormented by conscience? And yet why, on the other hand, do we stand joyous, firm, and unshaken in every good work? And why, if our good deed is hidden from general view, do we want it to be made publicly known? Yes why—unless because our very nature, serving as witness to itself, makes clear both its own goodness and its displeasure at evil, and taking confidence only in the doing of good, declares what is alone proper to itself as human nature? Thus it is that often the torments of conscience rage furiously in the doer of a crime, and even though the villain be undiscovered, the secret punishment of the mind pursues the lurking culprit. Nor is there any place of impunity after a crime when guilt itself is the punishment. And thus it is, following our argument above, that the innocent man, on the other hand, enjoys the composure of a good conscience even in the midst of torture, and, though he is fearful of the pain, glories in his innocence.

There is, I say, in our souls a certain natural holiness, so to speak, which presides as if in the apex of the soul and exercises judgment over evil and good. Just at it looks with approval on honorable and upright acts, so it condemns improper deeds, and in accordance with the testimony of conscience judges our conflicting inclinations by a certain interior law. This natural holiness does not deceive us—it is not in its own nature deceptive, nor does it flaunt a counterfeit brilliance of argument. It accuses or defends us reasonably by most trustworthy judgments and the most reliable of evidence. The Apostle in writing to the Romans makes mention of this law, which he claims is innate in all men, as if written on tables of the heart. He says, "When Gentiles who have not the law do by nature what the law requires, they are a law to themselves, even though they do not have the law. They show that what the law requires is written on their hearts, while their conscience also bears witness and their conflicting thoughts accuse or perhaps excuse them."[5] All those men between Adam and Moses were employing this law whom scripture records as living holy lives and pleasing God. Some of these, for the sake of example, must now be placed before you so that you may easily understand how great our natural goodness is, although by these examples you will discover also that scripture propounds righteousness as a law. . . . [Pelagius then proceeds to a discussion of a series of Old Testament figures lying between Adam and Moses—Abel, Enoch, Noah, Melchisedek, etc.—the point of which is to show that these were righteous and holy men who not only possessed natural goodness but conducted themselves in keeping with it. But a further point which Pelagius wishes to make is that these Old Testament men were keeping command-

[5] Rom. 2:14, 15.

ments enjoined by the New Testament, that they were "Gospel men" before the Gospel. His intention here is well illustrated by his words concerning Job: "O Gospel man before the Gospel, apostolic man before the apostolic commandments! Disciple of the apostles, opening up the hidden riches of human nature and bringing them out into the open, he has shown himself what all can do, and he has demonstrated how great is that treasure-vault of the soul which we possess without drawing on it. And that treasure which we do not wish to bring forth, we believe we do not possess." Realizing that scripture speaks of many who were not holy and righteous, Pelagius then goes on to cite texts from Old and New Testaments with the intent of proving that wickedness and faithlessness proceed not from any necessity inherent in human nature but from freedom of will. We take up the text of Pelagius again at approximately the point where this series of quotations leaves off.]

CHAPTER 8

We are not defending natural goodness in such a way as to say that it is not able to do evil; we emphatically say that it is capable of good and evil. We are only defending our nature against this one affront, [the charge of evil by natural necessity,] so that at least we will not seem to be impelled toward evil by that particular blemish—we who do neither good nor evil without our will. To us it is always open to do one of the two, since we are always able to do both. For why is it that some are to judge and some are to be judged, unless it be that in the same human nature there is a disparity of wills, unless it be that although we are all able to do the same, we in fact do different things? In order that the point may be more clearly luminous some examples must be brought forward. Adam was thrown out of paradise, Enoch was snatched away from the world.[6] In both cases the Lord demonstrated human freedom of choice. For just as the one who sinned had it within his power to please God, so the one who pleased God had it within his power to sin. By a *just* God Adam would not have deserved to be punished nor Enoch to be chosen unless both had had it within their power to be both punished and chosen. The same point is to be understood concerning the brothers Cain and Abel,[7] and the same also concerning the twins Jacob and Esau.[8] And it is to be further understood that the sole basis for God's choosing and

---

[6] See Genesis 3:23 and 5:24.

[7] See Genesis 4:2–16.

[8] For the Jacob and Esau stories see Genesis, chs. 25–36. It might be argued that it is difficult to see how Pelagius' point can be made to apply to these two, who offer a notorious example of Biblical disregard of human merit, unless Pelagius is perhaps thinking of such a verse as Gen. 36:2, which informs us that Esau took wives away from the Canaanites, whereas Jacob had made the journey east to take wives from among his mother's relatives.

rejecting is that of human will, since in the same human nature there is a diversity of merits. The righteous Noah stood as testimony to the guilt of that whole world that was destroyed in the flood because of its sins,[9] and the moral purity of Lot stood in judgment over the crimes of the Sodomites.[10]

For the purpose of proving our natural goodness the above is no weak argument, because those first men, through such long stretches of time, were without any admonition from the Law.[11] This was the case not, to be sure, because God at one time did not care about his creation, but because he knew that he had made human nature such that it was sufficient to men, by way of law, for the practice of righteousness. So long as human nature was more or less fresh and unspoiled, its proper use did indeed flourish; and before the long habit of sinning enveloped human reason, as it were, in a thick darkness, our nature was left on its own without the Law. But when that nature had become overlaid with excessive vices and tainted, so to speak, by the rust of ignorance, the Lord applied to it the file of the Law. Our nature was to be filed clean by frequent admonition and so enabled to return to its proper brilliance.

No other cause, in fact, is responsible for our difficulty in well doing than the long habit of sinning which infects us from childhood. Little by little that habit has corrupted us through many years, and finally it holds us so tied and bound to itself that it seems, in a way, to possess the very power of nature. The weight of that whole time now resists and opposes us—that whole time when our instruction was neglected, when we were educated for sin, when we studied to be evil, when innocence was led in folly to the allures of wickedness. Now old habit opposes new will. In the ignorance which has come upon us through sloth and laxity, we wonder why holiness is being imposed upon us as if from some alien source (we who make no habit of doing good since we have learned evil so long).

These observations concerning natural goodness have been hurriedly made, and as if in a separate work.[12] It was necessary for me to say these things so that I could lay before you a more level path to perfect righteousness, a path on which you may be able to make your way the more easily because you will know that on it there is nothing really troublesome, no height that is unapproachable. For if, as we have said, certain people are reported to have lived righteous and holy lives even before the giving of the Law and long before the coming of the Lord our Savior, how much more must it be believed that we are able so to live after the clear and brilliant example provided by his coming, since we have been instructed through the grace of

---

[9] Genesis, chs. 6–9.

[10] Genesis, ch. 19.

[11] i.e., the Law of Moses, the Torah.

[12] i.e., separate from the main body of his letter to the girl, which deals specifically with the vocation of a Christian virgin.

Christ and have been reborn into a better humanity.[13] We who have been purified and cleansed by his blood, and by his example have been aroused toward perfect righteousness, ought to be better than they who lived before the law; we ought to be better even than they who lived under the law. As the Apostle says: "Sin will now have no dominion over you, for you are not under law, but under grace."[14]

B. [Excerpts from] Expositions of Thirteen Epistles of St. Paul*

PELAGIUS

[1. On Original Sin: "But the free gift is not like the trespass. For if many died through one man's trespass, much more have the grace of God and the free gift in the grace of that one man Jesus Christ abounded for many." (Romans 5:15)]

Righteousness has had greater power in bringing life than sin in bringing death, because Adam brought death only to himself and to those coming after him, but Christ has brought freedom both to people alive at his time and to those coming after him. Those, however, who are against the lineal transmission of sin, endeavor to refute it in this way: "If the sin of Adam," they say, "harmed even those who do not sin,[15] therefore the righteousness of Christ is of benefit even to non-believers, because the apostle says that salvation is brought through one man in a similar way, nay even to a greater degree, than death previously had been brought through one man." Then they say, "If baptism cleans away that ancient sin, those who are born of two baptized persons ought to be free of this sin, for such baptized persons

---

* The translations are made by Professor Robert F. Evans of the University of Pennsylvania. All footnotes are his. Biblical references are to the Revised Standard Version. The Pauline commentary selections are translated from Alexander Souter, ed. of the Latin Text, Pelagius's *Expositions of Thirteen Epistles of St. Paul*, Vol. II. Cambridge University Press, 1926.

[13] Pelagius' phrase here is *in meliorem hominem renati*. Taken in conjunction with the immediately preceding mention of Christ, this suggests that Pelagius has in mind Christ himself who constitutes the "better man" or "better humanity" into which we are reborn.

[14] Rom. 6:14.

[15] i.e., infants, who, on the theory of original sin, do not commit actual sins of their own, but only bear the guilt and burden of original sin.

have not been able to pass on to their children what they themselves by no means possessed. And it further is the case, that if not the soul but only the flesh is inherited,[16] the flesh itself alone then possesses the inherited sin and it alone deserves punishment." They maintain it is unjust that a soul born today and not issuing from Adam's mass of humanity, should bear so ancient a sin and one that is foreign to itself, and they say also the admission is without rational foundation that God, who forgives a man's own sins, should reckon against a man's sins that do not belong to him.

[2. On Law and Grace: "And you show that you are a letter from Christ delivered by us, written not with ink but with the Spirit of the living God, not on tablets of stone but on tablets of human hearts." (II Corinthians 3:3)]

Here he (Paul) introduces the difference between law and grace. The Jews received the law in hard stone, signifying the hardness of their minds, just as the veil on the face of Moses portended the veil of their ignorance. But, although we do have the law of Christ written in the Gospels, still we took it to our heart in the first instance not from tables as if written in our absence but by hearing the words of the Lord spoken in our presence. The Gospels then were written down later according to the memory of those who came after. If therefore they who received the law in stone were without excuse, how much more so are we who have taken to ourselves the words of Christ, if we sin.

[3. On Justification by Faith: "For we hold that a man is justified by faith apart from works of the law." (Romans 3:28.)]

Certain people abuse this passage to the effect of destroying the works of righteousness, asserting that faith alone is able to suffice for him who has been baptized, although the same apostle says elsewhere, "And if I have all faith so as to remove mountains, but have not love, it profits me nothing."[17] In this love, he declares in another place, consists the fulfilling of the law, saying, "The fulfilling of the law is love."[18] Now if these two passages seem to be contrary in meaning to each other, without which works of the law, must one believe, has the Apostle said man is justified by faith? Undoubtedly

---

[16] i.e., in the creationist view of the soul's origin, according to which each human soul is a new creation of God, as opposed to the traducianist view that both soul and body are derived from parents. The creationist view was the more prevalent one and was the one upheld by Pelagius. Augustine leaned toward the traducianist view as more consonant with his theory of original sin but never made up his mind on the subject.

[17] I Corinthians 13:2.

[18] Romans 13:10.

it is the works of circumcision, sabbath observance, and other things of similar sort that are meant, but not apart from the works of righteousness [is man justified], concerning which blessed James says, "Faith without works is dead."[19] In this passage however,[20] Paul is talking about the man who in coming to Christ is saved by faith alone when he first believes. But by adding the phrase about works of the law he shows that it is works of grace which those who are baptized ought to perform.[21]

41 JOHN CASSIAN represented the semi-Pelagian or semi-Augustinian position, the latter term having more justification than the former. He was born about 360, probably in Gaul; little else is known about his family background or education. After some time in a monastery in Bethlehem, he visited monastic centers in Egypt. Among the Egyptian anchorites he met was Chaeremon, the monk whose conversations Cassian sought to record in the following selection. He remained in Egypt for several years and later travelled to Rome and then settled at Marseilles, where his reputation as one of the formative figures of Western monasticism was made secure.

In his later life, after the turn of the fifth century, he wrote his three major works: the *Institutes*, the *Conferences*, and *On the Incarnation Against Nestorius*. The *Conferences*, written long after the conversations they purport to record, probably 425–430, were, it is believed, representative of Cassian's position as well as the figure involved, in our case Chaeremon. In this period, Augustine's more severe tracts were being circulated and there were those who resisted the strong doctrine of predestination, unrelated to conduct, and Augustine's statement concerning the relation of grace and

---

[19] James 2:26.

[20] i.e., the verse from Romans on which Pelagius is commenting.

[21] The thought of the above passage is a bit confused and confusing; Pelagius is a bit nervous before this verse, but his meaning is fairly clear. In the first instance, and in relation to his baptism, the believer is justified by faith alone apart from works of any sort. But insofar as God's justifying activity applies to the continuing life of the Christian, justification is not possible without the "works of righteousness." That this is Pelagius' meaning can be ascertained by comparing his above comments with those on Rom. 3:24, 4:5f., and 10:9.

free will. In contrast to Augustine, Cassian insisted that man, unaided by the grace of God, could move toward his restoration from sin, though continually insisting on the cooperative relation between God's grace and man's will to restore man's status before God. By reacting more directly against Augustine, Cassian tended to state his position in terms that could be interpreted in a Pelagian fashion.

Though John Cassian has not been recognized as a saint by the Western church, he is regarded so in the Eastern church.

The Third Conference of Abbot Chaeremon*

JOHN CASSIAN

CHAPTER 8

. . . when He [God] sees in us some beginnings of a good will, He at once enlightens it and strengthens it and urges it on towards salvation, increasing that which He Himself implanted or which He sees to have arisen from our own efforts. For He says "Before they cry, I will hear them: While they are still speaking I will hear them;" and again: "As soon as He hears the voice of thy crying, He will answer thee." (Is. lxv. 24; xxx. 19). And in His goodness, not only does He inspire us with holy desires, but actually creates occasions for life and opportunities for good results, and shows to those in error the direction of the way of salvation.

CHAPTER 9

Whence human reason cannot easily decide how the Lord gives to those that ask, is found by those that seek, and opens to those that knock, and on the other hand is found by those that sought Him not, appears openly among those who asked not for Him, and all the day long stretches forth His hands to an unbelieving and gainsaying people, calls those who resist and stand afar off, draws men against their will to salvation, takes away from those who want to sin the faculty of carrying out their desire, in His

* From John Cassian, The Conferences, tr. by E. C. Gibson, A Select Library of Nicene and Post-Nicene Fathers, Vol. XI, Second series. Grand Rapids, Mich.: Wm. B. Eerdmans Publishing Co., 1955.

goodness stands in the way of those who are rushing into wickedness. But who can easily see how it is that the completion of our salvation is assigned to our own will, of which it is said: "If ye be willing, and hearken unto Me, ye shall eat the good things of the land," and how it is "not of him that willeth or runneth, but of God that hath mercy?" What too is this, that God "will render to every man according to his works;" and "it is God who worketh in you both to will and to do, of His good pleasure;" and "this is not of yourselves but it is the gift of God: not of works, that no man may boast?" What is this too which is said: "Draw near to the Lord, and He will draw near to you," and what He says elsewhere: "No man cometh unto Me except the Father who sent Me draw Him?" What is it that we find: "Make straight paths for your feet and direct your ways," and what is it that we say in our prayers: "Direct my way in Thy sight," and "establish my goings in Thy paths, that my footsteps be not moved?" . . . What is it that is said to us: "Enlighten yourselves with the light of knowledge;" and this which is said of God: "Who teacheth man knowledge;" and "the Lord enlightens the blind," or at any rate this, which we say in our prayers with the prophet: "Lighten mine eyes that I sleep not in death," unless in all these there is a declaration of the grace of God and the freedom of our will, because even of his own motion a man can be led to the quest of virtue, but always stands in need of the help of the Lord? For neither does anyone enjoy good health whenever he will, nor is he at his own will and pleasure set free from disease and sickness. But what good is it to have desired the blessing of health, unless God, who grants us the enjoyments of life itself, grant also vigorous and sound health? But that it may be still clearer that through the excellence of nature which is granted by the goodness of the Creator, sometimes the first beginnings of the good will arise, which however cannot attain to the complete performance of what is good unless it is guided by the Lord, the Apostle bears witness and says: "For to will is present with me, but to perform what is good I find not."

CHAPTER 10

For Holy Scripture supports the freedom of the will where it says: "Keep thy heart with all diligence," but the Apostle indicates its weakness by saying "The Lord keep your hearts and minds in Christ Jesus." David asserts the power of free will, where he says, "I have inclined my heart to do Thy righteous acts," but the same man in like manner teaches us its weakness, by praying and saying, "Incline my heart unto Thy testimonies and not to covetousness. . . ." The importance of our will is maintained by the Lord, when we find "Break the chains of thy neck, O captive daughter of Zion:" of its weakness the prophet sings, when he says: "The Lord looseth them that are bound:" and "Thou hast broken my chains: To Thee will I offer the sacrifice of praise." We hear in the gospel the Lord summoning us to come speedily to Him by our free will: "Come unto Me all ye that labour and are heavy laden, and I will refresh you," but the same Lord testifies to its weakness, by saying: "No man can come unto Me except the Father which sent Me draw him." The Apostle indicates our free will by saying: "So run that ye may obtain:" but to its weakness John Baptist bears witness where he says: "No man can receive anything of himself, except it be given him from above." We are commanded to keep our souls with all care, when the Prophet says: "Keep your souls," but by the same spirit another Prophet proclaims: "Except the Lord keep the city, the watchman waketh but in vain." The Apostle writing to the Philippians, to show that their will is free, says "Work out your own salvation with fear and trembling," but to point out its weakness, he adds: "For it is God that worketh in you both to will and to do of His good pleasure."

CHAPTER 11

And so these are somehow mixed up and indiscriminately confused, so that among many persons, which depends on the other is involved in great questionings, i.e., does God have compassion upon us because we have shown the beginning of a good will, or does the beginning of a good will follow because God has had compassion upon us? For many believing each of these and asserting them more widely than is right are entangled in all kinds of opposite errors. For if we say that the beginning of free will is in our own power, what about Paul the persecutor, what about Matthew the publican, of whom the one was drawn to salvation while eager for bloodshed and the punishment of the innocent, the other for violence and rapine? But if we say that the beginning of our free will is always due to the inspiration of the grace of God, what about the faith of Zaccheus, or what are we to say of the goodness of the thief on the cross, who by their own desires brought violence to bear on the kingdom of heaven and so prevented the special leadings of their vocation? But if we attribute the performance of virtuous acts, and the execution of God's commands to our own will, how do we pray: "Strengthen, O God, what Thou hast wrought in us;" and "The work of our hands establish Thou upon us? . . ." These two then; viz., the grace of God and free will seem opposed to each other, but really are in harmony, and we gather from the system of goodness that we ought to have both alike, lest if we withdraw one of them from man, we may seem to have broken the rule of the Church's faith; for when God sees us inclined to will what is good, He meets, guides, and strengthens us: for "At the voice of thy cry, as soon as He shall hear, He will answer thee;" and: "Call upon Me," He says, "in the day of tribulation and I will deliver thee, and thou shalt glorify Me." And again, if He finds that we are unwilling or have grown cold, He stirs our hearts with salutary exhortations, by which a good will is either renewed or formed in us.

CHAPTER 12

For we should not hold that God made man such that he can never will or be capable of what is good: or else He has not granted him a free will, if He has suffered him only to will or be capable of evil, but neither to will or be capable of what is good of himself. And, in this case how will that first statement of the Lord made about men after the fall stand: "Behold, Adam is become as one of us, knowing good and evil?" For we cannot think that before, he was such as to be altogether ignorant of good. Otherwise we should have to admit that he was formed like some irrational and insensate beast: which is sufficiently absurd and altogether alien from the Catholic faith. Moreover as the wisest Solomon says: "God made man upright," i.e., always to enjoy the knowledge of good only, "But they have sought out many imaginations," for they came, as has been said, to know good and evil. Adam therefore after the fall conceived a knowledge of evil which he had not previously, but did not lose the knowledge of good which had before. Finally the Apostle's words very clearly show that mankind did not lose after the fall of Adam the knowledge of good: as he says: "For when the Gentiles, which have not the law, do by nature the things of the law, these, though they have not the law, are a law to themselves, as they show the work of the law written in their hearts, their conscience bearing witness to these, and their thoughts within them either accusing or else excusing them, in the day in which God shall judge the secrets of men. . . ." Finally in order to denote that the possibility of good was in them, in chiding the Pharisees, He (the Lord) says: "But why of your own selves do ye not judge what is right?" And this he certainly would not have said to them, unless He knew that by their natural judgment they could discern what was fair. Wherefore we must take care not to refer all the merits of the saints to the Lord in such a way as to ascribe nothing but what is evil and perverse to human nature: in doing which we are confuted by the evidence of the most wise Solomon, or rather of the Lord Himself, Whose words these are; for when the building of the Temple was finished and he was praying, he spoke as follows: "And David my father would have built a house to the name of the Lord God of Israel: and the Lord said to David my father: Whereas thou hast thought in thine heart to build a house to My name, thou hast well done in having this same things in thy mind. Nevertheless thou shalt not build a house to My name." This thought then and this purpose of King David, are we to call it good and from God or bad and from man? For if that thought was good and from God, why did He by whom it was inspired refuse that it should be carried into effect? But if it is bad and from man, why is it praised by the Lord? It remains then that we must take it as good and from man. And in the same way we can take our own thoughts today. For it was not given only to David to think what is good of himself, nor is it denied to us naturally to think or imagine anything that is good. It cannot then be doubted that there are by nature some seeds of goodness in every soul implanted by the kindness of the Creator: but unless these are quickened by the assistance of God, they will not be able to attain to an increase of perfection, for, as the blessed Apostle says: "Neither is he that planteth anything nor he that watereth, but God that giveth the increase. . . ." And therefore the will always remains free in man, and can either neglect or delight in the grace of God. . . .

CHAPTER 13

And so the grace of God always co-operates with our will for its advantage, and in all things assists, protects, and defends it, in such a way as sometimes even to require and look for some efforts of good will from it that it may not appear to confer its gifts on one who is asleep or relaxed in sluggish ease, as it seeks opportunities to show that as the torpor of man's sluggishness is shaken off its bounty is not unreasonable, when it bestows it on account of some desire and efforts to gain it. And none the less does God's grace continue to be free grace while in return for some small and trivial efforts it bestows with priceless bounty such glory of immortality, and such gifts of eternal bliss. For because the faith of the thief on the cross came as the first thing, no one would say that therefore the blessed abode of Paradise was not promised to him as a free gift, nor could we hold that it was the penitence of King David's single word which he uttered: "I have sinned against the Lord," and not rather the mercy of God which removed those two grievous sins of his, so that it was vouchsafed to him to hear from the prophet Nathan: "The Lord also hath put away thine iniquity: thou shalt not die." The fact then that he added murder to adultery, was certainly due to free will: but that he was reproved by the prophet, this was the grace of Divine Compassion. Again it was his own doing that he was humbled and acknowledged his guilt; but that in a very short interval of time he was granted pardon for such sins, this was the gift of the merciful Lord. And what shall we say of this brief confession and of the incomparable infinity of Divine reward, when it is easy to see what the blessed Apostle, as he fixes his gaze on the greatness of future remuneration, announced on those countless persecutions of his? "for," says he, "our light affliction which is but for a moment worketh in us a far more exceeding and eternal weight of glory," of which elsewhere he constantly affirms, saying that "the sufferings of this present time are not worthy to be compared with the future glory which shall be revealed in us." However much then human weakness may survive, it cannot come up to the future reward, nor by its efforts so take off from Divine grace that it should not always remain a free gift. And therefore the aforesaid teacher of the Gentiles, though he bears his witness that he had obtained the grade of Apostolate by the grace of God, saying: "By the grace of God I am what I am," yet also declares that he himself had corresponded to Divine Grace, where he says: "And His Grace in me was not in vain; but I laboured more abundantly than they all: and yet not I, but the Grace of God with me." For when he says: "I laboured," he shows the effort of his own will; when he says: "yet not I, but the grace of God," he points out the value of Divine protection; when he says: "with me," he affirms that it co-operates with him when he was not idle or careless, but working and making an effort.

42   THE COUNCIL OF ORANGE dealt with the aftermath of the controversy between Augustine and Pelagius. The decision reached at Orange has frequently been labeled semi-Pelagianism, though more justification can be made for the term, semi-Augustinianism. Thoroughgoing Pelagianism is ruled out and a rigorous doctrine of predestination is disavowed. The thrust of this decision was to stress the centrality of the sacrament of baptism and good works resulting from the grace imparted in the sacrament.

Council of Orange, 529*

Canon 1. Whoever says that by the offence of the disobedience of Adam not the entire man, that is, in body and soul, was changed for the worse, but that the freedom of his soul remained uninjured, and his body only was subject to corruption, has been deceived by the error of Pelagius and opposes scripture [Ezek. 18:20; Rom. 6:16; II Peter 2:19].

Canon 2. Whoever asserts that the transgression of Adam injured himself only, and not his offspring, or that death only of the body, which is the

* Reprinted with the permission of Charles Scribner's Sons from A Source Book for Ancient Church by J. C. Ayer. Copyright 1913 Charles Scribner's Sons; renewal copyright 1941 J. C. Ayer.

penalty of sin, but not also sin, which is the death of the soul, passed by one man to the entire human race, wrongs God and contradicts the Apostle [Rom. 5:12].

Canon 3. Whoever says that the grace of God can be bestowed in reply to human petition, but not that the grace brings it about so that it is asked for by us, contradicts Isaiah the prophet and the Apostle [Is. 65:1; Rom. 10:20].

Canon 4. Whoever contends that our will, to be set free from sin, may anticipate God's action, and shall not confess that it is brought about by the infusion of the Holy Spirit and his operation in us, that we wish to be set free, resists that same Holy Spirit speaking through Solomon: "The will is prepared by the Lord" [Proverbs 8:35, cf. LXX; not so in Vulgate or Heb.], and the Apostle [Phil. 2:13].

Canon 5. Whoever says the increase, as also the beginning of faith and the desire of believing, by which we believe in Him who justifies the impious, and we come to the birth of holy baptism, is not by the free gift of grace, that is, by the inspiration of the Holy Spirit turning our will from unbelief to belief, from impiety to piety, but belongs naturally to us, is declared an adversary of the apostolic preaching [Phil. 1:6; Ephes. 2:8]. For they say that faith by which we believe in God is natural, and they declare that all those who are strangers to the Church of Christ in some way are believing.

Canon 6. Whoever says that to us who, without the grace of God, believe, will, desire, attempt, struggle for, watch, strive for, demand, ask, knock, mercy is divinely bestowed, and does not rather confess that it is brought about by the infusion and inspiration of the Holy Spirit in us that believe, will, and do all these other things as we ought, and annexes the help of grace to human humility and obedience, and does not admit that it is the gift of that same grace that we are obedient and humble, opposes the Apostle [I Cor. 4:7].

Canon 7. Whoever asserts that by the force of nature we can rightly think or choose anything good, which pertains to eternal life, or be saved, that is, assent to the evangelical preaching, without the illumination of the Holy Spirit, who gives to all grace to assent to and believe the truth, is deceived by an heretical spirit, not understanding the voice of the Lord [John 15:5], and of the Apostle [II Cor. 3:5].

Canon 8. Whoever asserts that some by mercy, others by free will, which in all who have been born since the transgression of the first man is evidently corrupt, are able to come to the grace of baptism, is proved an alien from the faith. For he asserts that the free will of all has not been weakened by the sin of the first man, or he evidently thinks that it has been so injured that some, however, are able without the revelation of God to attain, by their own power, to the mystery of eternal salvation. Because the

Lord himself shows how false this is, who declares that not some, but no one was able to come to Him unless the Father drew him [John 6:4], and said so to Peter [Matt. 16:17] and the Apostle [I Cor. 12:3]. . . .

And so according to the above sentences of the Holy Scriptures and definitions of ancient Fathers, by God's aid, we believe that we ought to believe and preach:

That by the sin of the first man, free will was so turned aside and weakened that afterward no one is able to love God as he ought, or believe in God, or do anything for God, which is good, except the grace of divine mercy comes first to him [Phil. 1:6, 29; Ephes. 2:8; I Cor. 4:7, 7:25; James 1:17; John 3:27]. . . .

We also believe this to be according to the Catholic faith, that grace having been received in baptism, all who have been baptised, can and ought, by the aid and support of Christ, to perform those things which belong to the salvation of the soul, if they labor faithfully.

But not only do we not believe that some have been predestinated to evil by the divine power, but also, if there are any who wish to believe so evil a thing, we say to them, with all detestation, anathema.

Also this we profitably confess and believe, that in every good we do not begin and afterward are assisted by the mercy of God, but without any good desert preceding, He first inspires in us faith and love in Him, so that we both faithfully seek the sacrament of baptism, and after baptism with His help are able to perform those things which are pleasing to Him. Whence it is most certainly to be believed that in the case of that thief, whom the Lord called to the fatherland of paradise, and Cornelius the Centurion, to whom an angel of the Lord was sent, and Zacchaeus, who was worthy of receiving the Lord himself, their so wonderful faith was not of nature, but was the gift of the divine bounty.

And because we desire and wish our definition of the ancient Fathers, written above, to be a medicine not only for the clergy but also for the laity, it has been decided that the illustrious and noble men, who have assembled with us at the aforesaid festival, shall subscribe it with their own hand.

43

THE INTERPRETATION of Peter Abailard (1079–1142) of the nature of man centered on his conviction that sin lies in the intention, not in the outward act. The work of Christ was to reorient the "intention" of man, to awaken a love for God.

Abailard's discussion of the atonement is intimately tied to his view of the nature of human sin.[1]

"Know Thyself"*

PETER ABAILARD

CHAPTER 11

We say, in fact, that an intention is good, that is, right in itself, but that an action is good, not because it acquires any kind of goodness in itself, but because it comes from a good intention. It follows from this that the same thing may be done by the same man at different times, and yet that the action may sometimes be called good, sometimes bad, because of a difference of intention, and thus its relation to good and evil seems to be altered. . . .

CHAPTER 12

This means that if your intention is right, the whole mass of deeds springing from it, which can be seen in the manner of corporeal things, will be worthy of light (that is, good), and contrariwise. Thus intention is not to be called good simply because it seems good, but because it really is what it is thought to be—as, for example, when it believes that what it is aiming at is pleasing to God, and in addition is not deceived at all in its judgment. Otherwise the very infidels would have good works, just as we do, since they, no less then we ourselves, believe that they are saved—or, if you will, please God—by their works.

CHAPTER 13

. . . If anyone asks, nonetheless, whether those who persecuted the martyrs or Christ sinned in that which they believed to be pleasing to God, or whether they could let pass without sin that which they thought should in no wise be let pass, certainly, in terms of our previous description of sin as contempt of God, or consent to that to which one believes that consent should not be given, we cannot say that they sinned in this, or that ignorance of anything, or even unbelief itself (in which no one can be saved), is

* From Peter Abailard, "Ethics or the Book Called 'Know Thyself,' " in, A Scholastic Miscellany, tr. by Eugene Fairweather, The Library of Christian Classics, Vol. X. London: Student Christian Movement Press; Philadelphia: Westminster Press, 1956.

1 See also, Exposition of the Epistle to the Romans, Selection 36.

sin. For those who do not know Christ, and on that account reject the Christian faith, because they believe that it is contrary to God, can hardly be said to show contempt of God in what they do for God's sake, and for that reason think that they do well—especially since the apostle says, "If our heart do not reprehend us, we have confidence before God,"[2] as if he were to say, Where we do not violate our own conscience, it is in vain that we fear being found guilty of sin before God. Yet if the ignorance of such men is not to be imputed for sin in any way, how is it that the Lord himself prays for those who crucify him, saying: "Father, forgive them, for they know not what they do"?[3] Or how is it that Stephen, taught by his example, entreats for those who are stoning him, saying, "Lord, lay not this sin to their charge"?[4] For it does not seem that forgiveness should be granted, if no sin has gone before, nor does forgiveness normally mean anything but the remission of the penalty deserved by sin. Besides, Stephen clearly calls what sprang from ignorance "sin."

CHAPTER 14

. . . But to reply to the objections more fully, one should know that the term "sin" is used in different ways. Properly, however, sin means actual contempt for God or consent to evil, as we mentioned above. From this little children are exempt, as well as the naturally simple-minded. Since these have no merits, because they lack reason, nothing can be imputed to them for sin, and they are saved by the sacraments alone. A victim offered for sin is also called "sin," as when the apostle speaks of Jesus Christ as having been "made sin." The penalty of sin is also called "sin" or a "curse," as when we say that sin is forgiven, meaning that the penalty is remitted, and that the Lord Jesus "bore our sins," meaning that he endured the penalty for our sins, or the penalties springing from them. But when we say that young children have "original sin," or that we all, as the apostle says, sinned in Adam, this amounts to saying that our punishment or the sentence of our condemnation takes its rise from his sin. The actual works of sin, also, or whatever we do not rightly know or will, we sometimes call "sins." For what does it mean for anyone to have committed sin, except that he has put his sin into effect? Nor is this strange, since conversely we refer to sins themselves[5] as deeds, as in the statement of Athanasius, when he says: "They shall give account for their own deeds. And they that have done good will go into life eternal, they that have done evil into eternal fire." For what does "for their own deeds" mean? Does it mean that judgment will only be

[2] I John 3:21.
[3] Luke 23:34.
[4] Acts 7:60.
[5] i.e., intentions.

returned for the intentions that were carried out in action, so that he who has more deeds to point to will receive a greater recompense? Does it mean that he who was unable to put his intention into effect will be exempt from condemnation, like the devil who did not obtain in effect what he had anticipated in desire?[6] It cannot mean this. "For their own deeds," then, refers to their consent to the things which they decided to carry out, that is, to the sins which with the Lord are reckoned as deeds done, since he punishes them as we punish deeds.

Now when Stephen speaks of the "sin" which the Jews were committing against him in ignorance, he means by "sin" the very penalty which he was suffering on account of the sin of our first parents (just as the term is applied to other penalties from the same source), or else he is referring to their unjust action in stoning him. He asked indeed that it should not be charged to them, or, in other words, that they should not be punished bodily on its account. For here God often punishes some persons corporally, when no fault of theirs requires it, and yet not without cause—as, for instance, when he sends afflictions to the just with a view to their purification or testing, or when he permits some to be afflicted, so that afterward they may be delivered and he may be glorified for the benefit he has conferred. This happened in the case of the blind man, of whom he himself said: "Neither hath this man sinned, nor his parents; but that the works of God should be made manifest in him."[7] Who will deny, either, that innocent children are sometimes imperiled or afflicted along with wicked parents, by the fault of the latter—as in the case of the men of Sodom and of a good many other peoples—so that greater terror may be inspired in the wicked by the wider extension of punishment? It was because he had carefully noted this that blessed Stephen prayed that "sin" (that is to say, the punishment he was enduring at the hands of the Jews, or that which they were wrongly doing) should not be charged to them, or, in other words, that they should not be punished physically because of it.

The Lord was also of this mind, when he said, "Father, forgive them," meaning, Do not avenge, even by physical punishment, this that they are doing against me. Such revenge could, in fact, have reasonably been taken, even if no fault of theirs had gone before, so that others who saw it, or even they themselves, might learn from the punishment that they had not acted rightly in this matter. But it was fitting for the Lord, by this example of his own prayer, to encourage us supremely to foster the virtue of patience and display the highest love, so that he should display to us in deed what he himself had taught us by word of mouth—namely, to pray also for our enemies. Therefore, when he said, "Forgive," this did not refer

[6] i.e., equality with God.
[7] John 9:3.

to any previous fault or contempt of God which they had in this matter, but had to do with the reasonableness of imposing a penalty, which, as we have said, could follow with good cause, even without any previous fault. This happened to the prophet who was sent against Samaria and by eating did what the Lord had forbidden. Since he did not presume to do anything in contempt of God, but was deceived by another prophet, he incurred death in his innocence, not so much from any guilty fault as from the actual doing of the deed. God indeed, as blessed Gregory recalls, sometimes changes his sentence, but never his purpose. That is to say, he often determines that what for some reason he had planned to command or to threaten shall not be carried out. But his purpose remains fixed, or, in other words, what in his own resolution he plans to do never lack efficacy. He did not, we know, adhere to what he had enjoined on Abraham concerning the sacrifice of his son, or to his threat against the Ninevites, and thus, as we have said, he changed his sentence. So the aforesaid prophet, whom he had forbidden to take food on his journey, believe that his sentence had been changed, and indeed that he would certainly be in the wrong if he did not listen to the other prophet, who claimed that he had been sent by the Lord for the very purpose of refreshing his weariness with food. He did this, therefore, without blame, since he was resolved to avoid blame. Nor did sudden death harm him, when it delivered him from the tribulations of this present life, while it was a profitable warning to many, since they saw a just man thus punished without fault, and observed the fulfillment in him of that which is elsewhere addressed to the Lord: "Thou, O God, forasmuch as thou art just, orderest all things justly, since him also who deserveth not to be punished thou dost condemn." This means: Thou dost condemn, not to eternal but to bodily death. For some, such as children, are saved without merits, and attain to eternal life by grace alone. Similarly, it is not absurd that some should endure bodily penalties which they have not deserved; this is certainly the case with young children who die without the grace of baptism, and are condemned to bodily as well as to eternal death. Many innocent persons, moreover, suffer affliction. What is strange, then, in the fact that those who crucified the Lord could reasonably incur temporal punishment by that unjust action, as we have said, even though ignorance excuses them from blame? It was for this reason that he said, "Forgive them"—in other words, Do not bring upon them the penalty which, as we have said, they could not unreasonably incur.

Moreover, if what they did through ignorance, or even the ignorance itself, is not properly called "sin" (that is, contempt of God), this applies to unbelief as well, even though the latter necessarily shuts off the entrance to eternal life from adults who have the use of reason. In fact, it is enough for eternal damnation not to believe the gospel, to be ignorant of Christ, not to receive the sacraments of the Church, even though this is done not so much by malice as by ignorance. Concerning such persons the truth also says: "He that doth not believe is already judged,"[8] while the apostle declares, "He who knows not shall not be known."[9] But when we say that we sin unwittingly—that is, that we do something which is not fitting— by "sin" we mean, not contempt, but the action. For the philosophers also equate sinning with doing or saying something in an unfitting way, even though there is nothing here that seems to have any bearing on an offense against God. Thus Aristotle, when he spoke of the faulty attribution of relations (in Ad aliquid), said: "But sometimes the relation will not seem to be reciprocal, unless it is attributed appropriately to that which is mentioned. For if he sins in making the attribution, as in speaking of the 'wing of a bird,' the connection is not reciprocal, as if one might speak of the 'bird of a wing.' " If, therefore, in this way we describe as "sin" everything that we do badly, or that we possess contrary to our salvation, then we shall certainly call "sins" both unbelief and ignorance of the things that must necessarily be believed for salvation, even though no contempt for God is in evidence. I think, nevertheless, that sin, properly speaking, is that which can never happen without blame. But ignorance of God, or unbelief, or actual deeds which are not done rightly, can occur without blame. For suppose that someone does not believe the gospel of Christ, because the proclamation has not reached him, as the text of the apostle indicates: "How shall they believe him, of whom they have not heard? And how shall they hear without a preacher?"[10] In that case, what blame can be attributed to him because he does not believe? Cornelius did not believe in Christ until Peter had been sent to him and had instructed him concerning this. Moreover, even though he previously knew and loved God by natural law, and so merited to be heard for his prayer, and to have his alms accepted by God, nevertheless, if by any chance he had departed from this light before he believed in Christ, we should not dare to make him any promise of life, however great his good works seemed. Nor should we number him with the faithful, but rather with unbelievers, no matter how great the zeal for salvation which had possessed him. Indeed, many of God's judgments are an abyss. Sometimes he draws those who resist, or at least are less concerned for their salvation, and repels those who present themselves, or at least are more ready to believe—all by the deepest counsel of his dispensation. For thus he rejected him who offered himself: "Master, I will follow thee whithersoever thou shalt go."[11] But when another excused himself on the ground of the solicitude he felt for his father, he did not tolerate this

---

8 John 3:18.
9 I Cor. 14:38.
10 Rom. 10:14.
11 Matt. 8:19.

dutiful excuse of his, even for an hour. Again, in rebuking the stubbornness of cities, he said: "Woe to thee, Chorazin, woe to thee, Bethsaida, for if in Tyre and Sidon had been wrought the miracles that have been wrought in you, they had long ago done penance in sackcloth and ashes."[12] You see, he tendered them not only his own preaching, but also a display of miracles, even though he already knew that they were not going to be believed. But as for the other cities of the Gentiles, though he was aware that they were ready to receive the faith, he did not deem them worthy of a visit from himself. And yet, when some of their citizens perished, deprived of the word of preaching—even though they were prepared to accept it—how can we blame them for that, when we see that it did not happen by any negligence of theirs? Nevertheless, we say that this their unbelief, in which they died, was enough to condemn them, although the cause of this blindness in which the Lord abandoned them is less clear to us.[13] Perhaps if anyone finds the cause in their sin, committed without guilt, it will be permitted, since he finds it absurd that they should be condemned without any sin at all.

Nonetheless, as we have often indicated, we think that the term "sin" can properly be applied to guilty negligence alone, and that this cannot exist in anyone, of any age whatever, without his deserving to be condemned. But I do not see how not believing in Christ, which is certainly a matter of unbelief, ought to be imputed as a fault to young children, or to those to whom belief in Christ has not been proclaimed. Nor do I see how blame attaches to anything that is done invincible ignorance, when we have not even been able to foresee it—for instance, if someone kills a man with an arrow because he does not see him in a wood, while he intends to shoot at wild beasts or birds. Nonetheless we say that he sins, but through ignorance, just as we sometimes admit that we sin, not only in consent but also in thought. But in this case we do not use the term properly, as equivalent to fault, but apply it loosely to that which it is not at all fitting for us to do, whether it is done by error or by negligence, or in any other unfitting way. This, then, is what it means to sin by ignorance: not to bear any blame, but to do what does not befit us—to sin in thought, that is, by willing what it is not at all fitting for us to will, or in speech or in act, that is, by saying or doing what should not be said or done, even if all these things happen to us involuntarily and by our ignorance. Thus we may also say that those who persecuted Christ or his people, whom they thought they ought to persecute, sinned in act. Nevertheless, they would have sinned more grievously if they had spared them against their own conscience.

---

[12] Matt. 11:21.
[13] Note the authentically Augustinian attitude.

44

THE FOLLOWING SELECTIONS from the *Summa Theologica* of Thomas Aquinas (1225–1274) consider the nature and effect of sin, the relation between human ability and God's grace, and the character and cause of faith.[1]

Summa Theologica[*]

THOMAS AQUINAS

Question Eighty-Two

THE ESSENCE OF ORIGINAL SIN

We must now consider the essence of original sin. There are four questions asked concerning it. 1. Whether original sin is a habit. 2. Whether original sin is one only, in any one man. 3. Whether original sin is desire. 4. Whether original sin is equally in all men.

Article One

WHETHER ORIGINAL SIN IS A HABIT

We proceed to the first article thus:

1. It seems that original sin is not a habit. As Anselm says (*De Conceptu Virginali* 2, 3, 26), original sin is the lack of original justice. It is therefore a kind of privation. But a privation is opposed to a habit. Hence original sin is not a habit.

2. Again, the character of guilt attaches to actual sin more than to original sin, since actual sin has more of the nature of the voluntary. But there is no guilt in the habit of actual sin. If there were, a man would sin guiltily while he slept. There cannot then be any guilt in a habit which is original.

3. Again, an act of sin always precedes the habit of it, because sinful

* From *Nature and Grace*, Vol. XI. LCC, tr. A. M. Fairweather. Published 1954, by the Westminster Press. Used by permission. Also with permission of Student Christian Movement Press, London.

1 See also *Summa Theologica*, Selection 6 and *On the Truth of the Catholic Faith*, Selection 60.

habits are always acquired, never infused. But there is no act which precedes original sin. Hence original sin is not a habit.

On the other hand: Augustine says (*De Baptismo Puer; De Peccat. Mer. et Remis.* I, ch. 39; *De Tempt., Sermo* 45); "because of original sin infants have a tendency to desire, even though they do not actually desire." Now we speak of a tendency where there is a habit. Original sin is therefore a habit.

I answer: as we said in Q. 50, Art. 1, there are two kinds of habit.[2] There is the habit which inclines a power to act, of the kind which enables us to say that sciences and virtues are habits. Original sin is not a habit of this kind. But we also give the name of habit to the disposition by which a composite nature is well or ill disposed in a certain way, especially when such a disposition has become almost second nature, as in the case of sickness or of health. Original sin is such a habit. It is the disordered disposition which has resulted from the dissolution of the harmony which was once the essence of original justice, just as bodily sickness is the disordered disposition of a body which has lost the equilibrium which is the essence of health. Original sin is accordingly called the languor of nature.

On the first point: just as sickness of the body involves positive disorder in the disposition of the humours, as well as privation of the equilibrium of health, so original sin involves disorder in the disposition of the parts of the soul, as well as the privation of original justice. It is more than mere privation. It is a corrupt habit.

On the second point: actual sin is the disorder of an act. But original sin is the disordered disposition of nature itself, since it is the sin of nature. Now this disordered disposition has the character of guilt in so far as it is inherited from our first parent, as we said in Q. 81, Art. 1. It also has the character of a habit, which the disordered disposition of an act has not. Original sin can therefore be a habit, though actual sin cannot be a habit.

On the third point: this objection argues about the kind of habit which inclines a power to act. Original sin is not a habit of this kind, although it does result in an inclination to disordered actions. It results in such inclination not directly but indirectly, through depriving us of the original justice which would have prevented disorderly actions, and once did prevent them. The inclination to disordered bodily functions results from sickness in the same indirect way. But we should not say that original sin is an infused habit, nor that it is acquired through action (unless the action of our first parent, but not that of any present person). It is inborn by reason of our corrupt origin. . . .

[2] A habit is defined as "a disposition of a subject which is in a state of potentiality either in respect of form or in respect of operation," but is distinguished from a "disposition" as being difficult to change. See "The Role of Habitus in the Thomistic Metaphysics of Potency and Act" in *Essays in Thomism,* Ed. R. E. Brennan.

Article Four

WHETHER ORIGINAL SIN IS IN ALL MEN EQUALLY

We proceed to the fourth article thus:

1. It seems that original sin is not in all men equally. It was said in the preceding article that original sin is inordinate desire. But all men are not equally subject to desire. It follows that original sin is not in all men equally.

2. Again, original sin is the disordered disposition of the soul, as sickness is the disordered disposition of the body. Now sickness admits of more or less. Therefore original sin also admits of more and less.

3. Again, Augustine says: "lust transmits original sin to posterity." (1 De Nup. et Concup. 23–24.) But the lust in generation may be greater in one than in another. Original sin may therefore be greater in one than in another.

On the other hand: it was said in the preceding article that original sin is the sin of nature. But nature is in all men equally. Original sin is therefore also in all men equally.

I answer: there are two things in original sin. One is the lack of original justice. The other is the relation of this lack to the sin of our first parent, from whom it is inherited through our corrupt origin. Now original sin cannot be greater or less in respect of the lack of original justice, since the whole gift of original justice has been taken away. Privations do not admit of more and less when they deprive us of something altogether, as we said of death and darkness in Q. 73, Art. 2. Nor can original sin be greater or less in respect of its relation to its origin. Everyone bears the same relation to the first beginning of the corrupt origin from which sin derives its guilt, and relations do not admit of greater and less. It is plain, then, that original sin cannot be greater in one man than in another.

On the first point: since man has lost the control of original justice which once kept all the powers of his soul in order, each power tends to follow its own natural movement, and to follow it more vehemently the stronger it is. Now some powers of the soul may be stronger in one man than in another, because bodily characteristic vary. That one man should be more subject to desire than another is not therefore the consequence of original sin, since all are equally deprived of the control of original justice, and the lower parts of the soul are equally left to themselves in all men. It is due to the different dispositions of their powers, as we have said.

On the second point: sickness of the body does not have an equal cause in all cases, even if it is of the same kind. For example, fever which results from putrefaction of the bile may be due to a greater or lesser putrefaction, or to one which is more or less removed from a vital principle.

But the cause of original sin is equal in respect of everyone. There is therefore no comparison.

On the third point: it is not actual lust that transmits original sin to posterity, for one would still transmit original sin even if it were divinely granted that one should feel no lust in generation. We must understand it to be habitual lust, on account of which the sensitive appetite is not subject to reason, now that the control of original justice is lost. Lust of this kind is equally in all. . . .

Question Eighty-Five

THE EFFECTS OF SIN

We must now consider the effects of sin. We must consider the corruption of natural good, concerning which there are six questions. 1. Whether natural good is diminished by sin. 2. Whether it is entirely destroyed by sin. 3. Of the four wounds which Bede names as the wounds inflicted on human nature as the result of sin. 4. Whether privation of mode, species, and order is the effect of sin. 5. Whether death and other bodily defects are the effects of sin. 6. Whether these are in some way natural to man.

Article Two

WHETHER THE WHOLE GOOD OF HUMAN NATURE CAN BE DESTROYED BY SIN

We proceed to the second article thus:

1. It seems that the whole good of human nature can be taken away by sin. The good of human nature is finite, since human nature itself is finite. Now a finite thing is removed altogether if it is continually reduced, and the good of human nature may be continually reduced by sin. It seems that it may finally be taken away altogether.

2. Again, what is simple in nature is the same in its wholeness as it is in its parts. This is obvious in the case of air, water, flesh, or any body whose parts are similar. Now the good of nature is altogether uniform. Hence since part of it may be taken away by sin, it seems that the whole of it may be taken away by sin.

3. Again, the natural good which is diminished by sin is the capacity for virtue. Sin destroys this capacity altogether in some persons. It obviously does so in the damned, who can no more recover virtue than a blind man can recover his sight. Thus sin may entirely destroy natural good.

On the other hand: Augustine says (Enchirid. 13, 14): "evil exists only in what is good." But the evil of guilt can be neither in the good of virtue nor in the good of grace, since these are contrary to it. It must therefore be in the good of nature. It cannot then totally destroy the good of nature.

I answer: we said in the preceding article that the natural good which sin diminishes is the natural inclination to virtue. Now the reason why man inclines to virtue is that he is rational. It is because he is rational that he acts in accordance with reason, and this is to act virtuously. But a man would not be able to sin without his rational nature. Sin cannot then deprive him of it altogether. It follows that his inclination to virtue cannot be entirely destroyed.

Since this natural good is found to be continually diminished by sin, some have sought to illustrate the diminution of it by the continuous reduction of a finite thing which is yet never entirely removed. As the philosopher says in 1 *Physics*, text 37, any finite magnitude will at length be exhausted if the same quantity is repeatedly taken from it—if I were to subtract a handbreadth from a finite quantity, for instance. But subtraction can go on indefinitely if the same proportion is subtracted instead of the same quantity. For example, if a quantity is divided in two, and the half taken from the half of it, subtraction can go on indefinitely, so long as each subsequent reduction is less than the preceding. This illustration, however, is irrelevant, because a subsequent sin diminishes the good of nature not less than a previous sin, but much more, if it be more serious.

We must say instead that the natural inclination to virtue is to be understood as a medium between two things. It depends on rational nature as its root, and inclines to the good of virtue as its term and end. The diminution of it may accordingly be understood either as referring to its root, or as referring to its term. Its root is not diminished by sin, because sin does not diminish nature itself, as we said in the preceding article. But it is diminished in respect of its term, in so far as an obstacle is put in the way of its attaining its end. If the natural inclination to virtue were diminished in respect of its root, it would be bound to be wholly destroyed in the end, along with the complete destruction of a man's rational nature. But since it is diminished by way of an obstacle preventing the attainment of its end, it is manifest that it can be diminished indefinitely. Obstacles can be interposed indefinitely. A man can add sin to sin without end. But it cannot be entirely destroyed, since the root of inclination always remains. The same sort of thing is apparent in the case of a diaphanous body, which has the inclination to take in light because it is diaphanous, and whose inclination or capacity to do so is diminished by intervening clouds, yet always remains rooted in its nature.

On the first point: this objection argues from diminution by subtraction. But the good of nature is diminished by way of an obstacle which is interposed, and which neither destroys nor diminishes the root of inclination, as we have said.

On the second point: natural inclination is indeed wholly uniform. But it is related both to its principle and to its end, and is diminished in one way and not in another because of this diversity of relation.

On the third point: the natural inclination to virtue remains even in the damned, who would not otherwise feel the remorse of conscience. The reason why it does not issue in act is that grace is withheld in accordance with divine justice. The capacity to see similarly remains in a blind man, at the root of his nature, in so far as he is an animal naturally possessed of sight, but fails to become actual because the cause which would enable it to do so, by forming the organ which sight requires, is lacking. . . .

Question One Hundred and Nine

CONCERNING THE EXTERNAL PRINCIPLE OF HUMAN ACTIONS, THAT IS, THE GRACE OF GOD

We must now consider the external principle of human actions, that is, God, in so far as we are helped by him to act rightly through grace. We shall consider first the grace of God, secondly its cause, and thirdly its effects. The first of these inquiries will be threefold, since we shall inquire first into the necessity of grace, second into the essence of grace itself, and third into the divisions of it.

There are ten questions concerning the necessity of grace. 1. Whether without grace a man can know any truth. 2. Whether without grace a man can do or will any good. 3. Whether without grace a man can love God above all things. 4. Whether without grace a man can keep the commandments of the law, by his own natural powers. 5. Whether without grace he can merit eternal life. 6. Whether without grace a man can prepare himself for grace. 7. Whether without grace he can rise from sin. 8. Whether without grace he can avoid sin. 9. Whether, having received grace, a man can do good and avoid sin without further divine help. 10 Whether he can persevere in good by himself.

Article One

WHETHER A MAN CAN KNOW ANY TRUTH WITHOUT GRACE

We proceed to the first article thus:

1. It seems that a man cannot know any truth without grace. The gloss by Ambrose on I Cor. 12:3, "no man can say that Jesus is the Lord, but by the Holy Ghost," says that "every truth, by whomsoever uttered, is by the Holy Ghost." Now the Holy Ghost dwells in us by grace. Hence we cannot know truth without grace.

2. Again, Augustine says (1 Soliloq. 6): "the most certain sciences are like things lit up by the sun so that they may be seen. But it is God who gives the light. Reason is in our minds as sight is in our eyes, and the eyes of the mind are the senses of the soul." Now however pure it be, bodily sense cannot see any visible thing without the light of the sun. Hence how-

ever perfect be the human mind, it cannot by reasoning know any truth without the light of God, which belongs to the aid of grace.

3. Again, the human mind cannot understand truth except by thinking, as Augustine explains (14 De Trin. 7). Now in II Cor. 3:5 the apostle says: "Not that we are sufficient of ourselves to think anything as of ourselves." Hence a man cannot know truth by himself, without the help of grace.

On the other hand: Augustine says (1 Retract. 4): "I do not now approve of having said in a prayer 'O God, who dost will that only the pure shall know truth.' For it may be replied that many who are impure know many truths." Now a man is made pure by grace, according to Ps. 51:10: "Create in me a clean heart, O God, and renew a right spirit within me." It follows that a man can know truth by himself, without the help of grace.

I answer: to know truth is a use or action of the intellectual light, since the apostle says that "whatever doth make manifest is light"[3] (Eph. 5:13), and every use involves movement, in the broad sense in which understanding and will are said to be movements, as the philosopher explains in 3 De Anima, text 28. In corporeal things, we see that any movement not only requires a formal principle of the movement or action itself, but also requires a motion of the first mover. Since the first mover in the order of material things is the heavenly body, fire could not cause change otherwise than through the motion of the heavenly body, even though it should possess perfect heat. It is plain, then, that just as every corporeal movement derives from the movement of the heavenly body as the first corporeal mover, so all movements, whether corporeal or spiritual, derive from the absolute prime mover, which is God. Hence no matter how perfect any corporeal or spiritual nature is supposed to be, it cannot issue in its act unless it is moved by God, whose moving is according to the plan of his providence, not necessitated by nature like the moving of the heavenly body. Now not only is every motion derived from God as first mover, but every formal perfection is likewise derived from God, as from the first act. It follows that an action of the intellect, or of any created thing, depends on God in two ways: first, in that it has from him the perfection or the form by means of which it acts, and second, in that it is moved to its act by him. Every power bestowed by God upon created things has the power to achieve some definite action by means of its own properties. But it cannot achieve anything further, unless through a form which is added to it. Water, for example, cannot heat unless it is itself heated by fire. So also the human intellect possesses the form of intellectual light, which by itself is sufficient for the knowledge of such intelligible things as we can learn through sense. But it cannot know intelligible things of a higher order unless it is perfected

---

[3] Migne: "All that is made manifest is light."

by a stronger light, such as the light of faith or prophecy, which is called "the light of glory" since it is added to nature.

We must therefore say that, if a man is to know any truth whatsoever, he needs divine help in order that his intellect may be moved to its act by God. But he does not need a new light added to his natural light in order to know the truth in all things, but only in such things as transcend his natural knowledge. Yet God sometimes instructs men miraculously by grace in matters which can be known through natural reasons, just as he sometimes achieves by miracle things which nature can do.

On the first point: "every truth, by whomsoever uttered, is by the Holy Ghost"—but as bestowing the natural light and as moving us to understand and to speak the truth, not as dwelling in us through sanctifying grace, or as bestowing any permanent gift superadded to nature. This is the case only with certain truths which must be known and spoken—especially with truths of faith, of which the apostle is speaking.

On the second point: the corporeal sun illumines externally, God internally. The natural light bestowed on the mind is God's light, by which we are enlightened to know such things as belong to natural knowledge. Other light is not required for this, but only for such things as transcend natural knowledge.

On the third point: we always need divine help for any thinking, in so far as God moves the intellect to act. For to think is to understand something actively, as Augustine explains (14 De Trin. 7).

Article Two

WHETHER A MAN CAN WILL OR DO GOOD WITHOUT GRACE

We proceed to the second article thus:

1. It seems that a man can will and do good without grace. For that of which he is master is within a man's power, and it was said previously that a man is master of his actions, especially of his willing. (Q. 1, Art. 1; Q. 13, Art. 6.) It follows that a man can will and do good by himself, without the help of grace.

2. Again, a man is master of what conforms with his nature more than of what is contrary to it. Now to sin is contrary to nature, as the Damascene says (2 De Fid. Orth. 30), whereas the practice of virtue conforms with nature, as was said in Q. 71, Art. 1. It seems, therefore, that since a man can sin by himself, he can much more will and do good by himself.

3. Again, "truth is the good of the intellect," as the philosopher says in 6 Ethics 2. Now the intellect can know truth by itself, just as any other thing can perform its natural action by itself. Much more, then, can a man will and do good by himself.

On the other hand: the apostle says in Rom. 9:16: "it is not of him that willeth, nor of him that runneth, but of God that sheweth mercy." Augustine, also, says that "men do absolutely nothing good without grace, whether by thought, will, love, or deed" (*De Corrept. et Grat.* 2).

I answer: man's nature may be considered in two ways, either in its purity, as it was in our first parent before sin, or as corrupt, as it is in ourselves after the sin of our first parent. In either state, human nature needs divine help in order to do or to will any good, since it needs a first mover, as we said in the preceding article. In regard to the sufficiency of his operative power, man in the state of pure nature could will and do, by his own natural power, the good proportionate to his nature, such as the good of acquired virtue, though not surpassing good such as the good of infused virtue. In the state of corrupt nature he falls short of what nature makes possible, so that he cannot by his own power fulfil the whole good that pertains to his nature. Human nature is not so entirely corrupted by sin, however, as to be deprived of natural good altogether. Consequently, even in the state of corrupt nature a man can do some particular good by the power of his own nature, such as build houses, plant vineyards, and things of this kind. But he cannot achieve the whole good natural to him, as if he lacked nothing. One who is infirm, similarly, can make some movements by himself, but cannot move himself naturally like a man in health, unless cured by the help of medicine.

Thus in the state of pure nature man needs a power added to his natural power by grace, for one reason, namely, in order to do and to will supernatural good. But in the state of corrupt nature he needs this for two reasons, in order to be healed, and in order to achieve the meritorious good of supernatural virtue. In both states, moreover, he needs the divine help by which he is moved to act well.

On the first point: it is because of the deliberation of his reason, which can turn to one side or the other, that a man is master of his actions, and of willing and not willing. But although he is thus master, it is only through a previous deliberation that he either deliberates or does not deliberate. Since this regress cannot be infinite, we are finally driven to say that a man's free will is moved by an external principle higher than the mind of man, that is, by God. The philosopher indeed proves this in his chapter on Good Fortune (7 *Mor. Euden.* 18). Thus even the mind of a healthy man is not so thoroughly master of its actions that it does not need to be moved by God. Much more so the free will of a man weakened by sin and thereby hindered from good by the corruption of nature.

On the second point: to sin is nothing other than to fall short of the good which befits one according to one's nature. Now just as every created thing has its being from another, and considered in itself is nothing, so also it must be preserved by another in the good which befits its nature. It can nevertheless through itself fall short of this good, just as it can through itself cease to exist, if it is not providentially preserved.

On the third point: as we said in Art. 1, a man cannot even know truth without divine help. Now his nature is impaired by sin more in the desire for good than in the knowledge of truth. . . .

Article Seven

WHETHER A MAN CAN RISE FROM SIN WITHOUT THE HELP OF GRACE

. . . a man can in no wise rise from sin by himself, without the help of grace. Sin endures as guilt, though it is transient as an action. (Q. 87, Art. 6.) To rise from sin, therefore, is not the same as to cease from the action of sin, but involves the restoration of what a man has lost through sinning. We have already shown that a man incurs a threefold loss through sin, namely, the stain on the soul, the corruption of natural good, and the debt of punishment (Qq. 85, 86, 87, Arts. 1). He incurs a stain, since the deformity of sin deprives him of the comeliness of grace; natural good is corrupted, since his nature is deranged by the insubordination of his will to the will of God, which disruption of the order of things leaves his whole nature disordered; finally, by mortal sin he merits eternal damnation as the debt of punishment. Now it is obvious that none of these can be restored except by God. The comeliness of grace cannot be restored unless God sheds his light anew, since it is derived from the shining of the divine light, and therefore depends on an enduring gift of the light of grace. Neither can the natural order of things be restored, in which a man's will is subordinated to the will of God, unless God draws his will to himself, as we said in the preceding article. Nor can the debt of punishment be forgiven save by God alone, against whom the offence is committed, and who is the judge of men. The help of grace is therefore indispensable if a man is to rise from sin. It is needed both as an enduring gift and as the inward moving of God. . . .

Article Eight

WHETHER A MAN CAN AVOID SIN, WITHOUT GRACE

We proceed to the eighth article thus:

1. It seems that a man can avoid sin without grace. Augustine says that "no man sins in respect of what he cannot avoid" (De Duab. Animabus, 10, 11; 3 De Lib. Arb. 18). Hence it appears that if a man cannot avoid sin while he lives in mortal sin, he does not sin while he sins. But this is impossible.

2. Again, one is chastised in order that one may not sin. But if a man who lived in mortal sin were unable to avoid sin, it seems that it would be useless to chastise him. But this is impossible.

3. Again, it is said in Ecclesiasticus 15:17: "Before man are life and death, good and evil; whatsoever he shall choose shall be given him." But when a man sins, he does not cease to be a man. It is therefore still within

his power to choose either good or evil. Hence one who lacks grace can avoid sin.

On the other hand: Augustine says (*De Perf. Just.* 21): "Whosoever denies that we ought to pray 'lead us not into temptation' (and he denies this who argues that a man does not need the help of God's grace in order not to sin) should assuredly be removed from every ear and anathematized by every mouth."

I answer: we may speak of man in two ways; either as in the state of pure nature, or as in the state of corrupt nature. In the state of pure nature, man could avoid both mortal and venial sin, without grace. For to sin is nothing other than to fall short of what befits one's nature, and a man in the state of pure nature could avoid this. Yet he could not avoid it without the help of God preserving him in good, without which help his nature itself would have ceased to exist. But in the state of corrupt nature a man needs grace to heal his nature continually, if he is to avoid sin entirely. In our present life this healing is accomplished first in the mind, the appetite of the flesh being not yet wholly cured. Hence the apostle, speaking as one who is restored, says in Rom. 7:25: "with the mind I myself serve the law of God, but with the flesh the law of sin." A man in this state can avoid all mortal sin, which has to do with his reason, as we said in Q. 74, Art. 5. But he cannot avoid all venial sin, owing to the corrupt sensuality of his lower appetite. Reason can indeed suppress the urges of the lower appetite severally, wherefore they are sinful and voluntary. But it cannot suppress all of them. For while a man endeavours to suppress one of them, another may arise. Moreover, as we said in Q. 74, Art. 10, reason cannot always be vigilant enough to suppress such urges.

But before his reason is restored through justifying grace, a man can likewise avoid severally, for some time, the mortal sins which have to do with his reason, since he is not bound by necessity actually to sin at all times. But he cannot continue without mortal sin for long. As Gregory says, "a sin which is not instantly blotted out by repentance drags us down to another by its weight" (*Hom. in Ezech.* 11; 25 *Moral.* 9). This is because reason ought to be subject to God, and ought to find in God the end which it desires, just as the lower appetite ought to be subject to reason. Every human action, indeed, ought to be regulated by this end, just as the urges of the lower appetite ought to be regulated by the judgment of reason. There are therefore bound to be many untoward actions of reason itself when reason is not entirely subject to God, just as there are bound to be uncontrolled movements of the sensitive appetite when the lower appetite is imperfectly subject to reason. When a man's heart is not so firmly fixed on God that he is unwilling to be separated from him for the sake of any good, or to avoid any evil, he forsakes God, and breaks his commandments in order to gain or to avoid many things. He thus sins mortally, especially since "he acts according to his preconceived end and previous habit whenever he is caught off his guard," as the philosopher says in 3 *Ethics* 8. Premeditation may perhaps enable him to do something better than his preconceived end requires, and better than that to which his habit inclines. But he cannot be always premeditating, and will not perchance continue for long before suiting his action to a will which is not controlled by God, unless he is quickly restored to right order by grace.

On the first point: as we have said, a man can avoid sinful actions taken singly, but he cannot avoid all of them, unless through grace. Yet his sin is not to be excused on the ground that he cannot avoid it without grace, because it is due to his own fault that he does not prepare himself for grace.

On the second point: as Augustine says (*De Corrept. et Grat.* 6): "chastisement is useful in order that the desire for regeneration may arise out of the pain of it. While the noise of chastisement resounds without, God may work within by an unseem inspiration, that one should so desire, if one be a son of promise." Chastisement is necessary because a man must desist from sin of his own will. But it is not enough without the help of God. Wherefore it is said in Eccl. 7:13: "Consider the work of God: for who can make that straight which he hath made crooked?"

On the third point: as Augustine says (or another, in *Hypognosticon* 3, cap. 1, 2), this saying must be understood as referring to man in the state of pure nature, not yet the slave of sin, able both to sin and not to sin. Whatever a man then desires is given him. It is nevertheless by the help of grace that he desires what is good. . . .

Question One Hundred and Eleven

THE DIVISIONS OF GRACE

We must now consider the division of grace, concerning which there are five questions. 1. Whether grace is appropriately divided into free grace and sanctifying grace. 2. Of the division of sanctifying grace into operative and co-operative grace. 3. Of the division of the same into prevenient and subsequent grace. 4. Of the division of free grace. 5. How sanctifying grace compares with free grace.

Article One
WHETHER GRACE IS APPROPRIATELY DIVIDED INTO SANCTIFYING GRACE AND FREE GRACE

. . . I answer: as the apostle says in Rom. 13:1, "the powers that be are ordained of God." Now the order of things is such that some things are led to God by means of others, as Dionysius says (*Coel. Hier.* 6, 7, 8). Hence grace, which is ordained to lead men to God, works in accordance with a certain order, in such a way that some men are led to God by means of other men. Grace is therefore twofold. There is grace through which a man is himself united to God, which is called sanctifying grace. There is also grace whereby one man co-operates with another to lead him to God. This latter gift is called "free grace," since it is beyond the capacity of nature to give, and beyond the merit of him to whom it is given. But it is not called sanctifying grace, since it is not given in order that a man may himself be justified by it, but in order that he may co-operate towards the justification of another. It is of such grace that the apostle speaks in I Cor. 12:7: "But the manifestation of the Spirit is given to every man to profit withal," that is, for the benefit of others. . . .

Article Two

WHETHER GRACE IS APPROPRIATELY DIVIDED INTO OPERATIVE AND CO-OPERATIVE GRACE

. . . I answer: . . . grace may be understood in two ways, as the divine help by which God moves us to do and to will what is good, and as a habitual gift divinely bestowed on us. In either sense grace is appropriately divided into operative and co-operative grace. An operation which is part of an effect is attributed to the mover, not to the thing moved. The operation is therefore attributed to God when God is the sole mover, and when the mind is moved but not a mover. We then speak of "operative grace." But when the soul is not only moved but also a mover, the operation is attributed to the soul as well as to God. We then speak of "co-operative grace." In this case there is a twofold action within us. There is an inward action of the will, in which the will is moved and God is the mover, especially when a will which previously willed evil begins to will good. We therefore speak of "operative grace," since God moves the human mind to this action. But there is also an outward action, in which operation is attributed to the will, since an outward action is commanded by the will, as we explained in Q. 17, Art. 9. We speak of "co-operative grace" in reference to actions of this kind, because God helps us even in outward actions, outwardly providing the capacity to act as well as inwardly strengthening the will to issue in act. Augustine accordingly adds, to the words quoted, "he operates to make us will, and when we will, he co-operates with us that we may be made perfect." Hence if grace is understood to mean the gracious moving by which God moves us to meritorious good, it is appropriately divided into operative and co-operative grace. . . .

Article Three

WHETHER GRACE IS APPROPRIATELY DIVIDED INTO PREVENIENT AND SUBSEQUENT GRACE

. . . I answer: just as grace is divided into operative and co-operative grace on account of its different effects, so is it divided into prevenient and subsequent grace on the same grounds. There are five effects of grace in us: first, that the soul is healed; second, that it wills what is good; third, that it carries out what it wills; fourth, that it perseveres in good; and fifth, that it attains to glory. Since grace causes the first effect in us, it is called prevenient in relation to the second effect. Since it causes the second effect in us, it is called subsequent in relation to the first effect. And since any particular effect follows one effect and precedes another, grace may be called both prevenient and subsequent in regard to the same effect as related to different effects. . . .

Treatise on the Theological Virtues

Question Two

THE ACT OF FAITH

We must now consider the act of faith, first the inward act, and second the outward act. There are ten questions concerning the inward act of faith. 1. In what belief consists, which is the inward act of faith. 2. In how many ways one may speak of belief. 3. Whether, for salvation, it is necessary to believe anything which is beyond natural reason. 4. Whether it is necessary to believe such things as are attainable by natural reason. 5. Whether, for salvation, it is necessary to believe anything explicity. 6. Whether explicit belief is required of all men equally. 7. Whether, for salvation, it is always necessary to have explicit belief concerning Christ. 8. Whether explicit belief in the Trinity is necessary for salvation. 9. Whether the act of faith is meritorious. 10. Whether a human reason diminishes the merit of faith.

Article One

WHETHER TO BELIEVE IS TO THINK WITH ASSENT

We proceed to the first article thus:

1. It seems that to believe is not to think with assent. For "to think" implies inquiry of some kind, the word being a contraction of "to consider together" (cogitare = coagitare = simul agitare). But the Damascene says that "faith is assent without inquiry" (4 De Fid. Orth. 1). It follows that the act of faith does not involve thinking.

2. Again, it will be shown in Q. 4, Art. 2, that faith belongs to reason. But it was said in Pt. I, Q. 78, Art. 4, that thinking is an act of the cogitative

power, which belongs to the sensitive part of the soul.[4] It follows that faith does not involve thinking.

3. Again, belief is an act of the intellect, since the object of belief is the true. Now it was said in 12ae, Q. 15, Art. 1, ad. 3 that assent is not an act of the intellect, but an act of the will, just as consent is an act of the will. It follows that to believe is not to think with assent.

On the other hand: "to believe" is thus defined by Augustine. (De Praed. Sanct. 2.)

I answer: "to think" can mean three things. Firstly, it means any deliberative intellectual act in general. This is what Augustine has in mind in 14 De Trin. 7, when he says: "what I now call understanding is that whereby we understand when we think." Secondly, and more precisely, it means the kind of intellectual deliberation which involves a degree of questioning, and which occurs before the intellect reaches perfection through the certainty of vision. This is what Augustine has in mind in 15 De Trin. 16, where he says: "The Son of God is not called the Thought of God, but the Word of God. When our thought has reached what we know and become formed by it, it becomes our word. The Word of God should therefore be conceived as without the thought of God, since it contains nothing which remains to be formed, and which could be unformed." In this sense, thought properly means the movement of a soul which deliberates, and which is not yet perfected by a full vision of the truth. But since such movement may be either deliberation about universal meanings, which are the concern of the intellect, or deliberation about particular meanings, which are the concern of the sensitive part of the soul, the word "to think" is used in this second sense to mean the intellectual act of deliberation, and in yet a third sense to mean an act of the cogitative power.

Now if "to think" is understood in the first or general sense, "to think with assent" does not express the whole meaning of "to believe." For a man thinks in this way even about what he knows and understands in science, and also gives his assent. But if it is understood in the second sense, then by means of this expression we understand the whole nature of the act of belief. There are some acts of the intellect, such as those whereby one contemplates what one knows and understands in science, in which assent is given with confidence, without any deliberation. There are also others in which thought is unformed, and in which there is no firm assent. One may incline to neither alternative, as one who doubts. Or one may incline to the one rather than to the other on the strength of slight evidence, as does one who suspects. Or, again, one may choose one alternative with misgivings about the other,

[4] The sensitive power operates through a corporeal organ, through which it perceives things which are actually present. The cogitative power perceives and preserves the "intention" or practical significance of particular things present or absent, by means of collating ideas. It is also called the "particular reason."

as does one who holds an opinion. Now the act which is "to believe" holds firmly to the one alternative. In this respect, belief is similar to science and understanding. Yet its thought is not perfected by clear vision, and in this respect belief is similar to doubt, suspicion, and opinion. To think with assent is thus the property of one who believes, and distinguishes the act of "belief" from all other acts of the intellect which are concerned with truth or falsity.

On the first point: faith does not make use of inquiry by natural reason to demonstrate what it believes. But it does inquire into the evidence by which a man is induced to believe, for example, into the circumstance that such things are spoken by God and confirmed by miracles.

On the second point: as we have said above, the word "to think" is here understood as it applies to the intellect, not as meaning an act of the cogitative power.

On the third point: the intellect of the believer is determined by the will, not by reason. Hence assent is here understood to mean the act of the intellect as determined by the will. . . .

Article Ten

WHETHER A REASON IN SUPPORT OF THE THINGS OF FAITH DIMINISHES THE MERIT OF FAITH

We proceed to the tenth article thus:

1. It seems that a reason in support of the things of faith diminishes the merit of faith. For Gregory says: "Faith has no merit when human reason proves it by test" (Hom. in Evang. 26). Thus a human reason excludes the merit of faith altogether, if it provides an adequate proof. It seems, therefore, that any kind of human reason in support of the things of faith diminishes the merit of faith.

2. Again, as the philosopher says in 1 Ethics 9, "happiness is the reward of virtue." Hence anything which diminishes the nature of a virtue diminishes the merit of it. Now a human reason seems to diminish the nature of the virtue of faith. For it is of the very nature of faith that its object is unseen, as was said in Q. 1, Arts. 4 and 5, and the more reasons are given in support of something, the less does it remain unseen. A human reason in support of the things of faith therefore diminishes the merit of faith.

3. Again, the causes of contraries are themselves contrary. Now anything which conduces to the contrary of faith, whether it be persecution in order to compel one to renounce it, or reasoning in order to persuade one to renounce it, increases the merit of faith. A reason which encourages faith therefore diminishes the merit of faith.

On the other hand: it is said in I Peter 3:15: "be ready always to give an answer to every man that asketh you a reason of the hope that is in you."[5]

[5] Migne: "of that faith and hope which is in you."

Now the apostle would not have given this advice if the merit of faith were to be diminished as a result of it. Hence a reason does not diminish the merit of faith.

I answer: as we said in the preceding article, the act of faith can be meritorious inasmuch as it depends on the will, in respect of assent and not only of practice. Now a human reason in support of the things of faith may relate to the will of the believer in two ways. In the first place, it may precede the will to believe, as it does when a man has no desire to believe, or has not a ready will to believe, unless he is induced to do so by some human reason. If it precedes in this way, a human reason diminishes the merit of faith. We have already said that a passion which precedes choice in moral virtues diminishes the worth of a virtuous action (12ae, Q. 24, Art. 4, ad 1; Q. 77, Art. 6, ad 6). Just as a man ought to perform acts of moral virtue on account of reasoned judgment, and not on account of passion, so ought he to believe the things of faith on account of divine authority, and not on account of human reason.

In the second place, a human reason may follow the will to believe. When a man has a ready will to believe, he rejoices in the truth which he believes, thinks about it, and turns it over in his mind to see whether he can find a reason for it. A human reason which thus follows the will to believe does not exclude merit. Rather is it a sign of greater merit, just as a passion which follows the will in moral virtues is a sign of greater readiness of will, as we said in 12ae, Q. 24, Art. 3, ad 1. This is the import of the words of the Samaritan to the woman, who signifies human reason (John 4:42): "Now we believe, not because of thy saying."

On the first point: Gregory is speaking of such as have no desire to believe the things of faith otherwise than on the evidence of reason. But when a man is willing to believe them on the authority of God alone, the merit of faith is neither excluded nor diminished if he also has demonstrative proof of some of them, such as that God is one.

On the second point: the reasons which are given in support of the authority of faith are not demonstrative reasons, such as could lead the human intellect to intellectual vision. Hence the things of faith do not cease to be unseen. Such reasons remove hindrances to faith, showing that what is proposed in faith is not impossible. They consequently diminish neither the nature nor the merit of faith. But although demonstrative reasons brought in support of the preambles to faith (not in support of the articles) may diminish the nature of faith by causing what is proposed to be seen, they do not diminish the nature of charity, through which the will is ready to believe the things of faith even though they should remain unseen. Hence the nature of merit is not diminished.

On the third point: whatever is hostile to the faith, whether it be the reasoning of a man or outward persecution, increases the merit of faith in so far as it shows that the will is readier and stronger in the faith. Martyrs had greater merit of faith, since they did not renounce the faith on account of persecutions. Men of wisdom also have greater merit, when they do not renounce it on account of reasons brought against it by philosophers or heretics. But things which encourage faith do not always diminish the readiness of the will to believe. Neither, therefore, do they always diminish the merit of faith. . . .

Question Six

THE CAUSE OF FAITH

We must now consider the cause of faith, concerning which there are two questions. 1. Whether faith is infused into man by God. 2. Whether unformed faith is a gift of God.

Article One

WHETHER FAITH IS INFUSED INTO MAN BY GOD

We proceed to the first article thus:

1. It seems that faith is not infused into man by God. For Augustine says (14 De Trin. 1): "by knowledge is faith begotten, nourished, defended, and strengthened in us." Now what is begotten in us by knowledge would seem to be acquired, rather than infused. Thus it appears that faith is not in us by divine infusion.

2. Again, what a man attains through hearing and seeing would seem to be acquired. Now a man comes to believe both through seeing miracles and through hearing the doctrine of the faith. Thus it is said in John 4:53: "So the father knew that it was at the same hour in which Jesus said unto him, Thy son liveth: and himself believed, and his whole house," and in Rom. 10:17: "faith cometh by hearing." Hence faith can be acquired.

3. Again, a man can acquire what depends on his will, and Augustine says that "faith depends on the will of those who believe" (De Praed. Sanct. 5). It follows that a man can acquire faith.

On the other hand: it is said in Eph. 2:8-9: "by grace are ye saved through faith; and that not of yourselves; it is the gift of God: . . . lest any man should boast."

I answer: for faith, two things are required. In the first place, the things which a man is to believe must be proposed to him. This is necessary if anything is to be believed explicitly. Secondly, the believer must give his assent to what is proposed. Now faith is bound to be from God as regards the first of these conditions. For the things of faith are beyond human reason, so that a man cannot know them unless God reveals them. They are revealed by God immediately to some, such as the apostles and the prophets, and mediately to others, through preachers of the faith who are sent by God according to Rom. 10:15: "And how shall they preach except they be sent?" The cause of the believer's assent to the things of faith is twofold. There is in the first place an external cause which induces him to believe, such as the sight of a miracle, or the persuasion of another who leads him to the faith. But neither of these is a sufficient cause. For of those who see one and the same miracle, or who hear the same prophecy, some will believe and others will not believe. We must therefore recognize that there is also an inward cause, which moves a man from within to assent to the things of faith.

The Pelagians attributed this inward cause solely to a man's own free will, and said accordingly that the beginning of faith lies with ourselves, since we prepare ourselves to assent to the things of faith, although the consummation of faith lies with God, who proposes to us such things as we ought to believe. But this is false. For when a man gives his assent to the things of faith, he is raised above his own nature, and this is possible only through a supernatural principle which moves him from within. This principle is God. The assent of faith, which is the principal act of faith, is therefore due to God, who moves us inwardly through grace.

On the first point: faith is begotten by knowledge, and is nourished by the external persuasion which knowledge provides. But the principal and proper cause of faith is that which inwardly moves us to give our assent.

On the second point: this reasoning argues from the cause whereby the things of faith are externally proposed, or whereby one is persuaded to believe them by means of word or deed.

On the third point: to believe does depend on the will of those who believe. But a man's will must be prepared by God through grace, in order that he may be raised to things which are above nature, as we have said, and as we have said also in Q. 2, Art. 3.

45 THESE ESSAYS of Martin Luther (1483–1546) offer different aspects of this reformer's view of the nature of man and the Christian faith. In a conciliatory letter to Pope Leo X, which prefaced *A Treatise on Christian Liberty*, (1520), Luther suggested that this short essay contained "the whole of Christion life in a brief form." His *Preface to the Epistle to the Romans* (1522) provides a remarkably concise statement of his understanding of the Christian faith. The *Preface* is

not an introduction to a Biblical book as much as it is a testimony of the man. His discussion of predestination, for example, displays his own conviction of comfort that comes from this affirmation rather than a logical or systematic defense of it as doctrine. *The Bondage of the Will* (1525) was written in response to an essay of Desiderius Erasmus on the freedom of the will. Erasmus, the humanist scholar, was not a rigorous theologian; Luther's rebuttal treatise was sharp in detail and language.[1]

A. A Treatise on Christian Liberty *

MARTIN LUTHER

Many have thought Christian faith to be an easy thing, and not a few have given it a place among the virtues. This they do because they have had no experience of it, and have never tasted what great virtue there is in faith. For it is impossible that anyone should write well of it or well understand what is correctly written of it, unless he has at some time tasted the courage faith gives a man when trials oppress him. But he who has had even a faint taste of it can never write, speak, meditate, or hear enough concerning it. For it is a living fountain springing up into life everlasting, as Christ calls it in John 4. For my part, although I have no wealth of faith to boast of and know how scant my store is, yet I hope that, driven about by great and various temptations, I have attained to a little faith, and that I can speak of it, if not more elegantly, certainly more to the point, than those literalists and all too subtle disputants have hitherto done, who have not even understood what they have written.

That I may make the way easier for the unlearned—for only such do I serve—I set down first these two propositions concerning the liberty and the bondage of the spirit:

A Christian man is a perfectly free lord of all, subject to none.

A Christian man is a perfectly dutiful servant of all, subject to all.

Although these two theses seem to contradict each other, yet, if they should be found to fit together they would serve our purpose beautifully. For they are both Paul's own, who says, in 1 Corinthians 9, "Whereas I was free, I made myself the servant of all," and Romans 8, "Owe no man

* From Martin Luther, *Three Treatises*, tr. by W. A. Lambert. Philadelphia: The Board of Publication of the Lutheran Church in America, 1943.

1 See also *The Letter and the Spirit*, Selection 8; *The Babylonian Captivity of the Chuch*, Selection 63.

anything, but to love one another." Now love by its very nature is ready to serve and to be subject to him who is loved. So Christ, although Lord of all, was made of a woman, made under the law, and hence was at the same time free and a servant, at the same time in the form of God and in the form of a servant.

Let us start, however, with something more remote from our subject, but more obvious. Man has a twofold nature, a spiritual and a bodily. According to the spiritual nature, which men call the soul, he is called a spiritual, or inner, or new man; according to the bodily nature, which men call the flesh, he is called a carnal, or outward, or old man, of whom the Apostle writes, in 2 Corinthians 4, "Though our outward man is corrupted, yet the inward man is renewed day by day." Because of this diversity of nature the scriptures assert contradictory things of the same man, since these two men in the same man contradict each other, since the flesh lusteth against the spirit and the spirit against the flesh (Galatians 5).

First, let us contemplate the inward man, to see how a righteous, free, and truly Christian man, that is, a new, spiritual, inward man, comes into being. It is evident that no external thing, whatsoever it be, has any influence whatever in producing Christian righteousness or liberty, nor in producing unrighteousness or bondage. A simple argument will furnish the proof. What can it profit the soul if the body fare well, be free and active, eat, drink, and do as it pleases? For in these things even the most godless slaves of all the vices fare well. On the other hand, how will ill health or imprisonment or hunger or thirst or any other external misfortune hurt the soul? With these things even the most godly men are afflicted, and those who because of a clear conscience are most free. None of these things touch either the liberty or the bondage of the soul. The soul receives no benefit if the body is adorned with the sacred robes of the priesthood, or dwells in sacred places, or is occupied with sacred duties, or prays, fasts, abstains from certain kinds of food, or does any work whatsoever that can be done by the body and in the body. The righteousness and the freedom of the soul demand something far different, since the things which have been mentioned could be done by any wicked man, and such works produce nothing but hypocrites. On the other hand, it will not hurt the soul if the body is clothed in secular dress, dwells in unconsecrated places, eats and drinks as others do, does not pray aloud, and neglects to do all the things mentioned above, which hypocrites can do.

Further, to put aside all manner of works, even contemplation, meditation, and all that the soul can do, avail nothing. One thing and one only is necessary for Christian life, righteousness, and liberty. That one thing is the most holy Word of God, the Gospel of Christ, as he says, John 11, "I am the resurrection and the life: he that believeth in me shall not die forever"; and John 8, "If the Son shall make you free, you shall be free indeed"; and

Matthew 4, "Not in bread alone doth man live; but in every word that proceedeth from the mouth of God." Let us then consider it certain and conclusively established that the soul can do without all things except the Word of God, and that where this is not there is no help for the soul in anything else whatever. But if it has the Word it is rich and lacks nothing, since this Word is the Word of life, of truth, of light, of peace, of righteousness, of salvation, of joy, of liberty, of wisdom, of power, of grace, of glory, and of every blessing beyond our power to estimate. This is why the prophet in the entire One Hundred and Nineteenth Psalm, and in many other places of scripture, with so many sighs yearns after the Word of God and applies so many names to it. On the other hand, there is no more terrible plague with which the wrath of God can smite men than a famine of the hearing of His Word, as He says in Amos, just as there is no greater mercy than when He sends forth His Word, as we read in Psalm 107, "He sent His word and healed them, and delivered them from their destructions." Nor was Christ sent into the world for any other ministry but that of the Word, and the whole spiritual estate, apostles, bishops and all the priests, has been called and instituted only for the ministry of the Word.

You ask, "What then is this Word of God, and how shall it be used, since there are so many words of God?" I answer, the Apostle explains that in Romans 1. The Word is the Gospel of God concerning His Son, who was made flesh, suffered, rose from the dead, and was glorified through the Spirit who sanctifies. For to preach Christ means to feed the soul, to make it righteous, to set it free, and to save it, if it believe the preaching. For faith alone is the saving and efficacious use of the Word of God, Romans 10, "If thou confess with thy mouth that Jesus is Lord, and believe with thy heart that God hath raised Him up from the dead, thou shalt be saved"; and again, "The end of the law is Christ, unto righteousness to everyone that believeth"; and, in Romans 1, "The just shall live by his faith." The Word of God cannot be received and cherished by any works whatever, but only by faith. Hence it is clear that, as the soul needs only the Word for its life and righteousness, so it is justified by faith alone and not by any works; for if it could be justified by anything else, it would not need the Word, and therefore it would not need faith. But this faith cannot at all exist in connection with works, that is to say, if you at the same time claim to be justified by works, whatever their character; for that would be to halt between two sides, to worship Baal and to kiss the hand, which, as Job says, is a very great iniquity. Therefore the moment you begin to believe, you learn that all things in you are altogether blameworthy, sinful, and damnable, as Romans 3 says, "For all have sinned and lack the glory of God"; and again, "there is none just, there is none that doeth good, all have turned out of the way: they are become unprofitable together." When you have learned this, you will know that you need Christ, who suffered and rose again for you, that, believing in Him, you may through this faith become a new man, in that all your sins are forgiven, and you are justified by the merits of another, namely, of Christ alone.

Since, therefore, this faith can rule only in the inward man, as Romans 10 says, "With the heart we believe unto righteousness"; and since faith alone justifies, it is clear that the inward man cannot be justified, made free, and be saved by any outward work or dealing whatsoever, and that works, whatever their character, have nothing to do with this inward man. On the other hand, only ungodliness and unbelief of heart, and no outward work, make him guilty and a damnable servant of sin. Wherefore it ought to be the first concern of every Christian to lay aside all trust in works, and more and more to strengthen faith alone, and through faith to grow in the knowledge, not of works, but of Christ Jesus, who suffered and rose for him, as Peter teaches, in the last chapter of his first Epistle; since no other work makes a Christian. Thus when the Jews asked Christ, John 6, what they should do that they might work the works of God, He brushed aside the multitude of works in which He saw that they abounded, and enjoined upon them a single work, saying, "This is the work of God, that you believe in Him whom He hath sent. For Him hath God the Father sealed. . . ."

Should you ask how it comes that faith alone justifies and without works offers us such a treasury of great benefits, when so many works, ceremonies, and laws are prescribed in the scriptures, I answer: First of all, remember what has been said: faith alone, without works, justifies, makes free and saves, as we shall later make still more clear. Here we must point out that all the scriptures of God are divided into two parts—commands and promises. The commands indeed teach things that are good, but the things taught are not done as soon as taught; for the commands show us what we ought to do, but do not give us the power to do it; they are intended to teach a man to know himself, that through them he may recognize his inability to do good and may despair of his powers. . . .

From what has been said it is easily seen whence faith has such great power, and why no good work nor all good works together can equal it: no work can cling to the Word of God nor be in the soul; in the soul faith alone and the Word have sway. As the Word is, so it makes the soul, as heated iron glows like fire because of the union of fire with it. It is clear then that a Christian man has in his faith all that he needs, and needs no works to justify him. And if he has no need of works, neither does he need the law; and if he has no need of the law, surely he is free from the law, and it is true, "the law is not made for a righteous man." And this is that Christian liberty, even our faith, which does not indeed cause us to live in idleness or in wickedness, but makes the law and works unnecessary for any man's righteousness and salavation. . . .

Now let us turn to the second part, to the outward man. Here we shall answer all those who, misled by the word "faith" and by all that has been said, now say: "If faith does all things and is alone sufficient unto righteousness, why then are good works commanded? We will take our ease and do no works, and be content with faith." I answer, Not so, ye wicked men, not so. That would indeed be proper, if we were wholly inward and perfectly spiritual men; but such we shall be only at the last day, the day of the resurrection of the dead. As long as we live in the flesh we only begin and make some progress in that which shall be perfected in the future life. For this reason the Apostle, in Romans 8, calls all that we attain in this life "the first fruits" of the spirit, because, forsooth, we shall receive the greater portion, even the fullness of the spirit, in the future. This is the place for that which was said above, that a Christian man is the servant of all and made subject to all. For in so far as he is free he does no works, but in so far as he is a servant he does all manner of works. How this is possible we shall see.

Although, as I have said, a man is abundantly justified by faith inwardly, in his spirit, and so has all that he ought to have, except in so far as this faith and riches must grow from day to day even unto the future life: yet he remains in this mortal life on earth, and in this life he must needs govern his own body and have dealings with men. Here the works begin; here a man cannot take his ease; here he must, indeed, take care to discipline his body by fastings, watchings, labors, and other reasonable discipline, and to make it subject to the spirit so that it will obey and conform to the inward man and to faith, and not revolt against faith and hinder the inward man, as it is the body's nature to do if it be not held in check. For the inward man, who by faith is created in the likeness of God, is both joyful and happy because of Christ in whom so many benefits are conferred upon him, and therefore it is his one occupation to serve God joyfully and for naught, in love that is not constrained.

While he is doing this, lo, he meets a contrary will in his own flesh, which strives to serve the world and to seek its own advantage. This the spirit of faith cannot tolerate, and with joyful zeal it attempts to put the body under and to hold it in check, as Paul says in Romans 7, "I delight in the law of God after the inward man; but I see another law in my members, warring against the law of my mind, and bringing me into captivity to the law of sin"; and, in another place, "I keep under my body, and bring it into subjection: lest by any means, when I have preached to others, I myself should be a castaway," and in Galatians, "They that are Christ's have crucified the flesh with its lusts."

In doing these works, however, we must not think that a man is justified before God by them: for that erroneous opinion faith, which alone is righteousness before God, cannot endure; but we must think that these works reduce the body to subjection and purify it of its evil lusts, and our whole purpose is to be directed only toward the driving out of lusts. For since by faith the soul is cleansed and made a lover of God, it desires that all things, and especially its own body, shall be as pure as itself, so that all things may join with it in loving and praising God. Hence a man cannot be idle, because the need of his body drives him and he is compelled to do many good works to reduce it to subjection. Nevertheless the works themselves do not justify him before God, but he does the works out of spontaneous love in obedience to God, and considers nothing except the approval of God, whom he would in all things most scrupulously obey. . . .

These two sayings, therefore, are true: "Good works do not make a good man, but a good man does good works; evil works do not make a wicked man, but a wicked man does evil works"; so that it is always necessary that the "substance" or person itself be good before there can be any good works, and that good works follow and proceed from the good person, as Christ also says, "A corrupt tree does not bring forth good fruit, a good tree does not bring forth evil fruit." It is clear that the fruits do not bear the tree, nor does the tree grow on the fruits, but, on the contrary, the trees bear the fruits and the fruits grow on the trees. As it is necessary, therefore, that the trees must exist before their fruits, and the fruits do not make trees either good or corrupt, but rather as the trees are so are the fruits they bear; so the person of a man must needs first be good or wicked before he does a good or a wicked work, and his works do not make him good or wicked, but he miself makes his works either good or wicked. . . .

Furthermore, no good work helps an unbeliever, so as to justify or save him. And, on the other hand, no evil work makes him wicked or damns him, but the unbelief which makes the person and the tree evil, does the evil and damnable works. Hence when a man is made good or evil, this is effected not by the works, but by faith or unbelief, as the Wise man says, "This is the beginning of sin, that a man falls away from God," which happens when he does not believe. And Paul, Hebrews 11, says, "He that cometh to God must believe." And Christ says the same: "Either make the tree good and his fruit good; or else make the tree corrupt and his fruit corrupt," as if He would say, "Let him who would have good fruit begin by planting a good tree." So let him who would do good works not begin with the doing of works, but with believing, which makes the person good. For nothing makes a man good except faith, nor evil except unbelief. . . .

So a Christian, like Christ, his Head, is filled and made rich by faith, and should be content with this form of God which he has obtained by faith; only, as I have said, he ought to increase this faith until it be made perfect. For this faith is his life, his righteousness, and his salvation: it saves him and makes him acceptable, and bestows upon him all things that are Christ's, as has been said above, and as Paul asserts in Galatians 2, when he says, "And the life which I now live in the flesh, I live by the faith of the Son of God."

Although the Christian is thus free from all works, he ought in this liberty to empty himself, to take upon himself the form of a servant, to be made in the likeness of men, to be found in fashion as a man, and to serve, help and in every way deal with his neighbor as he sees that God through Christ has dealt and still deals with himself. And this he should do freely, having regard to nothing except the divine approval. He ought to think: "Though I am an unworthy and condemned man, my God has given me in Christ all the riches of righteousness and salvation without any merit on my part, out of pure, free mercy, so that henceforth I need nothing whatever except faith which believes that this is true. Why should I not therefore freely, joyfully, with all my heart, and with an eager will, do all things which I know are pleasing and acceptable to such a Father, who has overwhelmed me with His inestimable riches? I will therefore give myself as a Christ to my neighbor, just as Christ offered Himself to me; I will do nothing in this life except what I see is necessary, profitable and salutary to my neighbor, since through faith I have an abundance of all good things in Christ. . . ."

We conclude, therefore, that a Christian man lives not in himself, but in Christ and in his neighbor. Otherwise he is not a Christian. He lives in Christ through faith, in his neighbor through love; by faith he is caught up beyond himself into God, by love he sinks down beneath himself into his neighbor; yet he always remains in God and in His love, as Christ says in John 1, "Verily, I say unto you, Hereafter ye shall see heaven open, and the angels of God ascending and descending upon the Son of man."

Enough now of liberty. As you see, it is a spiritual and true liberty, and makes our hearts free from all sins, laws and mandates, as Paul says, 1 Timothy 1, "The law is not made for a righteous man." It is more excellent than all other liberty which is external, as heaven is more excellent than earth. This liberty may Christ grant us both to understand and to preserve. Amen.

Finally, something must be added for the sake of those for whom nothing can be so well said that they will not spoil it by misunderstanding it, though it is a question whether they will understand even what shall here be said. There are very many who, when they hear of this liberty of faith, immediately turn it into an occasion for the flesh, and think that now all things are allowed them. They want to show that they are free men and Christians only by despising and finding fault with ceremonies, traditions, and human laws; as if they were Christians because on stated days they do not fast or eat meat when others fast, or because they do not use the accustomed prayers, and with upturned nose scoff at the precepts of men, although they utterly disregard all else that pertains to the Christian religion. The extreme opposite of these are those who rely for their salvation solely on their reverent observance of ceremonies, as if they would be saved because on certain days they fast or abstain from meats, or pray certain prayers; these make a boast of the precepts of the Church and of the Fathers, and care not a fig for the things which are of the essence of our faith. Plainly, both are in error, because they neglect the weightier things which are necessary to salvation, and quarrel so noisily about those trifling and unnecessary matters.

How much better is the teaching of the Apostle Paul, who bids us take a middle course, and condemns both sides when he says, "Let not him that eateth despise him that eateth not; and let not him which eateth not judge him that eateth." Here you see that they who neglect and disparage ceremonies, not out of piety, but out of mere contempt, are reproved, since the Apostle teaches us not to despise them. Such men are puffed up by knowledge. On the other hand, he teaches those who insist on the ceremonies not to judge the others, for neither party acts toward the other according to the love that edifies. Wherefore, we ought here to listen to the scriptures, which teach that we should not go aside to the right nor to the left, but follow the statutes of the Lord which are right, rejoicing the heart. For as a man is not righteous because he keeps and clings to the works and forms of the ceremonies, so also will a man not be counted righteous merely because he neglects and despises them.

B. Preface to the Epistle to the Romans*

MARTIN LUTHER

This Epistle is really the chief part of the New Testament and the very purest Gospel, and is worthy not only that every Christian should know it word for word, by heart, but occupy himself with it every day, as the daily bread of the soul. It can never be read or pondered too much, and the more it is dealt with the more precious it becomes, and the better it tastes.

Therefore, I, too, will do my best, so far as God has given me power, to open the way into it through this preface, so that it may be the better understood by everyone. For heretofore it has been evilly darkened with commentaries and all kinds of idle talk, though it is, in itself, a bright light, almost enough to illumine all the scripture.

* From Works of Martin Luther, Vol. IV, tr. by C. M. Jacobs. Philadelphia: A. J. Holman Co., 1932. Used by permission of The Board of Publication of the Lutheran Church in America.

To begin with we must have knowledge of its language and know what St. Paul means by the words, law, sin, grace, faith, righteousness, flesh, spirit, etc., otherwise no reading of it has any value.

The little word "law," you must not take here in human fashion, as a teaching about what works are to be done or not done. That is the way it is with human laws,—the law is fulfilled by works, even though there is no heart in them. But God judges according to what is at the bottom of the heart, and for this reason, His law makes its demands on the inmost heart and cannot be satisfied with works, but rather punishes works that are done otherwise than from the bottom of the heart, as hypocrisy and lies. Hence all men are called liars, in Psalm cxvi, for the reason that no one keeps or can keep God's law from the bottom of the heart, for everyone finds in himself displeasure in what is good and pleasure in what is bad. If, then, there is no willing pleasure in the good, then the inmost heart is not set on the law of God, then there is surely sin, and God's wrath is deserved, even though outwardly there seem to be many good works and an honorable life.

Hence St. Paul concludes, in chapter ii, that the Jews are all sinners, and says that only the doers of the law are righteous before God. He means by this that no one is, in his works, a doer of the law; on the contrary, he speaks to them thus, "Thou teachest not to commit adultery, but thou committest adultery"; and "Wherein thou judgest another, thou condemnest thyself, because thou doest the same thing that thou judgest"; as if to say, "You live a fine outward life in the works of the law, and judge those who do not so live, and know how to teach everyone; you see the splinter in the other's eye, but of the beam in your own eye you are not aware."

For even though you keep the law outwardly, with works, from fear of punishment or love of reward, nevertheless, you do all this without willingness and pleasure, and without love for the law; but rather with unwillingness, under compulsion; and you would rather do otherwise, if the law were not there. The conclusion is that at the bottom of your heart you hate the law. What matter, then, that you teach others not to steal, if you are a thief at heart, and would gladly be one outwardly, if you dared? Though, to be sure, the outward work is not far behind such hypocrites! Thus you teach others, but not yourself; and you yourself know not what you teach, and have never yet rightly understood the law. Nay, the law increases sin, as he says in chapter v, for the reason that the more the law demands what men cannot do, the more they hate the law.

For this reason he says, in chapter vii, "The law is spiritual." What is that? If the law were for the body, it could be satisfied with works; but since it is spiritual, no one can satisfy it, unless all that you do is done from the bottom of the heart. But such a heart is given only by God's Spirit, who makes a man equal to the law, so that he acquires a desire for the law in his heart, and henceforth does nothing out of fear and compulsion, but everything out of a willing heart. That law, then, is spiritual which will be loved and fulfilled with such a spiritual heart, and requires such a spirit. Where that spirit is not in the heart, there sin remains, and displeasure with the law, and enmity toward it; though the law is good and just and holy.

Accustom yourself, then, to this language, and you will find that doing the works of the law and fulfilling the law are two very different things. The work of the law is everything that one does, or can do toward keeping the law of his own free will or by his own powers. But since under all these works and along with them there remains in the heart dislike for the law and the compulsion to keep it, these works are all wasted and have no value. That is what St. Paul means in chapter iii, when he says, "By the works of the law no man becomes righteous before God." Hence you see that the wranglers and sophists are deceivers, when they teach men to prepare themselves for grace by means of works. How can a man prepare himself for good by means of works, if he does no good works without displeasure and unwillingness of heart? How shall a work please God, if it proceeds from a reluctant and resisting heart?

To fulfil the law, however, is to do its works with pleasure and love, and to live a godly and good life of one's own accord, without the compulsion of the law. This pleasure and love for the law is put into the heart by the Holy Ghost, as he says in chapter v. But the Holy Ghost is not given except in, with, and by faith in Jesus Christ, as he says in the introduction; and faith does not come, save only through God's Word or Gospel, which preaches Christ, that He is God's Son and a man, and has died and risen again for our sakes, as he says in chapters iii, iv and x.

Hence it comes that faith alone makes righteous and fulfils the law; for out of Christ's merit, it brings the Spirit, and the Spirit makes the heart glad and free, as the law requires that it shall be. Thus good works come out of faith. That is what he means in chapter iii, after he has rejected the works of the law, so that it sounds as though he would abolish the law by faith; "Nay," he says, "we establish the law by faith," that is, we fulfil it by faith.

Sin, in the scripture, means not only the outward works of the body, but all the activities that move men to the outward works, namely, the inmost heart, with all its powers. Thus the little word "do" ought to mean that a man falls all the way into sin and walks in sin. This is done by no outward work of sin, unless a man goes into sin altogether, body and soul. And the scriptures look especially into the heart and have regard to the root and source of all sin, which is unbelief in the inmost heart. As, therefore, faith alone makes righteous, and brings the Spirit, and produces pleasure in good, eternal works, so unbelief alone commits sin, and brings up the flesh, and produces pleasure in bad external works, as happened to Adam and Eve in Paradise.

Hence Christ calls unbelief the only sin, when he says, in John xvi, "The Spirit will rebuke the world for sin, because they believe not on me." For this reason, too, before good or bad works are done, which are the fruits, there must first be in the heart faith or unbelief, which is the root, the sap, the chief power of all sin. And this is called in the scriptures, the head of the serpent and of the old dragon, which the seed of the woman, Christ, must tread under foot, as was promised to Adam, in Genesis iii.

Between grace and gift there is this difference. Grace means properly God's favor, or the good-will God bears us, by which He is disposed to give us Christ and to pour into us the Holy Ghost, with His gifts. This is clear from chapter v, where he speaks of "the grace and gift in Christ." The gifts and the Spirit increase in us every day, though they are not yet perfect, and there remain in us the evil lust and sin that war against the Spirit, as he says in Romans vii and Galatians v, and the quarrel between the seed of the woman and the seed of the serpent is foretold in Genesis iii. Nevertheless, grace does so much that we are accounted wholly righteous before God. For His grace is not divided or broken up, as are the gifts, but it takes us entirely into favor, for the sake of Christ our Intercessor and Mediator, and because of that the gifts are begun in us.

In this sense, then, you understand chapter vii, in which St. Paul still calls himself a sinner, and yet says, in chapter viii, that there is nothing condemnable in those who are in Christ on account of the incompleteness of the gifts and of the Spirit. Because the flesh is not yet slain, we still are sinners; but because we believe and have a beginning of the Spirit, God is so favorable and gracious to us that He will not count the sin against us or judge us for it, but will deal with us according to our faith in Christ, until sin is slain.

Faith is not that human notion and dream that some hold for faith. Because they see that no betterment of life and no good works follow it, and yet they can hear and say much about faith, they fall into error, and say, "Faith is not enough; one must do works in order to be righteous and be saved." This is the reason that, when they hear the Gospel, they fall to— and make for themselves, by their own powers, an idea in their hearts, which says, "I believe." This they hold for true faith. But it is a human imagination and idea that never reaches the depths of the heart, and so nothing comes of it and no betterment follows it.

Faith, however, is a divine work in us. It changes us and makes us to be born anew of God (John i); it kills the old Adam and makes altogether different men, in heart and spirit and mind and powers, and it brings with it the Holy Ghost. O, it is a living, busy, active, mighty thing, this faith; and so it is impossible for it not to do good works incessantly. It does not ask whether there are good works to do, but before the question rises; it has already done them, and is always at the doing of them. He who does not these works is a faithless man. He gropes and looks about after faith and good works, and knows neither what faith is nor what good works are, though he talks and talks, with many words, about faith and good works.

Faith is a living, daring confidence in God's grace, so sure and certain that a man would stake his life on it a thousand times. This confidence in God's grace and knowledge of it makes men glad and bold and happy in dealing with God and with all His creatures; and this is the work of the Holy Ghost in faith. Hence a man is ready and glad, without compulsion, to do good to everyone, to serve everyone, to suffer everything, in love and praise of God, who has shown him his grace; and thus it is impossible to separate works from faith, quite as impossible as to separate heat and light from fire. Beware, therefore, of your own false notions and of the idle talkers, who would be wise enough to make decisions about faith and good works, and yet are the greatest fools. Pray God to work faith in you; else you will remain forever without faith, whatever you think or do.

Righteousness, then, is such a faith and is called "God's righteousness," or "the righteousness that avails before God," because God gives it and counts it as righteousness for the sake of Christ, our Mediator, and makes a man give to very man what he owes him. For through faith a man becomes sinless and comes to take pleasure in God's commandments; thus he gives to God the honor that is His and pays Him what he owes Him; but he also serves man willingly, by whatever means he can, and thus pays his debt to everyone. Such righteousness nature and free will and all our powers cannot bring into existence. No one can give himself faith, and no more can he take away his own unbelief; how, then, will he take away a single sin, even the very smallest? Therefore, all that is done apart from faith, or in unbelief, is false; it is hypocrisy and sin, no matter how good a show it makes (Romans xiv).

You must not so understand flesh and spirit as to think that flesh has to do only with unchastity and spirit only with what is inward, in the heart; but Paul, like Christ, in John iii, calls "flesh" everything that is born of the flesh; viz., the whole man, with body and soul, mind and senses, because everything about him longs for the flesh. Thus you should learn to call him "fleshly" who thinks, teaches, and talks a great deal about high spiritual matters, but without grace. From the "works of the flesh," in Galatians v, you can learn that Paul calls heresy and hatred "works of the flesh," and in Romans viii, he says that "the law was weak through the flesh," and this does not refer to unchastity, but to all sins, above all to unbelief, which is the most spiritual of all vices. On the other hand, he calls him a spiritual man who is occupied with the most external kind of works, as Christ, when He washed the disciples' feet, and Peter, when he steered his boat, and fished. Thus "the flesh" is a man who lives and works, inwardly and outwardly, in the service of the flesh's profit and of this temporal life;

"the spirit" is the man who lives and works, inwardly and outwardly, in the service of the Spirit and the future life.

Without such an understanding of these words, you will never understand this letter of St. Paul, or any other book of Holy Scripture. Therefore, beware of all teachers who use these words in a different sense, no matter who they are, even Jerome, Augustine, Ambrose, Origen, and men like them, or above them. Now we will take up the Epistle.

It is right for a preacher of the Gospel first, by a revelation of the law and of sin, to rebuke everything and make sin of everything that is not the living fruit of the Spirit and of faith in Christ, so that men may be led to know themselves and their own wretchedness, and become humble and ask for help. That is what St. Paul does. He begins in chapter i and rebukes the gross sin and unbelief that are plainly evident, as the sins of the heathen, who live without God's grace, were and still are. He says: The wrath of God is revealed from heaven, through the Gospel, upon all men because of their godless lives and their unrighteousness. For even though they know and daily recognize that there is a God, nevertheless, nature itself, without grace, is so bad that it neither thanks nor honors Him, but blinds itself, and goes continually from bad to worse, until at last, after idolatry, it commits the most shameful sins, with all the vices, and is not ashamed, and allows others to do these things unrebuked.

In chapter ii, he stretches this rebuke still farther and extends it to those who seem outwardly to be righteous, but commit sin in secret. Such were the Jews and such are all the hypocrites, who, without desire or love for the law of God, lead good lives, but hate God's law in their hearts, and yet are prone to judge other people. It is the nature of all the hypocrites to think themselves pure, and yet be full of covetousness, hatred, pride, and all uncleanness (Matthew xxiii). These are they who despise God's goodness and in their hardness heap wrath upon themselves. Thus St. Paul, as a true interpreter of the law, leaves no one without sin, but proclaims the wrath of God upon all who live good lives from nature or free will, and makes them appear no better than open sinners; indeed he says that they are hardened and unrepentant.

In chapter iii, he puts them all together in a heap, and says that one is like the other; they are all sinners before God, except that the Jews have had God's Word. Not many have believed on it, to be sure, but that does not mean that the faith and truth of God are exhausted; and he quotes a saying from Psalm li, that God remains righteous in His words. Afterwards he comes back to this again and proves by scripture that they are all sinners and that by the works of the law no man is justified, but that the law was given only that sin might be known.

Then he begins to teach the right way by which men must be justified and saved, and says, They are all sinners and without praise from God, but they must be justified, without merit, through faith in Christ, who has earned this for us by His blood, and has been made for us a mercy-seat by God, Who forgives us all former sins, proving thereby that were we aided only by His righteousness, which He gives in faith, which is revealed in this time through the Gospel and "testified before by the law and the prophets." Thus the law is set up by faith, though the works of the law are put down by it, together with the reputation that they give.

After the first three chapters, in which sin is revealed and faith's way to righteousness is taught, he begins, in chapter iv, to meet certain objections. And first he takes up the one that all men commonly make when they hear of faith, that it justifies, without works. They say, "Are men, then, to do no good works?" Therefore he himsself takes up the case of Abraham, and asks, "What did Abraham accomplish, then, with his good works? Were they all in vain? Were his works of no use?" He concludes that Abraham was justified by faith alone, without any works; nay, the scriptures, in Genesis xv, declare that he was justified by faith alone, even before the work of circumcision. But if the work of circumcision contributed nothing to his righteousness, though God commanded it and it was a good work of obedience; then, surely, no other good work will contribute anything to righteousness. On the other hand, if Abraham's circumsision was an external sign by which he showed the righteousness that was already his in faith, then all good works are only external signs which follow out of faith, and show, like good fruit, that a man is already inwardly righteous before God.

With this powerful illustration, out of the scriptures, St. Paul establishes the doctrine of faith which he had taught before, in chapter iii. He also brings forward another witness, viz., David, in Psalm xxxii, who says that a man is justified without works, although he does not remain without works when he has been justified. Then he gives the illustration a broader application, and concludes that the Jews cannot be Abraham's heirs merely because of their blood, still less because of the works of the law, but must be heirs of Abraham's faith, if they would be true heirs. For before the law—either the law of Moses or the law of circumcision—Abraham was justified by faith and called the father of believers; moreover, the law works wrath rather than grace, because no one keeps it out of love for it and pleasure in it, so that what comes by the works of the law is disgrace rather than grace. Therefore faith alone must obtain the grace promised to Abraham, for these examples were written for our sakes, that we, too, should believe.

In chapter v, he comes to the fruits and works of faith, such as peace, joy, love to God and to every man, and confidence, boldness, joy, courage, and hope in tribulation and suffering. For all this follows, if faith be true, because of the over-abundant goodness that God shows us in Christ, so that He caused Him to die for us before we could ask it, nay, while we were still His enemies. Thus we have it that faith justifies without any works; and yet it does not follow that men are, therefore, to do no good works, but rather that the true works will not be absent. Of these the work-righteous saints know nothing, but feign works of their own in which there is no peace, joy, confidence, love, hope, boldness, nor any of the qualities of true Christian works and faith.

After this, he breaks out, and makes a pleasant excursion, and tells whence come both sin and righteousness, death and life, and compares Adam and Christ. He says that Christ had to come, a second Adam, to bequeath His righteousness to us, through a new spiritual birth in faith, as the first Adam bequeathed sin to us, through the old, fleshly birth. Thus he declares, and confirms it, that no one, by his own works, can help himself out of sin into righteousness, any more than he can prevent the birth of his own body. This is proved by the fact that the divine law—which ought to help to righteousness, if anything can—has not only not helped, but has even increased sin; for the reason that the more the law forbids, the more our evil nature hates it, and the more it wants to give rein to its own lust. Thus the law makes Christ all the more necessary, and more grace is needed to help our nature.

In chapter vi, he takes up the special work of faith, the conflict of the spirit with the flesh, for the complete slaying of the sin and lust that remain after we are justified. He teaches us that by faith we are not so freed from sin that we can be idle, slack, and careless, as though there were no longer any sin in us. There is sin; but it is no longer counted for condemnation, because of the faith that strives against it. Therefore we have enough to do all our life long in taming the body, slaying its lust, and compelling its members to obey the spirit and not the lusts, thus making our lives like the death and resurrection of Christ and completing our baptism—which signifies the death of sin and the new life of grace—until we are entirely pure of sin, and even our bodies rise again with Christ and live forever.

And that we can do, he says, because we are in grace and not in the law. He himself explains that to mean that to be without the law is not the same thing as to have no laws and be able to do what one pleases; but we are under the law when, without grace, we occupy ourselves in the work of the law. Then sin assuredly rules by the law, for no one loves the law by nature; and that is great sin. Grace, however, makes the law dear to us, and then sin is no more there, and the law is no longer against us, but with us.

This is the true freedom from sin and the law, of which he writes, down to the end of this chapter, saying that it is liberty only to do good with pleasure and live a good life without the compulsion of the law. Therefore this liberty is a spiritual liberty, which does not abolish the law, but presents what the law demands; namely, pleasure and love. Thus the law is quieted, and no longer drives men or makes demands of them. It is just as if you owed a debt to your overlord and could not pay it. There are two ways in which you could rid yourself of the debt,—either he would take nothing from you and would tear up the account; or some good man would pay it for you, and give you the means to satisfy the account. It is in this latter way that Christ has made us free from the law. Our liberty is, therefore, no fleshly liberty, which is not obligated to do anything, but a liberty that does many works of all kinds, and thus is free from the demands and the debts of the law.

In chapter vii, he supports this with a parable of the married life. When a man dies, his wife is single, and thus the one is released from the other; not that the wife cannot or ought not take another husband, but rather that she is now really free to take another, which she could not do before she was free from her husband. So our conscience is bound to the law, under the old man; when he is slain by the Spirit, then the conscience is free; the one is released from the other; not that the conscience is to do nothing, but rather that it is now really free to cleave to Christ, the second husband, and bring forth the fruit of life.

Then he sketches out more broadly the nature of sin and the law, showing how, by means of the law sin now moves and is mighty. The old man hates the law the more because he cannot pay what the law demands, for sin is his nature and by himself he can do nothing but sin; therefore the law is death to him, and torment. Not that the law is bad, but his evil nature cannot endure the good, and the law demands good of him. So a sick man cannot endure it when he is required to run and jump and do the works of a well man.

Therefore St. Paul here concludes that the law, rightly understood and thoroughly comprehended, does nothing more than remind us of our sin, and slay us by it, and make us liable to eternal wrath; and all this is taught and experienced by our conscience, when it is really smitten by the law. Therefore a man must have something else than the law, and more than the law, to make him righteous and save him. But they who do not rightly understand the law are blind; they go ahead, in their presumption, and think to satisfy the law with their works, not knowing what the law demands, viz., a willing and happy heart. Therefore they do not see Moses clearly, the veil is put between them and him, and covers him.

Then he shows how spirit and flesh strive with one another in a man. He uses himself as an example, in order that we may learn rightly to understand the work of slaying sin within us. He calls both spirit and flesh "laws," for just as it is the nature of the divine law to drive men and make demands of them, so the flesh drives men and makes demands and rages against the spirit, and will have its own way. The spirit, too, drives men and makes demands contrary to the flesh, and will have its own way. This contention within us lasts as long as we live, though in one man it is greater, in another less, according as spirit or flesh is stronger. Nevertheless, the whole man is both spirit and flesh and he fights with himself until he becomes wholly spiritual.

In chapter viii, he encourages these fighters, telling them not to condemn the flesh; and he shows further what the nature of flesh and spirit is, and how the spirit comes from Christ, Who has given us His Holy Spirit to make us spiritual and subdue the flesh. He assures us that we are still God's children, however hard sin may rage within us, so long as we follow the spirit and resist sin, to slay it. Since, however, nothing else is so good for the mortifying of the flesh as the cross and suffering, he comforts us in suffering with the support of the Spirit of love, and of the whole creation. For the Spirit sighs within us and the creation longs with us that we may be rid of the flesh and of sin. So we see that these three chapters (vi–viii) deal with the one work of faith, which is to slay the old Adam and subdue the flesh.

In chapters ix, x, and xi, he teaches concerning God's eternal predestination, from which it originally comes that one believes or not, is rid of sin or not rid of it. Thus our becoming righteous is taken entirely out of our hands and put in the hand of God. And that is most highly necessary. We are so weak and uncertain that, if it were in our power, surely not one man would be saved, the devil would surely overpower us all; but since God is certain, and His predestination cannot fail, and no one can withstand Him, we still have hope against sin.

And here we must set a boundary for those audacious and high-climbing spirits, who first bring their own thinking to this matter and begin at the top to search the abyss of divine predestination, and worry in vain about whether they are predestinate. They must have a fall; either they will despair, or else they will take long risks.

But do you follow the order of this epistle. Worry first about Christ and the Gospel, that you may recognize your sin and His grace; then fight your sin, as the first eight chapters here have taught; then, when you have reached the eighth chapter, and are under the cross and suffering, that will teach you the right doctrine of predestination, in the ninth, tenth and eleventh chapters, and how comforting it is. For in the absence of suffering and the cross and the danger of death, one cannot deal with predestination without harm and without secret wrath against God. The old Adam must die before he can endure this subject and drink the strong wine of it. Therefore beware not to drink wine while you are still a suckling. There is a limit, a time, an age for every doctrine.

In chapter xii, he teaches what true worship is; and he makes all Christians priests, who are to offer not money and cattle, as under the law, but their own bodies, with a slaying of the lusts. Then he describes the outward conduct of Christians, under spiritual government, telling how they are to teach, preach, rule, serve, give, suffer, love, live, and act toward friend, foe and all men. These are the works that a Christian does; for, as has been said, faith takes no holidays.

In chapter xiii, he teaches honor and obedience to worldly government, which accomplishes much, although it does not make its people righteous before God. It is instituted in order that the good may have outward peace and protection, and that the wicked may not be free to do evil, without fear, in peace and quietness. Therefore the righteous are to honor it, though they do not need it. In the end he comprises it all in love, and includes it in the example of Christ, Who has done for us what we also are to do, following in His footsteps.

In chapter xiv, he teaches that weak consciences are to be led gently in faith and to be spared, so that Christians are not to use their liberty for doing harm, but for the furtherance of the weak. If that is not done, then discord follows and contempt for the Gospel; and the Gospel is the all-important thing. Thus it is better to yield a little to the weak in faith, until they grow stronger, than to have the doctrine of the Gospel come to nought. This is a peculiar work of love, for which there is great need even now, when with meat-eating and other liberties, men are rudely and roughly shaking weak consciences, before they know the truth.

In chapter xv, he sets up the example of Christ, to show that we are to suffer those who are weak in other ways,—those whose weakness lies in open sins or in unpleasing habits. These men are not to be cast off, but borne with till they grow better. For so Christ has done to us, and still does every day; He bears with our many faults and bad habits, and with all our imperfections, and helps us constantly.

Then, at the end, he prays for them, praises them and commends them to God; he speaks of his office and his preaching, and asks them gently for a contribution to the poor at Jerusalem; all that he speaks of or deals with is pure love.

The last chapter is a chapter of greetings, but he mingles with them a noble warning against doctrines of men, which are put in alongside the doctrine of the Gospel and cause offense. It is as though he had foreseen that out of Rome and through the Romans would come the seductive and offensive canons and decretals and the whole squirming mass of human laws and commandments, which have now drowned the whole world and wiped out this Epistle and all the Holy Scriptures, along with the Spirit and with faith, so that nothing has remained there except the idol, Belly, whose servants St. Paul here rebukes. God release us from them. Amen.

Thus in this Epistle we find most richly the things that a Christian ought to know; namely, what is law, Gospel, sin, punishment, grace, faith, righteousness, Christ, God, good works, love, hope, the cross, and also how we are to conduct ourselves toward everyone, whether righteous or sinner, strong or weak, friend or foe. All this is ably founded on scripture and proved by his own example and that of the prophets. Therefore it appears that St. Paul wanted to comprise briefly in this one epistle the whole Christian and evangelical doctrine and to prepare an introduction to the entire Old Testament; for, without doubt, he who has this epistle well in his heart, has the light and power of the Old Testament with him. Therefore let every Christian exercise himself in it habitually and continually. To this may God give His grace. Amen.

C. The Bondage of the Will*

MARTIN LUTHER

The "Form" of Christianity set forth by you, among other things, has this—"That we should strive with all our powers, have recourse to the remedy of repentance, and in all ways try to gain the mercy of God; without which, neither human will, nor endeavour, is effectual." Also, "that no one should despair of pardon from a God by nature most merciful."—

These statements of yours are without Christ, without the Spirit, and more cold than ice: so that, the beauty of your eloquence is really deformed by them. Perhaps a fear of the Popes and those tyrants, extorted them from you their miserable vassal, lest you should appear to them a perfect atheist. But what they assert is this—That there is ability in us; that there is a striving with all our powers; that there is mercy in God; that there are ways of gaining that mercy; that there is a God, by nature just, and most merciful, &c.—But if a man does not know what these powers are; what they can do, or in what they are to be passive; what their efficacy, or what their inefficacy is; what can such an one do? What will you set him about doing?

"It is irreligious, curious, and superfluous, (you say) to wish to know, whether our own will does any thing in those things which pertain unto eternal salvation, or whether it is wholly passive under the work of grace."— But here, you say the contrary: that it is Christian piety to "strive with all the powers;" and that, "without the mercy of God the will is ineffective."

Here you plainly assert, that the will does something in those things which pertain unto eternal salvation, when you speak of it as striving: and again, you assert that it is passive, when you say, that without the mercy of God it is ineffective. Though, at the same time, you do not define how far

* From Martin Luther, The Bondage of the Will, tr. by Henry Cole, with slight alteration from E. T. Vaughan. Corrected by Henry Atherton. Grand Rapids, Mich.: Wm. B. Eerdmans Publishing Co., 1931.

that doing, and being passive, is to be understood: thus, designedly keeping us in ignorance how far the mercy of God extends, and how far our own will extends; what our own will is to do, in that which you enjoin, and what the mercy of God is to do. Thus, that prudence of yours, carries you along; by which, you are resolved to hold with neither side, and to escape safely through Scylla and Charybdis; in order that, when you come into the open sea, and find yourself overwhelmed and confounded by the waves, you may have it in your power, to assert all that you now deny, and deny all that you now assert. . . .

But I will set your theology before your eyes by a few similitudes.— What if any one, intending to compose a poem, or an oration, should never think about, nor inquire into his abilities, what he could do, and what he could not do, nor what the subject undertaken required; and should utterly disregard that precept of Horace, "What the shoulders can sustain, and what they must sink under;" but should precipitately dash upon the undertaking and think thus—I must strive to get the work done; to inquire whether the learning I have, the eloquence I have, the force of genius I have, be equal to it, is curious and superfluous:—Or, if any one, desiring to have a plentiful crop from his land, should not be so curious as to take the superfluous care of examining the nature of the soil, (as Virgil curiously and in vain teaches in his Georgics,) but should rush on at once, thinking of nothing but the work, and plough the seashore, and cast in the seed wherever the soil was turned up, whether sand or mud:—Or if any one, about to make war, and desiring a glorious victory, or intending to render any other service to the state, should not be so curious as to deliberate upon what it was in his power to do; whether the treasury could furnish money, whether the soldiers were fit, whether any opportunity offered; and should pay no regard whatever to that of the historian, "Before you act, there must be deliberation, and when you have deliberated, speedy execution;" but should rush forward with his eyes blinded, and his ears stopped, only exclaiming war! war! and should be determined on the undertaking:—What, I ask you, Erasmus, would you think of such poets, such husbandmen, such generals, and such heads of affairs? I will add also that of the Gospel—If any one going to build a tower, sits not down first and counts the cost, whether he has enough to finish it,—What does Christ say of such an one? (Luke xiv. 28–32). . . .

Therefore, it is not irreligious, curious, or superfluous, but essentially wholesome and necessary, for a Christian to know, whether or not the will does any thing in those things which pertain unto Salvation. Nay, let me tell you, this is the very hinge upon which our discussion turns. It is the very heart of our subject. For our object is this: to inquire what "Free-will" can do, in what it is passive, and how it stands with reference to the grace of God. *If we know nothing of these things, we shall know nothing what-*

ever of Christian matters, and shall be far behind all people upon the earth.
He that does not feel this, let him confess that he is no Christian. And he
that despises and laughs at it, let him know that he is the Christian's greatest
enemy. For, if I know not how much I can do myself, how far my ability
extends, and what I can do God-wards; I shall be equally uncertain and
ignorant how much God is to do, how far His ability is to extend, and what
He is to do toward me: whereas it is "God that worketh all in all." (1 Cor.
xii. 6.) But if I know not the distinction between our working and the
power of God, I know not God Himself. And if I know not God, I cannot
worship Him, praise Him, give Him thanks, nor serve Him; for I shall not
know how much I ought to ascribe unto myself, and how much unto God.
It is necessary, therefore, to hold the most certain distinction, between the
power of God and our power, the working of God and our working, if we
would live in His fear. . . .

This, therefore, is . . . necessary and wholesome for Christians to
know: *that God foreknows nothing by contingency, but that He foresees,
purposes, and does all things according to His immutable, eternal, and infallible will.* By this thunderbolt, "Free-will" is thrown prostrate, and utterly
dashed to pieces. Those, therefore, who would assert "Free-will," must either
deny this thunderbolt, or pretend not to see it, or push it from them. But,
however, before I establish this point by any arguments of my own, and by
the authority of scripture, I will first set it forth in your words.

Are you not then the person, friend Erasmus, who just now asserted,
that God is by nature just, and by nature most merciful? If this be true, does
it not follow that He is *immutably* just and merciful? That, as His nature is
not changed to all eternity, so neither His justice nor His mercy? And what
is said concerning His justice and His mercy, must be said also concerning
His knowledge, His wisdom, His goodness, His will, and His other Attributes. If therefore these things are asserted religiously, piously, and wholesomely concerning God, as you say yourself, what has come to you, that,
contrary to your own self, you now assert, that it is irreligious, curious, and
vain, to say, that God foreknows of necessity? You openly declare that the
immutable *will* of God is to be known, but you forbid the knowledge of
His immutable *prescience.* Do you believe that He foreknows against His
will or that He wills in ignorance? If then, He foreknows, willing, His will is
eternal and immovable, because His nature is so: and, if He wills, fore-
knowing, His knowledge is eternal and immovable, because His nature is so.

From which it follows unalterably, that all things which we do, although they may appear to us to be done mutably and contingently, and
even may be done thus contingently by us, are yet, in reality, done necessarily and immutably, with respect to the will of God. For the will of God is
effective and cannot be hindered; because the very power of God is natural
to Him, and His wisdom is such that He cannot be deceived. And as His

will cannot be hindered, the work itself cannot be hindered from being done in the place, at the time, in the measure, and by whom He foresees and wills. If the will of God were such, that, when the work was done, the work remained but the will ceased, (as is the case with the will of men, which, when the house is built which they wished to build, ceases to will, as though it ended by death) then, indeed, it might be said, that things are done by contingency and mutability. But here, the case is the contrary; the work ceases, and the will remains. So far is it from possibility, that the doing of the work or its remaining, can be said to be from contingency or mutability. But, (that we may not be deceived in terms) being done by contingency, does not, in the Latin language, signify that the work itself which is done is contingent, but that it is done according to a contingent and mutable will—such a will as is not to be found in God! Moreover, a work cannot be called contingent, unless it be done by us unawares, by contingency, and, as it were, by chance; that is, by our will or hand catching at it, as presented by chance, we thinking nothing of it, nor willing any thing about it before. . . .

I could wish, indeed, that we were furnished with some better term for this discussion, than this commonly used term, necessity, which cannot rightly be used, either with reference to the human will, or the divine. It is of a signification too harsh and ill-suited for this subject, forcing upon the mind an idea of compulsion, and that which is altogether contrary to will; whereas, the subject which we are discussing, does not require such an idea: for Will, whether divine or human, does what it does, be it good or evil, not by any compulsion, but by mere willingness or desire, as it were, totally free. The will of God, nevertheless, which rules over our mutable will, is immutable and infallible; as Boëtius sings, "Immovable Thyself, Thou movement giv'st to all." And our own will, especially our corrupt will, cannot of itself do good; therefore, where the term fails to express the idea required, the understanding of the reader must make up the deficiency, knowing what is wished to be expressed—the immutable will of God, and the impotency of our depraved will; or, as some have expressed it, the necessity of immutability, though neither is that sufficiently grammatical, or sufficiently theological. . . .

If, therefore, we are taught, and if we believe, that we ought not to know the necessary prescience of God, and the necessity of the things that are to take place, Christian faith is utterly destroyed, and the promises of God and the whole Gospel entirely fall to the ground; for the greatest and only consolation of Christians in their adversities, is the knowing that God lies not, but does all things immutably, and that His will cannot be resisted, changed, or hindered. . . .

Do you now, then, only observe, friend Erasmus, to what that most moderate, and most peace-loving theology of yours would lead us. You call us off, and forbid our endeavouring to know the prescience of God, and the necessity that lies on men and things, and counsel us to leave such things, and to avoid and disregard them; and in so doing, you at the same time teach us your rash sentiments; that we should seek after an ignorance of God, (which comes upon us of its own accord, and is engendered in us), disregard faith, leave the promises of God, and account the consolations of the Spirit, and the assurances of conscience, nothing at all! Such counsel scarcely any Epicure himself would give! . . .

And now, what if I prove from your own words, on which you assert the freedom of the will, that there is no such thing as "Free-will" at all! What if I should make it manifest that you unknowingly deny that, which, with so much policy, you labour to affirm. And if I do not this, actually, I vow that I will consider all that I advance in this book against you, revoked; and all that your Diatribe advances against me, and aims at establishing, confirmed.

You make the power of "Free-will" to be—'that certain small degree of power, which, without the grace of God, is utterly ineffective.'

Do you not acknowledge this?—Now then, I ask and demand of you, if the grace of God be wanting, or, if it be taken away from that certain small degree of power, what can it do of itself? 'It is ineffective (you say) and can do nothing of good.' Therefore, it cannot do what God or His grace wills. And why? because we have now separated the grace of God from it; and what the grace of God does not, is not good. And hence it follows, that "Free-will," without the grace of God is, absolutely, not FREE; but, immutably, the servant and bond-slave of evil; because, it cannot turn itself unto good. This being determined, I will allow you to make the power of "Free-will," not only a certain small degree of power, but to make it evangelical if you will, or, if you can, to make it divine: provided that, you add to it this doleful appendage—that, without the grace of God, it is ineffective. Because, then you will at once take from it all power: for, what is ineffective power, but plainly, no power at all?

Therefore, to say, that the will is FREE, and that it has indeed power, but that it is ineffective, is what the sophists call 'a direct contrariety.' As if one should say, "Free-will" is that which is not free. Or as if one should term fire cold, and earth hot. For if fire had the power of heat, yea of the heat of hell, yet, if it did not burn or scorch, but were cold and produced cold, I should not call it fire, much less should I term it hot; unless, indeed, you were to mean an imaginary fire, or a fire represented in a picture.—But if we call the power of "Free-will" that, by which a man is fitted to be caught by the Spirit, or to be touched by the grace of God, as one created unto eternal life or eternal death, may be said to be; this power, that is, fitness, or, (as the Sophists term it) 'disposition-quality,' and 'passive aptitude,' this I also confess. And who does not know, that this is not in trees or beasts? For, (as they say) Heaven was not made for geese.

Therefore, it stands confirmed, even by your own testimony, that we do all things from necessity, not from "Free-will:" seeing that, the power of "Free-will" is nothing, and neither does, nor can do good, without grace. Unless you wish efficacy to bear a new signification, and to be understood as meaning *perfection:* that is, that "Free-will" can, indeed, will and begin, but cannot perfect: which I do not believe: and upon this I shall speak more at large hereafter.

It now then follows, that Free-will is plainly a divine term, and can be applicable to none but the divine Majesty only: for He alone "doth, (as the Psalm sings) what He will in Heaven and earth." (Ps. cxxxv. 6.) Whereas, if it be ascribed unto men, it is not more properly ascribed, than the divinity of God Himself would be ascribed unto them: which would be the greatest of all sacrilege. Wherefore, it becomes Theologians to refrain from the use of this term altogether, whenever they wish to speak of human ability, and to leave it to be applied to God only. And moreover, to take this same term out of the mouths and speech of men; and thus to assert, as it were, for their God, that which belongs to His own sacred and holy Name. . . .

But, if we do not like to leave out this term altogether, (which would be most safe, and also most religious) we may, nevertheless, with a good conscience teach, that it be used so far as to allow man a "Free-will," not in respect of those which are above him, but in respect only of those things which are below him: that is, he may be allowed to know, that he has, as to his goods and possessions the right of using, acting, and omitting, according to his "Free-will;" although, at the same time, that same "Free-will" is over-ruled by the Free-will of God alone, just as He pleases: but that, God-ward, or in things which pertain unto salvation or damnation, he has no "Free-will," but is a captive, slave, and servant, either to the will of God, or to the will of Satan. . . .

As to myself, I openly confess, that I should not wish "Free-will" to be granted me, even if it could be so, nor anything else to be left in my own hands, whereby I might endeavour something towards my own salvation. And that, not merely because in so many opposing dangers, and so many assaulting devils, I could not stand and hold it fast, (in which state no man could be saved, seeing that one devil is stronger than all men;) but because, even though there were no dangers, no conflicts, no devils, I should be compelled to labour under a continual uncertainty, and to beat the air only. Nor would my conscience, even if I should live and work to all eternity, ever come to a settled certainty, how much it ought to do in order to satisfy God. For whatever work should be done, there would still remain a scrupling, whether or not it pleased God, or whether He required any thing more; as is proved in the experience of all justiciaries, and as I myself learned to my bitter cost, through so many years of my own experience.

But now, since God has put my salvation out of the way of my will, and has taken it under *His own,* and has promised to save me, not according to my working or manner of life, but according to His own grace and mercy, I rest fully assured and persuaded that He is faithful, and will not lie, and moreover great and powerful, so that no devils, no adversities can destroy Him, or pluck me out of His hand. "No one (saith He) shall pluck them out of My hand, because My Father which gave them Me is greater than all." (John x. 27–28). Hence it is certain, that in this way, if all are not saved, yet some, yea, many shall be saved; whereas by the power of "Free-will," no one whatever could be saved, but all must perish together. And moreover, we are certain and persuaded, that in this way, we please God, not from the merit of our own works, but from the favour of His mercy promised unto us; and that, if we work less, or work badly, He does not impute it unto us, but, as a Father, pardons us and makes us better.—This is the glorying which all the saints have in their God!

46   JOHN CALVIN'S (1509–1564) SYSTEMATIC STATEMENT of Christian doctrine, *Institutes of the Christian Religion*, remains a work of major importance in the history of Christian thought. The following selections from Books II and III are divided into five sections: (1) The Condition of Man; (2) The Purpose of the Law; (3) Justification by Faith; (4) Christian Liberty; (5) Election.[1]

Institutes of the Christian Religion*

JOHN CALVIN

1. THE CONDITION OF MAN

There is much reason in the old adage, which so strongly recommends to man the knowledge of himself. For if it be thought disgraceful to be ignorant of whatever relates to the conduct of human life, ignorance of ourselves is much more shameful, which causes us, in deliberating on subjects

* From *The Institutes of the Christian Religion* by John Calvin. tr. John Allen. Published 1936, the Presbyterian Board of Christian Education. Used by permission. [The titles are supplied by the editor.]

[1] See also selections from The *Institutes*, Selection 9, 66.

of importance, to grope our way in miserable obscurity, or even in total darkness. But in proportion to the utility of this precept ought to be our caution not to make a preposterous use of it; as we see some philosophers have done. For while they exhort man to the knowledge of himself, the end they propose is, that he may not remain ignorant of his own dignity and excellence: nor do they wish him to contemplate in himself any thing but what may swell him with vain confidence, and inflate him with pride. But the knowledge of ourselves consists, first, in considering what was bestowed on us at our creation, and the favours we continually receive from the Divine benignity, that we may know how great the excellence of our nature would have been, if it had retained its integrity; yet, at the same time, recollecting that we have nothing properly our own, may feel our precarious tenure of all that God has conferred on us, so as always to place our dependence upon him. Secondly, we should contemplate our miserable condition since the fall of Adam, the sense of which tends to destroy all boasting and confidence, to overwhelm us with shame, and to fill us with real humility. For as God, at the beginning, formed us after his own image, that he might elevate our minds both to the practice of virtue, and to the contemplation of eternal life, so, to prevent the great excellence of our species, which distinguishes us from the brutes, from being buried in sottish indolence, it is worthy of observation, that the design of our being endued with reason and intelligence is, that, leading a holy and virtuous life, we may aspire to the mark set before us of a blessed immortality. But we cannot think upon that primeval dignity, without having our attention immediately called to the melancholy spectacle of our disgrace and ignominy, since in the person of the first man we are fallen from our original condition. Hence arise disapprobation and abhorrence of ourselves, and real humility; and we are inflamed with fresh ardour to seek after God, to recover in him those excellences of which we find ourselves utterly destitute. . . .

. . . since it could not have been a trivial offence, but must have been a detestable crime, that was so severely punished by God, we must consider the nature of Adam's sin, which kindled the dreadful flame of Divine wrath against the whole human race. The vulgar opinion concerning the intemperance of gluttony is quite puerile; as though the sum and substance of all virtues consisted in an abstinence from one particular kind of fruit, when there were diffused on every side all the delights which could possibly be desired, and the happy fecundity of the earth afforded an abundance and variety of dainties. We must therefore look further, because the prohibition of the tree of knowledge of good and evil was a test of obedience, that Adam might prove his willing submission to the Divine government. And the name itself shows that the precept was given for no other purpose than that he might be contented with his condition, and not aim with criminal cupidity at any higher. But the promise which authorized him to expect eternal life, as long as he should eat of the tree of life, and, on the other hand, the dreadful denunciation of death, as soon as he should taste of the tree of knowledge of good and evil, were calculated for the probation and exercise of his faith. Hence it is easy to infer by what means Adam provoked the wrath of God against him. Augustine, indeed, properly observes, that pride was the first of all evils; because, if ambition had not elated man beyond what was lawful and right, he might have continued in his honourable situation. . . .

As the spiritual life of Adam consisted in a union to his Maker, so an alienation from him was the death of his soul. Nor is it surprising that he ruined his posterity by his defection, which has perverted the whole order of nature in heaven and earth. "The creatures groan," says Paul, "being made subject to vanity, not willingly." If the cause be inquired, it is undoubtedly that they sustain part of the punishment due to the demerits of man, for whose use they were created. And his guilt being the origin of that curse which extends to every part of the world, it is reasonable to conclude its propagation to all his offspring. Therefore, when the Divine image in him was obliterated, and he was punished with the loss of wisdom, strength, sanctity, truth, and righteousness, with which he had been adorned, but which were succeeded by the dreadful pests of ignorance, impotence, impurity, vanity, and iniquity, he suffered not alone, but involved all his posterity with him, and plunged them into the same miseries. This is that hereditary corruption which the fathers called *original sin*; meaning by sin, the depravation of a nature previously good and pure; on which subject they had much contention, nothing being more remote from natural reason, than that all should be criminated on account of the guilt of one, and thus his sin become common; which seems to have been the reason why the most ancient doctors of the Church did but obscurely glance at this point, or at least explained it with less perspicuity than it required. Yet this timidity could not prevent Pelagius from arising, who profanely pretended, that the sin of Adam only ruined himself, and did not injure his descendants. By concealing the disease with this delusion, Satan attempted to render it incurable. But when it was evinced by the plain testimony of the scripture, that sin was communicated from the first man to all his posterity, he sophistically urged that it was communicated by imitation, not by propagation. Therefore good men, and beyond all others Augustine, have laboured to demonstrate that we are not corrupted by any adventitious means, but that we derive an innate depravity from our very birth. . . . Every descendant, therefore, from the impure source, is born infected with the contagion of sin; and even before we behold the light of life, we are in the sight of God defiled and polluted. For "who can bring a clean thing out of an unclean?" The book of Job tells us, "Not one."

We have heard that the impurity of the parents is so transmitted to the children, that all, without a single exception, are polluted as soon as they exist. But we shall not find the origin of this pollution, unless we ascend to the first parent of us all, as to the fountain which sends forth all the streams. Thus it is certain that Adam was not only the progenitor, but as it were the root of mankind, and therefore that all the race were necessarily vitiated in his corruption. The Apostle explains this by a comparison between him and Christ: "As," says he, "by one man sin entered into the world, and death by sin, and so death passed upon all men, for that all have sinned," so, by the grace of Christ, righteousness and life have been restored to us. What cavil will the Pelagians raise here? That the sin of Adam was propagated by imitation? Do we then receive no other advantage from the righteousness of Christ than the proposal of an example for our imitation? Who can bear such blasphemy? But if it cannot be controverted that the righteousness of Christ is ours by communication, and life as its consequence, it is equally evident that both were lost in Adam, in the same manner in which they were recovered in Christ, and that sin and death were introduced by Adam, in the same manner in which they are abolished by Christ. There is no obscurity in the declaration that many are made righteous by the obedience of Christ, as they had been made sinners by the disobedience of Adam. And, therefore, between these two persons there is this relation, that the one ruined us by involving us in his destruction, the other by his grace has restored us to salvation. Any more prolix or tedious proof of a truth supported by such clear evidence must, I think, be unnecessary. . . . No other explanation therefore can be given of our being said to be dead in Adam, than that his transgression not only procured misery and ruin for himself, but also precipitated our nature into similar destruction. And that not by his personal guilt as an individual, which pertains not to us, but because he infected all his descendants with the corruption into which he had fallen. Otherwise there would be no truth in the assertion of Paul, that all are by nature children of wrath, if they had not been already under the curse even before their birth. Now, it is easily inferred that our nature is there characterized, not as it was created by God, but as it was vitiated in Adam; because it would be unreasonable to make God the author of death. Adam, therefore, corrupted himself in such a manner, that the contagion has been communicated from him to all his offspring. And Christ himself, the heavenly Judge, declares, in the most unequivocal terms, that all are born in a state of pravity and corruption, when he teaches, that "whatsoever is born of the flesh is flesh," and that, therefore, the gate of life is closed against all who have not been regenerated. . . .

To remove all uncertainty and misunderstanding on this subject, let us define original sin. It is not my intention to discuss all the definitions given by writers; I shall only produce one, which I think perfectly consistent with the truth. Original sin, therefore, appears to be an hereditary pravity and corruption of our nature, diffused through all the parts of the soul, rendering us obnoxious to the Divine wrath, and producing in us those works which the scripture calls "works of the flesh." And this is indeed what Paul frequently denominates sin. The works which proceed thence, such as adulteries, fornications, thefts, hatreds, murders, revellings, he calls in the same manner "fruits of sin;" although they are also called "sins" in many passages of scripture, and even by himself. These two things therefore should be distinctly observed: first, that our nature being so totally vitiated and depraved, we are, on account of this very corruption, considered as convicted and justly condemned in the sight of God, to whom nothing is acceptable but righteousness, innocence, and purity. And this liableness to punishment arises not from the delinquency of another; for when it is said that the sin of Adam renders us obnoxious to the Divine judgment, it is not to be understood as if we, though innocent, were undeservedly loaded with the guilt of his sin; but, because we are all subject to a curse, in consequence of his transgression, he is therefore said to have involved us in guilt. Nevertheless we derive from him, not only the punishment, but also the pollution to which the punishment is justly due. Wherefore Augustine, though he frequently calls it the sin of another, the more clearly to indicate its transmission to us by propagation, yet, at the same time, also asserts it properly to belong to every individual. And the Apostle himself expressly declares, that "death has therefore passed upon all men, for that all have sinned;" that is, have been involved in original sin, and defiled with its blemishes. And therefore infants themselves, as they bring their condemnation into the world with them, are rendered obnoxious to punishment by their own sinfulness, not by the sinfulness of another. For though they have not yet produced the fruits of their iniquity, yet they have the seed of it within them; even their whole nature is as it were a seed of sin, and therefore cannot but be odious and abominable to God. Whence it follows, that it is properly accounted sin in the sight of God, because there could be no guilt without crime. The other thing to be remarked is, that this depravity never ceases in us, but is perpetually producing new fruits, those works of the flesh, which we have before described, like the emission of flame and sparks from a heated furnace, or like the streams of water from a never failing spring. Wherefore those who have defined original sin as a privation of the original righteousness, which we ought to possess, though they comprise the whole of the subject, yet have not used language sufficiently expressive of its operation and influence. For our nature is not only destitute of all good, but is so fertile in all evils that it cannot remain inactive. Those who have called it concupiscence have used an expression not improper, if it were only added, which is far from being conceded by most persons, that every thing in man, the understanding and will, the soul and body, is polluted and engrossed by this concupiscence; or, to express it more briefly, that man is of himself nothing else but concupiscence. . . .

And, indeed, I much approve of that common observation which has been borrowed from Augustine, that the natural talents in man have been corrupted by sin, but that of the supernatural ones he has been wholly deprived. For by the latter are intended, both the light of faith and righteousness, which would be sufficient for the attainment of a heavenly life and eternal felicity. Therefore, when he revolted from the Divine government, he was at the same time deprived of those supernatural endowments, which had been given him for the hope of eternal salvation. Hence it follows, that he is exiled from the kingdom of God, in such a manner, that all the affections relating to the happy life of the soul, are also extinguished in him, till he recovers them by the grace of regeneration. Such are faith, love to God, charity towards our neighbours, and an attachment to holiness and righteousness. All these things, being restored by Christ, are esteemed adventitious and preternatural; and therefore we conclude that they had been lost. Again, soundness of mind and rectitude of heart were also destroyed; and this is the corruption of the natural talents. For although we retain some portion of understanding and judgment together with the will, yet we cannot say that our mind is perfect and sound, which is oppressed with debility and immersed in profound darkness; and the depravity of our will is sufficiently known. Reason, therefore, by which man distinguishes between good and evil, by which he understands and judges, being a natural talent, could not be totally destroyed, but is partly debilitated, partly vitiated, so that it exhibits nothing but deformity and ruin. In this sense John says, that "the light" still "shineth in darkness," but that "the darkness comprehendeth it not." In this passage both these ideas are clearly expressed—that some sparks continue to shine in the nature of man, even in its corrupt and degenerate state, which prove him to be a rational creature, and different from the brutes, because he is endued with understanding; and yet that this light is smothered by so much ignorance, that it cannot act with any degree of efficacy. So the will, being inseparable from the nature of man, is not annihilated; but it is fettered by depraved and inordinate desires, so that it cannot aspire after any thing that is good. . . .

A question, nearly the same as we have already answered, here presents itself to us again. For in all ages there have been some persons, who, from the mere dictates of nature, have devoted their whole lives to the pursuit of virtue. And though many errors might perhaps be discovered in their conduct, yet by their pursuit of virtue they afforded a proof, that there was some degree of purity in their nature. The value attached to virtues of such a description before God, we shall more fully discuss when we come to treat of the merits of works; yet it must be stated also in this place, so far as is necessary for the elucidation of the present subject. These examples, then, seem to teach us that we should not consider human nature to be totally corrupted; since, from its instinctive bias, some men have not only been eminent for noble actions, but have uniformly conducted themselves in a most virtuous manner through the whole course of their lives. But here we ought to remember, that amidst this corruption of nature there is some room for Divine grace, not to purify it, but internally to restrain its operations. For should the Lord permit the minds of all men to give up the reins to every lawless passion, there certainly would not be an individual in the world, whose actions would not evince all the crimes, for which Paul condemns human nature in general, to be most truly applicable to him. For can you except yourself from the number of those whose feet are swift to shed blood, whose hands are polluted with rapine and murder, whose throats are like open sepulchres, whose tongues are deceitful, whose lips are envenomed, whose works are useless, iniquitous, corrupt, and deadly, whose souls are estranged from God, the inmost recesses of whose hearts are full of pravity, whose eyes are insidiously employed, whose minds are elated with insolence—in a word, all whose powers are prepared for the commission of atrocious and innumerable crimes? If every soul be subject to all these monstrous vices, as the Apostle fearlessly pronounces, we clearly see what would be the consequence, if the Lord should suffer the human passions to go all the lengths to which they are inclined. There is no furious beast, that would be agitated with such ungovernable rage; there is no river, though ever so rapid and violent, that would overflow its boundaries with such impetuosity. In his elect, the Lord heals these maladies by a method which we shall hereafter describe. In others, he restrains them, only to prevent their ebullitions so far as he sees to be necessary for the preservation of the universe. Hence some by shame, and some by fear of the laws, are prevented from running into many kinds of pollutions, though they cannot in any great degree dissemble their impurity; others, because they think that a virtuous course of life is advantageous, entertain some languid desires after it, others go further, and display more than common excellence, that by their majesty they may confine the vulgar to their duty. Thus God by his providence restrains the perverseness of our nature from breaking out into external acts, but does not purify it within. . . .

2. THE PURPOSE OF THE LAW

. . . the law was superadded about four hundred years after the death of Abraham, not to draw away the attention of the chosen people from Christ, but rather to keep their minds waiting for his advent, to inflame their desires and confirm their expectations, that they might not be discouraged by so long a delay. By the word law, I intend, not only the decalogue, which prescribes the rule of a pious and righteous life, but the form of religion delivered from God by the hands of Moses. For Moses was not made a legislator to abolish the blessing promised to the seed of Abraham;

on the contrary, we see him on every occasion reminding the Jews of that gracious covenant made with their fathers, to which they were heirs; as though the object of his mission had been to renew it. It was very clearly manifested in the ceremonies. For what could be more vain or frivolous than for men to offer the fetid stench arising from the fat of cattle, in order to reconcile themselves to God? or to resort to any aspersion of water or of blood, to cleanse themselves from pollution? In short, the whole legal worship, if it be considered in itself, and contain no shadows and figures of correspondent truths, will appear perfectly ridiculous. . . .

Therefore if we direct our views exclusively to the law, the effects upon our minds will only be despondency, confusion, and despair, since it condemns and curses us all, and keeps us far from that blessedness which it proposes to them who observe it. Does the Lord, then, you will say, in this case do nothing but mock us? For how little does it differ from mockery, to exhibit a hope of felicity, to invite and exhort to it, to declare that it is ready for our reception, whilst the way to it is closed and inaccessible! I reply, although the promises of the law, being conditional, depend on a perfect obedience to the law, which can nowhere be found, yet they have not been given in vain. For when we have learned that they will be vain and inefficacious to us, unless God embrace us with his gratuitous goodness, without any regard to our works, and unless we have also embraced by faith that goodness, as exhibited to us in the gospel,—then these promises are not without their use, even with the condition annexed to them. For then he gratuitously confers every thing upon us, so that he adds this also to the number of his favours, that not rejecting our imperfect obedience, but pardoning its deficiencies, he gives us to enjoy the benefit of the legal promises, just as if we had fulfilled the condition ourselves. . . .

. . . let us state, in a compendious order, the office and use of what is called the moral law. It is contained, as far as I understand it, in these three points. The first is, that while it discovers the righteousness of God, that is, the only righteousness which is acceptable to God, it warns every one of his own unrighteousness, places it beyond all doubt, convicts, and condemns him. For it is necessary that man, blinded and inebriated with self-love, should thus be driven into a knowledge of himself, and a confession of his own imbecility and impurity. Since, unless his vanity be evidently reproved, he is inflated with a foolish confidence in his strength, and can never be brought to perceive its feebleness as long as he measures it by the rule of his own fancy. But as soon as he begins to compare it to the difficulty of the law, he finds his insolence and pride immediately abate. . . .

Thus the law is like a mirror, in which we behold, first, our impotence; secondly, our iniquity, which proceeds from it; and lastly, the consequence of both, our obnoxiousness to the curse; just as a mirror represents to us the spots on our face. For when a man is destitute of power to practise righteousness, he must necessarily fall into the habits of sin. And sin is immediately followed by the curse. Therefore the greater the transgression of which the law convicts us, the more severe is the judgment with which it condemns us. This appears from the observation of the Apostle, that "by the law is the knowledge of sin." . . . if our will were wholly conformed to the law, and disposed to obey it, the mere knowledge of it would evidently be sufficient to salvation. But since our carnal and corrupt nature is in a state of hostility against the spirituality of the Divine law, and not amended by its discipline, it follows that the law, which was given for salvation, if it could have found adequate attention, becomes an occasion of sin and death. For since we are all convicted of having transgressed it, the more clearly it displays the righteousness of God, so, on the contrary, the more it detects our iniquity, and the more certainly it confirms the reward of life and salvation reserved for the righteous, so much the more certain it makes the perdition of the wicked. These expressions, therefore, are so far from being dishonourable to the law, that they serve more illustriously to recommend the Divine goodness. For hence it really appears, that our iniquity and depravity prevent us from enjoying that blessed life which is revealed to all men in the law. Hence the grace of God, which succours us without the assistance of the law, is rendered sweeter; and his mercy, which confers it on us, more amiable; from which we learn that he is never wearied with repeating his blessings and loading us with new favours. . . .

The second office of the law is, to cause those who, unless constrained, feel no concern for justice and rectitude, when they hear its terrible sanctions, to be at least restrained by a fear of its penalties. And they are restrained, not because it internally influences or affects their minds, but because, being chained, as it were, they refrain from external acts, and repress their depravity within them, which otherwise they would have wantonly discharged. This makes them neither better nor more righteous in the Divine view. For although, being prevented either by fear or by shame, they dare not execute what their minds have contrived, nor openly discover the fury of their passions, yet their hearts are not disposed to fear and obey God; and the more they restrain themselves, the more violently they are inflamed within; they ferment, they boil, ready to break out into any external acts, if they were not prevented by this dread of the law. . . .

The third use of the law, which is the principal one, and which is more nearly connected with the proper end of it, relates to the faithful, in whose hearts the Spirit of God already lives and reigns. For although the law is inscribed and engraven on their hearts by the finger of God,—that is, although they are so excited and animated by the direction of the Spirit, that they desire to obey God,—yet they derive a twofold advantage from the law. For they find it an excellent instrument to give them, from day to day, a better and more certain understanding of the Divine will to which they aspire, and to confirm them in the knowledge of it. As, though a servant be already influenced by the strongest desire of gaining the approbation of his master, yet it is necessary for him carefully to inquire and observe the orders of his master, in order to conform to them. Nor let any one of us exempt himself from this necessity; for no man has already acquired so much wisdom, that he could not by the daily instruction of the law make new advances into a purer knowledge of the Divine will. In the next place, as we need not only instruction, but also exhortation, the servant of God will derive this further advantage from the law; by frequent meditation on it he will be excited to obedience, he will be confirmed in it, and restrained from the slippery path of transgression. For in this manner should the saints stimulate themselves, because, with whatever alacrity they labour for the righteousness of God according to the Spirit, yet they are always burdened with the indolence of the flesh, which prevents their proceeding with due promptitude. To this flesh the law serves as a whip, urging it, like a dull and tardy animal, forwards to its work; and even to the spiritual man, who is not yet delivered from the burden of the flesh, it will be a perpetual spur, that will not permit him to loiter. . . .

3. JUSTIFICATION BY FAITH

I think I have already explained, with sufficient care, how that men, being subject to the curse of the law, have no means left of attaining salvation but through faith alone; and also what faith itself is, what Divine blessings it confers on man, and what effects it produces in him. The substance of what I have advanced is, that Christ, being given to us by the goodness of God, is apprehended and possessed by us by faith, by a participation of whom we receive especially two benefits. In the first place, being by his innocence reconciled to God, we have in heaven a propitious father instead of a judge; in the next place, being sanctified by his Spirit, we devote ourselves to innocence and purity of life. . . .

But that we may not stumble at the threshold, (which would be the case were we to enter on a disputation concerning a subject not understood by us,) let us first explain the meaning of these expressions To be justified in the sight of God, To be justified by faith or by works. He is said to be justified in the sight of God who in the Divine judgment is reputed righteous, and accepted on account of his righteousness; for as iniquity is abominable to God, so no sinner can find favour in his sight, as a sinner, or so long as he is considered as such. Wherever sin is, therefore, it is accompanied with the wrath and vengeance of God. He is justified who is considered not as a sinner, but as a righteous person, and on that account stands in safety before the tribunal of God, where all sinners are confounded and ruined. As, if an innocent man be brought under an accusation before the tribunal of a just judge, when judgment is passed according to his innocence, he is said to be justified or acquitted before the judge, so he is justified before God, who, not being numbered among sinners, has God for a witness and asserter of his righteousness. Thus he must be said, therefore, to be *justified by works,* whose life discovers such purity and holiness, as to deserve the character of righteousness before the throne of God; or who, by the integrity of his works, can answer and satisfy the divine judgment. On the other hand, he will be *justified by faith,* who, being excluded from the righteousness of works, apprehends by faith the righteousness of Christ, invested in which, he appears, in the sight of God, not as a sinner, but as a righteous man. Thus we simply explain justification to be an acceptance, by which God receives us into his favour, and esteems us as righteous persons; and we say that it consists in the remission of sins and the imputation of the righteousness of Christ. . . .

4. CHRISTIAN LIBERTY

We have now to treat of Christian liberty, an explanation of which ought not to be omitted in a treatise which is designed to comprehend a compendious summary of evangelical doctrine. . . .

Christian liberty, according to my judgment, consists of three parts. The first part is, that the consciences of believers, when seeking an assurance of their justification before God, should raise themselves above the law, and forget all the righteousness of the law. For since the law, as we have elsewhere demonstrated, leaves no man righteous, either we must be excluded from all hope of justification, or it is necessary for us to be delivered from it, and that so completely as not to have any dependence on works. For he who imagines, that in order to obtain righteousness he must produce any works, however small, can fix no limit or boundary, but renders himself a debtor to the whole law. Avoiding, therefore, all mention of the law, and dismissing all thought of our own works, in reference to justification, we must embrace the Divine mercy alone, and turning our eyes from ourselves, fix them solely on Christ. For the question is, not how we can be righteous, but how, though unrighteous and unworthy, we can be considered as righteous. And the conscience that desires to attain any certainty respecting this, must give no admission to the law. Nor will this authorize any one to conclude, that the law is of no use to believers, whom it still continues to instruct and exhort, and stimulate to duty, although it has no place in their consciences before the tribunal of God. For these two things, being very different, require to be properly and carefully distinguished by us. The whole life of Christians ought to be an exercise of piety, since they are called to sanctification. It is the office of the law to remind them of their duty, and thereby to excite them to the pursuit of holiness and integrity. But when their consciences are solicitous how God may be propitiated, what answer they shall make, and on what they shall rest their confidence, if called to his tribunal, there must then be no consideration of the requisitions of the law, but Christ alone must be proposed for righteousness, who exceeds all the perfection of the law. . . .

The second part of Christian liberty, which is dependent on the first, is, that their consciences do not observe the law, as being under any legal obligation; but that, being liberated from the yoke of the law, they yield a voluntary obedience to the will of God. For being possessed with perpetual terrors, as long as they remain under the dominion of the law, they will engage with alacrity and preemptitude in the service of God, unless they have previously received this liberty. . . .

The third part of Christian liberty teaches us, that we are bound by no obligation before God respecting external things, which in themselves are indifferent; but that we may indifferently sometimes use, and at other times omit them. And the knowledge of this liberty also is very necessary for us; for without it we shall have no tranquillity of conscience, nor will there be any end of superstitions. Many in the present age think it a folly to raise any dispute concerning the free use of meats, of days, and of habits, and similar subjects, considering these things as frivolous and nugatory; but they are of greater importance than is generally believed. For when the conscience has once fallen into the snare, it enters a long and inextricable labyrinth, from which it is afterwards difficult to escape; if a man begin to doubt the lawfulness of using flax in sheets, shirts, handkerchiefs, napkins, and table cloths, neither will he be certain respecting hemp, and at last he will doubt of the lawfulness of using tow; for he will consider with himself whether he cannot eat without table cloths or napkins, whether he cannot do without handkerchiefs. If any one imagine delicate food to be unlawful, he will ere long have no tranquillity before God in eating brown bread and common viands, while he remembers that he might support his body with meat of a quality still inferior. If he hesitate respecting good wine, he will afterwards be unable with any peace of conscience to drink the most vapid; and at last he will not presume even to touch purer and sweeter water than others. In short, he will come to think it criminal to step over a twig that lies across his path. For this is the commencement of no trival controversy; but the dispute is whether the use of certain things be agreeable to God, whose will ought to guide all our resolutions and all our actions. The necessary consequence is, that some are hurried by despair into a vortex of confusion, from which they see no way of escape; and some, despising God, and casting off all fear of him, make a way of ruin for themselves. For all, who are involved in such doubts, which way soever they turn their views, behold something offensive to their consciences presenting itself on every side. . . .

5. ELECTION

The covenant of life not being equally preached to all, and among those to whom it is preached not always finding the same reception, this diversity discovers the wonderful depth of the Divine judgment. Nor is it to be doubted that this variety also follows, subject to the decision of God's eternal election. If it be evidently the result of the Divine will, that salvation is freely offered to some, and others are prevented from attaining it,— this immediately gives rise to important and difficult questions, which are incapable of any other explication, than by the establishment of pious minds in what ought to be received concerning election and predestination—a question, in the opinion of many, full of perplexity; for they consider nothing more unreasonable, than that, of the common mass of mankind, some should be predestinated to salvation, and others to destruction. But how unreasonably they perplex themselves will afterwards appear from the sequel of our discourse. Besides, the very obscurity which excites such dread, not only displays the utility of this doctrine, but shows it to be productive of the most delightful benefit. We shall never be clearly convinced as we ought to be, that our salvation flows from the fountain of God's free mercy, till we are acquainted with his eternal election, which illustrates the grace of God by this comparison, that he adopts not all promiscuously to the hope of salvation, but gives to some what he refuses to others. Ignorance of this principle evidently detracts from the Divine glory, and diminishes real humility. . . . The discussion of predestination—a subject of itself rather intricate—is made very preplexed, and therefore dangerous, by human curiosity, which no barriers can restrain from wandering into forbidden labyrinths, and soaring beyond its sphere, as if determined to leave none of the Divine secrets unscrutinized or unexplored. As we see multitudes every where guilty of this arrogance and presumption, and among them some who are not censurable in other respects, it is proper to admonish them of the bounds of their duty on this subject. First, then, let them remember that when they inquire into predestination, they penetrate the inmost recesses of Divine wisdom, where the careless and confident intruder will obtain no satisfaction to his curiosity, but will enter a labyrinth from which he will find no way to depart. For it is unreasonable that man should scrutinize with impunity those things which the Lord has determined to be hidden in himself; and investigate, even from eternity, that sublimity of wisdom which God would have us to adore and not comprehend, to promote our admiration of his glory. The secrets of his will which he determined to reveal to us, he discovers in his word; and these are all that he foresaw would concern us or conduce to our advantage. . . .

Predestination, by which God adopts some to the hope of life, and adjudges others to eternal death, no one, desirous of the credit of piety, dares absolutely to deny. But it is involved in many cavils, especially by those who make foreknowledge the cause of it. We maintain, that both belong to God; but it is preposterous to represent one as dependent on the other. When we attribute foreknowledge to God, we mean that all things have ever been, and perpetually remain, before his eyes, so that to his knowledge nothing is future or past, but all things are present; and present in such a manner, that he does not merely conceive of them from ideas formed in his mind, as things remembered by us appear present to our minds, but really beholds and sees them as if actually placed before him. And this foreknowledge extends to the whole world, and to all the creatures. Presdestination we call the eternal decree of God, by which he has determined in himself, what he would have to become of every individual of mankind. For they are not all created with a similar destiny; but eternal life is foreordained for some, and eternal damnation for others. Every man, therefore, being created for one or the other of these ends, we say, he is predestinated either to life or to death. . . . In conformity, therefore, to the clear doctrine of the scripture, we assert, that by an eternal and immutable counsel, God has once for all determined, both whom he would admit to salvation, and whom he would condemn to destruction. We affirm that this counsel, as far as concerns the elect, is founded on his gratuitous mercy, totally irrespective of human merit; but that to those whom he devotes to condemnation, the gate of life is closed by a just and irreprehensible, but incomprehensible, judgment. In the elect, we consider calling as an evidence of election, and justification as another token of its manifestation, till they arrive in glory, which constitutes its completion. As God seals his elect by vocation and justification, so by excluding the reprobate from the knowledge of his name and the sanctification of his Spirit, he affords an indication of the judgment that awaits them. . . .

Wherefore some people falsely and wickedly charge God with a violation of equal justice, because, in his predestination, he observes not the same uniform course of proceeding towards all. If he finds all guilty, they say, let him punish all alike; if innocent, let him withhold the rigour of justice from all. But they deal with him just as if either mercy were forbidden him, or, when he chooses to show mercy, he were constrained wholly to renounce justice. What is it that they require? If all are guilty, that they shall all suffer the same punishment. We confess the guilt to be common, but we say, that some are relieved by Divine mercy. They say, Let it relieve all. But we reply, Justice requires that he should likewise show himself to be a just judge in the infliction of punishment. When they object to this, what is it but attempting to deprive God of the opportunity to manifest his mercy, or to grant it to him, at least, on the condition that he wholly abandon his justice? Wherefore there is the greatest propriety in these observations of Augustine: "The whole mass of mankind having fallen into condemnation in the first man, the vessels that are formed from it to honour, are not vessels of personal righteousness, but of Divine mercy; and the formation of others to dishonour, is to be attributed, not to iniquity, but to the Divine decree," &c. While God rewards those whom he rejects with deserved punishment, and to those whom he calls, freely gives undeserved grace, he is liable to no accusation, but may be compared to a creditor, who has power to release one, and enforce his demands on another. The Lord, therefore, may give grace to whom he will, because he is merciful, and yet not give it to all, because he is a just judge; may manifest his free grace, by giving to some what they never deserve, while, by not giving to all, he declares the demerit of all. For when Paul says, that "God hath concluded all under sin, that he might have mercy upon all," it must, at the same time, be added, that he is debtor to none; for no man "hath first given to him," to entitle him to demand a recompense.

Another argument often urged to overthrow predestination is, that its establishment would destroy all solicitude and exertion for rectitude of conduct. For who can hear, they say, that either life or death is appointed for him by God's eternal and immutable decree, without immediately concluding that it is of no importance how he conducts himself; since no action of his can in any respect either impede or promote the predestination of God? Thus all will abandon themselves to despair, and run into every excess to which their licentious propensities may lead them. And truly this objection is not altogether destitute of truth; for there are many impure persons who bespatter the doctrine of predestination with these vile blasphemies, and with this pretext elude all admonitions and reproofs: God knows what he has determinted to do with us: if he has decreed our salvation, he will bring us to it in his own time; if he has destined us to death, it will be in vain for us to strive against it. But the scripture, while it inculcates superior awe and reverence of mind in the consideration of so great a mystery, instructs the godly in a very different conclusion, and fully refutes the wicked and unreasonable inferences of these persons. For the design of what it contains respecting predestination is, not that, being excited to presumption, we may attempt, with nefarious temerity, to scrutinize the inaccessible secrets of God, but rather that, being humbled and dejected, we may learn to tremble at his justice and admire his mercy. At this object believers will aim. But the impure cavils of the wicked are justly restrained by Paul. They profess to go on securely in their vices; because if they are of the number of the elect, such conduct will not prevent their being finally brought into life. But Paul declares the end of our election to be, that we may lead a holy and blameless life. If the object of election be holiness of life, it should rather awaken and stimulate us to a cheerful practice of it, than be used as a pretext for slothfulness. But how inconsistent is it to cease from the practice of virtue because election is sufficient to salvation, while the end proposed in election is our diligent performance of virtuous actions! Away, then, with such corrupt and sacrilegious perversions of the whole order of election. They carry their blasphemies much further, by asserting, that any one who is reprobated by God will labour to no purpose if he endeavour to approve himself to him by innocence and integrity of life; but here they are convicted of a most impudent falsehood. For whence could such exertion originate but from election? Whoever are of the number of the reprobate, being vessels made to dishonour, cease not to provoke the Divine wrath against them by continual transgressions, and to confirm by evident proofs the judgment of God already denounced against them; so that their striving with him in vain is what can never happen. . . . Now, while many arguments are advanced on both sides, let our conclusion be to stand astonished with Paul at so great a mystery, and amidst the clamour of petulant tongues let us not be ashamed of exclaiming with him, "O man, who art thou that repliest against God?" For, as Augustine justly contends, it is acting a most perverse part, to set up the measure of human justice as the standard by which to measure the justice of God.

47   THIS TRACT, *Concerning the Satisfaction of Christ*, was prepared by the Swiss Anabaptists, probably between 1525 and 1530. Though its title indicates a discussion of the atonement, it may also be seen as a concise and representative statement of the Anabaptist understanding of the Christian life. The point of view is critical not only of Catholicism, but also of the more radical elements of the Reformation (for example, antinomianism) and other Protestant reformers. The reader may refer also to *The Schleitheim Confession of Faith* (see Selection 65), that was prepared by the same group.

Concerning the Satisfaction of Christ*

ANONYMOUS [ANABAPTIST]

Paul says to the Romans in the third chapter, [that] they are all together sinners and come short of the glory which God should have from them, [yet] apart from merit [they] shall be justified by His grace through the redemption which Christ accomplished, Whom God hath set forth as a mercy seat through faith in His blood, by which He sets forth the righteousness which avails before God, in that He forgives the sins which took place formerly under the divine patience, which He manifested, etc. He says; From which also ye are in Christ Jesus, who of God is made unto us wisdom, righteousness and sanctification and redemption. John the Baptist says, [in] John 1, Behold, That is the Lamb of God who takes upon Himself the sin of the world. John says [in] I John 2, And He is the reconciliation for our sins. Peter says [in] I Peter 2, Who offered Himself [for] our sin on the tree, that we might be without sin. As the prophet also speaks, [in] Isaiah 53, We are made well through His stripes. Isaiah 9, A child is born to us, to us a child is given, etc.

Such statements, I say, and others like them, the scribes interpret as if a person could be saved through Christ whether he do the works of faith or not. If such were the case, why then should Paul say [in] Romans 2 that God will render to everyone according to his works, namely eternal life to those who strive after glory, praise and immortality with perseverance in good works, but to those who are quarrelsome and are not obedient to the truth, but are obedient to the evil, there will come disfavor and wrath, tribulation and anxiety, [namely] upon all the souls of men who do evil. He says, [in] Romans 2, Not those who hear the Law are righteous, but those who do the Law. Paul says in Romans 3, He does not make void the law through faith; [rather] he establishes it. In Romans 8 he says, There is therefore now no condemnation to those who are in Christ Jesus, who walk not after the flesh but after the Spirit. For what the Law could not do, in that is was weak through the flesh, that God did and sent His Son in the form of sinful flesh and through sin condemned sin in the flesh, that the righteousness which the Law demands might be fulfilled in us who now walk not after the flesh but after the Spirit. If ye live after the flesh, ye shall die. Galatians 5 [states]: In Christ Jesus neither circumcision nor uncircumcision availeth [anything], but a faith which worketh by love. I Corinthians 13: If I had all faith so that I could

---

* The Mennonite Quarterly Review, Vol. XX, tr. by John C. Wenger, October 1946, pp. 247–254. The words enclosed in brackets were supplied by Professor Wenger.

remove mountains but have not love, I am nothing. Ephesians 5: For ye
know that no whoremonger nor impure person nor covetous man, who is
an idolater, hath any inheritance in the kingdom of Christ and of God.
Let no man deceive you with vain words. Ephesians 6: For ye know that
everyone will receive from the Lord that good which he hath done. II
Corinthians 5: For we must all appear before the judgment seat of Christ
that everyone may receive according to that which he hath done with his
body, whether it be good or evil. Peter [says in] I Peter 1: And since ye
call upon the Father, who without regarding the person, judgeth according
to each man's work so pass the time of your pilgrimage with fear. II Peter
1: And therefore offer, with highest diligence, through your faith, virtue;
through virtue, knowledge; through knowledge, moderation; through moderation, patience; through patience, godliness; through godliness, brotherly
love; through brotherly love, common love. For if such [virtues] abound
in you ye shall neither be lazy nor idle in the knowledge of our Lord
Jesus Christ. But he who lacketh these things is blind and doth grope.
John says [in] I John 1, If we should say that we have fellowship with
Him and walk in darkness we would lie and do not the truth. I John 2:
Hereby know we that we do know Him if we keep His commandment.
He who saith he knoweth Him and keepeth not His commandment is a
liar. He who saith he is in the light and hateth his brother is in darkness.
I John 3: Children, let no one deceive you. He who doeth righteousness
is righteous as He is righteous, but he who doeth sin is of the devil. He
who is born of God sinneth no more for his seed remaineth in him and
[he] is not able to sin for he is born of God. I will not mention what
Christ says [in] Matthew 4: Improve yourselves for the kingdom of heaven
is come near. [He] saith to Peter and to others: Follow me. Matthew 5:
Let your light shine for men that they may see your good works and
praise your Father [who is] in heaven. Ye ought not to think that I am
come to do away with the Law and the Prophets. I did not come to do
away with [them] but to fulfil. Matthew 7: Therefore he who heareth my
discourse and doeth it, him will I compare with a prudent man who built
his house upon a rock. And then a pelting rain fell and floods came and the
winds blew and beat upon the house but yet it fell not for it was founded
upon a rock. And he who heareth my word and doeth it not is like a
foolish man who built his house upon the sand. Matthew 10: He who
confesseth me before men, him will I confess before my Father in heaven.
He who loveth father or mother more than me is not worthy of me,
and he who loveth son or daughter more than me is not worthy of me.
And [consider] what He says of the good seed which falls into the good
earth. Matthew 16, Mark 8, Luke 9: If anyone wisheth to come after me,
let him deny himself and take up his cross upon himself and follow me.
For he who wisheth to preserve his life shall lose it, but he who loseth his

life for my sake will find it. Matthew 16: For it shall come to pass that the Son of Man will come in the glory of His Father, with His angels and then will He require each one according to his works. [In] Luke 10 Christ speaks to the scribe [that] he should love God with his whole heart and his neighbor as himself; thus would he live. Luke 13: Strive that ye may enter through the narrow door. Luke 14: If anyone come to me and hate not his father, mother, wife, children, brothers, sisters, and also his own life, he cannot be my disciple. And he who does not bear his cross and follow me cannot be my disciple. He who doth not renounce all that he hath cannot be my disciple. John 13: I have given you an example that ye should do as I have done to you. If ye know these things, blessed are ye if ye do them. A new commandment give I unto you that ye love one another as I have loved you. So shall all men know that ye are my disciples if ye have love among yourselves.

Further, as Christ therefore hath suffered for us (He did not have where he might lay His head, Matthew 8) [must] we never through faith in Him renounce [our] supposed possessions and our [own] selves, and suffer for His sake? Why then does He say [in] Matthew 19 to the young man who asked him how he might be saved, If thou desirest to be perfect, go, sell what thou hast and give to the poor, and thou shalt have treasure in heaven, and come, follow me? Why does He say, It is easier for a camel to go through the eye of a needle than for a rich man to enter into the kingdom of God? Yea, why does He say [in] Luke 5 to Peter and Andrew (as was said above), Follow me? [And] to Matthew, Follow Me? Did not Zacchaeus say [in] Luke 19, after he [came to] know the poor Jesus and had received Him, Behold, the half of my goods I give to the poor, and if I have defrauded anyone I will restore fourfold? It would then be the case that Christ had lied when He says [in] Matthew 6, We cannot serve God and mammon. And that which Luke writes [in] Acts 2 of the righteous Christian church which was once at Jerusalem, would not be true, But those who believed were together and had all things common. Yea, the article of the Christian Faith which says, A communion of the saints, would also be untrue. Why then does He say [in] Matthew 8, He who wisheth to come after me, let him deny himself, take his cross upon himself and follow me? [And,] He who wisheth to save his life shall lose it. Why does He say [in] Matthew 5, Blessed are they who are persecuted for righteousness' sake [And,] Blessed are ye when men revile you and persecute you and say all manner of evil against you for my sake, if they lie therein. Matthew 10, John 15: The disciple is not above his master, nor the servant above his Lord. It is enough for the disciple that he be as his master, and the servant as his lord. John 16: They will put you under the ban. The time cometh that he who killeth you will think that he doeth God a service therein.

Verily, verily, I say to you, Ye shall weep and lament, but the world shall rejoice. Does not Peter also say [in] I Peter 2, For hereunto were ye called: because Christ also suffered for us, and left us an example, that ye should follow His footsteps. Yea indeed, if Christ therefore did enough by his passion which He suffered at Jerusalem, and nothing was uncompleted of his suffering, why then does Paul say in Colossians 1, Now I rejoice in my suffering which I bear for you and fill up in my body that which is lacking in the afflictions of Christ? II Corinthians 1: But as we have tribulation or comfort it works out for your good. Ephesians 3: Therefore I, Paul, a prisoner of Jesus Christ for you Gentiles. Philippians 2: And if I be offered as an offering and service to God [for] your faith, I joy and rejoice with you all. In the same way, did not Christ chiefly establish the Lord's Supper for this reason, namely that they had to suffer as Christ their Head, and through death enter into glory, yea that their death should not be their's but the Lord's and that they like their Head should arise [from the dead]? And what about the dear apostles and prophets, yea even Christ Himself, and likewise the dear friends of God who suffer much at this time and who have testified (prophetiert) for so many years, —if the members of Christ must not suffer like their Head? Does Peter not say [in] I Peter 5, Humble yourselves under the mighty hand of God that He might exalt you at the right time? Cast upon Him all your care, for He careth for you. Be sober, watch ye, for your adversary, the slanderer, goeth about as a roaring lion, seeking whether he can devour someone, whom resist, fortified by faith, since ye know that through your brotherhood which is in the world the same suffering is accomplished.

And for this reason when Paul says [in] Romans 3 that those who are justified through Christ are justified without any merit or without the works of the Law he does not mean that a man can be saved without the works of faith [since Christ and the apostles demand such], but without those works which are done outside of faith and of the love of God,—such as circumcision and the like, which the Jews did that they might thereby be justified. Therefore whenever Paul and Christ apply the term justifying to works they do not mean that those works are of men; but [they are] of God and of Christ (through whose strength the man performs them). [Those justifying works] are not performed by the man as if he received something as his own, but [they are performed] because God wishes so to give the man such works that they are His works. And why is there a mercy seat with God except for His own through His will? Why should God make known His will, if He would not wish that a person do it? Yea, how could God be satisfied with anyone who neither wishes to hear the will of God concerning His mercy seat, or who having heard and knowing thereof wishes to hold it only with words? Will he not diminish his boast that the mercy seat exists for his sake? Yea, he gives his own word and says that he heard it from the mercy seat. Yea, he curses and persecutes everyone who refuses to believe him. Will such boasting not lead to his damnation? But if we would think like Paul [in] I Corinthians 1, where he calls Christ the righteousness and wisdom of the believers or Christians, does he mean the outward Christ without the inward, and not much more the inward with the outward [Christ]? Namely, since He is the Word of the Father He makes known to us the true obedience by which alone the Father is satisfied. He is the true Bread from heaven which comes down from above to feed the souls of men. He says, He who doth not renounce all that he possesseth cannot be His disciple. He says, He who wisheth to follow me, let him deny himself. No one cometh to the Father but by me. I am the door of the sheepfold. I am the light of the world. I am the way, the truth, and the life. He testifies all this in deed. I will not mention that Paul at this place is not speaking of Pharisees or scribes (as if they were the righteousness of Christ), but of him and those like him who accept Him in truth and keep their standing as His [disciples] according to that which faith eliminates and [that which it] demands. But what have they to do with it who boast to me so proudly of Christ? They allege that Paul wrote of them when they are the chief persecutors of Christ and of Paul.

How does it concern me that the emperor claims so many kingdoms, since I am a poor beggar? But when John the Baptist says [in] John 1, Christ is the Lamb which taketh upon Himself the sin of the world, he wishes to be understood: insofar as the world surrenders to Him in faith. And therefore he says also [in] John 3, He who believeth in the Son hath everlasting life; he who doth not believe in the Son shall not see life. In the same way also when John says [in] I John 2, He is our reconciliation, he wishes to be understood: namely, of those who so recognize Him. For although He is truly a reconciliation for the whole world, that does no one any good except those who recognize and accept Him by faith. And those who [accept Him] keep the commandments of Christ. But he who does not [keep the commandments] and yet boasts of Christ as being his reconciliation is a liar, inasmuch as he has never known Christ,—as John testifies. And do we think, when Peter says in I Peter 2, Who offered Himself for our sins in His body on the tree that we might be without sin, [that] he meant that Christ so offered Himself for the sins of men that through Him they are pronounced free, whether or not they believe on Him, whether or not they turn from sin, whether or not they have a change of mind, as the works-saints and scribes think? That is far [from the truth]! Why then would he say [in] I Peter 1, Whom having not seen ye love, in whom ye also believe although ye see Him not. And whereas ye call on the Father who, without regarding the person, judgeth according to every man's work, conduct your life in the time of your pilgrimage in fear. Blessed be God and the Father of our Lord Jesus Christ who according to His great mercy hath begotten us again to a living hope by the resurrection of Jesus Christ from the dead. Now those who are without faith, who have not ceased [from sin], those sinning even worse than before,[1] yea [those with] just as slavish and ugly a disposition toward God and their neighbor as they had before,—how can such people appropriate the words of Peter for themselves, since Peter did not write to them but to Christians? In the same way one understands also the two statements of Isaiah, for in Isaiah 28 God said concerning Christ, Behold, I lay a chosen, costly cornerstone in Zion and he who believes therein shall not be put to shame. The ruling Lord however shall be your fear and your dread, and He shall be to you for sanctification, for a stone of stumbling, and a rock of offense, for the two houses of Israel, etc.

How then did Christ do enough for our sins? Answer: [He did enough,] not only for ours, but also for the sins of the whole world, insofar as they believe on Him and follow Him according to the demands of faith, as was said. Yea, He has done enough as the Head of his church; He does no less for His members day by day so that He [continues to] do enough for those who are His; just as He has done from the beginning [so will He continue to do] until His Return. And therefore just as one speaks of justification through Christ so must one also speak of faith, [namely] that repentance is not apart from works, yea not apart from love (which is an unction), for only such an anointed faith as one receives from the resurrection from the dead is [at all a] Christian faith, and [it alone] is reckoned for righteousness, Romans 4. Again, one must not speak of works after the manner of the works-saints, [namely], works of the Law, but [one] must preach works of faith, that is a turning back from works, possessions, and yourself, through faith in Christ the crucified;—not as though a man could do this of himself but as he is able to do through the strength of faith, so that these ["works"] are not of man but of God, inasmuch as the will and the ability to turn back to God are not of man but the gift of God through Jesus Christ our Lord.

Truly happy then is the man who keeps on the middle path and does not yield to the work-saints[2] (who promise salvation or the forgiveness of sins through works apart from faith—that is through the supposed possession of works—and thus veer to the left, preaching works; paying no attention to a constant faith and not wishing to see or hear of a faith which

---

[1] The author is probably making a comparison between the moral level of the masses when still under Roman Catholicism and that which obtained after the inauguration of the Protestant reformation. It is a known fact that his charge is correct: the Reformation lowered the moral standards of the people for a time in some places.

[2] In his further discussion the author indicates that by "works-saints" he means Roman Catholics, while by "scribes" he means the Protestant reformers.

is sufficient unto salvation: all their works are like wild plums, that is, ceremonies devoid of faith) nor on the other hand to the scribes, who although they have kept clear of [building on] works yet veer to the right and under the name of gospel teach a faith without works, taking the poor and obedient Christ (who had not where to lay His head, Luke 9, and without either the murmuring complaints or the defense of men said, Luke 22, Nevertheless, Father, not my will but Thine be done) for their satisfaction but they do not wish to hear what he says [in] Luke 9, Come, follow me. Luke 14: He who doth not renounce all that he possesseth cannot be my disciple. Mark 8: He who wisheth to come after me, let him deny himself, take his cross upon himself, and follow me. Yea, the Father must also be a "fanatic" [to] them when He says, This is my beloved Son in whom I am well pleased, hear Him. They make of Christ, in His humanity, what the pope has made of the saints, namely a golden calf like the Jews of old, that is, they confess Christ as David's Son and [yet] they deny Him, yea make Him a "fanatic" because God's Word and Son were sent into the world to make known the obedience or right-eousness of His Father not only in words but also with "works," so that all who believe in Him might not perish in their death but be delivered from death. All their preaching and fruit are like prickly thistles; they have much to say regarding faith, and [yet] know neither what Christ nor faith are; they reject works without faith in order that they may set up faith without works. They wish to obey God only with the soul and not also with the body, in order that they may escape persecution. They think that faith is a false (fauler) and empty delusion. For this reason they are able to say that infants have faith although they give no evidence of works of faith, even when they come to years. It would then be the case that the work of faith and of the Holy Spirit would be cursing, when they are scarcely able to speak. And alas for the miserable blindness, although it is not be-cause they do not know better that they do not speak or write all this but because they wish to provide for the belly and preserve their honor.

And how well can one see here the beast that hath seven heads and ten horns, which hath again recovered from its deadly wound, inasmuch as the Romish school or Curia from which the bread-god and infant-baptism come originally, are again defended as the truth by the scribes. I will not mention many other things in which the scribes hypocritically imitate the papists and establish them as Christian. But thus must the second beast with the two horns—that is, the gang of the scribes—cause the earth and the people thereon to worship again the first beast, again establishing the papal oil-idol,—that is, popery,—casting down fire from heaven, banishing and cursing everyone who does not cleave to them,— everything just as John had said beforehand. This is also just as he had seen in Revelation 17 where the ten horns on the beast would hate the whore and make her desolate and naked, devour her flesh and burn her with fire, seeing that God had put it in their hearts. The kingdom would be given to the beast until the Word of God should be fulfilled. Yea, those ten horns who like kings should receive the kingdom after the beast, would be of one mind, would give authority to the beast, would make war with the Lamb, and the Lamb would overcome them. This is how there should arise scholars [scribes] in the last days from all the higher schools [of learning], awakened through the Spirit; and the Romish church or congregation of works-saints, possessed of great zeal, would bring everything on itself and burn up what it had accumulated of money, silver and food, and damn them [the awakened scholars] as heretics. But soon thereafter they would fall back to the beast,—that is, the Romish school,—and defend it, and the kingdom of God which had previously come to them they would again cast away. Yea these [apostate reformers] would defend the beast and those who cleave [to the beast], against the Word of God, and fight vehemently with the Lamb. Nevertheless, the Lamb who is a Lord of lords and the King of all kings will conquer them, together with [assisted by] His believers and called ones. And would not this, together with the papists, be the abomination of desolation of which Daniel in the ninth chapter, Paul [in] Second Thessalonians 2, Peter [in] Second Peter 2, yea also Christ [in] Matthew 24, Mark 13, [and] Luke 17, clearly have spoken, [namely] where that one sits in the holy place, allows himself to be worshipped either for gospel or for Christianity, according to which the works-saints say, Lo, here is Christ! The scribes cry, Lo, here is Christ! Therefore, happy is he who departs from Babylon, that is, [who] neither believes the works-saints nor the scribes, [but] submits with fear to the discipline of Christ, because the heavenly voice, [in] Revelation 18, Isaiah 52, II Corinthians 6, cries out and says, Come out of her, my people, that ye be not partakers of her sins, that ye receive not of her plagues, for her sins have resounded unto heaven.

48 THE FOLLOWING SELECTIONS from the sessions of the Council of Trent, the sixteenth-century council that defined Roman Catholic dogma, state the Church's position on sin, justification by faith, and the relation of faith and works.[1]

1 See also Council of Trent, Selections 10, 67.

The Council of Trent (1545-1563)*

FIFTH SESSION: JUNE 17, 1546

DECREE CONCERNING ORIGINAL SIN

That our Catholic "faith, without which it is impossible to please God", may, errors being purged away, continue in its own perfect and spotless integrity, and that the Christian people may not "be carried about with every wind of doctrine"; whereas that old serpent, the perpetual enemy of mankind, amongst the very many evils with which the Church of God is in these our times troubled, has also stirred up not only new, but even old, dissensions touching original sin, and the remedy thereof; the sacred and holy, ecumenical and general Synod of Trent,—lawfully assembled in the Holy Ghost, the three same legates of the Apostolic See presiding therein,—wishing now to come to the reclaiming of the erring, and the confirming of the wavering,—following the testimonies of the sacred scriptures, of the holy Fathers, of the most approved councils, and the judgment and consent of the Church itself, ordains, confesses, and declares these things touching the said original sin:

1. If any one does not confess that the first man, Adam, when he had transgressed the commandment of God in Paradise, immediately lost the holiness and justice wherein he had been constituted; and that he incurred, through the offense of that prevarication, the wrath and indignation of God, and consequently death, with which God had previously threatened him, and, together with death, captivity under his power who thenceforth "had the empire of death, that is to say, the devil", and that the entire Adam, through that offense of prevarication, was changed, in body and soul, for the worse; let him be anathema.

2. If any one asserts, that the prevarication of Adam injured himself alone, and not his posterity; and that the holiness and justice, received of God, which he lost, he lost for himself alone, and not for us also; or that he, being defiled by the sin of disobedience, has only transfused death and pains of the body into the whole human race, but not sin also, which is the death of the soul; let him be anathema:—whereas he contradicts the apostle who says: "By one man sin entered into the world, and by sin death, and so death passed upon all men, in whom all have sinned."

3. If any one asserts, that this sin of Adam,—which in its origin is one,

* From Philip Schaff, The Creeds of Christendom, Vol. II. New York: Harper and Row Publishers, 1919. Used by permission of Mary L. Schaff.

and being transfused into all by propagation, not by imitation, is in each one as his own,—is taken away either by the powers of human nature, or by any other remedy than the merit of the "one mediator, our Lord Jesus Christ, who hath reconciled us to God in his own blood, being made unto us justice, sanctification, and redemption"; or if he denies that the said merit of Jesus Christ is applied, both to adults and to infants, by the sacrament of baptism rightly administered in the form of the Church; let him be anathema: "For there is no other name under heaven given to men, whereby we must be saved." Whence that voice: "Behold the lamb of God, behold him who taketh away the sins of the world"; and that other: "As many as have been baptized, have put on Christ."

4. If any one denies, that infants, newly born from their mothers' wombs, even though they be sprung from baptized parents, are to be baptized; or says that they are "baptized" indeed "for the remission of sins", but that they derive nothing of original sin from Adam, which has need of being expiated by the laver of regeneration for obtaining life everlasting,—whence it follows as a consequence, that in them the form of baptism, "for the remission of sins", is understood to be not true, but false,—let him be anathema. For that which the apostle has said, "By one man sin entered into the world, and by sin death, and so death passed upon all men, in whom all have sinned", is not to be understood otherwise than as the Catholic Church spread everywhere hath always understood it. For, by reason of this rule of faith, from a tradition of the apostles, even infants, who could not as yet commit any sin of themselves, are for this cause truly "baptized for the remission of sins", that in them that may be cleansed away by regeneration, which they have contracted by generation. "For, unless a man be borne again of water and the Holy Ghost, he can not enter into the kingdom of God."

5. If any one denies, that, by the grace of our Lord Jesus Christ, which is conferred in baptism, the guilt of original sin is remitted; or even asserts that the whole of that which has the true and proper nature of sin is not taken away; but says that it is only rased, or not imputed; let him be anathema. For, in those who are "born again", there is nothing that God hates; because, "There is no condemnation to those who are" truly "buried together with Christ by baptism into death"; "who walk not according to the flesh", but, "putting off the old man, and putting on the new who is created according to God", are made innocent, immaculate, pure, harmless, and beloved of God, "heirs indeed of God, but joint heirs with Christ"; so that there is nothing whatever to retard their entrance into heaven. But this holy synod confesses and is sensible, that in the baptized there remains concupiscence, or an incentive (to sin); which, whereas it is left for our exercise, can not injure those who consent not, but resist manfully by the grace of Jesus Christ; yea, he who shall have "striven lawfully shall be

crowned." This concupiscence, which the apostle sometimes calls sin, the holy synod declares that the Catholic Church has never understood it to be called sin, as being truly and properly sin in those "born again", but because it is of sin, and inclines to sin. And if any one is of a contrary sentiment, let him be anathema.

This same holy synod doth nevertheless declare, that it is not its intention to include in this decree, where original sin is treated of, the blessed and immaculate Virgin Mary, the mother of God; but that the constitutions of Pope Sixtus IV., of happy memory, are to be observed, under the pains contained in the said constitutions, which it renews.

SIXTH SESSION: JANUARY 13, 1547

DECREE ON JUSTIFICATION

On the inability of nature and of the law to justify man

The holy synod declares first, that, for the correct and sound understanding of the doctrine of Justification, it is necessary that each one recognize and confess, that, whereas all men had lost their innocence in the prevarication of Adam,—having become unclean, and, as the apostle says, "by nature children of wrath", as (this synod) has set forth in the decree on original sin,—they were so far "the servants of sin", and under the power of the devil and of death, that not the Gentiles only by the force of nature, but not even the Jews by the very letter itself of the law of Moses, were able to be liberated, or to arise, therefrom; although freewill, attenuated as it was in its powers, and bent down, was by no means extinguished in them.

On the necessity, in adults, of preparation for justification, and whence it proceeds

The synod furthermore declares, that, in adults, the beginning of the said Justification is to be derived from the prevenient grace of God, through Jesus Christ, that is to say, from his vocation, whereby, without any merits existing on their parts, they are called; that so they, who by sins were alienated from God, may be disposed through his quickening and assisting grace, to convert themselves to their own justification, by freely assenting to and co-operating with that said grace: in such sort that, while God touches the heart of man by the illumination of the Holy Ghost, neither is man himself utterly inactive while he receives that inspiration, forasmuch as he is also able to reject it; yet is he not able, by his own free will, without the grace of God, to move himself unto justice in his sight. Whence, when it is said in the sacred writings: "Turn ye to me, and I will turn to you", we are admonished of our liberty; and when we answer: "Convert us, O Lord, to thee, and we shall be converted", we confess that we are prevented (anticipated) by the grace of God.

The manner of preparation

Now they [adults] are disposed unto the said justice, when, excited and assisted by divine grace, conceiving "faith by hearing", they are freely moved towards God, believing those things to be true which God has revealed and promised—and this especially, that God justifies the impious "by his grace, through the redemption that is in Christ Jesus"; and when, understanding themselves to be sinners, they, by turning themselves, from the fear of divine justice whereby they are profitably agitated, to consider the mercy of God, are raised unto hope, confiding that God will be propitious to them for Christ's sake; and they begin to love him as the fountain of all justice; and are therefore moved against sins by a certain hatred and detestation, to wit, by that penitence which must be performed before baptism: lastly, when they purpose to receive baptism, to begin a new life, and to "keep the commandments" of God. Concerning this disposition it is written: "He that cometh to God, must believe that he is, and is a rewarder to them that seek him"; and, "Be of good faith, son, thy sins are forgiven thee"; and, "The fear of the Lord driveth out sin"; and, "Do penance, and be baptized every one of you in the name of Jesus Christ, for the remission of your sins, and you shall receive the gift of the Holy Ghost"; and, "Going, therefore, teach ye all nations, baptizing them in the name of the Father, and of the Son, and of the Holy Ghost"; finally, "Prepare your hearts unto the Lord."

What the justification of the impious is, and what are the causes thereof

This disposition, or preparation, is followed by Justification itself, which is not remission of sins merely, but also the sanctification and renewal of the inward man, through the voluntary reception of the grace, and of the gifts, whereby man of unjust becomes just, and of an enemy a friend, that so he may be "an heir according to hope of life everlasting."

Of this Justification the causes are these: the final cause indeed is the glory of God and of Jesus Christ, and life everlasting; while the efficient cause is a merciful God who "washes and sanctifies" gratuitously, "signing", and anointing with the holy "Spirit of promise, who is the pledge of our inheritance"; but the meritorious cause is his most beloved only-begotten, our Lord Jesus Christ, who, when we were enemies, "for the exceeding charity wherewith he loved us", merited Justification for us by his most holy Passion on the wood of the cross, and made satisfaction for us unto God the Father; the instrumental cause is the sacrament of baptism, which is the sacrament of faith, without which [faith] no man was ever justified; lastly, the alone formal cause is the justice of God, not that whereby he himself is just, but that whereby he maketh us just, that, to wit, with which "we", being endowed by him, "are renewed in the spirit of our mind", and we are not only reputed, but are truly called, and are just, receiving justice within us, each one according to his own measure, "which the Holy Ghost distributes to every one as he wills", and according to each one's proper disposition and co-operation. For, although no one can be just, but he to whom the merits of the Passion of our Lord Jesus Christ are communicated, yet is this done in the said justification of the impious, when by the merit of that same most holy Passion, "the charity of God is poured forth", by the Holy Spirit, "in the hearts" of those that are justified, and is inherent therein: whence, man, through Jesus Christ, in whom he is ingrafted, receives, in the said justification, together with the remission of sins, all these [gifts] infused at once, faith, hope, and charity. For faith, unless hope and charity be added thereto, neither unites man perfectly with Christ, nor makes him a living member of his body. For which reason it is most truly said, that "Faith without works is dead" and profitless; and, "In Christ Jesus neither circumcision availeth any thing nor uncircumcision, but faith which worketh by charity." This faith, Catechumens beg of the Church—agreeably to a tradition of the apostles—previously to the sacrament of baptism; when they beg for the faith which bestows life everlasting, which, without hope and charity, faith can not bestow: whence also do they immediately hear that word of Christ: "If thou wilt enter into life, keep the commandments." Wherefore, when receiving true and Christian justice, they are bidden, immediately on being born again, to preserve it pure and spotless, as "the first robe" given them through Jesus Christ in lieu of that which Adam, by his disobedience, lost for himself and for us, that so they may bear it before the judgment-seat of our Lord Jesus Christ, and may have life eternal.

In what manner it is to be understood, that the impious is justified by faith, and gratuitously

And whereas the Apostle saith, that man is "justified by faith" and "freely", those words are to be understood in that sense which the perpetual consent of the Catholic Church hath held and expressed; to wit, that we are therefore said to be "justified by faith", because faith is the beginning of human salvation, the foundation, and the root of all Justification; "without which it is impossible to please God", and to come unto the fellowship of his sons: but we are therefore said to be justified "freely", because that none of those things which precede justification—whether faith or works—merit the grace itself of justification. For, "if it be a grace, it is not now by works", otherwise, as the same Apostle says, "grace is no more grace."

Against the vain confidence of heretics

But, although it is necessary to believe that sins neither are remitted, nor ever were remitted save gratuitously by the mercy of God for Christ's sake; yet is it not to be said, that sins are forgiven, or have been forgiven, to any one who boasts of his confidence and certainty of the remission of his sins, and rests on that alone; seeing that it may exist, yea does in our day exist, amongst heretics and schismatics; and with great vehemence is this vain confidence, and one alien from all godliness, preached up in opposition to the Catholic Church. But neither is this to be asserted—that they who are truly justified must needs, without any doubting whatever, settle within themselves that they are justified, and that no one is absolved from sins and justified, but he that believes for certain that he is absolved and justified; and that absolution and justification are effected by this faith alone: as though whoso has not this belief, doubts of the promises of God, and of the efficacy of the death and resurrection of Christ. For even as no pious person ought to doubt of the mercy of God, of the merit of Christ, and of the virtue and efficacy of the sacraments, even so each one, when he regards himself, and his own weakness and indisposition, may have fear and apprehension touching his own grace; seeing that no one can know with a certainty of faith, which can not be subject to error, that he has obtained the grace of God.

On the increase of justification received

Having, therefore, been thus justified, and made the friends and "domestics of God", advancing "from virtue to virtue", they are "renewed", as the Apostle says, "day by day"; that is, "by mortifying the members" of their own flesh, and "by presenting them as instruments of justice unto sanctification", they, through the observance of the commandments of God and of the Church, faith co-operating with good works, increase in that justice which they have received through the grace of Christ, and are still further justified, as it is written: "He that is just, let him be justified still"; and again, "Be not afraid to be justified even to death"; and also, "Do you see that by works a man is justified, and not by faith only." And this increase of justification holy Church begs, when she prays, 'Give unto us, O Lord, increase of faith, hope, and charity.'

That a rash presumptuousness in the matter of predestination is to be avoided

No one, moreover, so long as he is in this mortal life, ought so far to presume as regards the secret mystery of divine predestination, as to determine for certain that he is assuredly in the number of the predestinate; as if it were true, that he that is justified, either can not sin any more, or, if he do sin, that he ought to promise himself an assured repentance; for except by special revelation, it can not be known whom God hath chosen unto himself.

On the gift of perseverance

So also as regards the gift of perseverance, of which it is written, "He that shall persevere to the end, he shall be saved";—which gift can not be derived from any other but Him, who is able to establish him who standeth that he stand perseveringly, and to restore him who falleth:—let no one herein promise himself any thing as certain with an absolute certainty; though all ought to place and repose a most firm hope in God's help. For God, unless men be themselves wanting in his grace, "as he has begun the good work, so will he perfect it, working (in them) to will and to accomplish." Nevertheless, let those who "think themselves to stand, take heed lest they fall", and "with fear and trembling work out their salvation", in labors, in watchings, in almsdeeds, in prayers and oblations, in fastings and chastity: for, knowing that "they are born again unto a hope of glory", but not as yet unto glory, they ought to fear for the combat which yet remains with the flesh, with the world, with the devil, wherein they can not be victorious, unless they be with God's grace, obedient to the Apostle, who says: "We are debtors, not to the flesh, to live according to the flesh; for if you live according to the flesh, you shall die; but if by the spirit you mortify the deeds of the flesh, you shall live."

That, by every mortal sin, grace is lost, but not faith

In opposition also to the subtle wits of certain men, who, "by pleasing speeches and good words, seduce the hearts of the innocent", it is to be maintained, that the received grace of Justification is lost, not only by infidelity whereby even faith itself is lost, but also by any other mortal sin whatever, though faith be not lost; thus defending the doctrine of the divine law, which excludes from the kingdom of God not only the unbelieving, but the faithful also [who are] "fornicators, adulterers, effeminate, liers with mankind, thieves, covetous, drunkards, railers, extortioners", and all others who commit deadly sins; from which, with the help of divine grace, they can refrain, and on account of which they are separated from the grace of Christ.

On the fruit of justification, that is, on the merit of good works, and on the nature of that merit

Before men, therefore, who have been justified in this manner,—whether they have preserved uninterruptedly the grace received, or whether they have recovered it when lost,—are to be set the words of the Apostle: "Abound in every good work, knowing that your labor is not in vain in the Lord; for God is not unjust, that he should forget your work, and the love which you have shown in his name"; and, "do not lose your confidence, which hath a great reward." And, for this cause, life eternal is to be proposed to those working well "unto the end", and hoping in God, both as a grace mercifully promised to the sons of God through Jesus Christ, and as a reward which is according to the promise of God himself, to be faithfully rendered to their good works and merits. For this is that "crown of justice" which the Apostle declared was, after his "fight" and "course, laid up for him, to be rendered to him by the just Judge, and not only to him,

but also to all that love his coming." For, whereas Jesus Christ himself
continually infuses his virtue into the said justified,—as the head into the
members, and the vine into the branches,—and this virtue always precedes
and accompanies and follows their good works, which without it could not
in any wise be pleasing and meritorious before God,—we must believe that
nothing further is wanting to the justified, to prevent their being accounted
to have, by those very works which have been done in God, fully satisfied
the divine law according to the state of this life, and to have truly merited
eternal life, to be obtained also in its (due) time, if so be, however, that
they depart in grace: seeing that Christ, our Saviour, saith: "If any one
shall drink of the water that I will give him, he shall not thirst forever; but
it shall become in him a fountain of water springing up unto life everlasting." Thus, neither is our own justice "established as our own" as from
ourselves; nor is the justice of God ignored or repudiated: for that justice
which is called ours, because that we are justified from its being inherent
in us, that same is (the justice) of God, because that it is infused into us
of God, through the merit of Christ. Neither is this to be omitted,—that
although, in the sacred writings, so much is attributed to good works, that
Christ promises, that even "he that shall give a drink of cold water to one
of his least ones, shall not lose his reward"; and the Apostle testifies that,
"That which is at present momentary and light of our tribulation, worketh
for us above measure exceedingly an eternal weight of glory"; nevertheless
God forbid that a Christian should either trust or glory in himself, and
not in the Lord, whose bounty towards all men is so great, that he will
have the things which are his own gifts be their merits. And forasmuch as
"in many things we all offend", each one ought to have before his eyes, as
well the severity and judgment, as the mercy and goodness (of God);
neither ought any one "to judge himself, even though he be not conscious
to himself of any thing"; because the whole life of man is to be examined
and judged, not by the judgment of man, but of God, "who will bring to
light the hidden things of darkness, and will make manifest the counsels
of the hearts, and then shall every man have praise from God", who, as it
is written, "will render to every man according to his works."

After this Catholic doctrine on Justification, which whoso receiveth
not faithfully and firmly can not be justified, it hath seemed good to the
holy synod to subjoin these canons, that all may know not only what they
ought to hold and follow, but also what to avoid and shun.

On justification

Canon 1. If any one saith, that man may be justified before God by
his own works, whether done through the teaching of human nature, or
that of the law, without the grace of God through Jesus Christ: let him be
anathema. . . .

Canon 4. If any one saith, that man's free-will moved and excited by God, by assenting to God exciting and calling, nowise co-operates towards disposing and preparing itself for obtaining the grace of Justification; that it can not refuse its consent, if it would, but that, as something inanimate, it does nothing whatever and is merely passive: let him be anathema.

Canon 5. If any one saith, that, since Adam's sin, the free-will of man is lost and extinguished; or, that it is a thing with only a name, yea a name without a reality, a figment, in fine, introduced into the Church by Satan: let him be anathema. . . .

Canon 7. If any one saith, that all works done before Justification, in whatsoever way they be done, are truly sins, or merit the hatred of God; or that the more earnestly one strives to dispose himself for grace, the more grievously he sins: let him be anathema. . . .

Canon 24. If any one saith, that the justice received is not preserved and also increased before God through good works; but that the said works are merely the fruits and signs of Justification obtained, but not a cause of the increase thereof: let him be anathema. . . .

Canon 30. If any one saith, that, after the grace of Justification has been received, to every penitent sinner the guilt is remitted, and the debt of eternal punishment is blotted out in such wise that there remains not any debt of temporal punishment to be discharged either in this world, or in the next in Purgatory, before the entrance to the kingdom of heaven can be opened [to him]: let him be anathema.

Canon 31. If any one saith, that the justified sins when he performs good works with a view to an eternal recompense: let him be anathema.

Canon 32. If any one saith, that the good works of one that is justified are in such manner the gifts of God, that they are not also the good merits of him that is justified; or, that the said justified, by the good works which he performs through the grace of God and the merit of Jesus Christ, whose living member he is, does not truly merit increase of grace, eternal life, and the attainment of that eternal life,—if so be, however, that he depart in grace,—and also an increase of glory: let him be anathema.

49

JAMES ARMINIUS (1560–1609), Professor of Theology at Leyden, Holland, was the central figure in a theological controversy in the Dutch Reformed Church in the first decade of the seventeenth century. Arminius was appointed in the late sixteenth century to answer the attacks on stringent supralapsarian Calvinism then being circulated by Dirck

Coornhert (1522–1590). The supralapsarian position affirmed that God decreed the election of some men and the reprobation of others and then permitted the "fall" as the means by which the divine decree could be carried out. The infralapsarians theorized that God permitted the "fall" and then decreed that some would be elected and others damned. In the process of studying the issues for debate, Arminius was convinced of a less severe Calvinism than he had previously held and as a result was himself attacked by a leader of the supralapsarian school, Franz Gomarus (1563–1641).

The branch of Calvinism known as Arminianism became the dominant theological position in mid-eighteenth-century English theology and in early nineteenth-century American thought. It is noteworthy, however, that later Arminianism diverted sharply from the position of Arminius himself. Arminius was a loyal disciple of Calvin, and he regarded the dominant position of the Dutch Church in his day as heterodox. Later Arminianism stressed the freedom of the will and either recast or neglected the doctrines relating to election and predestination.

In the *Declaration of Sentiments*, Arminius outlined his position on some of the central issues of that day and delivered this statement to the States of Holland in October of 1608.

Declaration of Sentiments*

JAMES ARMINIUS

1. PREDESTINATION

I have hitherto been stating those opinions concerning the article of Predestination [supralapsarian] which are inculcated in our churches and in the University of Leyden, and of which I disapprove. I have at the same time produced my own reasons, why I form such an unfavorable judgment concerning them; and I will now declare my own opinions on this subject, which are of such a description as, according to my views, appear most conformable to the word of God.

1. The First absolute decree of God concerning the salvation of sinful man, is that by which he decreed to appoint his Son, Jesus Christ, for a

* From *The Works of James Arminius, D.D.*, Vol. I, tr. by James Nichols. Buffalo: Derby, Miller and Orton, 1853.

Mediator, Redeemer, Savior, Priest and King, who might destroy sin by his own death, might by his obedience obtain the salvation which had been lost, and might communicate it by his own virtue.

2. The Second precise and absolute decree of God, is that in which he decreed to receive into favor *those who repent and believe,* and, in Christ, for His sake and through Him, to effect the salvation of such penitents and believers as persevered to the end; but to leave in sin, and under wrath, all *impenitent persons and unbelievers,* and to damn them as aliens from Christ.

3. The Third divine decree is that by which God decreed to administer in a *sufficient and efficacious manner* the Means which were necessary for repentance and faith; and to have such administration instituted according to the *Divine Wisdom,* by which God knows what is proper and becoming both to his mercy and his severity, and according to *Divine Justice,* by which He is prepared to adopt whatever his wisdom may prescribe and put it in execution.

4. To these succeeds the Fourth decree, by which God decreed to save and damn certain particular persons. This decree has its foundation in the foreknowledge of God, by which he knew from all eternity those individuals who *would,* through his preventing grace, *believe,* and, through his subsequent grace *would persevere,* according to the before described administration of those means which are suitable and proper for conversion and faith; and, by which foreknowledge, he likewise knew those who *would* not believe and persevere. . . .

2. THE PROVIDENCE OF GOD

I consider *Divine Providence* to be "that solicitous, continued, and universally present inspection and oversight of God, according to which he exercises a general care over the whole world, but evinces a particular concern for all his [intelligent] creatures without any exception, with the design of preserving and governing them in their own essence, qualities, actions, and passions, in a manner that is at once worthy of Himself and suitable to them, to the praise of his name and the salvation of believers. In this definition of Divine Providence, I by no means deprive it of any particle of those properties which agree with it or belong to it; but I declare that it preserves, regulates, governs and directs all things, and that nothing in the world happens fortuitously or by chance. Beside this, I place in subjection to Divine Providence both the *free-will* and even the *actions of a rational creature,* so that nothing can be done without the will of God, not even any of those things which are done in opposition to it; only we must observe a distinction between good actions and evil ones, by saying, that "God both *wills* and *performs* good acts," but that "He only *freely permits* those which are evil." Still farther than this, I very readily grant, that even all actions whatever, concerning evil, that can possibly be devised or invented, may be attributed to Divine Providence—employing solely one caution, "not to conclude from this concession that God is the cause of sin." This I have testified with sufficient clearness, in a certain disputation concerning the Righteousness and Efficacy of Divine Providence concerning things that are evil, which was discussed at Leyden on two different occasions, as a divinity-act, at which I presided. In that disputation, I endeavored to ascribe to God whatever actions concerning sin I could possibly conclude from the scriptures to belong to him; and I proceeded to such a length in my attempt, that some persons thought proper on that account to charge me with having made God the author of sin. The same serious allegation has likewise been often produced against me, from the pulpit, in the city of Amsterdam, on account of those very theses; but with what show of justice such a charge was made, may be evident to any one, from the contents of my written answer to those Thirty-one Articles formerly mentioned, which have been falsely imputed to me, and of which this was one.

3. THE FREE-WILL OF MAN

This is my opinion concerning the Free-will of man: In his primitive condition as he came out of the hands of his Creator, man was endowed with such a portion of knowledge, holiness and power, as enabled him to understand, esteem, consider, will, and to perform The True Good, according to the commandment delivered to him. Yet none of these acts could he do, except through the assistance of Divine Grace. But in his lapsed and sinful state, man is not capable, of and by himself, either to think, to will, or to do that which is really good; but it is necessary for him to be regenerated and renewed in his intellect, affections or will, and in all his powers, by God in Christ through the Holy Spirit, that he may be qualified rightly to understand, esteem, consider, will, and perform whatever is truly good. When he is made a partaker of this regeneration or renovation, I consider that, since he is delivered from sin, he is capable of thinking, willing and doing that which is good, but yet not without the continued aids of Divine Grace.

4. THE GRACE OF GOD

In reference to Divine Grace, I believe, (1.) It is a gratuitous affection by which God is kindly affected towards a miserable sinner, and according to which he, in the first place, gives his Son, "that whosoever believeth in him might have eternal life," and, afterwards, he justifies him in Christ Jesus and for his sake, and adopts him into the right of sons, unto salvation.

(2.) It is an infusion (both into the human understanding and into the will and affections,) of all those gifts of the Holy Spirit which appertain to the regeneration and renewing of man—such as faith, hope, charity, etc.; for, without these gracious gifts, man is not sufficient to think, will, or do any thing that is good. (3.) It is that perpetual assistance and continued aid of the Holy Spirit, according to which He acts upon and excites to good the man who has been already renewed, by infusing into him salutary cogitations, and by inspiring him with good desires, that he may thus actually will whatever is good; and according to which God may then will and work together with man, that man may perform whatever he wills.

In this manner, I ascribe to grace The Commencement, The Continuance And the Consummation of All Good, and to such an extent do I carry its influence, that a man, though already regenerate, can neither conceive, will, nor do any good at all, nor resist any evil temptation, without this preventing and exciting, this following and co-operating grace. From this statement it will clearly appear, that I by no means do injustice to grace, by attributing, as it is reported of me, too much to man's free-will. For the whole controversy reduces itself to the solution of this question, "is the grace of God a certain irresistible force?" That is, the controversy does not relate to those actions or operations which may be ascribed to grace, (for I acknowledge and inculcate as many of these actions or operations as any man ever did,) but it relates solely to the mode of operation, whether it be irresistible or not. With respect to which, I believe, according to the scriptures, that many persons resist the Holy Spirit and reject the grace that is offered.

5. THE PERSEVERANCE OF THE SAINTS

My sentiments respecting the perseverance of the Saints are, that those persons who have been grafted into Christ by true faith, and have thus been make partakers of his life-giving Spirit, possess sufficient powers [or strength] to fight against Satan, sin, the world and their own flesh, and to gain the victory over these enemies—yet not without the assistance of the grace of the same Holy Spirit. Jesus Christ also by his Spirit assists them in all their temptations, and affords them the ready aid of his hand; and, provided they stand prepared for the battle, implore his help, and be not wanting to themselves, Christ preserves them from falling. So that it is not possible for them, by any of the cunning craftiness or power of Satan, to be either seduced or dragged out of the hands of Christ. But I think it is useful and will be quite necessary in our first convention, [or synod] to institute a diligent enquiry from the scriptures, whether it is not possible for some individuals through negligence to desert the commencement of their existence in Christ, to cleave again to the present evil world, to decline from the sound doctrine which was once delivered to them, to lose a good conscience, and to caused Divine grace to be ineffectual.

Though I here openly and ingenuously affirm, I never taught that a true believer can either totally or finally fall away from the faith, and perish; yet I will not conceal, that there are passages of scripture which seem to me to wear this aspect; and those answers to them which I have been permitted to see, are not of such a kind as to approve themselves on all points to my understanding. On the other hand, certain passages are produced for the contrary doctrine [of unconditional perseverance] which are worthy of much consideration.

6. THE ASSURANCE OF SALVATION

With regard to the certainty [or assurance] of salvation, my opinion is, that it is possible for him who believes in Jesus Christ to be certain and persuaded, and, *if his heart condemn him not*, he is now in reality assured, *that he is a Son of God, and stands in the grace of Jesus Christ*. Such a certainty is wrought in the mind, as well by the action of the Holy Spirit inwardly actuating the believer and by the fruits of faith, as from his own conscience, and the testimony of God's Spirit witnessing together with his conscience. I also believe, that it is possible for such a person, with an assured confidence in the grace of God and his mercy in Christ, to depart out of this life, and to appear before the throne of grace, without any anxious fear or terrific dread: and yet this person should constantly pray, *"O Lord, enter not into judgment with thy servant!"*

But, since "God is greater than our hearts, and knoweth all things," and since a man judges not his own self—yea, though a man know nothing by himself, yet is he not thereby justified, but he who judgeth him is the Lord, . . . , I dare not [on this account] place this assurance [or certainty] on an equality with that by which we know *there is a God, and that Christ is the Savior of the world*. Yet it will be proper to make *the extent of the boundaries of this assurance*, a subject of enquiry in our convention.

7. THE PERFECTION OF BELIEVERS IN THIS LIFE

Besides those doctrines on which I have treated, there is now much discussion among us respecting *the perfection of believers, or regenerate persons, in this life*; and it is reported, that I entertain sentiments on this subject, which are very improper, and nearly allied to those of the Pelagians, viz: "that it is possible for the regenerate in this life perfectly to keep God's precepts." To this I reply, though these might have been my sentiments, yet I ought not on this account to be considered a Pelagian, either partly or entirely, provided I had only added that "they could do this *by the Grace of Christ, and by no means without it*." But while I never asserted, that a believer could perfectly keep the precepts of Christ in this life, I never denied it, but always left it as a matter which has still to be decided. For I have contented myself with those sentiments which St. Augustine has expressed on this subject, whose words I have frequently quoted in the University, and have usually subjoined, that I had no addition to make to them.

Augustine says, "four questions may claim our attention on this topic. The first is, was there ever yet a man without sin, one who from the beginning of life to its termination never committed sin? The second, has there ever been, is there now, or can there possibly be, an individual who does not sin, that is, who has attained to such a state of perfection in this life as not to commit sin, but perfectly to fulfill the law of God? The third, is it possible for a man in this life to exist without sin? The fourth, if it be possible for a man to be without sin, why has such an individual never yet been found?" St. Augustine says, "that such a person as is described in the first question never yet lived, or will hereafter be brought into existence, with the exception of Jesus Christ. He does not think, that any man has attained to such perfection in this life as is protrayed in the second question. With regard to the third, he thinks it possible for a man to be without sin, by means of the grace of Christ and free-will. In answer to the fourth, man does not do what it is possible for him by the grace of Christ to perform, either because that which is good escapes his observation, or because in it he places no part of his delight." From this quotation it is apparent, that St. Augustine, one of the most strenuous adversaries of the Pelagian doctrine, retained this sentiment, that "it is possible for a man to live in this world without sin."

Besides this, the same Christian Father says, "Let Pelagius confess, that it is possible for man to be without sin, in no other way than by the grace of Christ, and we will be at peace with each other." The opinion of Pelagius appeared to St. Augustine to be this—"that man could fulfill the law of God by his own proper strength and ability; but with still "greater facility by means of the grace of Christ." I have already most abundantly stated the great distance at which I stand from such a sentiment; in addition to which I now declare, that I account this sentiment of Pelagius to be heretical, and diametrically opposed to these words of Christ, "Without me ye can do nothing:" (John XV, 5). It is likewise very destructive, and inflicts a most grievous wound on the glory of Christ.

8. THE DIVINITY OF THE SON OF GOD

. . . The word "God" . . . signifies, that He has the true Divine Essence; but the word "Son" signifies, that He has the Divine Essence from the Father. On this account, he is correctly denominated both God and the Son of God. But since He cannot be styled the Father, he cannot possibly be said to have the Divine Essence from himself or from no one. Yet much labor is devoted to the purpose of excusing these expressions, by saying, "that when the Son of God in reference to his being God is said to have his essence from himself, that form of speech signifies nothing more, than that the Divine Essence is not derived from any one." But if this be thought to be the most proper mode of action which should be adopted, there will be no depraved or erroneous sentiment which can be uttered that may not thus find a ready excuse. For though God and the Divine Essence do not differ substantially, yet whatever may be predicated of the Divine Essence can by no means be equally predicated of God; because they are distinguished from each other in our mode of framing conceptions, according to which mode all forms of speech ought to be examined, since they are employed only with a design that through them we should receive correct impressions. . . . Therefore, in no way whatever can this phrase, "The Son of God is autotheon," [God of himself," or "in his own right,"] be excused as a correct one, or as having been happily expressed. Nor can that be called a proper form of speech which says, "the Essence of God is common to three persons;" but it is improper, since the Divine Essence is declared to be communicated by one of them to another. . . .

9. THE JUSTIFICATION OF MAN BEFORE GOD

I am not conscious to myself, of having taught or entertained any other sentiments concerning the justification of man before God, than those which are held unanimously by the Reformed and Protestant Churches, and which are in complete agreement with their expressed opinions. . . .

For the present, I will only briefly say, "I believe that sinners are accounted righteous solely by the obedience of Christ; and that the righteousness of Christ is the only meritorious cause on account of which God pardons the sins of believers and reckons them as righteous as if they had perfectly fulfilled the law. But since God imputes the righteousness of Christ to none except believers, I conclude that, in this sense, it may be well and properly said, To a man who believes, Faith is imputed for righteousness through grace, because God hath set forth his Son, Jesus Christ, to be a propitiation, a throne of grace, [or mercy seat] through faith in his blood." Whatever interpretation may be put upon these expressions, none of our divines blames Calvin or considers him to be heterodox on this point; yet my opinion is not so widely different from his as to prevent me from employing the signature of my own hand in subscribing to those things which he has delivered on this subject, in the third book of his Institutes; this I am prepared to do at any time, and to give them my full approval.

Most noble and potent Lords, these are the principle articles, respecting which I have judged it necessary to declare my opinion before this august meeting, in obedience to your commands.

50

THE REMONSTRANCE, also known as "The Five Arminian Articles," was offered in 1610 by the leaders of the Arminian movement as a concise statement of their position. In contrast to the form of Calvinistic theology prevailing in the Dutch Church, the Remonstrants, as the group came to be known, affirmed that Christ died for all men, though only the believers receive the benefit of his death, that grace is not irresistible, that the assertion of the perseverance of the saints is unclear in scripture and a firm affirmation of this doctrine cannot be made. The Remonstrants brought the conflict between the two groups within the Dutch Church into open debate.

The Remonstrance: 1610*

ARTICLE 1

That God, by an eternal, unchangeable purpose in Jesus Christ his Son, before the foundation of the world, hath determined, out of the fallen, sinful race of men, to save in Christ, for Christ's sake, and through Christ, those who, through the grace of the Holy Ghost, shall believe on this his Son Jesus, and shall persevere in this faith and obedience of faith, through this grace, even to the end; and, on the other hand, to leave the incorrigible and unbelieving in sin and under wrath, and to condemn them as alienate from Christ, according to the word of the gospel in John iii.36: 'He that believeth on the Son hath everlasting life: and he that believeth not the Son shall not see life; but the wrath of God abideth on him,' and according to other passages of scripture also.

ARTICLE 2

That, agreeably thereto, Jesus Christ, the Saviour of the world, died for all men and for every man, so that he has obtained for them all, by his death on the cross, redemption and the forgiveness of sins; yet that no one

* From Philip Schaff, The Creeds of Christendom, Vol. III. New York: Harper and Row, Publishers, 1919. Used by permission of Mary L. Schaff.

actually enjoys this forgiveness of sins except the believer, according to the
word of the Gospel of John iii. 16: 'God so loved the world that he gave
his only-begotten Son, that whosoever believeth in him should not perish,
but have everlasting life.' And in the First Epistle of John ii. 2: 'And he
is the propitiation for our sins; and not for ours only, but also for the sins
of the whole world.'

ARTICLE 3

That man has not saving grace of himself, nor of the energy of his
free will, inasmuch as he, in the state of apostasy and sin, can of and by
himself neither think, will, nor do any thing that is truly good (such as
saving Faith eminently is); but that it is needful that he be born again of
God in Christ, through his Holy Spirit, and renewed in understanding,
inclination, or will, and all his powers, in order that he may rightly understand, think, will, and effect what is truly good, according to the Word
of Christ, John xv. 5: 'Without me ye can do nothing.'

ARTICLE 4

That this grace of God is the beginning, continuance, and accomplishment of all good, even to this extent, that the regenerate man himself, without prevenient or assisting, awakening, following and co-operative grace, can
neither think, will, nor do good, nor withstand any temptations to evil;
so that all good deeds or movements, that can be conceived, must be
ascribed to the grace of God in Christ. But as respects the mode of the
operation of this grace, it is not irresistible, inasmuch as it is written concerning many, that they have resisted the Holy Ghost. Acts vii, and elsewhere in many places.

ARTICLE 5

That those who are incorporated into Christ by a true faith, and
have thereby become partakers of his life-giving Spirit, have thereby full
power to strive against Satan, sin, the world, and their own flesh, and to
win the victory; it being well understood that it is ever through the assisting
grace of the Holy Ghost; and that Jesus Christ assists them through his
Spirit in all temptations, extends to them his hand, and if only they are
ready for the conflict, and desire his help, and are not inactive, keeps them
from falling, so that they, by no craft or power of Satan, can be misled nor
plucked out of Christ's hands, according to the Word of Christ, John x.
28: 'Neither shall any man pluck them out of my hand.' But whether they
are capable, through negligence, of forsaking again the first beginnings of

their life in Christ, of again returning to this present evil world, of turning away from the holy doctrine which was delivered them, of losing a good conscience, of becoming devoid of grace, that must be more particularly determined out of the Holy Scripture, before we ourselves can teach it with the full persuasion of our minds.

These Articles, thus set forth and taught, the Remonstrants deem agreeable to the Word of God, tending to edification, and, as regards this argument, sufficient for salvation, so that it is not necessary or edifying to rise higher or to descend deeper.

51 THE SYNOD OF DORT met from November of 1618 to May of 1619 to deal with the Arminian heresy. In addition to the delegates from the Dutch Church, Swiss, English, and other continental clerics attended and condemned the Arminian position bringing about the banishment of the Remonstrant ministers. Though the canons of the Synod of Dort do not express the clearly supralapsarian Calvinism of Franz Gomarus (1563–1641), the assembly marked the temporary victory of strict orthodoxy within the Reformed church.

The Canons of the Synod of Dort[*]

FIRST HEAD OF DOCTRINE

OF DIVINE PREDESTINATION

Article I. As all men have sinned in Adam, lie under the curse, and are obnoxious to eternal death, God would have done no injustice by leaving them all to perish, and delivering them over to condemnation on account of sin, according to the words of the Apostle (Rom. iii. 19), 'that every mouth may be stopped, and all the world may become guilty before God;' (ver. 23) 'for all have sinned, and come short of the glory of God;' and (vi. 23), 'for the wages of sin is death.'

* From Philip Schaff, *The Creeds of Christendom*, Vol. III. New York: Harper and Row Publishers, 1919. Used by permission of Mary L. Schaff.

Article II. But 'in this the love of God was manifested, that he sent his only-begotten Son into the world,' 'that whosoever believeth on him should not perish, but have everlasting life' (1 John iv. 9; John iii. 16).

Article III. And that men may be brought to believe, God mercifully sends the messengers of these most joyful tidings to whom he will, and at what time he pleaseth; by whose ministry men are called to repentance and faith in Christ crucified. 'How then shall they call on him in whom they have not believed? And how shall they believe in him of whom they have not heard? And how shall they hear without a preacher? And how shall they preach, except they be sent?' (Rom. x. 14, 15).

Article IV. The wrath of God abideth upon those who believe not this gospel; but such as receive it, and embrace Jesus the Saviour by a true and living faith, are by him delivered from the wrath of God and from destruction, and have the gift of eternal life conferred upon them.

Article V. The cause or guilt of this unbelief, as well as of all other sins, is nowise in God, but in man himself: whereas faith in Jesus Christ, and salvation through him is the free gift of God, as it is written, 'By grace ye are saved through faith, and that not of yourselves: it is the gift of God' (Eph. ii. 8); and, 'Unto you it is given in the behalf of Christ, not only to believe on him,' etc. (Phil. i. 29).

Article VI. That some receive the gift of faith from God, and others do not receive it, proceeds from God's eternal decree. 'For known unto God are all his works from the beginning of the world' (Acts xv. 18; Eph. i. 11). According to which decree he graciously softens the hearts of the elect, however obstinate, and inclines them to believe; while he leaves the non-elect in his just judgment to their own wickedness and obduracy. And herein is especially displayed the profound, the merciful, and at the same time the righteous discrimination between men, equally involved in ruin; or that decree of *election* and *reprobation*, revealed in the Word of God, which, though men of perverse, impure, and unstable minds wrest it to their own destruction, yet to holy and pious souls affords unspeakable consolation.

Article VII. Election is the unchangeable purpose of God, whereby, before the foundation of the world, he hath, out of mere grace, according to the sovereign good pleasure of his own will, chosen, from the whole human race, which had fallen through their own fault, from their primitive state of rectitude, into sin and destruction, a certain number of persons to redemption in Christ, whom he from eternity appointed the Mediator and head of the elect, and the foundation of salvation.

Article IX. This election was not founded upon foreseen faith, and the obedience of faith, holiness, or any other good quality or disposition in man, as the prerequisite, cause, or condition on which it depended; but men are chosen to faith and to the obedience of faith, holiness, etc. Therefore election is the fountain of every saving good; from which proceed faith, holiness, and the other gifts of salvation, and finally eternal life itself, as its fruits and effects, according to that of the Apostle. 'He hath chosen us [not because we were, but] that we should be holy and without blame before him in love' (Eph. i. 4).

Article X. The good pleasure of God is the sole cause of this gracious election; which doth not consist herein that God, foreseeing all possible qualities of human actions, elected certain of these as a condition of salvation, but that he was pleased out of the common mass of sinners to adopt some certain persons as a peculiar people to himself, as it is written, 'For the children being not yet born, neither having done any good or evil,' etc., 'it was said [namely, to Rebecca] the elder shall serve the younger; as it is written, Jacob have I loved, but Esau have I hated' (Rom. ix. 11–13); and, 'As many as were ordained to eternal life believed' (Acts xiii. 48).

Article XI. And as God himself is most wise, unchangeable, omniscient, and omnipotent, so the election made by him can neither be interrupted nor changed, recalled nor annulled; neither can the elect be cast away, nor their number diminished.

Article XV. What peculiarly tends to illustrate and recommend to us the eternal and unmerited grace of election is the express testimony of sacred scripture, that not all, but some only, are elected, while others are passed by in the eternal decree; whom God, out of his sovereign, most just, irreprehensible and unchangeable good pleasure, hath decreed to leave in the common misery into which they have willfully plunged themselves, and not to bestow upon them saving faith and the grace of conversion; but permitting them in his just judgment to follow their own way; at last, for the declaration of his justice, to condemn and punish them forever, not only on account of their unbelief, but also for all their other sins. And this is the decree of reprobation which by no means makes God the author of sin (the very thought of which is blasphemy), but declares him to be an awful, irreprehensible, and righteous judge and avenger.

SECOND HEAD OF DOCTRINE

OF THE DEATH OF CHRIST, AND THE REDEMPTION OF MEN THEREBY

Article I. God is not only supremely merciful, but also supremely just. And his justice requires (as he hath revealed himself in his Word) that our sins committed against his infinite majesty should be punished, not only with temporal, but with eternal punishments, both in body and soul; which we can not escape, unless satisfaction be made to the justice of God.

Article II. Since, therefore, we are unable to make that satisfaction in our own persons, or to deliver ourselves from the wrath of God, he hath been pleased of his infinite mercy to give his only-begotten Son for our surety, who was made sin, and became a curse for us and in our stead, that he might make satisfaction to divine justice on our behalf.

Article III. The death of the Son of God is the only and most perfect sacrifice and satisfaction for sin; is of infinite worth and value, abundantly sufficient to expiate the sins of the whole world.

Article VI. And, whereas many who are called by the gospel do not repent nor believe in Christ, but perish in unbelief; this is not owing to any defect or insufficiency in the sacrifice offered by Christ upon the cross, but is wholly to be imputed to themselves.

Article VII. But as many as truly believe, and are delivered and saved from sin and destruction through the death of Christ, are indebted for this benefit solely to the grace of God given them in Christ from everlasting, and not to any merit of their own.

Article VIII. For this was the sovereign counsel and most gracious will and purpose of God the Father, that the quickening and saving efficacy of the most precious death of his Son should extend to all the elect, for bestowing upon them alone the gift of justifying faith, thereby to bring them infallibly to salvation: that is, it was the will of God, that Christ by the blood of the cross, whereby he confirmed the new covenant, should effectually redeem out of every people, tribe, nation, and language, all those, and those only, who were from eternity chosen to salvation, and given to him by the Father; that he should confer upon them faith, which, together with all the other saving gifts of the Holy Spirit, he purchased for them by his death; should purge them from all sin, both original and actual, whether committed before or after believing; and having faithfully preserved them even to the end, should at last bring them free from every spot and blemish to the enjoyment of glory in his own presence forever.

Article IX. This purpose proceeding from everlasting love towards the elect, has, from the beginning of the world to this day, been powerfully accomplished, and will, henceforward, still continue to be accomplished, notwithstanding all the ineffectual opposition of the gates of hell; so that the elect in due time may be gathered together into one, and that there never may be wanting a Church composed of believers, the foundation of which is laid in the blood of Christ, which may steadfastly love and faithfully serve him as their Saviour, who, as the bridegroom for his bride, laid down his life for them upon the cross; and which may celebrate his praises here and through all eternity.

THIRD AND FOURTH HEADS OF DOCTRINE

OF THE CORRUPTION OF MAN, HIS CONVERSION TO GOD, AND THE MANNER THEREOF

Article I. Man was originally formed after the image of God. His understanding was adorned with a true and saving knowledge of his Creator, and of spirtual things: his heart and will were upright, all his affections pure, and the whole Man was holy; but revolting from God by the instigation of the devil, and abusing the freedom of his own will, he forfeited these excellent gifts, and on the contrary entailed on himself blindness of mind, horrible darkness, vanity, and perverseness of judgment; became wicked, rebellious, and obdurate in heart and will, and impure in [all] his affections.

Article II. Man after the fall begat children in his own likeness. A corrupt stock produced a corrupt offspring. Hence all the posterity of Adam, Christ only excepted, have derived corruption from their original parent, not by imitation, as the Pelagians of old asserted, but by the propagation of a vicious nature [in consequence of a just judgment of God].

Article III. Therefore all men are conceived in sin, and are by nature children of wrath, incapable of any saving good, prone to evil, dead in sin, and in bondage thereto; and, without the regenerating grace of the Holy Spirit, they are neither able nor willing to return to God, to reform the depravity of their nature, nor to dispose themselves to reformation.

Article IV. There remain, however, in man since the fall, the glimmerings of natural light, whereby he retains some knowledge of God, of natural things, and of the difference between good and evil, and discovers some regard for virtue, good order in society, and for maintaining an orderly external deportment. But so far is this light of nature from being sufficient to bring him to a saving knowledge of God, and to true conversion, that he is incapable of using it aright even in things natural and civil. Nay farther, this light, such as it is, man in various ways renders wholly polluted, and holds it [back] in unrighteousness; by doing which he becomes inexcusable before God.

Article IX. It is not the fault of the gospel, nor of Christ offered therein, nor of God, who calls men by the gospel, and confers upon them various gifts, that those who are called by the ministry of the Word refuse to come and be converted. The fault lies in themselves; some of whom when called, regardless of their danger, reject the Word of life; others, though they receive it, suffer it not to make a lasting impression on their heart; therefore, their joy, arising only from a temporary faith, soon vanishes, and they fall away; while others choke the seed of the Word by perplexing cares and the pleasures of this world, and produce no fruit. This our Saviour teaches in the parable of the sower (Matt. xiii.).

Article X. But that others who are called by the gospel obey the call and are converted, is not to be ascribed to the proper exercise of free-will, whereby one distinguishes himself above others equally furnished with grace sufficient for faith and conversion (as the proud heresy of Pelagius maintains); but it must be wholly ascribed to God, who, as he hath chosen his own from eternity in Christ, so he [calls them effectually in time] confers upon them faith and repentance, rescues them from the power of darkness, and translates them into the kingdom of his own Son, that they may show forth the praises of him who hath called them out of darkness into his marvelous light; and may glory not in themselves but in the Lord, according to the testimony of the Apostles in various places.

Article XI. But when God accomplishes his good pleasure in the elect, or works in them true conversion, he not only causes the gospel to be externally preached to them, and powerfully illuminates their minds by his Holy Spirit, that they may rightly understand and discern the things of the Spirit of God, but by the efficacy of the same regenerating Spirit he pervades the inmost recesses of the man; he opens the closed and softens the hardened heart, and circumcises that which was uncircumcised; infuses new qualities into the will, which, though heretofore dead, he quickens; from being evil, disobedient, and refractory, he renders it good, obedient, and pliable; actuates and strengthens it, that, like a good tree, it may bring forth the fruits of good actions.

Article XIV. Faith is therefore to be considered as the gift of God, not on account of its being offered by God to man, to be accepted or rejected at his pleasure, but because it is in reality conferred, breathed, and infused into him; nor even because God bestows the power or ability to believe, and then expects that man should, by the exercise of his own free will, consent to the terms of salvation, and actually believe in Christ; but because he who works in man both to will and to do, and indeed all things in all, produces both the will to believe and the act of believing also.

Article XVI. But as man by the fall did not cease to be a creature endowed with understanding and will, nor did sin, which pervaded the whole race of mankind, deprive him of the human nature, but brought upon him depravity and spiritual death; so also this grace of regeneration does not treat men as senseless stocks and blocks, nor take away their will and it properties, neither does violence thereto; but spiritually quickens, heals, corrects, and at the same time sweetly and powerfully bends it, that where carnal rebellion and resistance formerly prevailed a ready and sincere spiritual obedience begins to reign; in which the true and spiritual restoration and freedom of our will consist. Wherefore, unless the admirable Author of every good work wrought in us, man could have no hope of recovering from his fall by his own free will, by the abuse of which, in a state of innocence, he plunged himself into ruin.

Article XVII. As the almighty operation of God, whereby he prolongs and supports this our natural life, does not exclude, but requires the use of means, by which God of his infinite mercy and goodness hath chosen to exert his influence; so also the before-mentioned supernatural operation of God, by which we are regenerated, in nowise excludes or subverts the use of the gospel, which the most wise God has ordained to be the seed of regeneration and food of the soul. Wherefore as the Apostles, and the teachers who succeeded them, piously instructed the people concerning this grace of God, to his glory and the abasement of all pride, and in the meantime, however, neglected not to keep them by the sacred precepts of the gospel, in the exercise of the Word, the sacraments and discipline; so, even to this day, be it far from either instructors or instructed to presume to tempt God in the Church by separating what he of his good pleasure hath most intimately joined together. For grace is conferred by means of admonitions; and the more readily we perform our duty, the more eminent usually is this blessing of God working in us, and the more directly is his work advanced; to whom alone all the glory, both of means and their saving fruit and efficacy, is forever due. Amen.

FIFTH HEAD OF DOCTRINE

OF THE PERSEVERANCE OF THE SAINTS

Article I. Whom God calls, according to his purpose, to the communion of his Son our Lord Jesus Christ, and regenerates by the Holy Spirit, he delivers also from the dominion and slavery of sin in this life; though not altogether from the body of sin and from the infirmities of the flesh, so long as they continue in this world.

Article III. By reason of these remains of indwelling sin, and the temptations of sin and of the world, those who are converted could not persevere in a state of grace if left to their own strength. But God is faithful, who having conferred grace, mercifully confirms and powerfully preserves them therein, even to the end.

Article VIII. Thus, it is not in consequence of their own merits or strength, but of God's free mercy, that they do not totally fall from faith and grace, nor continue and perish finally in their backslidings; which, with respect to themselves is not only possible, but would undoubtedly happen; but with respect to God, it is utterly impossible, but would undoubtedly happen; but with respect to God, it is utterly impossible, since his counsel can not be changed, nor his promise fail, neither can the call according to his purpose be revoked, nor the merit, intercession, and preservation of Christ be rendered ineffectual, nor the sealing of the Holy Spirit be frustrated or obliterated.

Article IX. Of this preservation of the elect to salvation, and of their perseverance in the faith, true believers for themselves may and do obtain assurance according to the measure of their faith, whereby they arrive at the certain persuasion that they ever will continue true and living members of the Church; and that they experience forgiveness of sins, and will at last inherit eternal life.

Article XII. This certainty of perseverance, however, is so far from exciting in believers a spirit of pride, or of rendering them carnally secure, that, on the contrary, it is the real source of humility, filial reverence, true piety, patience in every tribulation, fervent prayers, constancy in suffering and in confessing the truth, and of solid rejoicing in God; so that the consideration of this benefit should serve as an incentive to the serious and constant practice of gratitude and good works, as appears from the testimonies of scripture and the examples of the saints.

Article XIII. Neither does renewed confidence of persevering produce licentiousness or a disregard to piety in those who are recovered from backsliding; but it renders them much more careful and solicitous to continue in the ways of the Lord, which he hath ordained, that they who walk therein may maintain an assurance of persevering; lest by abusing his fatherly kindness, God should turn away his gracious countenance from them (to behold which is to the godly dearer than life, the withdrawing whereof is more bitter than death), and they in consequence thereof should fall into more grievous torments of conscience.

Article XIV. And as it hath pleased God, by the preaching of the gospel, to begin this work of grace in us, so he preserves, continues, and perfects it by the hearing and reading of his Word, by meditation thereon, and by the exhortations, threatenings, and promises thereof, as well as by the use of the Sacraments.

Article XV. The carnal mind is unable to comprehend this doctrine of the perseverance of the saints, and the certainty thereof, which God hath most abundantly revealed in his Word, for the glory of his name and the consolation of pious souls, and which he impresses upon the hearts of the faithful. Satan abhors it; the world ridicules it; the ignorant and hypocrite abuse, and heretics oppose it. But the spouse of Christ hath always most tenderly loved and constantly defended it, as an inestimable treasure; and God, against whom neither counsel nor strength can prevail, will dispose her to continue this conduct to the end. Now to This One God, Father, Son, and Holy Spirit Be Honor and Glory Forever. Amen.

52 SHORTLY AFTER HIS ORDINATION in 1728 as a priest in the Church of England, John Wesley (1703–1791), together with his brother Charles and other Oxford students, formed what was derisively called the "Holy Club" to provide the means for developing the Christian life. A preacher of exceptional power, missionary to the New World, a loyal churchman, a friend of Moravian pietists, and a gifted organizer, Wesley gave a quickening to the religious fervor of

eighteenth-century England. As were others in the Church of England during this period, the Wesleyans (Methodists) were strongly, though not exclusively, Arminian in theology.[1] His zeal for the development of the regenerate Christian life and despair at the lack of religious fervor in the church brought, despite Wesley's resistance, a gradual separation of the Methodist Church from the Church of England.

The following sermons, *Free Grace*, and *The Scripture Way of Salvation*, are representative of his theological concerns and his understanding of the Christian life.

A. Free Grace[*]

JOHN WESLEY

"He that spared not his own Son, but delivered him up for us all, how shall he not with him also freely give us all things?"
ROMANS viii. 32.

How freely does God love the world! While we were yet sinners, "Christ died for the ungodly." While we were "dead in sin," God "spared not his own Son, but delivered him up for us all." And how freely with him does he "give us all things!" Verily, FREE GRACE is all in all!

The grace or love of God, whence cometh our salvation, is FREE IN ALL, and FREE FOR ALL.

First. It is free IN ALL to whom it is given. It does not depend on any power or merit in man; no, not in any degree, neither in whole, nor in part. It does not in any wise depend either on the good works or righteousness of the receiver; not on anything he has done, or anything he is. It does not depend on his endeavours. It does not depend on his good tempers, or good desires, or good purposes and intentions; for all these flow from the free grace of God; they are the streams only, not the fountain. They are the fruits of free grace, and not the root. They are not the cause, but the effects of it. Whatsoever, good is in man, or is done by man, God is the author and doer of it. Thus is his grace free in all; that is, no way depending on any power or merit in man, but on God alone, who freely gave us his own Son, and "with him freely giveth us all things."

[*] From John Wesley, *Sermons on Several Occasions*, Vol. II. London: Wesleyan Conference Office, 1865.

[1] See also *Declaration of Sentiments*, Section 49; *The Remonstrance: 1610*, Selection 50; *The Canons of the Synod of Dort*, Selection 51.

But is it free FOR ALL, as well as IN ALL? To this some have answered, "No: it is free only for those whom God hath ordained to life; and they are but a little flock. The greater part of mankind God hath ordained to death; and it is not free for them. Them God hateth; and, therefore, before they were born, decreed they should die eternally. And this he absolutely decreed; because so was his good pleasure; because it was his sovereign will. Accordingly, they are born for this,—to be destroyed body and soul in hell. And they grow up under the irrevocable curse of God, without any possibility of redemption; for what grace God gives, he gives only for this, to increase, not prevent, their damnation."

This is that decree of predestination. But methinks I hear one say, "This is not the predestination which I hold: I hold only the election of grace. What I believe is no more than this,—that God, before the foundation of the world, did elect a certain number of men to be justified, sanctified, and glorified. Now, all these will be saved, and none else; for the rest of mankind God leaves to themselves: so they follow the imaginations of their own hearts, which are only evil continually, and, waxing worse and worse, are at length justly punished with everlasting destruction."

Is this all the predestination which you hold? Consider; perhaps this is not all. Do not you believe God ordained them to this very thing? If so, you believe the whole decree; you hold predestination in the full sense which has been above described. But, it may be, you think you do not. Do not you then believe, God hardens the hearts of them that perish? Do not you believe, he (literally) hardened Pharaoh's heart; and that for this end he raised him up, or created him? Why, this amounts to just the same thing. If you believe Pharaoh, or any one man upon earth, was created for this end,—to be damned,—you hold all that has been said of predestination. And there is no need you should add, that God seconds his decree, which is supposed unchangeable and irresistible, by hardening the hearts of those vessels of wrath whom that decree had before fitted for destruction.

Well, but it may be you do not believe even this; you do not hold any decree of reprobation; you do not think God decrees any man to be damned, nor hardens, irresistibly fits him, for damnation; you only say, "God eternally decreed that all being dead in sin, he would say to some of the dry bones, Live, and to others he would not; that, consequently, these should be made alive, and those abide in death,—these should glorify God by their salvation, and those by their destruction."

Is not this what you mean by "the election of grace?" If it be, I would ask one or two question: Are any who are not thus elected saved? or were any, from the foundation of the world? Is it possible any man should be saved unless he be thus elected? If you say, "No," you are but where you was; you are not got one hair's breadth farther; you still believe, that, in consequence of an unchangeable, irresistible decree of God, the greater part of mankind abide in death, without any possibility of redemption; inasmuch as none can save them but God, and he will not save them. You believe he hath absolutely decreed not to save them; and what is this but decreeing to damn them? It is, in effect, neither more nor less; it comes to the same thing; for if you are dead, and altogether unable to make yourself alive, then, if God has absolutely decreed he will make only others alive, and not you, he hath absolutely decreed your everlasting death; you are absolutely consigned to damnation. So then, though you use softer words than some, you mean the self-same thing; and God's decree concerning the election of grace, according to your account of it, amounts to neither more nor less than what others call "God's decree of reprobation."

Call it therefore by whatever name you please, "election, preterition, predestination, or reprobation," it comes in the end to the same thing. The sense of all is plainly this,—by virtue of an eternal, unchangeable, irresistible decree of God, one part of mankind are infallibly saved, and the rest infallibly damned; it being impossible that any of the former should be damned, or that any of the latter should be saved.

But if this be so, then is all preaching vain. It is needless to them that are elected; for they, whether with preaching or without, will infallibly be saved. Therefore, the end of preaching—to save souls—is void with regard to them. And it is useless to them that are not elected; for they cannot possibly be saved: they, whether with preaching or without, will infallibly be damned. The end of preaching is therefore void with regard to them likewise. So that in either case our preaching is vain, as your hearing is also vain.

This, then, is a plain proof that the doctrine of predestination is not a doctrine of God, because it makes void the ordinance of God; and God is not divided against himself. A second is, that it directly tends to destroy that holiness which is the end of all the ordinances of God. I do not say, none who hold it are holy; (for God is of tender mercy to those who are unavoidably entangled in errors of any kind;) but that the doctrine itself,—that every man is either elected or not elected from eternity, and that the one must inevitably be saved, and the other inevitably damned,—has a manifest tendency to destroy holiness in general; for it wholly takes away those first motives to follow after it, so frequently proposed in scripture, the hope of future reward and fear of punishment, the hope of heaven and fear of hell. That these shall go away into everlasting punishment, and those into life eternal, is no motive to him to struggle for life who believes his lot is cast already; it is not reasonable for him so to do, if he thinks he is unalterably adjudged either to life or death. You will say, "But he knows not whether it is life or death." What then?—this helps not the matter; for if a sick man knows that he must unavoidably die, or unavoidably recover, though he knows not which, it is unreasonable for him to take any physic at all. He might justly say, (and so I have heard some speak, both in bodily sickness and in spiritual,) "If I am ordained to life, I shall live; if to death, I shall die; so I need not trouble myself about it." So directly does this doctrine tend to shut the very gate of holiness in general,—to hinder unholy men from ever approaching thereto, or striving to enter in thereat. . . .

Such blasphemy this, as one would think might make the ears of a Christian to tingle! But there is yet more behind; for just as it honours the Son, so doth this doctrine honour the Father. It destroys all his attributes at once: it overturns both his justice, mercy, and truth; yea it represents the most holy God as worse than the devil; as both more false, more cruel, and more unjust. More *false*; because the devil, liar as he is, hath never said, he willeth all men to be saved: more *unjust*; because the devil cannot, if he would, be guilty of such injustice as you ascribe to God, when you say that God condemned millions of souls to everlasting fire, prepared for the devil and his angels, for continuing in sin, which, for want of that grace *he will not* give them, they cannot avoid: and more *cruel*; because that unhappy spirit "seeketh rest and findeth none;" so that his own restless misery is a kind of temptation to him to tempt others. But God resteth in his high and holy place; so that to suppose him, of his own mere motion, of his pure will and pleasure, happy as he is, to doom his creatures, whether they will or no, to endless misery, is to impute such cruelty to him as we cannot impute even to the great enemy of God and man. It is to represent the most high God (he that hath ears to hear let him hear!) as more cruel, false, and unjust than the devil!

This is the blasphemy clearly contained in *the horrible decree* of predestination! And here I fix my foot. On this I join issue with every assertor of it. You represent God as worse than the devil; more false, more cruel, more unjust. But you say you will prove it by scripture. Hold! What will you prove by scripture? that God is worse than the devil? It cannot be. Whatever that scripture proves, it never can prove this; whatever its true meaning be, this cannot be its true meaning. Do you ask, "What is its true meaning then?" If I say, "I know not," you have gained nothing; for there are many scriptures the true sense whereof neither you nor I shall know till death is swallowed up in victory. But this I know, better it were to say it had no sense at all, than to say it had such a sense as this. It cannot mean, whatever it mean besides, that the God of truth is a liar. Let it mean what it will, it cannot mean that the Judge of all the world is unjust. No scripture can mean that God is not love, or that his mercy is not over all his works; that is, whatever it prove beside, no scripture can prove predestination. . . .

"I will set before the sons of men 'life and death, blessing and cursing.' And the soul that chooseth life shall live, as the soul that chooseth death shall die." This decree, whereby "whom God did foreknow, he did predestinate," was indeed from everlasting; this, whereby all who suffer Christ to make them alive are "elect according to the foreknowledge of God," now standeth fast, even as the moon, and as the faithful witnesses in heaven; and when heaven and earth shall pass away, yet this shall not pass away; for it is as unchangeable and eternal as is the being of God that gave it. This decree yields the strongest encouragement to abound in all good works, and in all holiness; and it is a well-spring of joy, of happiness also, to our great and endless comfort. This is worthy of God; it is every way consistent with all the perfections of his nature. It gives us the noblest view both of his justice, mercy, and truth. To this agrees the whole scope of the Christian Revelation, as well as all the parts thereof. To this Moses and all the Prophets bear witness, and our blessed Lord and all his Apostles. Thus Moses, in the name of his Lord: "I call heaven and earth to record against you this day, that I have set before you life and death, blessing and cursing; therefore choose life, that thou and thy seed may live." Thus Ezekiel: (to cite one Prophet for all:) "The soul that sinneth, it shall die: the son shall not bear" eternally "the iniquity of the father. The righteousness of the righteous shall be upon him, and the wickedness of the wicked shall be upon him." Thus our blessed Lord: "If any man thirst, let him come unto me, and drink." Thus his great Apostle, St. Paul: "God commandeth all men everywhere to repent;"—"all men everywhere;" every man in every place, without any exception either of place or person. Thus St. James: "If any of you lack wisdom, let him ask of God, who giveth to all men liberally, and upbraideth not; and it shall be given him." Thus St. Peter: "The Lord is not willing that any should perish, but that all should come to repentance." And thus St. John: "If any man sin, we have an Advocate with the Father; and he is the propitiation for our sins; and not for ours only, but for the sins of the whole world."

O hear ye this, ye that forget God! Ye cannot charge your death upon him! "Have I any pleasure at all that the wicked should die? saith the Lord God. Repent, and turn from all your transgressions; so iniquity shall not be your ruin. Cast away from you all your transgressions, whereby ye have transgressed,—for why will ye die, O house of Israel? For I have no pleasure in the death of him that dieth, saith the Lord God. Wherefore turn yourselves, and live ye." "As I live, saith the Lord God, I have no pleasure in the death of the wicked.—Turn ye, turn ye from your evil ways; for why will ye die, O house of Israel?"

B. The Scripture Way of Salvation*

JOHN WESLEY

"Ye are saved through faith."
EPH. ii. 8.

Nothing can be more intricate, complex, and hard to be understood, than religion, as it has been often described. And this is not only true concerning the religion of the Heathens, even many of the wisest of them, but concerning the religion of those also who were, in some sense, Christians; yea, and men of great name in the Christian world; men who seemed to be pillars thereof. Yet how easy to be understood, how plain and simple a thing, is the genuine religion of Jesus Christ; provided only that we take it in its native form, just as it is described in the oracles of God! It is exactly suited, by the wise Creator and Governor of the world, to the weak understanding and narrow capacity of man in his present state. How observable is this, both with regard to the end it proposes, and the means to attain that end! The end is, in one word, salvation; the means to attain it, faith.

It is easily discerned, that these two little words, I mean faith and salvation, include the substance of all the Bible, the marrow, as it were, of the whole scripture. So much the more should we take all possible care to avoid all mistake concerning them, and to form a true and accurate judgment concerning both the one and the other.

Let us then seriously inquire,

    I. WHAT IS SALVATION?
    II. WHAT IS THAT FAITH WHEREBY WE ARE SAVED? AND,
    III. HOW WE ARE SAVED BY IT?

I. And, first, let us inquire, What is salvation? The salvation which is here spoken of is not what is frequently understood by that word, the going to heaven, eternal happiness. It is not the soul's going to paradise, termed by our Lord, "Abraham's bosom." It is not a blessing which lies on the other side of death; or, as we usually speak, in the other world. The very words of the text itself put this beyond all question: "Ye are saved." It is not something at a distance: it is a present thing; a blessing which, through the free mercy of God, ye are now in possession of. Nay, the words may be rendered, and that with equal propriety, "Ye have been saved:" so that the salvation which is here spoken of might be extended to the entire work of

---

* From John Wesley, *Sermons on Several Occasions*, Vol. III. London: Wesleyan Conference Office, 1865.

God, from the first dawning of grace in the soul, till it is consummated in glory.

If we take this in its utmost extent, it will include all that is wrought in the soul by what is frequently termed "natural conscience," but more properly, "preventing grace;"—all the drawings of the Father; the desires after God, which, if we yield to them, increase more and more;—all that light wherewith the Son of God "enlighteneth every one that cometh into the world;" showing every man "to do justly, to love mercy, and to walk humbly with his God;"—all the convictions which his Spirit, from time to time, works in every child of man; although it is true, the generality of men stifle them as soon as possible, and after a while forget, or at least deny, that they even had them at all.

But we are at present concerned only with that salvation which the Apostle is directly speaking of. And this consists of two general parts,— justification and sanctification.

Justification is another word for pardon. It is the forgiveness of all our sins; and, what is necessarily implied therein, our acceptance with God. The price whereby this hath been procured for us, (commonly termed "the meritorious cause of our justification,") is the blood and righteousness of Christ; or, to express it a little more clearly, all that Christ hath done and suffered for us, till he "poured out his soul for the transgressors." The immediate effects of justification are, the peace of God, a "peace that passeth all understanding," and a "rejoicing in hope of the glory of God" "with joy unspeakable and full of glory."

And at the same time that we are justified, yea, in that very moment, sanctification begins. In that instant we are born again, born from above, born of the Spirit: there is a *real* as well as a *relative* change. We are inwardly renewed by the power of God. We feel "the love of God shed abroad in our heart by the Holy Ghost which is given unto us;" producing love to all mankind, and more especially to the children of God; expelling the love of the world, the love of pleasure, of ease, of honour, of money, together with pride, anger, self-will, and every other evil temper; in a word, changing the earthly, sensual, devilish mind, into "the mind which was in Christ Jesus."

How naturally do those who experience such a change imagine that all sin is gone; that it is utterly rooted out of their heart, and has no more any place therein! How easily do they draw that inference, "I feel no sin; therefore, I have *none*: it does not *stir*: therefore, it does not *exist*: it has no *motion*; therefore it has no *Being!*"

But it is seldom long before they are undeceived, finding sin was only suspended, not destroyed. Temptations return, and sin revives; showing it was but stunned before, not dead. They now feel two principles in themselves, plainly contrary to each other; "the flesh lusting against the Spirit;"

nature opposing the grace of God. They cannot deny, that although they still feel power to believe in Christ, and to love God; and although his "Spirit" still "witnesses with their spirits, that they are children of God;" yet they feel in themselves sometimes pride or self-will, sometimes anger or unbelief. They find one or more of these frequently *stirring* in their heart, though not conquering; yea, perhaps, "thrusting sore at them that they may fall;" but the Lord is their help. . . .

From the time of our being born again, the gradual work of sanctification takes place. We are enabled "by the Spirit" to "mortify the deeds of the body," of our evil nature; and as we are more and more dead to sin, we are more and more alive to God. We go on from grace to grace, while we are careful to "abstain from all appearance of evil," and are "zealous of good works," as we have opportunity, doing good to all men; while we walk in all His ordinances blameless, therein worshipping Him in spirit and in truth; while we take up our cross, and deny ourselves every pleasure that does not lead us to God.

It is thus that we wait for entire sanctification; for a full salvation from all our sins,—from pride, self-will, anger, unbelief; or, as the Apostle expresses it, "go on unto perfection." But what is perfection? The word has various senses: here it means perfect love. It is love excluding sin; love filling the heart, taking up the whole capacity of the soul. It is love "rejoicing evermore, praying without ceasing, in every thing giving thanks."

II. But what is that faith through which we are saved. This is the second point to be considered.

Faith, in general, is defined by the Apostle . . . *an evidence, a divine evidence and conviction,* (the word means both,) *of things not seen;* not visible, not perceivable either by sight, or by any other of the external senses. It implies both a supernatural *evidence* of God, and of the things of God; a kind of spiritual *light* exhibited to the soul, and a supernatural *sight* or perception thereof. Accordingly, the scripture speaks of God's giving sometimes light, sometimes a power of discerning it. So St. Paul: "God, who commanded light to shine out of darkness, hath shined in our hearts, to give us the light of the knowledge of the glory of God in the face of Jesus Christ." And elsewhere the same Apostle speaks of "the eyes of" our "understanding being opened." By this two-fold operation of the Holy Spirit, having the eyes of our soul both *opened* and *enlightened,* we see the things which the natural "eye hath not seen, neither the ear heard." We have a prospect of the invisible things of God; we see the *spiritual world,* which is all round about us, and yet no more discerned by our natural faculties than if it had no being. And we see the *eternal world;* piercing through the veil which hangs between time and eternity. Clouds and darkness then rest upon it no more, but we already see the glory which shall be revealed.

Taking the word in a more particular sense, faith is a divine *evidence* and *conviction* not only that "God was in Christ, reconciling the world unto himself," but also that Christ loved *me*, and gave himself for *me*. It is by this faith (whether we term it the *essence*, or rather a *property* thereof) that we *receive Christ*; that we receive him in all his offices, as our Prophet, Priest, and King. It is by this that he is "made of God unto us wisdom, and righteousness, and sanctification, and redemption."

"But is this the *faith of assurance*, or *faith of adherence?*" The scripture mentions no such distinction. The Apostle says, "There is one faith, and one hope of our calling;" one Christian, saving faith; "as there is one Lord," in whom we believe, and "one God and Father of us all." And it is certain, this faith necessarily implies an *assurance* (which is here only another word for *evidence*, it being hard to tell the difference between them) that Christ loved me, and gave himself for me. For "he that believeth" with the true living faith "hath the witness in himself:" "the Spirit witnesseth with his spirit that he is a child of God." "Because he is a son, God hath sent forth the Spirit of his Son into his heart, crying, Abba, Father;" giving him an assurance that he is so, and a childlike confidence in him. But let it be observed, that, in the very nature of the thing, the assurance goes before the confidence. For a man cannot have a childlike confidence in God till he knows he is a child of God. Therefore, confidence, trust, reliance, adherence, or whatever else it be called, is not the first, as some have supposed, but the second, branch or act of faith.

It is by this faith we are saved, justified, and sanctified; taking that word in its highest sense. But how are we justified and sanctified by faith? This is our third head of inquiry. And this being the main point in question, and a point of no ordinary importance, it will not be improper to give it a more distinct and particular consideration.

III. And, first, how are we justified by faith? In what sense is this to be understood? I answer, Faith is the condition, and the only condition, of justification. It is the *condition:* none is justified but he that believes: without faith no man is justified. And it is the *only condition:* this alone is sufficient for justification. Every one that believes is justified, whatever else he has or has not. In other words: no man is justified till he believes; every man when he believes is justified.

"But does not God command us to repent also? Yea, and to 'bring forth fruits meet for repentance?'—to cease, for instance, from doing evil, and learn to do well? And is not both the one and the other of the utmost necessity, insomuch that if we willingly neglect either, we cannot reasonably expect to be justified at all? But if this be so, how can it be said that faith is the only condition of justification?"

God does undoubtedly command us both to repent, and to bring forth fruits meet for repentance; which if we willingly neglect, we cannot reasonably expect to be justified at all: therefore both repentance, and fruits meet for repentance, are, in some sense, necessary to justification. But they are not necessary in the *same sense* with faith, nor in the *same degree*. Not in the *same degree*; for those fruits are only necessary *conditionally*; if there be time and opportunity for them. Otherwise a man may be justified without them, as was the *thief* upon the cross; (if we may call him so; for a late writer has discovered that he was no thief, but a very honest and respectable person!) but he cannot be justified without faith; this is impossible. Likewise, let a man have ever so much repentance, or ever so many of the fruits meet for repentance, yet all this does not at all avail; he is not justified till he believes. But the moment he believes, with or without those fruits, yea, with more or less repentance, he is justified.—Not in the same sense; for repentance and its fruits are only *remotely* necessary; necessary in order to faith; whereas faith is *immediately* and *directly* necessary to justification. It remains, that faith is the only condition which is *immediately* and *proximately* necessary to justification. . . .

I allow there is a repentance consequent upon, as well as a repentance previous to, justification. It is incumbent on all that are justified to be zealous of good works. And these are so necessary, that if a man willingly neglect them, he cannot reasonably expect that he shall ever be sanctified; he cannot grow in grace, in the image of God, the mind which was in Christ Jesus; nay, he cannot retain the grace he has received; he cannot continue in faith, or in the favour of God.

What is the inference we must draw herefrom? Why, that both repentance, rightly understood, and the practice of all good works,—works of piety, as well as works of mercy, (now properly so called, since they spring from faith,) are, in some sense, necessary to sanctification. . . .

Though it be allowed, that both this repentance and its fruits are necessary to full salvation; yet they are not necessary either in the same sense with faith, or in the same degree:—Not in the *same degree*; for these fruits are only necessary *conditionally*, if there be time and opportunity for them; otherwise a man may be sanctified without them. But he cannot be sanctified without faith. Likewise, let a man have ever so much of this repentance, or ever so many good works, yet all this does not at all avail: he is not sanctified till he believes. But the moment he believes, with or without those fruits, yea, with more or less of this repentance, he is sanctified.—Not in the *same sense*; for this repentance and these fruits are only *remotely* necessary,—necessary in order to the continuance of his faith, as well as the increase of it; whereas faith is *immediately* and *directly* necessary to sanctification. It remains, that faith is the only condition which is *immediately* and *proximately* necessary to sanctification. . . .

"But does God work this great work in the soul gradually or instantaneously?" Perhaps it may be gradually wrought in some; I mean in this sense,—they do not advert to the particular moment wherein sin ceases to be. But it is infinitely desirable, were it the will of God, that it should be done instantaneously; that the Lord should destroy sin "by the breath of his mouth," in a moment, in the twinkling of an eye. And so he generally does; a plain fact, of which there is evidence enough to satisfy any unprejudiced person. *Thou* therefore look for it every moment! Look for it in the way above described; in all those *good works* whereunto thou art "created anew in Christ Jesus." There is then no danger: you can be no worse, if you are no better, for that expectation. For were you to be disappointed of your hope, still you lose nothing. But you shall not be disappointed of your hope: it will come, and will not tarry. Look for it then every day, every hour, every moment! Why not this hour, this moment? Certainly you may look for it *now*, if you believe it is by faith. And by this token you may surely know whether you seek it by faith or by works. If by works, you want something to be done *first, before* you are sanctified. You think, I must first *be* or *do* thus or thus. Then you are seeking it by works unto this day. If you seek it by faith, you may expect it *as you are;* and if as you are, then expect it *now*. It is of importance to observe, that there is an inseparable connexion between these three points,—expect it *by faith*, expect it *as you are*; and expect it *now*. To deny one of them, is to deny them all; to allow one, is to allow them all. Do you believe we are sanctified by faith? Be true then to your principle; and look for this blessing just as you are, neither better nor worse; as a poor sinner that has still nothing to pay, nothing to plead, but "Christ died." And if you look for it as you are, then expect it *now*. Stay for nothing: why should you? Christ is ready; and he is all you want. He is waiting for you: he is at the door!

53   THESE TWO ESSAYS of the American Unitarian, William Ellery Channing, (1780–1842), are offered as an indication of the way in which Enlightenment thought affected the interpretation of human ability. Though Channing's rejection of Calvinism was due to many factors, he, like any theologian, was closely related to the intellectual context of his times. In *The Moral Argument Against Calvinism* (1820) he centered his attention on what seemed to him to be the debilitating effects of Calvinism; in *Likeness to God* (1828) he argued for the affinity between God and man.[1]

[1] See also *Unitarian Christianity*, Selection 11.

A. The Moral Argument Against Calvinism*

WILLIAM ELLERY CHANNING

. . . the principal argument against Calvinism, in the General View of Christian Doctrines,[2] is the *moral argument*, or that which is drawn from the inconsistency of the system with the divine perfections. It is plain that a doctrine which contradicts our best ideas of goodness and justice cannot come from the just and good God, or be a true representation of his character. This moral argument has always been powerful to the pulling down of the strongholds of Calvinism. Even in the dark period, when this system was shaped and finished at Geneva, its advocates often writhed under the weight of it; and we cannot but deem it a mark of the progress of society that Calvinists are more and more troubled with the palpable repugnance of their doctrines to God's nature, and accordingly labor to soften and explain them, until in many cases the name only is retained. If the stern reformer of Geneva could lift up his head and hear the mitigated tone in which some of his professed followers dispense his fearful doctrines, we fear that he could not lie down in peace until he had poured out his displeasure on their cowardice and degeneracy. He would tell them, with a frown, that *moderate Calvinism* was a solecism, a contradiction in terms, and would bid them in scorn to join their real friend Arminius. . . .[3]

Calvinists will tell us that because a doctrine opposes our convictions of rectitude it is not necessarily false; that apparent are not always real inconsistencies; that God is an infinite and incomprehensible Being, and not to be tried by our ideas of fitness and morality; that we bring their system to an incompetent tribunal when we submit it to the decision of human reason and conscience; that we are weak judges of what is right and wrong, good and evil, in the Deity; that the happiness of the universe may require an administration of human affairs which is very offensive to limited understanding; that we must follow revelation, not reason or moral feeling,

---

* From *The Works of William E. Channing*. Boston: American Unitarian Association, 1891.

2 The words, "General View of Christian Doctrines," refer to a volume published under that title in 1809 which was a compilation of the arguments of a Rev. Robert Fellows against Calvinism. Channing's essay, "Moral Argument Against Calvinism," was a review of that book.

3 James Arminius (1560–1609), a Dutch theologian, proposed a less severe form of Calvinism. See Selection 49.

and must consider doctrines which shock us in revelation as awful mysteries, which are dark through our ignorance, and which time will enlighten. How little, it is added, can man explain or understand God's ways! How inconsistent the miseries of life appear with goodness in the Creator! How prone, too, have men always been to confound good and evil, to call the just unjust! How presumptuous is it in such a being to sit in judgment upon God, and to question the rectitude of the divine administration, because it shocks *his* sense of rectitude! Such we conceive to be a fair statement of the manner in which the Calvinist frequently meets the objection that his system is at war with God's attributes; such the reasoning by which the voice of conscience and nature is stifled, and men are reconciled to doctrines which, if tried by the established principles of morality, would be rejected with horror. On this reasoning we purpose to offer some remarks; and we shall avail ourselves of the opportunities to give our views of *the confidence which is due to our rational and moral faculties in religion.*

That God is infinite, and that man often errs, we affirm as strongly as our Calvinistic brethren. We desire to think humbly of ourselves, and reverently of our Creator. In the strong language of scripture, "We now see through a glass darkly." "We cannot by searching find out God unto perfection. Clouds and darkness are round about him. His judgments are a great deep." God is great and good beyond utterance or thought. We have no disposition to idolize our own powers, or to penetrate the secret counsels of the Deity. But, on the other hand, we think it ungrateful to disparage the powers which our Creator has given us, or to question the certainty or importance of the knowledge which He has seen fit to place within our reach. There is an affected humility, we think, as dangerous as pride. We may rate our faculties too meanly, as well as too boastingly. The worst error in religion, after all, is that of the sceptic, who records triumphantly the weaknesses and wanderings of the human intellect, and maintains that no trust is due to the decisions of this erring reason. We by no means conceive that man's greatest danger springs from pride of understanding, though we think as badly of this vice as other Christians. The history of the church proves that men may trust their faculties too little as well as too much, and that the timidity which shrinks from investigation has injured the mind, and betrayed the interests of Christianity, as much as an irreverent boldness of thought.

It is an important truth, which we apprehend has not been sufficiently developed, that the ultimate reliance of a human being is and must be on his own mind. To confide in God, we must first confide in the faculties by which He is apprehended, and by which the proofs of his existence are weighed. A trust in our ability to distinguish between truth and falsehood is implied in every act of belief; for to question this ability would of necessity unsettle all belief. We cannot take a step in reasoning or action without a secret reliance on our own minds. Religion in particular implies that we have understandings endowed and qualified for the highest employments of intellect. In affirming the existence and perfections of God, we suppose and affirm the existence in ourselves of faculties which correspond to these sublime objects, and which are fitted to discern them. Religion is a conviction and an act of the human soul, so that in denying confidence to the one, we subvert the truth and claims of the other. Nothing is gained to piety by degrading human nature, for in the competency of this nature to know and judge of God all piety has its foundation. Our proneness to err instructs us, indeed, to use our powers with great caution, but not to contemn and neglect them. The occasional abuse of our faculties, be it ever so enormous, does not prove them unfit for their highest end, which is to form clear and consistent views of God. Because our eyes sometimes fail or deceive us, would a wise man pluck them out, or cover them with a bandage, and choose to walk and work in the dark? or, because they cannot distinguish distant objects, can they discern nothing clearly in their proper sphere, and is sight to be pronounced a fallacious guide? Men who, to support a creed, would shake our trust in the calm, deliberate, and distinct decisions of our rational and moral powers, endanger religion more than its open foes, and forge the deadliest weapon for the infidel. . . .

We grant that God is *incomprehensible.* . . . But He is not therefore *unintelligible*; and this distinction we conceive to be important. We do not pretend to know the *whole* nature and properties of God, but still we can form some *clear ideas* of him, and can reason from these ideas as justly as from any other. The truth is, that we cannot be said to comprehend any being whatever, not the simplest plant or animal. All have hidden properties. Our knowledge of all is limited. But have we therefore no distinct ideas of the objects around us, and is all our reasoning about them unworthy of trust? Because God is infinite, his name is not therefore a mere sound. It is a representative of some distinct conceptions of our Creator; and these conceptions are as sure, and important, and as proper materials for the reasoning faculty, as they would be if our views were indefinitely enlarged. . . . we maintain that God's attributes are intelligible, and that we can conceive as truly of his goodness and justice as of these qualities in men. In fact, these qualities are essentially the same in God and man, though differing in degree, in purity, and in extent of operation. We know not and we cannot conceive of any other justice or goodness than we learn from our own nature; and if God have not these, He is altogether unknown to us as a moral being; He offers nothing for esteem and love to rest upon; the objection of the infidel is just, that worship is wasted: "We worship we know not what. . . ."

We have thus endeavored to show that the testimony of our rational and moral faculties against Calvinism is worthy of trust. We know that this reasoning will be met by the question, What, then, becomes of Christianity? for this religion plainly teaches the doctrines you have condemned. Our answer is ready. Christianity contains no such doctrines. Christianity, reason, and conscience are perfectly harmonious on the subject under discussion. Our religion, fairly construed, gives no countenance to that system which has arrogated to itself the distinction of Evangelical. We cannot, however, enter this field at present. We will only say that the general spirit of Christianity affords a very strong presumption, that its records teach no such doctrines as we have opposed. This spirit is love, charity, benevolence. Christianity, we all agree, is designed to manifest God as perfect benevolence, and to bring men to love and imitate him. Now, is it probable that a religion, having this object, gives views of the Supreme Being from which our moral convictions and benevolent sentiments shrink with horror, and which, if made our pattern, would convert us into monsters? It is plain that, were a human parent to form himself on the Universal Father, as described by Calvinism, that is, were he to bring his children into life totally depraved, and then to pursue them with endless punishment, we should charge him with a cruelty not surpassed in the annals of the world; or, were a sovereign to incapacitate his subjects in any way whatever for obeying his laws, and then to torture them in dungeons of perpetual woe, we should say that history records no darker crime. And is it probable that a religion which aims to attract and assimilate us to God, considered as love, should hold him up to us in these heart-withering characters? We may confidently expect to find in such a system the brightest views of the divine nature; and the same objections lie against interpretations of its records, which savor of cruelty and injustice, as lie against the literal sense of passages which ascribe to God bodily wants and organs. Let the scriptures be read with a recollection of the spirit of Christianity, and with that modification of particular texts by this general spirit, which a just criticism requires, and Calvinism would no more enter the mind of the reader than Popery,—we had almost said, than Heathenism. . . .

Calvinism, we are persuaded, is giving place to better views. It has passed its meridian, and is sinking to rise no more. It has to contend with foes more formidable than theologians; with foes from whom it cannot shield itself in mystery and metaphysical subtilties,—we mean with the progress of the human mind, and with the progress of the spirit of the gospel. Society is going forward in intelligence and charity, and of course is leaving the theology of the sixteenth century behind it. We hail this revolution of opinion as a most auspicious event to the Christian cause. We hear much at present of efforts to spread the gospel. But Christianity is gaining more by the removal of degrading errors than it would by armies of missionaries who should carry with them a corrupted form of the religion. We think the decline of Calivinism one of the most encouraging facts in our passing history; for this system, by outraging conscience and reason, tends to array these high faculties against revelation. Its errors are peculiarly mournful, because they relate to the character of God. It darkens and stains his pure nature, spoils his character of its sacredness, loveliness, glory, and thus quenches the central light of the universe, makes existence a curse, and the extinction of it a consummation devoutly to be wished. We now speak of the *peculiarities* of this system, and of their natural influence, when not counteracted, as they always are in a greater or less degree, by better views, derived from the spirit and plain lessons of Christianity.

B. Likeness to God[*]

WILLIAM ELLERY CHANNING

I begin with observing, what all indeed will understand, that the likeness to God, of which I propose to speak, belongs to man's higher or spiritual nature. It has its foundation in the original and essential capacities of the mind. In proportion as these are unfolded by right and vigorous exertion, it is extended and brightened. In proportion as these lie dormant, it is obscured. In proportion as they are perverted and overpowered by the appetites and passions, it is blotted out. In truth, moral evil, if unresisted and habitual, may so blight and lay waste these capacities, that the image of God in man may seem to be wholly destroyed. . . .

It is only in proportion to this likeness that we can enjoy either God or the universe. That God can be known and enjoyed only through sympathy or kindred attributes, is a doctrine which even Gentile philosophy discerned. That the pure in heart can alone see and commune with the pure Divinity, was the sublime instruction of ancient sages as well as of inspired prophets. It is indeed the lesson of daily experience. To understand a great and good being, we must have the seeds of the same excellence. How quickly, by what an instinct, do accordant minds recognize one another! No attraction is so powerful as that which subsists between the truly wise and good; whilst the brightest excellence is lost on those who have nothing congenial in their own breasts. God becomes a real being to us in proportion as his own nature is unfolded within us. To a man who

* From *The Works of William E. Channing*. Boston: American Unitarian Association, 1891.

is growing in the likeness of God, faith begins even here to change into vision. He carries within himself a proof of a Deity, which can only be understood by experience. He more than believes he feels the Divine presence; and gradually rises to an intercourse with his Maker, to which it is not irreverent to apply the name of friendship and intimacy. The Apostle John intended to express this truth, when he tells us that he in whom a principle of divine charity or benevolence has become a habit and life "dwells in God and God in him."

It is plain, too, that likeness to God is the true and only preparation for the enjoyment of the universe. In proportion as we approach and resemble the mind of God, we are brought into harmony with the creation; for in that proportion we possess the principles from which the universe sprung; we carry within ourselves the perfections of which its beauty, magnificence, order, benevolent adaptations, and boundless purposes are the results and manifestations. God unfolds himself in his works to a kindred mind. . . .

I am aware that it may be said that the scriptures, in speaking of man as made in the image of God, and in calling us to imitate him, use bold and figurative language. It may be said that there is danger from too literal an interpretation; that God is an unapproachable being; that I am not warranted in ascribing to man a like nature to the divine; that we and all things illustrate the Creator by contrast, not by resemblance; that religion manifests itself chiefly in convictions and acknowledgements of utter worthlessness; and that to talk of the greatness and divinity of the human soul is to inflate that pride through which Satan fell, and through which man involves himself in that fallen spirit's ruin.

I answer that, to me, scripture and reason hold a different language. In Christianity, particularly, I meet perpetual testimonies to the divinity of human nature. This whole religion expresses an infinite concern of God for the human soul, and teaches that he deems no methods too expensive for its recovery and exaltation. Christianity, with one voice, calls me to turn my regards and care to the spirit within me, as of more worth than the whole outward world. It calls us to "be perfect as our Father in heaven is perfect;" and everywhere, in the sublimity of its precepts, it implies and recognizes the sublime capacities of the being to whom they are addressed. It assures us that human virtue is "in the sight of God of great price," and speaks of the return of a human being to virtue as an event which increases the joy of heaven. In the New Testament, Jesus Christ, the Son of God, the brightness of his glory, the express and unsullied image of the Divinity, is seen mingling with men as a friend and brother, offering himself as their example, and promising to his true followers a share in all his splendors and joys. In the New Testament God is said to communicate his own spirit and all his fulness to the human soul. In the New Testament man is exhorted to aspire after "honor, glory, and immortality;" and heaven, a word expressing the nearest approach to God and a divine happiness, is every-where proposed as the end of his being. In truth, the very essence of Christian faith is that we trust in God's mercy as revealed in Jesus Christ, for a state of celestial purity in which we shall grow for ever in the likeness and knowledge and enjoyment of the Infinite Father. Lofty views of the nature of man are bound up and interwoven with the whole Christian system. Say not that these are at war with humility; for who was ever humbler than Jesus, and yet who ever possessed such a consciousness of greatness and divinity? Say not that man's business is to think of his sin and not of his dignity; for great sin implies a great capacity; it is the abuse of a noble nature; and no man can be deeply and rationally contrite but he who feels that in wrong-doing he has resisted a divine voice, and warred against a divine principle in his own soul. I need not, I trust, pursue the argument from revelation. There is an argument from nature and reason which seems to me so convincing, and is at the same time so fitted to explain what I mean by man's possession of a like nature to God, that I shall pass at once to its exposition.

That man has a kindred nature with God, and may bear most important and ennobling relations to him, seems to me to be established by a striking proof. This proof you will understand by considering, for a moment, how we obtain our ideas of God. Whence come the conceptions which we include under that august name? Whence do we derive our knowledge of the attributes and perfections which constitute the Supreme Being? I answer, we derive them from our own souls. The divine attributes are first developed in ourselves, and thence transferred to our Creator. The idea of God, sublime and awful as it is, is the idea of our own spiritual nature, purified and enlarged to infinity. In ourselves are the elements of the Divinity. God, then, does not sustain a figurative resemblance to man. It is the resemblance of a parent to a child, the likeness of a kindred nature.

We call God a Mind. He has revealed himself as a Spirit. But what do we know of mind but through the unfolding of this principle in our own breasts? That unbounded spiritual energy which we call God is conceived by us only through consciousness, through the knowledge of ourselves. We ascribe thought or intelligence to the Deity, as one of his most glorious attributes. And what means this language? These terms we have framed to express operations or faculties of our own souls. The Infinite Light would be for ever hidden from us did not kindred rays dawn and brighten within us. God is another name for human intelligence raised above all error and imperfection, and extended to all possible truth.

The same is true of God's goodness. How do we understand this but by the principle of love implanted in the human breast? Whence is it that this divine attribute is so faintly comprehended, but from the feeble development of it in the multitude of men? Who can understand the strength, purity, fulness, and extent of divine philanthropy, but he in whom selfishness has been swallowed up in love?

The same is true of all the moral perfections of the Deity. These are comprehended by us only through our own moral nature. It is conscience within us which, by its approving and condemning voice, interprets to us God's love of virtue and hatred of sin; and without conscience, these glorious conceptions would never have opened on the mind. It is the law-giver in our own breasts which gives us the idea of divine authority, and binds us to obey it. The soul, by its sense of right, or its perception of moral distinctions, is clothed with sovereignty over itself, and through this alone it understands and recognizes the Sovereign of the universe. . . .

It will be said that these various attributes of which I have spoken exist in God in infinite perfection, and that this destroys all affinity between the human and the divine mind. To this I have two replies. In the first place, an attribute by becoming perfect does not part with its essence. Love, wisdom, power, and purity do not change their nature by enlargement. If they did, we should lose the Supreme Being through his very infinity. Our ideas of him would fade away into mere sounds. For example, if wisdom in God, because unbounded, have no affinity with that attribute in man, why apply to him that term? It must signify nothing. Let me ask what we mean when we say that we discern the marks of intelligence in the universe? We mean that we meet there the proofs of a mind like our own. We certainly discern proofs of no other; so that to deny this doctrine would be to deny the evidences of a God, and utterly to subvert the foundations of religious belief. What man can examine the structure of a plant or an animal, and see the adaptation of its parts to each other and to common ends, and not feel that it is the work of an intelligence akin to his own, and that he traces these marks of design by the same spiritual energy in which they had their origin?

But I would offer another answer to this objection, that God's infinity places him beyond the resemblance and approach of man. I affirm, and trust that I do not speak too strongly, that there are traces of infinity in the human mind; and that, in this very respect, it bears a likeness to God. The very conception of infinity is the mark of a nature to which no limit can be prescribed. This thought, indeed, comes to us not so much from abroad as from our own souls. We ascribe this attribute to God, because we possess capacities and wants which only an unbounded being can fill, and because we are conscious of a tendency in spiritual faculties to unlimited expansion. We believe in the divine infinity through something congenial with it in our own breasts. . . .

The views which I have given in this discourse respecting man's participation of the Divine nature, seem to me to receive strong confirmation from the title or relation most frequently applied to God in the New Testament; and I have reserved this as the last corroboration of this doctrine, because, to my own mind, it is singularly affecting. In the New Testament God is made known to us as a Father; and a brighter feature of that book cannot be named. Our worship is to be directed to him as our Father. Our whole religion is to take its character from this view of the Divinity. In this He is to rise always to our minds. And what is it to be a father? It is to communicate one's own nature, to give life to kindred beings; and the highest function of a father is to educate the mind of the child, and to impart to it what is noblest and happiest in his own mind. God is our Father, not merely because He created us, or because He gives us enjoyment; for He created the flower and the insect, yet we call him not their Father. This bond is a spiritual one. This name belongs to God, because He frames spirits like himself, and delights to give them what is most glorious and blessed in his own nature. Accordingly, Christianity is said with special propriety to reveal God as the Father, because it reveals him as sending his Son to cleanse the mind from every stain, and to replenish it for ever with the spirit and moral attributes of its Author. Seperate from God this idea of his creating and training up beings after his own likeness, and you rob him of the paternal character. This relation vanishes, and with it vanishes the glory of the gospel, and the dearest hopes of the human soul.

The greatest use which I would make of the principles laid down in this discourse, is to derive from them just and clear views of the nature of religion. What, then, is religion? I answer, it is not the adoration of a God with whom we have no common properties; of a distinct, foreign, separate being; but of an all-communicating Parent. It recognizes and adores God as a being whom we know through our own souls; who has made man in his own image; who is the perfection of our own spiritual nature; who has sympathies with us as kindred beings; who is near us, not in place only like this all-surrounding atmosphere, but by spiritual influence and love; who looks on us with parental interest, and whose great design it is to communicate to use for ever, and in freer and fuller streams, his own power, goodness, and joy. The conviction of this near and ennobling relation of God to the soul, and of his great purposes towards it, belongs to the very essence of true religion; and true religion manifests itself chiefly and most conspicuously in desires, hopes, and efforts, corresponding to this truth. It desires and seeks supremely the assimilation of the mind to God, or the perpetual unfolding and enlargement of those powers and virtues by which it is constituted his glorious image. The mind, in proportion as it is enlightened and penetrated by true religion, thirsts and labors for a godlike elevation. What else, indeed, can it seek if this good be placed within its reach? If I am capable of receiving and reflecting the intellectual and moral glory of my Creator, what else in comparison shall I desire? Shall I deem a property in the outward universe as the highest good, when I may become partaker of the very mind from which it springs, of the prompting love, the disposing wisdom, the quickening power, through which its order, beauty, and beneficent influences subsist? True religion is known by these high aspirations, hopes, and efforts. And this is the religion which most truly honors God. To honor him is not to tremble before him as an unapproachable sovereign, not to utter barren praise which leaves us as it found us. It is to become what we praise. It is to approach God as an inexhaustible fountain of light, power, and purity. It is to feel the quickening and transforming energy of his perfections. It is to thirst for the growth and invigoration of the divine principle within us. It is to seek the very spirit of God. It is to trust in, to bless, to thank him for that rich grace, mercy, love, which was revealed and proffered by Jesus Christ, and which proposes as its great end the perfection of the human soul.

PART IV

The Church
and the Sacraments

PART IV

The Church
and the Sacraments

54 CYPRIAN, BISHOP OF CARTHAGE (249–258), lived during a
time of severe persecutions. His two major tracts, *The
Lapsed* and *The Unity of the Catholic Church*, were written
after the first wave of persecutions under Decius, probably
in 251. Though Cyprian fled Carthage during this period, his
pastoral counsel was evident in his writing; later, in 258,
he suffered a martyr's death.

The problem facing the church in this period was the
question of the locus of authority in dealing with those who
succumbed to persecution and in resolving doctrinal controversy. Cyprian argued that all bishops shared in the authority that Christ gave to Peter, though the church of Rome
was of pre-eminence. Independent action by any one bishop
would threaten the unity of the church. His plea was for the
recognition that in the episcopate the unity of the church
is to be found.

The Unity of the Catholic Church[*]

CYPRIAN, BISHOP OF CARTHAGE

1. Our Lord solemnly warns us: 'You are the salt of the earth,' and
bids us in our love of good to be not only simple but prudent as well. Accordingly, dearest brethren, what else ought we to do but be on our guard
and watch vigilantly, in order to know the snares of our crafty foe and to
avoid them? Otherwise, after putting on Christ who is the Wisdom of God
the Father, we may be found to have failed in wisdom for the care of our
souls. It is not persecution alone that we ought to fear, nor those forces
that in open warfare range abroad to overthrow and defeat the servants of
God. It is easy enough to be on one's guard when the danger is obvious;
one can stir up one's courage for the fight when the Enemy shows himself
in his true colours. There is more need to fear and beware of the Enemy
when he creeps up secretly, when he beguiles us by a show of peace and
steals forward by those hidden approaches which have earned him the
name of the 'Serpent.' Such is ever his craft: lurking in the dark, he en-

* From St. Cyprian, *The Unity of the Catholic Church*, tr. by Maurice Bevenot,
S.J. Westminster, Maryland: The Newman Press; London: Longmans, Green and
Co. Ltd., 1957.

snares men by trickery. That was how at the very beginning of the world he deceived and by lying words of flattery beguiled the unguarded credulity of a simple soul; that was how he tried to tempt Our Lord Himself, approaching Him in disguise, as though he could once more creep upon his victim and deceive Him. But he was recognized and beaten back, and he was defeated precisely through being detected and unmasked.

2. Here we are given an example how to break company with the 'old man,' how to follow in the steps of Christ to victory, so that we may not carelessly stumble again into the snare of death, but being alive to the danger, hold fast to the immortality given us. And how can we hold fast to immortality unless we observe those commandments of Christ by which death is defeated and conquered? He Himself assures us: 'If thou wilt attain to life, keep the commandments'; and again: 'If ye do what I command you, I call you no longer servants but friends.' He says that it is those who so act that are strong and firm; it is they that are founded in massive security upon a rock, they that are established in unshakable solidity, proof against all the storms and hurricanes of the world. 'Him that heareth my words and doeth them,' He says, 'I will liken to the wise man who built his house upon the rock. The rain fell, the floods rose, the winds came and they crashed against that house: but it fell not. For it was founded upon the rock.'[1]

We must therefore carry out His words: whatsoever He taught and did, that must we learn and do ourselves. Indeed how can a man say he believes in Christ if he does not do what Christ commanded him to do? Or how shall a man who when under command will not keep faith, hope to receive the reward of faith? He who does not keep to the true way of salvation will inevitably falter and stray; caught up by some gust of error, he will be tossed about like windswept dust; walk as he may, he will make no advance towards his salvation. . . .

3. However, we must not only beware of all that is obvious and unmistakable, but also of all that can deceive by fraud and cunning. What could be more clever and cunning than the Enemy's moves after being unmasked and worsted by Christ's coming? Light had come to the gentiles and the lamp of salvation was shining for the deliverance of mankind, so that the deaf began to hearken to the Spirit's call of grace, the blind to open their eyes upon the Lord, the sick to recover their health unto eternity, the lame to make speed to the Church, and the dumb to raise their voice aloud in prayer. Thereupon the Enemy, seeing his idols abandoned and his temples and haunts deserted by the ever growing numbers of the faithful, devised a fresh deceit, using the Christian name itself to mislead the unwary. He invented heresies and schisms so as to undermine the faith, to corrupt the truth, to sunder our unity. Those whom he has failed to

[1] Matthew 7:24 ff.

keep in the blindness of their old ways he beguiles, and leads them up a new road of illusion. He snatches away people from within the Church herself, and while they think that coming close to the light they have now done with the night of the world, he plunges them unexpectedly into darkness of another kind. They still call themselves Christians after abandoning the Gospel of Christ and the observance of His law; though walking in darkness they think they still enjoy the light. The Enemy cajoles and deceives them; as the Apostle says, he transforms himself into an angel of light, and primes his servants to act as the servants of justice, to call the night day, and damnation salvation, to teach recklessness under the pretext of hope, disbelief under colour of the faith, Antichrist under the name of Christ, so that by lies that have all the appearance of truth, they undermine the truth with trickery. All this has come about, dearest brethren, because men do not go back to the origin of [the Christian] realities, because they do not look for their source, nor keep to the teaching of their heavenly Master.

4. But if anyone considers those things carefully, he will need no long discourse or arguments. The proof is simple and convincing, being summed up in a matter of fact. The Lord says to Peter: 'I say to thee, that thou art Peter and upon this rock I will build my Church, and the gates of hell shall not overcome it. I will give to thee the keys of the kingdom of heaven. And what thou shalt bind upon earth shall be bound also in heaven, and whatsoever thou shalt loose on earth shall be loosed also in heaven.'[2]

1st EDITION

[And He says to him again after the resurrection: 'Feed my sheep.' It is on him that He builds the Church, and to him that He entrusts the sheep to feed. And although He assigns a like power to all the Apostles, yet He founded a single Chair, thus establishing by His own authority the source and hallmark of the [Church's] oneness. No doubt the others were all that Peter was, but a primacy is given to Peter, and it is [thus] made clear that there is but one Church and one Chair. So too, even if they are all shepherds, we are shown but one flock which is to be fed by all the Apostles in common accord. If a man does not hold fast to this oneness of Peter, does he imagine the he still holds the faith? If he deserts the Chair of Peter upon whom the Church was built, has he still confidence that he is in the Church?]

[2] Matthew 16:18 ff. [editor. Historians have frequently urged that the "1st Edition" text of Chapter 4 is the original and the "2nd Edition" text is Cyprian's revision when confronted by a controversy with Stephen, Bishop of Rome (254–257) who suggested that baptism by heretics was effective if properly performed. Roman Catholic historians have insisted that if the revision was done by Cyprian, it does not alter the implicit recognition in the church of the primacy of the See of Peter.]

2nd EDITION

[It is on one man that He builds the Church, and although He assigns a like power to all the Apostles after His resurrection, saying: 'As the Father hath sent me, I also send you. . . . Receive ye the Holy Spirit: if you forgive any man his sins, they shall be forgiven him; if you retain any man's, they shall be retained,' yet, in order that the oneness might be unmistakable, He established by His own authority a source for that oneness having its origin in one man alone. No doubt the other Apostles were all that Peter was, endowed with equal dignity and power, but the start comes from him alone, in order to show that the Church of Christ is unique. Indeed this oneness of the Church is figured in the Canticle of Canticles when the Holy Spirit, speaking in Our Lord's name, says: 'One is my dove, my perfect one: to her mother she is the only one, the darling of her womb.' If a man does not hold fast to this oneness of the Church, does he imagine that he still holds the faith? If he resists and withstands the Church, has he still confidence that he is in the Church, when the blessed Apostle Paul gives us this very teaching and points to the mystery of Oneness saying: 'One body and one Spirit, one hope of your calling, one Lord, one Faith, one Baptism, one God'?

5. Now this oneness we must hold to firmly and insist on—especially we who are bishops and exercise authority in the Church—so as to demonstrate that the episcopal power is one and undivided too. Let none mislead the brethren with a lie, let none corrupt the true content of the faith by a faithless perversion of the truth.]

The authority of the bishops forms a unity, of which each holds his part in its totality. And the Church forms a unity, however far she spreads and multiplies by the progeny of her fecundity; just as the sun's rays are many, yet the light is one, and a tree's branches are many, yet the strength deriving from its sturdy root is one. So too, though many streams flow from a single spring, though its multiplicity seems scattered abroad by the copiousness of its welling waters, yet their oneness abides by reason of their starting point. Cut off one of the sun's rays—the unity of that body permits no [such] division of its light; break off a branch from the tree, it can bud no more; dam off a stream from its source, it dries up below the cut. So too Our Lord's Church is radiant with light and pours her rays over the whole world; but it is one and the same light which is spread everywhere, and the unity of her body suffers no division. She spreads her branches in generous growth over all the earth, she extends her abundant streams ever further; yet one is the head-spring, one the source, one the mother who is prolific in her offspring, generation after generation: of her womb are we born, of her milk are we fed, of her Spirit our souls draw their life-breath. . . .

6. The spouse of Christ cannot be defiled, she is inviolate and chaste; she knows one home alone, in all modesty she keeps faithfully to one only couch. It is she who rescues us for God, she who seals for the kingdom the sons whom she has borne. Whoever breaks with the Church and enters on an adulterous union, cuts himself off from the promises made to the Church; and he who has turned his back on the Church of Christ shall not come to the rewards of Christ: he is an alien, a worldling, an enemy. You cannot have God for your Father if you have not the Church for your mother. If there was escape for anyone who was outside the ark of Noe, there is escape too for one who is found to be outside the Church. Our Lord warns us when He says: *'He that is not with me is against me, and he that gathereth not with me, scattereth.'* Whoever breaks the peace and harmony of Christ acts aganst Christ; whoever gathers elsewhere than in the Church, scatters the Church of Christ. Our Lord says: *'I and the Father are One';* and again, of Father, Son, and Holy Spirit it is written: *And the three are One.* Does anyone think then that this oneness, which derives from the stability of God and is welded together after the celestial pattern, can be sundered in the Church and divided by the clash of discordant wills? If a man does not keep this unity, he is not keeping the law of God; he has lost his faith about Father and Son, he has lost his life and his soul.

7. This holy mystery of oneness, this unbreakable bond of close-knit harmony is portrayed in the Gospel by Our Lord Jesus Christ's coat, which was not divided or cut at all, but when they drew lots for the vesture of Christ to see which of them should put on Christ, it was the whole coat that was won, the garment was acquired unspoiled and undivided. These are the words of Holy Scripture: *Now as to His coat, because it was from the upper part woven throughout without a seam, they said to one another: Let us not divide it, but let us cast lots for it, whose it shall be.*[3] The 'oneness' with which He was clothed came 'from the upper part,' that is, from His Father in heaven, and could in no way be divided by any who came to acquire it: it retained its well-knit wholeness indivisibly. That man cannot possess the garment of Christ who rends and divides the Church of Christ. For this reason, by contrast, when Solomon was dying and his kingdom and people were to be divided, Achias the prophet on meeting king Jeroboam in the field tore his own garment into twelve pieces saying: *Take to thyself ten pieces, for thus saith the Lord: 'Behold I rend the kingdom of Solomon and I will give thee ten sceptres, and two sceptres shall be his for the sake of my servant David and for the sake of Jerusalem the city which I have chosen, . . . that I may place there my name.'* When the

[3] John 19:23 ff.

twelve tribes of Israel were being divided, Achias the prophet divided his own garment. But because Christ's people cannot be divided, His coat, woven compactly as it was throughout, is not divided by those who acquire it; indivisible, woven all of a piece, compact, it shows that we, who have put on Christ, form a people knit together in harmony. By the sacred symbolism of His garment was proclaimed the oneness of the Church.

8. Can anyone then be so criminal and faithless, so mad in his passion for quarrelling, as to believe it possible that the oneness of God, the garment of the Lord, the Church of Christ should be divided, or dare to divide it himself? Christ admonishes and teaches us in His Gospel: 'And they shall be one flock and one shepherd.' And does anyone think that in any one place there can be more than one shepherd or more than one flock? The Apostle Paul too commends this same oneness when he begs and exhorts us: I beseech you brethren by the name of Our Lord Jesus Christ, that you all speak the same thing and that there be no schisms among you; but that you be knit together, having the same mind and the same judgment. And again he says: Supporting one another with love, striving to keep the unity of the Spirit in the bond of peace. Do you think a man can hold his own or survive, when he leaves the Church and sets up a new place and a separate home for himself? Whereas it was said to Rahab, in whom the Church was prefigured: Gather to thyself in thy house thy father and thy mother and thy brethren and all thy father's household, and whosoever shall pass outside through the door of thy house, his blood shall be on his own head. So too the sacred meaning of the Pasch lies essentially in the fact, laid down in Exodus, that the lamb —slain as a type of Christ—should be eaten in one single home. God says the words: 'In one house shall it be eaten, ye shall not cast its flesh outside the house.' The flesh of Christ and the Lord's sacred body cannot be cast outside, nor have believers any other home but the one Church. This home, this dwelling of concord is indicated and foretold by the Holy Spirit when He says in the Psalms: God who maketh those who are of one mind to dwell in a house. In God's house, in the Church of Christ do those of one mind dwell, there they abide in concord and simplicity. . . .

12. Nor let certain people deceive themselves by foolish interpretation of Our Lord's words: 'Wherever two or three are gathered together in my name, I am with them.' Corruptors and false interpreters of the Gospel, they quote the end and ignore what has gone before, repeating part of it and dishonestly suppressing the rest; just as they have cut themselves off from the Church, so they cut up the sense of a single passage. For Our Lord was urging His disciples to unanimity and peace when He said: 'I say to you that if two of you agree on earth concerning anything whatsoever you shall ask, it shall be done for you by my Father who is in heaven. For wherever two or three are gathered together in my name, I am with

them.'—showing that it was not the number but the unanimity of those praying that counted most. 'If two of you,' He said, 'agree on earth': He put unanimity first, He gave the precedence to peace and concord; we must agree together loyally and sincerely—that was what He taught. But what sort of agreement will a man make with another if he is out of agreement with the body of the Church itself and with the brethren as a whole? How can two or three gather together in Christ's name, if they have obviously cut themselves off from Christ and His Gospel? For it is not we who have left them, but they who have left us, and by setting up conventicles in opposition and thus creating new sects and schisms, they have cut themselves off from the source and origin of [the Christian] realities.

No, Our Lord is speaking of His Church; He is telling those who are in the Church, that if they are of one mind, if, as He commanded and bade, even two or three gather and pray in unison, they shall, though but two or three, obtain from God's majesty what they ask for. 'Wherever two or three shall be,' He says, 'I am with them,' that is, with those who are without guile and peaceable, with those who fear God and obey His commands. He said that He would be with a mere 'two or three,' just as once He was with the three youths in the fiery furnace, and because they were guileless before God and persevered in harmony with one another, He refreshed them with a dew-laden breeze in the midst of the encircling flames. So too was He with His two imprisoned Apostles because they were guileless and in harmony; He Himself opened the bars of their prison and set His faithful preachers in the market place once more, to announce the word to the crowds. Therefore when He lays down in His commands: 'Wherever two or three shall be, I am with them,' He does not mean to take men away from the Church which He founded and built Himself, but He condemns the discord of the faithless; and with His own lips He commends concord to His faithful, by making clear that He is with two or three who pray in harmony, rather than with any number of dissenters, and that more can be obtained by the united prayers of a few than by the petitioning of many who are in disagreement.

55 IN HIS TREATISE *On Baptism*, Augustine (354–430) considered the issues that had arisen in the North African churches with the outbreak of the Donatist controversy. The Donatists, led by a schismatic bishop, Donatus of Carthage, insisted on the purity of the church and affirmed the necessity of rebaptism for those who succumbed to persecution and re-ordination for "lapsed" clergy. This raised the question for many, including Augustine, of the validity of original baptism. Augustine contended that the validity of the sacraments did not depend on the character of the clergy, that baptism should not be repeated, but its fruits should be developed in the right kind of community, the Catholic not the Donatist Church. It is this problem that Augustine considered in *On Baptism*, written about 400 A.D.

Augustine's *The City of God* is a work of major scope. It was composed as an apology for Christianity against those who attributed the fall of Rome (410) to the Christians' neglect of Roman gods. The following selections from Books 15 and 19 show Augustine's description of the plight of man, for in this world man is confronted by conflicting loyalties. The members of the City of God are submissive to the will of God; the citizens of the City of the World seek their own ends. Augustine viewed the decay of Roman society as due to the inherent conflict and division in the City of the World. Though this same tension is evident in the visible church, at the Last Judgment the separation between the members of the two cities will occur. This work was completed about 425 A.D., fifteen years after the sack of Rome by Aleric the Goth.[1]

A. On Baptism[*]

AUGUSTINE

. . . the sacrament of baptism is what the person possesses who is baptized; and the sacrament of conferring baptism is what he possesses who is ordained. And as the baptized person, if he depart from the unity of the Church, does not thereby lose the sacrament of baptism, so also he who is ordained, if he depart from the unity of the Church, does not lose the

[*] From *Writings in Connection with the Donatist Controversy*, tr. by J. R. King, Bk. I. Edinburgh: T. & T. Clark, 1872.

[1] See also, *Letter 120*, Selection 4A; "God—The Eternal Creator," *The City of God*, Selection 4B; *On the Trinity*, Selection 34A; *On the Gospel of John*, Selection 34B; *Letter 217*, Selection 39A; *A Treatise on Rebuke and Grace*, Selection 39B; *Against the Pelagians*, Selection 39C.

sacrament of conferring baptism. For neither sacrament may be wronged. If a sacrament necessarily becomes void in the case of the wicked, both must become void; if it remain valid with the wicked, this must be so with both. If, therefore, the baptism be acknowledged which he could not lose who severed himself from the unity of the Church, that baptism must also be acknowledged which was administered by one who by his secession had not lost the sacrament of conferring baptism. For as those who return to the Church, if they had been baptized before their secession, are not re-baptized, so those who return, having been ordained before their secession, are certainly not ordained again; but either they again exercise their former ministry, if the interests of the Church require it, or if they do not exercise it, at any rate they retain the sacrament of their ordination; and hence it is, that when hands are laid on them, to mark their reconciliation, they are not ranked with the laity. . . . And hence it is clear that they are guilty of impiety who endeavour to rebaptize those who are in Catholic unity; and we act rightly who do not dare to repudiate God's sacraments, even when administered in schism. For in all points in which they think with us, they also are in communion with us, and only are severed from us in those points in which they dissent from us. For contact and disunion are not to be measured by different laws in the case of material or spiritual affinities. For as union of bodies arises from continuity of position, so in the agreement of wills there is a kind of contact between souls. If, there-fore, a man who has severed himself from unity wishes to do anything different from that which had been impressed on him while in the state of unity, in this point he does sever himself, and is no longer a part of the united whole; but wherever he desires to conduct himself as is customary in the state of unity, in which he himself learned and received the lessons which he seeks to follow, in these points he remains a member, and is united to the corporate whole. . . .

And so the Donatists in some matters are with us; in some matters have gone out from us. Accordingly, those things wherein they agree with us we forbid them not to do; but in those things in which they differ from us, we earnestly endeavour that they should come and receive them from us, or return and recover them, as the case may be. We do not therefore say to them, "Abstain from giving baptism," but "Abstain from giving it in schism." Nor do we say to those whom we see them on the point of baptizing, "Do not receive the baptism," but "Do not receive it in schism." For if any one were compelled by urgent necessity, being unable to find a Catholic from whom to receive baptism, and so, while preserving Catho-lic peace in his heart, should receive from one without the pale of Catholic unity the sacrament which he was intending to receive within its pale, this man, should he forthwith depart this life, we deem to be none other than a Catholic. But if he should be delivered from the death of the body, on his restoring himself in bodily presence to that Catholic congregation from which in heart he had never departed, so far from blaming his conduct, we should praise it with the greatest truth and confidence; because he trusted that God was present to his heart, while he was striving to preserve unity, and was unwilling to depart this life without the sacrament of holy baptism, which he knew to be of God, and not of men, wherever he might find it. But if any one who has it in his power to receive baptism within the Catholic Church prefers, from some perversity of mind, to be baptized in schism, even if he afterwards bethinks himself to come to the Catholic Church, because he is assured that there that sacrament will profit him, which can indeed be received but cannot profit elsewhere, beyond all question he is perverse, and guilty of sin, and that the more flagrant in proportion as it was committed wilfully. For that he entertains no doubt that the sacrament is rightly received in the Church, is proved by his conviction that it is there that he must look for profit even from what he has received elsewhere. . . .

There are two propositions, moreover, which we affirm,—that baptism exists in the Catholic Church, and that in it alone can it be rightly received,—both of which the Donatists deny. Likewise there are two other propositions which we affirm,—that baptism exists among the Donatists, but that with them it is not rightly received,—of which two they strenuously confirm the former, that baptism exists with them; but they are unwilling to allow the latter, that in their Church it cannot be rightly received. Of these four propositions, three are peculiar to us; in one we both agree. For that baptism exists in the Catholic Church, that it is rightly received there, and that it is not rightly received among the Donatists, are assertions made only by ourselves; but that baptism exists also among the Donatists, is asserted by them and allowed by us. If any one, therefore, is desirous of being baptized, and is already convinced that he ought to choose our Church as a medium for Christian salvation, and that the baptism of Christ is only profitable in it, even when it has been received elsewhere, but yet wishes to be baptized in the schism of Donatus, because not they only, nor we only, but both parties alike say that baptism exists with them, let him pause and look to the other three points. For if he has made up his mind to follow us in the points which they deny, though he prefers what both of us acknowledge to what only we assert, it is enough for our purpose that he prefers what they do not affirm and we alone assert, to what they alone assert. That baptism exists in the Catholic Church, we assert and they deny. That it is rightly received in the Catholic Church, we assert and they deny. That it is not rightly received in the schism of Donatus, we assert and they deny. As, therefore, he is the more ready to believe what we alone assert should be believed, so let him be the more ready to do what we alone declare should be done. But let him believe more firmly, if he be so disposed, what both parties assert should be believed, than what we alone maintain. For he is inclined to believe more firmly that the baptism of Christ exists in the schism of Donatus, because that is acknowledged by both of us, than that is exists in the Catholic Church, an assertion made alone by the Catholics. But again, he is more ready to believe that the baptism of Christ exists also with us, as we alone assert, than that it does not exist with us, as they alone assert. For he has already determined and is fully convinced, that where we differ, our authority is to be preferred to theirs. So that he is more ready to believe what we alone assert, that baptism is rightly received with us, than that it is not rightly so received, since that rests only on their assertion. And, by the same rule, he is more ready to believe what we alone assert, that it is not rightly received with them, than as they alone assert, that it is rightly so received. He finds, therefore, that his confidence in being baptized among the Donatists is somewhat profitless, seeing that, though we both acknowledge that baptism exists with them, yet we do not both declare that it ought to be received from them. But he has made up his mind to cling rather to us in matters where we disagree. Let him therefore feel confidence in receiving baptism in our communion, where he is assured that it both exists and is rightly received; and let him not receive it in a communion, where those whose opinion he has determined to follow acknowledge indeed that it exists, but say that it cannot rightly be received. Nay, even if he should hold it to be a doubtful question, whether or no it is impossible for that to be rightly received among the Donatists which he is assured can rightly be received in the Catholic Church, he would commit a grievous sin, in matters concerning the salvation of his soul, in the mere fact of preferring uncertainty to certainty. At any rate, he must be quite sure that a man can be rightly baptized in the Catholic Church, from the mere fact that he has determined to come over to it, even if he be baptized elsewhere. But let him at least acknowledge it to be matter of uncertainty whether a man be not improperly baptized among the Donatists, when he finds this asserted by those whose opinion he is convinced should be preferred to theirs; and, preferring certainty to uncertainty, let him be baptized here, where he has good grounds for being assured that it is rightly done, in the fact that when he thought of doing it elsewhere, he had still determined that he ought afterwards to come over to this side.

B. The City of God*

AUGUSTINE

Of the bliss of Paradise, of Paradise itself, and of the life of our first parents there, and of their sin and punishment, many have thought much, spoken much, written much. We ourselves, too, have spoken of these things in the foregoing books, and have written either what we read in the Holy Scriptures, or what we could reasonably deduce from them. And were we to enter into a more detailed investigation of these matters, an endless number of endless questions would arise, which would involve us in a larger work than the present occasion admits. We cannot be expected to find room for replying to every question that may be started by unoccupied and captious men, who are ever more ready to ask questions than capable of understanding the answer. Yet I trust we have already done justice to these great and difficult questions regarding the beginning of the world, or of the soul, or of the human race itself. This race we have distributed into two parts, the one consisting of those who live according to man, the other of those who live according to God. And these we also mystically call the two cities, or the two communities of men, of which the one is predestined to reign eternally with God, and the other to suffer eternal punishment with the devil. This, however, is their end, and of it we are to speak afterwards. At present, as we have said enough about their origin, whether among the angels, whose numbers we know not, or in the two first human beings, it seems suitable to attempt an account of their career, from the time when our two first parents began to propagate the race until all human generation shall cease. For this whole time or worldage, in which the dying give place and those who are born succeed, is the career of these two cities concerning which we treat.

Of these two first parents of the human race, then, Cain was the first-born, and he belonged to the city of men; after him was born Abel, who belonged to the city of God. For as in the individual the truth of the apostle's statement is discerned, "that is not first which is spiritual, but that which is natural, and afterward that which is spiritual," whence it comes to pass that each man, being derived from a condemned stock, is first of all born of Adam evil and carnal, and becomes good and spiritual only afterwards, when he is grafted into Christ by regeneration: so was it in the human race as a whole. When these two cities began to run their course by a series of deaths and births, the citizen of this world was the first-born,

* From *The City of God*, Vol. II., tr. by Marcus Dods. Edinburgh: T. & T. Clark, 1872.

and after him the stranger in this world, the citizen of the city of God, predestinated by grace, elected by grace, by grace a stranger below, and by grace a citizen above. By grace—for so far as regards himself he is sprung from the same mass, all of which is condemned in its origin: but God, like a potter (for this comparison is introduced by the apostle judiciously, and not without thought), of the same lump made one vessel to honor, another to dishonor. But first the vessel to dishonor was made, and after it another to honor. For in each individual, as I have already said, there is first of all that which is reprobate, that from which we must begin, but in which we need not necessarily remain; afterwards is that which is well-approved, to which we may advancing attain, and in which, when we have reached it, we may abide. Not, indeed, that every wicked man shall be good, but that no one will be good who was not first of all wicked; but the sooner any one becomes a good man, the more speedily does he receive this title, and abolish the old name in the new. Accordingly, it is recorded of Cain that he built a city, but Abel, being a sojourner, built none. For the city of the saints is above, although here below it begets citizens, in whom it sojourns till the time of its reign arrives, when it shall gather together all in the day of the resurrection; and then shall the promised kingdom be given to them, in which they shall reign with their Prince, the King of the ages, time without end. . . .

There was indeed on earth, so long at it was needed, a symbol and foreshadowing image of this city, which served the purpose of reminding men that such a city was to be, rather than of making it present; and this image was itself called the holy city, as a symbol of the future city, though not itself the reality. Of this city which served as an image, and of that free city it typified, Paul writes to the Galatians in these terms: "Tell me, ye that desire to be under the law, do ye not hear the law? For it is written, that Abraham had two sons, the one by a bond maid, the other by a free woman. But he who was of the bond woman was born after the flesh, but he of the free woman was by promise. Which things are an allegory: for these are the two covenants; the one from the mount Sinai, which gendereth to bondage, which is Agar. For this Agar is mount Sinai in Arabia, and answereth to Jerusalem which now is, and is in bondage with her children. But Jerusalem which is above is free, which is the mother of us all. For it is written, Rejoice, thou barren that bearest not; break forth and cry, thou that travailest not for the desolate hath many more children than she which hath an husband. Now we, brethren, as Isaac was, are the children of promise. But as then he that was born after the flesh persecuted him that was born after the Spirit, even so it is now. Nevertheless, what saith the scripture? Cast out the bond woman and her son: for the son of the bond woman shall not be heir with the son of the free woman. And we, brethren, are not children of the bond woman, but of the free, in the liberty wherewith Christ hath made us free." This interpretation of the passage, handed down to us with apostolic authority, shows how we ought to understand the scriptures of the two covenants—the old and the new. One portion of the earthly city became an image of the heavenly city, not having a significance of its own, but signifying another city, and therefore serving, or "being in bondage." For it was founded not for its own sake, but to prefigure another city; and this shadow of a city was also itself foreshadowed by another preceding figure. For Sarah's handmaid Agar, and her son, were an image of this image. And as the shadows were to pass away when the full light came, Sarah, the free woman, who prefigured the free city (which again was also prefigured in another way by that shadow of a city Jerusalem), therefore said, "Cast out the bond woman and her son; for the son of the bond woman shall not be heir with my son Isaac," or, as the apostle says, "with the son of the free woman." In the earthly city, then, we find two things—its own obvious presence, and its symbolic presentation of the heavenly city. Now citizens are begotten to the earthly city by nature vitiated by sin, but to the heavenly city by grace freeing nature from sin; whence the former are called "vessels of wrath," the latter "vessels of mercy." And this was typified in the two sons of Abraham—Ishmael, the son of Agar the handmaid, being born according to the flesh, while Isaac was born of the free woman Sarah, according to the promise. Both, indeed, were of Abraham's seed; but the one was begotten by natural law, the other was given by gracious promise. In the one birth, human action is revealed; in the other, a divine kindness comes to light. . . .

But the earthly city, which shall not be everlasting (for it will no longer be a city when it has been committed to the extreme penalty), has its good in this world, and rejoices in it with such joy as such things can afford. But as this is not a good which can discharge its devotees of all distresses, this city is often divided against itself by litigations, wars, quarrels, and such victories as are either life-destroying or short-lived. For each part of it that arms against another part of it seeks to triumph over the nations through itself in bondage to vice. If, when it has conquered, it is inflated with pride, its victory is life-destroying; but if it turns its thoughts upon the common casualties of our mortal condition, and is rather anxious concerning the disasters that may befall it than elated with the successes already achieved, this victory, though of a higher kind, is still only short-lived; for it cannot abidingly rule over those whom it has victoriously subjugated. But the things which this city desires cannot justly be said to be evil, for it is itself, in its own kind, better than all other human good. For it desires earthly peace for the sake of enjoying earthly goods, and it makes war in order to attain to this peace; since, if it has conquered, and there remains no one to resist it, it enjoys a peace which it had not while there were opposing parties who contested for the enjoyment of those things which were too small to satisfy both. This peace is purchased by toilsome wars; it is obtained by what they style a glorious victory. Now, when victory remains with the party which had the juster cause, who hesitates to congratulate the victor, and style it a desirable peace? These things, then, are good things, and without doubt the gifts of God. But if they neglect the better things of the heavenly city, which are secured by eternal victory and peace never-ending, and so inordinately covet these present good things that they believe them to be the only desirable things, or love them better than those things which are believed to be better—if this be so, then it is necessary that misery follow and ever increase. . . .

Thus the founder of the earthly city was a fratricide. Overcome with envy, he slew his own brother, a citizen of the eternal city, and a sojourner on earth. So that we cannot be surprised that this first specimen, or, as the Greeks say, archetype of crime, should, long afterwards, find a corresponding crime at the foundation of that city which was destined to reign over so many nations, and be the head of this earthly city of which we speak. For of that city also, as one of their poets has mentioned, "the first walls were stained with a brother's blood," or, as Roman history records, Remus was slain by his brother Romulus. And thus there is no difference between the foundation of this city and of the earthly city, unless it be that Romulus and Remus were both citizens of the earthly city. Both desired to have the glory of founding the Roman republic, but both could not have as much glory as if one only claimed it; for he who wished to have the glory of ruling would certainly rule less if his power were shared by a living consort. In order, therefore, that the whole glory might be enjoyed by one, his consort was removed; and by this crime the empire was made larger indeed, but inferior, while otherwise it would have been less, but better. Now these brothers, Cain and Abel, were not both animated by the same earthly desires, nor did the murderer envy the other because he feared that, by both ruling, his own dominion would be curtailed—for Abel was not solicitous to rule in that city which his brother built—he was moved by that diabolical, envious hatred with which the evil regard the good, for no other reason than because they are good while themselves are evil. For the possession of goodness is by no means diminished by being shared with a partner either permanent or temporarily assumed; on the contrary, the possession of goodness is increased in proportion to the concord and charity of each of those who share it. In short, he who is unwilling to share this possession cannot have it; and he who is most willing to admit others to a share of it will have the greatest abundance to himself. The quarrel, then, between Romulus and Remus shows how the earthly city is divided against itself; that which fell out between Cain and Abel illustrated the hatred that subsists between the two cities, that of God and that of men. The wicked war with the wicked; the good also war with the wicked. But with the good, good men, or at least perfectly good men, cannot war; though, while only going on towards perfection, they war to this extent, that every good man resists others in those points in which he resists himself. And in each individual "the flesh lusteth against the spirit, and the spirit against the flesh." This spiritual lusting, therefore, can be at war with the carnal lust of another man; or carnal lust may be at war with the spiritual desires of another, in some such way as good and wicked men are at war; or, still more certainly, the carnal lusts of two men, good but not yet perfect, contend together, just as the wicked contend with the wicked, until the health of those who are under the treatment of grace attains final victory. . . .

But the families which do not live by faith seek their peace in the earthly advantages of this life; while the families which live by faith look for those eternal blessings which are promised, and use as pilgrims such advantages of time and of earth as do not fascinate and divert them from God, but rather aid them to endure with greater ease, and to keep down the number of those burdens of the corruptible body which weigh upon the soul. Thus the things necessary for this mortal life are used by both kinds of men and families alike, but each has its own peculiar and widely different aim in using them. The earthly city, which does not live by faith, seeks an earthly peace, and the end it proposes, in the well-ordered concord of civic obedience and rule, is the combination of men's wills to attain the things which are helpful to this life. The heavenly city, or rather the part of it which sojourns on earth and lives by faith, makes use of this peace only because it must, until this mortal condition which necessitates it shall pass away. Consequently, so long as it lives like a captive and a stranger in the earthly city, though it has already received the promise of redemption, and the gift of the Spirit as the earnest of it, it makes no scruple to obey the laws of the earthly city, whereby the things necessary for the maintenance of this mortal life are administered; and thus, as this life is common to both cities, so there is a harmony between them in regard to what belongs to it. But, as the earthly city has had some philosophers whose doctrine is condemned by the divine teaching, and who, being deceived either by their own conjectures or by demons, supposed that many gods must be invited to take an interest in human affairs, and assigned to each a separate function and a separate department—to one the body, to another the soul; and in the body itself, to one the head, to another the neck, and each of the other members to one of the gods; and in like manner, in the soul, to one god the natural capacity was assigned, to another education, to another anger, to another lust; and so the various affairs of life were assigned—cattle to one, corn to another, wine to another, oil to another, the woods to another, money to another, navigation to another, wars and victories to another, marriages to another, births and fecundity to another, and other things to other gods: and as the celestial city, on the other hand, knew that one God only was to be worshipped, and that to Him alone was due that service which the Greeks call λατρεία, and which can be given only to a god, it has come to pass that the two cities could not have common laws of religion, and that the heavenly city has been compelled in this matter to dissent, and to become obnoxious to those who think differently, and to stand the brunt of their anger and hatred and persecutions, except in so far as the minds of their enemies have been alarmed by the multitude of the Christians and quelled by the manifest protection of God accorded to them. This heavenly city, then, while it sojourns on earth, calls citizens out of all nations, and gathers together a society of pilgrims of all languages, not scrupling about diversities in the manners, laws, and institutions whereby earthly peace is secured and maintained, but recognizing that, however various these are, they all tend to one and the same end of earthly peace. It therefore is so far from rescinding and abolishing these diversities, that it even preserves and adopts them, so long only as no hindrance to the worship of the one supreme and true God is thus introduced. Even the heavenly city, therefore, while in its state of pilgrimage, avails itself of the peace of earth, and, so far as it can without injuring faith and godliness, desires and maintains a common agreement among men regarding the acquisition of the necessaries of life, and makes this earthly peace bear upon the peace of heaven; for this alone can be truly called and esteemed the peace of the reasonable creatures, consisting as it does in the perfectly ordered and harmonious enjoyment of God and of one another in God. When we shall have reached that peace, this mortal life shall give place to one that is eternal, and our body shall be no more this animal body which by its corruption weighs down the soul, but a spiritual body feeling no want, and in all its members subjected to the will. In its pilgrim state the heavenly city possesses this peace by faith; and by this faith it lives righteously when it refers to the attainment of that peace every good action towards God and man; for the life of the city is a social life.

56

THE DONATION OF CONSTANTINE was probably composed during the latter half of the eighth century. Though it purports to be the bequest of Constantine to Pope Sylvester (314–366) of supremacy over the other patriarchates and the Western provinces, and served to give authority to papal claims during the middle ages, its authenticity was challenged in the fifteenth century by Lorenzo Valla (1405–1457) and other humanist scholars.

The Donation of Constantine[*]

"We—together with all our satraps, and the whole senate and my
nobles, and also all the people subject to the government of glorious
Rome—considered it advisable, that as the Blessed Peter is seen to have
been constituted vicar of the Son of God on the earth, so the Pontiffs
who are the representatives of that same chief of the apostles, should obtain
from us and our empire the power of a supremacy greater than the
clemency of our earthly imperial serenity is seen to have conceded to it,
choosing that same chief of the apostles and his vicars to be our constant
intercessors with God. And to the extent of our earthly imperial power,
we have decreed that his holy Roman church shall be honored with veneration, and that more than our empire and earthly throne the most sacred
seat of the Blessed Peter shall be gloriously exalted, we giving to it power,
and dignity of glory, and vigor, and honor imperial. And we ordain and
decree that he shall have the supremacy as well over the four principal seats,
Alexandria, Antioch, Jerusalem, and Constantinople, as also over all the
churches of God in the whole earth. And the Pontiff, who at the time shall
be at the head of the holy Roman church itself, shall be more exalted
than, and chief over, all the priests of the whole world, and according to his
judgment everything which is provided for the service of God and for the
stability of the faith of Christians is to be administered. *And below:*
§. 1. On the churches of the blessed apostles Peter and Paul, for the providing of the lights, we have conferred landed estates of possessions, and have
enriched them with different objects, and through our sacred imperial
mandate we have granted him of our property in the east as well as in the
west, and even in the northern and the southern quarter; namely, in Judea,
Greece, Asia, Thrace, Africa, and Italy and the various islands; under this
condition indeed, that all shall be administered by the hand of our most
blessed father the supreme Pontiff, Sylvester, and his successors. *And
below:* §. 2. And to our Father, the Blessed Sylvester, supreme Pontiff and
Pope universal, of the city of Rome, and to all the Pontiffs, his successors,
who shall sit in the seat of the Blessed Peter even unto the end of the world,
we by this present do give our imperial Lateran palace, then the diadem,
that is, the crown of our head, and at the same time the tiara and also
the shoulder-band,—that is, the strap that usually surrounds our imperial
neck; and also the purple mantle and scarlet tunic, and all the im-

---

[*] From *The Treatise of Lorenzo Valla on the Donation of Constantine,* tr. by
Christopher B. Coleman. New Haven: Yale University Press, 1922.

perial raiment; and also the same rank as those presiding over the imperial cavalry, conferring also even the imperial scepters, and at the same time all the standards, and banners, and the different ornaments, and all the pomp of our imperial eminence, and the glory of our power. §. 3. We decree moreover, as to the most reverend men, the clergy of different orders who serve that same holy Roman church, that they have that same eminence, distinction, power and excellence, by the glory of which it seems proper for our most illustrious senate to be adorned; that is, that they be made patricians and consuls, and also we have proclaimed that they be decorated with the other imperial dignities. And even as the imperial militia is adorned, so also we decree that the clergy of the holy Roman church be adorned. And even as the imperial power is adorned with different offices, of chamberlains, indeed, and door-keepers, and all the guards, so we wish the holy Roman church also to be decorated. And in order that the pontifical glory may shine forth most fully, we decree this also; that the horses of the clergy of this same holy Roman church be decorated with saddle-cloths and linens, that is, of the whitest color, and that they are to so ride. And even as our senate uses shoes with felt socks, that is, distinguished by white linen, so the clergy also should use them, so that, even as the celestial orders, so also the terrestrial may be adorned to the glory of God. §. 4. Above all things, moreover, we give permission to that same most holy one our Father Sylvester and to his successors, from our edict, that he may make priest whomever he wishes, according to his own pleasure and counsel, and enroll him in the number of the religious clergy [i.e., regular, or monastic, clergy; or, perhaps, the cardinals], let no one whomsoever presume to act in a domineering way in this. §. 5. We also therefore decreed this, that he himself and his successors might use and bear upon their heads—to the praise of God for the honor of the Blessed Peter—the diadem, that is, the crown which we have granted him from our own head, of purest gold and precious gems. But since he himself, the most blessed Pope, did not at all allow that crown of gold to be used over the clerical crown which he wears to the glory of the Blessed Peter, we placed upon his most holy head, with our own hands, a glittering tiara of dazzling white representing the Lord's resurrection, and holding the bridle of his horse, out of reverence for the Blessed Peter, we performed for him the duty of groom, decreeing that all his successors, and they alone, use this same tiara in processions in imitation of our power. §. 6. Wherefore, in order that the supreme pontificate may not deteriorate, but may rather be adorned with glory and power even more than is the dignity of an earthly rule; behold, we give over and relinquish to the aforesaid our most blessed Pontiff, Sylvester, the universal Pope, as well our palace, as has been said, as also the city of Rome, and all the provinces, places and cities of Italy and the western regions, and we decree by this our godlike and pragmatic sanction that they are to be controlled by him and by his successors, and we grant that they shall remain under the law of the holy Roman church. §. 7. Wherefore we have perceived it to be fitting that our empire and the power of our kingdom should be transferred in the regions of the East, and that in the province of Byzantia, in the most fitting place, a city should be built in our name, and that our empire should there be established, for where the supremacy of priests and the head of the Christian religion has been established by the heavenly Emperor, it is not right that there an earthly emperor should have jurisdiction. §. 8. We decree, moreover, that all these things, which through this our sacred imperial [charter] and through other godlike decrees we have established and confirmed, remain inviolate and unshaken unto the end of the world. Wherefore, before the living God who commanded us to reign, and in the face of his terrible judgment, we entreat, through this our imperial sanction, all the emperors our successors, and all the nobles, the satraps also, the most glorious senate, and all the people in the whole world, now and in all times still to come subject to our rule, that no one of them in any way be allowed either to break these [decrees], or in any way overthrow them. If any one, moreover,—which we do not believe—prove a scorner or despiser in this matter, he shall be subject and bound over to eternal damnation, and shall feel the holy ones of God, the chief of the apostles, Peter and Paul, opposed to him in the present and in the future life, and he shall be burned in the lower hell and shall perish with the devil and all the impious. The page, moreover, of this our imperial decree, we, confirming it with our own hands, did place above the venerable body of the Blessed Peter, chief of the apostles. Given at Rome on the third day before the Kalends of April, our master the august Flavius Constantine, for the fourth time, and Gallicanus, most illustrious men, being consuls."

57 THE FOLLOWING LETTER of Gregory VII to Hermann, Bishop of Metz, was written in March of 1081. It served as a justification of Pope Gregory's assertion of papal power in his effort to dethrone Henry IV in 1076. It marks a significant step in the development of papal authority.

A Letter to Hermann, Bishop of Metz*

POPE GREGORY VII

Against those who foolishly say that the Emperor cannot be excommunicated by the Roman Pontiff.

Gregory, Bishop, slave of the slaves of God, to his beloved brother in Christ, Hermann, Bishop of Metz, greeting and apostolic blessing.

We do not doubt that it is by the Divine operation that, as we hear, thou art prepared to undergo troubles and dangers for the defence of the truth. . . . That thou shouldest have asked to be, as it were, aided by our writings and fortified against the folly of those, who with impious tongue babble that the authority of the holy and apostolic see does not suffice to excommunicate King Henry—a man who despises the Christian law, who destroys churches and the Empire and encourages and supports heretics—nor to absolve any man from his oath of fealty to Henry, seems to us hardly necessary in view of the many clear passages on this subject to be found in the pages of the sacred scriptures. . . . For, that we may quote a few sentences out of many, who does not know of the words of our Lord and Savious Jesus Christ in the gospel, 'Thou are Peter, and upon this rock I will build My church; and the gates of hell shall not prevail against it. And I will give unto thee the keys of the kingdom of heaven; and whatsoever thou shalt bind on earth shall be bound in heaven; and whatsoever thou shalt loose on earth shall be loosed in heaven'?[1] Is an exception here made in favour of kings? Or are they not amongst the sheep, whom God's Son committed to blessed Peter? Who, I ask, in view of this universal commission of binding and loosing, considers himself exempt from the power of Peter, except perhaps that unhappy man who will not endure the yoke of the Lord, but submits himself to the service of the devil and refuses to be of the number of Christ's sheep. . . .

The holy fathers, both in general councils and in other of their writings and acts, have called the holy Roman church the universal mother, accepting and maintaining this institution of the divine will, this guarantee of a dispensation to the church, this privilege given and confirmed by the decree of Heaven above all to blessed Peter, the chief of the apostles. And as they accepted its statements in confirmation of the faith and exposition of holy religion, so they received its judgements; agreeing and, as it were

* From R. G. D. Laffan, *Select Documents of European History 800–1492.* New York: Holt, Rinehart & Winston, Inc., 1930. Used by permission of Metheun and Co. Ltd., London, England.

[1] Matthew xvi. 18, 19.

with one spirit and one voice consenting to this—that all greater cases and matters of outstanding importance as well as judgements over all churches ought to be referred to it as to a mother and head, that from it there is no appeal, that its judgements ought not to be, and cannot be, withdrawn or reversed by any one. . . .

Should not an authority established by laymen, even by those ignorant of God, be subordinate to that authority which the providence of Almighty God established for His own honour and in His mercy gave to the world? For His Son is both firmly believed to be God and Man and also held to be the supreme priest, the head of all priests, seated at the right hand of the Father and ever interceding for us. Yet He despised a secular kingdom, whence arises the pride of the sons of this world, and of His own will sought the priesthood of the cross. But who does not know that kings and dukes are the successors of those, who, in ignorance of God, by pride, robbery, perfidy, homicide, in fact by almost every crime, at the instigation of the devil, the prince of this world, have striven with blind avarice and intolerable presumption to dominate their equals, their fellow-men? To whom can such men, when they try to drag down the priests of God to their ways, be more fitly compared than to him who is the head over all the sons of pride—he who tempted the supreme pontiff Himself, the head of all priests, the Son of the Most High, and promised Him all the kingdoms of the earth, saying, 'All these will I give Thee if Thou wilt fall down and worship me'?[2] Who will doubt that Christ's priests are to be held to be fathers and masters of kings and princes and of all the faithful? Is it not clearly pitiful folly if a son tries to subject his father to himself, or a disciple his master, or if any tries to bind with iniquitous bonds him by whom he believes that he can be bound or loosed not only on earth but also in heaven? . . .

Many pontiffs have excommunicated kings or emperors. For, if particular examples of princes be required, the blessed Pope Innocent excommunicated the Emperor Arcadius for consenting to the expulsion of St. John Chrysostom from his see. Another Roman pontiff, Zachary, deposed a king of the Franks, not so much for his misdeeds as because he was unfit for so great power, and in his place set up Pepin, father of the Emperor Charles the Great, releasing all the Franks from the oath of fealty which they had taken to the former king. . . .

Further, every Christian king when he comes to die, as a pitiful suppliant begs the help of a priest, that he may escape hell's prison, that out of darkness he may attain to light, that by God's judgement he may be loosed from the bonds of his sins. What layman—not to mention what priest—in his last hour has ever implored the aid of an earthly king for the salvation of his soul? What king or emperor is able, in virtue of his office,

2 Matthew iv. 9.

to snatch any Christian from the power of the devil by Holy Baptism, to place him amongst the sons of God and fortify him with Holy Unction? And who of them by his own word can make the Body and Blood of the Lord—the greatest thing in the Christian religion? And to which of them has been granted the power to bind and loose in heaven and on earth?—whence it is clearly seen how greatly the priestly dignity excels in power. Or who of them can ordain a clerk in Holy Church, much less depose him for any fault? For in ecclesiastical matters a greater power is needed to depose than to ordain. For bishops can ordain other bishops, but cannot depose them without the authority of the apostolic see. Who, therefore, of even moderate understanding will doubt that priests are above kings? And if kings are to be judged for their sins by priests, by whom can they be more rightly judged than by the Roman pontiff?

In fact any good Christians are much more rightly considered kings than are bad princes. For the former rule themselves strictly, seeking God's glory, while the latter, enemies to themselves, and seeking their own interests not God's, tyrannically oppress others. The former are of the body of the true king, Chirst; the latter, of the devil. . . .

Nor is it surprising that evil prelates are of one mind with an evil king, whom they love and fear, since they have wrongfully obtained honours at his hand. These men simoniacally ordain whom they please and so sell God even for a paltry sum. For as the elect are indissolubly united to their Head, so the reprobate are presistently banded together with him who is the head of evil, especially against the good. Rather than denounce them, we ought to lament for them with tears and weeping, that Almighty God may release them from the snares of Satan, in which they are held captive, and after their perils may bring them some day at last to the knowledge of the truth.

We speak of those kings and emperors, who rule not for God but for themselves, being puffed up by worldly glory. But since it is our duty to exhort all, according to the rank and dignity which they enjoy, under God's guidance we endeavour to provide emperors, kings and other princes with the armour of humility, that they may be able to subdue the waves of the sea[3] and the storms of pride. For we know that earthly glory and the cares of this world usually tempt men to pride, especially rulers, so that neglecting humility and seeking their own glory they ever desire to lord it over their brothers. Wherefore it is well, especially for emperors and kings, that whenever their minds are puffed up and delight in their own glory, they should discover means to humble themselves and should perceive that the cause of their self-satisfaction should be feared above all things. Therefore let them observe how perilous and awful is the imperial or royal dignity, the holders of which are rarely saved, while even those who by God's

[3] Ps. xciii.

mercy do come to salvation are not so honoured in Holy Church by the guidance of the Holy Spirit as are many of the poor. For from the beginning of the world till our own times in all true records we do not find seven emperors or kings whose lives were so conspicuous for piety or so adorned with the power of miracles as those of an innumerable multitude of those who despised this world, even though we believe many of them found mercy in the presence of Almighty God. For what emperor or king was so distinguished for miracles as blessed Martin, Antony and Benedict, not to mention the apostles and martyrs? What emperor or king has raised the dead, healed lepers, given sight to the blind? Holy Church praises and venerates the Emperor Constantine of pious memory, Theodosius and Honorius, Charles and Lewis, as lovers of justice, propogators of the Christian religion, defenders of churches; but it does not declare them to have been glorified by miracles. Further, to how many kings or emperors has Holy Church ordered basilicas or altars to be dedicated, or masses to be celebrated in their honour?

Kings and other princes should fear lest, as they rejoice in their elevation over others in this life, so they will be the more subjected to eternal fires. As it is written: 'Mighty men shall be searched out mightily.'[4] For they will give account to God for as many men as they have had under their rule. And if it is no small labour for a devout person to guard his own soul, how great is the labour of those who rule over many thousands of souls?

Further, if the sentence of Holy Church severely punishes a sinner for killing one man, what of those who for worldly glory send many thousands to death? Such men sometimes with their lips say 'Mea culpa,' because of a great slaughter, but in their hearts they rejoice at the extension of their 'fame.' They do not regret what they have done. Nor are they grieved at having sent their brethren down to Tartarus. As long as they do not repent with their whole heart nor agree to give up what they have acquired or kept through bloodshed, their repentance remains without the true fruit of penitence in God's eyes.

Therefore they should fear and often call to mind what we have said above, that out of the innumerable host of kings in all countries from the beginning of the world, very few are found to have been holy; whereas in one single see—the Roman—of bishops regularly succeeding each other, from the time of blessed Peter the Apostle, nearly one hundred are counted amongst the most holy. And why is this, unless because kings and princes, enticed by vain glory, prefer, as has been said, their own interests to spiritual issues, whereas the bishops of the church, despising vain glory, prefer God's will to earthly interests? The former quickly punish offences against themselves, but calmly tolerate those who sin against God. The latter readily pardon those who sin against themselves, but do not lightly forgive of-

4 Wisdom vi. 6.

fenders against God. The former, too bent on earthly achievements, think little of spiritual ones; the latter, earnestly meditating on heavenly things, despise the things of earth. . . .

Wherefore let those, whom Holy Church, of her own will and careful counsel, not for transitory fame but for the salvation of many, calls to rule or dominion, humbly obey. . . . And so, living humbly and loving God and their neighbour as they ought, they may count on His mercy who said, 'Learn of Me, for I am meek and lowly of heart.'[5] If they have humbly followed His example, they will pass from a servile and transitory kingdom to an eternal kingdom of true liberty.

58 PASCHASIUS RADBERTUS, the abbot of the monastery of Corbie (near Amiens) from 844–853, inaugurated a controversy concerning the Lord's Supper that was to recur during the next four centuries. His essay on the Eucharist presented a position that was similar to, though not precisely the same as, later Roman Catholic dogma enunciated at the Fourth Lateran Council in 1215. Radbertus insisted that the elements of the Eucharist, after consecration by the priest, became the true body and blood of Christ, though, contrary to later statements, he identified the body and blood of Christ in the sacrament with the visible body and blood of Christ on earth. A contemporary member of the same monastery, Ratramnus, developed a position that was in conflict with that of Radbertus (see Selection 59).

The Lord's Body and Blood[*]

PASCHASIUS RADBERTUS

III. 1. A sacrament is anything handed down to us in any divine celebration as a pledge of salvation, when what is visibly done accomplishes

* From *Early Medieval Theology*, Vol. IX, LCC. Tr. George E. McCracken. Published in 1957, The Westminster Press. Used by permission. Also with permission of Student Christian Movement Press, London.

5 Matthew xi. 29.

inwardly something far different, to be taken in a holy sense. They are called sacraments either because they are secret in that in the visible act divinity inwardly accomplishes something secretly through the corporeal appearance, or from the sanctifying consecration, because the Holy Spirit, remaining in the body of Christ, latently accomplishes for the salvation of the faithful all these mystical sacraments under the cover of things visible. By this divine power he teaches the souls of believers about things invisible more than if he visibly revealed what inwardly is effective for salvation: "For we walk by faith and not by sight."

2. Christ's sacraments in the church are baptism and anointing,[1] and the Lord's body and blood, which are called sacraments because under their visible appearance the divine flesh is secretly hallowed through power, so that they are inwardly in truth what they are outwardly believed to be by the power of faith. There is a legal sense of the word "sacrament," that is, an oath, in which after choosing sides each person takes an oath concerning what he has determined by his agreement. This is called a sacrament because secretly invisible faith, through consecration by prayer to God or through something sacred, is grasped, because outwardly by sight or hearing the voice of the one swearing is heard. The birth of Christ, therefore, and all that dispensation of humanity, becomes, as it were, a great sacrament, because in the visible man the divine majesty inwardly for the sake of our consecration worked invisibly those things which came into being secretly by his power. Thus the mystery or sacrament, which is God made man, is rightly so called, but the word "mystērion" is Greek for what has in it a hidden and secret character. It is a sacrament in the divine scriptures wherever the sacred Spirit accomplishes something in them inwardly by speaking. But instructed by the sacrament of the scriptures, we are divinely fed from within, and, being fed, we are instructed to fulfillment of Christ's teaching. In the sacrament of his birth and humanity, however, we are also redeemed unto pardon, and the scriptures are revealed unto understanding, and through it a way is shown to us and power is bestowed on us that we may pass from the condition of servants into that of adopted children. Furthermore, in the sacrament of baptism a door for entering into adoption is opened for believers, that thenceforth in Christ's members, through that same rebirth freed from evil, we may be made one body. In this baptism, of course, and afterward, the Holy Spirit is poured forth upon the soul of the one being reborn, so that the whole church of Christ may be quickened when a single spirit has been received, and it may be made one body. Because as all members of our body are animated and guided by

---

[1] In this sentence "anointing" is part of the baptismal rite. Radbertus recognizes but two sacraments, Baptism and the Eucharist. His contemporary Rabanus Maurus includes with these extreme unction. The list of seven sacraments came to acceptance only with the Scholastics under the influence of Peter Lombard (d. 1164).

one soul, so that from the union of the parts one body results, so the parts of the whole church are guided and animated by one Holy Spirit that they be made one body of Christ. "Because if any man have not the Spirit of Christ, he is not his."

3. No one therefore doubts that each of us, still in his mother's womb, receives a soul secretly, that is, to the end that he be made man with a living soul. So, meanwhile, the mother does not know when, through her, before birth, he enters life. In the same way, of course, no one ought to doubt that in the womb of baptism, before the babe rises from the fount, the Holy Spirit enters into one reborn, although not seen; that the divine power is no less provident and efficacious for the regeneration of holy adoption than it was previously in the birth by flesh, to quicken the sown members of a man, though conceived in sin. Wherefore, we have no doubt that God, who surveys all things and is powerful over them, always grants grace that is capable of preventing what he has ordained from being changed. If within the father's lust and the sin of the mother the seed of passion becomes the members of a living man, so in times and places when the Holy Spirit is present, because he fills the whole earth, he offers himself rather to everyone reborn through faith, so that through him the members of Christ may feel themselves one, and that all of them may become one body.

4. But on the journey through this life we only feed upon and drink the sacrament of the body and blood so that nourished from it we may be made one in Christ, that being invigorated by tasting him we may be prepared for things immortal and eternal. While we are now fed on angelic grace we may be quickened spiritually. For us, however, in all these sacraments the divine Spirit works. If, indeed, in the Holy Scriptures he illumines our hearts, because "neither he who plants nor he who waters is anything but it is God who gives the increase." Of this Ezekiel says: "For the Spirit of life was in the wheels," and John says: "Let him who has ears for hearing hear what the Spirit says to the churches." But in Christ the same Spirit is at work because Christ is believed to have been conceived from Him and the Virgin Mary. In like manner, in the baptism through the water we are from him all regenerated, and afterward we daily feed upon Christ's body and drink his blood by his power. No wonder that the Spirit which without seed created the man Christ in the womb of the Virgin, from the substance of bread and wine daily creates the flesh and blood of Christ by invisible power through the sanctification of his sacrament, though outwardly understood by neither sight nor taste. But because they are spiritual things, they are fully received as certainties by faith and understanding, as the Truth foretold.

IV. 1. That in truth the body and blood are created by the consecration of the mystery, no one doubts who believes the divine words when the

Truth says: "For my flesh is truly food, and my blood is truly drink." And that when his disciples did not rightly understand, he clearly identified what flesh he meant, what blood: "He who eats my flesh and drinks my blood, abides in me and I in him." Therefore, if it is truly food, it is true flesh, and if it is truly drink, it is true blood. How else will what he says be true: "The bread which I shall give, my flesh, is for the life of the world," unless it be true flesh? and the "bread which came down from heaven," true bread? But because it is not right to devour Christ with the teeth, he willed in the mystery that this bread and wine be created truly his flesh and blood through consecration by the power of the Holy Spirit, by daily creating it so that it might be mystically sacrificed for the life of the world; so that as from the Virgin through the Spirit true flesh is created without union of sex, so through the same, out of the substance of bread and wine, the same body and blood of Christ may be mystically consecrated. It is plainly of this flesh and blood that he says: "Verily, verily, I say to you, except you eat of the flesh of the Son of Man and drink his blood, you will not have eternal life in you." There, certainly, he is speaking about no other flesh than the true flesh and the true blood, that is, in a mystical sense. And because the sacrament is mystical, we cannot deny the figure, but if it is a figure, one must ask how it can be truth. For every figure is the figure of something, and always has reference to it in order that it might be a true thing of which it is the figure. That the figures of the Old Testament were shadows, no one who reads the sacred literature is in doubt, but this mystery is either truth or a figure and in the latter case a shadow. One should certainly inquire whether all this can be called truth without a shadow of falsity, though a mystery of this sort must be called a reality. But it seems to be a figure when it is "broken," when something is understood in visible appearance other than what is sensed by the sight and taste of the flesh, and when the blood in the cup is at the same time mixed with water. Furthermore, that sacrament of faith is rightly called truth; truth, therefore, when the body and blood of Christ is created by the power of the Spirit in his word out of the substance of bread and wine; but a figure when, through the agency of the priest at the altar, outwardly performing another thing, in memory of his sacred Passion, the Lamb is daily sacrificed as he was once for all.

2. If we truthfully examine the matter, it is rightly called both the truth and a figure, so that it is a figure or character of truth because it is outwardly sensed. Truth, however, is anything rightly understood or believed inwardly concerning this mystery. Not every figure is a shadow or falsity, whence Paul, speaking to the Hebrews about God's only Son, says, "Since he is the splendor of glory and the figure of his substance, bearing all things by the word of his power, making purification of sins." In these words, certainly, he declares that there are two substances in Christ, each of them

true. For when he says, "Since He is the splendor of the glory," of divinity, he proclaims him as consubstantial. But since the figure or character of his substance marks the human nature, where the fullness of divinity dwells corporeally, nevertheless, the one and true Christ is universally represented as God. For this reason he takes one thing for the demonstration of two substances and calls it the figure or character of substance, because as through characters or the figures of letters we as small children first progressed gradually to reading, later to the spiritual senses and understanding of the scriptures, so also there is a progression from the humanity of Christ to the divinity of the Father, and therefore it is rightly called the figure or character of his substance. What else are the figures of letters than their characters, that through them force and power and utterance of spirit are demonstrated to the eyes? So also the Word is formed flesh that through flesh we as small children may be nourished to the understanding of divinity. Yet the characters of the letters are not falsity, nor are they anything but letters. Neither can the man Christ be called false nor anything but God, with the result, of course, that the figure may rightly be called the character of the divinity's substance. Because he advances us small children through himself to things spiritual, which must be understood inwardly and by our senses, he shows himself in visible form while we receive what is in it. But because he, after the flesh had to penetrate to heavens, so that, through faith, those reborn in him might with greater boldness seek, he has left us this sacrament, a visible figure and character of flesh and blood, so that through them our soul and our flesh are richly nourished for grasping things invisible and spiritual by faith. This which is outwardly sensed is, however, the figure or character but wholly truth and no shadow, because intrinsically perceived, and for this reason nothing else henceforth than truth and the sacrament of his flesh is apparent.

3. As it is the true flesh of Christ which was crucified and buried, truly is it the sacrament of his flesh, which is divinely consecrated through the Holy Spirit on the altar by the agency of the priest in Christ's word. The Lord himself proclaims, "This is my body." Do not be surprised, O man, and do not ask about the order of nature here; but if you truly believe that that flesh was without seed created from the Virgin Mary in her womb by the power of the Holy Spirit, so that the Word might be made flesh, truly believe also that what is constructed in Christ's word through the Holy Spirit is his body from the Virgin. If you ask the method, who can explain or express it in words? Be assured, please, that the method resides in Christ's virtue, the knowledge in faith, the cause in power, but the effect in will, because the power of divinity over nature effectively works beyond the capacity of our reason. Therefore, let knowledge be held in the teaching of salvation, let faith be preserved in the mystery of truth, since in all these "we walk by faith and not by sight."

59 RATRAMNUS, A NINTH-CENTURY MONK, engaged in controversy with Radbertus concerning the Lord's Supper. It is probable that Ratramnus' essay, *Christ's Body and Blood*, was composed after that of Radbertus (see Selection 58) and at the request of Charles the Bald. Unlike Radbertus, Ratramnus regarded the elements, even after consecration, as retaining their visible character of bread and wine, though they served as symbols of the body and blood of Christ and conveyed a power through a faithful participation in the sacrament. Ratramnus' work, though neglected throughout most of the Middle Ages, excited new interest among some of the Protestant reformers.

Christ's Body and Blood*

RATRAMNUS

While certain of the faithful say that in the mystery of the body and the blood of Christ, daily celebrated in the church, nothing takes place under a figure, under a hidden symbol, but it is performed with a naked manifestation of truth[1] itself, others bear witness, however, that these elements are contained in the figure of a mystery, and that it is one thing which appears to the bodily sense and another which faith beholds. No small divergence is to be distinguished between them. And though the apostle writes to the faithful that they should all hold the same views and say the same things, and that no schism should appear among them, yet they are divided by great schism when they utter different views concerning the mystery of Christ's body and blood. . . .

Your majesty inquires whether that which in the church is received into the mouth of the faithful becomes the body and blood of Christ in a mystery or in truth. That is, whether it contains some hidden element which becomes patent only to the eyes of faith, or whether without con-

---

* From *Early Medieval Theology*, Vol. IX, LCC. Tr. George E. McCracken. Published in 1957, The Westminster Press. Used by permission. Also with permission of Student Christian Movement Press, London.

1 In this work *veritas* and its cognates appear always to connote truth in a completely physical sense as opposed to any figurative or symbolical sense, not opposed to falsity.

cealment of any mystery the appearance of the body is seen outwardly in what the mind's eyes see inwardly, so that everything which takes place becomes clearly visible; and whether it is that body which was born of Mary, suffered, died, and was buried, and which, rising again and ascending into heaven, sits on the right hand of the Father.

Let us examine the first of these two questions, and, to prevent our being stopped by ambiguity of language, let us define what we mean by "figure," what by "truth," so that keeping our gaze fixed on something quite certain, we may know in what path of reasoning we ought to direct our steps.

"Figure" means a kind of overshadowing that reveals its intent under some sort of veil. For example, when we wish to speak of the Word, we say "bread," as when in the Lord's Prayer we ask that daily bread be given us, or when Christ speaking in the Gospel says, "I am the living bread who came down from heaven"; or when he calls himself the vine and his disciples the branches. For all these passages say one thing and hint at another.

"Truth," on the other hand, is representation of clear fact, not obscured by any shadowy images, but uttered in pure and open, and to say it more plainly, in natural meanings, as, for example, when Christ is said to have been born of the Virgin, suffered, been crucified, died, and been buried. For nothing is here adumbrated by concealing metaphors, but the reality of the fact is represented in the ordinary senses of the words. Nothing else may be understood than what is said. In the instances mentioned above this was not the case. From the point of view of substance, the bread is not Christ, the vine is not Christ, the branches are not apostles. Therefore in this latter instance the figure, but in the former the truth, is represented by the statement, that is, the bare and obvious meaning.

Now let us go back to the matter which is the cause of what has been said, namely, the body and blood of Christ. For if that mystery is not performed in any figurative sense, then it is not rightly given the name of mystery. Since that cannot be called a mystery in which there is nothing hidden, nothing removed from the physical senses, nothing covered over with any veil. But that bread which through the ministry of the priest comes to be Christ's body exhibits one thing outwardly to human sense, and it proclaims another thing inwardly to the minds of the faithful. Outwardly it has the shape of bread which it had before, the color is exhibited, the flavor is received, but inwardly something far different, much more precious, much more excellent, becomes known, because something heavenly, something divine, that is, Christ's body, is revealed, which is not beheld, or received, or consumed by the fleshly senses but in the gaze of the believing soul.

The wine also, which through priestly consecration becomes the sacrament of Christ's blood, shows, so far as the surface goes, one thing; inwardly it contains something else. What else is to be seen on the surface than the substance of wine? Taste it, and it has the flavor of wine; smell it, and it has the aroma of wine; look at it, and the wine color is visible. But if you think of it inwardly, it is now to the minds of believers not the liquid of Christ's blood, and when tasted, it has flavor; when looked at, it has appearance; and when smelled, it is proved to be such. Since no one can deny that this is so, it is clear that that bread and wine are Christ's body and blood in a figurative sense. For as to outward appearance, the aspect of flesh is not recognized in that bread, nor in that wine is the liquid blood shown, when, however, they are, after the mystical consecration, no longer called bread or wine, but Christ's body and blood.

For if, as some would have it, nothing is here received figuratively, but everything is visible in truth, faith does not operate here, since nothing spiritual takes place, but whatever it is, it is wholly received according to its bodily sense. And since faith, according to the apostle, is "the evidence of things not appearing," that is, not of substances, visible but invisible, we shall here receive nothing according to faith since we distinguish what it is according to the senses of the body. Nothing is more absurd than to take bread as flesh and to say that wine is blood, and there will be no mystery in anything which contains nothing secret, nothing concealed. . . .

Christ's body and blood, viewed outwardly, are something created and subject to change and corruption. If, however, you weigh the power of the mystery, they are life, granting immortality to those who partake of them. Therefore, what are seen and what are believed are not the same. For with respect to what are seen, they, themselves corruptible, feed a corruptible body; but with respect to what they are believed to be, they, themselves immortal, feed souls which will live forever. . . .

And from the words of the Evangelist we learn that our Lord Jesus Christ before he suffered, "having taken bread, gave thanks, gave to his disciples, saying, 'This is my body which is given for you. Do this in remembrance of me.' Likewise also the cup, after he ate, saying, 'This is the cup, the New Testament, in my blood, which shall be shed for you.' "[2] We see that Christ had not yet suffered, but already the mystery of his body and blood was in effect.

We do not think that any of the faithful can doubt that that bread was made Christ's body because in giving it to his disciples he says, "This is my body which is given for you." Neither can he doubt that the cup contains Christ's blood, of which he himself says, "This is the cup, the New Testament, in my blood, which shall be shed for you." As, then, a little while before he suffered, he could change the substance of bread and the created wine into his own body which was about to suffer, and into his blood which was later to be shed, so also in the desert he had the power to

---

[2] Luke 22:19 f. (Vulgate of Matt. 26:28); Mark 14:24, used in part.

change the manna and water from the rock into his flesh and blood, and his flesh survived long afterward to be hanged on the cross for us, and his blood to be shed for our cleansing.

Here also we must consider the proper interpretation of his words: "Unless you shall eat the flesh of the Son of Man, and drink his blood, you shall not have life in you."[3] For he does not say that his flesh which hung on the cross would have to be cut to bits and eaten by his disciples, or that his blood which was to be shed for the redemption of the world would have to be given to his disciples to drink. This would have been a crime if, in accordance with what men outside the faith then understood, his blood were to be drunk or his flesh to be eaten by his disciples.

For this reason a little later in the same passage he says to his disciples who were receiving Christ's words, not as unbelievers but as believers, though hitherto it did not enter into their thoughts how those words would have to be understood: "Do you take offense at this? What if you should see the Son of Man ascending where he was before?" This is as if he were to say: "Do not think that you must eat in a bodily sense my flesh or drink my blood, distributed to you in pieces or having to be so distributed, since after the resurrection you will see me ascending into the heavens with the fullness of my entire body and of my blood. Then you will understand that my flesh does not have to be eaten by believers, as men without faith suppose, but the bread and wine, by the mystery truly changed into the substance of my body and blood, must be taken by believers."

And he goes on to say: "It is the Spirit which gives life; the flesh is of no avail."[4] He says that the flesh is of no avail in the sense in which those without faith understood. In some other way it bestows life as it is taken through the mystery by those with faith. And this, as he makes it clear by saying: "It is the Spirit which gives life." So in this mystery the effect of the body and blood is spiritual. It gives life, and without its effect the mysteries are of no avail, since they, indeed, feed the body but cannot feed the soul.

Here arises that question which many express when they say that these things do not happen in a figure but in truth. When they say this, they are shown to be out of harmony with writings of the holy fathers. . . .

From all that has thus far been said it has been shown that Christ's body and blood which are received in the mouth of the faithful in the church are figures according to their visible appearance, but according to their invisible substance, that is, the power of the divine Word, truly exist as Christ's body and blood. Therefore, with respect to visible creation, they feed the body; with reference to the power of a stronger substance, they feed and sanctify the souls of the faithful.

[3] John 6:53.
[4] John 6:63.

Now it is proposed to examine the second question and to see whether that very body which was born of Mary, suffered, died, and was buried, and which sits on the right hand of the Father, is what is daily taken in the church by the mouth of the faithful through the mystery of the sacraments.

. . . we teach that a great difference separates the body in which Christ suffered, and the blood which he shed from his side while hanging on the cross, from this body which daily in the mystery of Christ's Passion is celebrated by the faithful, and from that blood also which is taken into the mouth of the faithful to be the mystery of that blood by which the whole world was redeemed. For that bread and that drink are Christ's body or blood, not with respect to what they seem, but with respect to the fact that they spiritually support the substance of life. That body in which Christ suffered once and for all exhibited no different appearance from the one it really had. For it was what it truly seemed, what was touched, what was crucified, what was buried. Likewise, his blood, trickling from his side, did not appear one thing outwardly and conceal another thing inwardly, and so true blood flowed from the true side. But now the blood of Christ which the believers drink, and the body which they eat, are one thing in appearance and another thing in meaning—the one, what feeds the body on corporeal food; and the other, what nourishes the mind on the substance of life eternal. . . .

They are therefore not the same. For that flesh which was crucified was made from the flesh of the Virgin, of bones and sinews joined together and marked with the lineaments of human parts, quickened to life of its own and harmonious motions by the spirit of a rational soul. But the spiritual flesh which spiritually feeds the people who believe, consists, with respect to the appearance it outwardly bears, of grains of flour molded by the hand of an artisan, joined together without sinews and bones, having no characteristic variation of parts, animated by no rational substance, unable to move of its own accord. For whatever in it furnishes the substance of life is of spiritual might, invisible in efficacy, and divine power. With respect to its outward view it is far different in constitution from that which it is believed to be with respect to the mystery. Furthermore, the flesh of Christ which was crucified revealed nothing different outwardly from what it was inwardly, because it existed as true flesh of true man, a body really true having the appearance of a true body.

It must be considered that in that bread not only Christ's body but the body also of the people believing on him should be symbolized by the many grains of flour of which it is made because the body of the people who believe is increased by many faithful ones through Christ's word.

Wherefore, as in the mystery that bread is taken as Christ's body, so also in the mystery the members of the people who believe in Christ are suggested, and as that bread is called the body of the believers, not in a corporeal sense but in a spiritual, so of necessity Christ's body must also be understood not corporeally but spiritually.

As also in the wine which is called Christ's blood mixing with water is prescribed, the one element is not allowed to be offered without the other, because the people cannot exist without Christ, nor Christ without the people, so also can the head not exist without the body, nor the body without the head. So then, in that sacrament, the water represents the people. Therefore, if that wine which is consecrated by the liturgy of the ministers is changed into Christ's blood in a corporeal sense, the water, likewise, which is mixed with it, must of necessity be converted corporeally into the blood of the people who believe. For where there is one consecration, of a consequence there is one action, and where there is a like transaction, there is a like mystery. But we see that in the water nothing is changed with respect to the body, so also for this reason in the wine there is nothing corporeally exhibited. Whatever is meant in the water concerning the body of the people is accepted spiritually. Therefore it is necessary that whatever in the wine is suggested concerning Christ's blood should be accepted spiritually.

Likewise, things that differ from each other are not the same. Christ's body which died and rose again, and having become immortal "will now not die again, and death will have no further dominion over him," is eternal and no longer capable of suffering. That which is celebrated in the church is temporary, not eternal. It is corruptible, not incorrupted. It is on the road, not in its homeland. They, then, differ from each other, and are, for this reason, not the same.

But if they are not the same, how is it called the true body of Christ and the true blood? For if it is Christ's body and the statement that it is Christ's body is true, it is Christ's body in truth; and if it is in truth the body of Christ, the body of Christ is both incorruptible and incapable of suffering, and therefore eternal. Therefore, this body of Christ which is enacted in the church must necessarily be incorruptible and eternal. But it cannot be denied that what is divided into bits to be consumed is corrupted, and when ground by the teeth is transferred into body. It is one thing, however, which is outwardly done, but another which through faith is believed. What pertains to the sense of the body is corruptible, but what faith believes is incorruptible. Therefore, what appears outwardly is not the thing itself but the image of the thing, but what is felt and understood in the soul is the truth of the thing. . . .

Thus we see that a great difference separates the mystery of Christ's blood and body which now is taken by the faithful in the church from that which was born of the Virgin Mary, suffered, died, rose again, ascended to the heavens, sits on the right hand of the Father. For what is done on the way must be accepted spiritually, because faith, which does not see, believes and spiritually feeds the soul and gladdens the heart and provides life and incorruption, provided what feeds the body, what is pressed by the teeth, what is broken into bits, is not considered, but what is in faith received spiritually. But that body in which Christ suffered and rose again exists as his own body, assumed from the body of the Virgin Mary, capable of being touched or visible even after the resurrection, as he himself said to his disciples: "Touch and see that a spirit does not have flesh and bones such as you see I have."

60 ON THE TRUTH OF THE CATHOLIC FAITH [*Summa Contra Gentiles*], written by Thomas Aquinas (1225–1274) in 1258 and 1259, was designed to be used as a handbook for Christian missionaries to Jewish and Muslim communities in Spain. The work was divided into four books, treating: (1) the existence and perfections of God; (2) the nature of man and God's creative power; (3) the relation of God and the created order; (4) the doctrine of the Trinity and man's salvation. Aquinas' sacramental theory became normative for the Roman Catholic Church. Antecedent discussions of the Eucharist by Ratramnus (Selection 59) and Radbertus (Selection 58) and the subsequent decrees of the Council of Trent (Selection 67) serve to indicate the relation of Aquinas' position to the development of the Roman Catholic doctrine.[1]

On the Truth of the Catholic Faith*

[Summa Contra Gentiles]

THOMAS AQUINAS

ON THE NECESSITY OF THE SACRAMENTS

[1] . . . the death of Christ is, so to say, the universal cause of human salvation, and since a universal cause must be applied singly to each of its

* From *On the Truth of the Catholic Faith*. Book Four: Salvation, by Saint Thomas Aquinas, translated by Charles J. O'Neil. Copyright © 1957 by Doubleday & Company, Inc. Reprinted by permission of the publisher.

1 See also *Summa Theologica*, Selections 6, 44.

effects, it was necessary to show men some remedies through which the benefit of Christ's death could somehow be conjoined to them. It is of this sort, of course, that the sacraments of the Church are said to be.

[2]   Now, remedies of this kind had to be handed on with some visible signs.

[3]   First, indeed, because just as He does for all other things, so also for man, God provides according to his condition. Now, man's condition is such that he is brought to grasp the spiritual and intelligible naturally through the senses. Therefore, spiritual remedies had to be given to men under sensible signs.

[4]   Second, because instruments must be proportioned to their first cause. But the first and universal cause of human salvation is the incarnate Word, as is clear from the foregoing. Therefore, harmoniously the remedies by which the power of the universal cause reaches men had a likeness to that cause; that is, the divine power operates in them under visible signs.

[5]   Third, because man fell into sin by clinging unduly to visible things. Therefore, that one might not believe visible things evil of their nature, and that for this reason those clinging to them had sinned, it was fitting that through the visible things themselves the remedies of salvation be applied to men. Consequently, it would appear that visible things are good of their nature—as created by God—but they become damaging to men so far as one clings to them in a disordered way, and saving so far as one uses them in an ordered way.

[6]   Thus, of course, one excludes the error of certain heretics who want every visible thing of this kind removed from the sacraments of the Church. Nor need one marvel at this, for the very same men maintain that whatever is visible is evil in its nature, and is produced by an evil author. And this we rejected in Book II.

[7]   Nor is it unsuitable that by things visible and bodily a spiritual salvation is served. For visible things of this kind are the instruments, so to say, of a God who was made flesh and suffered. Now, an instrument does not operate by the power of its nature, but by the power of its principal agent who puts it into operation. Thus, also, then, do visible things of this kind work out a spiritual salvation—not by a property of their own nature, but by Christ's institution, and from the latter they receive their instrumental power. . . .

ON THE NUMBER OF THE SACRAMENTS
OF THE NEW LAW

[1]   However, since the spiritual remedies of salvation have been given to men under sensible signs, it was suitable also to distinguish the remedies provided for the spiritual life after the likeness of bodily life.

[2]   Now, in bodily life we find a twofold order: for some propagate and

order the bodily life in others; and some are propagated and ordered in the bodily life.

[3] Now, in a bodily and natural life three things are necessary of themselves, and a fourth incidentally. For first, by generation or birth a thing must receive life; second, by growth it must arrive at its due size and strength; third, both for the preservation of life acquired by generation and for growth nourishment is necessary. And these are of themselves necessities for natural life, because without these bodily life cannot be perfected; wherefore, one assigns to the vegetative soul which is the principle of life the three natural powers: that of generation, that of growth, and that of nourishment. But, since there can be an impediment to natural life from which the living thing grows weak, a fourth thing is incidentally necessary; this is the healing of the sick living thing.

[4] Thus, then, in the spiritual life, also, the first thing is spiritual generation: by baptism; the second is spiritual growth leading to perfect strength: by the sacrament of confirmation; the third is spiritual nourishment: by the sacrament of the Eucharist. A fourth remains, which is the spiritual healing; it takes place either in the soul alone through the sacrament of penance; or from the soul flows to the body when this is timely, through extreme unction. These, therefore, bear on those who are propagated and preserved in the spiritual life.

[5] Now, those who propagate and order in the bodily life are marked by two things: namely, natural origin, and this refers to parents; and the political regime by which the peaceful life of man is conserved, and this refers to kings and princes.

[6] It is, then, also like this in the spiritual life. For some propagate and conserve the spiritual life in a spiritual ministry only, and this belongs to the sacrament of orders; and some belong to the bodily and spiritual life simultaneously, which takes place in the sacrament of matrimony where a man and woman come together to beget offspring and to rear them in divine worship.

ON BAPTISM

[1] In this way, then, one can discern in the individual sacraments the proper effect of each one and the becoming matter. Now, first: Regarding the spiritual generation which takes place in baptism, one must consider that the generation of a living thing is a kind of change from non-living to life. But man in his origin was deprived of spiritual life by original sin, as was shown above; and still every single sin whatever which is added draws him away from life. Baptism, therefore, which is spiritual generation, had to have the power to take away both original sin and all the actual, committed sins.

[2]   Now, because the sensible sign of a sacrament must be harmonious with the representation of its spiritual effect, and since washing away filth in bodily things is done more easily and more commonly by water, baptism is, therefore, suitably conferred in water made holy by the Word of God.

[3]   And since the generation of one is the corruption of another, and since what is generated loses both its previous form and the properties consequent on that form; necessarily through baptism, which is a spiritual generation, not only are sins taken away—these are contrary to a spiritual life—but also every guilt of sins. For this reason, too, baptism not only washes away the fault, but also absolves from all guilt. Hence, no satisfaction for their sins is enjoined on the baptized.

[4]   Again, when by generation a thing acquires a form, it acquires at the same time the operation consequent on the form and the place in harmony with it. For fire, as soon as generated, tends upward as to its proper place. Accordingly, since baptism is a spiritual generation, the baptized are forthwith suited for spiritual actions—the reception of the other sacraments, for example, and other things of the sort—and forthwith there is due to them the place harmonious to the spiritual life, which is eternal beatitude. Hence, we say that "Baptism opens the gate of heaven."

[5]   One should also consider that one thing has but one generation. Hence, since baptism is a spiritual generation, a man is to be baptized once only.

[6]   Clearly, also, the infection which entered the world through Adam makes a man guilty but once. Hence, baptism, which is chiefly ordered against this infection, should not be repeated. There is also this common consideration: that, as long as a thing is once consecrated, it must not be consecrated again, so long as it endures, lest the consecration appear inefficacious. And so, since baptism is a kind of consecration of the one baptized, baptism must not be repeated. This excludes the error of the Donatists or Rebaptizers.

ON CONFIRMATION

[1]   The perfection of spiritual strength consists properly in a man's daring to confess the faith of Christ in the presence of anyone at all, and in a man's being not withdrawn therefrom either by confusion or by terror, for strength drives out inordinate terror. Therefore, the sacrament by which spiritual strength is conferred on the one born again makes him in some sense a front-line fighter for the faith of Christ. And because fighters under a prince carry his insignia, they who receive the sacrament of confirmation are signed with the sign of Christ; this is the sign of the cross by which He fought and conquered. This sign they receive on the forehead as a sign that without a blush they publicly confess the faith of Christ.

[2] This signing takes place with a mixture of oil and balm which is called chrism, and not without reason. For by the oil one designates the power of the Holy Spirit, from whom Christ, too, is called "anointed" (Ps. 44:8; Luke 4:18); and consequently from Christ they are called "Christians" (Acts 9:26), so to say, as fighting under Him. And by the balm, through its fragrance, good repute is indicated. For the public confession of faith in Christ this good repute must be had by those who dwell among men of this world, brought forth, so to say, from the hidden recesses of the Church onto the field of battle.

[3] Suitably, too, this sacrament is conferred only by bishops, who are in some sense the leaders of the Christian army. For even in secular military forces it is the prerogative of the army leader to select some men to be enrolled; so, also, those who receive this sacrament seem to be enrolled somehow in the spiritual military forces. Hence, also, a hand is laid upon them to designate the derivation of manliness from Christ.

ON THE EUCHARIST

[1] Now, bodily life needs material nourishment, not only for increase in quantity, but to maintain the nature of the body as well, lest it be dissolved by continuous resolutions and lose its power; in the same way it was necessary to have spiritual nourishment for the spiritual life that the reborn may both be conserved in virtues and grow in them.

[2] Spiritual effects were fittingly given under the likeness of things visible; therefore, spiritual nourishment of this kind is given to us under the appearances of the things which men rather commonly use for bodily nourishment. Bread and wine are of this sort. Accordingly, this sacrament is given under the appearances of bread and wine.

[3] But consider this: He who begets is joined to the begotten in one way, and nourishment is joined to the nourished in another way in bodily things. For the one who begets need not be conjoined to the begotten in substance, but in likeness and in power only. But nutriment must be conjoined to the one nourished in substance. Wherefore, that the spiritual effects may answer the bodily signs, the mystery of the incarnate Word is joined to us in one way in baptism which is a spiritual rebirth, and in another way in this sacrament of the Eucharist which is a spiritual nourishment. In baptism the Word incarnate is contained in His power only, but we hold that in the sacrament of the Eucharist He is contained in His substance.

[4] And since the fulfillment of our salvation took place through the passion and death of Christ, in which His blood was separated from His flesh, we are given the sacrament of His body separately under the appearance of bread, and of His blood under the appearance of wine; and so we

have in this sacrament both memory and the representation of our Lord's passion. And in this our Lord's words are fulfilled: "My flesh is meat indeed, and my blood is drink indeed" (John 6:56). . . .

SOLUTION OF THE DIFFICULTIES SET DOWN: FIRST, ABOUT THE CONVERSION OF THE BREAD INTO THE BODY OF CHRIST

[1] Although, of course, the divine power operates with a greater sublimity and secrecy in this sacrament than a man's inquiry can search out, nonetheless, lest the teaching of the Church regarding this sacrament appear impossible to unbelievers, one must make the endeavor to exclude every impossibility.

[2] The first consideration we meet, then, is that of the way in which the true body of Christ begins to be under this sacrament.

[3] It is impossible, of course, that this take place by a local motion of the body of Christ. One reason is that it would follow that He ceases to be in heaven whenever this sacrament is performed. Another reason is that this sacrament could not be performed at the same time except in one place, since a local motion is not ended except at one term. Another reason, also, is that local motion cannot be instantaneous, but requires time. Consecration, however, is perfected in the ultimate instant of the pronouncement of the words.

[4] Therefore, one concludes by saying that the true body of Christ begins to be in this sacrament by the fact that the substance of the bread is converted into the substance of the body of Christ, and the substance of the wine into the substance of His blood.

[5] But thus appears the falsity of the opinion: not only of those who say that the substance of the bread exists simultaneously with the substance of Christ in this sacrament, but also of those who hold that the substance of the bread is reduced to nothing or is resolved into prime matter. For on each of these positions it follows that the body of Christ does not begin to be in this sacrament except by local motion. And this is impossible, as we have shown.

Furthermore, if the substance of the bread is simultaneous in this sacrament with the true body of Christ, Christ should rather have said: "My body is here" than: "This is My body." For by "here" one points to the substance which is seen, and this is indeed the substance of the bread, if it remains in the sacrament with the body of Christ.

Similarly, also, it seems impossible that the substance of the bread returns to nothingness. For much of the bodily nature first created would have already returned into nothingness from the repetition of this mystery. Neither is it becoming that in a sacrament of salvation something be reduced to nothing by the divine power. Nor is it even possible that the substance of the bread is resolved into prime matter, since prime matter cannot be without form—except, perhaps, that one is to understand by "prime matter" the primary bodily elements. To be sure, if the substance of the bread were resolved into these, this very thing would necessarily be perceived by the senses, since the bodily elements are sensible. There would also be local transmutation in the place and bodily alteration of contraries. And these cannot be instantaneous.

[6]   Nonetheless, it must be recognized that the aforesaid conversion of the bread into the body of Christ is of another mode than any natural conversion whatever. For in any natural conversion a subject persists in which different forms succeed themselves: these are accidental—white, for example, is converted into black; or they are substantial—air, for example, is converted into fire; wherefore these are named *formal conversions*. But in the conversion under discussion a subject passes over into a subject, and the accidents persist; hence, this conversion is named *substantial*. Indeed, how these accidents persist, and why, must be closely examined later.

[7]   But now we must consider how a subject is converted into a subject. And this, to be sure, nature cannot do. For every operation of nature presupposes matter which individuates the substance; wherefore, nature cannot bring it about that this substance become that substance, that this finger, for example, become that finger. But matter is subject to the divine power, since the latter brings it into being. Hence, by divine power it can come about that this individual substance be converted into that preexisting substance. Now, just as the power of a natural agent whose operation extends to the change of a form only—and the existence of the subject is supposed—changes this whole into that whole in a variation of the species and the form—this air, let us say, into that generated fire—so the divine power, which does not presuppose matter, but produces matter, converts *this* matter into *that* matter, and, in consequence, this individual into that individual; for the principle of individuation is matter, just as form is the principle of species.

[8]   In this way, of course, it is clear that in the aforesaid conversion of bread into the body of Christ there is not a common subject persisting after the conversion, since a transmutation takes place in the first subject, and this is the principle of the individuation. It is necessary, for all that, that something persist to make true the words. "This is My Body"; the very words, in fact, which are significative and effective of this conversion. And the substance of the bread does not persist; neither does any prior matter (as was shown). Therefore, one necessarily says that what persists is other than the substance of the bread. Of this sort, of course, is the accident of the bread. Therefore, the accidents of the bread do persist even after the conversion mentioned.

[9] Among accidents, however, there is a certain order to be considered. For, among all the accidents, that inhering more closely to the substance is the quantity which tends to measure. Then the qualities are received in the substance with the quantity as medium—color, for example, with the surface as medium; hence, even by the division of the quantity they are incidentally divided. But, in addition, the qualities are the principles of actions and passions, as well as of certain relations—father and son, let us say, or master and servant, and others of this kind. Of course, some relations follow immediately on the quantities—greater and less, for instance, or doubled and halved, and similar relations. Therefore, one ought to hold that the accidents of the bread persist after the conversion mentioned in such wise that only the quantity which tends to measure subsists without a subject, and on it the qualities are based as on a subject, and so in consequence are the accidents, passions, and relations. Therefore, in this conversion what takes place is the contrary of what usually takes place in natural mutations, for in these the substance persists as the subject of the mutation, whereas the accidents are varied; but here, conversely, the accident persists, the substance passes.

[10] Of course, a conversion of this kind cannot properly be called *motion* as that is considered by the natural philosopher, since that requires a subject, but it is a kind of *substantial succession*; so there is in creation a succession of being and non-being, as was said in Book II.

[11] This, then, is one reason why the accident of the bread must remain: that something be discoverable which persists in the conversion under discussion.

[12] But it is necessary for another reason. For, if the substance of the bread were converted into the body of Christ and the accidents were to pass on, it would not follow from such a conversion that the body of Christ in His substance would be where first there was bread, for no relationship between the body of Christ and the aforesaid place would be left. But since, after the conversion, the quantity of the bread which tends to measure does remain, and through this the bread acquired this place, the substance of the bread changed into the body of Christ becomes the body of Christ under the bread's quantity tending to measure; in consequence, the body of Christ in some way acquires the place of the bread, with the measurements of the bread, nonetheless, mediating.

[13] Other reasons can also be given: respecting the essentials of faith, which deals with the invisible; respecting also its merit, which is so much the greater in connection with this sacrament, since it deals with the more invisible, for the body of Christ is hidden under the accidents of the bread; respecting, also, the more appropriate and worthy use of this sacrament, for it would be horrible for the receivers, and an abomination to those looking on, if the body of Christ were received by the faithful in its

own appearance. Hence, it is under the appearance of bread and wine, which men use rather commonly for meat and drink, that the body of Christ is set forth to be eaten and His blood to be drunk. . . .

ON THE SACRAMENT OF PENANCE, AND, FIRST, THAT MEN AFTER RECEIVING SACRAMENTAL GRACE ARE ABLE TO SIN

[1] Now, although grace is bestowed upon men by the aforesaid sacraments, they are not, for all that, rendered incapable of sin.

[2] For gratuitous gifts are received in the soul as habitual dispositions; it is not always, then, that a man acts according to those gifts. Nothing stops him who has a habit from acting in accord with the habit or against it; thus, a grammarian can in accord with grammar speak rightly, or even against grammar speak awkwardly. It is also like this with the habits of the moral virtues, for one who has the habit of justice can also act against justice. This is the case because the use of habits in us depends on the will, but the will is related to each of two opposites. Manifestly, then, he who receives gratuitous gifts can sin by acting against grace.

[3] What is more, there can be no impeccability in a man unless there is immutability of will. But immutability of will does not become man except so far as he attains his ultimate end. For what renders the will immutable is its complete fulfillment, so that it has no way to turn away from that on which it is made firm. But the fulfillment of will is not proportioned to a man except as attaining his ultimate end, for, as long as something remains to be desired, the will has not been fulfilled. Thus, then, impeccability is not proper for a man before he arrives at the ultimate end. And this, to be sure, is not given man in the grace which is bestowed in the sacraments, because the sacraments are for man's assistance along the road to the end. Therefore, no one is rendered impeccable from the grace received in the sacraments.

[4] Furthermore, every sin comes about from a kind of ignorance. Thus, the Philosopher says that "every evil man is ignorant";[2] and we read in Proverbs (14:22): "They err that work evil." Therefore, then, a man can be secure from sin in the will, only when his intellect is secure from ignorance and from error. But, manifestly, a man is not rendered immune from every ignorance and error by the grace received in the sacraments; for such is a man whose intellect is beholding that truth which is the certitude of all truths; and this very beholding is the ultimate end of man, as was shown in Book III. It is not, then, by the grace of the sacraments that man is rendered impeccable. . . .

---

2 Aristotle, *Nicomachean Ethics*, III, 1 (1110b 28).

ON THE NECESSITY OF PENANCE AND OF ITS PARTS

[1]   From this, then, it is evident that if a man sins after baptism he cannot have the remedy against his sin in baptism. And since the abundance of the divine mercy and the effectiveness of Christ's grace do not suffer him to be dismissed without a remedy, there was established another sacramental remedy by which sins are washed away. And this is the sacrament of penance, which is spiritual healing of a sort. For just as those who receive a natural life by generation can, if they incur some disease which is contrary to the perfection of life, be cured of their disease: not, indeed, so as to be born a second time, but healed by a kind of alteration; so baptism, which is a spiritual regeneration, is not given a second time against sins committed after baptism, but they are healed by penance which is a kind of spiritual alteration. . . .

[4]   Therefore, the first thing required in penance is the ordering of the mind; namely, that the mind be turned toward God, and turned away from sin, grieving at its commission, and proposing not to commit it; and this belongs essentially to contrition.

[8]   . . . after the fault is taken away by contrition and the guilt of eternal punishment is relieved (as was said), there sometimes persists an obligation to some punishment to maintain the justice of God which requires that fault be ordered by punishment.

[9]   Since, however, to undergo punishment for a fault calls for a kind of judgment, the penitent who has committed himself to Christ for healing must look to Christ's judgment for fixing the punishment; and this, indeed, Christ does through His ministers, just as He does in the other sacraments. But no one can judge of faults which he does not know. It was necessary, then, that confession be instituted, the second part of this sacrament, so to say, in order to make the fault of the penitent known to the minister of Christ.

[10]   The minister, therefore, to whom confession is made must have judiciary power representing Christ, "who was appointed to be judge of the living and the dead" (Acts 10:42). For judiciary power two things are required: namely, the authority to know about the fault, and the power to absolve or condemn. And these two are called the "two keys of the Church," namely, the knowledge to discern and the power to bind and loose which our Lord committed to Peter as Matthew (16:19) has it: "I will give to thee the keys of the kingdom of heaven." He is not understood to have committed these to Peter so that he alone might have them, but so that they might through him be passed on to others; otherwise, sufficient provision for the salvation of the faithful would not have been made. . . .

[12]   In this way one avoids the error of some who held that a man can achieve forgiveness of sins without confession and without the purpose of confessing, and that the prelates of the Church can dispense one from the obligation of confessing. For the prelates of the Church are unable "to make vain the keys of the Church" in which their entire power consists, and they cannot bring it about that one achieve the remission of his sins apart from a sacrament which has power from the passion of Christ. This belongs only to Christ, who established the sacraments and is their author. Thus, then, as there can be no dispensation from the prelates of the Church allowing one to be saved without baptism, neither can there be one allowing a man to achieve the remission of his sins without confession and absolution. . . .

ON THE SACRAMENT OF EXTREME UNCTION

[1]   Now, the body is the instrument of the soul, and an instrument is for the use of the principal agent: therefore, the disposition of the instrument necessarily must be such as becomes the principal agent. Hence, the body is disposed in harmony with the soul. Therefore, from the infirmity of the soul which is sin infirmity sometimes flows into the body, when the divine judgment so disposes. To be sure, this bodily infirmity is at times useful for the soundness of the soul: so far as a man bears bodily infirmity humbly and patiently, and so far as it is reckoned as satisfying punishment for him. At times, also, it tends to hinder spiritual health: so far as bodily infirmity hinders the virtues. Therefore, it was suitable to employ some spiritual medicine against sin, in accord with the fact that bodily infirmity flows out of sin; indeed, this spiritual medicine cures the bodily infirmity at times, namely, when this is helpful to salvation. And for this a sacrament was established—extreme unction, about which James (5:14-15) says: "Is any man sick among you? Let him bring in the priests of the Church, and let them pray over him, anointing him with oil in the name of the Lord. And the prayer of faith shall heal the sick man."

[2]   Nor is the power of this sacrament prejudiced if at times the sick on whom it is conferred are not wholly cured of this bodily infirmity, for the restoration of bodily health—even in those who receive the sacrament worthily—sometimes is not useful for salvation. And they do not, for all that, receive it in vain, although bodily health may not follow on it. For, since this sacrament is set against bodily infirmity so far as this follows on sin, this sacrament manifestly was established against the other consequences of sin, which are proneness to evil and difficulty in good, and it is set so much the more as the soul's infirmities of this sort are closer neighbors to sin than bodily infirmity is. Indeed, spiritual infirmities of this

sort are to be cured by penance, in that the works of virtue which the penitent performs when he makes satisfaction withdraw him from evils and incline him to good. But, since man, whether due to negligence, or to the changing occupations of life, or even to the shortness of time, or to something else of the sort, does not perfectly heal within himself the weaknesses mentioned, a healthful provision for him is made by this sacrament: it completes the healing aforesaid, and it delivers him from the guilt of temporal punishment; as a result, nothing remains in him when the soul leaves the body which can obstruct the soul in the perception of glory. And therefore James adds: "And the Lord shall raise him up." Perhaps, also, a man has neither awareness nor memory of all the sins which he has committed, so that they may be washed away individually by penance. There are also those daily sins without which one does not lead this present life. And from these a man ought to be cleansed at his departure by this sacrament, so that nothing be found in him which would clash with the perception of glory. And therefore James adds: "If he be in sins, they shall be forgiven him."

[3]   Hence, it is clear that this sacrament is the last, that it somehow tends to consummate the entire spiritual healing, and that in it a man is, as it were, prepared for the perception of glory. For this reason also it is named *extreme unction.* . . .

ON THE SACRAMENT OF ORDERS

[1]   It is, of course, clear from what has been said that in all the sacraments dealt with a spiritual grace is conferred in a mystery of visible things. But every action ought to be proportioned to its agent. Therefore, the sacraments mentioned must be dispensed by visible men who have spiritual power. For angels are not competent to dispense the sacraments; this belongs to men clothed in visible flesh. Hence, the Apostle says: "Every high priest taken from among men is ordained for men in the things that appertain to God" (Heb. 5:1).

[2]   This argument can be derived in another way. The institution and the power of the sacraments has its beginning in Christ. For the Apostle says of Him: "Christ loved the Church and delivered Himself up for it: that He might sanctify it, cleansing it by the laver of water in the word of life" (Eph. 5:25–26). It is also clear that Christ gave the sacrament of His body and blood at the Last Supper, and ordered it to be frequented; and these are the principal sacraments. Therefore, since Christ was about to withdraw His bodily presence from the Church, it was necessary that Christ should establish other ministers in His place who would dispense the sacraments to the faithful; in the Apostle's words: "Let a man so

account of us as ministers of Christ and dispensers of the mysteries of God" (I Cor. 4:1). And so He committed the consecration of His body and blood to the disciples, saying: "Do this in commemoration of Me" (Luke 22:19); the same received the power of forgiving sins, in the words of John (20:23): "Whose sins you shall forgive, they are forgiven them"; the same also were given the duty of teaching and baptizing, when He said: "Going, therefore, teach ye all nations, baptizing them" (Matt. 28:19). But a minister is compared to his lord as an instrument to its principal agent, for, as an instrument is moved by the agent for making something, so the minister is moved by his lord's command to accomplish something. Of course, the instrument must be proportionate to the agent. Hence, the ministers of Christ must be in conformity with Him. But Christ, as the Lord, by His very own authority and power wrought our salvation, in that He was God and man: so far as He was man, in order to suffer for our redemption; and, so far as He was God, to make His suffering salutary for us. Therefore, the ministers of Christ must not only be men, but must participate somehow in His divinity through some spiritual power, for an instrument shares in the power of its principal agent. Now, it is this power that the Apostle calls "the power which the Lord hath given me unto edification and not unto destruction" (II Cor. 13:10). . . .

THAT THE SACRAMENTS CAN BE DISPENSED BY EVIL MINISTERS

[1] From what we have premised it is clear that the ministers of the Church, when they receive their orders, receive a certain power for dispensing the sacraments.
[2] But what is acquired by a thing through consecration persists in that thing forever; hence, nothing consecrated is consecrated a second time. Therefore, the power of their orders persists in the ministers of the Church perpetually. Therefore, it is not taken away by sin. Therefore, even sinners and evil men, provided they have orders, are able to confer the sacraments of the Church.
[3] Then, too, nothing has power over that which exceeds its capacities unless the power be received from some other source. This is clear in natural as well as in civil matters: Water cannot heat unless it receives the power of heating from fire, nor can a bailiff coerce citizens unless he receives power from a king. But the things accomplished in sacraments exceed human capacity, as the foregoing made clear. Therefore, no man can dispense the sacraments, no matter how good he is, unless he receives the power to dispense them. Now, goodness is in man the opposite of malice and sin. Therefore, one who has received the power to dispense the sacraments is not blocked by sin from dispensing them. . . .

ON THE SACRAMENT OF MATRIMONY

[1]   Now, we grant that by the sacraments men are restored to grace; nonetheless, they are not immediately restored to immortality. We have given the reason for this. But things which are corruptible cannot be perpetuated except by generation. Since, then, the people of the faithful had to be perpetuated unto the end of the world, this had to be done by generation, by which, also, the human species is perpetuated.

[2]   But let us consider this: When something is ordered to different ends there must be differing principles directing it to the end, for the end is proportioned to the agent. Human generation, of course, is ordered to many things; namely, to the perpetuity of the species and to the perpetuity of some political good—the perpetuity of a people in some state for example. It is also ordered to the perpetuity of the Church, which consists in the collection of the faithful. Accordingly, generation of this kind must be subject to a diversity of directions. Therefore, so far as it is ordered to the good of nature, which is the perpetuity of the species, it is directed to the end by nature inclining to this end; thus, one calls it a duty of nature. But, so far as generation is ordered to a political good, it is subject to the ordering of civil law. Then, so far as it is ordered to the good of the Church, it must be subject to the government of the Church. But things which are dispensed to the people by the ministers of the Church are called sacraments. Matrimony, then, in that it consists in the union of a husband and wife purposing to generate and educate offspring for the worship of God, is a sacrament of the Church; hence, also, a certain blessing on those marrying is given by the ministers of the Church.

[3]   And as in the other sacraments by the thing done outwardly a sign is made of a spiritual thing, so, too, in this sacrament by the union of husband and wife a sign of the union of Christ and the Church is made; in the Apostle's words: "This is a great sacrament; but I speak in Christ and in the church" (Eph. 5:32).

[4]   And because the sacraments effect that of which they are made signs, one must believe that in this sacrament a grace is conferred on those marrying, and that by this grace they are included in the union of Christ and the Church, which is most especially necessary to them, that in this way in fleshly and earthly things they may purpose not to be disunited from Christ and the Church. . . .

[6]   Thus, then, there are three goods of matrimony as a sacrament of the Church: namely, offspring to be accepted and educated for the worship of God; fidelity by which one man is bound to one wife; and the sacrament— and, in accord with this—there is indivisibility in the marriage union, in so far as it is a sacrament of the union of Christ and the Church.

61

THE BULL, *Unam Sanctam*, issued by Pope Boniface VIII in 1302, marked the high point of papal claim to supremacy over civil power. The bull was delivered in answer to Philip IV of France who refused to acknowledge the papal authority. In the bull, Boniface insisted that temporal powers are subject to a higher spiritual authority.

Unam Sanctam*

BONIFACE VII

Boniface, Bishop, Servant of the servants of God. For perpetual remembrance. Urged on by our faith, we are compelled to believe and hold that there is One Holy Catholic and Apostolic Church and we firmly believe and clearly profess that outside of her there is neither salvation nor remission of sins as the bridegroom declares in the Canticles, my dove, my undefiled is one; she is the only one of her mother, the chosen one of her that bare her. And she represents the mystical body of Christ whose head is Christ and God the head of Christ. In her there is one Lord, one faith, one baptism. For, in the time of the flood there was the single ark of Noah which prefigures the one Church, and was finished according to the measurement of one cubit and had one Noah for pilot and captain, and outside of it every living creature on the earth, as we read, was destroyed. And this Church we revere as the only one even as the Lord said to the prophet, Deliver my soul from the sword, my darling from the power of the dog. Ps. xxii, 20. He prayed for his life that is for himself, head and body. And this body, that is the Church, he called one—unicam—on account of the one bridegroom; and the oneness of the faith, the sacraments and the love in the Church. She is that seamless shirt of the Lord which was not rent but was allotted by the casting of lots. Therefore, this one and only Church has one head and not two heads,—for had she two heads, she would be a monster—that is, Christ and Christ's vicar, Peter and Peter's successor. For the Lord said to Peter himself, Feed my sheep. "My," he said (using the plural) that is all, not individuals, these and those; and by this he is understood to have committed to him all the sheep

* From Philip Schaff, *The Creeds of Christendom*, Vol. II. New York: Harper and Row Publishers, 1919. Used by permission of Mary L. Schaff.

—*oves universas.* When, therefore, either the Greeks or others say that they were not committed to the care of Peter and his successors, they must confess that they are not of Christ's sheep, even as the Lord says in John, There is one fold and one shepherd, John x, 10.

That in this Church and within her power are the two swords, we are taught in the Gospels, namely, the spiritual sword and the temporal sword. For when the Apostle said, Lo here—that is in the Church—are two swords the Lord did not reply to the Apostles, It is too much, but It is enough. For, certainly, he who denies that the temporal sword is in Peter's power, listens badly to the Lord's words Put up thy sword into its sheath. Matthew xxvi, 52. Therefore, both are in the power of the Church, namely, the spiritual sword and the temporal sword—the latter to be used for the Church, the former by the Church; the former by the hand of the priest, the latter by the hand of princes and kings, but at the nod and instance of the priest. The one sword must of necessity be subject to the other, and the temporal power to the spiritual power. For the Apostle said, There is no power but of God and the powers that be are ordained of God, Romans xiii, 1, but not ordained except as sword is subjected to sword and so the inferior is brought by the other to the highest end. For, according to St. Dionysius, it is a divine law that the lowest things are made by mediocre things to attain to the highest. Therefore, it is not according to the order of the universe that all things in an equal way and directly should reach their end, but the lowest through the mediocre and the lower through the higher; and, that the spiritual power excels the earthly power in dignity and worth, we will the more clearly acknowledge in the proportion that the spiritual is higher than the temporal. This we perceive quite distinctly from the donation of the tithe and the functions of benediction and sanctification, from the mode in which power itself is received and the government of things themselves. Truth being the witness, the spiritual power has the function of establishing the temporal power and sitting in judgment on it if it should prove not to be good. And to the Church, and the Church's power, Jeremiah's prophecy, i, 9, applies: See I have set thee this day over the nations and the kingdoms to pluck up and to break down, to destroy and to overthrow, to build and to plant.

And, if the earthly power deviates from the right path, it is judged by the spiritual power, but if a minor spiritual power deviate from the right path, the minor is judged by the superior power, but if the supreme power [the papacy or the Church] deviate, it can be judged not by man but by God only. And so the Apostle testifies, He which is spiritual judges all things but he himself is judged of no man, I Cor., ii, 15. But this authority, although it is given to a man and exercised by a man, is not a human power, nay, much rather a divine power given by the divine lips to Peter, to Peter himself and to his successors in Christ, whom Peter confessed when the Rock was established—*petra firmata*—when the Lord said unto him, Whatsoever thou shalt bind, etc., Matt., xvi, 19.

Whoever, therefore, resists this power ordained by God, resists God's ordinance, unless perchance he imagines two principles to exist, as did Manichaeus, a thing which we pronounce false and heretical because, as Moses testified, "God created the heaven and the earth not in the beginnings, but 'in the beginning.'"

Further, we declare, say, define and pronounce it to be altogether necessary for salvation for every human creature that he be subject to the Roman pontiff.

62 JOHN HUSS (1373–1415), the Bohemian reformer, was involved in the conciliar movement in tragic ways. His concerns, frequently similar to those of the English reformer, John Wycliff (d. 1384), achieved widespread following in the churches of Bohemia, especially after his excommunication in 1410. During Huss' lifetime, efforts to effect a reform of abuses in the church were being made. The Council of Constance, called to meet in 1414, sought a thorough reformation of the church. Huss' treatise, *The Church* (*de Ecclesia*), written between 1413 and 1415, was an attack on the prevailing ecclesiastical system. The Council of Constance summoned Huss to investigate his position and though he was granted safe conduct, he was imprisoned and put to death for heresy on July 6, 1415.

The conciliar movement was short lived. In 1460, Pius II, in his *Bull Execrabilis*, put an end to conciliar reform. His document reads in part: "An execrable abuse, unheard of in former ages, has grown up in our time. Some persons . . . presume to appeal to a future council from the Roman Pontiff, the vicar of Jesus Christ. . . . Anyone not wholly ignorant of the laws can see how contrary this is to the sacred canons and how injurious to Christendom. And who will not pronounce it ridiculous that appeal should be made to what does not exist and the time of whose future existence is unknown? (1) Therefore . . . we condemn such appeals and denounce them as erroneous and detestable. . . .

(2) If anyone . . . shall act contrariwise, he shall *ipso facto* incur sentence of execration, from which he cannot be absolved but by the Roman Pontiff and when at the point of death."

John Huss' *The Church* served not only as an incentive to reforming groups in the fifteenth century but also as a model for many Protestant reformers.

The Church*

JOHN HUSS

[I. CHRIST THE ONLY HEAD OF THE CHURCH]

Christ alone is the head of the universal church, which church is not a part of anything else. This is clear because, if any one is the head of the universal church, then is he made better than the angels and than any blessed created spirit, Heb. 1:4; but this befits Christ alone, for it behooved him to be the first-born among many brethren, Romans 8:29, and consequently it behooves him to be the chief by the right of the law of primogeniture, Col. 1:15. This conclusion also follows from the apostle's words, Eph. 1:20: "Which God wrought in Christ when he raised him from the dead and made him to sit at his right hand in the heavenly places, far above all rule and authority, power and dominion, and every name which is named not only in this world but also in the world which is to come, and has put all things under his feet and gave him to be head over all things to the church, which is his body." From this it is clear that, if any Christian were to be the head of the universal church with Christ (for the church cannot be a monster having two heads, as is set forth in Boniface VIII's bull, beginning *Unam sanctam*; therefore, the bull says, "the church is one body and has one head, not two heads, like a monster"), it would be necessary to concede that the Christian who was the head of that church was Christ himself, or otherwise it would be necessary to concede that Christ is inferior to that Christian and a lowly member of him. The conclusion shows that the thing is impossible. Hence, the holy apostles agreed in confessing that they were servants of that one Head and humble ministers of the church, his bride. No one of the apostles ever presumed to claim that he was the head or the bridegroom of the church, for this

* Reprinted with the permission of Charles Scribner's Sons from *The Church* by John Huss, translated by David S. Schaff. (Charles Scribner's Sons, 1915.) [The titles are supplied by the editor.]

would have meant to adulterate with the queen of heaven and to arrogate the name of dignity and office—the dignity by which, according to the eternal predestination, and the office through which, by eternal appointment, God ordained that Christ should be supreme ruler of his bride. This also appears from St. Augustine's letter to Dardanus [Migne's ed., 33:832 sqq.], where he says: "She only has one head, namely him who rules over her, excelling all and typifying in one union the spiritual and secular rule."

Therefore, it is possible to understand the "Head of the Church" in a twofold sense: inward and outward. In the inward sense, as the chief person of his church, and he is this in two ways: either by superintendence over the material goods of his church or by ruling over its spiritual things. As outward head he is a person that superintends persons inferior to his nature, but he is called the head to those outside of this number whom he rules by his influence in virtue of his nature. And so Christ is the outward head of every particular church and of the universal church by virtue of his divinity, and he is the inward head of the universal church by virtue of his humanity; and these two natures, divinity and humanity, are one Christ, who is the only head of his bride, the universal church, and this is the totality of the predestinate. For this divinity is the man who descended from heaven and who ascended again into heaven, as is said in John 3:13, not the whole of the divinity considered as divinity, but according to the headship whose descent was not a local movement but an incarnation or self-emptying. And the ascent was a local movement by which he took with himself the other parts of the body.

Hence, it is plain that there is nothing inconsistent in a particular church having several heads. For it may have three heads, namely the divinity of Christ, his humanity, and the chief appointed by God to rule over it. But there are degrees of subordination in these heads, because the divinity is supreme, Christ's humanity is intermediate, and the chief is the lowest. But the universal church, as has been said, has two heads, the outward head which is the divinity and the inward which is the humanity.

Further, from these things it is seen that Christ from the very beginning of the world down to his incarnation was, in virtue of his divinity, the outward head of the church, but from the incarnation on he is the inward head of the church, by virtue of his humanity. And so the whole holy catholic church always has had and now has Christ as its head, from whom it cannot fall away, for she is the bride knit to him, her head, by a love that never ends, for the bridegroom says to the church herself, Jer. 31:3: "I have loved thee with an everlasting love, therefore with loving kindness have I drawn thee." Therefore, always, from the very beginning, the bridegroom has been present with the whole church by virtue of his divinity, who later was with the holy fathers by virtue of his humanity. Hence Augustine says, commenting on Psalm 37:25, "I have been young [junior, younger] and now I am old": "The Lord himself in his heart, that is, his church, was younger than the first men. And, behold, now that he is old, ye know and do not know, and ye understand because ye are fixed in this, and so ye have believed, because Christ is our head, we are the body of the head. Are we alone the body and not those also who were before us? All who were righteous from the beginning of the world have Christ for their head. For they believed that he was for to come whom we now believe to have come, and in the faith in him they were healed, in which faith we also are healed; that he verily might be the head of the whole city of Jerusalem, all the faithful being included from the beginning even unto the end, and all the legions and armies of the angels being also added— that so there might be one city under one king, and one province under one emperor, happy, lauding God in its never-ending peace and salvation, and blessed without end. Christ's body, which is the church, is, as it were, like a young man. And now in the end of the world the church is of plump old age, because, with reference to this, it was said of her: 'They shall be multiplied in her plump old age.' She has been multiplied among all nations." So much Augustine, in whose words it appears how Christ is the head of the holy church, in whom the fathers believed as the one who was for to come in virtue of his humanity that he might be their head in his humanity as he had always been present with them in his divinity. And in this head all the elect are united, together with the holy angels. . . .

[II. THE CHURCH UNIVERSAL]

It has been said that Christ is the sole Head of the holy universal church and all the predestinate, past and future, are his mystical body and every one of them members of that body. It remains now briefly to examine whether the Roman church is that holy universal church, the bride of Christ. This seems to be the case because the holy catholic apostolic church is one, and this is none other than the Roman church. What seemed a matter of question is therefore true. The first part of the statement appears from Pope Boniface's bull: "By the urgency of faith we are compelled to believe and hold that the holy catholic apostolic church is one."[1] Likewise, the second statement appears from the same decretal, which says: "Of the one and only church there is one body, one head, and not two heads like a monster, namely, Christ and Christ's vicar, Peter, and Peter's successors, even as, when the Lord said to Peter himself, 'Feed my sheep,' he spoke in a general sense, not of individuals, of these or those sheep. It is plain that he regarded all the sheep as committed to him. Therefore, if the Greeks and others say that they were not committed to Peter and his successors, they thereby confess that it is not necessary to be

[1] Unam Sanctam.

of Christ's sheep; for did not the Lord say, in John: 'They shall become one fold and one shepherd'?" Is it not evident, therefore, that the holy Roman church is that holy universal church, because all are Christ's sheep, and the one fold is of one shepherd? This is the meaning of the aforesaid decretal of Boniface, which closes with these words: "Further we declare, say and determine that to be subject to the Roman pontiff is for every human being altogether necessary for salvation." If, therefore, every man is of necessity subjected by this declaration to the Roman pontiff, the aforesaid proposition will follow as true, and, on the other hand, the proposition that the Roman church is the church, whose head is the pope and whose body the cardinals, and these together constitute that church. But that church is not the holy catholic and apostolic church. Therefore, what seemed a matter of doubt is false. The first proposition is made out by the statements of certain doctors—among the statements being that the pope is the head of the Roman church and the body is the college of cardinals. The second is manifest from the fact that the pope with the cardinals is not the totality of all the elect.

For the understanding of this subject the notable passage of the Gospel must be meditated upon, namely, Matt. 16:16–19: "And Simon Peter answered and said, Thou art the Christ, the Son of the living God. And Jesus answered and said, Blessed art thou, Simon Bar-Jonah: for flesh and blood hath not revealed it unto thee, but my Father which is in heaven. And I also say unto thee, that thou art Peter, and upon this rock I will build my church; and the gates of hell shall not prevail against it. I will give unto thee the keys of the kingdom of heaven: and whatsoever thou shalt bind on earth shall be bound in heaven: and whatsoever thou shalt loose on earth shall be loosed in heaven." In this passage are designated Christ's church, its faith, the foundation, and the authority. In these words Christ's church is designated, "I will build my church"; in these Peter's faith, "Thou art the Christ, the Son of the living God"; in these the foundation, "on this rock I will build"; and in these the authority, "I will give unto thee the keys of the kingdom of heaven." These four are to be touched upon briefly, namely, the church, faith, the foundation, the church's power.

[A. THE CHURCH]

As for the first point, in view of the things set forth above the proposition is to be laid down that, if we put aside the church, nominally so called and as she is generally esteemed to be, then the church is said to be threefold. In one sense it is the congregation or company of the faithful in respect to what is for a time or in respect to present righteousness alone, and in this sense the reprobate are of the church for the time in which they are in grace. But this church is not Christ's mystical body nor the holy catholic church nor any part of it. In the second sense the church is taken to be the admixture of the predestinate and the reprobate while they are in grace in respect to present righteousness. And this church is in part but not in whole identical with God's holy church. And this church is called mixed in character—grain and chaff, wheat and tares—the kingdom of heaven like unto a net cast into the sea and gathering fish of every kind and the kingdom of heaven like unto ten virgins, of whom five were foolish and five wise. . . . For the reprobate are not the body of the Lord or any part of it.

In the third sense the church is taken for the company of the predestinate, whether they are in grace in respect to present righteousness or not. In this sense the church is an article of faith, about which the apostle was speaking when he said, Eph. 5:26: "Christ loved the church and gave himself for it, cleansing it by the washing of water in the word of life, that he might present it to himself a glorious church not having spot or wrinkle or any such thing, but that it might be holy and without spot."

This church the Saviour calls his church in the Gospel quoted, when he said: "On this rock I will build my church." And that he means this church is plain from the words which follow: "And the gates of hell shall not prevail against it." For seeing that Christ is the rock of that church and also the foundation on whom she is builded in respect to predestination, she cannot finally be overthrown by the gates of hell, that is, by the power and the assaults of tyrants who persecute her or the assaults of wicked spirits. For mightier is Christ the king of heaven, the bridegroom of the church, than the prince of this world. Therefore, in order to show his power and foreknowledge and the predestination wherewith he builds, protects, foreknows, and predestinates his church, and to give persevering hope to his church, he added: "And the gates of hell shall not prevail against it. . . ."

From the aforesaid words of Christ it is evident that the church is taken to mean all, in a special sense, who after his resurrection were to be built upon him and in him by faith and perfecting grace. . . . The conclusion, therefore, is that there is one holy church of Christ, which in Greek is *katholike* and in Latin *universalis*. She is also called apostolic, *apostolike*, because she was established by the words and deeds of the apostles and founded upon the Rock, Christ. . . .

In view of these things it is plain what ought to be said with regard to the doubtful statement made [above]. For it should be granted that the Roman church is the holy mother, the catholic church, the bride of Christ. To the argument in favor of the opposite, by which it is argued that the Roman church is the church of which the pope is the head and the cardinals the body—this is said by way of concession and by defining the church in the second way, that is, as the pope—whoever he may be—in conjunction with the cardinals—whoever they may be and wheresoever they may live. But it is denied that this church is the holy, catholic and apostolic church. And so both parts of the argument are granted, but the conclusion is denied. But if this be said, namely, "I lay down that the pope is holy together with all the twelve cardinals living with him," this being laid down and admitted as highly possible, it follows that the pope himself in conjunction with the cardinals is the holy, catholic and apostolic church. This conclusion is denied, but it follows well that a holy pope in conjunction with holy cardinals are a holy church which is a part of the holy, catholic and apostolic church. Therefore Christ's faithful must hold firmly as a matter of faith to the first conclusion and not to the second; for the first is confirmed by Christ's words: "The gates of hell shall not prevail against it." But the second is a matter of doubt to me and to every other pilgrim, unless a divine revelation makes it plain. Hence neither is the pope the head nor are the cardinals the whole body of the holy, universal, catholic church. For Christ alone is the head of that church, and his predestinate are the body and each one is a member, because his bride is one person with Jesus Christ. . . .

[B. THE FAITH]

. . . believing is an act of faith, that is, to put trust in—*fidere*—therefore know that to believe that which is necessary for a man to secure blessedness is to adhere firmly and without wavering to the truth spoken as by God. For this truth, because of its certitude, a man ought to expose his life to the danger of death. And, in this way, every Christian is expected to believe explicitly and implicitly all the truth which the Holy Spirit has put in scripture, and in this way a man is not bound to believe the sayings of the saints which are apart from scripture, nor should he believe papal bulls, except in so far as they speak out of scripture, or in so far as what they say is founded in scripture simply. But a man may believe bulls as probable, for both the pope and his curia make mistakes from ignorance of the truth. And, with reference to this ignorance, it can be substantiated that the pope makes mistakes and may be deceived. Lucre deceives the pope, and he is deceived through ignorance. How far, however, faith ought to be placed in the letters of princes, the instruments of notaries, and the descriptions of men, experience, which is the teacher of things, teaches. For she teaches that these three often make mistakes. Of one kind is the faith which is placed in God. He cannot deceive or be deceived; of another is the faith placed in the pope, who may deceive and be deceived. Of one kind is the faith placed in Holy Scripture; and another, faith in a bull thought out in a human way. For to Holy Scripture exception may not be taken, nor may it be gainsaid; but it is proper at times to take exception to bulls and gainsay them when they either commend the unworthy or put them in authority, or savor of avarice, or honor the unrighteous or oppress the innocent, or implicitly contradict the commands or counsels of God.

It is, therefore, plain which faith is the foundation of the church—the faith with which the church is built upon the Rock, Christ Jesus, for it is that by which the church confesses that "Jesus Christ is the Son of the living God." For Peter spoke for all the faithful, when he said: "Thou art the Christ, the Son of the living God." "This is the victory," says John, "which overcometh the world—even our faith. Who is he that overcometh the world but he that believeth that Jesus is the Son of God?" I John 5:4.

[C. THE FOUNDATION]

The third foundation, included in the proposition (Matt. 16:18) is touched upon in the words: "On this rock I will build my church." And in view of the fact that in their utterances the popes most of all use this saying of Christ, wishing to draw from it that they themselves are the rock or the foundation upon which the church stands, namely upon Peter, to whom it was said, "Thou art Peter,"—in view of this fact, in order to understand the Lord's word it must be noted that the foundation of the church by whom it is founded is touched upon in the words: "I will build," and the foundation in which it is laid is referred to in the words, "on this Rock," and the foundation wherewith the church is founded is referred to in the words, "Thou art the Christ, the Son of the living God." Christ is therefore the foundation by whom primarily and in whom primarily the holy catholic church is founded, and faith is the foundation with which it is founded—that faith which works through love, which Peter set forth when he said: "Thou art the Christ, the Son of the living God." The foundation, therefore, of the church is Christ, and he said: "Apart from me ye can do nothing," John 15:5; that is, apart from me as the prime and principal foundation. But Christ grounds and builds his church on himself, the Rock, when he so influences her that she hears and does his words, for then the gates of hell do not prevail against her. . . .

[D. AUTHORITY]

Hence the spiritual power, which is sacerdotal, excels the royal in age, dignity, and usefulness. In age it excels, because the priesthood was instituted by God's command, as appears from Ex. 28. Later at God's command the kingly power was instituted by the priesthood, as appears from Deut. 17 and I Sam. 12. In dignity it excels, as already said, because the priest as the greater blesses, consecrates and anoints the king. And the usefulness is evidently greater for the reason that the spiritual power is in and of itself sufficient for the ruling of the people, as appears from the history of Israel, which down to the time of Saul was salubriously administered independent of the kingly authority. Therefore, the spiritual power, inasmuch as it concerns the best things—things having their sufficiency in themselves—excels the earthly power, since the latter is of no avail independent of the spiritual power which is the chief regulative force. On the other hand, the spiritual power may act by itself without the aid of the earthly power. And, for this reason, the priests who abuse this power, which is so exalted, by pride or other open sin, fall all the lower with the devil into hell, and this is in accord with the rule of St. Gregory and other saints: "The higher the position the deeper the fall."

And it is to be noted, that power now means absolutely the ability to regulate and rule and now collectively such ability through authoritative notification and announcement. And when these senses are equally known, it is evident, there is nothing contradictory in the principles that there is no power but of God and yet to give power from God, that is, make an authoritative announcement before the church that a created being has from God power of this sort. Indeed such a bestowal, so far as part of it is concerned, is given by man but not unless God primarily authorizes it. And from this we may further understand that power is not relaxed or stiffened, increased or diminished, so far as its essence goes, but only in respect to the exercise of the act which proceeds from the power itself. And this exercise ought only to be used when a reasonable ground exists for it from the side of God. . . .

Hence, when Christ said to Peter: "I will give thee the keys of the kingdom of heaven," that is the power of binding and loosing sins, he said in the person of Peter to the whole church militant, that not does any person whatever of the church without distinction hold those keys, but that the whole church, as made up of its individual parts, as far as they are suitable for this, holds the keys. These keys, however, are not material things, but they are spiritual power and acquaintance with evangelical knowledge, and it was on account of this power and knowledge, as we believe, that Christ used the plural "keys. . . ." These keys are the wisdom of discernment and the power of judging, whereby the ecclesiastical judge is bound to receive the worthy and exclude the unworthy from the kingdom." And it is to be noted, that to the Trinity alone does it belong to have the chief power of this kind. And the humanity of Christ alone has chief subordinate power from within himself, for Christ is at the same time God and man. Nevertheless, prelates of the church have committed unto them instrumental or ministerial power, which is a judicial power, consisting chiefly of two things, namely, the power of knowing how to discriminate, and the power of judging judicially. The former of these is called in the court of penance the key of the conscience, reasonably disposing the mind to the exercise of the second function, that is, the judicial;

for no one legally has the power of pronouncing a definite sentence unless he has the prior power of discerning in a case in which he is called upon to discriminate and pronounce sentence. . . .

But God's act of binding or loosing is absolutely first. And it is evident, it would be blasphemy to assert that a man may remit an offense done to so great a Lord, with the Lord himself approving the remission. For by the universal law and practice followed by the Lord, He himself must loose or bind first, if any vicar looses or binds. And for us no article of the faith ought to be more certain than the impossibility of any one of the church militant to absolve or bind except in so far as he is conformed to the head of the church, our Lord Jesus Christ. . . .

[III. THE ROMAN PONTIFF]

Further, the aforesaid doctors[2] lay down in their writing that "the pope is head of the Roman church and the college of cardinals the body, and that they are very successors and princes of the apostle Peter and the college of Christ's other apostles in ecclesiastical office for the purpose of discerning and defining all catholic and church matters, correcting and purging all errors in respect to them and, in all these matters, to have the care of all the churches and of all the faithful of Christ. For in order to govern the church throughout the whole world it is fitting there should always continue to be such manifest and true successors in the office of Peter, the prince of the apostles, and of the college of the other apostles of Christ. And such successors cannot be found or procured on the earth other than the pope, the existing head, and the college of cardinals, the existing body, of the aforesaid Roman church."

These follies, long drawn out, which, I think, proceeded for the most part from the brain of Stanislaus, overcome and terrified by the Roman curia, involve many points. And in regard to these, I note that in their writing the church is taken to mean all Christian pilgrims. They seem to admit this when they say that "the body of the clergy in the kingdom of Bohemia, not only with the whole body of clergy in the world but also with the whole body of Christendom, always feels and believes as the faith dictates, just as the Roman church does." Or, secondly, these doctors call the pope, together with his cardinals, alone the Roman church, when they say that they believe just as the Roman church believes and not otherwise, the pope being the head of this Roman church and the cardinals the body. In these ways only, so far as I can see, do the doctors designate the church in their writing.

I assume that the pope stands for that spiritual bishop who, in the highest way and in the most similar way, occupies the place of Christ,

[2] The names are referred to in Chapter XI of Huss' treatise.

just as Peter did after the ascension. But if any person whatsoever is to be called pope—whom the Western church accepts as Roman bishop—appointed to decide as the final court ecclesiastical cases and to teach the faithful whatever he wishes, then there is an abuse of the term, because according to this view, it would be necessary in cases to concede that the most unlettered layman or a female, or a heretic and antichrist, may be pope. This is plain, for Constantine II, an unlettered layman, was suddenly ordained a priest and through ambition made pope and then was deposed and all the things which he ordained were declared invalid, about A.D. 707. And the same is plain from the case of Gregory, who was unlettered and consecrated another in addition to himself. And as the people were displeased with the act, a third pope was superinduced. Then these quarrelling among themselves, the emperor came to Rome and elected another as sole pope.[3] . . .

As for a heretic occupying the papal chair we have an instance in Liberius, . . . [who] was exiled for three years because he wished to favor the Arians. At the counsel of the same Constantius, the Roman clergy ordained Felix pope who, during the sessions of a synod condemned and cast out two Arian presbyters, Ursacius and Valens, and when this became known, Liberius was recalled from exile, and being wearied by his long exile and exhilarated by the reoccupation of the papal chair, he yielded to heretical depravity; and when Felix was cast down, Liberius with violence held the church of Peter and Paul and St. Lawrence so that the clergy and priests who favored Felix were murdered in the church, and Felix was martyred, Liberius not preventing.

As for antichrist occupying the papal chair, it is evident that a pope living contrary to Christ, like any other perverted person, is called by common consent antichrist. In accordance with John 2:22, many are become antichrists. And the faithful will not dare to deny persistently that it is possible for the man of sin to sit in the holy place. Of him the Saviour prophesied when he said: "When ye see the abomination of desolation, which is spoken of by Daniel, standing in the holy place," Matt. 24:15. The apostle also says: "Let no man beguile you in any wise, for it will not be except the falling away come first and the man of sin be revealed, the son of perdition; he that opposeth and exalteth himself against all that is

---

[3] Huss seems to refer to Gregory VI, 1045–1046, although a part of his statement cannot be verified. Gregory bought the papacy from the flagitious Benedict IX for one thousand or, according to another account, two thousand pounds silver. There were then three popes, Benedict IX, Sylvester III, and Gregory, all three elected by the Roman people. At the Synod of Sutri, 1046, two of these popes were deposed and Gregory abdicated and, at the instance of the Emperor Henry III, the bishop of Bamberg was elected and took the name Clement II. Gregory was taken to Germany as a prisoner and died about 1048.

called God or is worshipped; so that he sitteth in the temple of God setting himself forth as God," II Thess. 2:3–4. And it is apparent from the *Chronicles* how the papal dignity has sunk. . . .

In regard to these follies of the Unlearned—*indoctorum*—I find these points: (1) The pope is the head of the holy Roman church. (2) The college of cardinals is the body of the holy Roman church. (3) The pope is manifestly and truly the successor of the prince of the apostles, Peter. (4) Cardinals are manifest and true successors of the college of Christ's other apostles. (5) For the government of the church throughout the whole world, there should always be manifest and true successors of the same kind in the office of the prince of the apostles and in the office of Christ's other apostles. (6) Such successors are not to be found or procured on the earth, other than the pope, the existing head and the college of cardinals, the existing body of the church.

Against all these six points, the argument in brief runs thus: all truth in the religion of Christ is to be followed and only that is truth which is known by the bodily senses, or discovered by an infallible intelligence, or made known through revelation, or laid down in sacred scripture. But none of these six points is truth known by the bodily senses or discovered by an infallible intelligence or known through revelation, or laid down in divine scripture. Therefore, no one of these six points is truth in the religion of Jesus Christ.

. . . it is not of necessity to salvation for all Christians, living together, that they should believe expressly that any one is head of any church whatsoever unless his evangelical life and works plainly moved them to believe this. For it would be all too much presumption to affirm that we are heads of any particular church which perhaps might be a part of holy mother church. How, therefore, may any one of us without revelation presume to assert of himself or of another that he is the head, since it is said truly, Ecclesiasticus 9, that "no one knows, so far as predestination goes, whether one is worthy of love or hatred. . . ."

From these and other sayings it is evident that no pope is the manifest and true successor of Peter, the prince of the apostles, if in morals he lives at variance with the principles of Peter; and, if he is avaricious, then is he the vicar of Judas, who loved the reward of iniquity and sold Jesus Christ. And by the same kind of proof the cardinals are not the manifest and true successors of the college of Christ's other apostles unless the cardinals live after the manner of the apostles and keep the commands and counsels of our Lord Jesus Christ. For, if they climb up by another way than by the door of our Lord Jesus Christ, then are they thieves and robbers, just as the Saviour himself declared when of all such he said: "All that came before me are thieves and robbers," John 10:8. Whosoever, therefore, say that they are Christ's true and manifest vicars, knowing that they are living in sin, lie. Therefore the apostle says: How "do they of the synagogue of Satan say that they are Jews, and they are not, but lie"? [Rev. 2:9.]

Hence, if the cardinals heap up to themselves ecclesiastical livings and barter with them and take money for their sale either themselves or through others, and so devour and consume in luxurious living the goods of the poor, and if they do not do miracles or preach the Word of God to the people or pray sincerely or fill the place of deacons—whom the apostles appointed, Acts 6—by not performing their duties or living their lives— in how far, I ask, are they the vicars of the apostles? In this that they heap up livings or, like Gehazi, seize upon gifts, or because very early in the morning they come into the pope's presence clad in the most splendid apparel, and attended with the most sumptuous retinue of horsemen—thus attended, not on account of the distance of place or difficulty of the journey but to show their magnificence to the world and their contrariety to Christ and his apostles, who went about among the towns, cities, and castles clad in humble garb, on foot, preaching—evangelizando—the king- dom of God. . . .

Likewise all bishops of Christ's church, who follow Christ in their lives, they are true vicars of the apostles and they are not pope or cardinals. Therefore, other true successors of the apostles can be found and given besides the pope and the cardinals. . . .

[IV. THE RIGHT OF REBELLION]

. . . to rebel against an erring pope is to obey Christ the Lord, be- cause in making his provisions he chiefly makes those which savor of personal affection. Therefore, I call the world to witness that the papal distribution of benefices sows in the church hirelings all too widely. On the part of the popes, it gives them occasion to exalt their vicarial power, to put an excessive value on the world's dignity and to make an extravagant show of a fantastic sanctity. But these doctors, who are looking for tem- poral remuneration from the pope or servilely fear his power, and also are saying that he has mysterious power and is impeccable and inerrant and that he may do lawfully whatsoever pleases him—these doctors are pseudo- prophets and pseudo-apostles of antichrist.

From the things already said, it is clear that the apostolic seat is the authority to judge and teach Christ's law, or secondly, as has been said, it is the family of holy popes who are successors to Christ. In this sense the apostolic seat is understood, where Pope Anacletus says: "This apostolic seat has been established as the head and hinge by the Lord and not by another; and just as a gate is ruled by the hinge, so by the authority of the holy apostolic seat all the other churches are ruled, subject to the government of the Lord." That pope intended that he himself should be the head and hinge, the head in presiding and the hinge in ruling, but he has a weak enough argument for proving his purpose. For he argues from things that are alike, when he says: "As a gate is ruled by its hinge, so by the authority of the holy apostolic see all the churches are ruled." It would have been sufficient to argue that the pope and cardinals rule themselves well.

For as by one hinge only one door is ruled, so it would be a good thing if by their doctrine and authority they were ruled well themselves, so that afterwards other churches should be well ruled. . . .

All rational creatures, according to the method practised by the Roman curia, are subject to the curia's command, for every human creature is subject to the Roman pontiff, so it is said in the *Extravagante* of Boniface VIII [the bull *Unam sanctam*], namely: "Further we declare, say and define that it is altogether necessary for salvation for every human creature to be subject to the Roman pontiff." Similarly, the angelic world is subject to the Roman pontiff, as appears in the bull of Pope Clement: "We command the angels of paradise that they lead to the glory of paradise the soul of him who has been wholly absolved from purgatory."

Since, therefore, according to this method of the curia, every rational creature—angel and man—is subject to the commands of the Roman Pontiff, and since the method in the processes of the same curia states that "whatsoever place, privileged or unprivileged, to which John Huss shall go, and as long as he may be there, we do subject them to the ecclesiastical interdict"—it follows that if, by the highest possibility, John Huss, according to God's absolute power, reached by death the heavenly Jerusalem, that city would be subject to the ecclesiastical interdict. But blessed be God Almighty, who has ordered that the angels and all the saints in that heavenly Jerusalem are not subject to an interdict of this sort! Blessed also be Christ, the chief Roman pontiff, who has given grace to his faithful ones that, when there is no Roman pontiff for a given time, they may, under Christ as their leader, arrive in the heavenly country! For who would say that while the woman Agnes, to all appearances, was for two years and five months the only pope, no one then could be saved? Or again, who would say that after a pope's death and in the interval between the pope's death and the election of his successor, no man dying in that period could be saved? Blessed also be God Almighty, who ordains that His militant church shall have such life that, when a pope is dead, she is not on that account without a head or dead! Because not upon the pope but upon the head, Christ, does her life depend. And blessed be God that, when a pope is insane or become a heretic, the church militant remains the faithful spouse of the Lord Jesus Christ! Blessed also be the Lord, the one living head of the church, who preserves her so effectually in unity that, even now, while there are three so-called papal heads, she remains the one spouse of the Lord Jesus Christ!

63 MARTIN LUTHER's (1483–1546) *The Babylonian Captivity of the Church* (1520) was written at a crucial period in the early years of the Protestant Reformation. The essay dealt with the sacramental theory of Roman Catholicism. Luther's conviction that scriptual justification must be found for the sacraments led him to affirm two, baptism and the Lord's Supper, not the seven of Roman Catholicism, though he reserved a special place for penance. He was severely critical of the practice that denied the cup to the laity and the "scholastic" elements of the doctrine of transubstantiation. This essay was written before the lines of the Protestant Reformation became clear, though its publication made sharp Luther's differing theological position.

The Babylonian Captivity of the Church[*]

MARTIN LUTHER

At the outset I must deny that there are seven sacraments, and hold for the present[1] to but three—baptism, penance, and the bread.[2] These three have been subjected to a miserable captivity by the Roman curia, and the Church has been deprived of all her liberty. To be sure, if I desired to use the term in its scriptural sense, I should allow but a single sacrament,[3]

[*] From Martin Luther, *Three Treatises*, tr. by A. T. W. Steinhaeuser. Philadelphia: The Board of Publication of the Lutheran Church in America, 1943.

[1] The present did not last very long; see below.
[2] So called because of the withholding of the wine from the laity in the Lord's Supper.
[3] Cf. I Timothy 3:16.

with three sacramental signs; but of this I shall treat more fully at the proper time.

THE SACRAMENT OF THE BREAD

Let me tell you what progress I have made in my studies on the administration of this sacrament. For when I published my treatise on the Eucharist,[4] I clung to the common usage, being in no wise concerned with the question of the right or wrong of the papacy. But now, challenged and attacked, nay, forcibly thrust into the arena, I shall freely speak my mind, let all the papists laugh or weep together.

In the first place, John 6 is to be entirely excluded from this discussion, since it does not refer in a single syllable to the sacrament. For not only was the sacrament not yet instituted, but the whole context plainly shows that Christ is speaking of faith in the Word made flesh, as I have said above. For He says, "My words are spirit, and they are life," which shows that He is speaking of a spiritual eating, whereby whoever eats has life, whereas the Jews understood Him to be speaking of bodily eating and therefore disputed with Him. But no eating can give life save the eating which is by faith, for that is the truly spiritual and living eating. As Augustine also says: "Why make ready teeth and stomach? Believe, and thou hast eaten." For the sacramental eating does not give life, since many eat unworthily. Therefore, He cannot be understood as speaking of the sacrament in this passage. . . .

In the Lord's Supper, I say, the whole sacrament, or communion in both kinds, is given only to the priests or else it is given also to the laity. If it is given only to the priests, as they would have it, then it is not right to give it to the laity in either kind; for it must not be rashly given to any to whom Christ did not give it when He instituted it. For if we permit one institution of Christ to be changed, we make all of His laws invalid, and everyone will boldly claim that he is not bound by any law or institution of His. For a single exception, especially in the scriptures, invalidates the whole. But if it is given also to the laity, then it inevitably follows that it ought not to be withheld from them in either form. And if any do withhold it from them when they desire it, they act impiously and contrary to the work, example and institution of Christ. . . .

What carries most weight with me, however, and quite decides me is this. Christ says: "This is my blood, which is shed for you and for many for the remission of sins." Here we see very plainly that the blood is given to all those for whose sins it was shed. But who will dare to say it was not shed for the laity? Do you not see whom He addresses when He gives the cup? Does He not give it to all? Does He not say that it is shed for all?

[4] *The Treatise on the Blessed Sacrament,* 1519.

"For you," He says—well: we will let these be the priests—"and for many" —these cannot be priests; and yet He says, "Drink ye all of it." I too could easily trifle here and with my words make a mockery of Christ's words, . . . but they who rely on the scriptures in opposing us must be refuted by the scriptures. This is what has prevented me from condemning the Bohemians, who, be they wicked men or good, certainly have the word and act of Christ on their side, while we have neither, but only that hollow device of men—"the Church has appointed it." It was not the Church that appointed these things, but the tyrants of the churches, without the consent of the Church, which is the people of God.

But where in all the world is the necessity, where the religious duty, where the practical use, of denying both kinds, i.e., the visible sign, to the laity, when everyone concedes to them the grace[5] of the sacrament without the sign? If they concede the grace, which is the greater, why not the sign, which is the lesser? For in every sacrament the sign as such is of far less importance than the thing signified. What then is to prevent them from conceding the lesser, when they concede the greater? I can see but one reason; it has come about by the permission of an angry God in order to give occasion for a schism in the Church, to bring home to us how, having long ago lost the grace of the sacrament, we contend for the sign, which is the lesser, against that which is the most important and the chief thing; just as some men for the sake of ceremonies contend against love. Nay, this monstrous perversion seems to date from the time when we began for the sake of the riches of this world to rage against Christian love. Thus God would show us, by this terrible sign, how we esteem signs more than the things they signify. How preposterous would it be to admit that the faith of baptism is granted the candidate for baptism, and yet to deny him the sign of this faith, namely, the water! . . .

Come hither then, you popish flatterers, one and all! Fall to and defend yourselves against the charge of godlessness, tyranny, lese majesty against the Gospel, and the crime of slandering your brethren—you that decry as heretics those who will not be wise after the vaporings of your own brains, in the face of such patent and potent words of scripture. If any are to be called heretics and schismatics, it is not the Bohemians nor the Greeks, for they take their stand upon the Gospel; but you Romans are the heretics and godless schismatics, for you presume upon your own fictions and fly in the face of the clear scriptures of God. Parry that stroke, if you can! . . .

The first captivity of this sacrament, therefore, concerns its substance or completeness, of which we have been deprived by the despotism of

[5] The res sacramenti. The sacrament consisted of these two parts—(1) the sacramentum, or external sign, and (2) the res sacramenti, or the thing signified, the sacramental grace. Another distinction is that between (1) materia, or the external sign, and (2) forma, or the words of institution or administration.

Rome. Not that they sin against Christ, who use the one kind, for Christ did not command the use of either kind, but left it to everyone's free will, when He said: "As oft as ye do this, do it in remembrance of me." But they sin who forbid the giving of both kinds to such as desire to exercise this free will. The fault lies not with the laity, but with the priests. The sacrament does not belong to the priests, but to all, and the priests are not lords but ministers, in duty bound to administer both kinds to those who desire them, and as oft as they desire them. . . .

The second captivity of this sacrament is less grievous so far as the conscience is concerned, yet the very gravest danger threatens the man who would attack it, to say nothing of condemning it.

. . . it is an absurd and unheard-of juggling with words, to understand "bread" to mean "the form, or accidents of bread," and "wine" to mean "the form, or accidents of wine." Why do they not also understand all other things to mean their forms, or accidents? And even if this might be done with all other things, it would yet not be right thus to emasculate the words of God and arbitrarily to empty them of their meaning.

. . . why could not Christ include His body in the substance of the bread just as well as in the accidents? The two substances of fire and iron are so mingled in the heated iron that every part is both iron and fire. Why could not much rather Christ's body be thus contained in every part of the substance of the bread? . . .

Let us not, however, dabble too much in philosophy. Does not Christ appear to have admirably anticipated such curiosity by saying of the wine, not, "Hoc est sanguis meus," but "Hic est sanguis meus"? And yet more clearly, by bringing in the word "cup," when He said, "This cup is the new testament in my blood." Does it not seem as though He desired to keep us in a simple faith, so that we might but believe His blood to be in the cup? For my part, if I cannot fathom how the bread is the body of Christ I will take my reason captive to the obedience of Christ, and clinging simply to His word, firmly believe not only that the body of Christ is in the bread, but that the bread is the body of Christ. For in this I am borne out by the words, "He took bread, and giving thanks, He brake it and said, Take, eat; this [i.e., this bread which He took and brake] is my body" And Paul says: "The bread which we break, is it not the communion of the body of Christ?" He says not in the bread, but the bread itself, is the communion of the body of Christ. What matters it if philosophy cannot fathom this? The Holy Spirit is greater than Aristotle. Does philosophy fathom that transubstantiation of theirs, of which they themselves admit that here all philosophy breaks down? But the agreement of the pronoun "this" with "body," in Greek and Latin, is owing to the fact that in these languages the two words are of the same gender. But in the Hebrew language, which has no neuter gender, "this" agrees with "bread," so that it would be proper to say, "*Hic* est corpus meum." This is proved also by the use of language and by common sense; the subject, forsooth, points to the bread, not to the body, when He says, "*Hoc* est corpus meum," "*Das ist mein Leib*"—i.e., This bread is my body.

Therefore it is with the sacrament even as it is with Christ. In order that the Godhead may dwell in Him, it is not necessary that the human nature be transubstantiated and the Godhead be contained under its accidents; but both natures are there in their entirety, and it is truly said, "This man is God," and "This God is man." Even though philosophy cannot grasp this, faith grasps it, and the authority of God's Word is greater than the grasp of our intellect. Even so, in order that the real body and the real blood of Christ may be present in the sacrament, it is not necessary that the bread and wine be transubstantiated and Christ be contained under their accidents; but both remain there together, and it is truly said, "This bread is my body, this wine is my blood," and *vice versa*. Thus I will for the nonce understand it, for the honor of the holy words of God, which I will not suffer any petty human arguments to override or wrest to meanings foreign to them. . . .

The third captivity of this sacrament is that most wicked abuse of all, in consequence of which there is today no more generally accepted and firmly believed opinion in the Church than this, that the mass is a good work and a sacrifice. And this abuse has brought an endless host of others in its train, so that the faith of this sacrament has become utterly extinct and the holy sacrament has been turned into a veritable fair, tavern, and place of merchandise. Hence participations, brotherhoods, intercessions, merits, anniversaries, memorial days, and the like wares are bought and sold, traded and bartered in the Church, and from this priests and monks derive their whole living.

I am attacking a difficult matter, and one perhaps impossible to abate, since it has become so firmly entrenched through century-long custom and the common consent of men that it would be necessary to abolish most of the books now in vogue, to alter well-nigh the whole external form of the churches, and to introduce, or rather reintroduce, a totally different kind of ceremonies. But my Christ lives; and we must be careful to give more heed to the Word of God than to all the thoughts of men and of angels. . . .

In the first place, in order to attain safely and fortunately to a true and unbiased knowledge of this sacrament, we must above all else be careful to put aside whatever has been added by the zeal and devotion of men to the original, simple institution of this sacrament—such things as vestments, ornaments, chants, prayers, organs, candles, and the whole pageantry of outward things; we must turn our eyes and hearts simply to the institution of Christ and to this alone, and set naught before us but the very word of

Christ by which He instituted this sacrament, made it perfect, and committed it to us. For in that word, and in that word alone, reside the power, the nature, and the whole substance of the mass. All else is the work of man, added to the word of Christ; and the mass can be held and remain a mass just as well without it. Now the words of Christ, in which He instituted this sacrament, are these:

"And whilst they were at supper, Jesus took bread, and blessed, and brake: and gave to His disciples, and said: Take ye and eat. This is my body, which shall be given for you. And taking the chalice, He gave thanks, and gave to them, saying: Drink ye all of this. This is the chalice, the new testament in my blood, which shall be shed for you and for many unto remission of sins. This do for the commemoration of me."[6]

These words the Apostle also delivers and more fully expounds in I Corinthians 11. On them we must lean and build as on a firm foundation, if we would not be carried about with every wind of doctrine, even as we have hitherto been carried about by the wicked doctrines of men, who turn aside the truth. For in these words nothing is omitted that pertains to the completeness, the use, and the blessing of this sacrament; and nothing is included that is superfluous and not necessary for us to know. Whoever sets them aside and meditates or teaches concerning the mass, will teach monstrous and wicked doctrines, as they have done who made of the sacrament an *opus operatum*[7] and a sacrifice.

Therefore let this stand at the outset as our infallibly certain proposition: The mass, or sacrament of the altar, is Christ's testament which He left behind Him at His death, to be distributed among His believers. For that is the meaning of His word, "This is the chalice, the new testament in my blood." Let this truth stand, I say, as the immovable foundation on which we shall base all that we have to say, for we are going to overthrow, as you will see, all the godless opinions of men imported into this most precious sacrament. Christ, who is the Truth, says truly that this is the new testament in His blood, which is shed for us. Not without reason do I dwell on this sentence; the matter is of no small moment, and must be most deeply impressed upon us.

Let us inquire, therefore, what a testament is, and we shall learn at the same time what the mass is, what its use and blessing, and what its abuse. A testament, as every one knows, is a promise made by one about to die, in which he designates his bequest and appoints his heirs. Therefore a testament involves, first, the death of the testator, and secondly, the promise of the bequest and the naming of the heir. Thus St. Paul discusses at length the nature of a testament in Romans 4, Galatians 3 and 4, and Hebrews 9. The same thing is also clearly seen in these words of Christ.

6 The Douay version has here been followed.

7 A work that is done without reference to the doer of it.

Christ testifies concerning His death when He says: "This is my body, which shall be given; this is my blood, which shall be shed." He designates the bequest when He says: "Unto remission of sins." And He appoints the heirs when He says: "For you, and for many," i.e., for such as accept and believe the promise of the testator; for here it is faith that makes men heirs, as we shall see.

You see, therefore, that what we call the mass is the promise of remission of sins made to us by God; and such a promise as has been confirmed by the death of the Son of God. For the one difference between a promise and a testament is that a testament is a promise which implies the death of him who makes it. A testator is a man making a promise who is about to die; whilst he that makes a promise is, if I may so put it, a testator who is not about to die. This testament of Christ was foreshadowed in all the promises of God from the beginning of the world; nay, whatever value those olden promises possessed was altogether derived from this new promise that was to come in Christ. Hence the words "covenant" and "testament of the Lord" occur so frequently in the scriptures, which words signified that God would one day die. For where there is a testament, the death of the testator must needs follow (Hebrew 9). Now God made a testament: therefore it was necessary that He should die. But God could not die unless He became man. Thus both the incarnation and the death of Christ are briefly comprehended in this one word "testament."

From the above it will at once be seen what is the right and what the wrong use of the mass, what is the worthy and what the unworthy preparation for it. If the mass is a promise, as has been said, it is to be approached, not with any work or strength or merit, but with faith alone. For where there is the word of God who makes the promise, there must be the faith of man who takes it. It is plain, therefore, that the first step in our salvation is faith, which clings to the word of the promise made by God, who without any effort on our part, in free and unmerited mercy, makes a beginning and offers us the word of His promise. For He sent His Word, and by it healed them. He did not accept our work and thus heal us. God's Word is the beginning of all; on it follows faith, and on faith charity; then charity works every good work, for it worketh no ill, nay, it is the fulfilling of the law. In no other way can man come to God and deal with Him than through faith; that is, not man, by any work of his, but God, by His promise, is the author of salvation, so that all things depend on the word of His power, and are upheld and preserved by it, with which word He begat us, that we should be a kind of first fruits of His creatures. . . .

The mass, according to its substance, is, therefore, nothing else than the aforesaid words of Christ—"Take and eat"; as if He said: "Behold, O sinful man and condemned out of pure and unmerited love wherewith I love thee, and by the will of the Father of all mercies, I promise thee in these words, or ever thou canst desire or deserve them, the forgiveness of all thy sins and life everlasting. And, that thou mayest be most certainly assured of this my irrevocable promise, I give my body and shed my blood, thus by my very death confirming this promise, and leaving thee my body and blood as a sign and memorial of this same promise. As oft, therefore, as thou partakest of them, remember me, and praise, magnify, and give thanks for my love and largess toward thee."

Herefrom you will see that nothing else is needed for a worthy holding of mass than a faith that confidently relies on this promise, believes Christ to be true in these words of His, and doubts not that these infinite blessings have been bestowed upon it. Hard on this faith there follows, of itself, a most sweet stirring of the heart, whereby the spirit of man is enlarged and waxes fat—that is love, given by the Holy Spirit through faith in Christ—so that he is drawn unto Christ, that gracious and good testator, and made quite another and a new man. Who would not shed tears of gladness, nay well-nigh faint, for the joy he hath toward Christ, if he believed with unshaken faith that this inestimable promise of Christ belonged to him! How could one help loving so great a benefactor, who offers, promises and grants, all unbidden, such great riches, and this eternal inheritance, to one unworthy and deserving of something far different? . . .

For anyone can easily see that these two—the promise and faith—must go together. For without the promise there is nothing to believe, while without faith the promise remains without effect; for it is established and fulfilled through faith. From this everyone will readily gather that the mass, which is nothing else than the promise, is approached and observed only in this faith, without which whatever prayers, preparations, works, signs of the cross, or genuflections are brought to it, are incitements to impiety rather than exercises of piety; for they who come thus prepared are wont to imagine themselves on that account justly entitled to approach the altar, when in reality they are less prepared than at any other time and in any other work, by reason of the unbelief which they bring with them. How many priests will you find every day offering the sacrifice of the mass, who accuse themselves of a horrible crime if they—wretched men!—commit a trifling blunder, such as putting on the wrong robe or forgetting to wash their hands or stumbling over their prayers; but that they neither regard nor believe the mass itself, namely, the divine promise—this causes them not the slightest qualms of conscience. O worthless religion of this our age, the most godless and thankless of all ages!

Hence the only worthy preparation and proper use of the mass is faith in the mass, that is to say, in the divine promise. Whoever, therefore, is minded to approach the altar and to receive the sacrament, let him beware of appearing empty before the Lord God. But he will appear empty unless he has faith in the mass, or this new testament. What godless work that he could commit would be a more grievous crime against the truth of God, than this unbelief of his, by which, as much as in him lies, he convicts God of being a liar and a maker of empty promises? The safest course, therefore, will be to go to mass in the same spirit in which you would go to hear any other promise of God; that is, not to be ready to perform and bring many works, but to believe and receive all that is there promised, or proclaimed by the priest as having been promised to you. If you do not go in this spirit, beware of going at all; you will surely go to your condemnation.

I was right then in saying that the whole power of the mass consists in the words of Christ, in which He testifies that the remission of sins is bestowed on all those who believe that His body is given and His blood shed for them. For this reason nothing is more important for those who go to hear mass than diligently and in full faith to ponder these words. Unless they do this, all else that they do is in vain. . . .

THE SACRAMENT OF BAPTISM

. . . Now, the first thing in baptism to be considered is the divine promise, which says: "He that believeth and is baptized shall be saved." This promise must be set far above all the glitter of works, vows, religious orders, and whatever man has added thereto; for on it all our salvation depends. But we must so consider it as to exercise our faith therein, and in no wise doubt that we are saved when we are baptized. For unless this faith be present or be conferred in baptism, baptism will profit us nothing, nay, it becomes a hindrance to us, not only in the moment of its reception, but all the days of our life; for such unbelief accuses God's promise of being a lie, and this is the blackest of all sins. If we set ourselves to this exercise of faith, we shall at once perceive how difficult it is to believe this promise of God. For our human weakness, conscious of its sins, finds nothing more difficult to believe than that it is saved or will be saved; and yet unless it does believe this, it cannot be saved, because it does not believe the truth of God that promiseth salvation.

This message should have been untiringly impressed upon the people and this promise dinned without ceasing in their ears; their baptism should have been called again and again to their mind, and faith constantly awakened and nourished. For, just as the truth of this divine promise, once pronounced over us, continues unto death, so our faith in the same ought never to cease, but to be nourished and strengthened until death, by the continual remembrance of this promise made to us in baptism. Therefore, when we rise from sins or repent, we do but return to the power and the faith of baptism from whence we fell, and find our way back to the promise then made to us, from which we departed when we sinned. For the truth of the promise once made remains steadfast, ever ready to receive us back with open arms when we return. This, if I mistake not, is the real meaning of the obscure saying, that baptism is the beginning and foundation of all the sacraments, without which none of the others may be received. . . .

Lo, how rich therefore is a Christian, or one who is baptized! Even if he would, he cannot lose his salvation, however much he sin, unless he will not believe. For no sin can condemn him save unbelief alone. All other sins—if faith in God's promise made in baptism return or remain —all other sins, I say, are immediately blotted out through that same faith, or rather through the truth of God, because He cannot deny Himself if you but confess Him and cling believing to Him that promises. But as for contrition, confession of sins, and satisfaction[8]—with all those carefully thought-out exercises of men—if you turn your attention to them and neglect this truth of God, they will suddenly fail you and leave you more wretched than before. For whatever is done without faith in the truth of God is vanity of vanities and vexation of spirit. . . .

Hence it is indeed correct to say that baptism is a washing from sins, but that expression is too weak and mild to bring out the full significance of baptism, which is rather a symbol of death and resurrection. For this reason I would have the candidates for baptism completely immersed in the water, as the word says and as the sacrament signifies. Not that I deem this necessary, but it were well to give to so perfect and complete a thing a perfect and complete sign; thus it was also doubtless instituted by Christ. The sinner does not so much need to be washed as he needs to die, in order to be wholly renewed and made another creature, and to be conformed to the death and resurrection of Christ, with whom, through baptism, he dies and rises again. Although you may properly say that Christ was washed clean of mortality when He died and rose again, yet that is a weaker way of putting it than if you said He was completely changed and renewed. In the same way it is far more forceful to say that baptism signifies our utter dying and rising to eternal life, than to say that it signifies merely our being washed clean from sins.

Here, again, you see that the sacrament of baptism, even in respect to its sign, is not the matter of a moment, but continues for all time. Although its administration is soon over, yet the thing it signifies continues until we die, nay, until we rise at the last day. For as long as we live we are continually doing that which our baptism signifies: we die and rise again. We die, that is, not only spiritually and in our affections, by renouncing the sins and vanities of this world, but we die in very truth, we begin to leave this bodily life and to lay hold on the life to come; so that there is, as they say, a real and even a bodily going out of this world to the Father. . . .

[8] The three parts of penance.

In contradiction of what has been said, some will perhaps point to the baptism of infants, who do not grasp the promise of God and cannot have the faith of baptism; so that either faith is not necessary or else infant baptism is without effect. Here I say what all say: Infants are aided by the faith of others, namely, those who bring them to baptism.[9] For the Word of God is powerful, when it is uttered, to change even a godless heart, which is no less deaf and helpless than any infant. Even so the infant is changed, cleansed and renewed by inpoured faith, through the prayer of the Church that presents it for baptism and believes, to which prayer all things are possible. Nor should I doubt that even a godless adult might be changed, in any of the sacraments, if the same Church prayed and presented him; as we read in the Gospel of the man sick of the palsy, who was healed through the faith of others. I should be ready to admit that in this sense the sacraments of the New Law are efficacious to confer grace, not only to those who do not, but even to those who do most obstinately, oppose a bar. What obstacle will not the faith of the Church and the prayer of faith remove? Do we not believe that Stephen by this powerful means converted Paul the Apostle? But then the sacraments accomplish what they do not by their own power, but by the power of faith, without which they accomplish nothing at all, as has been said. . . .

THE SACRAMENT OF PENANCE

. . . Now let us see what they have put in the place of the promise and the faith which they have blotted out and overthrown. Three parts have they made of penance: contrition, confession, and satisfaction; yet so as to destroy whatever of good there might be in any of them and to establish here also their covetousness and tyranny.

In the first place, they teach that contrition precedes faith in the promise; they hold it much too cheap, making it not a work of faith, but a merit; nay, they do not mention it at all. So deep are they sunk in works and in those instances of scripture that show how many obtained grace by reason of their contrition and humility of heart; but they take no account of the faith which wrought such contrition and sorrow of heart, as it is written of the men of Nineveh in Jonah 3, "And the men of Nineveh believed in God: and they proclaimed a fast," etc. Others, again, more bold and wicked, have invented a so-called "attrition," which is converted into contrition by virtue of the power of the keys, of which they know nothing. This attrition they grant to the wicked and unbelieving and thus abolish contrition altogether. O the intolerable wrath of God, that such things should be taught in the Church of Christ! Thus, with both faith and

[9] The position of Thomas Aquinas, going back to Augustine, and ratified by Clement V at the Council of Vienna, 1311–12.

its work destroyed, we go on secure in the doctrines and opinions of men—yea, we go on to our destruction. A contrite heart is a precious thing, but it is found only where there is a lively faith in the promises and the threats of God. Such faith, intent on the immutable truth of God, startles and terrifies the conscience and thus renders it contrite, and afterwards, when it is contrite, raises it up, consoles and preserves it; so that the truth of God's threatening is the cause of contrition, and the truth of His promise the cause of consolation, if it be believed. By such faith a man merits the forgiveness of sins. Therefore faith should be taught and aroused before all else; and when faith is obtained, contrition and consolation will follow inevitably and of themselves.

Therefore, although there is something of truth in their teaching that contrition is to be attained by what they call the recollection and contemplation of sins, yet their teaching is perilous and perverse so long as they do not teach first of all the beginning and cause of contrition—the immutable truth of God's theatening and promise, to the awakening of faith—so that men may learn to pay more heed to the truth of God, whereby they are cast down and lifted up, than to the multitude of their sins, which will rather irritate and increase the sinful desires than lead to contrition, if they be regarded apart from the truth of God. I will say nothing now of the intolerable burden they have bound upon us with their demand that we should frame a contrition for every sin. That is impossible; we can know only the smaller part of our sins, and even our good works are found to be sins, according to Psalm 143, "Enter not into judgment with thy servant; for in thy sight shall no man living be justified." It is enough to lament the sins which at the present moment distress our conscience, as well as those which we can readily call to mind. Whoever is in this frame of mind is without doubt ready to grieve and fear for all his sins, and will do so whenever they are brought to his knowledge in the future.

Beware, then, of putting your trust in your own contrition and of ascribing the forgiveness of sins to your own sorrow. God does not have respect to you because of that, but because of the faith by which you have believed His threatenings and promises, and which wrought such sorrow within you. Thus we owe whatever of good there may be in our penance, not to our scrupulous enumeration of sins, but to the truth of God and to our faith. All other things are the works and fruits of this, which follow of their own accord, and do not make a man good, but are done by a man already made good through faith in the truth of God. Even so, "a smoke goeth up in His wrath, because He is angry and troubleth the mountains and kindleth them," as it is said in Psalm 18. First comes the terror of His threatening, which burns up the wicked; then faith, accepting this, sends up the cloud of contrition, etc.

Contrition, however, is less exposed to tyranny and gain than wholly given over to wickedness and pestilent teaching. But confession and satisfaction have become the chief workshop of greed and violence. Let us first take up confession. There is no doubt that confession is necessary and commanded of God. . . . But most effectively of all does Matthew 18 prove the institution of confession, in which passage Christ teaches that a sinning brother should be rebuked, haled before the Church, accused and, if he will not hear, excommunicated. But he hears when, heeding the rebuke, he acknowledges and confesses his sin.

Of private confession, which is now observed, I am heartily in favor, even though it cannot be proved from the scriptures; it is useful and necessary, nor would I have it abolished—nay, I rejoice that it exists in the Church of Christ, for it is a cure without an equal for distressed consciences. For when we have laid bare our conscience to our brother and privately made known to him the evil that lurked within, we receive from our brother's lips the word of comfort spoken by God Himself; and, if we accept it in faith, we find peace in the mercy of God speaking to us through our brother. This alone do I abominate—that this confession has been subjected to the despotism and extortion of the pontiffs. They reserve to themselves even hidden sins, and command that they be made known to confessors named by them, only to trouble the consciences of men. They merely play the pontiff, while they utterly despise the true duties of pontiffs, which are to preach the Gospel and to care for the poor. Yea, the godless despots leave the great sins to the plain priests, and reserve to themselves those sins only which are of less consequence. . . .

Hence, I have no doubt but that everyone is absolved from his hidden sins when he has made confession, either of his own accord or after being rebuked, has sought pardon and amended his ways, privately before any brother, however much the violence of the pontiffs may rage against it; for Christ has given to everyone of His believers the power to absolve even open sins. Add yet this little point: If any reservation of hidden sins were valid, so that one could not be saved unless they were forgiven, then a man's salvation would be prevented most of all by those aforementioned good works and idolatries, which are nowadays taught by the popes. But if these most grievous sins do not prevent one's salvation, how foolish it is to reserve those lighter sins! Verily, it is the foolishness and blindness of the pastors that produce these monstrous things in the Church. Therefore I would admonish these princes of Babylon and bishops of Bethaven to refrain from reserving any cases whatsoever. Let them, moreover, permit all brothers and sisters freely to hear the confession of hidden sins, so that the sinner may make his sins known to whomever he will and seek pardon and comfort, that is, the word of Christ, by the mouth of his neighbor. For with these presumptions of theirs they only ensnare the consciences of the weak without necessity, establish their wicked despotism, and fatten their avarice on the sins and ruin of their brethren. Thus they stain their hands with the blood of souls, sons are devoured by their parents, Ephraim devours Judah, and Syria Israel with open mouth, as Isaiah says. . . .

How unworthily they have dealt with satisfaction, I have abundantly shown in the controversies concerning indulgences. They have grossly abused it, to the ruin of Christians in body and soul. To begin with, they taught it in such a manner that the people never learned what satisfaction really is, namely, the renewal of a man's life. Then, they so continually harp on it and emphasize its necessity, that they leave no room for faith in Christ. With these scruples they torture poor consciences to death, and one runs to Rome, one to this place, another to that, this one to Chartreuse, that one to some other place, one scourges himself with rods, another ruins his body with fasts and vigils, and all cry with the same mad zeal, "Lo here is Christ! lo there!" believing that the kingdom of heaven, which is within us, will come with observation.

For these monstrous things we are indebted to thee, O Roman See, and thy murderous laws and ceremonies, with which thou hast corrupted all mankind, so that they think by works to make satisfaction for sin to God, who can be satisfied only by the faith of a contrite heart! This faith thou not only keepest silent with this uproar of thine, but even oppressest, only so thy insatiable horseleech have those to whom it may say, "Bring, bring!" and may traffic in sins. . . .

THE SACRAMENT OF CONFIRMATION

I wonder what could have possessed them to make a sacrament of confirmation out of the laying on of hands, which Christ employed when He blessed young children, and the apostles when they imparted the Holy Spirit, ordained elders and cured the sick, as the Apostle writes to Timothy, "Lay hands suddenly on no man." Why have they not also turned the sacrament of the bread into confirmation? For it is written in Acts 9, "And when he had taken meat he was strengthened," and in Psalm 104, "And that bread may cheer man's heart." Confirmation would thus include three sacraments—the bread, ordination, and confirmation itself. But if everything the apostles did is a sacrament, why have they not rather made preaching a sacrament?

I do not say this because I condemn the seven sacraments, but because I deny that they can be proved from the scriptures. Would to God we had in the Church such a laying on of hands as there was in apostolic times, whether we called it confirmation or healing! But there is nothing left of it now but what we ourselves have invented to adorn the office of the bishops, that they may have at least something to do in the Church. For after they relinquished to their inferiors those arduous sacraments together with the Word, as being too common for themselves—since, forsooth, whatever the divine Majesty has instituted must needs be despised of men!—it was no more than right that we should discover something easy and not too burdensome for such delicate and great heroes to do, and should by no means entrust it to the lower clergy as something common —for whatever human wisdom has decreed must needs be held in honor among men! Therefore, as are the priests, so let their ministry and duty be. For a bishop who does not preach the Gospel or care for souls, what is he but an idol in the world, having but the name and appearance of a bishop?

But we seek, instead of this, sacraments that have been divinely instituted, among which we see no reason for numbering confirmation. For, in order that there be a sacrament, there is required above all things a word of divine promise, whereby faith may be trained. But we read nowhere that Christ ever gave a promise concerning confirmation, although He laid hands on many and included the laying on of hands among the signs in Mark 16: "They shall lay their hands on the sick, and they shall recover." Yet no one referred this to a sacrament, nor can this be done. Hence it is sufficient to regard confirmation as a certain churchly rite or sacramental ceremony, similar to other ceremonies, such as the blessing of holy water and the like. For if every other creature is sanctified by the word and by prayer, why should not much rather man be sanctified by the same means? Still, these things cannot be called sacraments of faith, because there is no divine promise connected with them, neither do they save; but sacraments do save those who believe the divine promise.

THE SACRAMENT OF MARRIAGE

Not only is marriage regarded as a sacrament without the least warrant of scripture, but the very traditions which extol it as a sacrament have turned it into a farce. Let me explain.

We said that there is in every sacrament a word of divine promise, to be believed by whoever receives the sign, and that the sign alone cannot be a sacrament. Now we read nowhere that the man who marries a wife receives any grace of God. Nay, there is not even a divinely instituted sign in marriage, for nowhere do we read that marriage was instituted by God to be a sign of anything. To be sure, whatever takes place in a visible manner may be regarded as a type or figure of something invisible; but types and figures are not sacraments in the sense in which we use this term.

Furthermore, since marriage existed from the beginning of the world and is still found among unbelievers, it cannot possibly be called a sacrament of the New Law and the exclusive possession of the Church. The marriages of the ancients were no less sacred than are ours, nor are those of unbelievers less true marriages than those of believers, and yet they are not regarded as sacraments. Besides, there are even among believers married folk who are wicked and worse than any heathen; why should marriage be called a sacrament in their case and not among the heathen? Or are we going to prate so foolishly of baptism and the Church as to hold that marriage is a sacrament only in the Church, just as some make the mad claim that temporal power exists only in the Church? That is childish and foolish talk, by which we expose our ignorance and our arrogance to the ridicule of unbelievers.

. . . we grant that marriage is a type of Christ and the Church, and a sacrament, yet not divinely instituted, but invented by men in the Church, carried away by their ignorance both of the word and of the thing. Which ignorance, since it does not conflict with the faith, is to be charitably borne with, just as many other practices of human weakness and ignorance are borne with in the Church, so long as they do not conflict with the faith and with the Word of God. But we are now dealing with the certainty and purity of the faith and the scriptures; so that our faith be not exposed to ridicule, when after affirming that a certain thing is contained in the Sacred Scriptures and in the articles of our faith, we are refuted and shown that it is not contained therein, and, being found ignorant of our own affairs, become a stumbling-block to our opponents and to the weak; nay, that we destroy not the authority of the Holy Scriptures. For those things which have been delivered to us by God in the Sacred Scriptures must be sharply distinguished from those that have been invented by men in the Church, it matters not how eminent they be for saintliness and scholarship. . . .

THE SACRAMENT OF ORDINATION

Of this sacrament the Church of Christ knows nothing; it is an invention of the church of the pope. Not only is there nowhere any promise of grace attached to it, but there is not the least mention of it in the whole New Testament. Now it is ridiculous to put forth as a sacrament of God that which cannot be proved to have been instituted by God. I do not hold that this rite, which has been observed for so many centuries, should be condemned; but in sacred things I am opposed to the invention of human fictions, nor is it right to give out as divinely instituted what was not divinely instituted, lest we become a laughing-stock to our opponents. We ought to see to it that every article of faith of which we boast be certain, pure, and based on clear passages of scripture. But that we are utterly unable to do in the case of the sacrament under consideration. . . .

The Church can give no promises of grace; that is the work of God alone. Therefore she cannot institute a sacrament. But even if she could, it yet would not follow that ordination is a sacrament. For who knows which is the Church that has the Spirit? since when such decisions are

made there are usually only a few bishops or scholars present; it is possible
that these may not be really of the Church, and that all may err, as
councils have repeatedly erred, particularly the Council of Constance,[10]
which fell into the most wicked error of all. Only that which has the approval of the Church universal, and not of the Roman church alone, rests
on a trustworthy foundation. I therefore admit that ordination is a certain
churchly rite, on a par with many others introduced by the Church
Fathers, such as the blessing of vases, houses, vestments, water, salt, candles,
herbs, wine, and the like. No one calls any of these a sacrament, nor is there
in them any promise. In the same maner, to anoint a man's hands with oil,
or to shave his head, and the like, is not to administer a sacrament, since
there is no promise given to those things; he is simply prepared, like a
vessel or an instrument, for a certain work. . . .

THE SACRAMENT OF EXTREME UNCTION

To the rite of anointing the sick our theologians have made two
additions which are worthy of them: first, they call it a sacrament, and
secondly, they make it the last sacrament. So that it is now the *sacrament
of extreme* unction, which may be administered only to such as are at the
point of death. Being such subtle dialecticians, perchance they have done
this in order to relate it to the first unction of baptism and the two succeeding unctions of confirmation and ordination. But here they are able to cast
in my teeth, that in the case of this sacrament there are, on the authority of
James the Apostle, both promise and sign, which, as I have all along maintained, constitute a sacrament. For does not James say: "Is any man sick
among you? Let him bring in the priests of the church, and let them pray
over him, anointing him with oil in the name of the Lord. And the prayer
of faith shall raise him up: and if he be in sins, they shall be forgiven
him." There, say they, you have the promise of the forgivenes of sins, and
the sign of the oil.

But I reply: If ever there was a mad conceit, here is one indeed. I will
say nothing of the fact that many assert with much probability that this
Epistle is not by James the Apostle, nor worthy of an apostolic spirit, although, whoever be its author, it has come to be esteemed as authoritative.
But even if the Apostle James did write it, I yet should say, no Apostle has
the right on his own authority to institute a sacrament, that is, to give a
divine promise with a sign attached; for this belongs to Christ alone. Thus
Paul says that he received from the Lord the sacrament of the Eucharist,
and that he was not sent to baptize but to preach the Gospel. And we read
nowhere in the Gospel of this sacrament of extreme unction. . . .

Now I do not condemn this our sacrament of extreme unction, but I
firmly deny that it is what the Apostle James prescribes; for his unction

[10] The council that condemned and burned John Huss (1414–18).

agrees with ours in neither form, use, power, nor purpose. Nevertheless we shall number it among those sacraments which we have instituted, such as the blessing and sprinkling of salt and holy water. For we cannot deny that every creature is sanctified by the word and by prayer, as the Apostle Paul teaches us. We do not deny, therefore, that forgiveness of sins and peace are granted through extreme unction; not because it is a sacrament divinely instituted, but because he who receives it believes that these blessings are granted to him. For the faith of the recipient does not err, however much the minister may err. For one who baptizes or absolves in jest, that is, does not absolve so far as the minister is concerned, does yet truly absolve and baptize if the person he baptizes or absolves believe. How much more will one who administers extreme unction confer peace, even though he does not really confer peace, so far as his ministry is concerned, since there is no sacrament there. The faith of the one anointed receives even that which the minister either could not or did not intend to give; it is sufficient for him to hear and believe the Word. For whatever we believe we shall receive, that we do really receive, it matters not what the minister may do or not do, or whether he dissemble or jest. The saying of Christ stands fast, "All things are possible to him that believeth," and, "Be it unto thee even as thou hast believed." But in treating the sacraments our sophists say nothing at all of this faith, but only babble with all their might of the virtues of the sacraments themselves—"ever learning, and never attaining to the knowledge of the truth. . . ."

There are yet a few other things it might seem possible to regard as sacraments; namely, all those to which a divine promise has been given, such as prayer, the Word, and the cross. Christ promised, in many places, that those who pray should be heard; especially in Luke 11, where He invites us in many parables to pray. Of the Word He says: "Blessed are they that hear the word of God, and keep it." And who will tell how often He promises aid and glory to such as are afflicted, suffer, and are cast down? Nay, who will recount all the promises of God? The whole scripture is concerned with provoking us to faith; now driving us with precepts and threats, now drawing us with promises and consolations. Indeed, whatever things are written are either precepts or promises; the precepts humble the proud with their demands, the promises exalt the humble with their forgiveness.

Nevertheless, it has seemed best to restrict the name of sacrament to such promises as have signs attached to them. The remainder, not being bound to signs, are bare promises. Hence there are, strictly speaking, but two sacraments in the Church of God—baptism and bread; for only in these two do we find both the divinely instituted sign and the promise of forgiveness of sins. The sacrament of penance, which I added to these two, lacks the divinely instituted visible sign, and is, as I have said, nothing but a return to baptism. Nor can the scholastics say that their definition fits penance, for they too ascribe to the sacrament a visible sign, which is to impress upon the senses the form of that which it effects invisibly. But penance, or absolution, has no such sign; wherefore they are constrained by their own definition, either to admit that penance is not a sacrament, and thus to reduce the number of sacraments, or else to bring forward another definition.

Baptism, however, which we have applied to the whole of life, will truly be a sufficient substitute for all the sacraments we might need as long as we live. And the bread is truly the sacrament of the dying; for in it we commemorate the passing of Christ out of this world, that we may imitate Him. Thus we may apportion these two sacraments as follows: baptism belongs to the beginning and the entire course of life, the bread belongs to the end and to death. And the Christian should use them both as long as he is in this poor body, until, fully baptized and strengthened, he passes out of this world and is born unto the new life of eternity, to eat with Christ in the Kingdom of His Father, as He promised at the Last Supper, "Amen I say to you, I will not drink from henceforth of this fruit of the vine, until it is fulfilled in the kingdom of God." Thus He seems clearly to have instituted the sacrament of the bread with a view to our entrance into the life to come. Then, when the meaning of both sacraments is fulfilled, baptism and bread will cease.

Herewith I conclude this prelude, and freely and gladly offer it to all pious souls who desire to know the genuine sense of the scriptures and the proper use of the sacraments. For it is a gift of no mean importance, to know the things that are given us, as it is said in I Corinthians 2, and what use we ought to make of them. Endowed with this spiritual judgment, we shall not mistakenly rely on that which does not belong here. These two things our theologians never taught us, nay, methinks they took particular pains to conceal them from us. If I have not taught them, I certainly did not conceal them, and have given occasion to others to think out something better. It has at least been my endeavor to set forth these two things. Nevertheless, not all can do all things. To the godless, on the other hand, and those who in obstinate tyranny force on us their own teachings instead of God's, I confidently and freely oppose these pages, utterly indifferent to their senseless fury. Yet I wish even them a sound mind, and do not despise their efforts, but only distinguish them from such as are sound and truly Christian.

I hear a rumor of new bulls and papal maledictions sent out against me, in which I am urged to recant or be declared a heretic. If that is true, I desire this book to be a portion of the recantation I shall make; so that these tyrants may not complain of having had their pains for nothing. The remainder I will publish ere long, and it will, please Christ, be such as the Roman See has hitherto neither seen nor heard. I shall give ample proof of my obedience. In the name of our Lord Jesus Christ. Amen.

64

HULDREICH ZWINGLI (1484–1531) was one of the leaders of the Protestant Reformation in Switzerland. An early indication of Zwingli's reform pattern was his deviation from the practice of preaching from assigned texts and instead beginning with the Gospel of Matthew and proceeding through the New Testament. His education from humanist scholars at the Universities of Vienna and Basel encouraged his primary stress on the scriptures, the source of the faith, and a life long distrust of the externals (for example, dietary regulations and the use of images) of the church. In his interpretation of the sacrament of the Lord's Supper as an act of faithful commemoration, he differed sharply from both the Roman Catholic position and that of Martin Luther. The Anabaptist movement and its characteristic emphasis on the separation of church and state, which began in Zurich in the 1520s, brought Zwingli's defense of civil government as ordained by God to preserve the order of church and society. His willingness to assume arms in defense and propagation of the Zurich reform against the Catholic cantons resulted in his death at the Battle of Kappel in 1531.

The *Exposition of the Christian Faith* was written in 1531 for King Francis I of France in defense of Zwingli's position.

Exposition of the Christian Faith [*]

HULDREICH ZWINGLI

REGARDING GOD AND HIS WORSHIP

I. All the things that are are either created or uncreated. The one and only uncreated thing is God, for there can be but one uncreated thing. If there were several uncreated things, there would be several eternals, for the uncreated and the eternal are so closely allied that as one is so is also the other. For if there were several eternals, there would be several infinites, for these are so like unto and allied with each other that whatever is eternal is

[*] From *The Latin Works of Huldreich Zwingli*, Vol. II., William J. Hinke, ed. Philadelphia: Heidelberg Press, 1922. Used by permission of the American Society of Church History.

also infinite and whatever is infinite is also eternal. Now, since there can be only one infinite (for as soon as we admit two infinite substances each becomes finite), it is certain that the one and only uncreated thing is God. On this depends also the origin, source and foundation of the first article of our faith, that is, when we say, "I believe in one God, the Father Almighty, Creator of heaven and earth," we confess and declare that we have an infallible faith, since it is one resting securely upon one only Creator. The heathen and the unbelievers who trust in created things are forced to confess that they may be deceived in their faith or belief, seeing that they trust in created things. But they that trust in the Creator and Source of all things, who never began to be, but called all other things into existence, these cannot be convicted of error. This also is certain, that nothing which is a created thing can be the object and basis of that unwavering and indubitable power which is faith. For whatever has begun to be at some time was not. When, therefore, it was not, how could anyone have trusted in what did not yet exist? Things, then, that have had a beginning cannot be the natural object or basis of faith. Only the eternal, infinite, and uncreated Good, therefore, is the true basis of faith.

Hence, all that confidence falls to the ground by which certain people lean thoughtlessly upon even the most sacred of created things or the most holy of sacraments. For that in which one should trust with absolute assurance must be God. But if one should trust in a created thing, then the created thing would have to be the Creator, and if in sacraments, then the sacraments would have to be God, so that not only the sacrament of the Eucharist, but baptism and the laying on of hands also would be God. How absurd that is to learned, to say nothing of pious men, not only the learned but any one endowed with intelligence can judge. In order, therefore, to help the theologians reach the truth, I shall gladly hold this torch before them. When they say, created things are to be employed but only God enjoyed, they say nothing else than what I also say, if they do not unthinkingly put a foreign meaning into their own words. For if God alone is to be enjoyed, He alone also is to be trusted, for that is to be trusted which is to be enjoyed, not that which is to be employed.

II. From this, most gracious King, you see clearly that we do not dismiss the saints nor the sacraments, nor move them from their place, as some men say that we do, but that we keep and guard them in their proper place and dignity, that no man may use them wrongly. We do not insult Mary, the Virgin Mother of God, when we forbid that she be adored with divine honors; but when we would attribute to her the majesty and power of the Creator, she herself would not permit such adoration. For true piety has one and the same character among all men and is the same in all, because it originates by one and the same Spirit. It cannot even be imagined, therefore, that any created being should at the same time be pious and suffer the worship due the Deity to be offered to himself. So also the Virgin Mother of God will as much the less accept the worship due the Deity as she is high above all created beings and reverently devoted to God, her Son. It is a mark of insanity in godless men and demons when they allow divine honors to be paid to them. This is proved by the images of demons and the arrogance of Herod, of whom the first, by teaching worship of themselves, deceived the world to its destruction, and the second, not refusing the divine honors offered him, was struck with phthiriasis, that he might learn to recognize the feebleness of man.

But we venerate and cherish the sacraments as signs and symbols of sacred things, not as if they were themselves the things of which they are signs. For who can be so ignorant as to say that a sign is the thing it signifies? In that case the word "ape," which I write here would place before the eyes of Your Majesty a real live ape. But because the sacraments signify real things, which really and naturally happened at some time, I say they represent these things, call them to mind and, as it were, set them before our eyes. Understand me correctly, I beg, O King! Christ by His death atoned for our sins. The Eucharist is a commemoration of this thing, as He Himself said—"This do in remembrance of me." By this commemoration all the benefits are presented which God has vouchsafed unto us through His Son. Furthermore, by the symbols themselves, namely the bread and wine, Christ Himself is, as it were, presented to our eyes, so that not only the ears but the eyes and the mouth see and perceive the Christ whom the soul has present within and rejoices in. This, therefore, we say and teach is the legitimate worship of the saints and the sacraments, which Christ Himself transmitted and taught us. "If ye are the children of Abraham," He said [John 8:37], "do the works of Abraham." This is, therefore, the example that we ought to follow in the case of all saints and holy men. Thus, if any of the prophets or holy men gave us divine warnings to drink, as it were, we should receive what has been given and set forth to us by the divine Spirit with the same religious devotion with which they received and imparted it. If they adorned religious devotion by sanctity of life, we should follow in their footsteps and be pious, holy, and innocent as they were.

In regard to baptism He says, "Baptize them in the name of the Father and of the Son and of the Holy Ghost" [Matth. 28:19]; in regard to the Eucharist, "This do in remembrance of me" [Luke 22:17]; and by the mouth of Paul, "We are all one bread and one body of the faithful" [I Cor. 10:17]. It is not hinted here, either in regard to the worship of the saints or in regard to the institution of the sacraments, that they have the power and grace which belongs to God alone. Since, then, the Deity has never conferred on created things the power which we attribute to them, it is clearly frivolous for us to teach that either the saints or the sacraments remove sins and bestow grace upon us. For who remitteth sins save God alone? Or from whom is every perfect gift, as St. James puts it [James 1:17], save from the Father of lights and of all good? We teach, therefore, that the sacraments should be cherished as sacred things signifying the most holy things, both such as have been done and such as we ought to do and show forth. Thus baptism signifies both that Christ has washed us by His blood, and that we ought to put Him on, as Paul teaches [Gal. 3:27], that is, live according to His example. In like manner the Eucharist signifies both all that has been given to us by divine bounty through Christ, and that we ought in gratitude to embrace our brethren with that Christian love with which Christ has taken us to Himself, cared for us, and secured salvation for us. But whether the natural body of Christ is eaten in the Eucharist will be discussed at length later.

To sum up:—This is the fountainhead of my religion, to recognize God as the uncreated Creator of all things, who solely and alone has all things in His power and freely giveth us all things. They, therefore, overthrow this first foundation of faith, who attribute to the creature what is the Creator's alone. For we confess in the creed that it is the Creator in whom we believe. It cannot, therefore, be the creature in whom we should put our trust. . . .

THE PRESENCE OF CHRIST'S BODY IN THE SUPPER

The other thing which I have undertaken to set forth here is this,— that that natural, material body of Christ's, in which He suffered here and now sitteth in heaven at the right hand of the Father, is not eaten literally and in its essence, but only spiritually, in the Lord's Supper, and that the teaching of the Papists, that Christ's body is eaten by us having the size and the exact qualities and nature it had when He was born, suffered, and died, is not only frivolous and stupid but impious and blasphemous.

. . . upon the Holy Scriptures it is established that Christ's body must in a natural, literal and true sense be in one place, unless we venture foolishly and impiously to assert that our bodies also are in many places, we have wrung from our opponents the admission that Christ's body, according to its essence, in itself, naturally and truly sits at the right hand of the Father, and it is not in this way in the Supper, so that those who teach the contrary drag Christ down from heaven and the Father's throne. For all the learned have condemned as exploded and impious the opinion which some have ventured to maintain, that Christ's body is just as much everywhere as His divinity.[1] For it cannot be everywhere unless in virtue of being infinite in nature, and what is infinite is also eternal. Christ's

---

[1] Namely the Lutherans, who teach the ubiquity of Christ's body.

humanity is not eternal; therefore it is not infinite. If it is not infinite, it must be finite. If it is finite, it is not everywhere. But putting aside these things, which I have introduced in order not to fail to meet the demands of philosophical argumentation, if you should happen to come upon such, O King, let me come to the impregnable testimonies of scripture.

I have made it plain enough before that whatever is said in the sacred scriptures of Christ is said in such way of the whole and entire Christ that even if it may be easily detected to which of His natures the thing said applies, yet Christ is not divided into two persons, however much each nature possesses its own peculiarity. For having two natures does not sever unity of person, as is clear in the case of man. And again, even if the things that belong to Christ's divinity are attributed to His humanity, and, on the other hand, the things that belong to His humanity to His divinity, yet the natures are not confused, as if the divinity had degenerated and been weakened to humanity, or the humanity changed into divinity. . . . Therefore the view is irreligious that maintains that Christ's body is eaten in the Supper in a bodily, literal, substantial and even quantitative sense, because such view is opposed to the truth, and what is opposed to the truth is impious and irreligious. These few brief remarks will be enough, I think, to enable your wisdom, which in its ready skill can estimate the whole from one of its parts, to see that out of the mouth of the Lord we are forced to consider how Christ's body is present in the Supper. Oecolampadius and I have treated the matter at length elsewhere and in many writings to various people, indeed, have waged long war, but it would be distasteful to repeat all this. But truth is carrying off the victory and breaking through daily more and more. Now that I may set forth what it is to eat spiritually and sacramentally, I shall make a digression.

To eat the body of Christ spiritually is nothing else than to trust in spirit and heart upon the mercy and goodness of God through Christ, that is, to be sure with unshaken faith that God is going to give us pardon for our sins and the joy of everlasting blessedness on account of His Son, who was made wholly ours, was offered for us, and reconciled the divine righteousness to us. For what can He refuse who gave His only begotten Son?

To eat the body of Christ sacramentally, if we wish to speak accurately, is to eat the body of Christ in heart and spirit with the accompaniment of the sacrament. I wish to set the whole matter, before the eyes of Your Highness, O King. You eat the body of Christ spiritually, though not sacramentally, every time you comfort your heart in its anxious query:— "How will you be saved? You sin daily, and yet are daily hastening towards death. After this life there is another, for how could this soul be destroyed with which we are endowed here and which is so solicitous about the hereafter? How could all this light and knowledge be turned into darkness and forgetfulness? Since, then, the life of the soul is everlasting, what sort of

life is coming to my dear soul? A happy or a miserable life? I will examine
my life and search out what it deserves, to be happy or miserable." Then
when you see such a host of things that we men are in the habit of doing
from passion and desire, you shudder and as far as your own righteousness
and integrity are concerned declare yourself in your own opinion unworthy
of everlasting happiness, and straightway despair of it. When, I say, you
comfort your troubled heart thus:—"God is good; he that is good must be
righteous and merciful and equitable, for righteousness without equity or
mercy is the height of injustice; mercy without righteousness is indifference,
wantonness and the destruction of all discipline. Since, therefore, God is
righteous, His righteousness must receive satisfaction for my sins. Since
He is merciful, I must not despair of forgiveness. I have an infallible pledge
of both of these in His only begotten Son, our Lord Jesus Christ, whom
He has given to us out of His mercy to be ours. And He has sacrificed himself to the Father for us, to appease His eternal righteousness. Thus we are
sure of His mercy and of the atonement for our sins made to His righteousness by none other than His own Son whom He has given to us out of
love." When with this confidence you cheer up your soul, tossed on the
floods of fear and despair, saying, "Why art thou sad, my soul? God, who
alone bestows blessedness, is thine, and thou art His. For when thou wast
His work and creation, and yet hadst perished by thy sin, He sent His Son
to thee, and made Him like thee, sin excepted, that, relying upon the rights
and privileges of this great brother and companion, thou mightest dare
even to demand everlasting salvation as thy right. What devil can frighten
me so that I shall fear him, when He is at hand to help me? Who shall
take from me what God Himself has bestowed, in giving His Son as pledge
and surety?"—When you comfort yourself thus, I say, you eat His body
spiritually, that is, you stand unterrified in God against all the attacks of
despair, through confidence in the humanity He took upon Himself for
you.

But when you come to the Lord's Supper with this spiritual participation and give thanks unto the Lord for His great kindness, for the deliverance of your soul, through which you have been delivered from the destruction of despair, and for the pledge by which you have been made sure of
everlasting blessedness, and along with the brethren partake of the bread
and wine which are the symbols of the body of Christ, then you eat Him
sacramentally, in the proper sense of the term, when you do internally
what you represent externally, when your heart is refreshed by this faith to
which you bear witness by these symbols.

But those are improperly said to eat sacramentally who eat the visible
sacrament or symbol in public assembly to be sure, but have not faith in
their hearts. These, therefore, call down judgment, that is, the vengeance
of God, upon themselves by eating, because they hold not in the same
high esteem, in which it is rightly held by the pious, the body of Christ,

that is, the whole mystery of the incarnation and passion, and even the Church itself of Christ. For a man ought to test himself before he partakes of the Supper, that is, examine himself and ask both whether he so recognizes and has received Christ as the Son of God and his own Deliverer and Saviour that he trusts Him as the infallible author and giver of salvation, and whether he rejoices that he is a member of the Church of which Christ is the head. If as an unbeliever he unites with the Church in the Supper, as if he had faith in these things, is he not guilty of the body and blood of the Lord? Not because he has eaten them in the literal, material sense, but because he has borne false witness to the Church that he has eaten them spiritually when he has never tasted them spiritually. Those, therefore, are said to eat merely sacramentally, who use the symbols of thanksgiving, to be sure, in the Supper, but have not faith. For this they are in more terrible condemnation than the rest of the unbelievers, because those simply do not acknowledge Christ's Supper, while these pretend to acknowledge it. He sins doubly who without faith celebrates the Supper. He is faithless and presumptuous, while the mere unbeliever is destroyed through his unbelief like the fool through his folly.

Furthermore, there has for some time been a sharp controversy among us as to what the sacraments or symbols do or can do in the Supper; our opponents contending that the sacraments give faith, and bring to us the natural body of Christ, causing it to be eaten in real presence. We hold a different view not without authoritative support. First, because none but the Holy Spirit giveth faith, which is confidence in God, and no external thing giveth it. Yet the sacraments do work faith, historical faith; for all festivals, trophies, nay, monuments and statues, work historical faith: that is, call to mind that a certain thing once took place, the memory of which is thus refreshed, as was the case with the festival of the Passover, among the Hebrews. . . . In this way, then, the Lord's Supper worketh faith, that is, signifies as certain that Christ was born and suffered. But to whom does it signify this? To the believer and the unbeliever alike. For it signifies to all that which belongs to the meaning of the sacrament, namely, that Christ suffered, whether they receive it or not, but that He suffered for us, it signifies to the pious believer only. For no one knows or believes that Christ suffered for us, save those whom the Spirit within has taught to recognize the mystery of divine goodness. For such alone receive Christ. Hence nothing gives confidence in God except the Spirit. No one cometh to Christ except the Father draweth him. Furthermore, Paul also decides this whole quarrel by one sentence when he says, "But let a man examine himself, and so let him eat of that bread, and drink of that cup" [I Cor. 11:28]. Since, then, a man ought to examine his faith before he approaches the table, it cannot be that faith is given in the Supper, for it must be there before you draw near.

I have opposed a second error on the part of our adversaries. They say that by the symbols of bread and wine the natural body of Christ is brought before us because this is the force and meaning of the words, "This is my body." But what I have said above about the words of Christ that showed that His body was to be no longer in the world, contradicts this view. Moreover, if the words could do that, they would bring before us Christ's body that was capable of suffering. For when He spoke these words, He still had a mortal body. Therefore, the apostles would have eaten His mortal body, for He did not have two bodies of which one was immortal and exempt from physical sensation, the other mortal. If, then, the apostles had eaten His mortal body, what would we be eating now? Of course, His mortal body. But that body is now immortal and incorruptible which before was mortal. If, then, we would now be eating His mortal body, He would, again, have a mortal and at the same time immortal body, and since this impossible (for it cannot be mortal and immortal at the same time), it would follow that He had two bodies, one mortal, which we would eat as well as the apostles, the other immortal, which would sit on the right hand of God, and not to move thence. Otherwise we would have to say that the apostles, indeed, ate His mortal but we eat His immortal body. Anyone can see how absurd that is.

Finally, I opposed our adversaries in their assertion that the natural, substantial body of Christ is eaten in real presence, because piety denies that also. When Peter perceived that there was divine power in Christ in the marvelous catch of fishes, he said, "Depart from me; for I am a sinful man, O Lord. For he was amazed" [Luke 5:8]. Now, do we long to eat Him physically, like cannibals? As if anyone's love for his children were such that he wished to devour and eat them! Or, as if among all men those were not adjudged the most savage who feed upon human flesh! The centurion said, "I am not worthy that thou shouldest come under my roof" [Matth. 8:8]. But Christ Himself bore witness of him that He had not found such faith in all Israel. Therefore, the greater and holier faith is, the more is it content with spiritual participation, and the more thoroughly that satisfies it, the more does a religious heart shrink from bodily manducation. Ministering women were wont to show their adoration by bathing and anointing Christ's body, not by eating it. The noble counsellor Joseph and the pious, secret disciple, Nicodemus, wrapped it in linen and spices and laid it in a sepulchre, but did not eat it physically.

THE VIRTUE OF THE SACRAMENTS

These difficulties, therefore, O King, plainly show that we ought not, under the guise of piety, to assign to the Eucharist or to Baptism qualities that bring faith and truth into danger. What then? Have the sacraments no virtue?

First virtue:—They are sacred and venerable rites, having been instituted and employed by Christ, the Great High Priest. For He not only instituted baptism; but Himself received it, and He not only bade us celebrate the Eucharist, but celebrated it Himself first of all.

Second virtue:—They bear witness to an accomplished fact, for all laws, customs, and institutions proclaim their authors and beginnings. Since, then, baptism proclaims by representation Christ's death and resurrection, these events must indeed have taken place.

Third virtue:—They take the place of the things they signify, whence also they get their names. The passover or passing by, through which God spared the children of Israel, cannot be placed before the eye, but a lamb is placed before the eye instead of this event as a symbol of it. Neither can the body of Christ and all that was accomplished in it be put before our eyes; the bread and wine are set before us to be eaten in place of it.

Fourth:—They signify sublime things. Now the value of every sign increases with the worth of the thing of which it is the sign, so that if the thing be great, precious, and sublime, its sign is, therefore, accounted the greater. The ring of the queen, your consort, with which Your Majesty was betrothed to her, is not valued by her at the price of the gold, but is beyond all price, however much it is gold, if you regard its material—for it is the symbol of her royal husband. . . . So the bread and wine are the symbols of that friendship by which God has been reconciled to the human race through His Son, and we value them not according to the price of the material but according to the greatness of the thing signified, so that the bread is no longer common, but sacred, and has not only the name of bread but of the body of Christ also, nay, is the body of Christ, but in name and significance, or, as the more recent theologians say, sacramentally.

The fifth virtue is the analogy between the symbols and the thing signified. The Eucharist has a two-fold analogy, first as applying to Christ, for as bread sustains and supports human life, as wine cheers man, so Christ alone restores, sustains and makes glad the heart bereft of all hope. For who can pine away in despair any longer when he sees the Son of God made his own, and holds Him in his soul like a treasure which cannot be torn from him and through which he can obtain all things from the Father? It has a second analogy as applying to us, for as bread is made of many grains, and wine is made of many grapes, so the body of the Church is cemented together and grows into one body from countless members, through common trust in Christ, proceeding from one Spirit, so that a true temple and body of the indwelling Holy Spirit, comes into existence.

Sixth, the sacraments bring increase and support to faith, and this the Eucharist does above all others. You know, O King, that our faith is constantly tried and tempted, for Satan sifts us like wheat, as he did the apostles. But how does he attack us? Through treachery in the camp, for he busies himself with trying to overwhelm us through the body as through an old wall of our defense ready to tumble down, setting up the scaling-ladders of the desires against our senses. When, therefore, the senses are diverted elsewhere, so as not to give ear to him, his schemes are less successful. Now in the sacraments the senses are not only made deaf to the wiles of Satan but bound over to faith, so that like handmaidens they do nothing but what their mistress, faith, does and directs. Hence they aid faith. I will speak plainly. In the Eucharist the four most powerful senses, nay, all the senses, are as it were, reclaimed and redeemed from fleshly desires, and drawn into obedience to faith. The hearing no longer hears the melodious harmony of varied strings and voices, but the heavenly words, "God so loved the world that He gave His only begotten for its life." We are present, therefore, as brethren, to give thanks for this bounty to us. For we do this rightly at the command of the Son Himself, who on the eve of His death instituted this thanksgiving, that He might leave us a lasting memorial and pledge of His love towards us. "And He took bread, and gave thanks, and brake it, and gave unto the disciples," uttering from His most holy lips these holy words, "This is my body" [Luke 22:19]. "Likewise also He took the cup," etc.—when, I say, the hearing takes in these words, is it not struck and does it not give itself up wholly in admiring wonder to this one thing that is proclaimed? It hears of God, and His love, and the Son delivered up to death for us. And when it gives itself up to this, does it not do what faith does? For faith is that which leans on God through Christ. When, therefore, the hearing looks to the same thing, it becomes the handmaiden of faith, and troubles faith no more with its own frivolous imaginings and interests. When the sight sees the bread and the cup which in place of Christ signify His goodness and inherent character, does it not also aid faith? For it sees Christ, as it were, before the eyes, as the heart, kindled by His beauty, languishes for Him. The touch takes the bread into its hands—the bread which is no longer bread but Christ by representation. The taste and smell are brought in to scent the sweetness of the Lord and the happiness of him that trusteth in Him. For as they rejoice in food and are quickened, so the heart, having tasted the sweetness of the heavenly hope, leaps and exults. The sacraments, then, aid the contemplation of faith, and harmonize it with the longings of the heart, as without the use of the sacraments could not be done at all so completely.

In baptism, sight, hearing, and touch, are summoned to the aid of faith. For faith, whether that of the Church or that of him who is baptized, recognizes that Christ endured death for His Church, rose again, and triumphed. The same thing is heard, seen, and touched in baptism. The sacraments, then, are a sort of bridles by which the senses, when on the point of dashing way to their own desires, are checked and brought back to the service of the heart and of faith.

The seventh power of the sacraments is that they fill the office of an oath of allegiance. For "sacramentum" is used by the Latin writers instead of "ius iurandum," i. e., "oath." For those who use one and the same oath, become one and the same race and sacred alliance, unite into one body and one people, and he who betrays it is false to his oath. When, therefore, the people of Christ by eating His body sacramentally become united into one body, he who without faith ventures to obtrude himself upon this company betrays the body of Christ, as well in its head as in its members, because he does not "discern," that is, does not properly value the body of the Lord, either as having been delivered up by Him for us, or as having been made free by His death. For we are one body with Him.

We are forced, then, whether we will or no, to acknowledge that the words, "This is my body," etc., are not to be understood literally and according to the primary meaning of the words, but symbolically, sacramentally, metaphorically, or, as a metonymy, thus:—"This is my body," that is, "this is the sacrament of my body," or, "this is my sacramental or mystical body, that is, the sacramental and vicarious symbol of that body which I really took and exposed to death."

But it is now time to pass to other things, lest I offend Your Majesty forgetting to be brief. What I have said, however, is so certain, most brave King, that no one, however many have tried to rebut it, has thus far been able to affect it one jot. Therefore, be not troubled if they that are more ready with their tongues than with substantial scripture, cry out that the view is irreligious. This they boast, indeed, in bold but empty words, though when they come to facts they are more empty than a cast-off serpent's skin.

THE CHURCH

I believe also that there is one holy Catholic, that is, universal Church, and that this is either visible or invisible. The invisible, as Paul teaches, is that which comes down from heaven, that is, which recognizes and embraces God through the enlightenment of the Holy Spirit. To this Church belong all those that believe throughout the whole world. And it is called invisible not as if they that believe were invisible, but because it is not evident to human eyes who do believe. The faithful are known to God and themselves alone. And the visible Church is not the Roman pontiff and the rest of them that wear the tiara, but all throughout the whole world who have enrolled themselves under Christ [through baptism]. Among these are all who are called Christians, even though falsely, seeing that they have no faith within. There are, therefore, in the visible Church some who are not members of the elect and invisible Church. For some men eat and drink judgment unto themselves in the Supper, yet all the brethren know them not. Since, therefore, this Church which is visible contains many rebellious and traitorous members who having no faith care nothing if they be a hundred times cast out of the Church, there is need of a government, whether of princes or of nobles, to restrain shameless sinners. For the magistrate carries the sword not in vain [Rom. 13:4]. Since, then, there are shepherds in the Church, who, as may be seen in Jeremiah [23:4 ff.], have also the rank of princes it is clear that without a temporal government the Church is crippled and incomplete. So far are we, most pious King, from rejecting government and thinking it should be done away with, as some men charge us with doing, that we even teach that it is necessary to the completeness of the ecclesiastical body. But hear our teaching about this briefly.

GOVERNMENTS

The Greeks recognize these three kinds of governments with their three degenerate forms: Monarchy, which the Latins call "regnum, kingdom," where one man stands alone as the head of the state under the guidance of piety and justice. The opposite and degenerate form is a tyranny, which the Latins less fittingly call "vis" or "violentia," "force" or "violence," or rather, not having quite the proper word themselves, they generally use "tyrannis," borrowing the word from the Greeks. This exists when piety is scorned, justice is trodden under foot, and all things are done by force, while the ruler holds that anything he pleases is lawful for him. Secondly, they recognize an aristocracy, which the Latins call "optimatium potentia, the power of the best people," where the best men are at the head of things, observing justice and piety towards the people. When this form degenerates it passes into an oligarchy, which the Latins call literally "paucorum potentia, the power of the few." Here a few of the nobles rise up and gain influence who, caring not for the general good but for private advantage, trample upon the public weal and serve their own ends. Finally they recognize a democracy, which the Latins render by "res publica, republic," a word of broader meaning than democracy, where affairs, that is, the supreme power, are in the hands of the people in general, the entire people; and all the civil offices, honors, and public functions are in the hands of the whole people. When this form degenerates, the Greeks call it . . . a state of sedition, conspiracy, and disturbance, where no man suffers himself to be held in check, and instead each one, asserting that he is a part and a member of the people, claims the power of the state as his own, and each one follows his own reckless desires. Hence there arise unrestrained conspiracies and factions, followed by bloodshed, plundering, injustice and all the other evils of treason and sedition.

These distinct forms of government of the Greeks I recognize with the following corrections: If a king or prince rules, I teach that he is to be honored and obeyed, according to Christ's command, "Render unto Caesar the things that are Caesar's and unto God the things that are God's" [Luke 20:25]. For by "Caesar" I understand every ruler upon whom power has been conferred or bestowed, either by hereditary right and custom or by election. But if the king or prince becomes a tyrant, I correct his reckless- ness and inveigh against it in season and out of season. For thus saith the Lord to Jeremiah, "See, I have . . . set thee over the nations and over the kingdoms," etc. [Jer. 1:10]. If he listens to the warning, I have gained a father for the whole kingdom and fatherland, but if he becomes more rebelliously violent, I teach that even a wicked ruler is to be obeyed until the Lord shall remove him from his office and power or a means be found to enable those whose duty it is to deprive him of his functions and restore order. In the same way we are watchful and on the alert, if an aristocracy begins to degenerate into an oligarchy or a democracy into a σύστρεμμα, mob. We have examples in scripture, from which we learn what we teach and demand,—Samuel endured Saul until the Lord deprived him of his kingdom along with his life. David returned to his senses at the rebuke of Nathan, and remained on the throne under much trial and temptation. Ahab lost his life because he would not turn from wickedness when Elijah reproved him. John dauntlessly unbraided Herod when he felt no shame at his incestuous conduct. But it would be a long task to bring forward all the examples in scripture. The learned and pious know from what source we draw what we say.

To sum up, in the Church of Christ government is just as necessary as preaching, although this latter occupies the first place. For as a man cannot exist except as composed of both body and soul, however much the body is the humbler and lower part, so the Church cannot exist with- out the civil government, though the government attends to and looks after the more material things that have not to do with the spirit. Since, then two particularly bright lights of our faith, Jeremiah and Paul, bid us pray to the Lord for our rulers that they may permit us to lead a life worthy of God, how much more ought all in whatever kingdom or people to bear and to do all things to guard the Christian peace! Hence we teach that tribute, taxes, dues, tithes, debts, loans, and all promises to pay of every kind should be paid and the laws of the state in general be obeyed in these things.

65

THE SCHLEITHEIM CONFESSION OF FAITH, prepared in 1527 by the Swiss Anabaptists, served as a summary statement of their position on seven dominant issues of the time. It is a clear, persuasive, and humble testimony of an early and important group in Protestantism and clearly marked them off from the more radical aspects of the "left wing" of the Reformation. See also *Concerning the Satisfaction of Christ* (Selection 47), a tract prepared by the same group.

The Schleitheim Confession of Faith*

SWISS ANABAPTISTS

May joy, peace and mercy from our Father through the atonement of the blood of Christ Jesus, together with the gifts of the Spirit—Who is sent from the Father to all believers for their strength and comfort and for their perseverence in all tribulation until the end, Amen—be to all those who love God, who are the children of light, and who are scattered everywhere as it has been ordained of God our Father, where they are with one mind assembled together in one God and Father of us all: Grace and peace of heart be with you all, Amen.

Beloved brethren and sisters in the Lord: First and supremely we are always concerned for your consolation and the assurance of your conscience (which was previously misled) so that you may not always remain foreigners to us and by right almost completely excluded, but that you may turn again to the true implanted members of Christ, who have been armed through patience and knowledge of themselves, and have therefore again been united with us in the strength of a godly Christian spirit and zeal for God.

It is also apparent with what cunning the devil has turned us aside, so that he might destroy and bring to an end the work of God which in mercy and grace has been partly begun in us. But Christ, the true Shepherd of our souls, Who has begun this in us, will certainly direct the same and teach [us] to His honor and our salvation, Amen.

Dear brethren and sisters, we who have been assembled in the Lord at Schleitheim on the Border, make known in points and articles to all who love God that as concerns us we are of one mind to abide in the Lord as

* The Mennonite Quarterly Review, Vol. XIX, tr. by John C. Wenger, October 1945, pp. 247–253. [The words enclosed in brackets were supplied by Professor Wenger.]

God's obedient children, [His] sons and daughters, we who have been and shall be separated from the world in everything, [and] completely at peace. To God alone be praise and glory without the contradiction of any brethren. In this we have perceived the oneness of the Spirit of our Father and of our common Christ with us. For the Lord is the Lord of peace and not of quarreling, as Paul points out. That you may understand in what articles this has been formulated you should observe and note [the following].

A very great offense has been introduced by certain false brethren among us, so that some have turned aside from the faith, in the way they intend to practice and observe the freedom of the Spirit and of Christ. But such have missed the truth and to their condemnation are given over to the lasciviousness and self-indulgence of the flesh. They think faith and love may do and permit everything, and nothing will harm them nor condemn them, since they are believers.

Observe, you who are God's members in Christ Jesus, that faith in the Heavenly Father through Jesus Christ does not take such form. It does not produce and result in such things as these false brethren and sisters do and teach. Guard yourselves and be warned of such people, for they do not serve our Father, but their father, the devil.

But you are not that way. For they that are Christ's have crucified the flesh with its passions and lusts. You understand me well and [know] the brethren whom we mean. Separate yourselves from them for they are perverted. Petition the Lord that they may have the knowledge which leads to repentance, and [pray] for us that we may have constancy to persevere in the way which we have espoused, for the honor of God and of Christ, His Son, Amen.

The articles which we discussed and on which we were of one mind are these 1. Baptism; 2. The Ban [Excommunication]; 3. Breaking of Bread; 4. Separation from the Abomination; 5. Pastors in the Church; 6. The Sword; and 7. The Oath.

First. Observe concerning baptism: Baptism shall be given to all those who have learned repentance and amendment of life, and who believe truly that their sins are taken away by Christ, and to all those who walk in the resurrection of Jesus Christ, and wish to be buried with Him in death, so that they may be resurrected with Him, and to all those who with this significance request it [baptism] of us and demand it for themselves. This excludes all infant baptism, the highest and chief abomination of the pope. In this you have the foundation and testimony of the apostles. Mt. 28, Mk. 16, Acts 2, 8, 16, 19. This we wish to hold simply, yet firmly and with assurance.

Second. We are agreed as follows on the ban: The ban shall be employed with all those who have given themselves to the Lord, to walk in His commandments, and with all those who are baptized into the one body

of Christ and who are called brethren or sisters, and yet who slip sometimes and fall into error and sin, being inadvertently overtaken. The same
shall be admonished twice in secret and the third time openly disciplined
or banned according to the command of Christ. Mt. 18. But this shall be
done according to the regulation of the Spirit (Mt. 5) before the breaking
of bread, so that we may break and eat one bread, with one mind and in
one love, and may drink of one cup.

Third. In the breaking of bread we are of one mind and are agreed
[as follows]: All those who wish to break one bread in remembrance of
the broken body of Christ, and all who wish to drink of one drink as a
remembrance of the shed blood of Christ, shall be united beforehand by
baptism in one body of Christ which is the church of God and whose Head
is Christ. For as Paul points out we cannot at the same time be partakers
of the Lord's table and the table of devils; we cannot at the same time drink
the cup of the Lord and the cup of the devil. That is, all those who have
fellowship with the dead works of darkness have no part in the light. Therefore all who follow the devil and the world have no part with those who are
called unto God out of the world. All who lie in evil have no part in the
good.

Therefore it is and must be [thus]: Whoever has not been called by
one God to one faith, to one baptism, to one Spirit, to one body, with all
the children of God's church, cannot be made [into] one bread with them,
as indeed must be done if one is truly to break bread according to the command of Christ.

Fourth. We are agreed [as follows] on separation: A separation shall
be made from the evil and from the wickedness which the devil planted in
the world; in this manner, simply that we shall not have fellowship with
them [the wicked] and not run with them in the multitude of their
abominations. This is the way it is: Since all who do not walk in the
obedience of faith, and have not united themselves with God so that they
wish to do His will, are a great abomination before God, it is not possible
for anything to grow or issue from them except abominable things. For
truly all creatures are in but two classes, good and bad, believing and unbelieving, darkness and light, the world and those who [have come] out of
the world, God's temple and idols, Christ and Belial; and none can have
part with the other.

To us then the command of the Lord is clear when He calls upon us to
be separate from the evil and thus He will be our God and we shall be His
sons and daughters.

He further admonishes us to withdraw from Babylon and the earthly
Egypt that we may not be partakers of the pain and suffering which the
Lord will bring upon them.

From all this we should learn that everything which is not united with

our God and Christ cannot be other than an abomination which we should
shun and flee from. By this is meant all popish and antipopish works and
church services, meetings and church attendance,[1] drinking houses, civic
affairs, the commitments [made in] unbelief and other things of that kind,
which are highly regarded by the world and yet are carried on in flat contradiction to the command of God, in accordance with all the unrighteousness which is in the world. From all these things we shall be separated and
have no part with them for they are nothing but an abomination, and they
are the cause of our being hated before our Christ Jesus, Who has set us
free from the slavery of the flesh and fitted us for the service of God
through the Spirit Whom He has given us.

Therefore there will also unquestionably fall from us the unchristian,
devilish weapons of force—such as sword, armor and the like, and all their
use [either] for friends or against one's enemies—by virtue of the word of
Christ, Resist not [him that is] evil.

Fifth. We are agreed as follows on pastors in the church of God: The
pastor in the church of God shall, as Paul has prescribed, be one who out-
and-out has a good report of those who are outside the faith. This office
shall be to read, to admonish and teach, to warn, to discipline, to ban in the
church, to lead out in prayer for the advancement of all the brethren and
sisters, to lift up the bread when it is to be broken, and in all things to see
to the care of the body of Christ, in order that it may be built up and
developed, and the mouth of the slanderer be stopped.

This one moreover shall be supported of the church which has chosen
him, wherein he may be in need, so that he who serves the Gospel may live
of the Gospel as the Lord has ordained. But if a pastor should do something
requiring discipline, he shall not be dealt with except [on the testimony of]
two or three witnesses. And when they sin they shall be disciplined before
all in order that the others may fear.

But should it happen that through the cross this pastor should be
banished or led to the Lord [through martyrdom] another shall be ordained
in his place in the same hour so that God's little flock and people may not
be destroyed.

Sixth. We are agreed as follows concerning the sword: The sword is
ordained of God outside the perfection of Christ. It punishes and puts to
death the wicked, and guards and protects the good. In the Law the sword

---

[1] This severe judgment on the state churches must be understood in the light of
sixteenth century conditions. The state clergymen were in many cases careless and carnal
men. All citizens in a given province were considered members of the state church because they had been made Christians ("christened") by infant baptism. Also, in 1527
Zurich had begun to use capital punishment on the Swiss Brethren, with the full approval
of the state church leaders. Sattler himself was burned at the stake less than three
months after the Schleitheim conference. [Michael Sattler was the probable author of
the Schleitheim Confession. Ed.]

was ordained for the punishment of the wicked and for their death, and the same [sword] is [now] ordained to be used by the worldly magistrates.

In the perfection of Christ, however, only the ban is used for a warning and for the excommunication of the one who has sinned, without putting the flesh to death,—simply the warning and the command to sin no more.

Now it will be asked by many who do not recognize [this as] the will of Christ for us, whether a Christian may or should employ the sword against the wicked for the defense and protection of the good, or for the sake of love.

Our reply is unanimously as follows: Christ teaches and commands us to learn of Him, for He is meek and lowly in heart and so shall we find rest to our souls. Also Christ says to the heathenish woman who was taken in adultery, not that one should stone her according to the law of His Father (and yet He says, As the Father has commanded me, thus I do), but in mercy and forgiveness and warning, to sin no more. Such [an attitude] we also ought to take completely according to the rule of the ban.

Secondly, it will be asked concerning the sword, whether a Christian shall pass sentence in worldly dispute and strife such as unbelievers have with one another. This is our united answer: Christ did not wish to decide or pass judgment between brother and brother in the case of the inheritance, but refused to do so. Therefore we should do likewise.

Thirdly, it will be asked concerning the sword, Shall one be a magistrate if one should be chosen as such? The answer is as follows: They wished to make Christ king, but He fled and did not view it as the arrangement of His Father. Thus shall we do as He did, and follow Him, and so shall we not walk in darkness. For He Himself says, He who wishes to come after me, let him deny himself and take up his cross and follow me. Also, He Himself forbids the [employment of] the force of the sword saying, The worldly princes lord it over them, etc., but not so shall it be with you. Further, Paul says, Whom God did foreknow He also did predestinate to be conformed to the image of His Son, etc. Also Peter says, Christ has suffered (not ruled) and left us an example, that ye should follow His steps.

Finally it will be observed that it is not appropriate for a Christian to serve as a magistrate because of these points: The government magistracy is according to the flesh,[2] but the Christians' is according to the Spirit; their houses and dwelling remain in this world, but the Christians' are in heaven; their citizenship is in this world, but the Christians' citizenship is in heaven; the weapons of their conflict and war are carnal and against the flesh only, but the Chrstians' weapons are spiritual, against the fortification of the devil. The worldlings are armed with steel and iron, but the Chris-

---

[2] Being "according to the flesh" does not refer to carnality proper, but to attachment to the world, a lack of separation from the "world."

tians are armed with the armor of God, with truth, righteousness, peace faith, salvation and the Word of God. In brief, as is the mind of Christ toward us, so shall the mind of the members of the body of Christ be through Him in all things, that there may be no schism in the body through which it would be destroyed. For every kingdom divided against itself will be destroyed. Now since Christ is as it is written of Him, His members must also be the same, that His body may remain complete and united to its own advancement and upbuilding.

Seventh. We are agreed as follows concerning the oath: The oath is a confirmation among those who are quarreling or making promises. In the Law it is commanded to be performed in God's Name, but only in truth, not falsely. Christ, who teaches the perfection of the Law, prohibits all swearing to His [followers], whether true or false,—neither by heaven, nor by the earth, nor by Jerusalem, nor by our head,—and that for the reason which He shortly thereafter gives, For you are not able to make one hair white or black. So you see it is for this reason that all swearing is forbidden: we cannot fulfill that which we promise when we swear, for we cannot change [even] the very least thing on us.

Now there are some who do not give credence to the simple command of God, but object with this question: Well now, did not God swear to Abraham by Himself (since He was God) when He promised him that He would be with him and that He would be his God if he would keep His commandments,—why then should I not also swear when I promise to someone? Answer: Hear what the scripture says: God, since He wished more abundantly to show unto the heirs the immutability of His counsel, inserted an oath, that by two immutable things (in which it is impossible for God to lie) we might have a strong consolation. Observe the meaning of this scripture: What God forbids you to do, He has power to do, for everything is possible for Him. God swore an oath to Abraham, says the scripture, so that He might show that His counsel is immutable. That is, no one can withstand nor thwart His will; therefore He can keep His oath. But we can do nothing, as is said above by Christ, to keep or perform [our oaths]: therefore we shall not swear at all [nichts schweren].

Then others further say as follows: It is not forbidden of God to swear in the New Testament, when it is actually commanded in the Old, but it is forbidden only to swear by heaven, earth, Jerusalem and our head. Answer: Hear the scripture, He who swears by heaven swears by God's throne and by Him who sitteth thereon. Observe: it is forbidden to swear by heaven, which is only the throne of God: how much more is it forbidden [to swear] by God Himself! Ye fools and blind, which is greater, the throne or Him that sitteth thereon?

Further some say, Because evil is now [in the world, and] because man needs God for [the establishment of] the truth, so did the apostles

Peter and Paul also swear. Answer: Peter and Paul only testify of that which God promised to Abraham with the oath. They themselves promise nothing, as the example indicates clearly. Testifying and swearing are two different things. For when a person swears he is in the first place promising future things, as Christ was promised to Abraham Whom we a long time afterwards received. But when a person bears testimony he is testifying about the present, whether it is good or evil, as Simeon spoke to Mary about Christ and testified, Behold this (child) is set for the fall and rising of many in Israel, and for a sign which shall be spoken against.

Christ also taught us along the same line when He said, Let your communication be Yea, yea; Nay, nay; for whatsoever is more than these cometh of evil. He says, Your speech or word shall be yea and nay. (However) when one does not wish to understand, he remains closed to the meaning. Christ is simply Yea and Nay, and all those who seek Him simply will understand His Word. Amen.

Dear brethren and sisters in the Lord: These are the articles of certain brethren who had heretofore been in error and who had failed to agree in the true understanding, so that many weaker consciences were perplexed, causing the Name of God to be greatly slandered. Therefore there has been a great need for us to become of one mind in the Lord, which has come to pass. To God be praise and glory!

Now since you have so well understood the will of God which has been made known by us, it will be necessary for you to achieve perseveringly, without interruption, the known will of God. For you know well what the servant who sinned knowingly heard as his recompense.

Everything which you have unwittingly done and confessed as evil doing is forgiven you through the believing prayer which is offered by us in our meeting for all our shortcomings and guilt. [This state is yours] through the gracious forgiveness of God and through the blood of Jesus Christ. Amen.

Keep watch on all who do not walk according to the simplicity of the divine truth which is stated in this letter from [the decisions of] our meeting, so that everyone among us will be governed by the rule of the ban and henceforth the entry of false brethren and sisters among us may be prevented.

Eliminate from you that which is evil and the Lord will be your God and you will be His sons and daughters.

Dear brethren, keep in mind what Paul admonishes Timothy when he says, The grace of God that bringeth salvation hath appeared to all men, teaching us that, denying ungodliness and worldly lusts, we should live soberly, righteously, and godly, in this present world; looking for that blessed hope, and the glorious appearing of the great God and our Saviour Jesus Christ; Who gave Himself for us, that He might redeem us from all iniquity, and purify unto Himself a people of His own, zealous of good works. Think on this and exercise yourselves therein and the God of peace will be with you.

May the Name of God be hallowed eternally and highly praised, Amen. May the Lord give you His peace, Amen.

The Acts of Schleitheim on the Border [Canton Schaffhausen, Switzerland], on Matthias' [Day],[3] Anno MDXXVII.

66

FROM JOHN CALVIN'S (1509–1564) *Institutes of the Christian Religion* stemmed much of the basis for the doctrine of the church within the Reformed tradition of Protestantism. The following selections from Book IV are divided into five sections: (1) The Purpose of the Church; (2) The Visible Church; (3) The Ministry; (4) The Sacraments (a.) Baptism; (b.) Lord's Supper; (5) The Church and Civil Government.[1]

Institutes of the Christian Religion[*]

JOHN CALVIN

1. THE PURPOSE OF THE CHURCH

. . . as our ignorance and slothfulness, and, I may add, the vanity of our minds, require external aids, in order to the production of faith in our hearts, and its increase and progressive advance even to its completion, God has provided such aids in compassion to our infirmity; and that the preaching of the gospel might be maintained, he has deposited this treasure with the Church. He has appointed pastors and teachers, that his people might be taught by their lips; he has invested them with authority; in short, he has omitted nothing that could contribute to a holy unity of faith, and to the establishment of good order. . . .

---

* From *Institutes of the Christian Religion*, Vol. II, tr. by John Allen. Philadelphia: Presbyterian Board of Christian Education, 1936. [The titles are supplied by the editor.]

3 February 24.

1 See also selections from the *Institutes*, Selections 9, 46.

That article of the Creed, in which we profess to believe THE CHURCH, refers not only to the visible Church of which we are now speaking, but likewise to all the elect of God, including the dead as well as the living. The word BELIEVE is used, because it is often impossible to discover any difference between the children of God and the ungodly, between his peculiar flock and wild beasts. The particle IN, interpolated by many, is not supported by any probable reason. I confess that it is generally adopted at present, and is not destitute of the suffrage of antiquity, being found in the Nicene Creed, as it is transmitted to us in ecclesiastical history. Yet it is evident from the writings of the fathers, that it was anciently admitted without controversy to say, "I believe the Church," not "in the Church. . . ." For we declare that we believe in God because our mind depends upon him as true, and our confidence rests in him. But this would not be applicable to the Church, any more than to "the remission of sins," or the "resurrection of the body." Therefore, though I am averse to contentions about words, yet I would rather adopt a proper phraseology adapted to express the subject than affect forms of expression by which the subject would be unnecessarily involved in obscurity. The design of this clause is to teach us, that though the devil moves every engine to destroy the grace of Christ, and all the enemies of God exert the most furious violence in the same attempt, yet his grace cannot possibly be extinguished, nor can his blood be rendered barren, so as not to produce some fruit. Here we must regard both the secret election of God, and his internal vocation; because he alone "knoweth them that are his;" and keeps them enclosed under his "seal," to use the expression of Paul; except that they bear his impression, by which they may be distinguished from the reprobate. But because a small and contemptible number is concealed among a vast multitude, and a few grains of wheat are covered with a heap of chaff, we must leave to God alone the knowledge of his Church whose foundation is his secret election. Nor is it sufficient to include in our thoughts and minds the whole multitude of the elect, unless we conceive of such a unity of the Church, into which we know ourselves to be truly ingrafted. For unless we are united with all the other members under Christ our Head, we can have no hope of the future inheritance. Therefore the Church is called CATHOLIC, or universal; because there could not be two or three churches, without Christ being divided, which is impossible. But all the elect of God are so connected with each other in Christ, that as they depend upon one head, so they grow up together as into one body, compacted together like members of the same body; being made truly one, as living by one faith, hope, and charity, through the same Divine Spirit, being called not only to the same inheritance of eternal life, but also to a participation of one God and Christ. Therefore, though the melancholy desolation which surrounds us, seems to proclaim that there is nothing left of the Church, let us remember that the death of Christ is fruitful, and that God wonderfully preserves his Church as it were in hiding-places; according to what he said in Elijah: "I have reserved to myself seven thousand men, who have not bowed the knee to Baal."

This article of the creed, however, relates in some measure to the external Church, that every one of us may maintain a brotherly agreement with all the children of God, may pay due deference to the authority of the Church, and, in a word, may conduct himself as one of the flock. Therefore we add THE COMMUNION OF SAINTS—a clause which, though generally omitted by the ancients, ought not to be neglected, because it excellently expresses the character of the Church; as though it had been said that the saints are united in the fellowship of Christ on this condition, that whatever benefits God confers upon them, they should mutually communicate to each other. This destroys not the diversity of grace, for we know that the gifts of the Spirit are variously distributed; nor does it disturb the order of civil polity, which secures to every individual the exclusive enjoyment of his property, as it is necessary for the preservation of the peace of society that men should have peculiar and distinct possessions. But the community asserted is such as Luke describes, that "the multitude of them that believed were of one heart and of one soul;" and Paul, when he exhorts the Ephesians to be "one body, and one spirit, even as they were called in one hope." Nor is it possible, if they are truly persuaded that God is a common Father to them all, and Christ their common Head, but that, being united in brotherly affection, they should mutually communicate their advantages to each other. Now, it highly concerns us to know what benefit we receive from this. For we believe the Church, in order to have a certain assurance that we are members of it. For thus our salvation rests on firm and solid foundations, so that it cannot fall into ruin, though the whole fabric of the world should be dissolved. First, it is founded on the election of God, and can be liable to no variation or failure but with the subversion of his eternal providence. In the next place, it is united with the stability of Christ, who will no more suffer his faithful people to be severed from him, than his members to be torn in pieces. Besides, we are certain, as long as we continue in the bosom of the Church, that we shall remain in possession of the truth. Lastly, we understand these promises to belong to us: "In mount Zion shall be deliverance." "God is in the midst of her; she shall not be moved." Such is the effect of union with the Church, that it retains us in the fellowship of God. The very word communion likewise contains abundant consolation; for while it is certain that whatever the Lord confers upon his members and ours belong to us, our hope is confirmed by all the benefits which they enjoy. But in order to embrace the unity of the Church in this manner, it is unnecessary, as we have observed, to see the Church with our eyes, or feel it with our hands; on the contrary, from its being an object of faith, we are taught that it is no less to be considered as existing, when it escapes our observation, than if it were evident to our eyes. Nor is our faith the worse, because it acknowledges the Church which we do not fully comprehend; for we are not commanded here to distinguish the reprobate from the elect, which is not our province, but that of God alone; we are only required to be assured in our minds, that all those who, by the mercy of God the Father, through the efficacious influence of the Holy Spirit, have attained to the participation of Christ, are separated as the peculiar possession and portion of God; and that being numbered among them, we are partakers of such great grace. . . .

2. THE VISIBLE CHURCH

From what has been said, I conceive it must now be evident what judgment we ought to form respecting the Church, which is visible to our eyes, and falls under our knowledge. For we have remarked that the word *Church* is used in the sacred scriptures in two senses. Sometimes, when they mention the Church, they intend that which is really such in the sight of God, into which none are received but those who by adoption and grace are the children of God, and by the sanctification of the Spirit are the true members of Christ. And then it comprehends not only the saints at any one time resident on earth, but all the elect who have lived from the beginning of the world. But the word *Church* is frequently used in the scriptures to designate the whole multitude, dispersed all over the world, who profess to worship one God and Jesus Christ, who are initiated into his faith by baptism, who testify their unity in true doctrine and charity by a participation of the sacred supper, who consent to the word of the Lord, and preserve the ministry which Christ has instituted for the purpose of preaching it. In this Church are included many hypocrites, who have nothing of Christ but the name and appearance; many persons ambitious, avaricious, envious, slanderous, and dissolute in their lives, who are tolerated for a time, either because they cannot be convicted by a legitimate process, or because discipline is not always maintained with sufficient vigour. As it is necessary, therefore, to believe that Church, which is invisible to us, and known to God alone, so this Church, which is visible to men, we are commanded to honour, and to maintain communion with it.

As far, therefore, as was important for us to know it, the Lord has described it by certain marks and characters. It is the peculiar prerogative of God himself to "know them that are his," as we have already stated from Paul. And to guard against human presumption ever going to such an extreme, the experience of every day teaches us how very far his secret judgments transcend all our apprehensions. For those who seemed the most abandoned, and were generally considered past all hope, are recalled by his goodness into the right way; while some, who seemed to stand better than others, fall into perdition. "According to the secret predestination of God," therefore as Augustine observes, "there are many sheep without the pale of the Church, and many wolves within." For he knows and seals those who know not either him or themselves. Of those who externally bear his seal, his eyes alone can discern who are unfeignedly holy, and will persevere to the end; which is the completion of salvation. On the other hand, as he saw it to be in some measure requisite that we should know who ought to be considered as his children, he has in this respect accommodated himself to our capacity. And as it was not necessary that on this point we should have an assurance of faith, he has substituted in its place a judgment of charity, according to which we ought to acknowledge as members of the Church all those who by a confession of faith, an exemplary life, and a participation of the sacraments, profess the same God and Christ with ourselves. But the knowledge of the body itself being more necessary to our salvation, he has distinguished it by more clear and certain characters.

Hence the visible Church rises conspicuous to our view. For wherever we find the word of God purely preached and heard, and the sacraments administered according to the institution of Christ, there, it is not to be doubted, is a Church of God; for his promise can never deceive—"where two or three are gathered together in my name, there am I in the midst of them. . . ."

We have stated that the marks by which the Church is to be distinguished, are, the preaching of the word and the administration of the sacraments. For these can nowhere exist without bringing forth fruit, and being prospered with the blessing of God. I assert not that wherever the word is preached, the good effects of it immediately appear; but that it is never received so as to obtain a permanent establishment, without displaying some efficacy. However this may be, where the word is heard with reverence, and the sacraments are not neglected, there we discover, while that is the case, an appearance of the Church, which is liable to no suspicion of uncertainty, of which no one can safely despise the authority or reject the admonitions, or resist the counsels, or slight the censures, much less separate from it and break up its unity. For so highly does the Lord esteem the communion of his Church, that he considers every one as a traitor and apostate from religion, who perversely withdraws himself from any Christian society which preserves the true ministry of the word and sacraments. He commends the authority of the Church, in such a manner as to account every violation of it an infringement of his own. For it is not a trivial circumstance, that the Church is called "the house of God, the pillar and ground of truth." For in these words Paul signifies that in order to keep the truth of God from being lost in the world, the Church is its faithful guardian; because it has been the will of God, by the ministry of the Church, to preserve the pure preaching of his word, and to manifest himself as our affectionate Father, while he nourishes us with spiritual food, and provides all things conducive to our salvation. . . .

3. THE MINISTRY

We must now treat of the order which it has been the Lord's will to appoint for the government of his Church. For although he alone ought to rule and reign in the Church, and to have all preëminence in it, and this government ought to be exercised and administered solely by his word,— yet, as he dwells not among us by a visible presence, so as to make an audible declaration of his will to us, we have stated, that for this purpose he uses the ministry of men whom he employs as his delegates, not to transfer his right and honour to them, but only that he may himself do his work by their lips; just as an artificer makes use of an instrument in the performance of his work. Some observations which I have made already, are necessary to be repeated here. It is true that he might do this either by himself, without any means or instruments, or even by angels; but there are many reasons why he prefers making use of men. For, in the first place, by this method he declares his kindness towards us, since he chooses from among men those who are to be his ambassadors to the world, to be the interpreters of his secret will, and even to act as his personal representa- tives. And thus he affords an actual proof, that when he so frequently calls us his temples, it is not an unmeaning appellation, since he gives answers to men, even from the mouths of men, as from a sanctuary. In the second place, this is a most excellent and beneficial method to train us to humility since he accustoms us to obey his word, though it is preached to us by men like ourselves, and sometimes even of inferior rank. If he were himself to speak from heaven, there would be no wonder if his sacred oracles were instantly received with reverence, by the ears and hearts of all mankind. For who would not be awed by his present power? who would not fall pros- trate at the first view of infinite Majesty? who would not be confounded by that overpowering splendour? But when a contemptible mortal, who had just emerged from the dust, addresses us in the name of God, we give the best evidence of our piety and reverence towards God himself, if we readily submit to be instructed by his minister, who possesses no personal su- periority to ourselves. For this reason, also, he has deposited the treasure of his heavenly wisdom in frail and earthen vessels, in order to afford a better proof of the estimation in which we hold it. Besides, nothing was more adapted to promote brotherly love, than a mutual connection of men by this bond, while one is constituted the pastor to teach all the rest, and they who are commanded to be disciples, receive one common doctrine from the same mouth. For if each person were sufficient for himself, and had no need of the assistance of another, such is the pride of human nature, every one would despise others, and would also be despised by them. The Lord, therefore, has connected his Church together, by that which he foresaw would be the strongest bond for the preservation of their union, when he committed the doctrine of eternal life and salvation to men, that by their hands it might be communicated to others. . . .

Now, the discussion of this subject includes four branches: what are the qualifications of ministers; in what manner they are to be chosen; by whom they ought to be appointed; and with what rite or ceremony they are to be introduced into their office. I speak of the external and solemn call, which belongs to the public order of the Church; passing over that secret call, of which every minister is conscious to himself before God, but which is not known to the Church. This secret call, however, is the honest testimony of our heart, that we accept the office offered to us, not from ambition or avarice, or any other unlawful motive, but from a sincere fear of God, and an ardent zeal for the edification of the Church. This, as I have hinted, is indispensable to every one of us, if we would approve our ministry in the sight of God. In the view of the Church, however, he who enters on his office with an evil conscience, is nevertheless duly called, provided his iniquity be not discovered. It is even common to speak of private persons as called to the ministry, who appear to be adapted and qualified for the discharge of its duties; because learning, connected with piety and other endowments of a good pastor, constitutes a kind of preparation for it. For those whom the Lord has destined to so important an office, he first furnishes with those talents which are requisite to its execution, that they may not enter upon it empty and unprepared. Hence Paul, in his Epistle to the Corinthians, when he intended to treat of the offices themselves, first enumerated the gifts which ought to be possessed by the persons who sustain those offices. But as this is the first of the four points which I have proposed, let us now proceed to it.

The qualifications of those who ought to be chosen bishops, are stated at large by Paul in two passages. The sum of all he says is, that none are to be chosen but men of sound doctrine and a holy life, not chargeable with any fault that may destroy their authority, or disgrace their ministry. The same rule is laid down for the deacons and governors. Constant care is required, that they be not unequal to the burden imposed upon them, or, in other words, that they be endowed with those talents which are necessary to the discharge of their duty. . . .

The third inquiry we proposed was, by whom ministers are to be chosen. Now, for this no certain rule can be gathered from the appointment of the apostles, which was a case somewhat different from the common call of other ministers. For as theirs was an extraordinary office, it was necessary, in order to render it conspicuous by some eminent character, that they who were to sustain it should be called and appointed by the mouth of the Lord himself. The apostles, therefore, entered upon their work, not in consequence of any human election, but empowered by the sole command of God and Christ. . . .

But that the election and appointment of bishops by men is necessary to constitute a legitimate call to the office, no sober person will deny, while there are so many testimonies of scripture to establish it. Nor is it contradicted by that declaration of Paul, that he was "an apostle, not of men, nor by man," since he is not speaking in that passage of the ordinary election of ministers, but claiming to himself what was the special privilege of the apostles. The immediate designation of Paul, by the Lord himself, to this peculiar privilege, was nevertheless accompanied with the form of an ecclesiastical call, for Luke states, that "As they ministered to the Lord, and fasted, the Holy Ghost said, Separate me Barnabas and Saul for the work whereunto I have called them." What end could be answered by this separation and imposition of hands after the Holy Spirit had testified their election, unless it was the preservation of the order of the Church in designating ministers by men? God could not sanction that order, therefore, by a more illustrious example than when, after having declared that he had constituted Paul the apostle of the Gentiles, he nevertheless directed him to be designated by the Church. . . . We find, therefore, that it is a legitimate ministry according to the word of God, when those who appear suitable persons are appointed with the consent and approbation of the people; but that other pastors ought to preside over the election, to guard the multitude from falling into any improprieties, through inconstancy, intrigue, or confusion.

There remains the Form of ordination, which is the last point that we have mentioned relative to the call of ministers. Now, it appears that when the apostles introduced any one into the ministry, they used no other ceremony than imposition of hands. This rite, I believe, descended from the custom of the Hebrews, who, when they wished to bless and consecrate anything, presented it to God by imposition of hands. Thus, when Jacob blessed Ephraim and Manasseh, he laid his hands upon their heads. This custom was followed by our Lord, when he prayed over infants. It was with the same design, I apprehend, that the Jews were directed in the law to lay their hands upon their sacrifices. Wherefore the imposition of the hands of the apostle was an indication that they offered to God the person whom they introduced into the ministry. They used the same ceremony over those on whom they conferred the visible gifts of the Spirit. But, be that as it may, this was the solemn rite invariably practised, whenever any one was called to the ministry of the Church. Thus they ordained pastors and teachers, and thus they ordained deacons. Now, though there is no express precept for the imposition of hands, yet since we find it to have been constantly used by the apostles, such a punctual observance of it by them ought to have the force of a precept with us. And certainly this ceremony is highly useful both to recommend to the people the dignity of the ministry, and to admonish the person ordained that he is no longer his own master, but devoted to the service of God and the Church. . . .

4. THE SACRAMENTS

Connected with the preaching of the gospel, another assistance and support for our faith is presented to us in the sacraments; on the subject of which it is highly important to lay down some certain doctrine, that we may learn for what end they were instituted, and how they ought to be used. In the first place, it is necessary to consider what a sacrament is. Now, I think it will be a simple and appropriate definition, if we say that it is an outward sign, by which the Lord seals in our consciences the promises of his good-will towards us, to support the weakness of our faith; and we on our part testify our piety towards him, in his presence and that of angels, as well as before men. It may, however, be more briefly defined, in other words, by calling it a testimony of the grace of God towards us, confirmed by an outward sign, with a reciprocal attestation of our piety towards him. . . . Sacraments, therefore, are exercises, which increase and strengthen our faith in the word of God; and because we are corporeal, they are exhibited under corporeal symbols, to instruct us according to our dull capacities, and to lead us by the hand as so many young children. For this reason Augustine calls a sacrament "a visible work;" because it represents the promises of God portrayed as in a picture, and places before our eyes an image of them, in which every lineament is strikingly expressed. Other similitudes may also be adduced for the better elucidation of the nature of sacraments; as if we call them *pillars of our faith*; for as an edifice rests on its foundation, and yet, from the addition of pillars placed under it, receive an increase of stability, so faith rests on the word of God as its foundation; but when the sacraments are added to it as pillars, they bring with them an accession of strength. Or if we call them *mirrors*, in which we may contemplate the riches of grace which God imparts to us; for in the sacraments, as we have already observed, he manifests himself to us as far as our dulness is capable of knowing him, and testifies his benevolence and love towards us more expressly than he does by his word. . . .

Wherefore let us abide by this conclusion, that the office of the sacraments is precisely the same as that of the word of God; which is to offer and present Christ to us, and in him the treasures of his heavenly grace; but they confer no advantage or profit without being received by faith; just as wine, or oil, or any other liquor, though it be poured plentifully on a vessel, yet will it overflow and be lost, unless the mouth of the vessel be open; and the vessel itself, though wet on the outside, will remain dry and empty within. It is also necessary to guard against being drawn into an error allied to this, from reading the extravagant language used by the fathers with a view to exalt the dignity of the sacraments; lest we should suppose there is some secret power annexed and attached to the sacraments, so that they communicate the grace of the Holy Spirit, just as wine is given in the cup; whereas the only office assigned to them by God, is to testify and confirm his benevolence towards us; nor do they impart any benefit, unless they are accompanied by the Holy Spirit to open our minds and hearts, and render us capable of receiving this testimony: and here, also, several distinct favours of God are eminently displayed. For the sacraments, as we have before hinted, fulfil to us, on the part of God, the same office as messengers of joyful intelligence, or earnests for the confirmation of covenants on the part of men; they communicate no grace from themselves, but announce and show, and, as earnests and pledges, ratify, the things which are given to us by the goodness of God. The Holy Spirit, whom the sacraments do not promiscuously impart to all but whom God, by a peculiar privilege, confers upon his servants, is he who brings with him the graces of God, who gives the sacraments admission into our hearts, and causes them to bring forth fruit in us. Now, though we do not deny that God himself accompanies his institution by the very present power of his Spirit, that the administration of the sacraments which he has ordained may not be vain and unfruitful, yet we assert the necessity of a separate consideration and contemplation of the internal grace of the Spirit, as it is distinguished from the external ministry. Whatever God promises and adumbrates in signs, therefore, he really performs; and the signs are not without their effect, to prove the veracity and fidelity of their Author. The only question here is, whether God works by a proper and intrinsic power, as it is expressed, or resigns the office to external symbols. Now, we contend, that whatever instruments he employs, this derogates nothing from his supreme operation. When this doctrine is maintained respecting the sacraments, their dignity is sufficiently announced, their use plainly signified, their utility abundantly declared, and a proper moderation is preserved in all these particulars, so that nothing is attributed, which ought not to be attributed to them, and nothing that belongs to them is denied; while there is no admission of the figment, which places the cause of justification and the power of the Spirit in the sacramental elements, as in so many vehicles; and that peculiar power which has been omitted by others is clearly expressed. Here, also, it must be remarked, that God accomplishes within, that which the minister represents and testifies by the external act; that we may not attribute to a moral man what God challenges exclusively to himself. . . .

A. BAPTISM

Baptism is a sign of initiation, by which we are admitted into the society of the Church, in order that, being incorporated into Christ, we may be numbered among the children of God. Now, it has been given to us by God for these ends, which I have shown to be common to all sacraments: first, to promote our faith towards him; secondly, to testify our confession before men. We shall treat of both these ends of its institution in order. To begin with the first: from baptism our faith derives three advantages, which require to be distinctly considered. The first is, that it is proposed to us by the Lord, as a symbol and token of our purification; or, to express my meaning more fully, it resembles a legal instrument properly attested, by which he assures us that all our sins are cancelled, effaced, and obliterated, so that they will never appear in his sight, or come into his remembrance, or be imputed to us. For he commands all who believe to be baptized for the remission of their sins. Therefore those who have imagined that baptism is nothing more than a mark or sign by which we profess our religion before men, as soldiers wear the insignia of their sovereign as a mark of their profession, have not considered that which was the principal thing in baptism; which is, that we ought to receive it with this promise, "He that believeth and is baptized shall be saved. . . ."

Nor must it be supposed that baptism is administered only for the time past, so that for sins into which we fall after baptism it would be necessary to seek other new remedies of expiation in I know not what other sacraments, as if the virtue of baptism were become obsolete. In consequence of this error, it happened, in former ages, that some persons would not be baptized except at the close of their life, and almost in the moment of their death, that so they might obtain pardon for their whole life—a preposterous caution, which is frequently censured in the writings of the ancient bishops. But we ought to conclude, that at whatever time we are baptized, we are washed and purified for the whole of life. Whenever we have fallen, therefore, we must recur to the remembrance of baptism, and arm our minds with the consideration of it, that we may be always certified and assured of the remission of our sins. For though, when it has been once administered, it appears to be past, yet it is not abolished by subsequent sins. For the purity of Christ is offered to us in it; and that always retains its virtue is never overcome by any blemishes, but purifies and obliterates all our defilements. Now, from this doctrine we ought not to take a license for the commission of future sins; for it is very far from inculcating such presumption; it is only delivered to those who, when they have sinned, groan under the fatigue and oppression of their transgressions; in order to afford them some relief and consolation and to preserve them from sinking into confusion and despair. . . .

The last advantage which our faith receives from baptism, is the certain testimony it affords us, that we are not only ingrafted into the life and death of Christ, but are so united as to be partakers of all his benefits. For this reason he dedicated and sanctified baptism in his own body, that he might have it in common with us, as a most firm bond of the union and society which he has condescended to form with us; so that Paul proves from it, that we are the children of God, because we have put on Christ in baptism. . . .

Now, if it be inquired, whether baptism may rightly be administered to infants, shall we not pronounce it an excess of folly, and even madness, in any one who resolves to dwell entirely on the element of water and the external observance, and cannot bear to direct his thoughts to the spiritual mystery; a due consideration of which will prove, beyond all doubt, that baptism is justly administered to infants, as that to which they are fully entitled? For the Lord, in former ages, did not favour them with circumcision without making them partakers of all those things which were then signified by circumcision. Otherwise, he must have deluded his people with mere impostures, if he deceived them by fallacious symbols; which it is dreadful even to hear. For he expressly pronounces that the circumcision of a little infant should serve as a seal for the confirmation of the covenant. But if the covenant remains firm and unmoved, it belongs to the children of Christians now, as much as it did to the infants of the Jews under the Old Testament. But if they are partakers of the thing signified, why shall they be excluded from the sign? If they obtain the truth, why shall they be debarred from the figure? Though the external sign in the sacrament is so connected with the word, as not to be separated from it, yet if it be distinguished, which shall we esteem of the greater importance? Certainly, when we see that the sign is subservient to the word, we shall pronounce it to be inferior to it, and assign it the subordinate place. While the word of baptism, then, is directed to infants, why shall the sign, which is an appendix to the word, be prohibited to them? This one reason, if there were no others, would be abundantly sufficient for the refutation of all opposers. The objection that there was a particular day fixed for circumcision, is a mere evasion. We admit that we are not now bound to certain days, like the Jews; but when the Lord, though he prescribes no particular day, yet declares it to be his pleasure that infants shall be received into his covenant by a solemn rite, what do we want more? . . .

Let those, therefore, who embrace the promise of God that he will perpetuate his mercy to their offspring, consider it their duty to present them to the Church to be signed with the symbol of mercy, and thereby to animate their minds to stronger confidence, when they actually see the covenant of the Lord engraven on the bodies of their children. The children also receive some advantage from their baptism, their ingrafting into the body of the Church being a more peculiar recommendation of them to the other members; and afterwards, when they grow to years of maturity, it operates upon them as a powerful stimulus to a serious attention to the worship of God, by whom they were accepted as his children by the solemn symbol of adoption, before they were capable of knowing him as their Father. . . .

B. THE LORD'S SUPPER

After God has once received us into his family, and not only so as to admit us among his servants, but to number us with his children,—in order to fulfil the part of a most excellent father, solicitous for his offspring, he also undertakes to sustain and nourish us as long as we live; and not content with this, he has been pleased to give us a pledge, as a further assurance of this never-ceasing liberality. For this purpose, therefore, by the hand of his only begotten Son, he has favoured his Church with another sacrament, a spiritual banquet, in which Christ testifies himself to be the bread of life, to feed our souls for a true and blessed immortality. Now, as the knowledge of so great a mystery is highly necessary, and on account of its importance, requires an accurate explication; and, on the other hand, as Satan, in order to deprive the Church of this inestimable treasure, long ago endeavoured, first by mists, and afterwards by thicker shades, to obscure its lustre, and then raised disputes and contentions to alienate the minds of the simple from a relish for this sacred food, and in our time also has attempted the same artifice; after having exhibited a summary of what relates to the subject, adapted to the capacity of the unlearned, I will disentangle it from those sophistries with which Satan has been labouring to deceive the world. In the first place, the signs are bread and wine, which represent to us the invisible nourishment which we receive from the body and blood of Christ. For as in baptism God regenerates us, incorporates us into the society of his Church, and makes us his children by adoption, so we have said, that he acts towards us the part of a provident father of a family, in constantly supplying us with food, to sustain and preserve us in that life to which he has begotten us by his word. Now, the only food of our souls is Christ; and to him, therefore, our heavenly Father invites us, that being refreshed by a participation of him, we may gain fresh vigour from day to day, till we arrive at the heavenly immortality. And because this mystery of the secret union of Christ with believers is incomprehensible by nature, he exhibits a figure and image of it in visible signs, peculiarly adapted to our feeble capacity; and, as it were, by giving tokens and pledges, renders it equally as certain to us as if we beheld it with our eyes; for the dullest minds understand this very familiar similitude, that our souls are nourished by Christ, just as the life of the body is supported by bread and wine. We see, then, for what end this mystical benediction is designed; namely, to assure us that the body of the Lord was once offered as a sacrifice for us, so that we may now feed upon it, and, feeding on it, may experience within us the efficacy of that one sacrifice; and that his blood was once shed for us, so that it is our perpetual drink. And this is the import of the words of the promise annexed to it: "Take, eat; this is my body, which is given for you." The body, therefore, which was once offered for our salvation, we are commanded to take and eat; that seeing ourselves made partakers of it, we may certainly conclude, that the virtue of that life-giving death will be efficacious within us. Hence, also, he calls the cup "the new testament," or rather covenant, in his blood. For the covenant which he once ratified with his blood, he in some measure renews, or rather continues, as far as relates to the confirmation of our faith, whenever he presents us that sacred blood to drink. . . .

The principal object of the sacrament, therefore, is not to present us the body of Christ, simply, and without any ulterior consideration, but rather to seal and confirm that promise, where he declares that his "flesh is meat indeed, and" his "blood drink indeed," by which we are nourished to eternal life; where he affirms that he is "the bread of life," and that "he that eateth of this bread shall live for ever;" to seal and confirm that promise, I say; and, in order to do this, it sends us to the cross of Christ, where the promise has been fully verified, and entirely accomplished. For we never rightly and advantageously feed on Christ, except as crucified, and when we have a lively apprehension of the efficacy of his death. And, indeed, when Christ called himself "the bread of life," he did not use that appelation on account of the sacrament, as some persons erroneously imagine, but because he had been given to us as such by the Father, and showed himself to be such, when, becoming a partaker of our human mortality, he made us partakers of his Divine immortality; when, offering himself a sacrifice, he sustained our curse, to fill us with his blessing; when, by his death, he destroyed and swallowed up death; when, in his resurrection, this corruptible flesh of ours, which he had assumed, was raised up by him, in a state of incorruption and glory. . . .

We conclude, that our souls are fed by the flesh and blood of Christ, just as our corporeal life is preserved and sustained by bread and wine. For otherwise there would be no suitableness in the analogy of the sign, if our souls did not find their food in Christ; which cannot be the case unless Christ truly becomes one with us, and refreshes us by the eating of his flesh and the drinking of his blood. Though it appears incredible for the flesh of Christ, from such an immense local distance, to reach us, so as to become our food, we should remember how much the secret power of the Holy Spirit transcends all our senses, and what folly it is to apply any measure of ours to his immensity. Let our faith receive, therefore, what our understanding is not able to comprehend, that the Spirit really unites things which are separated by local distance. Now, that holy participation of his flesh and blood, by which Christ communicates his life to us, just as if he actually penetrated every part of our frame, in the sacred supper he also testifies and seals; and that not by the exhibition of a vain or ineffectual sign, but by the exertion of the energy of his Spirit, by which he accomplishes that which he promises. And the thing signified he exhibits and offers to all who come to that spiritual banquet; though it is advantageously enjoyed by believers alone, who receive such great goodness with true faith and gratitude of mind. For which reason the apostle said, "The cup of blessing which we bless, is it not the communion of the blood of Christ? The bread which we break, is it not the communion of the body of Christ?" Nor is there any cause to object, that it is a figurative expression, by which the name of the thing signified is given to the sign. I grant, indeed, that the breaking of the bread is symbolical, and not the substance itself: yet, this being admitted, from the exhibition of the symbol we may justly infer the exhibition of the substance; for, unless any one would call God a deceiver, he can never presume to affirm that he sets before us an empty sign. Therefore, if, by the breaking of the bread, the Lord truly represents the participation of his body, it ought not to be doubted that he truly presents and communicates it. And it must always be a rule with believers, whenever they see the signs instituted by the Lord, to assure and persuade themselves that they are also accompanied with the truth of the thing signified. For to what end would the Lord deliver into our hands the symbol of his body, except to assure us of a real participation of it? If it be true that the visible sign is given to us to seal the donation of the invisible substance, we ought to entertain a confident assurance, that in receiving the symbol of his body, we at the same time truly receive the body itself. . . .

5. THE CHURCH AND CIVIL GOVERNMENT

Here it is necessary to state in a brief manner the nature of the office of magistracy, as described in the word of God, and wherein it consists. If the scripture did not teach that this office extends to both tables of the law, we might learn it from heathen writers; for not one of them has treated of the office of magistrates, of legislation, and civil government, without beginning with religion and Divine worship. And thus they have all confessed that no government can be happily constituted, unless its first object be the promotion of piety, and that all laws are preposterous which neglect the claims of God, and merely provide for the interests of men. Therefore, as religion holds the first place among all the philosophers, and as this has always been regarded by the universal consent of all nations,

Christian princes and magistrates ought to be ashamed of their indolence, if they do not make it the object of their most serious care. . . . this duty is particularly enjoined upon them by God; for it is reasonable that they should employ their utmost efforts in asserting and defending the honour of him, whose vicegerents they are, and by whose favour they govern. And the principal commendations given in the scripture to the good kings are for having restored the worship of God when it had been corrupted or abolished, or for having devoted their attention to religion, that it might flourish in purity and safety under their reigns. On the contrary, the sacred history represents it as one of the evils arising from anarchy, or a want of good government, that when "there was no king in Israel, every man did that which was right in his own eyes." These things evince the folly of those who would wish magistrates to neglect all thoughts of God, and to confine themselves entirely to the administration of justice among men; as though God appointed governors in his name to decide secular contro-versies, and disregarded that which is of far greater importance—the pure worship of himself according to the rule of his law. . . .

But here, it seems, arises an important and difficult question. If by the law of God all Christians are forbidden to kill, and the prophet predicts respecting the Church, that "they shall not hurt nor destroy in all my holy mountain, saith the Lord," how can it be compatible with piety for magistrates to shed blood? But if we understand, that in the infliction of punishments, the magistrate does not act at all from himself, but merely executes the judgments of God, we shall not be embarrassed with this scruple. The law of the Lord commands, "Thou shalt not kill;" but that homicide may not go unpunished, the legislator himself puts the sword into the hands of his ministers, to be used against all homicides. To hurt and to destroy are incompatible with the character of the godly; but to avenge the afflictions of the righteous at the command of God, is neither to hurt nor to destroy. Therefore it is easy to conclude that in this respect magistrates are not subject to the common law; by which, though the Lord binds the hands of men, he does not bind his own justice, which he exer-cises by the hands of magistrates. So, when a prince forbids all his subjects to strike or wound any one, he does not prohibit his officers from executing that justice which is particularly committed to them. I sincerely wish that this consideration were constantly in our recollection, that nothing is done here by the temerity of men, but every thing by the authority of God, who commands it, and under whose guidance we never err from the right way. For we can find no valid objection to the infliction of public vengeance, unless the justice of God be restrained from the punishment of crimes. But if it be unlawful for us to impose restraints upon him, why do we calumniate his ministers? Paul says to the magistrate, that "He beareth not the sword in vain; for he is the minister of God, a revenger to execute wrath upon him that doeth evil." Therefore, if princes and other governors know that nothing will be more acceptable to God than their obedience, and if they desire to approve their piety, justice, and integrity before God, let them devote themselves to this duty. . . .

What I have said will be more clearly understood, if in all laws we properly consider these two things—the constitution of the law and its equity, on the reason of which the constitution itself is founded and rests. Equity, being natural, is the same to all mankind; and consequently all laws, on every subject, ought to have the same equity for their end. Particular enactments and regulations, being connected with circumstances, and partly dependent upon them, may be different in different cases without any impropriety, provided they are all equally directed to the same object of equity. Now, as it is certain that the law of God, which we call the moral law, is no other than a declaration of natural law, and of that conscience which has been engraven by God on the minds of men, the whole rule of this equity, of which we now speak, is prescribed in it. This equity, therefore, must alone be the scope, and rule, and end, of all laws. Whatever laws shall be framed according to that rule, directed to that object, and limited to that end, there is no reason why we should censure them, however they may differ from the Jewish law or from each other. . . .

But in the obedience which we have shown to be due to the authority of governors, it is always necessary to make one exception, and that is entitled to our first attention,—that it do not seduce us from obedience to him, to whose will the desires of all kings ought to be subject, to whose decrees all their commands ought to yield, to whose majesty all their sceptres ought to submit. And, indeed, how preposterous it would be for us, with a view to satisfy men, to incur the displeasure of him on whose account we yield obedience to men! The Lord, therefore, is the King of kings; who, when he has opened his sacred mouth, is to be heard alone, above all, for all, and before all; in the next place, we are subject to those men who preside over us; but no otherwise than in him. If they command any thing against him, it ought not to have the least attention; nor, in this case, ought we to pay any regard to all that dignity attached to magistrates; to which no injury is done when it is subjected to the unrivalled and supreme power of God. . . . this edict has been proclaimed by that celestial herald, Peter, "We ought to obey God rather than men,"—let us console ourselves with this thought, that we truly perform the obedience which God requires of us, when we suffer any thing rather than deviate from piety. And that our hearts may not fail us, Paul stimulates us with another consideration—that Christ has redeemed us at the immense price which our redemption cost him, that we may not be submissive to the corrupt desires of men, much less be slaves to their impiety.

6 7   THE DECISIONS of the Roman Catholic Church at the Council
           of Trent (1545–1563) brought firm structure to the doctrinal
           affirmations of Catholicism. As reaction to challenges of
           Protestant reformers and in fulfillment of a long needed
           definition of dogma, Pope Paul III summoned this major
           church council. In the following selections we have state-
           ments of the Roman Catholic Church on the seven sacra-
           ments and on the additional subjects of purgatory, indul-
           gences, and the use of images.[1]

The Council of Trent*

SEVENTH SESSION: MARCH 3, 1547

DECREE ON THE SACRAMENTS

For the completion of the salutary doctrine on Justification, which
was promulgated with the unanimous consent of the Fathers in the last
preceding Session, it hath seemed suitable to treat of the most holy
Sacraments of the Church, through which all true justice either begins, or
being begun is increased, or being lost is repaired. With this view, in order
to destroy the errors and to extirpate the heresies which have appeared in
these our days on the subject of the said most holy sacraments,—as well
as those which have been revived from the heresies condemned of old by
our Fathers, as also those newly invented, and which are exceedingly
prejudicial to the purity of the Catholic Church, and to the salvation of
souls,—the sacred and holy, oecumenical and general Synod of Trent, lawfully assembled in the Holy Ghost, the same legates of the Apostolic See
presiding therein, adhering to the doctrine of the Holy Scriptures, to the
apostolic traditions, and to the consent of other councils and of the
Fathers, has thought fit that these present canons be established and
decreed; intending, the divine Spirit aiding, to publish later the remaining
canons which are wanting for the completion of the work which it has
begun.

* From Philip Schaff, The Creeds of Christendom, Vol. II. New York: Harper and
Row Publishers, 1919. Used by permission of Mary L. Schaff.

1 See also Council of Trent, Selections 10, 48.

ON THE SACRAMENTS IN GENERAL

Canon I. If any one saith, that the sacraments of the New Law were not all instituted by Jesus Christ, our Lord; or, that they are more, or less, than seven, to wit, Baptism, Confirmation, the Eucharist, Penance, Extreme Unction, Order, and Matrimony; or even that any one of these seven is not truly and properly a sacrament: let him be anathema.

Canon IV. If any one saith, that the sacraments of the New Law are not necessary unto salvation, but superfluous; and that, without them, or without the desire thereof, men obtain of God, through faith alone, the grace of justification;—though all [the sacraments] are not indeed necessary for every individual: let him be anathema.

Canon VIII. If any one saith, that by the said sacraments of the New Law grace is not conferred through the act performed, but that faith alone in the divine promise suffices for the obtaining of grace: let him be anathema.

Canon IX. If any one saith, that, in the three sacraments, to wit, Baptism, Confirmation, and Order, there is not imprinted in the soul a character, that is, a certain spiritual and indelible sign, on account of which they can not be repeated: let him be anathema.

Canon XI. If any one saith, that, in ministers, when they effect, and confer the sacraments, there is not required the intention at least of doing what the Church does: let him be anathema.

Canon XII. If any one saith, that a minister, being in mortal sin,—if so be that he observe all the essentials which belong to the effecting, or conferring of, the sacrament,—neither effects, nor confers the sacrament: let him be anathema.

THIRTEENTH SESSION: OCTOBER 11, 1551

DECREE CONCERNING THE MOST HOLY SACRAMENT OF THE EUCHARIST

On the real presence of our Lord Jesus Christ in the most holy sacrament of the Eucharist

In the first place, the holy synod teaches, and openly and simply professes, that, in the august sacrament of the holy Eucharist, after the consecration of the bread and wine, our Lord Jesus Christ, true God and man, is truly, really, and substantially contained under the species of those sensible things. For neither are these things mutually repugnant,— that our Saviour himself always sitteth at the right hand of the Father in heaven, according to the natural mode of existing, and that, nevertheless, he be, in many other places, sacramentally present to us in his own substance, by a manner of existing, which, though we can scarcely express it in words, yet can we, by the understanding illuminated by faith, conceive, and we ought most firmly to believe, to be possible unto God: for thus all our forefathers, as many as were in the true Church of Christ, who have treated of this most holy Sacrament, have most openly professed, that our Redeemer instituted this so admirable a sacrament at the last supper, when, after the blessing of the bread and wine, he testified, in express and clear words, that he gave them his own very body, and his own blood, words which,—recorded by the holy Evangelists, and afterwards repeated by Saint Paul, whereas they carry with them that proper and most manifest meaning in which they were understood by the Fathers,—it is indeed a crime the most unworthy that they should be wrested, by certain contentious and wicked men, to fictitious and imaginary tropes, whereby the verity of the flesh and blood of Christ is denied, contrary to the universal sense of the Church, which, as "the pillar and ground of truth," has detested, as satanical, these inventions devised by impious men; she recognizing, with a mind ever grateful and unforgetting, the most excellent benefit of Christ.

On the excellency of the most holy Eucharist over the rest of the sacraments

The most holy Eucharist has indeed this in common with the rest of the sacraments, that it is a symbol of a sacred thing, and is a visible form of an invisible grace; but there is found in the Eucharist this excellent and peculiar thing, that the other sacraments have then first the power of sanctifying when one uses them, whereas in the Eucharist, before being used, there is the Author himself of sanctity. For the apostles had not as yet received the Eucharist from the hand of the Lord, when nevertheless himself affirmed with truth that to be his own body which he presented [to them]. And this faith has ever been in the Church of God, that, immediately after the consecration, the veritable body of our Lord, and his veritable blood, together with his soul and divinity, are under the species of bread and wine; but the body indeed under the species of bread, and the blood under the species of wine, by the force of the words; but the body itself under the species of wine, and the blood under the species of bread, and the soul under both, by the force of that natural connection and concomitancy whereby the parts of Christ our Lord, "who hath now risen from the dead, to die no more," are united together; and the divinity, furthermore, on account of the admirable hypostatical union thereof with his body and soul. Wherefore it is most true, that as much is contained under either species as under both; for Christ whole and entire is under the species of bread, and under any part whatsoever of that species; likewise the whole (Christ) is under the species of wine, and under the parts thereof.

On Transubstantiation

And because that Christ, our Redeemer, declared that which he offered under the species of bread to be truly his own body, therefore has it ever been a firm belief in the Church of God, and this holy synod doth now declare it anew, that, by the consecration of the bread and of the wine, a conversion is made of the whole substance of the bread into the substance of the body of Christ our Lord, and of the whole substance of the wine into the substance of his blood; which conversion is, by the holy Catholic Church, suitably and properly called Transubstantiation.

On the preparation to be given that one may worthily receive the sacred Eucharist

If it is unbeseeming for any one to approach to any of the sacred functions, unless he approach holily; assuredly, the more the holiness and divinity of this heavenly sacrament are understood by a Christian, the more diligently ought he to give heed that he approach not to receive it but with great reverence and holiness, especially as we read in the Apostle those words full of terror: "He that eateth and drinketh unworthily, eateth and drinketh judgment to himself." Wherefore, he who would communicate, ought to recall to mind the precept of the Apostle: "Let a man prove himself." Now ecclesiastical usage declares that necessary proof to be, that no one, conscious to himself of mortal sin, how contrite soever he may seem to himself, ought to approach to the sacred Eucharist without previous sacramental confession. This the holy synod hath decreed is to be invariably observed by all Christians, even by those priests on whom it may be incumbent by their office to celebrate, provided the opportunity of a confessor do not fail them; but if, in an urgent necessity, a priest should celebrate without previous confession, let him confess as soon as possible.

ON THE MOST HOLY SACRAMENT OF THE EUCHARIST

Canon I. If any one denieth, that, in the sacrament of the most holy Eucharist, are contained truly, really, and substantially, the body and blood together with the soul and divinity of our Lord Jesus Christ, and consequently the whole Christ; but saith that he is only therein as in a sign, or in figure, or virtue: let him be anathema. . . .

Canon VI. If any one saith, that, in the holy sacrament of the Eucharist, Christ, the only-begotten Son of God, is not to be adored with the worship, even external of latria; and is, consequently, neither to be venerated with a special festive solemnity, nor to be solemnly borne about in procession, according to the laudable and universal rite and custom of holy

Church; or, is not to be proposed publicly to the people to be adored, and that the adorers thereof are idolators: let him be anathema. . . .

Canon VIII. If any one saith, that Christ, given in the Eucharist, is eaten spiritually only, and not also sacramentally and really: let him be anathema.

Canon IX. If any one denieth, that all and each of Christ's faithful of both sexes are bound, when they have attained to years of discretion, to communicate every year, at least at Easter, in accordance with the precept of holy Mother Church: let him be anathema. . . .

Canon XI. If any one saith, that faith alone is a sufficient preparation for receiving the sacrament of the most holy Eucharist: let him be anathema. And for fear lest so great a sacrament may be received unworthily, and so unto death and condemnation, this holy synod ordains and declares, that sacramental confession, when a confessor may be had, is of necessity to be made beforehand, by those whose conscience is burthened with mortal sin, how contrite even soever they may think themselves. But if any one shall presume to teach, preach, or obstinately to assert, or even in public disputation to defend the contrary, he shall be thereupon excommunicated.

FOURTEENTH SESSION: NOVEMBER 25, 1551

ON THE MOST HOLY SACRAMENTS OF PENANCE AND EXTREME UNCTION

On the necessity, and on the institution of the Sacrament of Penance

If such, in all the regenerate, were their gratitude towards God, as that they constantly preserved the justice received in baptism by his bounty and grace, there would not have been need for another sacrament, besides that of baptism itself, to be instituted for the remission of sins. But because God, "rich in mercy, knows our frame," he hath bestowed a remedy of life even on those who may, after baptism, have delivered themselves up to the servitude of sin and the power of the devil,—the sacrament to wit of Penance, by which the benefit of the death of Christ is applied to those who have fallen after baptism. Penitence was indeed at all times necessary, in order to attain to grace and justice, for all men who had defiled themselves by any mortal sin, even for those who begged to be washed by the sacrament of baptism; that so, their perverseness renounced and amended, they might, with a hatred of sin and a godly sorrow of mind, detest so great an offense of God. Wherefore the prophet says: "Be converted and do penance for all your iniquities, and iniquity shall not be your ruin." The Lord also said: "Except you do penance, you shall also likewise perish"; and Peter, the prince of the apostles, recommending penitence to sinners who were about to be initiated by baptism, said: "Do penance, and be baptized every one of you." Nevertheless, neither before the coming of Christ was penitence a sacrament, nor is it such, since his coming, to any previously to baptism. But the Lord then principally instituted the sacrament of penance, when, being raised from the dead, he breathed upon his disciples, saying: "Receive ye the Holy Ghost: whose sins you shall forgive, they are forgiven them, and whose sins you shall retain, they are retained." [John XX, 23] By which action so signal, and words so clear, the consent of all the Fathers has ever understood that the power of "forgiving and retaining sins" was communicated to the apostles and their lawful successors, for the reconciling of the faithful who have fallen after baptism. And the Catholic Church with great reason repudiated and condemned as heretics the Novatians, who of old obstinately denied that power of forgiving. Wherefore, this holy synod, approving of and receiving as most true this meaning of those words of our Lord, condemns the fanciful interpretations of those who, in opposition to the institution of this sacrament, falsely wrest those words to the power of preaching the Word of God, and of announcing the Gospel of Christ.

On the parts and on the fruit of this sacrament

The holy synod doth furthermore teach, that the form of the sacrament of Penance, wherein its force principally consists, is placed in those words of the minister: "I absolve thee," etc.; to which words indeed certain prayers are, according to the custom of holy Church, laudably joined, which nevertheless by no means regard the essence of that form, neither are they necessary for the administration of the sacrament itself. But the acts of the penitent himself, to wit, contrition, confession, and satisfaction, are as it were the matter of this sacrament. Which acts, inasmuch as they are, by God's institution, required in the penitent for the integrity of the sacrament, and for the full and perfect remission of sins, are for this reason called the parts of penance. But the thing signified indeed, and the effect of this sacrament, as far as regards its force and efficacy, is reconciliation with God, which sometimes, in persons who are pious and who receive this sacrament with devotion, is wont to be followed by peace and serenity of conscience, with exceeding consolation of spirit. The holy synod, whilst delivering these things touching the parts and the effect of this sacrament, condemns at the same time the opinions of those who contend that the terrors which agitate the conscience, and faith, are the parts of penance.

On the ministry of this sacrament, and on Absolution

But, as regards the minister of this sacrament, the holy synod declares all those doctrines to be false, and utterly alien from the truth of the Gospel, which perniciously extend the ministry of the keys to any others soever besides bishops and priests; imagining, contrary to the institution of this sacrament, that those words of our Lord, "Whatsoever you shall bind upon earth, shall be bound also in heaven, and whatsoever you shall loose upon earth shall be loosed also in heaven," and, "Whose sins you shall forgive, they are forgiven them, and whose sins you shall retain, they are retained," were in such wise addressed to all the faithful of Christ indifferently and indiscriminately, as that every one has the power of forgiving sins,—public sins to wit by rebuke, provided he that is rebuked shall acquiesce, and secret sins by a voluntary confession made to any individual whatsoever. It also teaches, that even priests, who are in mortal sin, exercise, through the virtue of the Holy Ghost which was bestowed in ordination, the office of forgiving sins, as the ministers of Christ; and that their sentiment is erroneous who contend that this power exists not in bad priests. But although the absolution of the priest is the dispensation of another's bounty, yet is it not a bare ministry only, whether of announcing the Gospel, or of declaring that sins are forgiven, but is after the manner of a judicial act, whereby sentence is pronounced by the priest as by a judge; and therefore the penitent ought not so to confide in his own personal faith as to think that,—even though there be no contrition on his part, or no intention on the part of the priest of acting seriously and absolving truly,—he is nevertheless truly and in God's sight absolved, on account of his faith alone. For neither would faith without penance bestow any remission of sins, nor would he be otherwise than most careless of his own salvation, who, knowing that a priest but absolved him in jest, should not carefully seek for another who would act in earnest.

On works of satisfaction

The synod teaches furthermore, that so great is the liberality of the divine munificence, that we are able through Jesus Christ to make satisfaction to God the Father, not only by punishments voluntarily undertaken of ourselves for the punishment of sin, or by those imposed at the discretion of the priest according to the measure of our delinquency, but also, which is a very great proof of love, by the temporal scourges inflicted of God, and borne patiently by us.

ON THE SACRAMENT OF EXTREME UNCTION

It hath also seemed good to the holy synod, to subjoin to the preceding doctrine on Penance, the following on the sacrament of Extreme Unction, which by the Fathers was regarded as being the completion, not only of penance, but also of the whole Christian life, which ought to be a perpetual penance. First, therefore, as regards its institution, it declares and teaches, that our most gracious Redeemer,—who would have his servants at all times provided with salutary remedies against all the weapons of all their enemies,—as, in the other sacraments, he prepared the greatest aids, whereby, during life, Christians may preserve themselves whole from every more grievous spiritual evil, so did he guard the close of life, by the sacrament of Extreme Unction, as with a most firm defense. For though "our adversary" seeks and seizes opportunities, all our life long, to be able in any way "to devour" our souls; yet is there no time wherein he strains more vehemently all the powers of his craft to ruin us utterly, and, if he can possibly, to make us fall even from trust in the mercy of God, than when he perceives the end of our life to be at hand.

On the institution of the sacrament of Extreme Unction

Now, this sacred unction of the sick was instituted by Christ our Lord, as truly and properly a sacrament of the new law, insinuated indeed in Mark, but recommended and promulgated to the faithful by James the Apostle, and brother of the Lord. "Is any man," he saith, "sick among you? Let him bring in the priests of the Church, and let them pray over him, anointing him with oil in the name of the Lord: and the prayer of faith shall save the sick man; and the Lord shall raise him up; and if he be in sins, they shall be forgiven him." In which words, as the Church has learned from apostolic tradition, received from hand to hand, he teaches the matter, the form, the proper minister, and the effect of this salutary sacrament. For the Church has understood the matter thereof to be oil blessed by a bishop. For the unction very aptly represents the grace of the Holy Ghost, with which the soul of the sick person is invisibly anointed; and furthermore that those words, 'By this unction,' etc., are the form.

On the effect of this Sacrament

Moreover, the thing signified, and the effect of this sacrament, are explained in those words: "And the prayer of faith shall save the sick man, and the Lord shall raise him up, and if he be in sins they shall be forgiven him." For the thing here signified is the grace of the Holy Ghost; whose anointing cleanses away sins, if there be any still to be expiated, as also the remains of sins; "and raises up" and strengthens the soul of the sick person, by exciting in him a great confidence in the divine mercy; whereby the sick being supported, bears more easily the inconveniences and pains of his sickness; and more readily resists the temptations of the devil who "lies in wait for his heel"; and at times obtains bodily health, when expedient for the welfare of the soul.

TWENTY-FIRST SESSION: JULY 16, 1562

DOCTRINE CONCERNING THE COMMUNION UNDER BOTH SPECIES, AND OF LITTLE CHILDREN

That laymen and clerics, when not sacrificing, are not bound, of divine right, to communion under both species

Wherefore, this holy synod,—instructed by the Holy "Spirit", who is "the spirit of wisdom and of understanding, the spirit of counsel and of godliness", and following the judgment and usage of the Church itself, —declares and teaches, that laymen, and clerics when not consecrating, are not obliged, by any divine percept, to receive the sacrament of the Eucharist under both species; and that neither can it by any means be doubted, without injury to faith, that communion under either species is sufficient for them unto salvation. For, although Christ, the Lord, in the Last Supper, instituted and delivered to the apostles, this venerable sacrament in the species of bread and wine; not therefore do that institution and delivery tend thereunto, that all the faithful of the Church be bound, by the institution of the Lord, to receive both species. But neither is it rightly gathered, from that discourse which is in the sixth of John,—however according to the various interpretations of holy Fathers and Doctors it be understood—that the communion of both species was enjoined by the Lord; for he who said, "Except you eat the flesh of the Son of man and drink his blood, you shall not have life in you" (v. 54), also said: "He that eateth this bread shall live forever (v. 59); also said: "He that eateth my flesh and drinketh my blood hath everlasting life" (v. 55), also said: "The bread that I will give is my flesh for the life of the world" (v. 52); and, in fine, he who said, "He that eateth my flesh and drinketh my blood, abideth in me and I in him" (v. 57), said, nevertheless, "He that eateth this bread shall live forever" (v. 59).

That Christ whole and entire and a true sacrament are received under either species

It moreover declares, that although, as hath been already said, our Redeemer, in that last supper, instituted, and delivered to the apostles, this sacrament in two species, yet is to be acknowledged, that Christ whole and entire and a true sacrament are received under either species alone; and that therefore, as regards the fruit thereof, they, who receive one species alone are not defrauded of any grace necessary to salvation.

TWENTY-SECOND SESSION: SEPTEMBER 17, 1562

DOCTRINE ON THE SACRIFICE OF THE MASS

On the institution of the most holy Sacrifice of the Mass

Forasmuch as, under the former Testament, according to the testimony of the Apostle Paul, there was no "perfection, because of the weakness of the Levitical priesthood"; there was need, God, the Father of mercies, so ordaining, that "another priest should rise, according to the order of Melchisedech," our Lord Jesus Christ, who might consummate, and lead to what is perfect, as many as were to be sanctified. He, therefore, our God and Lord, though he was about to offer himself once on the altar of the cross unto God the Father, "by means of his death," there to operate "an eternal redemption"; nevertheless, because that his priesthood was not to be extinguished by his death, in the Last Supper, on the night in which he was betrayed,—that he might leave, to his own beloved Spouse the Church, a visible sacrifice, such as the nature of man requires, whereby that bloody sacrifice, once to be accomplished on the cross, might be represented, and the memory thereof remain even unto the end of the world, and its salutary virtue be applied to the remission of those sins which we daily commit,—declaring himself constituted "a priest forever, according to the order of Melchisedech," he offered up to God the Father his own body and blood under the species of bread and wine; and, under the symbols of those same things, he delivered [his own body and blood] to be received by his apostles, whom he then constituted priests of the New Testament; and by those words, "Do this in commemoration of me," he commanded them and their successors in the priesthood to offer [them]; even as the Catholic Church has always understood and taught. For, having celebrated the ancient Passover, which the multitude of the children of Israel immolated in memory of their going out of Egypt, he instituted the new Passover [to wit], himself to be immolated, under visible signs, by the Church through [the ministry of] priests, in memory of his own passage from this world unto the Father, when by the effusion of his own blood he redeemed us, "and delivered us from the power of darkness, and translated us into his kingdom." And this is indeed that clean oblation, which can not be defiled by any unworthiness, or malice of those that offer [it]; which the Lord foretold by Malachias was to be "offered in every place, clean to his name, which was to be great amongst the Gentiles"; and which the Apostle Paul, writing to the Corinthians, has not obscurely indicated, when he says, that they who are defiled by "the participation of the table of devils, can not be partakers of the table of the Lord"; by "the table," meaning in both places the altar. This, in fine, is that oblation which was prefigured by various types of sacrifices, during the period of nature, and of the law; inasmuch as it comprises all the good things signified by those sacrifices, as being the consummation and perfection of them all.

That the Sacrifice of the Mass is propitiatory, both for the living and the dead

And forasmuch as, in this divine sacrifice which is celebrated in the mass, that same Christ is contained and immolated in an unbloody manner who once offered himself in a bloody manner on the altar of the cross; the holy synod teaches, that this sacrifice is truly propitiatory, and that by means thereof this is effected, that we obtain mercy, and find grace "in seasonable aid," if we draw nigh unto God, contrite and penitent, with a sincere heart and upright faith, with fear and reverence. For the Lord, appeased by the oblation thereof, and granting the grace and gift of penitence, forgives even heinous crimes and sins. For the victim is one and the same, the same now offering by the ministry of priests, who then offered himself on the cross, the manner alone of offering being different. The fruits indeed of which oblation, of that bloody one to wit, are received most plentifully through this unbloody one; so far is this [latter] from derogating in any way from that [former oblation]. Wherefore, not only for the sins, punishments, satisfactions, and other necessities of the faithful who are living, but also for those who are departed in Christ, and who are not as yet fully purified, is it rightly offered, agreeably to a tradition of the apostles.

TWENTY-THIRD SESSION: JULY 15, 1563

THE TRUE AND CATHOLIC DOCTRINE CONCERNING THE SACRAMENT OF ORDER

On the Ecclesiastical hierarchy, and on Ordination

But, forasmuch as in the sacrament of Order, as also in Baptism and Confirmation, a character is imprinted which can neither be effaced nor taken away, the holy synod with reason condemns the opinion of those who assert that the priests of the New Testament have only a temporary power; and that those who have once been rightly ordained can again become laymen, if they do not exercise the ministry of the Word of God. And if any one affirm, that all Christians indiscriminately are priests of the New Testament, or that they are all mutually endowed with an equal spiritual power, he clearly does nothing but confound the ecclesiastical hierarchy, which is "as an army set in array;" as if, contrary to the doctrine of blessed Paul, "all" were "apostles, all prophets, all evangelists, all pastors, all doctors." Wherefore, the holy synod declares that, besides the other ecclesiastical degrees, bishops, who have succeeded to the place of the Apostles, principally belong to this hierarchical order; that they are "placed," as the same apostle says, "by the Holy Ghost, to rule the Church of God"; that they are superior to priests; administer the sacrament of Confirmation; ordain the ministers of the Church; and that they can perform very many other things; over which functions others of an inferior order have no power. Furthermore, the sacred and holy synod teaches, that, in the ordination of bishops, priests, and of the other orders, neither the consent, nor vocation, nor authority, whether of the people, or of any civil power or magistrate whatsoever, is required in such wise as that, without this, the ordination is invalid: yea rather doth it decree, that all those who, being only called and instituted by the people, or by the civil power and magistrate, ascend to the exercise of these ministrations, and those who of their own rashness assume them to themselves, are not ministers of the Church, but are to be looked upon as "thieves and robbers, who have not entered by the door." These are the things which it hath seemed good to the sacred synod to teach the faithful of Christ, in general terms, touching the sacrament of Order. But it hath resolved to condemn whatsoever things are contrary thereunto, in express and specific canons,[2] in the manner following; in order that all men, with the help of Christ, using the rule of faith, may, in the midst of the darkness of so many errors, more easily be able to recognize and to hold Catholic truth.

TWENTY-FOURTH SESSION: NOVEMBER 11, 1563

DOCTRINE ON THE SACRAMENT OF MATRIMONY

The first parent of the human race, under the influence of the Divine Spirit, pronounced the bond of matrimony perpetual and indissoluble, when he said: "This now is bone of my bones, and flesh of my flesh. Wherefore a man shall leave father and mother, and shall cleave to his wife, and they shall be two in one flesh."

But, that by this bond two only are united and joined together, our Lord taught more plainly, when, rehearsing those last words as having been uttered by God, he said: "Therefore now they are not two, but one flesh"; and straightway confirmed the firmness of that tie, proclaimed so long before by Adam, by these words: "What therefore God hath joined together, let no man put asunder."

But the grace which might perfect that natural love, and confirm that indissoluble union, and sanctify the married, Christ himself, the institutor and perfecter of the venerable sacraments, merited for us by his passion; as the Apostle Paul intimates, saying, "Husbands love your wives, as Christ also loved the Church, and delivered himself up for it"; adding shortly after, "This is a great sacrament, but I speak in Christ and in the Church."

Whereas therefore matrimony, in the evangelical law, excels in grace, through Christ, the ancient marriages, with reason have our holy Fathers, the Councils, and the tradition of the universal Church, always taught, that it is to be numbered amongst the sacraments of the new law; against which, impious men of this age raging, have not only had false notions touching this venerable sacrament, but, introducing according to their wont, under the pretext of the Gospel, a carnal liberty, they have by word and writing asserted, not without great injury to the faithful of Christ, many things alien from the sentiment of the Catholic Church, and from the usage approved of since the times of the Apostles; the holy and universal synod, wishing to meet the rashness of these men, has taught it proper, let their pernicious contagion may draw more after it, that the more remarkable heresies and errors of the above-named schismatics be exterminated, by decreeing against the said heretics and their errors the following anathemas.[3]

[2] [The canons are omitted. Ed.]

[3] [The anathemas are omitted. Ed.]

TWENTY-FIFTH SESSION: DECEMBER 4, 1563

DECREE CONCERNING PURGATORY

Whereas the Catholic Church, instructed by the Holy Ghost, has, from the Sacred Writings and the ancient tradition of the Fathers, taught, in sacred Councils, and very recently in this oecumenical synod, that there is a Purgatory, and that the souls there detained are helped by the suffrages of the faithful, but principally by the acceptable sacrifice of the altar,—the holy synod enjoins on bishops that they diligently endeavor that the sound doctrine concerning Purgatory, transmitted by the holy Fathers and sacred Councils, be believed, maintained, taught, and every where proclaimed by the faithful of Christ. But let the more difficult and subtle questions, and which tend not to edification, and from which for the most part there is no increase of piety, be excluded from popular discourses before the uneducated multitude. In like manner, such things as are uncertain, or which labor under an appearance of error, let them not allow to be made public and treated of. While those things which tend to a certain kind of curiosity or superstition, or which savor of filthy lucre, let them prohibit as scandals and stumbling-blocks of the faithful. But let the bishops take care that the suffrages of the faithful who are living, to wit, the sacrifices of masses, prayers, alms, and other works of piety, which have been wont to be performed by the faithful for the other faithful departed, be piously and devoutly performed, in accordance with the institutes of the Church; and that whatsoever is due on their behalf, from the endowments of testators, or in other way, be discharged, not in a perfunctory manner, but diligently and accurately, by the priests and ministers of the Church, and others who are bound to render this [service].

ON THE INVOCATION, VENERATION, AND RELICS OF SAINTS, AND ON SACRED IMAGES

The holy synod enjoins on all bishops, and others who sustain the office and charge of teaching, that, agreeably to the usage of the Catholic and Apostolic Church, received from the primitive times of the Christian religion, and agreeably to the consent of the holy Fathers, and to the decrees of sacred Councils, they especially instruct the faithful diligently concerning the intercession and invocation of saints; the honor [paid] to relics; and the legitimate use of images: teaching them, that the saints, who reign together with Christ, offer up their own prayers to God for men; that it is good and useful suppliantly to invoke them, and to have recourse to their prayers, aid, [and] help for obtaining benefits from God, through his Son, Jesus Christ our Lord, who is our alone Redeemer and Saviour; but that they think impiously who deny that the saint, who enjoy eternal happiness in heaven, are to be invocated; or who assert either that they do not pray for men; or that the invocation of them to pray for each of us even in particular is idolatry; or that it is repugnant to the Word of God, and is opposed to the honor of the "one mediator of God and men, Christ Jesus;" or that it is foolish to supplicate, vocally or mentally, those who reign in heaven.

Also, that the holy bodies of holy martyrs, and of others now living with Christ,—which bodies were the living members of Christ, and "the temple of the Holy Ghost," and which are by him to be raised unto eternal life, and to be glorified,—are to be venerated by the faithful; through which [bodies] many benefits are bestowed by God on men; so that they who affirm that veneration and honor are not due to the relics of saints; or that these, and other sacred monuments, are uselessly honored by the faithful; and that the places dedicated to the memories of the saints are in vain visited with the view of obtaining their aid, are wholly to be condemned, as the Church has already long since condemned, and now also condemns them.

Moreover, that the images of Christ, of the Virgin Mother of God, and of the other saints, are to be had and retained particularly in temples, and that due honor and veneration are to be given them; not that any divinity, or virtue, is believed to be in them, on account of which they are to be worshipped; or that any thing is to be asked of them; or that trust is to be reposed in images, as was of old done by the Gentiles, who placed their hope in idols; but because the honor which is shown them is referred to the prototypes which those images represent; in such wise that by the images which we kiss, and before which we uncover the head, and prostrate ourselves, we adore Christ, and we venerate the saints, whose similitude they bear: as, by the decrees of Councils, and especially of the second Synod of Nicaea, has been defined against the opponents of images.

And the bishops shall carefully teach this,—that, by means of the histories of the mysteries of our Redemption, portrayed by paintings or other representations, the people is instructed, and confirmed in [the habit of] remembering, and continually revolving in mind the articles of faith; as also that great profit is derived from all sacred images, not only because the people are thereby admonished of the benefits and gifts bestowed upon them by Christ, but also because the miracles which God has performed by means of the saints, and their salutary examples, are set before the eyes of the faithful; that so they may give God thanks for those things; may order their own lives and manners in imitation of the saints; and may be excited to adore and love God, and to cultivate piety. But if any one shall teach or entertain sentiments contrary to these decrees: let him be anathema. . . .

Moreover, in the invocation of saints, the veneration of relics, and the sacred use of images, every superstition shall be removed, all filthy lucre be abolished; finally, all lasciviousness be avoided; in such wise that figures shall not be painted or adorned with a beauty exciting to lust; nor the celebration of the saints and the visitation of relics be by any perverted into revelings and drunkenness; as if festivals were celebrated to the honor of the saints by luxury and wantonness.

In fine, let so great care and diligence be used herein by bishops, as that there be nothing seen that is disorderly, or that is unbecomingly or confusedly arranged, nothing that is profane, nothing indecorous, seeing that "holiness becometh the house of God. . . ."

DECREE CONCERNING INDULGENCES

Whereas the power of conferring Indulgences was granted by Christ to the Church, and she has, even in the most ancient times, used the said power delivered unto her of God, the sacred holy synod teaches and enjoins that the use of Indulgences, for the Christian people most salutary, and approved of by the authority of sacred Councils, is to be retained in the Church; and it condemns with anathema those who either assert that they are useless, or who deny that there is in the Church the power of granting them. In granting them, however, it desires that, in accordance with the ancient and approved custom in the Church, moderation be observed; lest, by excessive facility, ecclesiastical discipline be enervated. And being desirous that the abuses which have crept therein, and by occasion of which this honorable name of Indulgences is blasphemed by heretics, be amended and corrected, it ordains generally by this decree, that all evil gains for the obtaining thereof,—whence a most prolific cause of abuses amongst the Christian people has been derived,—be wholly abolished. But as regards the other abuses which have proceeded from superstition, ignorance, irreverence, or from whatsoever other source, since, by reason of the manifold corruptions in the places and provinces where the said abuses are committed, they can not conveniently be specially prohibited, it commands all bishops diligently to collect, each in his own Church, all abuses of this nature, and to report them in the first provincial synod; that, after having been reviewed by the opinions of the other bishops also, they may forthwith be referred to the Sovereign Roman Pontiff, by whose authority and prudence that which may be expedient for the universal Church will be ordained; that thus the gift of holy Indulgences may be dispensed to all the faithful, piously, holily, and incorruptly.

68

THE PROFESSION OF THE TRIDENTINE FAITH, prepared by Pope Paul IV in 1564, was designed as a summary of the decisions of the Council of Trent, including, in addition, an oath of obedience to the Roman pontiff. The statement was made binding on Roman Catholic priests and teachers in Catholic schools.

Profession of the Tridentine Faith*

I. I. . . ., with a firm faith believe and profess all and every one of the things contained in that creed which the holy Roman Church makes use of:

'I believe in one God, the Father Almighty,' etc. [The Nicene Creed.]

II. I most steadfastly admit and embrace apostolic and ecclesiastic traditions, and all other observances and constitutions of the same Church.

III. I also admit the Holy Scriptures, according to that sense which our holy mother Church has held and does hold, to which it belongs to judge of the true sense and interpretation of the scriptures; neither will I ever take and interpret them otherwise than according to the unanimous consent of the Fathers.

IV. I also profess that there are truly and properly seven sacraments of the new law, instituted by Jesus Christ our Lord, and necessary for the salvation of mankind, though not all for every one, to wit: baptism, confirmation, the Eucharist, penance, extreme unction, holy orders, and matrimony; and that they confer grace; and that of these, baptism, confirmation, and ordination can not be reiterated without sacrilege. I also receive and admit the received and approved ceremonies of the Catholic Church, used in the solemn administration of the aforesaid sacraments.

V. I embrace and receive all and every one of the things which have been defined and declared in the holy Council of Trent concerning original sin and justification.

VI. I profess, likewise, that in the mass there is offered to God a true, proper, and propitiatory sacrifice for the living and the dead; and that in the most holy sacrament of the Eucharist there is truly, really, and substantially,

* From Philip Schaff, The Creeds of Christendom, Vol. II. New York: Harper and Row Publishers, 1919. Used by permission of Mary L. Schaff.

the body and blood, together with the soul and divinity of our Lord Jesus Christ; and that there is made a change of the whole essence of the bread into the body, and of the whole essence of the wine into the blood; which change the Catholic Church calls transubstantiation.

VII. I also confess that under either kind alone Christ is received whole and entire, and a true sacrament.

VIII. I firmly hold that there is a purgatory, and that the souls therein detained are helped by the suffrages of the faithful. Likewise, that the saints reigning with Christ are to be honored and invoked, and that they offer up prayers to God for us, and that their relics are to be held in veneration.

IX. I most firmly assert that the images of Christ, and of the perpetual Virgin the Mother of God, and also of other saints, ought to be had and retained, and that due honor and veneration are to be given them. I also affirm that the power of indulgences was left by Christ in the Church, and that the use of them is most wholesome to Christian people.

X. I acknowledge the holy Catholic Apostolic Roman Church for the mother and mistress of all churches; and I promise and swear true obedience to the Bishop of Rome, successor to St. Peter, Prince of the Apostles, and Vicar of Jesus Christ.

XI. I likewise undoubtingly receive and profess all other things delivered, defined, and declared by the Sacred Canons and General Councils, and particularly by the holy Council of Trent; and I condemn, reject, and anathematize all things contrary thereto, and all heresies which the Church has condemned, rejected, and anathematized.

XII. I do, at this present, freely profess and truly hold this true Catholic faith, without which no one can be saved; and I promise most constantly to retain and confess the same entire and inviolate, with God's assistance, to the end of my life. And I will take care, as far as in me lies, that it shall be held, taught, and preached by my subjects, or by those the care of whom shall appertain to me in my office. This I promise, vow, and swear—so help me God, and these holy Gospels of God.

69   MENNO SIMONS (1496–1561), the founder of the Mennonite Church, was one of the major figures in the "left wing" of the Reformation. He was ordained a Catholic priest in 1524 and after serving in a Netherlands parish for twelve years, he joined the Anabaptist group led by Obbe Philips.

During the 1530's the Anabaptist movement encountered

harsh resistance. Some of its more extreme elements prompted Roman Catholic and Protestant reformers to use physical violence to prevent the spread of Anabaptist groups, most of whom are remembered for their humane, though intense, character.

Menno Simons and his tradition sought to recapture the simplicity and purity of the early Christian communities and, as part of their distinctive teachings, advocated the separation of church and state, the union of faith and works, toleration for differing theological perspectives, and, characteristically, adult baptism. The following selection, written in 1539, offers this reformer's statement of reasons for a position that was similar to others in the "left wing" of the reformation.

Foundation of Christian Doctrine[*]

[On Baptism]

MENNO SIMONS

Christ, after His resurrection, commanded His apostles saying, Go ye therefore, and teach all nations, baptizing them in the name of the Father, and of the Son, and the Holy Ghost; teaching them to observe all things whatsoever I have commanded you; and, lo, I am with you always, even unto the end of the world. Amen.

Here we have the Lord's commandment concerning baptism, as to when according to the ordinance of God it shall be administered and received; namely, that the Gospel must first be preached, and then those baptized who believe it, as Christ says: Go ye into all the world, and preach the gospel to every creature; he that believeth and is baptized shall be saved, but he that believeth not, shall be damned. Thus has the Lord commanded and ordained; therefore, no other baptism may be taught or practiced forever. The Word of God abideth forever.

Young children are without understanding and unteachable; therefore baptism cannot be administered to them without perverting the ordinance of the Lord, misusing His exalted name, and doing violence to His holy

* From "Foundation of Christian Doctrine" in The Complete Writings of Menno Simons, John C. Wenger, ed. Scottdale, Penn.: Herald Press, 1956.

Word. In the New Testament no ceremonies for infants are enjoined, for it treats both in doctrines and sacraments with those who have ears to hear and hearts to understand. Even as Christ commanded, so the holy apostles also taught and practiced, as may be plainly perceived in many parts of the New Testament. Peter said, Repent and be baptized every one of you in the name of Jesus Christ for the remission of sins, and ye shall receive the gift of the Holy Ghost. And Philip said to the eunuch, If thou believest with all thine heart, thou mayest. Faith does not follow from baptism, but baptism follows from faith.

In this manner Christ has commanded baptism and received it Himself, as follows: When the time had come and the hour had approached in which He would fulfill the commission given Him to preach the Word and make known His Father's holy name, He came to John to the Jordan and desired to be baptized of him, that He might fulfill all righteousness. He prepared Himself to meet temptation, misery, the cross, and death, and as a willing, obedient child resigned Himself to the will of His almighty Father, as He Himself said that He came down from heaven, not to do His own will, but the will of Him that sent Him. He was baptized of John, witnessed to by the Holy Ghost, and acknowledged by the Father to be a beloved Son.

Beloved, so runs Christ's command, so Christ was baptized, so the apostles taught and practiced. Who now will confront the Lord and say it shall not be done so? Who will teach and instruct Wisdom? Who will rebuke apostles and evangelists for falsehood? It would be entirely unbecoming for a child, would it not, to command and judge his father, or a servant his master, and it is much more unbecoming for the creature to exalt himself above his Creator. But now it is manifest that the whole world with its unprofitable doctrines and commandments of men, with its anti-Christian customs, usages of long standing, and by its tyrannical, murderous judgment of the sword over Christ and His Word pronounces the truths of Christ lies; His wisdom, foolishness; His light, darkness, and His Gospel a perverted and false sect. In short Christ must be silent and passive.

Probably it will be said that this was necessary in the beginning of the Gospel because at that time there were no believers whose children might be baptized, but now if the parents are believers then are the children also to be baptized, just as when Abraham believed his children were circumcised. Oh, no, this does not follow; for although Abraham believed God only one half of his seed was circumcised, namely, the male children and not the female, though he was the father of the female as well as of the male children, of which by the grace of God, more shall be said below in the reply.

That in the beginning the Gospel was to be preached and that then faith came by hearing, and that baptism was to ensue upon faith, is undeniable, for scriptures teach this. But that the children of believers should be baptized because Abraham's children were circumcised, can in no wise be sustained by scripture. But even if it could be, which it cannot, then there would be but few children baptized, for the number of true believers is, sad to say, very small, as anyone may see.

Not all are Christians of whom it is boasted. But those who have the Spirit of Christ are true Christians, though I do not know where one might find very many. Yes, what more shall we say? All who with Abel bring an acceptable sacrifice, all who with Isaac are born of the free woman, and with Jacob have received the birthright and the paternal blessing; these must be slain by bloodthirsty Cain, mocked by Ishmael, and hated by Esau, even as also we may hear and see on every hand.

This then is the Word and will of the Lord, that all who hear and believe the Word of God shall be baptized as related above. Thereby they profess their faith and declare that they will henceforth live not according to their own will, but according to the will of God. For the testimony of Jesus they are prepared to forsake their homes, possessions, lands, and lives and to suffer hunger, affliction, oppression, persecution, the cross and death for the same; yes, they desire to bury the flesh with its lusts and arise with Christ to newness of life, even as Paul says: Know ye not that so many of us as were baptized into Christ Jesus were baptized into his death? Therefore we are buried with him in baptism into death; that like as Christ was raised up from the dead by the glory of the Father, even so we also should walk in newness of life.

Beloved reader, take heed to the Word of the Lord, Paul who did not receive his Gospel from men, but from the Lord Himself, teaches that even as Christ died and was buried, so also ought we to die unto our sins, and be buried with Christ in baptism. Not that we are to do this for the first time after baptism, but we must have begun all this beforehand, as Paul says: For if we have been planted together in the likeness of his death, we shall also be in the likeness of his resurrection. Knowing this that our old man is crucified with him, that the body of sin might be destroyed, that henceforth we should not serve sin. For he that is dead is freed from sin. For even as Christ has died, has taken way sin, and lives unto God, so true Christians die unto sin and live unto God.

Think not that we teach that Christians are to die unto sin to such an extent as to sense it no longer. Not by any means. But they die unto sin so as to be no longer subjects to their impure lusts. As Paul says, Let not sin therefore reign in your mortal body, that ye should obey it in the lusts thereof. Whosoever is born of God doth not commit sin; for his seed remaineth in him; and he cannot sin because he is born of God.

For even as the death of our Lord would not have profited us had He not risen from the power of death to the praise of His Father, so it will not avail us anything to bury our sins in baptism if we do not arise with Christ Jesus from the power of sin unto a new life to the praise of the Lord. For in that he died, he died unto sin once, says Paul; but in that he liveth, he liveth unto God. Likewise, reckon yourselves to be dead indeed unto sin but alive unto God through Christ Jesus. And as ye have yielded your members servants to uncleanness, and iniquity unto iniquity, even so now yield your members servants to righteousness and holiness. For being made free from sin, ye became the servants of righteousness and have your fruit unto holiness and the end everlasting life.

Here you notice, sensible reader, you who desire to know the truth and seek the salvation of your soul, what the great and holy apostle Paul has taught. If you believe his word, doctrine, and testimony to be true, you will no doubt readily perceive from these assertions and from many other passages in his writings that baptism is as much in place in the case of infants as circumcision was in the case of females of the Israelites. For we are no more commanded to baptize infants than Israel was to circumcise female children. It is also impossible for little children to die to sin as long as it has not become alive in them. Neither can they rise to a new life, as long as they are not born of God through faith, and by the Spirit of God led into righteousness. Therefore beware, for the symbolism of baptism is to bury sin, and to rise with Christ in a new life, things which can by no means be said of infants. Therefore consider at length what the Word of the Lord teaches you on this subject.

Paul also calls baptism the washing of regeneration. O dear Lord, how lamentably Thy holy Word is abused! Is it not most lamentable that men attempt with these plain passages to support their idolatrous and invented baptism of infants, asserting that infants are regenerated in baptism, as if regeneration were simply a matter of immersing in water. Oh, no! Regeneration is not such an hyprocrisy but it is an inward change which converts a man by the power of God through faith from evil to good, from carnality to spirituality, from unrighteousness to righteousness, out of Adam unto Christ. This is a matter which can in no wise take place with infants, for the regenerated live by the power of the new life; they crucify the flesh with its evil lusts; they put off the old Adam with his deeds; they avoid every appearance of evil; they are taught, ruled, and driven by the Holy Ghost.

Behold, this is the true new birth with its fruits, of which the scriptures speak and which comes forth from the Word of God through faith, without which no one, that is, no one who has come to years of understanding, can be saved. . . .

Observe, all of you who persecute the Word of the Lord and His people: this is our doctrine, position, and belief concerning baptism according to the instruction of the words of Christ; namely, that we must first hear the Word of God, believe it, and then upon our faith be baptized. Not because we seek sedition and want to fight; not because we want to practice polygamy or expect a kingdom on earth.[1] Oh, no, God be eternally praised, we know very well what the Word of the Lord teaches and implies on this matter. This Word of the Lord commands it. We with a sincere heart desire to die to sin, to bury our sins with Christ, and with Him to rise to a new life, even as baptism signifies. We seek to walk humbly and uprightly in Christ Jesus, in the covenant of His grace, in His eternal peace, and to have a pious and peaceful conscience before the Lord, even as the mouth of the Lord has commanded, as His example attests, and as the pure doctrines and practices of the apostles teach and indicate.

70

THE THIRTY-NINE ARTICLES have served as the statement of faith of the Church of England. Written and ratified in 1562, during the reign of Elizabeth, the Articles were a revision of the *Forty-Two Articles* of 1553, issued during the reign of Edward VI. The English translation of the *Thirty-Nine Articles* was approved in 1571 and given royal support. The influence of Reformed doctrine is apparent not only in the articles dealing with original sin, predestination, justification by faith (not included in the following selection), but also in the articles dealing with the Lord's Supper. The excerpts that follow are taken from the American Revision of 1801 that differs from the 1571 edition only in the omission in Article VIII of reference to the Athanasian Creed as an essential doctrinal statement, the omission of Article XXI that dealt with the power of General Councils, and a radical revision of Article XXXVII. The wording of Article XXXVII in the English edition of 1571 and American revision of 1801 are included below, though the Old English has been modernized by the editor.

[1] Menno Simons was critical of the more extreme elements within the "left wing" of the reformation, particularly the Munsterites. Ed.

The Thirty-nine Articles of the Church of England[*]

XIX. Of the Church

The visible Church of Christ is a congregation of faithful men, in the which the pure Word of God is preached, and the Sacraments be duly ministered according to Christ's ordinance, in all those things that of necessity are requisite to the same.

As the church of Jerusalem, Alexandria, and Antioch, have erred; so also the church of Rome hath erred, not only in their living and manner of Ceremonies, but also in matters of Faith.

XX. Of the Authority of the Church

The Church hath power to decree Rites or Ceremonies, and authority in Controversies of Faith: and yet it is not lawful for the Church to ordain any thing that is contrary to God's Word written, neither may it so expound one place of scripture, that it be repugnant to another. Wherefore, although the Church be a witness and a keeper of Holy Writ, yet, as it ought not to decree any thing against the same, so besides the same ought it not to enforce any thing to be believed for necessity of Salvation. . . .

XXIII. Of Ministering in the Congregation

It is not lawful for any man to take upon him the office of public preaching, or ministering the Sacraments in the Congregation, before he be lawfully called, and sent to execute the same. And those we ought to judge lawfully called and sent, which be chosen and called to this work by men who have public authority given unto them in the Congregation, to call and send Ministers into the Lord's vineyard. . . .

XXV. Of the Sacraments

Sacraments ordained of Christ be not only badges or tokens of Christian men's profession, but rather they be certain sure witnesses, and effectual sings of grace, and God's good will towards us, by the which he

* From Philip Schaff, The Creeds of Christendom, Vol. III. New York: Harper and Row Publishers, 1919. Used by permission of Mary L. Schaff.

doth work invisibly in us, and doth not only quicken, but also strengthen and confirm our Faith in him.

There are two Sacraments ordained of Christ our Lord in the Gospel, that is to say, Baptism, and the Supper of the Lord.

Those five commonly called Sacraments, that is to say, Confirmation, Penance, Orders, Matrimony, and Extreme Unction, are not to be counted for Sacraments of the Gospel, being such as have grown partly of the corrupt following of the Apostles, partly are states of life allowed in the Scriptures; but yet have not like nature of Sacraments with Baptism, and the Lord's Supper, for that they have not any visible sign or ceremony ordained of God.

The Sacraments were not ordained of Christ to be gazed upon, or to be carried about, but that we should duly use them. And in such only as worthily receive the same, they have a wholesome effect or operation: but they that receive them unworthily, purchase to themselves damnation, as Saint Paul saith.

XXVI. Of the Unworthiness of the Ministers which hinders not the effect of the Sacraments

Although in the visible Church the evil be ever mingled with the good, and sometimes the evil have chief authority in the Ministration of the Word and Sacraments, yet forasmuch as they do not the same in their own name, but in Christ's, and do minister by his commission and authority, we may use their Ministry, both in hearing the Word of God, and in receiving the Sacraments. Neither is the effect of Christ's ordinance taken away by their wickedness, nor the grace of God's gifts diminished from such as by faith, and rightly, do receive the Sacraments ministered unto them; which be effectual, because of Christ's institution and promise, although they be ministered by evil men.

Nevertheless, it appertaineth to the discipline of the Church, that inquiry be made of evil Ministers, and that they be accused by those that have knowledge of their offences; and finally, being found guilty, by just judgment be deposed.

XXVII. Of Baptism

Baptism is not only a sign of profession, and mark of difference, whereby Christian men are discerned from others that be not christened, but it is also a sign of Regeneration or New-Birth, whereby, as by an instrument, they that receive baptism rightly are grafted into the Church; the promises of the forgiveness of sin, and of our adoption to be the sons of God by the Holy Ghost, are visibly signed and sealed; Faith is confirmed, and Grace increased by virtue of prayer unto God.

The baptism of young children is in any wise to be retained in the Church, as most agreeable with the institution of Christ.

XXVIII. Of the Lord's Supper

The Supper of the Lord is not only a sign of the love that Christians ought to have among themselves one to another; but rather it is a Sacrament of our Redemption by Christ's death: insomuch that to such as rightly, worthily, and with faith, receive the same, the Bread which we break is a partaking of the Body of Christ; and likewise the Cup of Blessing is a partaking of the Blood of Christ.

Transubstantiation (or the change of the substance of Bread and Wine) in the Supper of the Lord, can not be proved by Holy Writ; but is repugnant to the plain words of scripture, overthroweth the nature of a Sacrament, and hath given occasion to many superstitions.

The Body of Christ is given, taken, and eaten, in the Supper, only after an heavenly and spiritual manner. And the mean whereby the Body of Christ is received and eaten in the Supper, is Faith.

The Sacrament of the Lord's Supper was not by Christ's ordinance reserved, carried about, lifted up, or worshiped.

XXIX. Of the Wicked, which eat not the Body of Christ in the use of the Lord's Supper

The Wicked, and such as be void of a lively faith, although they do carnally and visibly press with their teeth (as Saint Augustine saith) the Sacrament of the Body and Blood of Christ; yet in no wise are they partakers of Christ: but rather, to their condemnation, do eat and drink the sign or Sacrament of so great a thing.

XXX. Of both Kinds

The Cup of the Lord is not to be denied to the Lay-people: for both the parts of the Lord's Sacrament, by Christ's ordinance and commandment, ought to be ministered to all Christian men alike.

XXXI. Of the one Oblation of Christ finished upon the Cross

The Offering of Christ once made is that [the] perfect redemption, propitiation, and satisfaction, for all the sins of the whole world, both original and actual; and there is none other satisfaction for sin, but that alone. Wherefore the sacrifices of Masses, in the which it was commonly said that the Priest did offer Christ for the quick and the dead, to have remission of pain or guilt, were blasphemous fables, and dangerous deceits.

XXXII. Of the Marriage of Priests

Bishops, Priests, and Deacons, are not commanded by God's Law, either to vow the estate of single life, or to abstain from marriage: therefore it is lawful for them, as for all other Christian men, to marry at their own discretion, as they shall judge the same to serve better to godliness. . . .

XXXIV. *Of the Traditions of the Church*

It is not necessary that Traditions and Ceremonies be in all places one, or utterly like; for at all times they have been divers, and may be changed according to the diversity of countries, times, and men's manners, so that nothing be ordained against God's Word.

Whosoever, through his private judgement, willingly and purposely, doth openly break the Traditions and Ceremonies of the Church, which be not repugnant to the Word of God, and be ordained and approved by common authority, ought to be rebuked openly (that others may fear to do the like), as he that offendeth against the common order of the Church, and hurteth the authority of the Magistrate, and woundeth the consciences of the weak brethren.

Every particular or national Church hath authority to ordain, change, and abolish, Ceremonies or Rites of the Church ordained only by man's authority, so that all things be done to edifying. . . .

XXXVII. *Of the Power of the Civil Magistrates*

The Power of the Civil Magistrate extendeth to all men, as well Clergy as Laity, in all things temporal; but hath no authority in things purely spiritual. And we hold it to be the duty of all men who are professors of the Gospel, to pay respectful obedience to the Civil Authority, regularly and legitimately constituted.

[XXXVII, 1571] [*Of the Civil Magistrates*]

[The Queen's Majesty hath the chief power in this Realm of England, and her other dominions, unto whom the chief government of all estates of this Realm, whether they be Ecclesiastical or Civil, on all causes doth appertain, and is not, nor ought to be subject to any foreign jurisdiction.

Where we attribute to the Queen's Majesty the chief government, by which title we understand the minds of some slanderous folks to be offended: we give not to our princes the ministering either of God's word, or of Sacraments, the which thing the injunctions also lately set forth by Elizabeth our Queen, doth most plainly testify: But only that prerogative which we see to have been given always to all godly Princes in Holy Scriptures by God himself, that is, that they should rule all estates and degrees committed to their charge by God, whether they be Ecclesiastical or Temporal, and restrain with the civil sword the stubborn and evil doers.

The Bishop of Rome hath no jurisdiction in this Realm of England.

The laws of the Realm may punish Christian men with death, for heinous and grievous offences.

It is lawful for Christian men, at the command of the Magistrate, to wear weapons, and serve in the wars.]

71 RICHARD HOOKER (1553?–1600) published the *Laws of Ecclesiastical Polity* in 1594. His work was a defense of the Anglican communion and directed against those who urged a more radical reformation. The attacks of the Puritans were ably challenged by Hooker in this notable treatise. Hooker's response to the Puritan's "scriptural" arguments and his reasonable advocacy of the ecclesiastical orders has remained a major work of the Anglican church.

Laws of Ecclesiastical Polity*

RICHARD HOOKER

By the Church . . . we understand no other than only the visible Church. For preservation of Christianity there is not any thing more needful, than that such as are of the visible Church have mutual fellowship and society one with another. In which consideration, as the main body of the sea being one, yet within divers precincts hath divers names; so the Catholic Church is in like sort divided into a number of distinct Societies, everyone of which is termed a Church within itself. In this sense the Church is always a visible society of men; not an assembly, but a society. For although the name of the Church be given unto Christian assemblies, although any multitude of Christian men congregated may be termed by the name of a Church, yet assemblies properly are rather things that belong to a Church. Men are assembled for performance of public actions; which actions being ended, the assembly dissolveth itself and is no longer in being, whereas the Church which was assembled doth no less continue afterwards than before. . . .

What the Church of God standeth bound to know or do, the same in part nature teacheth. And because nature can teach them but only in part, neither so fully as is requisite for man's salvation, nor so easily as to make the way plain and expedite enough that many may come to the knowledge of it, and so be saved; therefore in scripture hath God both collected the most necessary things that the school of nature teacheth unto that end, and revealeth also whatsoever we neither could with safety be ignorant of, nor at all be instructed in but by supernatural revelation

* From *The Works of Richard Hooker*, Vols. I and III, arr. by John Keble. London: Oxford University Press, 1841.

from him. So that scripture containing all things that are in this kind any way needful for the Church, and the principal of the other sort, this is the next thing wherewith we are charged as with an error: we teach that whatsoever is unto salvation termed necessary by way of excellency, whatsoever it standeth all men upon to know or do that they may be saved, whatsoever there is whereof it may truly be said, "This not to believe is eternal death and damnation," or, "This every soul that will live must duly observe;" of which sort the articles of Christian faith and the sacraments of the Church of Christ are: all such things of scripture did not comprehend, the Church of God should not be able to measure out the length and the breadth of that way wherein for ever she is to walk, heretics and schismatics never ceasing some to abridge, some to enlarge, all to pervert and obscure the same. But as for those things that are accessory hereunto, those things that so belong to the way of salvation, as to alter them is no otherwise to change that way, than a path is changed by altering only the uppermost face thereof; which be it laid with gravel, or set with grass, or paved with stone, remaineth still the same path; in such things because discretion may teach the Church what is convenient, we hold not the the Church further tied herein unto scripture, than that against scripture nothing be admitted in the Church, lest that path which ought always to be kept even, do thereby come to be overgrown with brambles and thorns.

. . . so I trust that to mention what the scripture of God leaveth unto the Church's discretion in some things, is not in any thing to impair the honour which the Church of God yieldeth to the sacred scripture's perfection. Wherein seeing that no more is by us maintained, than only that scripture must needs teach the Church whatsoever is in such sort necessary as hath been set down; and that it is no more disgrace for scripture to have left a number of other things free to be ordered at the discretion of the Church, than for nature to have left it unto the wit of man to devise his own attire, and not to look for it as the beasts of the field have theirs: if neither this can import, nor any other proof sufficient be brought forth, that we either will at any time or ever did affirm the sacred scripture to comprehend no more than only those bare necessaries; if we acknowledge that as well for particular application to special occasions, as also in other manifold respects, infinite treasures of wisdom are over and besides abundantly to be found in the Holy Scripture; yea that scarcely there is any noble part of knowledge, worthy the mind of man, but from thence it may have some direction and light; yea, that although there be no necessity it should of purpose prescribe any one particular form of church government, yet touching the manner of governing in general the precepts that scripture setteth down are not few, and the examples many which it proposeth for all church governors even in particularities to follow; yea, that those things finally which are of principal weight in the very particular form of church polity (although not that form which they imagine, but that which we against them uphold) are in the selfsame scriptures contained: if all this be willingly granted by us which are accused to pin the word of God in so narrow room, as that it should be able to direct us but in principal points of our religion; or as though the substance of religion or some rude and unfashioned matter of building the Church were uttered in them, and those things left out that should pertain to the form and fashion of it; let the cause of the accused be referred to the accuser's own conscience, and let that judge whether this accusation be deserved where it hath been laid.

But so easy it is for every man living to err, and so hard to wrest from any man's mouth the plain acknowledgment of error, that what hath been once inconsiderately defended, the same is commonly persisted in, as long as wit by whetting itself is able to find out any shift, be it never so sleight, whereby to escape out of the hands of present contradiction. So that it cometh herein to pass with men unadvisedly fallen into error, as with them whose state hath no ground to uphold it, but only the help which by subtile conveyance they draw out of casual events arising from day to day, till at length they be clean spent. They which first gave out, that "nothing ought to be established in the Church which is not commanded by the word of God," thought this principle plainly warranted by the manifest words of the Law, "Ye shall put nothing unto the word which I command you, neither shall you take aught therefrom, that ye may keep the commandments of the Lord your God, which I command you." Wherefore having an eye to a number of rites and orders in the Church of England, as marrying with a ring, crossing in the one sacrament, kneeling at the other, observing of festival days more than only that which is called the Lord's day, enjoining abstinence at certain times from some kinds of meat, churching of women after childbirth, degrees taken by divines in universities, sundry church offices, dignities, and callings, for which they found no commandment in the Holy Scripture, they thought by the one only stroke of that axiom to have cut them off. But that which they took for an oracle being sifted was repelled. True it is concerning the word of God, whether it be by misconstruction of the sense or by falsification of the words, wittingly to endeavour that any thing may seem divine which is not, or any thing not seem which is, were plainly to abuse, and even to falsify divine evidence; which injury offered but unto men, is most worthily counted heinous. Which point I wish they did well observe, with whom nothing is more familiar than to plead in these causes, "the law of God," "the word of the Lord;" who notwithstanding when they come to allege what word and what law they mean, their common ordinary practice is to quote by-speeches in some historical narration or other, and to urge them as if they were written in most exact form of law. What is to add to the law of God if this be not? When that which the word of God doth but deliver historically, we construe without any warrant as if it were legally meant, and so urge it further than we can prove that it was intended; do we not add to the laws of God, and make them in number seem more than they are? It standeth us upon to be careful in this case. For the sentence of God is heavy against them that wittingly shall presume thus to use the scripture. . . .

[Thus] the question is only how far the bounds of the Church's liberty do reach. We hold, that the power which the Church hath lawfully to make laws and orders for itself doth extend unto sundry things of ecclesiastical jurisdiction, and such other matters, whereto their opinion is that the Church's authority and power doth not reach. Whereas therefore in disputing against us about this point, they take their compass a great deal wider than the truth of things can afford; producing reasons and arguments by way of generality, to prove that Christ hath set down all things belonging any way unto the form of ordering his Church, and hath absolutely forbidden change by addition or diminution, great or small: (for so their manner of disputing is:) we are constrained to make our defence, by shewing that Christ hath not deprived his Church so far of all liberty in making orders and laws for itself, and that they themselves do not think he hath so done. For are they able to shew that all particular customs, rites, and orders of reformed churches have been appointed by Christ himself? No: they grant that in matter of circumstance they alter that which they have received, but in things of substance they keep the laws of Christ without change. If we say the same in our own behalf (which surely we may do with a great deal more truth) then must they cancel all that hath been before alleged, and begin to inquire afresh, whether we retain the laws that Christ hath delivered concerning matters of substance, yea or no. For our constant persuasion in this point is as theirs, that we have no where altered the laws of Christ farther than in such particularities only as have the nature of things changeable according to the difference of times, places, persons, and other the like circumstances. Christ hath commanded prayers to be made, sacraments to be ministered, his Church to be carefully taught and guided. Concerning every of these somewhat Christ hath commanded which must be kept till the world's end. On the contrary side, in every of them somewhat there may be added, as the Church shall judge it expedient. So that if they will speak to purpose, all which hitherto hath been disputed of they must give over, and stand upon such particulars only as they can shew we have either added or abrogated otherwise than we ought, in the matter of church polity. Whatsoever Christ hath commanded for ever to be kept in his Church, the same we take not upon us to abrogate; and whatsoever our laws have thereunto added besides, of such quality we hope it is as no law of Christ doth any where condemn. . . .

The matters wherein church polity is conversant are the public religious duties of the Church, as the administration of the word and sacraments, prayers, spiritual censures, and the like. To these the Church standeth always bound. Laws of polity, are laws which appoint in what manner these duties shall be performed.

In performance whereof because all that are of the Church cannot jointly and equally work, the first thing in polity required is a difference of persons in the Church, without which difference those functions cannot in orderly sort be executed. Hereupon we hold that God's clergy are a state, which hath been and will be, as long as there is a Church upon earth, necessary by the plain word of God himself; a state whereunto the rest of God's people must be subject as touching things that appertain to their soul's health. For where polity is, it cannot but appoint some to be leaders of others, and some to be led by others. "If the blind lead the "blind, they both perish." It is with the clergy, if their persons be respected, even as it is with other men; their quality many times far beneath that which the dignity of their place requireth. Howbeit according to the order of polity, they being the "lights of the world," others (though better and wiser) must that way be subject unto them.

Again, forasmuch as where the clergy are any great multitude, order doth necessarily require that by degrees they be distinguished; we hold there have ever been and ever ought to be in such case at leastwise two sorts of ecclesiastical persons, the one subordinate unto the other; as to the Apostles in the beginning, and to the Bishops always since, we find plainly both in scripture and in all ecclesiastical records, other ministers of the word and sacraments have been.

Moreover, it cannot enter into any man's conceit to think it lawful, that every man which listeth should take upon him charge in the Church. . . .

A thousand five hundred years and upward the Church of Christ hath now continued under the sacred regiment of bishops. Neither for so long hath Christianity been ever planted in any kingdom throughout the world but with this kind of government alone; which to have been ordained of God, I am for mine own part even as resolutely persuaded, as that any kind of government in the world whatsoever is of God. In this realm of England, before Normans, yea before Saxons, there being Christians, the chief pastors of their souls were bishops. This order from about the first establishment of Christian religion, which was publicly begun through the virtuous disposition of King Lucie not fully two hundred years after Christ, continued till the coming in of the Saxons; by whom Paganism being every where else replanted, only one part of the island, whereinto the ancient natural inhabitants the Britons were driven, retained constantly the faith of Christ, together with the same form of spiritual regiment, which their fathers had before received. Wherefore in the histories of the Church we find very ancient mention made of our own bishops. At the Council of Ariminum, about the year three hundred and fifty-nine, Britain had three of her bishops present. At the arrival of Augustine the monk, whom Gregory sent hither to reclaim the Saxons from Gentility about six hundred years after Christ, the Britons he found observers still of the selfsame government by bishops over the rest of the clergy; under this form Christianity took root again, where it had been exiled. Under the selfsame form it remained till the days of the Norman conqueror. By him and his successors thereunto sworn, it hath from that time till now by the space of five hundred years more been upheld.

O nation utterly without knowledge, without sense! We are not through error of mind deceived, but some wicked thing hath undoubtedly bewitched us, if we forsake that government, the use whereof universal experience hath for so many years approved, and betake ourselves unto a regiment neither appointed of God himself, as they who favour it pretend, nor till yesterday ever heard of among men. By the Jews Festus was much complained of, as being a governor marvellous corrupt, and almost intolerable: such notwithstanding were they who came after him, that men which thought the public condition most afflicted under Festus, began to wish they had him again, and to esteem him a ruler commendable. Great things are hoped for at the hands of these new presidents, whom reformation would bring in: notwithstanding the time may come, when bishops whose regiment doth now seem a yoke so heavy to bear, will be longed for again even by them that are the readiest to have it taken off their necks.

But in the hands of Divine Providence we leave the ordering of all such events, and come now to the question itself which is raised concerning bishops. For the better understanding whereof we must beforehand set down what is meant, when in this question we name a bishop.

For whatsoever we bring from antiquity, by way of defence in this cause of bishops, it is cast off as impertinent matter, all is wiped away with an odd kind of shifting answer, "That the bishops which now are, be not like unto them which were." We therefore beseech all indifferent judges to weigh sincerely with themselves how the case doth stand. If it should be at this day a controversy whether kingly regiment were lawful or no, peradventure in defence thereof, the long continuance which it hath had since the first beginning might be alleged; mention perhaps might be made what kings there were of old even in Abraham's time, what sovereign princes both before and after. Suppose that herein some man purposely bending his wit against sovereignty, should think to elude all such allegations by making ample discovery through a number of particularities, wherein the kings that are do differ from those that have been, and should therefore in the end conclude, that such ancient examples are no convenient proofs of that royalty which is now in use. Surely for decision of truth in this case there were no remedy, but only to shew the nature of sovereignty, to sever it from accidental properties, make it clear that ancient and present regality are one and the same in substance, how great odds soever otherwise may seem to be between them. In like manner, whereas a question of late hath grown, whether ecclesiastical regiment by bishops be lawful in the Church of Christ or no: in which question, they that hold the negative being pressed with that general received order, according whereunto the most renowned lights of the Christian world have governed the same in every age as bishops; seeing their manner is to reply, that such bishops as those ancient were, ours are not; there is no remedy but to shew, that to be a bishop is now the selfsame thing which it hath been; that one definition agreeth fully and truly as well to those elder, as to these latter bishops. Sundry dissimilitudes we grant there are, which notwithstanding are not such that they cause any equivocation in the name, whereby we should think a bishop in those times to have had a clean other definition than doth rightly agree unto bishops as they are now. Many things there are in the state of bishops, which the times have changed; many a parsonage at this day is larger than some ancient bishoprics were; many an ancient bishop poorer than at this day sundry under them in degree. The simple hereupon lacking judgment and knowledge to discern between the nature of things which changeth not, and these outward variable accidents, are made believe that a bishop heretofore and now are things in their very nature so distinct that they cannot be judged the same. Yet to men that have any part of skill, what more evident and plain in bishops, than that augmentation or diminution in their precincts, allowances, privileges, and such like, do make a difference indeed, but no essential difference between one bishop and another? As for those things in regard whereof we use properly to term them bishops, those things whereby they essentially differ from other pastors, those things which the natural definition of a bishop must contain; what one of them is there more or less appliable unto bishops now than of old?

The name Bishop hath been borrowed from the Grecians, with whom it signifieth one which hath principal charge to guide and oversee others. The same word in ecclesiastical writings being applied unto church governors, at the first unto all and not unto the chiefest only, grew in short time peculiar and proper to signify such episcopal authority alone, as the chiefest governors exercised over the rest. For with all names this is usual, that inasmuch as they are not given till the things whereunto they are given have been sometime first observed, therefore generally things are ancienter than the names whereby they are called. . . .

A Bishop is a minister of God, unto whom with permanent continuance there is given not only power of administering the Word and Sacraments, which power other Presbyters have; but also a further power to ordain ecclesiastical persons, and a power of chiefty in government over Presbyters as well as Laymen, a power to be by way of jurisdiction a Pastor even to Pastors themselves. So that this office, as he is a Presbyter or Pastor, consisteth in those things which are common unto him with other pastors, as in ministering the Word and Sacraments: but those things incident unto his office, which do properly make him a Bishop, cannot be common unto him with other Pastors.

Now even as pastors, so likewise bishops being principal pastors, are either at large or else with restraint: at large, when the subject of their regiment is indefinite, and not tied to any certain place; bishops with restraint are they whose regiment over the Church is contained within some definite, local compass, beyond which compass their jurisdiction reacheth not. Such therefore we always mean when we speak of that regiment by bishops which we hold a thing most lawful, divine and holy in the Church of Christ. . . .

Thus we see that prelacy must needs be acknowledged exceedingly beneficial in the Church; and yet for more perspicuity's sake, it shall not be pains superfluously taken, if the manner how be also declared at large. For this one thing not understood by the vulgar sort, causeth all contempt to be offered unto higher powers, not only ecclesiastical, but civil: whom when proud men have disgraced, and are therefore reproved by such as carry some dutiful affection of mind, the usual apologies which they make for themselves are these: "What more virtue in these great ones than in others? We see no such eminent good which they do above other men."

We grant indeed, that the good which higher governors do is not so immediate and near unto every of us, as many times the meaner labours of others under them, and this doth make it to be less esteemed. But we must note, that it is in this case as in a ship; he that sitteth at the stern is quiet, he moveth not, he seemeth in a manner to do little or nothing in comparison of them that sweat about other toil, yet that which he doth is in value and force more than all the labours of the residue laid together. The influence of the heavens above worketh infinitely more to our good, and yet appeareth not half so sensible as the force doth of things below. We consider not what it is which we reap by the authority of our chiefest spiritual governors, nor are likely to enter into any consideration thereof, till we want them; and that is the cause why they are at our hands so unthankfully rewarded.

Authority is a constraining power, which power were needless if we were all such as we should be, willing to do the things we ought to do without constraint. But because generally we are otherwise, therefore we all reap singular benefit by that authority which permitteth no men, though they would, to slack their duty. It doth not suffice, that the lord of an household appoint labourers what they should do, unless he set over them some chief workmen to see they do it. Constitutions and canons made for the ordering of church affairs are dead taskmasters. The due execution of laws spiritual dependeth most upon the vigilant care of the chiefest spiritual governors, whose charge is to see that such laws be kept by the clergy and people under them: with those duties which the law of God and the ecclesiastical canons require in the clergy, lay governors are neither for the most part so well acquainted, nor so deeply and nearly touched. Requisite therefore it is, that ecclesiastical persons have authority in such things; which kind of authority maketh them that have it prelates. If then it be a thing confessed, as by all good men it needs must be, to have prayers read in all churches, to have the sacraments of God administered, to have the mysteries of salvation painfully taught, to have God every where devoutly worshipped, and all this perpetually, and with quietness, bringeth unto the whole Church, and unto every member thereof, inestimable good; how can that authority which hath been proved the ordinance of God for preservation of these duties in the Church, how can it choose but deserve to be held a thing publicly most beneficial?

72 THE RACOVIAN CATECHISM (1605), the theological *Credo* of the sixteenth-century Socinians, sought to offer a systematic statement of Christian theology. In the following selection we have the Socinian view of the Lord's Supper, cast in terms that reject not only the Roman Catholic interpretation but also that of major traditions within Protestantism. The Lord's Supper, as baptism, possesses a symbolic value and because it was instituted by Christ serves to encourage Christian piety and devotion.[1]

[1] See also, *The Racovian Catechism*, Selection 37.

The Racovian Catechism*

SECTION V. OF THE PROPHETIC OFFICE OF CHRIST

CHAPTER IV. THE LORD'S SUPPER

Of the breaking of the holy bread

What is the rite of breaking bread?

It is an institution of the Lord Christ, that believers in him should break and eat bread, and drink of a cup together, with the view of commemorating him, or of showing forth his death;—which institution ought to continue until his coming.

Do you then consider the commemoration of Christ to be the same as showing forth his death?

They are the same; as the apostle Paul clearly explains that commemoration in this sense (1 Cor. xi. 26), "For as often as ye eat this bread, and drink this cup, ye do show the Lord's death till he come." For as to those persons who by commemoration, in the words of Christ, wherein he instituted this rite, understand recollection, or use the latter term for the former,—conceiving that this sacred rite was instituted in order that it might recall the death of Christ to our memory,—they do in this manifestly err. For he who would rightly comply with this ordinance, and in this way show the death of the Lord, ought to have the death of Christ familiarly and at all times in his mind.

What is meant, then, by showing the Lord's death?

It is, in the observance of this rite, to celebrate the great kindness of Christ, in that, from his unspeakable love towards us, he suffered his body to be tormented and lacerated, and thus in a manner broken, and his blood to be shed: or solemnly to testify by this act how great that kindness is, and how beneficial and salutary to us, to the glory of his name, and the perpetual commemoration of so distinguished a blessing.

But why does our Lord wish the remembrance of this to be above all other things celebrated in his Church?

Because of all the actions of Christ, which he undertook with a view to our salvation, this was the most difficult, exhibited the strongest proof of his love towards us, and was the most proper to him. For the resurrection of Christ from the dead, and his exaltation, were the work of God the Father, and not of Christ himself.

* From *The Racovian Catechism*, tr. by Thomas Rees. London: Longman, Horst, Rees, Orme, and Brown, 1818.

Is there no other stronger reason, on account of which the Lord Jesus instituted this ordinance?

There is no stronger reason,—although some assert that he instituted it, in order that from the observance of it the remission of sins and the confirmation of our Faith might follow; and others, that it is a sacrifice for the living and the dead.

What is to be thought of these opinions?

That they cannot be maintained. For as to the first, since this rite is to be observed for the purpose of commemorating or showing forth the kindness manifested by Christ towards us, and no other end besides this is intimated by Christ, it is evident that it was not instituted with the view that we might receive any benefit from Christ at the celebration of it, except in so far as it is worthily observed it forms a part of Christian piety. And as to the confirmation of our faith, so far is our faith from being confirmed by the mere use of the bread and wine, that he who would worthily partake of them ought to be already assured of the remission of his sins on the part of God; and the more certain he is of this, the more worthily will he be able to comply with this ordinance.

What is to be thought of the opinion that the Lord's Supper is a sacrifice for the living and the dead?

That it is altogether a great and pernicious error: for the scripture testifies (Heb. viii. 2, 3, 4; ix. 24) that the offering of the body of Christ, which followed his death, was made in heaven, and could not have been made on earth; and that the body of Christ now dwells not on earth, but in heaven. Besides, as Christ is himself both the priest and the victim, it follows that no one can offer Christ but himself. Let it be added, that it were absurd to suppose that he who has offered himself to God could be offered by another. Lastly; since the scripture asserts (Heb. vii. 27; x. 14) that the sacrifice of Christ is but one, and that it was so perfect that "by this one offering he perfected for ever them that are sanctified," it neither ought to be, nor can be, repeated; otherwise it would be neither a perfect, nor yet a single, offering.

What is the meaning of these words, "This is my body?"

They are not understood by all persons in the same sense: for some think that the bread is actually changed into the body, and the wine into the blood of Christ, which change they denominate transubstantiation. Others imagine that the body of Christ is in the bread, or under it, or with it. And there are some who suppose that in the Lord's Supper they are partakers, but nevertheless spiritually, of the body and the blood of the Lord: all which opinions are erroneous and false.

How do you prove this in respect to the first of these opinions?

As follows—Because it might otherwise be in like manner maintained that the cup is changed into the testament, or that the testament was in, under, and with the cup, or was drunk spiritually: since it is written by Luke and Paul, "This cup is the new testament in my blood," as absolutely as it is before said, "this is my body,"—the words from which these persons deduce their opinion. Moreover, in respect to this transubstantiation, as it is called, since the scriptures designate the bread we take by the name of bread in the very use of it, (as is clear from the words of Paul, 1 Cor. x. 16; xi. 26, 27, 28), it is evident that the bread remains there, without any transmutation whatever into the body of the Lord. The scripture, besides, testifies (Acts iii. 21) that the body of Christ is in heaven, and must abide there "until the time of the restitution of all things." He cannot therefore be any more existing on earth. Whence it is that the Holy Scriptures assert that the Lord Jesus will descend and come to us from heaven: but if he be now here under the form of bread and wine, he can no more come; for no one can come to the place where he already is. The body of Christ, moreover, is only one; whereas the bread, or the hosts, as they call them, are many, and indeed infinite in number. It would follow, therefore, that the body of Christ is at the same time both numerically one, and many and infinite in number. It would also follow, that this one body of Christ was at one and the same time seen and not seen by the same person, was eaten by him and not eaten, was within him and not within him; that it is at the same time superior and inferior to itself, is greater and less than itself; that it retains its stature and does not retain it;—all which things overturn one another, and are clearly self-contradictory. It is above all most absurd, as common sense itself shows, that the immortal body of Christ should be capable of being chewed and masticated by our teeth, as the host is chewed and masticated; and also that it should be capable of being burnt, and in many other ways destroyed. It is evident in the next place, that Christ speaks of that body of his wherein he was crucified, which was a terrestrial and animal body;—but that which he now has is neither terrestrial nor animal, but celestial and spiritual, as clearly appears from Paul (1 Cor. xv. 44–49). And besides, in instituting this rite, he considers his body, and proposes it for our commemoration, as, on account of suffering, without life and blood; and therefore appoints a peculiar commemoration, by the use of the cup, of his blood drawn from his body. But the body of Christ is now living, and no longer obnoxious to any pains or to death. Let it be added, that that which now exists, cannot be made out of any thing else;—but the body of Christ now exists, therefore it cannot be made out of bread.

How do you prove the second opinion to be erroneous and false?

That this opinion cannot stand, appears from most of the reasons already stated, and principally from hence, that the body of Christ dwells in heaven, and that this opinion takes away altogether from the body of Christ the properties of a body, and thus becomes self-contradictory.

How do you prove the same in respect to the third opinion.

This opinion also cannot stand; since it can by no means happen that the very substance of the body of Christ, abiding in heaven, can be actually taken by us, who dwell on earth; and this too in an infinite number of places at the same instant. For this real partaking requires that the ones should be actually brought into contact with the other. But if they should assert that this is done by faith, which looks to the substance of Christ, existing in heaven, as its object, and through this, as a medium, derives a certain efficacy or advantage flowing from Christ to mankind;—it may be replied, first, that this is not a real participation of the body of Christ; since, according to this, the substance itself is not partaken, but the fruits of it: and they themselves affirm, that the real participation of the body of Christ is such that it cannot be comprehended by the mind, nor expressed by the tongue; whereas that participation which has just been noticed, may be both understood by the mind and expressed in words. In the next place, this may be done without this eucharistic rite, as well as by it. Besides, if this was the intention of Christ in the words "this is my body," they could not have been spoken either of the bread or of this act absolutely; but only with this condition, that those who came to the Lord's table were possessed of this faith. As, however, those persons observe the ordinance who are without this faith,—and sometimes all may be of this description who eat this sacred bread together,—neither the bread nor the act can have any such conjunction with the body of Christ as they desire: not to repeat at this time other things tending to the refutation of this opinion. . . .

Explain to me, then, the true and genuine sense of these words, "This is my body?"

This you will easily understand, if you only bear in mind that, in the sacred writings, and indeed in common practice, figures, images, and commemorating signs, are called by the names of those things of which they are the figures, images, and memorials. Wherefore, when Christ designed that in this rite his bloody death should be declared by us, under a kind of shadow or representation, he said that this bread which is broken is his body, delivered for us: that is to say, is a commemorating sign, a kind of emblem of his body to be shortly, on our account, broken, that is, lacerated, pierced, wounded, and tortured: and also, in like manner, that the cup, or the wine contained in it, was for the same reason his blood, to be shortly shed for us. For the wine is no otherwise in the cup than as it is poured out of his vessel, or at least drawn from his grapes. It is by way of figure or emblem only that it is said in Ezekiel (chap. v. ver. 1–5) concerning the hair, whereof a part was to be cut, a part burnt, a part scattered, and a part preserved, to be afterwards consumed: "THIS IS JERUSALEM:" that is, this is an emblem of Jerusalem, or a shadow of what she is to become. As to what is stated in the account of Luke and Paul,—that this cup is the new testament in the blood of Christ,—this must be understood as if they had said, This is a certain memorial, or commemorating sign, of the New Covenant confirmed by the blood of Christ. In like manner circumcision also was formerly called a Covenant (Gen. xvii. 13), namely, between God and Abraham; that is, was a kind of commemorating token of the Covenant, as the scriptures themselves explain it (Gen. xvii. 11). So likewise the sabbath is called (Exod. xxxi. 16) a Covenant between God and the Israelites; that is, a sign of that Covenant, as the scriptures in like manner explain, Exod. xxxi. 13 and 17. For a similar reason it is said concerning that remarkable rite of eating the paschal lamb (Exod. xii. 11), that "it is the Lord's passover," by which name, PASCHA, or rather PESACH, the passover, namely, of the Lord, the lamb itself also is called, because it was the memorial of his passover. In like manner both the rite itself of breaking bread, and the bread and the cup, may be denominated the body and the blood of Christ.

But if such be the case, why does Paul say (1 Cor. xi. 9) that "whosoever shall eat this bread and drink this cup unworthily, shall be guilty of the body and blood of the Lord;" and (ver. 29) that "he does not discern the Lord's body?"

Paul does not thus speak because such a person takes the very body or blood of Christ, which, as far as it can be taken by us, can be taken only worthily:—but because that while he eats this bread and drinks of the cup of the Lord, unworthily, he offends against the very body and blood of Christ, and is guilty of his sufferings, whereof this rite is the memorial or emblem, and for the proclaiming and commemorating of which it was instituted. This Paul himself intimates, when from this circumstance— that as often as we eat this bread, and drink this cup, we do show forth the Lord's death—he draws this conclusion, that whosoever eats and drinks unworthily, is guilty of the body and blood of the Lord. Nor do the words "not discerning the Lord's body" imply any thing else than that he does not value and esteem, as highly as he ought, the singular dignity of the body of Christ, delivered to death on our account; nor distinguish those sacred symbols, the representations of Christ's body, or the act appointed for the celebration of it, from ordinary and profane food, and the eating of such food; nor treat the one with any more religious respect than the other.

What is meant, then, by eating this bread and drinking this cup unworthily?

It is not to observe this ordinance with due reverence and piety, or in such a way as we ought, and the reason of its appointment demands. Whence may easily be understood what is meant by observing it worthily.

I wish you to explain this to me a little more at large?

In order to the worthy observation of this ordinance, it is requisite, first, that you carefully consider what is to be done in it, for what purpose it was instituted, and is to be observed by you; that you devoutly reflect how severely Christ suffered; what great blessings he has procured for you by his agonies and death, and how resplendently the love both of Christ and of God shines forth here; that, in this manner, you excite your mind to venerate and worship God and Christ, and to offer them thanksgivings; that you do this continually in this rite; and that you cautiously avoid doing any thing, which is not accompanied by the highest reverence of God and Christ. And because we testify in this ordinance that we have the body of Christ, crucified on our account, for the spiritual food of our souls, and his blood shed, for our saving drink; also that we have communion with him, and thus belong to the New Covenant, and together with other Christians are members of one body (all which demand a faith working by love), we ought at the same time, and above all things, to study to be what in this ordinance we profess ourselves to be, that we may not lie to God and Christ: and if, as yet, we are not such, we should at all events resolve to become such as soon as possible; and not suffer this determination of our mind to be afterwards of none effect. In order that we may accomplish all this, Paul commands us to examine and judge ourselves, and so observe the ordinance.

What is meant by examining and judging ourselves?

Carefully to scrutinize ourselves and our actions: not those actions alone which are passed, as if we would punish what was criminal in them, amend them, and pray God to forgive them; but those also which are present; carefully to deliberate upon whatever we undertake, that we may not in any thing offend God, but conduct ourselves in all our proceedings as we ought, and the divine commands require.

73 THE CAMBRIDGE PLATFORM was the work of a synod of New England Churches held intermittently from 1646–1648. Here clergy and laymen devised the form of church government that became the norm for Congregationalism in Massachusetts throughout the colonial period. The document may be seen as the concrete application of the covenant theology of the Puritans (see John Winthrop, Selection 74). In addition, the synod adopted the Confession of Faith that was being issued concurrently by the Westminster Assembly.

The Cambridge Platform*

CHAPTER 1

Of the form of church-government; and that it is one, immutable, and prescribed in the Word of God

Ecclesiastical Polity or Church Government, or discipline is nothing else, but that Form & order that is to be observed in the Church of Christ upon earth, both for the Constitution of it, and all the Administrations that therein are to be performed.

2. Church-Government is Considered in a double respect either in regard of the parts of Government themselves, or necessary Circumstances thereof. The parts of Government are prescribed in the word, because the Lord Jesus Christ the King and Law-giver of his Church, is no less faithful in the house of God than was Moses, who from the Lord delivered a form and pattern of Government to the Children of Israel in the old Testament: And the Holy Scriptures are now also so perfect, as they are able to make the man of God perfect and thoroughly furnished unto every good work; and therefore doubtless to the well ordering of the house of God.

3. The parts of Church-Government are all of them exactly described in the word of God being parts or means of Instituted worship according to the second Commandment: and therefore to continue one and the same, unto the appearing of our Lord Jesus Christ as a kingdom that cannot be shaken, until he shall deliver it up unto God, even the Father. So that it is not left in the power of men, officers, Churches, or any state in the world to add, or diminish, or alter any thing in the least measure therein. . . .

CHAPTER 2

Of the nature of the Catholic Church in general, and in special, of a particular visible church

The Catholic Church, is the whole company of those that are elected, redeemed, and in time effectually called from the state of sin and death unto a state of Grace, and salvation in Jesus Christ.

2. This church is either Triumphant, or Militant. Triumphant, the

* From Williston Walker, *The Creeds and Platforms of Congregationalism*. New York: Scribner's and Sons, 1893. [The spelling has been modernized by the editor.]

number of them who are Gloryfied in heaven: Militant, the number of them who are conflicting with their enemies upon earth.

3. This Militant Church is to be considered as Invisible, and Visible. Invisible, in respect of their relation wherein they stand to Christ, as a body unto the head, being united unto him, by the spirit of God, and faith in their hearts: Visible, in respect of the profession of their faith, in their persons, and in particular Churches: and so there may be acknowledged an universal visible Church.

4. The members of the Militant visible Church, considered either as not yet in church-order, or as walking according to the church-order of the Gospel. In order, and so besides the spiritual union, and communion, common to all believers, they enjoy moreover a union and communion ecclesiastical-Political. So we deny a universal visible church.

5. The state the members of the Militant visible church walking in order, was either before the law, economical, that is in families; or under the law, National: or, since the coming of Christ, only congregational: (The term Independent, we approve not.) Therefore neither national, provincial, nor classical.

6. A Congregational-church, is by the institution of Christ a part of the Militant-visible-church, consisting of a company of Saints by calling, united into one body, by a holy covenant, for the public worship of God, and the mutual edification one of another, in the Fellowship of the Lord Jesus.

CHAPTER 3

Of the matter of the visible church both in respect of quality and quantity

The matter of a visible church are *Saints* by calling.

2. By Saints, we understand, 1. Such, as have not only attained the knowledge of the principles of Religion, and are free from gross and open scandals, but also do together with the profession of their faith and Repentance, walk in blameless obedience to the word, so as that in charitable discretion they may be accounted Saints by calling. . . . 2. The children of such, who are also holy.

3. The members of churches though orderly constituted, may in time degenerate, and grow corrupt and scandalous, which though they ought not to be tolerated in the church, yet their continuance therein, through the defect of the execution of discipline and Just censures, doth not immediately dissolve the being of the church, as appears in the church of Israel, and the churches of *Galatia* and *Corinth, Pergamus* and *Thyatira.*

4. The matter of the Church in respect of its *quantity* ought not to be of greater number than may ordinarily meet together conveniently in one place: nor ordinarily fewer, than may conveniently carry on Church-work. . . .

5. Nor can it with reason be thought but that every church appointed and ordained by *Christ*, had a ministry ordained and appointed for the same: and yet plain it is, that there were no ordinary officers appointed by Christ for any other, than *Congregational* churches: Elders being appointed to feed, not all flocks, but the particular flock of God over which the Holy Ghost had made them the overseers, and that flock they must attend, even the whole flock: and one *Congregation* being as much as any ordinary Elders can attend, therefore there is no greater Church than a Congregation, which may ordinarily meet in one place.

CHAPTER 4

Of the form of a visible church and of church covenant

Saints by Calling, must have a Visible-Political-Union amongst themselves, or else they are not yet a particular church: as those similitudes hold forth, which scripture makes use of, to show the nature of particular Churches: As a *Body*, A *building*, or *House*, *Hands*, *Eyes*, *Feet*, and other members must be united, or else, remaining separate are not a body. *Stones*, *Timber*, though squared, hewn and polished, are not a house, until they are compacted and united: so Saints or believers in judgment of charity, are not a church, unless Orderly knit together.

2. Particular churches cannot be distinguished one from another but by their forms. *Ephesus* is not *Smyrna*, and *Pergamus Thyatira*, but each one a distinct society of itself, having officers of their own, which had not the charge of others: Virtues of their own, for which others are not praised: Corruptions of their own, for which others are not blamed.

3. This *Form* is the *Visible Covenant*, Agreement, or consent whereby they give up themselves unto the Lord, to the observing of the ordinances of Christ together in the same society, which is usually called the *Church-Covenant*; For we see not otherwise how members can have *Church-power* one over another mutually. . . .

The *Covenant*, as it was that which made the Family of Abraham and children of Israel to be a church and people unto God, so it is that which now makes the several societies of Gentile believers to be churches in these days. . . .

CHAPTER 5

Of the first subject of church power or, to whom church power doth first belong

The first subject of church power, is either *Supreme* or *Subordinate*, and *Ministerial*. The *Supreme* (by way of gift from the father) is the Lord Jesus Christ. The *Ministerial*, is either extraordinary; as the *Apostles*,

Prophets, and *Evangelists*: or *Ordinary*; as every particular *Congregational* church.

2. *Ordinary* church power, is either the power of office, that is such as is proper to the eldership: or, power of privilege, such as belongs unto the brotherhood. The latter is in the brethren formally, and immediately from Christ, that is, so as it may according to order be acted or exercised immediately by themselves: the former, is not in them formally or immediately, and therefore cannot be acted or exercised immediately by them, but is said to be in them, in that they design the persons unto office, who only are to act, or to exercise this power.

CHAPTER 6

Of the officers of the church and especially of pastors and teachers

A Church being a company of people combined together by covenant for the worship of God, it appeareth thereby, that there may be the essence and being of a church without any officers, seeing there is both the form and matter of a church, which is implied when it is said, the Apostles ordained elders in every church.

2. Nevertheless, though officers be not absolutely necessary, to the simple being of churches, when they be called: yet ordinarily to their calling they are, and to their well being: and therefore the Lord Jesus out of his tender compassion hath appointed, and ordained officers which he would not have done, if they had not been useful and needful for the church; yea, being Ascended into heaven, he received gifts for men, and gave gifts to men, whereof officers for the church are Justly accounted no small parts; they being to continue to the end of the world, and for the perfecting of all the Saints.

3. The officers were either extraordinary, or ordinary, extraordinary as *Apostles, Prophets, Evangelists*. ordinary as *Elders and Deacons*.

The *Apostles, Prophets*, and *Evangelists*, as they were called extraordinarily by Christ, so their office ended with themselves whence it is that *Paul* directing *Timothy* how to carry along Church-Administrations, Giveth no direction about the choice or course of *Apostles, Prophets*, or *Evangelists*, but only of *Elders and Deacons*; and when *Paul* was to take his last leave of the church of *Ephesus*, he committed the care of feeding the church to no other, but unto the Elders of that church. The like charge doth *Peter* commit to the Elders.

4. Of *Elders* (who are also in scripture called *Bishops*) Some attend chiefly to the ministry of the word, As the *Pastors and Teachers Others*, attend especially unto *Rule*, who are therefore called *Ruling Elders*.

5. The office of *Pastor and Teacher*, appears to be distinct. The *Pastor's* special work is, to attend to *exhortation*: and therein to Administer a

word of *Wisdom:* the *Teacher* is to attend to *Doctrine*, and therein to Administer a word of *Knowledge:* and either of them to administer the *Seals* of that Covenant, unto the dispensation whereof they are alike called: as also to execute the *Censures*, being but a kind of application of the word, the preaching of which, together with the application thereof they are alike charged withall. . . .

CHAPTER 7

Of ruling elders and deacons

. . . 2. The *Ruling Elder's* work is to join with the *Pastor and Teacher* in those acts of spiritual *Rule* which are distinct from the ministry of the word and Sacraments committed to them. . . .

3. The office of a *Deacon* is Instituted in the church by the Lord Jesus. Sometime they are called *Helps.*

The scripture telleth us, how they should be qualified: *Grave, not double tongued, not given too much to wine, not given to filthy lucre.* They must first be *proved* and then use the office of a *Deacon*, being found *Blameless.*

The office and work of the *Deacons* is to receive the offerings of the church, gifts given to the church, and to keep the treasury of the church: and therewith to serve the *Tables* which the church is to provide for: as the *Lord's Table*, the table of the *ministers*, and of such as are in *necessity*, to whom they are to distribute in simplicity. . . .

7. The Lord hath appointed *ancient widows* (where they may be had) to minister in the church, in giving attendance to the sick, and to give succour unto them, and others in the like necessities.

CHAPTER 8

Of the election of church-officers

No man may take the honour of a Church-Officer unto himself, but he that was *called* of God, as was Aaron.

2. *Calling* unto office is either *Immediate*, by Christ himself: such was the call of the Apostles, and Prophets: this manner of calling ended with them, as hath been said: or *Mediate*, by the church.

3. It is meet, that before any be ordained or chosen officers, they should first be *Tried and proved;* because hands are not suddenly to be laid upon any, and both *Elders and Deacons* must be of honest and good report. . . .

5. Officers are to be *called by such Churches*, where unto they are to minister, of such moment is the preservation of this power, that the churches exercised it in the presence of the Apostles.

6. A church being free cannot become subject to any, but by a free election; Yet when such a people do choose any to be over them in the Lord, then do they become subject, and most willingly submit to their ministry in the Lord, whom they have so chosen.

7. And if the church have power to choose their officers and ministers, then in case of manifest unworthiness, and delinquency they have power also to depose them. For to open, and shut: to choose and refuse; to constitute in office, and remove from office: are acts belonging unto the same power.

8. We judge it much conducing to the well-being, and communion of churches, that where it may conveniently be done, neighbour-churches be advised withall, and their help made use of in the trial of church-officers, in order to their choice.

9. The choice of such Church-officers belongeth not to the civil-magistrates, as such, or diocesan-bishops, or patrons: for of these or any such like, the scripture is wholly silent, as having any power therein.

CHAPTER 9

Of ordination, and imposition of hands

Church-officers are not only to be chosen by the Church, but also to be ordained by Imposition of hands, and prayer. with which at ordination of Elders, Fasting also is to be joined.

2. This ordination we account nothing else, but the solemn putting of a man into his place and office in the Church whereunto he had right before by election, being like the installing of a magistrate in the common-wealth.

Ordination therefore is not to go before, but to follow election. The essence and substance of the outward calling of an ordinary officer in the Church, doth not consist in his ordination, but in his voluntary and free election by the Church, and in his accepting of that election. Whereupon is founded the relation between Pastor and flock, between such a minister, and such a people.

Ordination does not constitute an officer, nor give him the essentials of his office. The Apostles were elders, without Imposition of hands by men: Paul and Barnabas were officers, before that Imposition of hands. Acts. 13.3. The posterity of Levi were Priests, and Levites, before hands were laid on them by the Children of Israel. . . .

4. In such Churches where there are no Elders, Imposition of hands may be performed by some of the Brethren orderly chosen by the church thereunto. . . .

5. Nevertheless in such Churches where there are no Elders, and

the Church so desire, we see not why *Imposition of hands* may not be performed by the *Elders of other Churches.* . . .

6. *Church Officers*, are officers to one church, even that particular, over which the Holy Ghost hath made them overseers. . . .

7. He that is clearly loosed from his office-relation unto that church whereof he was a minister, cannot be looked at as an officer, nor perform any act of *Office* in any other church, unless he be again orderly called unto *Office*: which when it shall be, we know nothing to hinder, but *Imposition of hands* also in his *Ordination* ought to be used towards him again. . . .

CHAPTER 10

Of the power of the church, and its presbytery

Supreme and Lordly power over all the Churches upon earth, doth only belong unto Jesus Christ, who is King of the church, and the head thereof. He hath the Government upon his shoulders, and hath all power given to him, both in heaven and earth.

2. A company of professed believers *Ecclesiastically Confederate*, as they are a church before they have officers, and without them; so even in that estate, *subordinate Church-power* under Christ delegated to them by him, doth belong to them, in such a manner as is before expressed . . . and as flowing from the very nature and Essence of a church: It being natural to all bodies, and so unto a church body, to be furnished with sufficient power, for its own preservation and subsistence.

3. This *Government* of the church, is a mixed Government (and so hath been acknowledged long before the term of Independency was heard of:) In respect of *Christ*, the head and King of the church, and the Sovereign power residing in him, and exercised by him, it is a *Monarchy*: In respect of the body, or *Brotherhood* of the church, and power from Christ granted unto them, it resembles a *Democracy*, In respect of the *Presbytery* and power committed to them, it is an *Aristocracy*. . . .

5. The power granted by Christ unto the body of the church and *Brotherhood*, is a prerogative or privilege which the church doth exercise: I In *Choosing* their own officers, whether Elders, or Deacons. II In *admission* of their own members and therefore there is great reason they should have power to *Remove* any from their fellowship again. . . .

6. In case an Elder offend incorrigibly, the matter so requiring, as the church had power to call him to office, so they have power according to order (the counsel of other churches where it may be had, directing thereto to remove him from his *Office*: and being now but a member, in case he add contumacy to his sin, the Church that had power to receive him into their fellowship, hath also the same power to cast him out, that they have concerning any other member. . . .

CHAPTER 11

Of the maintenance of church officers

The Apostle concludes, that necessary and sufficient maintenance is due unto the ministers of the word: from the law of nature and nations, from the law of Moses, the equity thereof, as also the rule of common reason. . . .

4. Not only members of Churches, but *all that are taught in the word*, are to contribute unto him that teacheth, in all good things. In case that Congregations are defective in their contributions, the Deacons are to call upon them to do their duty: if their call sufficeth not, the church by her power is to require it of their members, and where church-power through the corruption of men, doth not, or cannot attain the end, the Magistrate is to see ministry be duely provided for, as appears from the commended example of Nehemiah. The Magistrates are nursing fathers, and nursing mothers, and stand charged with the custody of both Tables; because it is better to prevent a scandal, that it may not come and easier also, than to remove it when it is given. . . .

CHAPTER 12

Of admission of members into the church

The *doors* of the Churches of Christ upon earth, do not by God's appointment stand so wide open, that all sorts of people good or bad, may freely enter therein at their pleasure; but such as are admitted thereto, as members ought to be *examined and tried* first: whether they be fit and meet to be received into church-society, or not. The Eunuch of Ethiopia, before his admission was examined by Philip, whether he did believe on Jesus Christ with all his heart the Angel of the church at Ephesus is commended, for trying such as said they were Apostles and were not. There is like reason for trying of them that profess themselves to be believers.

The officers are charged with the keeping of the doors of the Church, and therefore are in a special manner to make trial of the fitness of such who enter. Twelve Angels are set at the gates of the Temple, lest such as were Ceremonially *unclean* should enter thereinto.

2. The things which are requisite to be found in all church members, are, *Repentance* from sin, and *faith* in Jesus Christ. . . .

3. The weakest *measure* of faith is to be accepted in those that desire to be admitted into the church: because weak christians if *sincere*, have the substance of that faith, repentance and holiness which is required in church members: and such have most *need* of the ordinances for their confirmation and growth in grace. . . .

4. In case any through excessive fear, or other infirmity, be unable to make their personal relation of their spiritual estate in public, it is sufficient that the Elders having received private satisfaction, make relation thereof in public before the church, they testifying their assents thereunto; this being the way that tendeth most to edification. . . .

7. The like trial is to be required from such members of the church, as were born in the same, or received their membership, and were baptized in their infancy, or minority, by virtue of the covenant of their parents, when being grown up unto years of discretion, they shall desire to be made partakers of the Lord's supper: unto which, because holy things must not be given unto the unworthy, therefore it is requisite, that these as well as others, should come to their trial and examination, and manifest their faith and repentance by an open profession thereof, before they are received to the Lord's supper, and otherwise not to be admitted thereunto.

Yet these church-members that were so born, or received in their childhood, before they are capable of being made partakers of full communion, have many privileges which others (not church-members) have not: they are in covenant with God; have the seal thereof upon them, viz. baptism; and so if not regenerated, yet are in a more hopeful way of attaining regenerating grace, and all the spiritual blessings both of the covenant and seal; they are also under Church-watch, and consequently subject, to the reprehensions, admonitions, and censures thereof, for their healing and amendment, as need shall require.

CHAPTER 13

Of church-members their removal from one church to another, and of letters of recommendation and dismission

Church-members may not remove or depart from the Church, and so one from another as they please, nor without just and weighty cause but ought to live and dwell together: for as much as they are commanded, not to forsake the assembling of themselves together. . . .

2. It is therefore the duty of Church-members, in such times and places when counsel may be had, to consult with the Church whereof they are members, about their removal, that accordingly they have their approbation, may be encouraged, or otherwise desist. They who are joined with consent, should not depart without consent, except forced thereunto. . . .

7. Order requires, that a member thus removing, have letters testimonial; and of dismission from the church whereof he yet is, unto the church whereunto he desireth to be joined, lest the church should be deluded; that the church may receive him in faith; and not be corrupted by receiving deceivers, and false brethren. Until the person dismissed be

received into another church, he ceaseth not by his letters of dismission to be a member of the church whereof he was. The church cannot make a member no member but by excommunication.

CHAPTER 14

Of excommunication and other censures

The Censures of the church, are appointed by Christ, for the preventing, removing, and healing of offences in the Church: for the reclaiming and gaining of offending brethren: for the deterring others from the like offences: for purging out the leaven which may infect the whole lump: for vindicating the honour of Christ, and of his church, and the holy profession of the gospel: and for preventing the wrath of God, that may justly fall upon the church, if they should suffer his covenant, and the seals thereof, to be profaned by notorious and obstinate offenders. . . .

4. In dealing with an offender, great care is to be taken, that we be neither overstrict or rigorous, nor too indulgent or remiss; our proceeding herein ought to be with a spirit of meekness, considering ourselves, lest we also be tempted; and that the best of us have need of much forgiveness from the Lord. Yet the winning and healing of the offender's soul, being the end of these endeavours, we must not daub with untempered mortar, nor heal the wounds of our brethren slightly: on some have compassion, others save with fear.

5. While the offender remains excommunicate, the Church is to refrain from all member-like communion with him in spiritual things, and also from all familiar communion with him in civil things, farther than the necessity of natural, or domestic, or civil relations do require: and are therefore to forbear to eat and drink with him, that he may be ashamed.

6. Excommunication being a spiritual punishment, it doth not prejudice the excommunicate in, nor deprive him of his civil rights, and therefore toucheth not princes, or other magistrates, in point of their civil dignity or authority. . . .

CHAPTER 15

Of the communion of churches one with another

Although Churches be distinct, and therefore may not be confounded one with another: and equal, and therefore have not dominion one over another: yet all the churches ought to preserve Church-communion one with another, because they are all united unto Christ, not only as a mystical, but as a political head; whence is derived a communion suitable thereunto. . . .

CHAPTER 16

Of synods

Synods orderly assembled, and rightly proceeding according to the pattern, we acknowledge as the ordinance of Christ: and though not absolutely necessary to the being, yet many times, through the iniquity of men, and perverseness of times, necessary to the well being of churches, for the establishment of truth, and peace therein. . . .

3. Magistrates, have power to call a synod, by calling to the Churches to send forth their Elders and other messengers, to counsel and assist them in matters of religion: but yet the constituting of a synod, is a church act, and may be transacted by the churches, even when civil magistrates may be enemies, to churches and to church assemblies.

4. It belongeth unto synods and counsels, to debate and determine controversies of faith, and cases of conscience; to clear from the holy directions for the holy worship of God, and good government of the church; to bear witness against mal-administration and Corruption in doctrine or manners in any particular Church, and to give directions for the reformation thereof: Not to exercise Church-censures in way of discipline, nor any other act of church-authority or jurisdiction: which that presidential synod did forbear. . . .

CHAPTER 17

Of the civil magistrates power in matters ecclesiastical

It is lawful, profitable, and necessary for christians to gather themselves into Church estate, and therein to exercise all the ordinances of Christ according unto the word, although the consent of Magistrate could not be had thereunto, because the Apostles and Christians in their time did frequently thus practice, when the Magistrates being all of them Jewish or pagan, and mostly persecuting enemies, would give no countenance or consent to such matters.

2. Church-government stands in no opposition to civil government of commonwealths, nor any intrencheth upon the authority of Civil Magistrates in their jurisdictions; nor any whit weakeneth their hands in governing; but rather strengtheneth them, and furthereth the people in yielding more hearty and conscionable obedience unto them. . . .

4. It is not in the power of Magistrates to compel their subjects to become church-members, and to partake at the Lord's table: . . .

5. As it is unlawful for church-officers to meddle with the sword of the Magistrate, so it is unlawful for the Magistrate to meddle with the work proper to church-officers. . . .

6. It is the duty of the Magistrate, to take care of matters of religion, and to improve his civil authority for the observing of the duties commanded in the first, as well as for observing of the duties commanded in the second table. . . .

8. Idolatry, Blasphemy, Heresy, venting corrupt and pernicious opinions, that destroy the foundation, open contempt of the word preached, profanation of the Lord's day, disturbing the peaceable administration and exercise of the worship and holy things of God, and the like, are to be restrained, and punished by civil authority.

9. If any church one or more shall grow schismatical, rending itself from the communion of other churches, or shall walk incorrigibly or obstinately in any corrupt way of their own, contrary to the rule of the word; in such case, the Magistrate is to put forth his coercive power, as the matter shall require.

74

JOHN WINTHROP (1588–1649), a leading figure in the Massachusetts Bay Colony, led a group of Puritans within the Church of England to the New World in 1630. His *A Model of Christian Charity* was composed aboard the Arbella as the small group approached the shores of Massachusetts. Here the design of the Puritan theocracy is laid out, based on the covenant theme that dominated early Puritan theology.

A Model of Christian Charity*

JOHN WINTHROP

God Almighty in his most holy and wise providence hath so disposed of the Condition of mankind, as in all times some must be rich some poor, some high and eminent in power and dignity; others mean and in subjection.

The reason hereof:

1. *First*, to hold conformity with the rest of his works, being delighted to show forth the glory of his wisdom in the variety and difference of the

* From *Winthrop Papers*, Vol. II. The Massachusetts Historical Society, 1931. [The spelling has been modernized by the editor.]

Creatures and the glory of his power, in ordering all these differences for the preservation and good of the whole, and the glory of his greatness that as it is the glory of princes to have many officers, so this great King will have many Stewards counting himself more honoured in dispensing his gifts to man by man, than if he did it by his own immediate hand.

2. *Secondly,* That he might have the more occasion to manifest the work of his Spirit: first, upon the wicked in moderating and restraining them: so that the rich and mighty should not eat up the poor, nor the poor, and despised rise up against their superiors, and shake off their yoke; secondly in the regenerate in exercising his graces in them, as in the great ones, their love, mercy, gentleness, temperance etc., in the poor and inferior sort, their faith patience, obedience etc:

3. *Thirdly,* That every man might have need of other, and from hence they might be all knit more nearly together in the Bond of brotherly affection: from hence it appears plainly that no man is made more honorable than another or more wealthy etc., out of any particular and singular respect to himself but for the glory of his Creator and the Common good of the Creature, Man; Therefore God still reserves the property of these gifts to himself, he there [Ezek. xvi, 17] calls wealth his gold and his silver etc. [Prov. iii, 9]. He claims their service as his due honor the Lord with thy riches etc. All men being thus (by divine providence) ranked into two sorts, rich and poor; under the first, are comprehended all such as are able to live comfortably by their own means duely improved; and all others are poor according to the former distribution. There are two rules whereby we are to walk one towards another: JUSTICE and MERCY. These are always distinguished in their Act and in their object, yet may they both concur in the same Subject in each respect; as sometimes there may be an occasion of showing mercy to a rich man, in some sudden danger of distress, and also doing of mere Justice to a poor man in regard of some particular contract etc. There is likewise a double Law by which we are regulated in our conversation one towards another: in both the former respects, the law of nature and the law of grace, or the moral law or the law of the gospel, to omit the rule of Justice as not properly belonging to this purpose otherwise then it may fall into consideration in some particular Cases: By the first of these laws man as he was enabled so withall [is] commanded to love his neighbor as himself upon this ground stands all the precepts of the moral law, which concerns our dealings with men. To apply this to the works of mercy this law requires two things first that every man afford his help to another in every want or distress; Secondly, That he perform this out of the same affection, which makes him careful of his own good according to that of our Savior, "Whatsoever ye would that men should do to you" [Matt. vii, 12]. This was practised by Abraham and Lot in entertaining the Angels and the old man of Gibea.

The Law of Grace or the Gospel hath some difference from the former as in these respects: first the law of nature was given to man in the estate of innocency; this of the gospel in the estate of regeneracy: secondly, the former propounds one man to another, as the same flesh and Image of God, this as a brother in Christ also, and in the Communion of the same spirit and so teacheth us to put a difference between Christians and others. Do good to all especially to the household of faith; upon this ground the Israelites were to put a difference between the brethren of such as were strangers though not of the Canaanites. Thirdly, The Law of nature could give no rules for dealing with enemies for all are to be considered as friends in the estate of innocency, but the Gospel commands love to an enemy. Proof! "If thine Enemy hunger feed him; Love your Enemies, do good to them that hate you." [Matt. v, 44.]

This Law of the Gospel propounds likewise a difference of seasons and occasions. There is a time when a christian must sell all and give to the poor as they did in the Apostles' times. There is a time also when a christian (though they give not all yet) must give beyond their ability, as they of Macedonia. Likewise, community of perils calls for extraordinary liberality and so doth Community in some special service for the Church. Lastly, when there is no other means whereby our Christian brother may be relieved in this distress, we must help him beyond our ability, rather than tempt God, in putting him upon help by miraculous or extraordinary means. . . .

The Apostle tells us that this love is the fulfilling of the law, not that it is enough to love our brother and so no further, but in regard of the excellency of his parts giving any motion to the other as the Soul to the body and the power it hath to set all the faculties on work in the outward exercise of this duty, as when we bid one make the clock strike he doth not lay hand on the hammer which is the immediate instrument of the sound but sets on work the first mover or main wheel, knowing that will certainly produce the sound which he intends; so the way to draw men to the works of mercy is not by force of Argument from the goodness or necessity of the work, for though this course may enforce a rational mind to some present Act of mercy as is frequent in experience, yet it cannot work such a habit in a Soul as shall make it prompt upon all occasions to produce the same effect but by framing these affections of love in the heart which will as natively bring forth the other, as any cause doth produce the effect.

The definition which the scripture gives us of love is this Love is the bond of perfection. First, it is a bond, or ligament. Secondly, it makes the work perfect. There is no body but consists of parts and that which knits these parts together gives the body its perfection, because it makes each part so contiguous to others as thereby they do mutually participate with each other, both in strength and infirmity in pleasure and pain, to instance in the most perfect of all bodies, Christ and his church make one body: the several parts of this body considered apart before they were united were as disproportionate and as much disordering as so many contrary qualities or elements but when Christ comes and by his spirit and love knits all these parts to himself and each to other, it is become the most perfect and best proportioned body in the world. [Eph.: iv, 16.] "Christ by whom all the body being knit together by every joint for the furniture thereof according to the effectual power which is in the measure of every perfection of parts a glorious body without spot or wrinkle the ligaments hereof being Christ or his love for Christ is love." [I John: iv, 8.] So this definition is right Love is the bond of perfection.

From hence we may frame these Conclusions.

First, all true Christians are of one body in Christ. . . .

Secondly, The ligaments of this body which knit together are love.

Thirdly, No body can be perfect which wants its proper ligaments.

Fourthly, All the parts of this body being thus united are made so contiguous in a special relation as they must needs partake of each others strength and infirmity, joy, and sorrow, weal and woe. If one member suffers all suffer with it, if one be in honor, all rejoice with it.

Fifthly, This sensibleness and Sympathy of each others Conditions will necessarily infuse into each part a native desire and endeavour, to strengthen defend preserve and comfort the other. . . .

It rests now to make some application of this discourse by the present design which gave the occasion of writing of it. Herein are 4 things to be propounded: first, the persons; secondly, the work; thirdly, the end; fourthly, the means.

First, for the persons, we are a Company professing ourselves fellow members of Christ, In which respect only though we were absent from each other many miles, and had our employments as far distant, yet we ought to account ourselves knit together by this bond of love, and live in the exercise of it, if we would have comfort of our being in Christ. . . .

Secondly, for the work we have in hand, it is by a mutual consent through a special overruling providence, and a more than an ordinary approbation of the Churches of Christ to seek out a place of Cohabitation and Consortship under a due form of Government both civil and ecclesiastical. In such cases as this the care of the public must oversway all private respects, by which not only conscience, but mere Civil policy doth bind us; for it is a true rule that particular estates cannot subsist in the ruin of the public.

Thirdly, the end is to improve our lives to do more service to the Lord the comfort and increase of the body of Christ whereof we are members, that ourselves and posterity may be the better preserved from the Common corruptions of this evil world to serve the Lord and work out our Salvation under the power and purity of his holy Ordinances.

Fourthly, for the means whereby this must be effected, they are two-fold: a Conformity with the work and end we aim at; these we see are extraordinary, therefore we must not content ourselves with usual ordinary means. Whatsoever we did or ought to have done when we lived in England, the same must we do and more also where we go. That which the most in their Churches maintain as a truth in profession only, we must bring into familiar and constant practice; as in this duty of love we must love brotherly without dissimulation, we must love one another with a pure heart fervently, we must bear one another's burdens, we must not look only on our own things, but also on the things of our brethren. Neither must we think that the Lord will bear with such failings at our hands as he doth from those among whom we have lived, and that for three Reasons. I. In regard of the more near bond of marriage between him and us, wherein he hath taken us to be his after a most strict and peculiar manner which will make him the more Jealous of our love and obedience, so he tells the people of Israel: "you only have I known of all the families of the Earth therefore will I punish you for your Trangressions." II. Because the Lord will be sanctified in them that come near him. We know that there were many that corrupted the service of the Lord some setting up Altars before his own, others offering both strange fire and strange Sacrifices also; yet there came no fire from heaven, or other sudden Judgement upon them as did upon Nadab and Abihu, who yet we may think did not sin presumptuously. III. When God gives a special Commission he looks to have it strictly observed in every Article. When he gave Saul a Commission to destroy Amaleck, he indented with him upon certain Articles, and because he failed in one of the least, and that upon a fair pretence, it lost him the kingdom which should have been his reward, if he had observed his Commission. Thus stands the cause between God and us. We are entered into Covenant with him for this work, we have taken out a Commission, the Lord hath given us leave to draw our own Articles. We have professed to enterprise these Actions upon these and these ends, we have hereupon besought him of favor and blessing. Now if the Lord shall please to hear us, and bring us in peace to the place we desire, then hath he ratified this Covenant and sealed our Commission, [and] will expect a strict performance of the Articles contained in it; but if we shall neglect the observation of these Articles which are the ends we have propounded, and dissembling with our God, shall fall to embrace this present world and prosecute our carnal intentions, seeking great things for ourselves and our posterity, the Lord will surely break out in wrath against us, be revenged of such a perjured people, and make us know the price of the breach of such a Covenant.

Now the only way to avoid this shipwreck and to provide for our posterity is to follow the Counsel of Micah, to do Justly, to love mercy, to walk humbly with our God. For this end, we must be knit together in this work as one man; we must entertain each other in brotherly Affection; we must be willing to abridge ourselves of our superfluities, for the supply of others' necessities; we must uphold a familiar Commerce together in all meekness, gentleness, patience and liberality; we must delight in each other, make others' Conditions our own, rejoice together, mourn together, labor and suffer together, always having before our eyes our Commission and Community in the work, our Community as members of the same body. So shall we keep the unity of the spirit in the bond of peace. The Lord will be our God and delight to dwell among us, as his own people and will command a blessing upon us in all our ways, so that we shall see much more of his wisdom, power, goodness, and truth than formerly we have been acquainted with. We shall find that the God of Israel is among us, when ten of us shall be able to resist a thousand of our enemies, when he shall make us a praise and glory, that men shall say of succeeding plantations: the Lord make it like that of New England. For we must Consider that we shall be as a City upon a Hill, the eyes of all people are upon us. So that if we shall deal falsely with our God in this work we have undertaken and so cause him to withdraw his present help from us, we shall be made a story and a by-word through the world; we shall open the mouths of enemies to speak evil of the ways of God and all professors for God's sake; we shall shame the faces of many of God's worthy servants, and cause their prayers to be turned into Curses upon us till we be consumed out of the good land whither we are going. And to shut up this discourse with that exhortation of Moses, that faithful servant of the Lord, in his last farewell to Israel, [Deut. xxx]. . . . Beloved there is now set before us life and good, death and evil in that we are Commanded this day to love the Lord our God, and to love one another, to walk in his ways and to keep his Commandments and his Ordinance and his laws and the Articles of our Covenant with him, that we may live and be multiplied, and that the Lord our God may bless us in the land whither we go to possess it. But if our hearts shall turn away so that we will not obey, but shall be seduced and worship . . . other gods, our pleasures, and profits, and serve them, it is propounded unto us this day, we shall surely perish out of the good Land whither we pass over this vast Sea to possess it.

> Therefore, let us choose life,
> that we, and our Seed,
> may live; by obeying his
> voice, and cleaving to him,
> for he is our life, and
> our prosperity.

Bibliography

BIBLIOGRAPHY

General

1. SOURCES

The Ante-Nicene Fathers, Edinburgh ed., rev. by A. Coxe, 10 Vols. Buffalo: Christian Literature, 1884–1886.

BAILLE, J., J. T. McNEILL, and H. P. VAN DUSEN, eds., *The Library of Christian Classics*. Philadelphia: The Westminster Press, 1953–1961.

BETTENSON, H., *Documents of the Christian Church*. New York: Oxford University Press, 1956.

KIDD, B. J., ed., *Documents Illustrative of the History of the Church*, 3 Vols. New York: The Macmillan Company, 1920–1941.

*LEITH, J. ed., *Creeds of the Churches: A Reader in Christian Doctrine from the Bible to the Present*. New York: Garden City Books, 1963.

The Nicene and Post-Nicene Fathers, First series, 14 Vols. Buffalo: Christian Literature, 1886–1894; Second series, 12 Vols. Buffalo: Christian Literature, 1890–1895.

PETRY, R., ed., *A History of Christianity: Readings in the History of the Early and Medieval Church*. Englewood Cliffs, N.J.: Prentice-Hall, Inc., 1962.

SCHAFF, P., *The Creeds of Christendom*, 6th ed., 3 Vols. New York: Harper and Row Publishers, 1919.

2. HISTORIES

DENZINGER, H. J., *The Sources of Catholic Dogma*, tr. by R. J. Deferrari. St. Louis: B. Herder Book Company, 1957.

*HARNACK, A., *A History of Dogma*, 7 Vols. London: Williams and Norgate, Ltd., 1896–1899.

LATOURETTE, K. S., *A History of Christianity*. New York: Harper and Row Publishers, 1953.

McGIFFERT, A. C., *A History of Christian Thought*, 2 Vols. New York: Charles Scribner's Sons, 1932–1933.

SEEBERG, R., *Textbook of the History of Doctrines*, tr. by C. E. Hay. Grand Rapids, Mich.: Baker Book House, 1952.

*TROELTSCH, E., *The Social Teachings of the Christian Churches*, tr. by O. Wyon, 2 Vols. New York: The Macmillan Company, 1931.

WALKER, W., *A History of the Christian Church*, rev. by C. C. Richardson, W. Pauck, and R. T. Handy. New York: Charles Scribner's Sons, 1959.

* available in paper edition.

Patristic Period

1. SOURCES

AYER, J. C., *A Source Book for Ancient Church History, from the Apostolic Age to the Close of the Conciliar Period*. New York: Charles Scribner's Sons, 1949.

*BAINTON, R. H., *Early Christianity*. Princeton, N.J.: D. Van Nostrand Company, Inc., 1960.

BETTENSON, H., ed., *The Early Christian Fathers*. New York: Oxford University Press, 1956.

GRANT, R. M., *Gnosticism: A Source Book of Heretical Writings from the Early Christian Period*. New York: Harper and Row Publishers, 1961.

*HAZELTON, R., *Selected Writings of Saint Augustine*. Cleveland: The World Publishing Company, 1962.

OATES, W. J., ed., *Basic Writings of Saint Augustine*, 2 Vols. New York: Random House, Inc., 1948.

SHOTWELL, J. T., and L. LOOMIS, *The See of Peter*. New York: Columbia University Press, 1927.

2. HISTORIES

BETHUNE-BAKER, J., *An Introduction to the Early History of Christian Doctrine*, 9th ed. London: Methuen & Co., Ltd. 1951.

*COCHRANE, A. N., *Christianity and Classical Culture*. New York: Oxford University Press, 1944.

HEFELE, K. J., *A History of the Councils of the Church*, 5 Vols. Edinburgh: T. & T. Clark, 1883–1896.

KELLY, J. D., *Early Christian Creeds*. New York: David McKay Company, Inc., 1950.

————, *Early Christian Doctrines*. New York: Harper and Row Publishers, 1958.

KIDD, B. J., *A History of the Church to A.D. 461*, 3 Vols. New York: Oxford University Press, 1922.

LIETZMANN, H., *The Beginnings of the Christian Church*. New York: Charles Scribner's Sons, 1937.

————, *The Founding of the Church Universal*. New York: Charles Scribner's Sons, 1938.

————, *From Constantine to Julian*. New York: Charles Scribner's Sons, 1950.

————, *The Era of the Church Fathers*. New York: Charles Scribner's Sons, 1952.

McGIFFERT, A. C., *A History of Christianity in the Apostolic Age*. New York: Charles Scribner's Sons, 1928.

MEER, F., VAN DER, and C. MOHRMANN, *Atlas of the Early Christian World*, tr. and ed. by M. F. Hedlund and H. H. Rowley. New York: Thomas Nelson & Sons, 1958.

* available in paper edition.

WAND, J. W. C., A History of the Early Church to A.D. 500, 3rd ed. London: Methuen & Co., Ltd., 1954.

*WEISS, J., Earliest Christianity: A History of the Period A.D. 30–150, 2 Vols. New York: Harper and Row Publishers, 1959.

WOLFSON, H., The Philosophy of the Early Church Fathers. Cambridge, Mass.: Harvard University Press, 1956.

3. TOPIC STUDIES

BAINTON, R. H., Early and Medieval Christianity. Boston: The Beacon Press, 1962.

BATTENHOUSE, R., ed., A Companion to the Study of St. Augustine. New York: Oxford University Press, 1955.

BIGG, C., The Christian Platonists of Alexandria. New York: Oxford University Press, 1913.

CORWIN, V., St. Ignatius and Christianity in Antioch. New Haven, Conn.: Yale University Press, 1960.

*D'ARCY, M. C., and others, St. Augustine: His Age, His Life and Thought, New York: Meridian Books, Inc., 1957.

DANIELOU, J., Origen, tr. by W. Mitchell. New York: Sheed & Ward, Inc., 1955.

DAVIES, W. D., Christian Origins and Judaism. Philadelphia: The Westminster Press, 1962.

*ENSLIN, M. S., Christian Beginnings. New York: Harper and Row Publishers, 1938.

FLESSEMAN-VAN LEER, E., Tradition and Scripture in the Early Church. Assen, Netherlands: Van Gorcum, 1954.

GRANT, R. M., Gnosticism and Early Christianity. New York: Columbia University Press, 1959.

GWATKIN, H. M., The Arian Controversy. New York: David McKay Company, Inc., 1898.

LAWSON, J., A Theological and Historical Introduction to the Apostolic Fathers. New York: The Macmillan Company, 1961.

McGIFFERT, A. C., The Apostles Creed. New York: Charles Scribner's Sons, 1902.

————, God of the Early Christians. New York: Charles Scribner's Sons, 1924.

MEER, F. VAN DER, Augustine the Bishop. New York: Sheed & Ward, Inc., 1962.

QUASTEN, J., Patrology, 3 Vols. Utrecht: Spectrum Publishers, 1950–1960.

RAVEN, C. E., Apollinarianism. London: Cambridge University Press, 1923.

SELLARS, R. V., Two Ancient Christologies; A Study in the Christological Thought of the Schools of Alexandria and Antioch. London: SPCK, 1954.

TOLLINTON, R. B., Clement of Alexandria, 2 Vols. London: Williams and Norgate, Ltd., 1914.

WARFIELD, B., Studies in Tertullian and Augustine. New York: Oxford University Press, 1930.

* available in paper edition.

Medieval Period

1. SOURCES

COLLEDGE, E., ed., *The Medieval Mystics of England.* New York: Charles Scribner's Sons, 1961.

McKEON, R. P., *Selections from Medieval Philosophers,* 2 Vols. New York: Charles Scribner's Sons, 1929.

PEGIS, A. C., ed., *Basic Writings of St. Thomas Aquinas,* 2 Vols. New York: Random House, Inc., 1944.

Ross, J. B., ed., *The Portable Medieval Reader.* New York: The Viking Press, Inc., 1949.

2. HISTORIES

CANNON, W. R., *A History of Christianity in the Middle Ages.* Nashville, Tenn.: Abingdon Press, 1960.

COULTON, G. G., *Five Centuries of Religion,* 4 Vols. London: Cambridge University Press, 1923–1950.

DEANESLY, M., *A History of the Medieval Church, 590–1500,* 6th ed. London: Methuen & Co., Ltd., 1950.

FLICK, A., *The Decline of the Medieval Church,* 2 Vols. New York: Alfred A. Knopf, Inc., 1930.

GILSON, E., *A History of Christian Philosophy in the Middle Ages.* New York: Random House, Inc., 1955.

*_____, *Reason and Revelation in the Middle Ages.* New York: Charles Scribner's Sons, 1938.

*LEFF, G., *Medieval Thought: St. Augustine to Ockham.* Baltimore: Penguin Book, Inc., 1958.

TAYLOR, H. O., *The Medieval Mind,* 4th ed., 2 Vols. Cambridge, Mass.: Harvard University Press, 1949.

WORKMAN, H. B., *Christian Thought to the Reformation.* London: Gerald Duckworth & Co., Ltd., 1911.

3. TOPIC STUDIES

*COPLESTON, F. C., *Aquinas.* Baltimore: Penguin Books, Inc., 1955.

*HUIZINGA, J., *The Waning of the Middle Ages.* New York: David McKay Company, Inc., 1948.

HYMA, A., *The Christian Renaissance: A History of the "Devotio Moderna."* Grand Rapids: The Reformed Press, 1924.

POOLE, R. L., *Illustrations of Medieval Thought and Learning,* 2nd rev. ed. New York: Dover Publications, 1960.

SPINKA, M., *John Hus and the Czech Reform.* Chicago: University of Chicago Press, 1941.

WORKMAN, H. B., *John Wycliff, a Study of the English Medieval Church,* 2 Vols. New York: Oxford University Press, 1926.

* available in paper edition.

Reformation Period

1. SOURCES

*Bainton, R. H., *The Age of the Reformation*. Princeton, N.J.: D. Van Nostrand Company, Inc., 1956.
*Dillenberger, J., ed., *Martin Luther: Selections from His Writings*. New York: Garden City Books, 1961.
Ferm, V., *Classics of Protestantism*. New York: Philosophical Library, Inc., 1959.
Fosdick, H. E., *Great Voices of the Reformation*. New York: Random House, Inc., 1952.
Gee, H., and W. J. Hardy, *Documents Illustrative of English Church History*. New York: The Macmillan Company, 1896.
Kidd, B. J., *Documents Illustrative of the Continental Reformation*. New York: Oxford University Press, 1911.
Schroeder, H. J., *Canons and Decrees of the Council of Trent*. St. Louis: B. Herder Book Company, 1941.
Torrance, T. F., ed., *The School of Faith: The Catechisms of the Reformed Church*. New York: Harper and Row Publishers, 1959.

2. HISTORIES

*Bainton, R. H., *The Reformation of the Sixteenth Century*. Boston: The Beacon Press, 1952.
*Harbison, E. H., *The Age of the Reformation*. Ithaca, N.Y.: Cornell University Press, 1955.
Lindsay, T. M., *A History of the Reformation*, 2d ed., 2 Vols. Edinburgh: T. & T. Clark, 1907–1908.
Pauck, W., *The Heritage of the Reformation*, 2d ed. New York: The Free Press of Glencoe, Inc., 1961.

3. TOPIC STUDIES

*Bainton, R. H., *Here I Stand: The Life of Martin Luther*. Nashville, Tenn.: Abingdon Press, 1950.
*Boehmer, H., *Martin Luther: Road to Reformation*. Philadelphia: The Board of Publication of the Lutheran Church of America, 1946.
Bornkamm, H., *Luther's World of Thought*. St. Louis: Concordia Publishing House, 1958.
Church, F. C., *The Italian Reformers, 1534–1564*. New York: Columbia University Press, 1932.
Constant, G., *The Reformation in England*, 2 Vols. New York: Sheed & Ward, Inc., 1934–1941.
Doernberg, E., *Henry VIII and Luther: An Account of Their Personal Relations*. Stanford, Calif.: Stanford University Press, 1961.
Dowey, E., *The Knowledge of God in Calvin's Theology*. New York: Columbia University Press, 1952.

* available in paper edition.

FARNER, O., Zwingli the Reformer. New York: Philosophical Library, Inc., 1952.

FORSTMAN, H. J., Word and Spirit: Calvin's Doctrine of Biblical Authority. Stanford, Calif.: Stanford University Press, 1962.

GEORGE, C. H., and K. GEORGE, The Protestant Mind of the English Reformation. Princeton, N.J.: Princeton University Press, 1961.

GERRISH, B., Grace and Reason: A Study in the Theology of Luther. New York: Oxford University Press, 1962.

HEPPE, H., Reformed Dogmatics. London: George Allen & Unwin, Ltd., 1950.

*HUIZINGA, J., Erasmus and the Age of the Reformation. New York: Harper and Row Publishers, 1957.

KOT, S., Socinianism in Poland. Boston: The Beacon Press, 1957.

LITTELL, F. H., The Anabaptist View of the Church, 2d ed., Boston: Starr King Press, 1958.

MACKINNON, J., Luther and the Reformation, 4 Vols. London: Longmans, Green & Co., Ltd., 1925–1930.

MCNEILL, J. T., The History and Character of Calvinism. New York: Oxford University Press, 1954.

MANSCHRECK, C., Melancthon, the Quiet Reformer. Nashville, Tenn.: Abingdon Press, 1958.

NIESEL, W., The Theology of Calvin. Philadelphia: The Westminster Press, 1958.

RUPP, E. G., The English Protestant Tradition. New York: Cambridge University Press, 1949.

SCHLINK, E., Theology of the Lutheran Confessions, tr. by P. F. Koehneke and H. S. A. Bouman. Philadelphia: The Board of Publication of the Lutheran Church of America, 1961.

SMITH, P., Erasmus. New York: Harper and Row Publishers, 1923.

SMITHSON, R. J., The Anabaptists. London: James C. Clarke & Co., Ltd., 1935.

TORRANCE, T. F., Kingdom and Church: A Study in the Theology of the Reformation. Edinburgh and London: Oliver and Boyd, Ltd., 1956.

WATKIN, E. I., Roman Catholicism in England from the Reformation to 1950. New York: Oxford University Press, 1957.

WILLIAMS, G., The Radical Reformation. Philadelphia: The Westminster Press, 1962.

Post-Reformation to 1800

1. SOURCES

*MILLER, P., and T. H. JOHNSON, eds., The Puritans. New York: American Book Company, 1938.

WALKER, W., The Creeds and Platforms of Congregationalism. New York: Charles Scribner's Sons, 1893.

2. HISTORIES

BAUMER, F., Religion and the Rise of Scepticism. New York: Harcourt, Brace & World, Inc., 1960.

* available in paper edition.

*CASSIRER, E., *The Philosophy of the Enlightenment*. Boston: The Beacon Press, 1955.

*CRAGG, G. R., *The Church and the Age of Reason, 1678–1789*. Baltimore: Penguin Books, Inc., 1960.

————, *From Puritanism to the Age of Reason: A Study of Changes in Religious Thought within the Church of England, 1660–1700*. London: Cambridge University Press, 1950.

HAZARD, P., *European Thought in the Eighteenth Century*. New Haven, Conn.: Yale University Press, 1954.

————, *The European Mind, 1680–1715*. New Haven: Yale University Press, 1953.

McGIFFERT, A. C., *Protestant Thought Before Kant*. New York: Charles Scribner's Sons, 1911.

STEPHEN, L., *History of English Thought in the Eighteenth Century*, 2 Vols. London: Smith, Elder, 1881.

3. TOPIC STUDIES

CAMERON, R. M., *The Rise of Methodism*. New York: Philosophical Library, Inc., 1954.

CANNON, W. R., *The Theology of John Wesley*. Nashville, Tenn.: Abingdon Press, 1946.

DESCHNER, J., *Wesley's Christology: An Interpretation*. Dallas, Tex.: Southern Methodist University Press, 1960.

*HALLER, W., *The Rise of Puritanism*. New York: Columbia University Press, 1938.

HARRISON, A. W., *Arminianism*. London: Gerald Duckworth & Co., Ltd., 1937.

KNAPPEN, M. M., *Tudor Puritanism*. Chicago: University of Chicago Press, 1939.

MILLER, P., *Errand into the Wilderness*. Cambridge, Mass.: Belknap Press of Harvard University Press, 1956.

NUTTALL, G. F., *Visible Saints: The Congregational Way, 1640–1660*. Oxford: Basil Blackwell & Mott, Ltd., 1957.

STROMBERG, R. N., *Religious Liberalism in Eighteenth Century England*. London: Oxford University Press, 1954.

WESTFALL, R. S., *Science and Religion in Seventeenth Century England*. New Haven, Conn.: Yale University Press, 1958.

WRIGHT, C., *The Beginnings of Unitarianism in America*. Boston: Starr King Press, 1955.

* available in paper edition.